MOON OUTDOORS

WITHDRAWN

MONTANA, WYOMING & IDAHO CAMPING

BECKY LOMAX

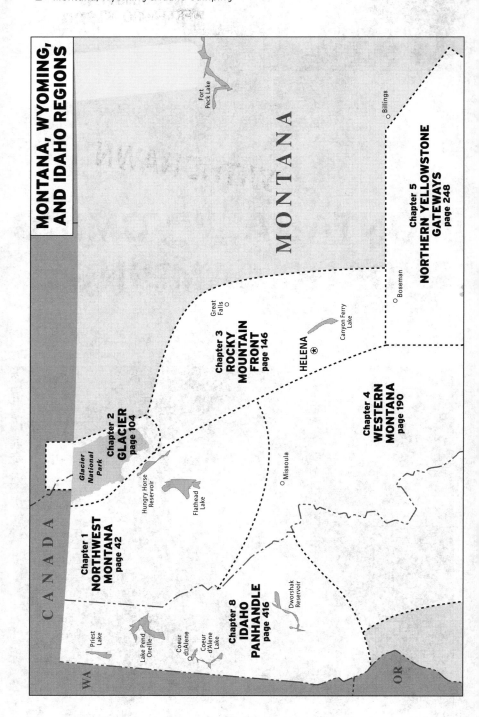

MONTANA, WYOMING, AND IDAHO REGIONS

CANADA

WA

OR

MONTANA

Glacier National Park

Fort Peck Lake

○ Billings

○ Great Falls

○ Boseman

HELENA ✦

Canyon Ferry Lake

Hungry Horse Reservoir

Flathead Lake

○ Missoula

Priest Lake

Lake Pend Oreille

Coeur d'Alene ○

Coeur d'Alene Lake

Dworshak Reservoir

Chapter 1
NORTHWEST MONTANA
page 42

Chapter 2
GLACIER
page 104

Chapter 3
ROCKY MOUNTAIN FRONT
page 146

Chapter 4
WESTERN MONTANA
page 190

Chapter 5
NORTHERN YELLOWSTONE GATEWAYS
page 248

Chapter 8
IDAHO PANHANDLE
page 416

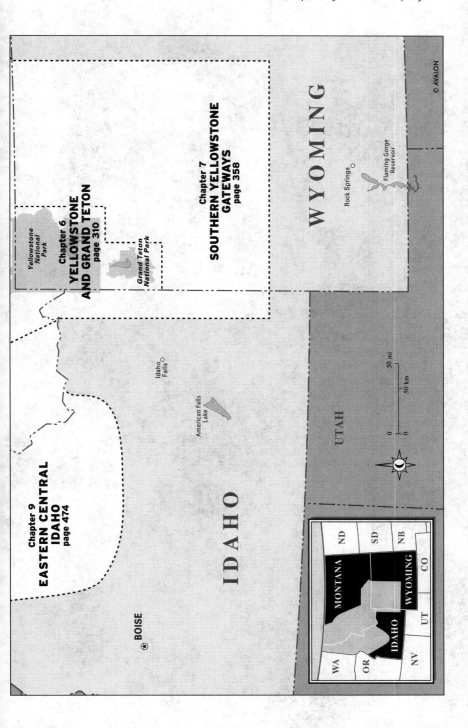

Contents

How to Use This Book

ABOUT THE CAMPGROUND PROFILES

The campgrounds are listed in a consistent, easy-to-read format to help you choose the ideal camping spot. If you already know the name of the specific campground you want to visit, or the name of the surrounding geological area or nearby feature (town, national or state park, forest, mountain, lake, river, etc.), look it up in the index and turn to the corresponding page. Here is a sample profile:

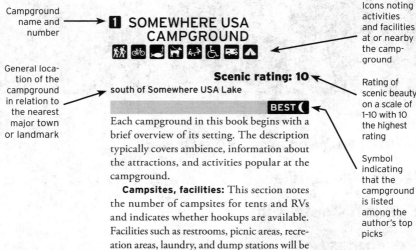

Campground name and number

General location of the campground in relation to the nearest major town or landmark

1 SOMEWHERE USA CAMPGROUND

Icons noting activities and facilities at or nearby the campground

Scenic rating: 10

south of Somewhere USA Lake

Rating of scenic beauty on a scale of 1-10 with 10 the highest rating

BEST (

Symbol indicating that the campground is listed among the author's top picks

Each campground in this book begins with a brief overview of its setting. The description typically covers ambience, information about the attractions, and activities popular at the campground.

Campsites, facilities: This section notes the number of campsites for tents and RVs and indicates whether hookups are available. Facilities such as restrooms, picnic areas, recreation areas, laundry, and dump stations will be addressed, as well as the availability of piped water, showers, playgrounds, stores, and other amenities. The campground's pet policy and wheelchair accessibility is also mentioned here.

Reservations, fees: This section notes whether reservations are accepted, and provides rates for tent sites and RV sites. If there are additional fees for parking or pets, or discounted weekly or seasonal rates, they will also be noted here.

Directions: This section provides mile-by-mile driving directions to the campground from the nearest major town or highway.

Contact: This section provides an address, phone number, and website, if available, for the campground.

ABOUT THE ICONS

The icons in this book are designed to provide at-a-glance information on activities, facilities, and services available on-site or within walking distance of each campground.

- 🏃 Hiking trails
- 🚲 Biking trails
- 🏊 Swimming
- 🎣 Fishing
- 🚤 Boating
- 🛶 Canoeing and/or kayaking
- 🏹 Hunting

- ❄️ Winter sports
- ♨️ Hot springs
- 🐾 Pets permitted
- 🛝 Playground
- ♿ Wheelchair accessible
- 🚐 RV sites
- ⛺ Tent sites

ABOUT THE SCENIC RATING

Each campground profile employs a scenic rating on a scale of 1 to 10, with 1 being the least scenic and 10 being the most scenic. A scenic rating measures only the overall beauty of the campground and environs; it does not take into account noise level, facilities, maintenance, recreation options, or campground management. The setting of a campground with a lower scenic rating may simply not be as picturesque that of as a higher rated campground, however other factors that can influence a trip, such as noise or recreation access, can still affect or enhance your camping trip. Consider both the scenic rating and the profile description before deciding which campground is perfect for you.

MAP SYMBOLS

▦▦▦ Expressway	(80) Interstate Freeway	✗ Airfield
▬▬▬ Primary Road	(101) U.S. Highway	✈ Airport
▦▦▦ Secondary Road	(21) State Highway	O City/Town
▫ ▫ ▫ Unpaved Road	(66) County Highway	▲ Mountain
·········· Ferry	Lake	🛡 Park
▬ ▪ ▬ National Border	Dry Lake	)(Pass
▬ ▪▪ ▬ State Border	Seasonal Lake	◉ State Capital

INTRODUCTION

Author's Note

Fire and ice dominate the Montana, Wyoming, and Idaho mountain corridor of the Northern Rockies. The earth fumes into boiling geysers from one of the biggest supervolcanoes in the world while craggy peaks cradle centuries-old ice. Yellowstone, the nation's first national park, resounds with the roar of vents spewing steam, and Glacier, the nation's tenth national park, retains fast-melting vestiges of ice snuggled in a scoured, jagged landscape that exposes some of the oldest sedimentary rocks in North America. In addition, Grand Teton National Park contributes a toothy landscape, with much younger mountains. Wrapped in winter cloaks of snow for half the year, the parks draw campers in summer because of their wildlife, beauty, and singularity.

As a bonus, 14 national forests, 9 national wildlife refuges, 38 state parks, and countless fishing accesses give campers loads of places to explore. Multistate trails include the historic routes of Lewis and Clark, the Nez Perce, and the new Ice Age Floods National Geologic Trail. Multiple national historic sites and monuments provide a breadth of experiences from the pioneer West to solidified lava.

The Northern Rockies corridor also forms a citadel for nature at its wildest. The region houses 16 wilderness areas, pristine swaths of mountains that have seen minimal impact by humans, including the largest roadless wilderness in the Lower 48. You can camp so far off the grid that you may not see another person for days.

With cell reception unavailable in many places, the mountainous spine through Montana, Wyoming, and Idaho provides places to put aside our technological umbilical cords. Relish the moments to listen to the wind chattering aspen leaves, a great horned owl hooting at dusk, or a bullfrog bellowing in a pond. Or soak up the silence.

The nation's largest carnivores make the Northern Rockies home along with wild native trout while one of the country's biggest migration flyways cruises overhead. Grizzly bears and gray wolves top the food chain, just as they did in Lewis and Clark's day. Moose, elk, antelope, and bison browse the meadowlands while bighorn sheep, mountain goats, and wolverines stand as icons of the alpine. Blue-ribbon streams abound where anglers can catch native westslope cutthroat trout. Overhead, the Rocky Mountain flyway crowds twice a year with golden eagles, raptors, and songbirds.

With less than 1 percent of the nation's population dotted across the three states in cow towns and blink-and-you'll-miss-it rural villages, the region offers big expanses of public land where you won't see a house for miles. Contrary to other states where private homes rim every inch of rivers and lakes, waterways in the Northern Rockies abound with easy public access. Montana houses Flathead Lake, the largest freshwater lake in the West, and some of the West's largest rivers—the Yellowstone, Missouri, Snake, and Salmon—find their headwaters in the mountains of Montana, Wyoming, and Idaho. Fed by chilly waters from snowmelt and glaciers, lakes provide campers with scenic places to boat, fish, paddle, water-ski, and swim, while rivers bring on small riffles for fishing and floating as well as frothy white water.

Montana, Wyoming, and Idaho are huge places. Many first-time visitors assume they can pop between Glacier and Yellowstone National Parks in a couple of hours, but the distance requires a full day's drive, minimum. For an enjoyable visit, plan camping trips that cover reasonable distances and include plenty of days; you'll have time to enjoy roasting marshmallows on the campfire by avoiding marathon drives. Many campground gems hide on remote gravel roads; plan on slower travel to reach them.

The corridor between the Glacier and Yellowstone-Teton country harbors black and grizzly bears. As black bears thrive across the United States, grizzly bears have been squeezed into 1 percent of their traditional range in the Lower 48. In the Northern Rockies, grizzly populations are rebounding enough to make wildlife officials work toward delisting the bears from the Endangered Species List. Camping in bear country demands conscientious habits for storing food and garbage. Although some campgrounds staple reminders to picnic tables and levy substantial fines for failure to keep a bear-proof camp, others do not. A few campgrounds listed in this book haven't seen a bear in decades; others do so frequently. To keep both you and the bears safe, assume you are in bear country at all campgrounds in the Northern Rockies.

Although I've made every endeavor to provide accurate information in this guide, the status of campgrounds changes fast. Storms, snows, floods, and fires destroy campgrounds. Even as new campgrounds are constructed, depleted federal maintenance budgets are forcing shorter seasons and closures of some lesser used campgrounds. Federal budget crunches have pressured national parks and the Forest Service to increase pricing, shrink services, and shorten seasons.

One small creature, however, is changing the face of campgrounds faster than anything else. Pine bark beetles are rampantly killing trees across western mountains—up to 40 percent in some national forests. Recognize their presence by rust-colored pines. Many national forests have adopted spraying programs to protect campground trees. When an infestation causes dead trees to pose a danger to the public, campgrounds close, so logging companies can thin the dead timber. Logging out the bug-infested trees converts deep shade campgrounds into sunny wide-open sites.

While private RV campgrounds spread across the Northern Rockies, only select ones are included in this book: those nearest the national parks, those that offer access to recreation, and those on travel corridors. Public campgrounds in national parks and national forests make up the bulk of the book's selections. Primitive campsites—a personal favorite—are also included for those who prefer the quiet, solitude, and seclusion they provide.

Ultimate memories from camping are forged not just from stunning views and spotting wildlife. They come from rare experiences—listening to raucous tent-shaking thunderclaps in Montana's Swan Valley, gagging on the stench from Yellowstone's mud pots, standing in utter blackness in the Lewis and Clark Caverns, spying a pair of wolverines romping in Glacier, and watching the sunrise glow on the Tetons. The best camping memories also come from sharing the experience. Among the indelible camping images etched in my memory, I have visions of paddling the sluggish Marge the Barge with my youngest sister up the Priest River Thoroughfare, mountain biking the Hiawatha rail trail with my intrepid 10-year-old niece, gazing with my college roommate at a sky blazing with stars on the remote North Fork of the Clearwater River, and hiking with friends through a wealth of yellow, purple, and red wildflowers in the Beartooth Mountains.

Regardless of the adventure, all camping trips have one thing in common—they increase the desire to camp again. The Northern Rockies are a place to smell rich pines, taste the dry air, and cool hot hiking feet in ice-cold streams. Bring the toys—hiking boots, boats, rafts, kayaks, canoes, and mountain bikes—to enjoy all that camping has to offer.

Best Campgrounds

BEST❰ of Montana
Big Therriault Lake, Northwest Montana, page 68.
Spotted Bear, Northwest Montana, page 100.
Bowman Lake, Glacier, page 109.
Rising Sun, Glacier, page 124.
Cave Mountain, Rocky Mountain Front, page 150.
Devil's Elbow, Rocky Mountain Front, page 171.
Missouri Headwaters State Park, Northern Yellowstone Gateways, page 250.
Lewis and Clark Caverns State Park, Northern Yellowstone Gateways, page 251.
Red Mountain, Northern Yellowstone Gateways, page 254.
Beaver Creek, Northern Yellowstone Gateways, page 266.

BEST❰ of Wyoming
Beartooth Lake, Northern Yellowstone Gateways, page 302.
Madison, Yellowstone and Tetons, page 329.
Cave Falls, Yellowstone and Tetons, page 338.
Grassy Lake Primitive, Yellowstone and Tetons, page 340.
Signal Mountain, Yellowstone and Tetons, page 348.
Brooks Lake, Southern Yellowstone Gateways, page 392.
Pinnacles, Southern Yellowstone Gateways, page 393.
Clearwater, Southern Yellowstone Gateways, page 405.

BEST❰ of Idaho
Big Springs, Southern Yellowstone Gateways, page 361.
Grandview, Southern Yellowstone Gateways, page 367.
Indian Creek, Idaho Panhandle, page 427.
Priest River Recreation Area (Mudhole), Idaho Panhandle, page 434.
North Fork of the Clearwater River Primitive, Idaho Panhandle, page 466.
Wilderness Gateway, Eastern Central Idaho, page 479.
Stanley Lake Inlet, Eastern Central Idaho, page 504.
Sockeye, Eastern Central Idaho, page 512.
Lava Flow, Eastern Central Idaho, page 521.

BEST❰ Boat-In Camping
Elk Island, Northwest Montana, page 98.
Head of Kintla Lake, Glacier, page 107.
Head of Bowman Lake, Glacier, page 110.
Boundary Bay, Glacier, page 141.
Coulter, Rocky Mountain Front, page 169.
Flat Mountain, South, and Southeast Arms, Yellowstone and Tetons, page 336.
Shoshone Lake, Yellowstone and Tetons, page 337.
Navigation, Idaho Panhandle, page 417.
Kalispell Island, Idaho Panhandle, page 423.
Redfish Inlet, Eastern Central Idaho, page 513.

BEST⟨ Fishing

Russell Gates Memorial, Western Montana, page 198.
Divide Bridge, Western Montana, page 237.
Palisades (Madison River), Northern Yellowstone Gateways, page 260.
Wade Lake, Northern Yellowstone Gateways, page 262.
Lewis Lake, Yellowstone and Tetons, page 338.
Riverside, Southern Yellowstone Gateways, page 366.
Green River Warren Bridge Access Area, Southern Yellowstone Gateways,
   page 385.
Shadowy St. Joe, Idaho Panhandle, page 453.
Johnson Bar, Eastern Central Idaho, page 482.
Salmon River, Eastern Central Idaho, page 504.

BEST⟨ Hiking

Little Therriault Lake, Northwest Montana, page 67.
Holland Lake, Northwest Montana, page 85.
Many Glacier, Glacier, page 127.
Two Medicine, Glacier, page 131.
Mill Falls, Rocky Mountain Front, page 151.
East Rosebud, Northern Yellowstone Gateways, page 293.
Island Lake, Northern Yellowstone Gateways, page 302.
Jenny Lake, Yellowstone and Tetons, page 350.
Big Sandy, Southern Yellowstone Gateways, page 390.
Iron Creek, Eastern Central Idaho, page 506.
Pettit Lake, Eastern Central Idaho, page 513.

BEST⟨ Hot Springs

Cascade, Northwest Montana, page 67.
Lolo Hot Springs Resort, Western Montana, page 203.
Lost Trail Hot Springs Resort, Western Montana, page 219.
Fairmont RV Park, Western Montana, page 235.
Norris Hot Springs, Northern Yellowstone Gateways, page 254.
Bozeman KOA, Northern Yellowstone Gateways, page 268.
Mammoth, Yellowstone and Tetons, page 314.
Granite Creek, Southern Yellowstone Gateways, page 380.
Wendover and Whitehouse, Eastern Central Idaho, page 478.
Easley and Boulder View, Eastern Central Idaho, page 516.

BEST⟨ Lake Camping

Big Arm State Park, Northwest Montana, page 80.
Kintla Lake, Glacier, page 106.
Sprague Creek, Glacier, page 123.
Cliff Point, Northern Yellowstone Gateways, page 263.
Grant Village, Yellowstone and Tetons, page 334.
Beaver Creek, Idaho Panhandle, page 420.
Sam Owen Recreation Area, Idaho Panhandle, page 437.

Hawley's Landing, Idaho Panhandle, page 452.
Dent Acres, Idaho Panhandle, page 463.
Outlet, Eastern Central Idaho, page 510.

BEST(River Camping
Bull River, Northwest Montana, page 62.
Big Creek, Glacier, page 112.
Dalles, Western Montana, page 224.
Warm River, Southern Yellowstone Gateways, page 368.
Aquarius Creek, Idaho Panhandle, page 466.
Washington Creek, Idaho Panhandle, page 467.
Wild Goose, Eastern Central Idaho, page 481.
O'Hara Bar, Eastern Central Idaho, page 483.
Upper and Lower O'Brien, Eastern Central Idaho, page 498.
Mormon Bend, Eastern Central Idaho, page 502.

BEST(Wildlife-Watching
Swan Lake, Northwest Montana, page 85.
Freezeout Lake, Rocky Mountain Front, page 156.
Departure Point, Rocky Mountain Front, page 167.
Brown's Lake, Western Montana, page 200.
Upper Red Rock Lake, Northern Yellowstone Gateways, page 264.
Indian Creek, Yellowstone and Tetons, page 315.
Slough Creek, Yellowstone and Tetons, page 317.
Pebble Creek, Yellowstone and Tetons, page 318.
Canyon, Yellowstone and Tetons, page 331.
Albeni Cove Recreation Area, Idaho Panhandle, page 434.

Camping Tips

TRAVELING THE NORTHERN ROCKIES
Roads and Routes

When traveling the Northern Rockies of Montana, Wyoming, and Idaho, you're in big country with minimal roads: Interstates are few and far between. Dirt roads are as ubiquitous as pavement. Rough, narrow, paved two laners are common.

HIGHWAYS AND INTERSTATES

Only two interstate highways bisect the region. I-15 runs through Montana and Idaho, connecting Calgary with Salt Lake City, and I-90 crosses Montana en route from Seattle to Chicago and Boston. State highways crisscross the region, providing the main thoroughfares. Some can have four lanes, but most will be two laners. To navigate the area, use a current detailed map that shows pavement and gravel roads.

CROSSING THE CONTINENTAL DIVIDE AND HIGH PASSES

The Continental Divide skitters along the highest summits of the Rocky Mountains, making the division between water flowing to the Atlantic versus the Pacific. For campers, driving over the Continental Divide provides a challenge. In winter, some high passes are closed for several months, while others struggle with intermittent closures due to avalanches. The Beartooth Highway, Glacier National Park's Going-to-the-Sun Road, and much of Yellowstone National Park closes for winter, and remote Forest Service roads convert to snowmobile routes.

But even in summer, you can encounter snow on the higher passes through the mountains from Glacier to the Tetons. Wyoming's Beartooth Pass tops out at 10,947 feet, and Togwotee Pass is 9,658 feet. Both have amassed snow in August. The most notorious is Teton Pass on the south end of Grand Teton National Park. Although it only touches 8,431 feet high, its 10 percent grade proves a grunt for RVs and those hauling camping trailers. Make a practice of downshifting into second gear for descents rather than burning your brakes.

Current pass conditions are available on each state's Department of Transportation website. Some even have webcams on the summits to check the weather.

DIRT ROADS

Many of the prized campgrounds in the Northern Rockies are accessed via dirt or gravel roads. The best roads—wide, graveled, double laners with regular maintenance—hold the washboards to a minimum. Others jounce along with large washboards, rocks, eroded streambeds, and small potholes. The worst contain monstrous chuckholes that can nearly swallow small cars and grab trailer hitches. Do not bring prized paint jobs on dirt roads! Take a hint from locals, who all drive rigs with dings and window chips. Rigs with four-wheel drive are helpful to get out of rough spots, but they are not required to reach any of the campgrounds in this book. If you are concerned about your vehicle's ability to navigate a certain dirt road, call the appropriate national forest for status.

DISTANCES

Many campers visiting the Northern Rockies for the first time expect to whiz between Glacier and Yellowstone National Parks in a few hours. The distance between the two is the same as driving from San Francisco to Los Angeles or from Boston to Baltimore, only without an interstate most of the way. To drive between the two parks, most campers take a full day without stopping or sightseeing.

GAS

Don't wait until you're empty to look for gas. Always plan ahead for filling up, as gas stations sometimes can be 60 miles or more away. Gas

ENTRY FEES

While many national forests and public lands require no entry fee, national parks, national historic sites, and some special federal sites charge entry fees. Rates vary by site.

NATIONAL PARKS

Entry for one private vehicle to Glacier, Grand Teton, or Yellowstone National Park costs $25 for a seven-day pass. No single-day passes are sold. Passes for Yellowstone or Grand Teton National Park are good for both parks. Entry on foot or by bicycle costs $12. A motorcycle can enter Glacier for $12, but entry to Yellowstone and Grand Teton costs $20.

Yellowstone has the same fees year-round, but Glacier reduces the entry fee in winter to $15, and Grand Teton reduces it to $5. You can enter all three national parks free on special days: Martin Luther King Jr. Day, National Park Week in late April, the birthday of the National Park Service in late August, National Public Lands Day in late September, and Veterans Day.

For those camping longer than seven days, annual passes are available, too, for each of the parks. A combined annual Yellowstone-Teton pass costs $50, and the Glacier annual pass costs $35. These are available for purchase at entrance stations.

INTERAGENCY PASSES

The **America the Beautiful Interagency Pass**, which costs $80, is a nontransferable annual pass that grants entrance to federal sites. This pass is valid at sites run by the National Park Service, Fish and Wildlife Service, Bureau of Land Management, Bureau of Reclamation, and the U.S. Forest Service. The pass does not cover camping fees or fees charged by concessionaires. The pass covers up to four adults and all children in a single, noncommercial vehicle. At walk-up entrance sites, the pass is good for the pass holder plus three adults. Children under 16 get free admission. Passes are available at entrance stations or online (store.usgs.gov/pass). The pass is available free for active military personnel and their dependents.

Seniors (U.S. citizens or permanent residents age 62 and older) can purchase lifetime nontransferable interagency passes for $10, available in person at park entrances. Bring proof of age (state driver's license, birth certificate, passport, etc.). The lifetime senior pass provides a 50 percent discount on some campgrounds.

U.S. citizens or permanent residents with permanent disabilities can get a free interagency pass, called an Access Pass, available only in person at entrance stations with proof of medical disability or eligibility for receiving federal benefits. The Access Pass provides a 50 percent discount on many campgrounds.

---

prices tend to be cheaper in Wyoming than in Montana or Idaho; they are also cheaper in cities compared to small rural stations.

REPAIRS

Repairs to vehicles and RVs are available. Even in the national parks or on remote national forest roads, mechanics can come take a look at your vehicle and tow it back to the shop. In some places, mobile repair services are available. Most repair services coming to your campsite will charge by the hour for their services rather than by the mile, to account for their time spent driving slow dirt roads and scenic byways to reach you.

RVs

Most RVers are well aware that different campgrounds have size restrictions based on the size of parking pads and configuration of the campground road. However, RVers will want to consider the road status in their choices of campgrounds, too. Dirt national forest roads do not usually post warnings on status. Call the local ranger station to check on conditions before driving. Most paved roads, except for the Logan Pass stretch of Glacier's Going-to-the-Sun Road, are suitable for any size RV. In Glacier, the Logan Pass stretch prohibits vehicles over 21 feet in length, taller than 10 feet, and wider than 8 feet.

MOTORCYCLES

Montana, Wyoming, and Idaho are popular for motorcycle touring. Many bikers haul their tents and mini trailers to camp in the national parks and ride the high scenic passes. None of the three states require helmets—except for those 17 years old and younger. Motorcyclists riding the high passes should be prepared for inclement weather and cold temperatures even in August.

Navigational Tools

MAPS

The dirt roads into many campgrounds in the Northern Rockies do not even appear on the state road maps. More detailed maps will provide you with a better view of where you are driving. Overall, U.S.G.S. seven-minute maps yield the most detail for driving forest roads, hiking, and camping; however, the dollars can rack up fast on a big trip requiring a load of maps. *National Geographic Trails Illustrated* maps (800/962-1643, www.natgeomaps.com) are available for Glacier, Grand Teton, and Yellowstone National Parks. Each national forest

also sells huge maps with one-mile grids; find these at ranger stations or purchase online (www.nationalforeststore.com). Beartooth Publishing (406/585-7205 or 800/838-1058, www.beartoothpublishing.com) produces regional recreation maps for southern Montana, northwestern Wyoming, and eastern Idaho; maps include latitude and longitude grids, trail mileages, and campgrounds.

GPS, COMPASSES, AND PERSONAL LOCATING DEVICES

GPS units and compasses are useful for navigation but require knowledge on how to use them. Learn to use them before you depart on a trip where your safety may rely on them. Vehicle GPS units work well on most areas accessed by paved roads, but some remote Forest Service roads fail to appear on screen. Both vehicle and handheld GPS units rely on access to satellites; in deep canyons, you may not be able to pick up enough of a satellite signal for them to work. A compass, which always works, can provide a good backup.

While personal locating devices will

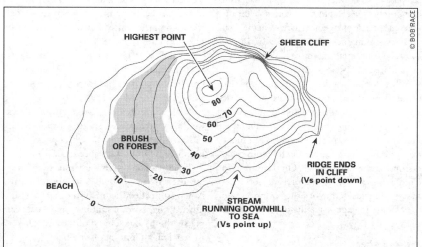

The **topographical map** is easier to read than many believe. Lines close together mean steep gradients; lines farther apart mean gentle gradients; V-shaped sets of lines pointing to higher elevations mean gulleys or stream-beds; V-shaped sets of lines pointing to lower elevations mean ridges.

transmit everywhere a GPS works, they require conscientious use. Across the West, rescue organizations are being called out for frivolous reasons or accidentally sent signals—risking the lives of the rescuers. Signals should only be transmitted in life-threatening situations. Personal locating devices should not be used as tickets to hike, climb, bike, or boat beyond one's abilities; go to only those places you would visit without one and plan self-rescue options.

Cell Phones

Visitors to the Northern Rockies expect cell phones to work everywhere as they do in virtually all populated areas. But dead zones are vast. Even though a cell tower sits near Old Faithful in Yellowstone National Park, much of the mountainous terrain across the Northern Rockies plummets into narrow canyons prohibiting signals. Don't expect to find reception deep in the forests, in canyons, or in the mountains. Most national forest and national park campgrounds do not get reception.

One of the best inventions for emergencies, cell phones allow immediate access to help. But do not rely on a cell phone as your sole means of rescue in case of an emergency. Whether you are backpacking in a wilderness or driving 20 dirt road miles snaking into a national forest, be prepared to rescue yourself.

When cell phones do work in campgrounds, use of them requires etiquette. Turn off ringers: Phone noise catapults hikers and campers from a natural experience back into the hubbub of modern life. If you must make a call, move away from campsites and other hikers to avoid disrupting their experience. On trails, refrain from using phones in the presence of other hikers. Be considerate of other campers and their desire to experience the outdoors rather than technology.

CLIMATE

The Northern Rockies from Glacier to Yellowstone sit on a collision course between Arctic Continental and Pacific Maritime weather.

Storms race inland from the Pacific, with accompanying moderate temperatures and precipitation. They crash into weather systems from the north that bring cold temperatures, resulting in snow in the high mountains—even in August. Yet when maritime jet streams chug north into Canada, southern heat waves creep into Montana, Idaho, and Wyoming, shooting the summer thermometer into the 90s or above.

The Northern Rockies region is a land of weather extremes. North of Helena, Montana, Rogers Pass ranks in the top 10 coldest places in the world, alongside Antarctica and Siberia. From Glacier National Park to Helena, the Rocky Mountain Front frequently makes the record books for extreme winds, cold, and heat. Loma recorded the most extreme temperature change in a 24-hour period in the United States when the January thermometer yo-yoed over 100 degrees—from -54°F to 49°F. Lander, Wyoming, ranks in the top 10 snowiest cities in the country. Of all 50 states, Montana holds the record for the most variation in extremes—a 187-degree difference between its record high and low, and Great Falls holds the record for the most rapid temperature change recorded in the United States—47 degrees in seven minutes.

Although precipitation drops equally on both sides of the Continental Divide, wind produces more weather extremes on the east side. While winter winds often blow snow from slopes, providing forage for ungulates, they also have pushed trains off their tracks in East Glacier, Montana. Chinook winds—high warm winds with speeds reaching over 90 miles per hour—blow any time of the year, but they are most obvious in winter. Native Americans called them "snow eaters" for rapidly melting snow. In summer, high passes can rage with unpredictable winds, causing hikers to crawl on all fours across them.

Seasons

The mountains of Montana, Idaho, and Wyoming enjoy four distinct seasons, each with its own quirks. With the appropriate equipment and preparation, you can enjoy camping year-round, even in snow.

SPRING

Spring first enters the lower elevations beginning in late March and April. Winter snow melts, turning miles of dirt roads into mud. Despite March, April, and May typically being appealing off-season months to travel, in the Northern Rockies they are wet and cold, still clinging to winter. Weather bounces between soggy rains one day and 70-degree blue skies the next. Snow buries the high country, including scenic routes such as Going-to-the-Sun Road in Glacier National Park and the Beartooth Highway to Yellowstone National Park. May still brings tempestuous storms to the mountains, with rains and snows increasing the potential for avalanches and mudslides, but stretches of sunny days hint at summer. Spring temperatures range from the mid-50s to the mid-70s with nighttime lows 20-40°F.

SUMMER

Summer brings the most campers to the national parks and forests, but the mountainous terrain of the Northern Rockies often reels with its own weather agenda. While cool breezes are welcome on baking summer days, they can also bring snows to the mountains in August. During summer months, June habitually has monsoons, but July and August usher in warmer, drier skies. Temperatures run at a pleasant 70-80°F with very little humidity. Most areas will see several days each summer in the 90s (locals consider anything over 90°F to be sweltering), but rarely does the thermometer stretch up to triple digits. Nighttime lows dip into the 40s and 50s.

FALL

The first frosts usually descend in September. Autumn's cool nights usher in warm, bug-free days. While shades of gold paint aspen and larch trees, temperatures bounce through

extremes—from warm shorts-wearing weather during the day to below freezing at night. Plenty of 70-degree days keep summer outdoor recreation alive as schizophrenic weather jerks between rain with snow at higher elevations for a few days followed by clear, warming trends. Daytime highs vacillate between the 40s and 60s, and nighttime lows dip to the 20s.

WINTER

Although winter temperatures vary by elevation, most of the Northern Rockies hang in the 10-25°F range, producing voluminous snows. Yellowstone National Park sees about 150 inches of snowfall, but Logan Pass in Glacier National Park is buried under 350-700 inches of snow. Temperatures can spike above freezing, with its companion rain, or plummet below zero for several days with an arctic front.

DAYLIGHT AND TIME

Given the northern latitude and placement of Montana and Wyoming on the Mountain Time Zone's west edge, hours of daylight fluctuate wildly during the year. In June, more than 16 hours of daylight floods the mountains. First light fades in around 5am, and dark doesn't descend until almost 11pm. By late August, darkness drops by 9pm with daylight cruising on a shorter ride until December's slim 8.5 hours of daylight. Around the winter solstice, the sun rises around 8am and sets at 4:30pm. The Idaho Panhandle, which operates on Pacific time, sees both daylight and darkness an hour earlier.

ELEVATION

Because of the mountainous terrain, temperatures vary by elevation. Mountaintops are cooler than valley floors—up to 15 degrees cooler. Boaters may enjoy 82-degree weather camping on Montana's Flathead Lake in August, while hikers less than 60 air miles away in Glacier National Park hit trails with temperatures in the high 60s. Yellowstone National Park sits on a high-elevation plateau with most of the park above 7,500 feet, and the highest campgrounds on Wyoming's Beartooth Plateau top out at 9,600 feet. Campgrounds in these locations are substantially cooler than those at lower elevations, such as Montana's Missouri Headwaters State Park at 4,045 feet.

Weather

Locals have a saying about the weather in the Northern Rockies: "Wait five minutes, and the weather will change." The mountain terrain lends itself to wild swings in weather. You can begin hiking in shorts but by afternoon be pulling on gloves and fleece hats as gray clouds lob down sheets of sleet. Calm, glassy lakes can give way to four-foot whitecaps as storms blow in.

LIGHTNING AND THUNDERSTORMS

Afternoon thundershowers and lightning storms are common across much of the Northern Rocky Mountains. In some locations—particularly around Yellowstone National Park and Wyoming's Beartooth Plateau—they roll in daily in late afternoon, almost like clockwork. During lightning storms, boaters should exit the water, and those enjoying beaches should move to sheltered locations. Hikers should descend from summits, ridges, and exposed slopes, and stay away from isolated trees. Some thunderstorms bring hail; others dump pelting rains.

WINDS

The Continental Divide causes high winds. With eastern air masses trying to equalize with western jet streams, the result is strong winds optimal for wind farms. But the open, eastern slopes of the Continental Divide can pose tricky driving for large RVs, with wind gusts threatening to push them off the road. Likewise, treeless campgrounds on the prairie often bluster with winds. Montana's Rocky Mountain Front and the Absaroka Front receive the most notorious winds, on an average day blowing 7-20 mph with gusts up to 50 mph.

PRECIPITATION

While Montana, Wyoming, and Idaho are drier than the Pacific Northwest, their mountain areas receive substantial precipitation. The amount depends largely upon topography. Across the area, most snow falls November-March, but heavy snowstorms can occur as early as mid-September or as late as May—especially in the high mountains. Annual snowfall averages 300 inches in many of the mountain ranges—hence the region's numerous ski resorts. Valley floors receive about 50 inches of snowfall. Nearly half of the region's annual average precipitation falls from May through July in the form of valley rain, sleet, or snow. Heavy rains falling during the spring thaw contribute to early summer avalanches and flooding.

FOREST FIRES

Like snow, wind, or rain, lightning-caused fire is a natural process. It is healthy for the ecosystem, removing bug infestations, reducing deadfall and nonnative plants, releasing nutrients into the soil like a good fertilizer, and maintaining a natural mix of vegetation. Following decades of heavy fire suppression, forest fuels have built up across the Northern Rockies. Some forests suffer under severe attacks from pine beetles and blister rust. Those conditions kill trees and make them ripe for fire. You can check on current forest fire locations and their status at www.inciweb.org.

CAMPING CONCERNS
Camping Regulations and Red Tape

NATIONAL PARKS

National parks are set aside for their historical, geological, cultural, or biological significance, and geared toward public recreation. Hunting is not permitted; neither is picking wildflowers nor picking berries for commercial use. Dogs are not allowed on trails; neither are mountain bikes. Camping is limited to designated campgrounds with 7-14 days in one campsite, unless otherwise posted. Permits are needed for backcountry camping. National parks require entrance fees, and each campground requires fees.

Waterton Lakes National Park in Canada borders Glacier National Park and is used to access parts of Glacier. U.S. national park passes are not valid in Waterton. In fact, passports are required to drive to Waterton, and passports are required to boat or walk down Waterton Lake to hike from Goat Haunt USA.

NATIONAL FORESTS

National forests are used for their resources, with timber harvesting, commercial berry picking, mushroom harvesting, mining, and recreation permitted. Hunting is permitted with licenses administered by each state. Trails permit dogs and mountain bikes as long as no special designation says otherwise. Designated campgrounds usually allow stays up to 14-16 days in the same campsite; a few high-use areas employ shorter limits. Unless otherwise designated, primitive camping is usually permitted anywhere outside of developed campgrounds. Permits are not needed for backcountry camping. National forests usually do not charge entrance fees, but some specific visitor sites do. Some developed campgrounds require fees; others are free, as is primitive camping.

Wilderness areas are administered usually by the national forest that contains the wilderness. They permit no mechanical transports, including mountain bikes. Hunting is permitted. Fido can go along on the trail, and permits are not needed for backcountry camping, which is free.

OTHER GOVERNMENT LANDS

Bureau of Land Management and Bureau of Reclamation terrain operates much like national forest land, with most developed campgrounds charging fees. Entrance fees are usually not charged; however, some sites charge day-use fees. Stays are limited to 14 days in the same spot, unless posted otherwise. Free primitive camping is permitted outside of developed campgrounds.

Montana, Wyoming, and Idaho **state parks** vary in campgrounds and amenities under the auspices of each state. State parks charge fees for day use and camping. Most campground fees include day use, too. Camping is permitted in a Montana or Wyoming state park for 14 days; in Idaho, the limit is 15 days.

Camping with Children

Children learn to enjoy camping when they can participate in activities. Have them help with camp chores—building fires, collecting garbage, and bear-proofing the camp.

Kids can earn **Junior Ranger Badges** by completing self-guided activities in Glacier, Yellowstone, and Teton National Parks. Activities, which target ages 5-12, vary by park but are an excellent way to help children learn about the park and wildlife. Junior Ranger activity books or newspapers are available at all visitors centers in the parks. They can also be downloaded online under each national park (www.nps.gov). When kids return the completed newspaper to any visitors center, they are sworn in as Junior Rangers and receive park-specific badges.

Plan ahead with kids by taking along extra clothing and shoes. If kids can get wet, they will. Replacing wet soggy clothing with warm dry gear improves their attitude and their enjoyment of camping. When hiking, even for short walks, take along water and snacks to maintain the energy level for children.

Camping with Pets
NATIONAL PARKS

Pets are allowed in national parks, but only in limited areas. They are allowed in campgrounds, roadsides, and parking lots on a six-foot or shorter leash or in a cage. With the exception of Waterton Lakes National Park north of Glacier, pets are not permitted on national park trails, to protect fragile vegetation or thermal areas and to prevent conflicts with wildlife. Bears are a major argument for leaving the pooch home. Pets are also not permitted in visitors centers or at beaches. Pets can stay in your vehicle while you are viewing roadside attractions, but you must provide ventilation for the animal's survival.

NATIONAL FORESTS

National forests permit pets on most trails. (Read trailhead signs as some trails do not permit pets.) Keep in mind that many hikers in the Northern Rockies have heightened sensitivity to movement, as they're on alert for bears. To prevent bear conflicts and to avoid scaring other hikers with a dog charging down the trail, keep Fido on a leash. Pets are also allowed in campgrounds, but they must be leashed, rather than running free.

In bear country, store pet food, bowls, and toys in a hard-sided vehicle or bear box when not in use. Like humans, pets should leave no trace other than footprints. Clean up and dispose of all pet feces in the garbage.

Camping Ethics

Protection of public lands and campgrounds is up to those of us who use them. Be respectful of nature and campground facilities, taking care of them as if they were your own. Follow Leave No Trace ethics when camping in developed campgrounds or the backcountry.

LEAVE NO TRACE

Visitors to the Northern Rockies need to take an active role in maintaining the environment.

Plan ahead and prepare. Plan ahead for camping by keeping in mind fluctuating weather, and choose appropriate hiking routes for mileage and elevation gain. Carry hiking essentials.

Travel and camp on durable surfaces. In both developed and backcountry campgrounds, camp in designated sites only. Protect fragile trailside plants by staying on the trail, refusing to cut switchbacks, and walking single file on trails even in the mud. If you must walk off-trail, step on rocks, snow, or dry grasses rather than on wet soils and fragile plants.

Leave what you find. Flowers, rocks, and goat fur tufts on shrubs are protected resources in national parks. Even on other public lands, they should be left for others to enjoy. For lunch stops and camping, sit on rocks or logs where you find them rather than moving them to accommodate your camp.

Properly dispose of waste. Whatever you bring in, you must pack out or deposit in garbage receptacles. Do not burn garbage in fire pits. If toilets are not available, urinate on rocks, logs, gravel, or snow to protect fragile soils and plants from salt-starved wildlife. Bury feces 6-8 inches deep at least 200 feet from water. Pack out used toilet paper in your trash.

Minimize campfire impacts. Make fires in designated fire pits only. Use small, wrist-size dead and down wood, not live branches. Be aware that fires or firewood collecting is not permitted in many places in national parks.

Respect wildlife. Bring along binoculars, spotting scopes, and telephoto lenses to aid in watching wildlife. Keep your distance. Do not feed any wildlife, even ground squirrels. Once fed, they become more aggressive. Maintain a distance of a football-field length from bears and wolves and 25 yards from all other wildlife.

Be considerate of other visitors. Minimize use of electronics, generators, and other noisemakers in campgrounds, and keep dogs from barking. Follow posted quiet hours, departing and arriving as silently as possible before or after hours.

RECREATION
Hiking

The Northern Rockies are crisscrossed with hiking trails—some short day-hike destinations and others stringing long miles back into remote wilderness areas. Montana's Bob Marshall Wilderness and Yellowstone National Park each contain over 1,000 miles of trails, while Glacier National Park contains over 700 miles of trails. Outfitters are available for guided hiking and backpacking in Glacier, Grand Teton, and Yellowstone National Parks. Though links still remain to be built, the Continental Divide Trail forms the longest trail system, running through Wyoming's Wind River Range, Yellowstone National Park, several national forests and wilderness areas in Montana, and Glacier National Park.

TRAILS AND SIGNS

Conditions on trails vary depending on the season, elevation, weather, and wildlife. In places where swinging or plank bridges are removed annually across rivers and creeks, crews reinstall them in late May or early June. Steep snowfields inhibit hiking at higher elevations until July. Avalanches and severe storms—wind microbursts, heavy snows, and torrential rains—can cause miles of downed trees across trails. Depending on the location, crews may or may not be available for immediate clearing. Some trails in Glacier, Grand Teton, and Yellowstone National Parks are closed temporarily because of increased bear activity. Yellowstone also has annual closures in feeding areas. To find out about trail conditions before hiking, stop at ranger stations and visitors centers for updates. In general, trails in the national parks are maintained in better condition than in national forests, which lack funding for bigger trail crews.

National park trails tend to be well signed with direction and mileage. Some signs, however, may be in kilometers, rather than miles. (To convert kilometers to miles, multiply the kilometers listed by 0.6.) National forests and wilderness areas tend to have less specific signage and fewer signs. Carry a good map and a compass or GPS to navigate the maze of trails. In the Northern Rockies, some trails have names while others use numbers with or without names. The numbers, which are assigned by the Forest Service, identify the trails on USFS maps and many topographical maps of the region.

In the national parks, where the concentration of bears is high, you may also see **bear warning signs.** Use extreme caution and all your bear country savvy when bears frequent a trail. Obey closures: They usually mean that

hikers on the Piegan Trail in Glacier National Park

a bear has been aggressive or is feeding on a carcass, which it will forcefully defend.

BACKCOUNTRY CAMPING

Backcountry camping is by permit only in Glacier, Grand Teton, and Yellowstone National Parks. Backcountry campgrounds vary in size, but most separate sleeping sites from communal cooking areas. No food, garbage, toiletries, or cookware should ever be kept in the tent sites. Near the cook sites, a bear pole, bar, or box allows for safe food storage. Take along a 30-foot rope and stuff bags to hang your food in Glacier and Yellowstone; backpackers in Grand Teton are required to carry bear-resistant food containers, available for free. Many backcountry campsites do not allow fires. Carry a lightweight stove for cooking.

To plan backcountry camping trips by foot, horseback, or boat in Glacier, Grand Teton, or Yellowstone National Park, follow the directions in each park's Backcountry Trip Planner, available online (www.nps.gov/glac, www.nps.gov/grte, www.nps.gov/yell). Permits may be

HIKING ESSENTIALS

Hiking in the Northern Rockies of Montana, Wyoming, and Idaho demands preparedness. High elevations, unpredictable winds, fast-changing weather, and summer snowstorms can catapult a lazy day walk into a nightmare if one is not prepared. Take the following:

Extra clothing: Rain pants and jackets can double as wind protection while gloves and a lightweight warm hat will save fingers and ears. Carry at least one extra water-wicking layer for warmth. Avoid cotton fabrics that stay soggy and fail to retain body heat, opting instead for synthetics.

Extra food and water: Take lunch and snacks, like compact high-energy food bars. Low-odor foods will not attract animals. Heat, wind, and elevation dehydrate hikers quickly; always carry extra water. Don't drink directly from streams or lakes because of the bacteria; always filter or treat water sources before drinking.

Navigation: Although national park trails are well signed, national forest and wilderness trails are not. Take a detailed topographical map of the area to ascertain the distance traveled and location. A compass or GPS will also help, but only if you know how to use them.

Flashlight: Carry a small flashlight or headlamp with extra batteries. In an after-dark emergency, the light becomes invaluable.

First-aid kit: Two Band-Aids are not enough! Carry a fully equipped standard first-aid kit with blister remedies. Don't forget personal requirements such as bee-sting kits and allergy medications.

Sun protection: Altitude, snow, ice, and lakes all increase ultraviolet radiation. Protect yourself with 30 SPF sunscreen, sunglasses, and a sunhat or baseball cap.

Emergency bathroom supplies: To accommodate alfresco bathrooms, carry a small trowel, plastic bags, and toilet paper. Move at least 200 feet away from water sources. For urinating, aim for a durable surface, such as rocks, logs, gravel, or snow, rather than fragile plants, campsites, or trails. Bury feces 6-8 inches deep in soil. Pack the toilet paper out in a Ziploc bag.

Feminine hygiene: Carry heavy-duty Ziploc bags for packing tampons and pads out rather than burying them.

Insect repellent: Insect repellents containing 50 percent DEET work best with the mosquitoes and black flies. Purchase applications that rub or spray in a close range rather than aerosols that become airborne onto other people, plants, and animals.

Pepper spray: Use an eight-ounce can of pepper spray for charging bears, but do not bother unless you know how to use it and what influences its effectiveness. It is not to be used like bug repellent.

Cell phones: Take the cell phone along for emergencies, but don't rely on it for rescue. In many mountains and canyons, cell phones do not work. Plan to self-rescue. If you do carry a cell phone, turn it off to save the batteries for an emergency and to avoid offending fellow hikers who seek solitude, quiet, and the sounds of nature.

Miscellaneous: Pack along a knife, a few feet of nylon cord, and duct tape wrapped around a flashlight handle. Many hikers have repaired boots and packs with duct tape and a little ingenuity.

reserved by mail for $25-30 (a limited number of sites are assigned this way, and you still have to pay your per person fee when you pick up the actual permit), or you can pick up permits in person, no more than 24 hours in advance. Permits are not issued over the phone. Permits are free except in Glacier ($5 per person per night). Permits are not needed for backpacking in national forests or wilderness areas.

In addition to a rope for hanging food, backcountry campers should take a small screen or strainer for sifting food particles out of gray water, a water purifier, and a small trowel for human waste when a pit toilet is unavailable.

Mountaineering and Climbing

The peaks of Montana, Idaho, and Wyoming draw mountaineers for their rugged, challenging routes to the summits. The quality of the rock varies between crumbling sedimentary shales in the north and harder granitic rocks in the south, making the type of climbing different. Ice routes, too, are shrinking because of the rapid melting of the region's glaciers. Mountaineers shimmy routes up through most of the region's mountain ranges, but a few specific locales gain above-average reputations. Area-specific books include route descriptions of popular ascents.

While technical rock-climbing routes are available in Glacier National Park, the bulk of the summits are reached via Class 3 or 4 scrambles. Long, loose scree fields lead to tight goat walks along cliffs. Even though more technical routes exist, all six summits over 10,000 feet can be reached via scrambles. You're on your own, though, as the park has no permitted guides for off-trail scrambles.

Teton National Park harbors the region's best technical rock-climbing opportunities. With over 50 major routes to the summit, the Grand Teton tops the Northern Rockies' highest elevation at 13,770 feet. Two companies in Jackson offer instruction and guided trips to Teton summits—including the Grand. Other popular rock-climbing routes string down the Wind River Mountains, particularly Cirque of the Towers in the Popo Agie Wilderness.

With the glaciers across the Northern Rockies fast melting into extinction, the routes that utilize ice are changing. However, winter ascents on skis and ice climbing are available.

Bicycling
ROAD BIKING
Road bicyclists relish the Northern Rockies for the long dramatic climbs over the Continental Divide and the miles of pedal-free descents. The **TransAmerica Trail** cuts through the region as does the **Lewis and Clark Trail,** among other long-distance rides. Route descriptions and maps are available from Missoula's Adventure Cycling Association (800/721-8719, www.adventurecycling.org).

Narrow, curvy roads with no shoulders and drivers gawking at scenery instead of the road all shove the biker into a precarious position. Wear a helmet and bright colors to ensure your safety.

Two scenic byways rank with bicyclists for their challenge and their scenery. In Glacier National Park, the 52-mile **Going-to-the-Sun Road** is a biker must-do. Early-season up-and-back riding is available in spring and fall while plowing and road construction has the route closed to vehicles. Once the road is open (mid-June-mid-Sept.), bicycling restrictions close two narrow sections of the road on the west side 11am-4pm until Labor Day. Eastbound riders must be at Logan Pass by 11am or dismount and wait.

Starting from Red Lodge, Montana, the 68-mile **Beartooth Highway** climbs a lung-busting route up to 10,947 feet to cross Beartooth Pass on a high tundra plateau. Riding westbound toward Yellowstone National Park lets you get the full wow of the snowcapped peaks of the Absaroka Range. The route, which bounces from Montana into Wyoming and back into Montana, passes scads of lakes, which produce mosquito swarms into August that plague bicyclists. Snow buries the highway much of the year, but it usually is open late May to mid-October.

For riders looking for flat spins instead, Idaho's 72-mile paved **Trail of the Coeur d'Alenes** runs from Mullan to Plummer, following rivers, passing wetlands brimming with wildlife, and crossing the Chacolet Bridge. Interpretive signs, picnic areas, and rest stations dot the route, which changes so little in elevation that you're never sure if you're riding uphill or down. The trail is usually snow-free April-November. Several resort locations also have extensive paved bike trail systems, including Sun Valley and Jackson Hole.

Glacier, Yellowstone, and Grand Teton National Parks maintain a few campsites at most of their campgrounds for bicyclists. The shared first-come, first-served campsites ($5-8 per person) have bear boxes for storing food and room for several small tents.

bicyclists on Going-to-the-Sun Road in Glacier National Park

MOUNTAIN BIKING

As single-track mountain bike trails are sprouting up around the region faster than weeds, rail trail projects are converting defunct tracks into wide bike paths. Idaho's 15-mile **Route of the Hiawatha** (208/744-1301, www.ridethehiawatha.com), the region's most popular mountain bike trail, crosses seven trestles and rides through nine dark tunnels, with the longest (1.7 miles) running under the Idaho-Montana state line. The Route of the Hiawatha (open late May-early Oct.) also offers a shuttle for those who only want to ride downhill. Eastern Idaho's 42-mile **Railroad Right of Way Trail** also runs from Warm River to West Yellowstone.

Many national forest trails permit bicycles, except in wildernesses or areas with special designations. Mountain bikes are not permitted on national park trails, except for special routes designated in each national park. Ski resorts, such as Big Sky, Whitefish, Sun Valley, and Jackson Hole, also have mountain biking trails, some with lift-served access for downhill riding.

Fishing

The movie *A River Runs Through It* catapulted Montana's rivers into the national consciousness with dreams of clear waters and wild trout. But that's the true nature of fly-fishing in the Northern Rockies, which harbor 18 blue-ribbon trout streams populated with rainbow, brown, brook, Yellowstone cutthroat, westslope cutthroat, and bull trout—many wild. Lowland lakes also fill with lake trout (mackinaw), kokanee salmon, northern pike, and bass.

NATIONAL PARK FISHING

Each of the national parks has different licensing regulations for fishing. Glacier requires no license. Yellowstone requires a fishing permit for anglers 16 years and older ($18 for three days, $25 for seven days, or $40 for a season); anglers 15 and younger may fish free under a supervising adult's permit or their own permit. Grand Teton requires a Wyoming fishing license. Waterton requires a national park fishing license (one day C$10 or annual C$35).

Buy national park fishing licenses at ranger stations and visitors centers.

Each park has slightly different fishing regulations with seasons, catch-and-release laws, closure locations, and creel limits designed to protect the resources. You'll need to be able to identify species that are catch-and-release only—especially the endangered bull trout. Fishing regulations are available online and at ranger stations and visitors centers.

STATE FISHING LICENSES

Outside the national parks, state fishing licenses are required. Some states offer discounts for seniors and those who are disabled. Kids often can fish free. Licenses are available online and at sporting goods stores. The one exception is on Indian reservations; each has its own tribal fishing permits and rates.

Montana fishing licenses (http://fwp.mt.gov) cost $13 for two days or $26 per season for resident adults ages 15-61. Teens ages 15-17 can get a season license for $16. Resident seniors age 62 and older and kids ages 12-14 only need an $8 conservation license. Nonresident licenses for ages 15 and older, including seniors, cost $25 for two days, $54 for 10 days, or $60 for the season. Additional permits are required for warm-water game fish, paddlefish, and bull trout.

Idaho fishing licenses (http://fishandgame.idaho.gov) for residents cost $11.50 for a single day and $5 for each consecutive day; for the season, they cost $14 for ages 14-17 and $26 for adults. Nonresident licenses cost $13 for one day and $6 for each consecutive day, or season licenses cost $22 for ages 14-17 and $99 for adults. Nonresidents can also purchase a three-day salmon/steelhead license for $38.

Wyoming fishing licenses (http://wgfd.wyo.gov) cost $6 per day for residents; for the season, they cost $3 for youth and $24 for adults. For nonresidents, a one-day adult license costs $14 and an annual license costs $92. Nonresident youth pay $15 for an annual license.

© BECKY LOMAX

Kids can enjoy fishing in the Northern Rockies.

Boating

Small reservoirs dot the Northern Rockies, but big lakes command most of the boating interest from visitors. Montana's Flathead Lake is the largest freshwater lake west of the Mississippi. Montana, Wyoming, and Idaho require boats to be registered. Rates vary depending on the state and the size of boat. Boats may also need to undergo checks in various waters for aquatic invasive species.

In **Montana,** motorized boats, personal watercraft, and sailboats over 12 feet long must be registered. Nonmotorized smaller sailboats, rowboats, rafts, canoes, and kayaks are exempt. Boats from out of state or country may be used in Montana for up to 90 consecutive days without registering.

Wyoming requires motorized boats to be registered. Motorboats that are properly registered in another state may be used on Wyoming's waters for up to 90 consecutive days without registration.

Idaho requires boats with mechanical

propulsion to be registered. Boats currently registered in another state may be used on Idaho's waterways for 60 consecutive days or less without registering.

National parks have their own boating permits, but costs vary depending on the park. Glacier and Waterton parks issue free permits to boats that pass the aquatic invasive species inspection. Boat permits cost $5-10 in Yellowstone or $20-40 in Grand Teton.

WATERSKIING

Water-skiers from warm-water areas often are shocked by their first contact with the chilly Northern Rockies. Water is cold—frigid in places. The ice-fed deep lakes maintain a chill even in summer. Surface water may only heat up in August into the low 60s, if that. Bring a wetsuit for more enjoyable waterskiing. Yellowstone does not permit waterskiing, and Jet skis are not allowed in Glacier, Yellowstone, or Grand Teton parks.

Swimming

You can swim in any lake in the Northern Rockies; however, buoy-rimmed swimming areas with lifeguards are rare. In most lakes, you swim at your own risk. Prepare for frigid cold water, even in midsummer, as snowmelt and glacial runoff feed the lakes. Plus, they are only ice-free for a portion of the year.

Use caution when swimming in rivers. Slick algae-covered rocks and swift-moving currents can be lethal. In Glacier National Park, drowning is the number one cause of accidental death.

Rafting

The Northern Rockies spill with Class III-V white water, frothy waves with big holes. Other Class I-II rivers make for more leisurely float trips. Thirteen major rivers contain Class III and above white-water sections that you can run on your own if you have the expertise or go with local guides. In Montana, head for the Clark Fork, Middle Fork of the Flathead, Yellowstone, Gallatin, Madison, or Stillwater River for white-water thrills. Where Wyoming's Shoshone, Green, and Snake Rivers squeeze through canyons, you can bounce

rafting on the Middle Fork of the Flathead River in Montana

© BECKY LOMAX

through rapids. In Idaho, the Lochsa, Selway, and Main Salmon provide single-day options for white water, but the Middle Fork of the Salmon requires a multiday trip through the Frank Church-River of No Return Wilderness. Most of these rivers have nearby drive-to campgrounds available, and some are lined with primitive campgrounds for overnight float trips. Check on current water levels through state hydrology departments or American Whitewater (www.americanwhitewater.org).

Floating most of these rivers on an overnight trip does not require a permit. However, Idaho's Selway, Middle Fork of the Salmon, and Main Salmon Rivers do. These are acquired via an annual computerized lottery drawing. You can apply for all three rivers with one application (877/444-6777, www.recreation.gov). Permits are not available by phone, except for acquiring permits from cancelled launches after the annual drawing.

Outfitters guide trips on most of the Northern Rockies' major rivers and some of their tributaries. Trips include half-day, full-day, and multiday excursions. Locate outfitters in the towns nearest the rivers. Check with state agencies to be sure they are licensed.

Canoeing and Kayaking

The Northern Rockies also harbor lakes and slow-moving rivers—gems for multiday paddling trips. In Montana, the Missouri River through Gates of the Mountains offers paddling along the route of Lewis and Clark, plus hiking and camping. Connected lakes, such as Idaho's Priest Lake and Upper Priest Lake, include camping on islands as well as paddling the two-mile Thoroughfare to the upper lake. A paddle route around Montana's Flathead Lake makes use of six state parks. Glacier, Yellowstone, and Teton National Parks offer large lakes with overnight paddling campgrounds.

Canoes and kayaks are available to rent in select places, but to guarantee you have a boat, bring your own or call ahead to reserve the rental. Rentals and guided paddle trips are available in Yellowstone and Grand Teton National Parks; Glacier has only rentals.

National parks require permits for non-motorized watercraft. Glacier requires a free self-inspection permit. Permits cost $5-10 in Yellowstone or $10-20 in Grand Teton.

GEAR SELECTION AND MAINTENANCE

Camping in the Northern Rocky Mountains requires planning for all types of weather and conditions. The proper equipment can make the difference between enjoying a trip when the temperatures plummet or the air drips soggy and hating the experience.

Tents

Tents come in a variety of shapes, sizes, weights, and prices—tailored to different types of camping. Any reputable outdoor store will provide comparative ratings for their tents. Considering elevation, erratic weather, and the potential for snow even in August, tents for the Northern Rockies should be double walled—with a tent wall and a rain fly that covers the complete tent to the ground. Purchase a tent with sealed seams to prevent water seeping into the tent. Bug netting is also essential for the voracious mosquitoes and black flies that proliferate during June and July. While many campers go without footprints or tarps below their tents, in wet, muddy conditions or snow, ground cloths can keep the tent floor dry. They also will prolong the life of a tent. Three-season tents work the best in the Northern Rockies for camping in summer, spring, or fall. But for winter camping, invest in a four-season tent.

After use, dry tents completely before storing to prevent mildew. They also should be stored in a dry location rather than a damp garage, attic, or crawl space. If possible, store them loose rather than folded or rolled up tight to prevent breakdown of the fabric on the folds.

© BECKY LOMAX

Daypacks should be large enough to carry essentials, first aid, and extra clothing.

Sleeping Bags and Pads

Sleeping bags are sold with synthetic or goose down insulation. Either works well in the Northern Rockies, although goose-down bag owners need to take extra precaution to keep the bags dry to prevent the down from losing its insulation value. Invest in a waterproof stuff sack to keep sleeping bags dry. Bags for summer camping should be rated to 20°F; however, if you plan on camping in spring or fall in the Northern Rockies, you'll be more prepared for the weather mood swings with a bag rated to zero. Mummy bag cuts as opposed to rectangular bags will allow your body to heat up the space faster.

A sleeping bag alone will not keep you warm without an insulating layer between the ground and your body. Sleeping pads range from a thin 0.5-inch layer of foam to large thick air mattresses that require a compressor to inflate. Assess your needs before purchasing. If backpacking, go for the lightest weight in foam or inflatable. If car camping, you can afford to pack along more weight. Self-inflating

and blow-up air mattresses allow you to camp more quietly than if you must turn on an air compressor.

Both sleeping bags and pads should be stored loose to extend their life as long as possible. A tall closet works well for hanging both. Launder sleeping bags according to the manufacturer's instruction.

Day Packs

If you plan on hiking on your camping trip, bring along a day pack. While you can get away with carrying just a water bottle for a one-hour hike, you should be prepared for the weather to change on longer day hikes. Mountain weather can mutate from blue skies to rain squalls, raging winds, hail, and even snow during summer. Bring a day pack that can fit extra clothing—rain jacket and pants, warm hat, gloves, and a light fleece layer. Your pack should also be able to fit lunch, snacks, first-aid kit, sunscreen, bug juice, headlamp, and water. Consider the size of optional items you may enjoy, such as a camera and binoculars.

Good day packs will include small padded hip belts to keep the weight from pulling on your neck. Hip belts also work for attaching pepper spray holders for bears. Try day packs on for size in the store, as different brands work better for different body types. Air out packs after use and store them in a dry location.

Food and Cooking Gear

Cooking while camping can be as simple as boiling water for quick instant freeze-dried meals or as involved as slow roasting on the fire. Your mode of travel will most likely dictate choices in cooking. If backpacking, bicycling, kayaking, or canoeing, quick-cooking meals require less gas, they weigh less, and they need fewer pots. Slow roasting on the fire requires aluminum foil, aluminum pots, or Dutch ovens. Traveling by RV, car, or boat allows for more room to pack along meals that are entertaining to cook. Virtually any recipe can be adapted to cooking outdoors with a little ingenuity. In bear country, low-odor foods mean less scent to attract wildlife.

Stoves and cooking pots also come in a variety of sizes to suit different uses. Smaller versions are available for backpacking, kayaking, and canoeing, while larger, heavier options are only suitable for vehicle-assisted camping. Most stoves are heated with white gas or propane, easy to find in the Northern Rockies. Butane canisters are convenient, but replacements may not be as easy to find, and they add to landfills. Most outdoor lightweight cooking pots are now available with nonstick surfaces.

Water Treatment

While the water in developed campgrounds is usually safe to drink, most streams and lakes in the West run the risk of carrying giardia and cryptosporidium, the two most common cysts. At campgrounds where potable water is not available, purify or boil water to kill potential trouble causers.

Boiling water requires no extra equipment—just a stove and extra fuel. The Wilderness Medical Society recommends heating the water to a rapid boil for one minute to kill microorganisms.

Water filters and purifiers pump water by hand through filters that are rated to strain out certain sizes of critters. A 1.0-micron filter will remove giardia and cryptosporidium, but a 0.2-micron filter will also remove bacteria while a 0.0004-micron purifier will remove viruses, too.

Chemical treatments include the use of chlorine or iodine tablets, crystals, or liquid. Follow the manufacturer's instructions for their use, most of which require waiting 30 minutes before drinking. While many campers dislike the taste left from iodine, it can work as a backup in an emergency.

UV light is now available in a compact instrument about the size of an electric toothbrush for killing microorganisms. Immerse the light tube into the water for 60 seconds. Batteries are required.

What to Wear
LAYERS
Dress in layers to adapt to the quick-changing

© SABRINA YOUNG

a standard Coleman propane stove

mountain conditions and weather. Mornings can start with blue skies and temperatures for T-shirts and shorts, but by afternoon, winds can usher in storm fronts delivering hail and even snow. The opposite can happen, too, with frosty mornings warming by afternoon. Layers allow adapting to the changing conditions by putting on additional clothing for protection from the elements or taking a layer off to cool down. Prepare for mountain extremes by packing a fleece or wool hat and gloves.

SUN PROTECTION
The sun's intensity increases at high elevations. With much of the Northern Rocky Mountains stretching above 6,000 feet in elevation, protection from the glaring sun is important for preventing blistering sunburns. Add white snowfields and glaciers to the elevation, and the sun's rays wax more intense. Ball caps or sun hats protect the face from the sun's scorching rays, and sunglasses will protect the eyes from burns and snow blindness.

RAIN GEAR
Breathable rain gear is essential camp clothing for the Northern Rockies. Breathable rain fabrics let you recreate outdoors without getting as wet beneath your jacket as outside of it. Both rain shells and pants are useful, especially when hiking in brushy meadows laden with moisture. Armpit zippers let you adjust the ventilation of shells. Hoods allow for closing off the neck area to chilling wet winds, and ankle zippers on pants allow for putting them on and taking them off without removing your hiking boots.

SHOES, SOCKS, AND FOOT CARE
Footwear needs to adapt to the activities you plan to do while camping. Hikers need boots with a sturdy tread, which are available in lightweight, waterproof, and leather options. Ill-fitting shoes and incorrect socks cause blisters—preventable by shoe choice and fit. Squished toes and loose heels are the biggest culprits for blisters. To prevent toes from blistering by rubbing on each other, a shoe with a larger toe box is essential. If heels fit too loosely, two remedies can prevent blisters: Wearing one liner sock inside a heavier sock allows socks to rub against each other rather than against the heels, and footbeds (either custom or market-ready) will absorb excess space and provide more support for the foot.

Appropriate socks can also prevent blisters. Although cotton socks feel good, they aren't the best choice for hiking. Cotton absorbs water from the feet and holds it, providing a surface for friction. Synthetic, silk, or wool blend socks wick water away from the skin. Socks should fit smoothly over the feet with no added bunching. A comfortable fit, but not loose, is paramount for preventing blisters.

Those including water sports in their itineraries should also bring sturdy water sandals or shoes that will protect the feet on rough algae-slick rocks. Flip-flops do not protect the feet; use sandals or water shoes with a thick, solid tread. During spring and fall, booties will keep the feet warm in chilly waters.

SAFETY AND FIRST AID
Plants
POISON IVY
Montana, Wyoming, and Idaho have pockets of poison ivy. Recognize the below-knee-height plant by its three leaves, often tinged with red and clustering in river corridors. If your skin comes into contact with poison ivy, wash immediately with soap and water. Do not scratch infected areas as it can spread. Avoid contact with eyes, mouth, and open sores. If you have a reaction, an antihistamine can relieve symptoms. Seek medical help.

NETTLES AND COW PARSNIP
Lush, forested slopes of the Northern Rockies sprout with two irritating plants. Stinging nettles vary in height 2-4 feet. Recognize them by the serrated-edged leaves and minuscule flowers hanging on a drooping stem. If skin comes into contact with nettles, you can use sting-relief products such as those for

mosquito bites. Calamine lotion also provides relief. Some people react to cow parsnip. Recognize the plants by their 10-inch-diameter heads of white flowers and gigantic leaves shaped like maple leaves. Reactions can vary from redness to blistering. For the latter, seek medical help.

Mosquitoes and Ticks

Bugs are irritants, but more importantly, they can carry diseases such as West Nile virus and Rocky Mountain spotted fever. Protect yourself by wearing long sleeves and pants as well as using bug repellents in spring and summer when mosquitoes and ticks are common. Also, avoid areas heavily trafficked by ungulates (deer, sheep, elk), which transport ticks. If a tick bites you, remove it and disinfect the bite; keep your eye on it for lesions or a rash, consulting a doctor if either appears.

Wildlife

Bears

Safety in bear country starts with knowledge and appropriate behavior. With the exception of Alaska and Canada, the Northern Rockies harbor the highest density of grizzly bears, and black bears find likable habitat here, too. For safety while watching bears, maintain the distance of a football field between you.

Hike safely by making vocal noise on the trails. Do not rely on the bells sold in gift shops to alert bears to your presence. Guides jokingly call them "dinner bells." Bells are ineffective and incur wrathful glares from hikers who loathe them. To check the bells' effectiveness out hiking, see how close you are to oncoming hikers before you hear their ringing. Sometimes, it's too close! Bear bells are best as a souvenir, not as a substitution for human noise on the trail. Talk, sing, hoot, and holler. You'll feel silly at first, but after a while, you'll realize it's something everyone does.

Many hikers carry **pepper spray** to deter aggressive, attacking bears. They are not repellents like bug sprays to be sprayed on the human body, tents, or gear. Instead, spray the capsicum derivative directly into a bear's face, aiming for the eyes and nose. While pepper sprays have repelled some attacking bears, wind and rain may reduce effectiveness, as will the product's age. Small, purse-sized pepper sprays are not adequate for bears; carry an eight-ounce can, which can be purchased in most outdoor stores in the Northern Rockies, and practice how to use it. Pepper spray is not protection: Carrying it does not lessen the need for making noise in bear country. Pepper sprays are not allowed by airlines unless checked in luggage, and only brands with USEPA labels may cross through Canadian customs.

Bears are dangerous around food—be it a carcass a bruin may be guarding in the woods or a cooler left in a campsite. Protecting bears and protecting yourself starts with being conscious of food, including wrappers and crumbs. Tidbits dropped along the trail attract wildlife, as do "biodegradable" apple cores chucked into the forest. Pick up what you drop and pack out all garbage, so you will not be leaving a Hansel and Gretel trail for bears.

Mountain Lions

Mostly unseen because of their nocturnal wanderings, these large cats are a sight to behold in daylight. They rarely prey on humans, but they can—especially small kids. While hiking, make noise to avoid surprising a lion. Hike with others, and keep kids close. If you do stumble upon a lion, do not run. Be calm. Group together and look big, waving arms overhead. Look at the cat from peripheral vision rather than staring straight on as you back slowly away. If the lion attacks, fight back with everything: rocks, sticks, or kicking.

Bison, Moose, and Other Wildlife

Bison can be as dangerous as bears. Gorings frequently occur despite the docile appearance of the animals. Moose also can be lethal with both antlers and hooves. For safety, maintain a distance of 25 yards from most wildlife and 100 yards from bears and wolves.

CAMPING IN BEAR COUNTRY

Prime grizzly bear habitat and black bear territory makes up most of the Northern Rocky Mountains. Where bears are plentiful, campgrounds require strict food- and garbage-management practices. Even in areas with less frequent bear visitation, properly storing food and garbage prevents problems with other wildlife, such as deer, squirrels, jays, and rodents.

- When not in immediate use, store all food, meat, cooking appliances, utensils, pots, pans, canned foods, toiletries, and empty or full food storage containers in a closed, hard-sided vehicle during the day and at night. Coolers and beverage containers should also be stored inside vehicles, as should garbage.

- For campers traveling on bicycles, motorcycles, or open vehicles, many campgrounds provide brown metal food lockers or **bear boxes** for storing food. Use these to store food, cooking gear, toiletries, and garbage, but do not leave the garbage in the bear box. Dispose of it properly in a bear-resistant trash container. In case bear boxes are not available, carry 30 feet of rope for hanging food supplies. Hang food 20 feet from the ground and 10 feet from the trunk of a tree.

- Store all pet items that may attract or provide a reward to wildlife inside vehicles. This includes pet food, empty food dishes, and toys. Stock feed should also be stowed in hard-sided vehicles.

- When hiking or walking in the woods, make noise. To avoid surprising a bear, use your voice. Sing loudly, hoot, holler, or clap your hands. Bears tend to recognize human sounds as ones to avoid and usually scoot off if they hear people approaching. Consciously make loud noise in thick brushy areas, around blind corners, near babbling streams, and against the wind.

- Hike with other people in broad daylight, avoiding early mornings, late evenings,

First Aid

DEHYDRATION
Many first-time visitors find the Northern Rockies to be surprisingly arid, despite the green appearance. Fight fluid loss by drinking plenty of water—especially when hiking. Altitude, sun exposure, wind, and exercise can all lead to dehydration, which manifests in yellow urine (rather than clear), lightheadedness, headaches, dizziness, rapid breathing and heart rate, and fatigue. If you feel a headache coming on, try drinking water. If you hike with children, monitor their fluid intake. For mild dehydration, sports drinks can restore the balance of body fluids, electrolytes, and salt. Severe cases of dehydration may need intravenous fluids; treat these as a medical emergency and get to a hospital.

GIARDIA
Lakes and streams can carry parasites such as *Giardia lamblia,* which if ingested causes cramping, nausea, and severe diarrhea for an exceptionally long period of time. Tap water in the park campgrounds and picnic areas has been treated (you'll definitely taste the strong chlorine in some systems), but if you drink untreated water from streams and lakes, you run the risk of ingesting the cysts. Seek medical attention if you suspect a case of giardia.

WATER HAZARDS
Contrary to popular opinion, grizzly bears are not the number one cause of death and accidents in the Northern Rockies—drowning is. Be cautious around lakes, streams, and waterfalls. Waters are swift, frigid, full of submerged obstacles, and unforgiving. Be especially careful on rocks and logs around fast-moving streams; moss and algae can make the rocks slippery.

Yellowstone's gorgeous hydrothermic features can be deadly, too. In many, water and night. Avoid hiking alone. Keep children near.

- Avoid bears' feeding areas. Since bears must gain weight before winter, eating is imperative. Often, bears will pack in 20,000 calories in a day. In the early season, glacier lily bulbs attract grizzlies for their high nutritional value. By midseason, cow parsnip patches provide sustenance, in between high-protein carrion. If you stumble across an animal carcass, leave the area immediately and notify a ranger. In August, huckleberry patches provide high amounts of sugar. Detour widely around feeding bears.

- Never approach a bear. Watch its body language: A bear that stands on hind legs may just be trying to get a good smell or better viewpoint. On the other hand, head swaying, teeth clacking, laid-back ears, a lowered head, and huffing or woofing are signs of agitation. Clear out!

- If you do surprise a bear, back away.

Contrary to all inclinations, do not run! Instead, walk backward slowly, talking quietly and turning sideways or bending your knees to appear smaller and non-threatening. Avoid direct eye contact, as the animal kingdom interprets eye contact as a challenge; instead, avert your eyes. Leave your pack on; it can protect you if the bear attacks.

- In case of an attack by a bear you surprised, use pepper spray if you have it. Protect yourself and your vulnerable parts by assuming a fetal position on the ground with your hands around the back of your neck. Play dead. Only move again when you are sure the bear has vacated the area.

- If a bear stalks you as food, which is rare, or attacks at night, fight back, using any means at hand. Grab pepper spray, shout, hit with sticks, or throw rocks to show the bear you are not an easy food source. Try to escape up something, like a building or tree.

bubbles above boiling, and what looks like solid ground may only be a thin crust that can give way with the weight of a human. Stay on designated boardwalks and trails. Toxic gases spew in some of the geyser basins. If you feel sick, leave the area immediately.

ALTITUDE

The Northern Rockies climb in elevation. Some visitors from coastal regions may feel the effects of altitude—a lightheadedness, headache, or shortness of breath—in high zones like Logan Pass in Glacier, the Yellowstone plateau, and the Beartooth Highway. In most cases, slowing down a hiking pace helps, along with drinking lots of fluids and giving the body time to acclimatize. If symptoms are more dramatic, descend in elevation as soon as possible.

Altitude also increases the effects of UV radiation. Above the tree line, you can actually feel cool but still redden with sunburn.

Use a strong sunscreen to prevent burning. Sunglasses and a hat will also add protection.

CREVASSES AND SNOWBRIDGES

While ice can look solid to step on, it harbors unseen caverns beneath. Crevasses (large vertical cracks) are difficult to see, and snowbridges can collapse with the weight of a person. Unless you have training in glacier travel, stay off the ice. Even Glacier National Park's tiny ice fields have caused fatalities. Snowfields also demand respect. Steep slopes can run out into rocks, trees, or over cliffs. If sliding for fun, choose a location with a safe runout. Do not travel across steep snowfields unless appropriately equipped with an ice axe and the knowledge of how to use it.

HYPOTHERMIA AND FROSTBITE

Because mountain weather can deteriorate from a summer balm to a winter snowstorm, hypothermia is a very real threat. At onset, the body's inner core loses heat, thus reducing mental and physical functions. It's insidious and progressively subtle: Watch for uncontrolled shivering, incoherence, poor judgment, fumbling, mumbling, and slurred speech. Exhausted, physically unprepared, and ill-clad hikers are most at risk. You can avoid becoming hypothermic by donning rain gear and warm layers. Don't let yourself get wet. Also, leave the cotton clothing back in the car; instead wear moisture-wicking layers that you can adjust to stay dry.

If someone in your party is hypothermic, get him or her sheltered and into dry clothing. Warm liquid can help heat the body, but be sure it's nonalcoholic and noncaffeinated. Build a fire for warmth. If the victim cannot regain body warmth, crawl into a sleeping bag for skin-to-skin contact with the victim. Seek medical help.

Frostbite, which usually affects extremities when exposed to very cold temperatures, causes the tissues to freeze, resulting in hard, pale, and cold skin. As the area thaws, the flesh becomes red and painful. Prevent frostbite by watching the hands, feet, nose, and ears for discoloration and wearing appropriate clothing. Warm the hands in armpits, and cover the nose and ears with dry, gloved hands. If frostbitten, do not rub the affected skin, let thawed areas refreeze, or thaw frozen areas if a chance of refreezing exists. Seek medical help.

BLISTERS

Blister prevention starts with recognition of "hot spots" or rubs. Before any blister forms, apply Moleskin or New Skin to the sensitive area. Both act as another layer of skin. Moleskin adheres to the skin, like a thick Band-Aid, with its fuzzy covering absorbing friction. New Skin, looking and smelling like fingernail polish, rubs off gradually, absorbing friction instead of the skin. Be aware that New Skin must be reapplied frequently and should not be used on open sores. In a pinch, duct tape can be slapped on potential trouble spots.

Once a blister occurs, apply Second Skin, a product developed for burns that cools the blister off and cushions it. Cover Second Skin with Moleskin, which absorbs future rubbing and holds the Second Skin in place. Also, marketed under several brand names, specialty blister bandages promote healing. Apply the adhesive bandage carefully with hand heat to mold it to the foot surface. Leave it in place until the blister begins to callus. Check placement often, as these bandages and moleskin tend to migrate away from the blister.

HANTAVIRUS

The hantavirus infection is contracted by inhaling the dust from deer mice urine and droppings. Once infected, you'll feel flu-like symptoms set in; seek medical attention if you suspect contact with the virus. To protect yourself, avoid areas thick with rodents, their burrows, and woodpiles. Store all food in rodent-proof containers. If you find rodent dust in your gear or tent, spray with a mix of water and bleach (1.5 cups bleach to one gallon water).

CAMPING EQUIPMENT CHECKLIST

GROUP GEAR

- 30-foot bear pole rope
- Aluminum foil
- Camp chairs
- Camp table
- Can opener
- Coffee cone and filters
- Cooking utensils
- Cooler
- Corkscrew
- Dishwashing tubs
- Duct tape
- Eating utensils
- Firewood
- Food
- Fuel for stove
- Garbage bags
- Ground tarp or tent footprint
- Hatchet
- Kindling and newspaper
- Lanterns
- Lighter and matches
- Maps, GPS, and compass
- Mugs, plates, bowls
- Parachute cord for tarps
- Pot holder
- Pots and pans with lids
- Rain tarps
- Salt, pepper, and spices
- Soap and sponge
- Stove
- Tent with rain-fly
- Toilet paper and trowel
- Utility knife
- Water filter
- Water jugs
- Ziploc bags

SAFETY

- First-aid kit
- Insect repellent
- Pepper spray
- Sunscreen

PERSONAL GEAR

- Bandana
- Batteries
- Flashlight or headlamp
- Fleece top and pants
- Gloves
- Hiking boots
- Rain jacket and pants
- Sleeping bag and pad
- Sunglasses
- Sun hat or ball cap
- Swimsuit
- Toiletries
- Warm hat and gloves
- Water bottle
- Water sandals

RECREATIONAL GEAR

- Binoculars and spotting scopes
- Camera
- Cribbage board
- Day pack
- Fishing rod and tackle
- Kayak, raft, or canoe
- Mountain bike and helmet
- Paddles and personal flotation devices
- Playing cards
- Trekking poles

NORTHWEST MONTANA

Seven mountain ranges, five wilderness areas, four

national forests, and two special hiking areas gain Northwest Montana a reputation as a camping mecca. Add more than 500 lakes, three major rivers, three huge reservoirs, and 3,000 miles of streams, and the options for camping multiply even further. Rarely do campgrounds swell to over 50 campsites, and many are small, free sites with room for only a few tents. The most popular camping areas cluster around lakes. Flathead Lake includes five state parks with campgrounds rimming its shoreline. East of Flathead Lake, Hungry Horse Reservoir squeezes between two mountain ranges with 14 campgrounds. Several islands dot the 35-mile-long reservoir—two contain campgrounds. Stretching into Canada, the 90-mile-long Lake Koocanusa rims with campgrounds. All three lakes offer prime boating and fishing.

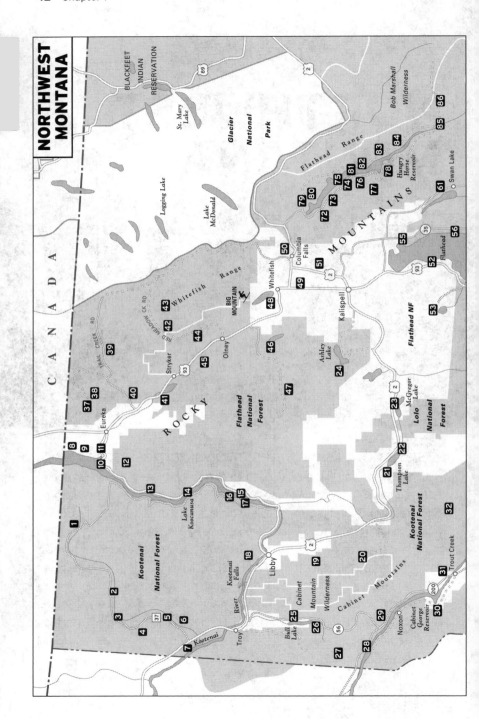

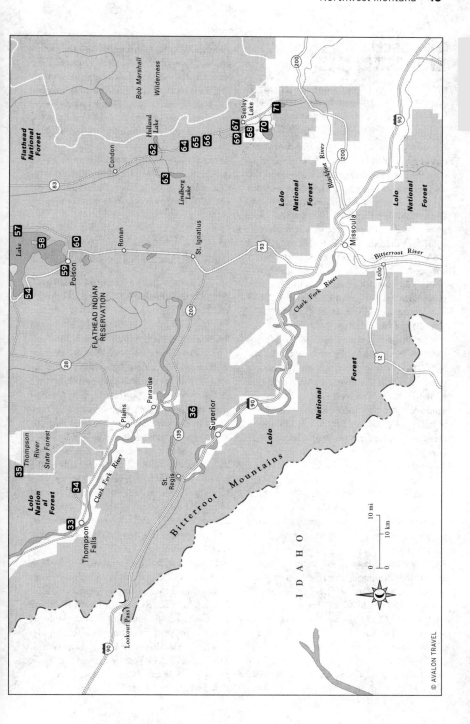

1 CARIBOU

🚶 🎣 🛶 📷 ❄️ 🐕 🚐 ⛺

Scenic rating: 7

in the Purcell Mountains in Kootenai National Forest

At 3,644 feet, Caribou Campground requires a long dirt road drive through logging country. Caribou Creek runs adjacent to the campground, which sits only 3.5 miles from the Canadian border. You can fish the creek. Upper Yaak Falls is about 10 miles west, and much of the area along the road provides good wildlife-watching. The nearby Caribou Trail (#56) traverses Caribou Mountain and peters out near the border. The Vinal-Mount Henry-Boulder National Recreation Trail sits in the mountains south of the campground. Trails 7 and 17 lead to Mount Henry Lakes and the summit of Mount Henry.

The tiny secluded campground is the epitome of quiet. Located miles from pavement, the forest road passing the campground produces minimal traffic and none at night. The creek, which flows on the west side of the campground, is the only sound you'll hear beside wildlife: owls, coyotes, and ravens. Campsites rim a meadow surrounded by a loose forest of conifers.

Campsites, facilities: The campground has three RV or tent campsites set around a small parking lot. Facilities include picnic tables, fire rings, and a vault toilet. Pack out your trash. No drinking water is available. Bring your own, or treat creek water. Leashed pets are permitted.

Reservations, fees: Reservations are not available. Campsites are free. Open year-round, but access may be limited because of snow until May and after September.

Directions: On Highway 2, drive 10 miles west from Troy or four miles east from the Idaho-Montana border. Turn north onto the Highway 508 (Yaak River Road) and drive for 30 miles to Yaak, where the road becomes dirt and changes to Forest Road 92. Drive 19 more miles and turn north into the campground. From the Eureka area, cross the Lake Koocanusa Bridge and drive six miles north on Forest Road 92 and turn left after crossing Sullivan Creek, driving about 19 miles west on Forest Road 92.

GPS Coordinates: N 48° 56.919' W 115° 30.229'

Contact: Kootenai National Forest, Three Rivers Ranger District, Troy Ranger Station, 12858 Hwy. 2, Troy, MT 59935-8750, 406/295-4693, www.fs.usda.gov/kootenai.

2 PETE CREEK

🚶 🚵 🛶 🛥️ 🎣 📷 ❄️ 🐕 ♿ 🚐 ⛺

Scenic rating: 7

in the Purcell Mountains in Kootenai National Forest

Pete Creek Campground sits at 2,966 feet, where Pete Creek and the Yaak River join. With a primitive boat launch available for rafts, kayaks, and canoes, you can float three miles from the campground to Whitetail Campground. Watch for logjams. The Yaak River harbors rainbow and brook trout. To explore the 19,100-acre Northwest Peak Scenic Area, drive 19 miles north on nearby Forest Road 338 and hike the 2.3-mile path to the top of 7,705-foot Northwest Peak for views of Canada and the Cabinet Mountains. Plenty of logging roads are available for mountain biking, hunting, and winter snowmobiling. The campground is also the closest to Yaak, a tiny, backwoods community.

Dense, tall conifers and lush undergrowth lend both shade and privacy to this intimate campground tucked between the road, Pete Creek, and Yaak River. With both the creek and the river, the sound of flowing water is heard at most of the campsites. Rock walls provide bouldering right in the campground. Three sites overlook Pete Creek, and two small, private walk-in campsites are best for tenters.

Campsites, facilities: The campground has

11 RV or tent campsites, plus two walk-in campsites for tents. RVs are limited to 32 feet. Facilities include picnic tables, fire rings, vault toilet (wheelchair-accessible), drinking water, campground hosts, firewood for sale, and boat ramp. Leashed pets are permitted.

Reservations, fees: Reservations are not available. Campsites cost $7. Cash or check. Open year-round, with limited services and weather-dependent access September-May.

Directions: On Highway 2, drive 10 miles west from Troy or four miles east from the Idaho-Montana border. Turn north onto the paved Highway 508 (Yaak River Road) and drive for 27 miles to the campground, which is on the south side of the road. From Yaak, the campground is 2.5 miles to the west.

GPS Coordinates: N 48° 49.843' W 115° 45.978'

Contact: Kootenai National Forest, Three Rivers Ranger District, Troy Ranger Station, 12858 Hwy. 2, Troy, MT 59935-8750, 406/295-4693, www.fs.usda.gov/kootenai.

❸ WHITETAIL

Scenic rating: 7

in the Purcell Mountains in Kootenai National Forest

Sitting at 2,913 feet, Whitetail is one of four campgrounds accessed by pavement along the lower Yaak River. The river is good for floating the six miles from the Yaak Bridge in the town of Yaak to the campground. This slow-flowing stretch works for canoes, inflatable kayaks, small rafts, and drift boats. Use large rafts only from Pete Creek to the campground. The river gets logjams, so keep alert. The campground has a primitive boat ramp, and the river harbors rainbow and brook trout. Forest Road 4354 leads to a trailhead into the Northwest Peak Scenic Area, and mountain bikers can ride to Mount Baldy Lookout.

A loose coniferous forest lends partial shade to the campground, which tucks between the road and the river on a gravel loop. Thick, lush brush and grass envelops the shoreline, but trails weave through it to reach the water. Sites are spread out for privacy, and a few of them overlook the river. Some also back into the hillside against the road. At night, the sound of the river is pervasive, and you might spot moose.

Campsites, facilities: The campground has 12 RV or tent campsites. RVs are limited to 32 feet. Facilities include picnic tables, fire rings with grills, vault toilet (wheelchair-accessible), drinking water, campground hosts, primitive boat ramp, and firewood for sale. Leashed pets are permitted.

Reservations, fees: Reservations are not available. Campsites cost $7. Cash or check. Open year-round, with limited services and weather-dependent access September-May.

Directions: On Highway 2, drive 10 miles west from Troy or four miles east from the Idaho-Montana border. Turn north onto the paved Highway 508 (Yaak River Road) and drive for 24 miles to the campground, located on the south side of the road. From Yaak, the campground is 5.5 miles to the west.

GPS Coordinates: N 48° 49.664' W 115° 49.010'

Contact: Kootenai National Forest, Three Rivers Ranger District, Troy Ranger Station, 12858 Hwy. 2, Troy, MT 59935-8750, 406/295-4693, www.fs.usda.gov/kootenai.

❹ RED TOP

Scenic rating: 6

in the Purcell Mountains in Kootenai National Forest

Sitting at 2,837 feet below Red Top Mountain, Red Top Campground is used mostly by those touring the Yaak River drainage. The campground does not sit on the river, but rather across the road on Red Top Creek. Fishing is available in Red Top Creek, but with private land flanking the Yaak River near the campground, use fishing accesses to the north and south.

Dense conifers shade the tiny campground, which is bordered on the north side by the creek. Its location on the road to Yaak allows for road noise to enter the campground, but at night, traffic quiets, so you can hear the creek. The dirt campground road is narrow, affording limited maneuvering space for trailers and large RVs.

Campsites, facilities: The campground has three RV or tent campsites. RVs are limited to 32 feet. Facilities include picnic tables, fire rings with grills, and a vault toilet, but no drinking water. Bring water with you, or haul it from Red Top Creek. Pack out your trash. Leashed pets are permitted.

Reservations, fees: Reservations are not available. Campsites are free. Open year-round, but with limited services and weather-dependent access September-May.

Directions: On Highway 2, drive 10 miles west from Troy or five miles east from the Idaho-Montana border to Highway 508 (Yaak River Road). Turn north onto the paved road and drive for 16 miles. Turn west into the campground. GPS Coordinates: N 48° 45.652' W 115° 55.051'

Contact: Kootenai National Forest, Three Rivers Ranger District, Troy Ranger Station, 12858 Hwy. 2, Troy, MT 59935-8750, 406/295-4693, www.fs.usda.gov/kootenai.

⁵ YAAK FALLS

Scenic rating: 7

in the Purcell Mountains in Kootenai National Forest

Sitting at 2,400 feet on the 53-mile Yaak River, this campground is named for the nearby falls 0.3 mile to the north. The falls, which honor the Yaak Indians who once populated the area, cascade through some of the oldest rock in the

North America—slabs up to 1.5 billion years old. They make good viewing locations for the two falls, which roar during high water. Above the falls, pools work for trout fly-fishing with easy access created by the road's proximity. White-water rafters and kayakers with experience navigating boulders float the Yaak. Below the falls, the canyon holds expert Class IV-V drops. Above the falls, the rapids rank Class II-III.

The campground receives filtered sunlight through larch and cedar trees. Underbrush alternates with open rocky areas, granting some sites privacy. You can hear the river in the campground.

Campsites, facilities: The campground has seven RV or tent campsites. RVs are limited to 32 feet. Facilities include picnic tables, fire rings, and a vault toilet, but no drinking water. Bring water with you, or treat river water. Pack out your trash. Leashed pets are permitted.

Reservations, fees: Reservations are not available. Campsites are free. Open year-round, but with limited services and weather-dependent access September-May.

Directions: On Highway 2, drive 10 miles west from Troy or four miles east from the Idaho-Montana border. Turn north onto Highway 508, a paved road also known as the Yaak River Road, and drive for seven miles. Turn right into the campground. GPS Coordinates: N 48° 38.682' W 115° 53.176'

Contact: Kootenai National Forest, Three Rivers Ranger District, Troy Ranger Station, 12858 Hwy. 2, Troy, MT 59935-8750, 406/295-4693, www.fs.usda.gov/kootenai.

⁶ KILBRENNAN LAKE

Scenic rating: 7

in the Purcell Mountains in Kootenai National Forest

Located at 2,917 feet, this small campground

tucks at the head of shallow Kilbrennan Lake, which only reaches about 40 feet at its deepest point. For anglers, the 55-acre lake harbors brook trout, some 12 inches, and bullhead catfish. Fishing is best from small motorboats, canoes, and kayaks, which can be launched from a primitive ramp. In fall, hunters go for grouse and deer in the Yaak.

The tiny campground sits at the north end of the lake with a natural dirt road and spur parking areas. Campsites hide under a thick canopy of firs, providing shade for all sites. The campground's main asset is its utter quiet. You'll hear only the creek, birds, and perhaps the wind in the trees.

Campsites, facilities: The campground has seven RV or tent campsites. RVs are limited to 32 feet. Facilities include picnic tables, fire rings with grills, and vault toilets, but no drinking water. Pack out your trash. Leashed pets are permitted.

Reservations, fees: Reservations are not available. Campsites cost $10. Cash or check. Open year-round, with limited services and weather-dependent access September-May.

Directions: From Troy, drive west on Highway 2. After crossing the bridge over the Kootenai River, continue 1.5 miles and veer right onto the East Side Road (Forest Road 176) for two miles heading north. Turn right onto Kilbrennen Lake Cutoff Road, which will soon join Kilbrennan Lake Road (Forest Road 2394). Drive north about 8.5 miles to the campground entrance on the left. From the Yaak River, access the Kilbrennan Lake Road via the 17-Mile Creek Road (Forest Road 471) bridge. Drive 0.3 mile and turn right onto the Kilbrennan Lake Road for eight miles to the campground entrance.

GPS Coordinates: N 48° 35.761' W 115° 53.228'

Contact: Kootenai National Forest, Three Rivers Ranger District, Troy Ranger Station, 12858 Hwy. 2, Troy, MT 59935-8750, 406/295-4693, www.fs.usda.gov/kootenai.

7 YAAK RIVER

Scenic rating: 8

in the Purcell Mountains in Kootenai National Forest

At 1,846 feet, the Kootenai and Yaak Rivers join with the popular Yaak River Campground providing the only developed Forest Service riverside campground between the Idaho border and Libby. It is also the lowest elevation campground in Montana. The 53-mile Yaak River, draining the Purcell Mountains, holds rainbow trout, mountain whitefish, and brook trout. After spring runoff, the river turns crystal clear. With only a few riffles, the lower Kootenai River is a favorite for floating rafts or kayaks and fishing in drift boats. Put in at the Troy Bridge to float nine miles to the campground.

The campground, which has two paved loops, sits on both sides of the Yaak River, with turnoffs north and south of the Yaak River Bridge. Shaded by tall larches and cedars, both loops have access to the Yaak and Kootenai Rivers, although the north loop has a larger sandy beach. Campsites are spaced out for privacy, with tall brush between sites with paved parking pads, several which are double-wide. You'll hear some highway trucks.

Campsites, facilities: The campground has 44 RV or tent campsites. RVs are limited to 32 feet. Facilities include picnic tables, fire rings with grills, vault toilets (wheelchair accessible), drinking water, garbage service, primitive boat ramp, and campground hosts. Leashed pets are permitted.

Reservations, fees: Reservations are not available. Campsites cost $10. Cash or check. Open year-round, with limited services and weather-dependent access September-May.

Directions: From Troy, drive on Highway 2 northwest for seven miles, or from the Idaho border, drive about seven miles southeast. Turn west off the highway into the campground. The two entrances flank the Yaak River

Bridge; however, the fee station and campground hosts are on the south campground loop.

GPS Coordinates: N 48° 33.658' W 115° 58.338'

Contact: Kootenai National Forest, Three Rivers Ranger District, Troy Ranger Station, 12858 Hwy. 2, Troy, MT 59935-8750, 406/295-4693, www.fs.usda.gov/kootenai.

8 GATEWAY BOAT

Scenic rating: 7

on Lake Koocanusa in Kootenai National Forest

Located at 2,475 feet, Gateway Boat Camp hovers on the east shore of Lake Koocanusa less than 0.2-mile south of the Canadian border. Access to the camp is only via boat or trail. Boaters must motor or paddle 6.5 miles to reach the camp. Hikers and equestrians can get to the campground via six miles of dusty trail that was once old road. Lake Koocanusa is popular with anglers for its sport fish, especially kokanee salmon and trout. Boaters also water-ski when the water is calm. No docking facilities are available at the campground; boaters should beach or secure boats, canoes, and kayaks for overnighting in case winds arise. The mixed sand and rock shoreline provides a swimming beach that plunges steeply underwater.

Surrounded by grasslands and loose arid forest with no understory, the campground perches on a hillside overlooking the lake. Views look across the lake into the Purcell Mountains, providing a good sunset-watching location. While little downed timber is available, plenty of driftwood can be collected on the beach for building fires.

Campsites, facilities: The tent-only campground has five campsites. Facilities include picnic tables, fire rings, pit toilet, and hitching rail. No drinking water is available. Bring your own, or treat lake water. Pack out your trash. Leashed pets are permitted.

Reservations, fees: Reservations are not available. Campsites are free. Open year-round, though winter access depends upon weather conditions.

Directions: Boaters must launch in Rexford, west of Eureka. Launch at Rexford Bench Campground, located on Highway 37 five miles west of Eureka. Follow the shoreline north for 6.5 miles to the campground. Hikers or equestrians can reach the camp from Eureka by driving Highway 37 west for one mile to Airport Road. Turn right and go for six miles to Road 15653. Turn left and drive for 0.7 miles to the trailhead.

GPS Coordinates: N 48° 59.818' W 115° 9.878'

Contact: Kootenai National Forest, Rexford Ranger District, Eureka Ranger Station, 949 Hwy. 93 N., Eureka, MT 59917-9550, 406/296-2536, www.fs.usda.gov/kootenai.

9 SWISHER LAKE

Scenic rating: 8

northwest of Eureka in Kootenai National Forest

Located at 2,510 feet, Swisher Lake is one of several small pothole ponds sitting northwest of Eureka. Surrounded by grasslands and forest, the tiny nine-acre lake is within two miles of Lake Koocanusa and two miles from the Canadian border. A 0.4-mile foot and horse trail leads to the campsites on the northwest shore of the lake. The campground includes a primitive boat ramp with a dock, and the lake harbors brook, westslope cutthroat trout, and regularly stocked rainbow trout. You can haul in small inflatable rafts and light canoes for floating. Because of its small size, the water heats up for pleasant swimming. For hiking and trail riding, the Swisher Lake Trail makes a 1.3-mile loop.

© BECKY LOMAX

Walk across the long span of the Koocanusa Bridge.

Swisher Lake is a walk-in campground for tents only. Parking is available for only four vehicles at the trailhead. The quiet campground sits on the grassy shore of the lake in a mixed open forest—a good location for spotting wildlife.

Campsites, facilities: The tent-only campground has four campsites. Facilities include picnic tables, fire rings, a vault toilet, hitching rail, and boat ramp. No drinking water is available. Bring your own, or treat lake water. Pack out your trash. Leashed pets are permitted. ATVs and motorbikes are not permitted on the access road.

Reservations, fees: Reservations are not available. Campsites are free. Open year-round, though winter access depends upon weather conditions.

Directions: North of Eureka, turn west on Highway 37 and drive one mile to the junction with Airport Road. Turn right and drive 3.1 miles north to Tetrault Lake Road. Turn left and drive 1.8 miles to Sophie Lake Road. Turn right for one mile and veer right onto Swisher Lake Road. Turn right to reach the parking area.

GPS Coordinates: N 48° 58.150' W 115° 7.922'
Contact: Kootenai National Forest, Rexford Ranger District, Eureka Ranger Station, 949 Hwy. 93 N., Eureka, MT 59917-9550, 406/296-2536, www.fs.usda.gov/kootenai.

10 REXFORD BENCH COMPLEX

Scenic rating: 8
on Lake Koocanusa in Kootenai National Forest

The Rexford Bench Complex is not wilderness. The popular steep hillside campground packs out in summer. It accesses Lake Koocanusa, a 90-mile-long reservoir crossing the international boundary. (Hence, the invented name that combines KOOtenai, CANada, and USA.) The Libby Dam formed the lake when it was completed in 1974. The huge lake garners recreational boaters around bays, but the main lake always seems empty. During droughts, late summer draw-downs drop the lake low, sometimes prohibiting launching boats. The complex includes a boat launch with low- and high-water concrete ramps, docks, fish-cleaning stations, trailer parking, and a buoyed sandy swimming beach. The beach sits on a narrow, sheltered side bay that is popular for waterskiing, canoeing, and fishing for kokanee salmon. Summer interpretive programs are available, and a short 0.5-mile nature trail overlooks sandstone hoodoos.

A paved road loops through the campground, which is shaded by a mix of pines. The campsites have no views of the lake, and the open understory permits visibility of neighboring campers. Vehicle noise from the highway floats through the campground. Six campsites have pull-through parking pads, and many have tent pads.

Campsites, facilities: The campground has 34 RV or tent campsites and 20 campsites for tents only. RVs are limited to 40 feet. Facilities include picnic tables, fire rings with grills, flush toilets (wheelchair-accessible), drinking water, garbage service, campground hosts, disposal station, boat ramp, swimming beach, and overflow overnight parking for RVs, but no hookups. Without designated parking spaces, the Kamloops Terrace overflow area fits about 25 RVs and has flush toilets, drinking water, tables, and fire rings. Leashed pets are permitted.

Reservations, fees: Reservations are highly recommended for summer (877/444-6777, www.recreation.gov). Campsites cost $12. Overflow camping costs $9. Cash, check, or credit card. Open year-round, but with limited services and weather-dependent access September-May. The boat launch is only available when reservoir water levels allow launching. Off-season camping is only in the Kamloops Terrace overflow area.

Directions: From Highway 93 north of Eureka, drive five miles west on Highway 37 to reach Rexford. Turn north off the highway into the campground. From the Lake Koocanusa Bridge, drive eight miles northeast.

GPS Coordinates: N 48° 53.961' W 115° 9.596'
Contact: Kootenai National Forest, Rexford Ranger District, Eureka Ranger Station, 949 Hwy. 93 N., Eureka, MT 59917-9550, 406/296-2536, www.fs.usda.gov/kootenai.

11 TOBACCO RIVER

Scenic rating: 6
on the Tobacco River in Kootenai National Forest

West of Eureka, the rustic Tobacco River Campground perches on a hillside above the mouth of the Tobacco River where it flows into a bay of Lake Koocanusa. Campers can use the nearby Rexford Bench Complex beach and boat launch facilities for swimming, fishing, waterskiing, and boat touring. The campground has a primitive boat launch for rowboats, kayaks, and canoes that can start on the river. In late summer when lake water levels drop, the bay becomes a dry bed with the small river. Hikers can access a short 0.5-mile nature trail that overlooks sandstone hoodoos.

A gravel road loops through the campground, which is partially shaded by evergreens. Some sites overlook the river. The sites spread out for privacy. Vehicle noise from the highway floats through the campground.

Campsites, facilities: The campground has six RV or tent campsites tucked on a steep hillside in a loose arid forest. RVs are limited to 20 feet. Facilities include picnic tables, fire rings, and vault toilet (wheelchair-accessible). Drinking water is not available. While you can opt to treat river water, bringing your own saves hiking up and down to the river. Pack out your trash. Leashed pets are permitted.

Reservations, fees: Reservations are not available. Campsites are free. Open year-round, but may have limited access in winter because of mud, ice, or snow.

Directions: From Eureka, drive four miles west on Highway 37 to Pidgeon Bridge Road

(Forest Road 7182). Turn north off the highway and drive one mile on the gravel road to the campground entrance.

GPS Coordinates: N 48° 53.662' W 115° 8.100'

Contact: Kootenai National Forest, Rexford Ranger District, Eureka Ranger Station, 949 Hwy. 93 N., Eureka, MT 59917-9550, 406/296-2536, www.fs.usda.gov/kootenai.

12 CAMP 32

Scenic rating: 5

east of Lake Koocanusa in Kootenai National Forest

The turnoff to Camp 32 sits 1.5 miles northwest of the Lake Koocanusa Bridge, the longest and tallest bridge in Montana. The bridge, built in 1970, is 2,437 feet long. You can park in the lot just south of the bridge and walk across the half-mile span. To get to the campground, the road follows Pinkham Creek, which draws anglers going after rainbow trout. The campground still has several buildings from when it served as a logging camp and homestead. The narrow, rough access road also offers several large secluded dispersed camping sites along the creek.

With its remote location, the campground is ultra quiet. At 2,750 feet, it circles one loop under Douglas firs, with small vine maples and wild rosebushes forming privacy barriers between campsites. The back-in sites are small. A large field parallels the entrance to the campground. Two campsites with less privacy back up to the entrance road rather than the creek.

Campsites, facilities: The campground has eight RV or tent campsites. The sites can accommodate a maximum RV size of 20 feet, and trailers are not recommended. Facilities include picnic tables, fire rings, vault toilets (wheelchair accessible), drinking water from a hand pump, and sometimes firewood. Pack out your trash. Leashed pets are permitted.

Reservations, fees: Reservations are not accepted. Campsites are free. Open year-round, but with limited services and weather-dependent access September-May.

Directions: From Highway 93 north of Eureka, drive 12 miles southwest on Highway 37. Turn east onto the dirt Rondo Road (Forest Road 7182). Drive 2.5 miles on the single-lane, narrow, potholed road to the campground. From the Lake Koocanusa Bridge, the signed turnoff sits 1.5 miles northeast.

GPS Coordinates: N 48° 50.192' W 115° 11.479'

Contact: Kootenai National Forest, Rexford Ranger District, Eureka Ranger Station, 949 Hwy. 93 N., Eureka, MT 59917-9550, 406/296-2536, www.fs.usda.gov/kootenai.

13 PECK GULCH

Scenic rating: 9

on Lake Koocanusa in Kootenai National Forest

Peck Gulch is a unique campground. People either love it or hate it. At 2,468 feet on the reservoir's east side, the campground sits on a flat, wide, treeless sandbar jutting several hundred feet out into the lake. Between Peck Gulch and the Lake Koocanusa Bridge, rocky cliffs broken with open grassy areas provide excellent habitat for bighorn sheep and routes for rock climbers. From the campground, a steep 0.5-mile trail climbs to Peck Gulch. Boating facilities include a high- and low-water ramp, boat dock, and paved trailer parking. For anglers, the reservoir harbors a variety of sport fish.

Raised grassy areas circle the campground around four large, round gravel parking lots with no designated parking strips or campsite boundaries. No vegetation—no trees, no bushes—grows on the sandbar. That means no privacy or wind blocks. Sidle up to a place that looks good and claim it. Many of the campsites sit right on the edge of the bar, with unobstructed views of the reservoir and the Purcell Mountains rising from the opposite shore.

Campsites, facilities: The campground spreads campsites on a flat, open, dirt, table-like sandbar with room for 22 RV or tent camping units. A few tent pads are available. RVs over 32 feet are not permitted. Facilities include picnic tables, fire rings with grills, vault toilets (wheelchair accessible), drinking water, and a campground host. Firewood is often available, but not in the off-season. Leashed pets are permitted.

Reservations, fees: Reservations are not accepted. Campsites cost $9. Cash or check. Open year-round, but with limited services and weather-dependent access September-May.

Directions: From Highway 93 north of Eureka, drive 21 miles southwest on Highway 37, or from Libby, drive 48 miles northeast on Highway 37. Turn west off the highway at the sign, which leads to a narrow, steep, paved single-lane road with a hairpin turn that drops to the campground.

GPS Coordinates: N 48° 43.431' W 115° 18.445'

Contact: Kootenai National Forest, Rexford Ranger District, Eureka Ranger Station, 949 Hwy. 93 N., Eureka, MT 59917-9550, 406/296-2536, www.fs.usda.gov/kootenai.

14 ROCKY GORGE

Scenic rating: 8

on Lake Koocanusa in Kootenai National Forest

Located at 2,500 feet on the east shore of 90-mile-long Lake Koocanusa, Rocky Gorge Campground clings to one of the narrowest stretches of the reservoir. A cement boat launch allows for getting onto the reservoir. At low pool (when water level is at its lowest seasonal levels), plenty of beach opens up with its combination of clay sand and rocks. Watch for bald eagle nests and ospreys fishing along this side of the reservoir. For anglers, the reservoir has trout, kokanee salmon, and other sport fish.

Islands of bushes, yellow arrowleaf balsamroot, and trees divide up the campground, but the rough-paved, parking lot effect is evident. No designated parking spaces denote campsites. Just roll in and claim a spot that looks good. The campground sits under ponderosa pines, but little privacy is available. Sites along the west perimeter have peek-a-boo views of the reservoir and work better for those with tents. Two walk-in tent sites sit right on the bluff with broad views of the reservoir. Recent thinning added more views, too.

Campsites, facilities: The campground has undesignated campsites with room for 60 RV or tent camping units. The maximum vehicle length is 32 feet. Facilities include picnic tables, fire rings with grills, vault toilets (wheelchair accessible), and a campground host. Bring your own drinking water, or treat lake water. Pack out your trash. Leashed pets are permitted.

Reservations, fees: Reservations are not accepted. Campsites cost $9. Cash or check. Open year-round, but with limited services and weather-dependent access September-May.

Directions: From Highway 93 north of Eureka, drive 31 miles southwest on Highway 37, or from Libby, drive 40 miles northeast on Highway 37. Turn west off the highway into the campground entrance.

GPS Coordinates: N 48° 39.120' W 115° 18.680'

Contact: Kootenai National Forest, Rexford Ranger District, Eureka Ranger Station, 949 Hwy. 93 N., Eureka, MT 59917-9550, 406/296-2536, www.fs.usda.gov/kootenai.

15 KOOCANUSA RESORT AND MARINA

Scenic rating: 7

on Lake Koocanusa in Kootenai National Forest

Lake Koocanusa Resort and Marina sits five miles north of Libby Dam on the east side of the lake. It is the only marina on the southern end of the 90-mile reservoir. The resort and campground perch high on a forested bluff with a steep road descending to the lake, marina, boat dock, boat rentals (aluminum and pontoon boats), and beach for swimming. The marina sits in a narrow sheltered bay, which offers calmer waters for swimming or canoeing than the windier reservoir channel. Two wave breakers also add protection. The resort attracts serious anglers, especially for its May fishing derby, and the lake teems with rainbow trout, kokanee salmon, and other sport fish. A walking trail to Warland Flats departs from the campground.

The two campground loops sit under a fir tree canopy providing filtered sunlight and shade. Loose natural underbrush or lack thereof creates sites that are open to each other with little privacy. The larger RV campground loop circles around a restroom building, while the smaller loop requires walking to the larger loop or the main lodge for restrooms. The lodge houses a camp store, restaurant, bar, and deck overlooking the marina. The new shower house, restrooms, and launderette are adjacent to the lodge.

Campsites, facilities: The campground has 78 RV or tent campsites. Some RV sites can fit the big rigs. Hookups include water, sewer, and electricity up to 30 amps. Facilities include some picnic tables, fire rings, flush toilets, drinking water, showers, boat ramp, marina, and a swimming beach. Leashed pets are permitted. Overflow camping in RVs is available in large parking lots—one paved and one gravel.

Reservations, fees: Reservations are accepted. Campsites cost $20 for tents and $31 for RVs. Overflow camping costs $12. Cash or credit card. Open daily mid-April-November, Fridays through Sundays mid-February-mid-April. A seven percent Montana bed tax will be added.

Directions: From Libby, drive 23 miles north on Highway 37, or from Eureka, drive 43 miles south on Highway 37. Turn west into the resort at the signed entrance.

GPS Coordinates: N 48° 28.996' W 115° 16.175'

Contact: Koocanusa Resort and Marina, 23911 Hwy. 37, Libby, MT 59923, 406/293-7474, www.koocanusaresort.com.

16 BARRON FLATS

Scenic rating: 7

on Lake Koocanusa in Kootenai National Forest

On Lake Koocanusa, known for its kokanee salmon fishery, Barron Flats sits at 2,500 feet on the reservoir's west side. A snowmobile destination in winter and a quiet getaway in summer, the campground serves as a west-side stop on the Koocanusa Scenic Byway, which loops 67 miles around the reservoir via the Lake Koocanusa Bridge on the north and Libby Dam on the south. The west-side road, which is closed in winter, usually melts out by April and receives snow again in November. Take binoculars—the region provides habitat for bighorn sheep, black bears, and bald eagles. A concrete boat launch allows launching powerboats, kayaks, and canoes. The reservoir is a sport fishery. Fall big game hunting brings on one of the busiest seasons here.

The upper campground sprawls across a large, grassy meadow rimmed by forest with undesignated sites; just pull over next to a patch of grass. You can camp in the open with views of the surrounding terrain or tuck adjacent to the forest with a semblance of privacy. The lower campground has four campsites on a paved, forested loop.

Campsites, facilities: The campground has seven RV or tent sites. Upper sites can fit RVs up to 40 feet. Facilities include vault toilets (wheelchair accessible) and some fire rings. No drinking water is provided. Plan on bringing your own, or treat lake water. Pack out your trash. Leashed pets are permitted.

Reservations, fees: Reservations are not accepted. Campsites are free. Open year-round, but with limited services and weather-dependent access September-May.

Directions: From the north, approach the campground via the Koocanusa Bridge, about an hour's drive on the curvy but paved Forest Road 228. At milepost 12.5, turn east onto the paved road into the boat launch and campground. From the south, turn off Highway 37 one mile northeast of the Canoe Gulch Ranger Station and drive 13 miles north.

GPS Coordinates: N 48° 30.946' W 115° 17.641'

Contact: Kootenai National Forest, Libby Ranger District, Canoe Gulch Ranger Station, 12557 Hwy. 37, Libby, MT 59923-8212, 406/293-7773, www.fs.usda.gov/kootenai.

17 MCGILLIVRAY

Scenic rating: 7

on Lake Koocanusa in Kootenai National Forest

On Lake Koocanusa's west side, McGillivray is the closest designated Forest Service campground to Libby Dam. The Libby Dam Visitor Center opens between Memorial Day and Labor Day. Four dam tours depart daily for 90-minute guided walks through the dam and powerhouse. The 422-foot-tall dam retains 90 miles of water in Lake Koocanusa, with 48 of the lake's miles in the United States and the other miles over the international border in Canada. Near the dam, the Souse Gulch picnic area is home to nesting bald eagles. At McGillivray, two boat ramps accommodate high and low reservoir levels with a dock, fish cleaning station, and boat trailer parking available. Trails loop around bluffs for views of the reservoir and Salish Mountains. A narrow inlet forms the swimming beach, only usable at high water. It is a snowmobile destination in winter on the snow-covered west-side road.

The two ultra-quiet campground loops sit under thick ponderosas and firs with no views. Recent thinning has opened up some of the campground to filtered sunlight, but most of the campsites are shaded. Campsites are spread apart for privacy.

Campsites, facilities: The campground has 33 RV or tent campsites. The maximum vehicle length is 40 feet. Facilities include picnic tables, fire rings with grills, vault toilets (wheelchair accessible), drinking water, campground hosts, boat ramp, covered picnic shelter, and swimming beach. Leashed pets are permitted.

Reservations, fees: Reservations are not accepted. Campsites cost $10. Cash or check. Open year-round, but limited services and weather-dependent access October-May.

Directions: From the north side of the Lake Koocanusa Bridge, drive south on the curvy, paved Forest Road 228 for about an hour to milepost 10.1. Turn east into the campground. From the south, turn north onto Forest Road 228 one mile northeast of Canoe Gulch Ranger Station and drive 10 miles north.

GPS Coordinates: N 48° 29.127' W 115° 18.232'

Contact: Kootenai National Forest, Libby Ranger District, Canoe Gulch Ranger Station, 12557 Hwy. 37, Libby, MT 59923-8212, 406/293-7773, www.fs.usda.gov/kootenai.

18 LOON LAKE

Scenic rating: 6
north of Libby in Kootenai National Forest

Loon Lake isn't so much of a lake as it is a long pool on a mountain stream. Sitting north of Libby below Turner Mountain, the local ski area, the lake and campground attract mostly anglers. At 3,600 feet, the long skinny shallow lake runs an average of five feet deep, making for propitious growth of algae and water foliage. Nevertheless, the 26-acre lake attracts some canoers to paddle its 0.7-mile serene length. Considering the brushy shoreline, anglers can fish better from a small boat or float tube for native westslope cutthroat trout. With a primitive path for lake access, only hand-carried watercrafts are recommended. Miles of gravel road access the campground, which deters some.

The ultra-quiet campground tucks at the bottom of a narrow heavily forested valley. Campsites spread out under conifers for shade.
Campsites, facilities: The campground has four RV or tent campsites. Two campsites have tent pads; the other two can accommodate small RVs up to 20 feet. Facilities include picnic tables, fire rings, and vault toilet (wheelchair-accessible). Drinking water is not available. Bring your own, or treat lake water. Pack out your trash. Leashed pets are permitted.
Reservations, fees: Reservations are not accepted. Campsites are free. Open year-round, but with limited services and access limited by snow in winter.
Directions: From Libby, drive north on Highway 37 to Pipe Creek Road, located 0.4 miles north of the bridge over the Kootenai River. Drive for 17 miles and turn left onto Seventeen Mile Road (Forest Road 471) for three miles. Turn left into the campground.
GPS Coordinates: N 48° 35.838' W 115° 40.253'
Contact: Kootenai National Forest, Libby Ranger District, Canoe Gulch Ranger Station, 12557 Hwy. 37, Libby, MT 59923-8212, 406/293-7773, www.fs.usda.gov/kootenai.

19 HOWARD LAKE

Scenic rating: 8
in the Cabinet Mountains in Kootenai National Forest

Tiny Howard Lake, a local Libby fishing hole stocked with rainbow trout, sits serene in a deep pocket amid a thick, mature cedar and spruce forest. At 4,100 feet, the lake is only 33 acres in size, making it best for canoeing and fishing from small boats. The Gold Panning Recreation Area is one mile from the lake, and nearby hiking trails climb up creek drainages into the Cabinet Mountain Wilderness. Unfortunately, the most popular hiking trail requires a long drive back out to the highway and a nine-mile drive up Bear Creek Road to the Leigh Lake Trailhead. The 1.5-mile trail climbs a steep ascent, gaining 1,000 feet past Leigh Falls and following rock cairns to find the easiest route into the alpine bowl where Leigh Lake clings. At the campground, a trail circles the lake.

The ultra-quiet campground sits half under big shade-producing conifers and half on the open edge of the forest adjacent to the lake. The campground's one road loops between the campsites and the lake, with a boat ramp that doubles as a swimming beach. Because it has little underbrush and several open sites, you will see neighbors.
Campsites, facilities: The campground has 10 RV or tent campsites. Three of them accommodate small RVs up to 20 feet in pull-through sites; five are tent sites that will not fit RVs. Facilities include picnic tables, fire rings, a vault toilet (wheelchair-accessible), campground hosts, and drinking water from a hand pump. Leashed pets are permitted.
Reservations, fees: Reservations are not

accepted. Campsites cost $8. Cash or check. Open May-November, but full services only late May-early September.

Directions: From Libby, head south on Highway 2 for 12 miles or from Kalispell, drive 75 miles west to the junction of Libby Creek Road (Forest Road 231). Turn south onto this road, which turns into dirt, and drive 14 miles to the campground sign. As you drive, stay on the well-traveled route, veering left at all junctions. At the junction with the campground sign, go right on Forest Road 4779, climbing up the hill and driving about one mile. The campground entrance sits on the left.

GPS Coordinates: N 48° 6.026' W 115° 31.829'

Contact: Kootenai National Forest, Libby Ranger District, Canoe Gulch Ranger Station, 12557 Hwy. 37, Libby, MT 59923-8212, 406/293-7773, www.fs.usda.gov/kootenai.

20 LAKE CREEK

Scenic rating: 7
in the Cabinet Mountains in Kootenai National Forest

At 3,360 feet, Lake Creek Campground sits at the confluence of Lake and Bramlet Creeks on the east flanks of the Cabinet Mountains. For stream anglers going after mountain whitefish and rainbow trout, nearby rivers also include Fourth of July and West Fisher, accessed via narrow forest roads or trails. The best hike goes to Geiger Lakes, a pair of subalpine pools in the Cabinet Mountains Wilderness. Locate the trailhead two miles from the campground on Forest Road 6748. A steady grade climbs through lodgepole pines to the first lake, rimmed with large boulders on a peninsula, before ascending 600 more feet to the second lake in a scenic alpine meadow below Lost Buck Pass. A longer drive on the Silver Butte Road leads to Baree Lake Trailhead for a three-mile climb to a lake known for its wealth of

huckleberries in July and August. The campground lures big game hunters in fall.

The tiny campground tucks into a conifer forest, offering seclusion and utter quiet with only the sound of the creek filtering through the trees. The campground's one small loop spreads out the campsites for privacy.

Campsites, facilities: The campground has four RV and tent campsites. RVs are limited to 32 feet. Four additional primitive sites are in the area, too. Facilities include picnic tables, fire rings, tent pads, and a vault toilet. Bring your own water, or treat the creek water. Pack out your trash. Leashed pets are permitted.

Reservations, fees: Reservations are not accepted. Campsites are free. Open year-round, but serviced only late May-early September. Snow may preclude access in winter.

Directions: On Highway 2, drive 22 miles southeast from Libby or 66 miles west from Kalispell to the junction with West Fisher Road (Forest Road 231). Turn onto this dirt road and drive approximately six miles, swinging left onto Bramlet Creek Road (Forest Road 2332) at the fork. Drive 0.8 mile to the campground entrance.

GPS Coordinates: N 48° 2.328' W 115° 29.338'

Contact: Kootenai National Forest, Libby Ranger District, Canoe Gulch Ranger Station, 12557 Hwy. 37, Libby, MT 59923-8212, 406/293-7773, www.fs.usda.gov/kootenai.

21 THOMPSON CHAIN OF LAKES COMPLEX

Scenic rating: 7
on Thompson Chain of Lakes in the Salish Mountains

The Thompson Chain of Lakes consists of 4,655 acres of land containing 18 lakes running in a 20-mile string along Highway 2 between Libby and Kalispell. Some of the lakes are small four-acre ponds; the largest lake tops

1,500 acres. Receding glaciers formed the lakes in a trail of water pockets separated by moraines. Crystal, Horseshoe, and Loon comprise the smaller lakes at the west end. The three Thompson Lakes (Upper, Middle, and Lower) cover the most miles, while McGregor Lake is the largest. The lakes are popular for trout and bass fishing as well as magnets for wildlife. Wake up to the call of loons and watch ospreys dive for fish. Concrete boat ramps for motorboats, canoes, and kayaks are located at Little McGregor, McGregor, Lower Thompson, Upper Thompson, Horseshoe, and Loon Lakes. Some of the lakes have no-wake speed limits. The lakes are loaded with sport fish, such as pike, rainbow trout, bass, and kokanee salmon.

Campsites are sprinkled along the shorelines singly or in pairs or groups on both sides of the lakes. Some are very primitive. To locate the Thompson Chain of Lakes campsites, pick up a map at one of the eight pay stations on the road entrances to the lakes. Those campsites adjacent to the highway are the most popular. Most of the campsites are accessed via narrow potholed dirt roads unsuitable for anything larger than a truck camper; however, some of those adjacent to the highway can fit larger rigs.

Campsites, facilities: Thompson Chain of Lakes has 83 primitive campsites and eight group campsites. Sites can have a maximum of two tents, trailers, or RVs, but many can only fit one. Where campsites are concentrated together, a vault toilet is available, but not at the single sites. Facilities include fire rings and some picnic tables. No drinking water is available. Bring your own, or treat lake water. Leashed pets are permitted.

Reservations, fees: Reservations are not accepted. Campsites cost $7 for those who already have Montana fishing licenses. Otherwise, camping costs $12. Cash or check. Open year-round unless snowbound.

Directions: From Kalispell, drive between 35 and 55 miles westward on Highway 2 to reach Thompson Chain of Lakes.

GPS Coordinates: N 48° 1.451' W 115° 2.446'
Contact: Montana Fish, Wildlife, and Parks, Region 1, 490 N. Meridian Rd., Kalispell, MT 59901, 406/752-5501, http://fwp.mt.gov.

22 LOGAN STATE PARK

Scenic rating: 8
on Middle Thompson Lake in the Salish Mountains

Sitting midway between Libby and Kalispell on the Highway 2 corridor at 3,300 feet, the Thompson Chain of Lakes strings the Upper, Middle, and Lower Thompson Lakes together with sloughs to make up about 3,000 acres for water recreation. The lakes garner their share of locals, especially on weekends and holidays, and are popular for waterskiing, paddling, and largemouth bass fishing. The bass can range 1-3 pounds in size. Logan Campground sits on the north shore of the middle lake, with a cement boat ramp, dock, trailer parking, and a swimming beach. A half-mile hiking trail leads along the lakeshore to good bird-watching spots to see herons, ospreys, and waterfowl. Loons nest on the lakes, too.

The 17-acre grassy campground circles its two loops under a canopy of western larch, ponderosa pine, and Douglas fir. Without underbrush, the campsites do not have much privacy from each other. Loop B sits closer to the swimming beach and boat launch. Loop A, which leads to the hiking trail, has the playground and showers. Squeezed between the lake and the highway, the campground picks up noise from passing vehicles on the highway.

Campsites, facilities: The campground has 37 RV or tent campsites. RVs are limited to 30 feet. Facilities include picnic tables, fire rings with grills, flush toilets, showers, drinking water, playground, boat launch, swimming beach, campground hosts, disposal station, firewood for sale, and horseshoe pit. Leashed pets are permitted. Wheelchair-accessible facilities include a toilet and two campsites.

Reservations, fees: Reservations are accepted online or by phone (855-922-6768). Campsites cost $15 for Montana residents (seniors and disabled get half price) and $23 for nonresidents Memorial Day weekend-Labor Day, or $12 for Montana residents and $20 for nonresidents September-May. Campsites with electrical hookups cost $17-28, depending on season and residency. Nonresidents with a Non-Resident Entrance Pass ($25) get a $5 discount on camping fees. Cash, check, or credit card. Open year-round, but drinking water and showers are only available May-September.

Directions: From Kalispell, drive 44 miles west on Highway 2, or from Libby, drive 45 miles southeast on Highway 2. Turn south at the signed entrance to the campground at 77518 Highway 2.

GPS Coordinates: N 48° 1.972' W 115° 3.976'

Contact: Montana Fish, Wildlife, and Parks, Region 1, 490 N. Meridian Rd., Kalispell, MT 59901, 406/752-5501, http://stateparks.mt.gov.

23 MCGREGOR LAKE

Scenic rating: 8
on McGregor Lake in Kootenai National Forest

At 3,900 feet, McGregor Lake is the easternmost lake in a long chain of easily accessed valley lakes strung along Highway 2. McGregor Lake Campground sits on the west end of the 1,522-acre lake. With a 35-minute drive from Flathead Valley, the lake is surrounded by summer homes and a small resort. On weekends, it's packed with water-skiers, boaters, paddlers, and anglers trolling for lake trout or stocked rainbow trout. The campground has a paved boat ramp, dock, trailer parking, and beach for swimming. Surrounding the campground, a patchwork of Kootenai National Forest and state lands offer mountain biking and hiking,

but not to exceptionally scenic destinations. The three-mile-long McGregor Lake Shoreline Trail tours the lake.

Young pine trees surround the campground, allowing most of the sites to receive a good deal of sunlight. A few campsites sit closer to the water, but not on the shoreline. Those rimming the shore are more open and less private than those shaded under trees away from the shore. Four tent sites sit right on the water near the boat ramp. Because of the proximity to the highway, truck noise seeps into the campground at night.

Campsites, facilities: The campground has 27 RV or tent campsites plus four tent-only sites. RVs are limited to 32 feet. Facilities include picnic tables, fire rings, vault toilets (wheelchair accessible), drinking water, a boat ramp, campground hosts, firewood for sale, and group campsite. Leashed pets are permitted.

Reservations, fees: Reservations are not accepted. Campsites cost $12. Cash or check. Open year-round, but with limited services and weather-dependent access September-May.

Directions: From Kalispell, drive 32 miles westward on Highway 2, or from Libby, drive 53 miles southeast on Highway 2. Turn south off the highway onto Forest Road 6770 to enter the campground.

GPS Coordinates: N 48° 1.908' W 114° 54.142'

Contact: Kootenai National Forest, Libby Ranger District, Canoe Gulch Ranger Station, 12557 Hwy. 37, Libby, MT 59923-8212, 406/293-7773, www.fs.usda.gov/kootenai.

24 ASHLEY LAKE

Scenic rating: 6
in the Salish Mountains in Flathead National Forest

West of Kalispell, Ashley Lake sits at 4,000 feet surrounded by multimillion dollar summer homes. Campers head to Ashley Lake for swimming, canoeing, fishing, and waterskiing. The lake, which is about five miles long and one mile wide, gets substantial day use from locals. Anglers go after kokanee salmon, west-slope cutthroat trout, yellow perch, and large rainbow trout. Some of the rainbow-cutthroat hybrids can get up to five pounds. Swimmers enjoy the lake because of the shallow shoreline that warms the water midsummer. Mountain bikers tour the scads of forest roads that criss-cross the area, and bird-watchers catch sight of loons and other waterfowl.

The campground is split between a north unit and a south unit, plus a few campsites are available at the boat ramp. All are small, huddling under conifers for shade. The north unit is located 0.5-mile west of the boat launch area. The south unit requires carrying canoes or float boats to the shore. Once the personal watercraft leave the lake at night, the campgrounds turn quiet. Sites are spread out for privacy, but neighboring campers are visible.

Campsites, facilities: The north side campground has five RV or tent campsites with a length limit of 25 feet on RVs or trailer combinations. The south side campground has two campsites for tents. The boat launch campground has four RV or tent campsites with RVs limited to 12 feet. Facilities include picnic tables, fire rings, vault toilets (wheelchair accessible), and campground host (north unit only). Drinking water is not available, so bring your own or treat lake water. Pack out all garbage. Leashed pets are permitted.

Reservations, fees: Reservations are not accepted, and camping is free. Open late May-September.

Directions: From Highway 93 in Kalispell, drive west on Highway 2 for 16 miles. Turn north onto the gravel Ashley Lake Road (Forest Road 912) and drive 7.4 miles to a fork. For the north campground, veer right around the north side of the lake for six miles to the campground entrance. For the south campground, veer left at the fork for 1.7 miles to the entrance.

North GPS Coordinates: N 48° 12.176' W 114° 37.996'
South GPS Coordinates: N 48° 12.697' W 114° 34.089'
Boat Launch GPS Coordinates: N 48° 12.810' W 114° 36.989'
Contact: Flathead National Forest, Talley Lake Ranger District, 650 Wolfpack Way, Kalispell, MT 59901, 406/758-5204, www.fs.usda.gov/flathead/.

25 DORR SKEELS

Scenic rating: 9
on Bull Lake in Kootenai National Forest

Bull Lake, which sits at 2,350 feet in elevation, tucked between the Cabinet Mountains and Scotchman Peaks, runs 4.5 miles in length. It harbors rainbow trout, kokanee salmon, and largemouth bass. While the lake borders public land on its west shore, the east shore contains private land and homes. The campground sits on the north end of the lake, with a warm, sunny, south-facing buoyed sand-and-pebble swimming beach. The day-use area sees heavy weekend visitation from locals, especially water-skiers. At the campground, a concrete ramp and dock aid those launching boats, kayaks, and canoes, and several boat tie-up anchors are available near the campsites. This is the closest campground for hiking to Kootenai Falls on the Kootenai River, made famous in *The River Wild*. A trail drops to the falls via a bridge and stairway over the railroad. Below the falls, a swinging bridge crosses the river canyon. Hikers can also access the northern Cabinet Mountain Wilderness. The closest big-view hikes have you climb to Cedar Lake and Scenery Mountain (11-mile loop) and Leigh Lake (2.6 miles).

Sitting on a forested bluff under cedars and firs, the shaded tent campsites have peek-a-boo views of the lake. Sites 6 and 7 offer the most privacy. Some of the flat sleeping spaces will accommodate only two-person tents. The self-contained RV campsites consist of a parking lot with no privacy and no hookups.

Campsites, facilities: The campground has five walk-in tent campsites and two RV campsites that can fit trailer combinations up to 32 feet. Facilities include picnic tables and fire rings with grills at tent sites only, vault toilets (wheelchair accessible), campground hosts, drinking water, garbage service, a boat launch, and swimming beach. Leashed pets are permitted.

Reservations, fees: Reservations are not accepted. Campsites cost $7. Open year-round, but services such as water are only available late May-early September. Snow may inhibit winter access.

Directions: On Highway 2, from Libby, drive 15.2 miles west, or from Troy, drive three miles east. Turn south onto Highway 56 and drive 13 miles. Turn west onto the 0.5-mile Dorr Skeels Road (Forest Road 1117), which leads to the campground. From Highway 200, drive 21.6 miles north on Highway 53 to the campground turnoff on the left.

GPS Coordinates: N 48° 16.041' W 115° 51.246'

Contact: Kootenai National Forest, Three Rivers Ranger District, Troy Ranger Station, 12858 Hwy. 2, Troy, MT 59935-8750, 406/295-4693, www.fs.usda.gov/kootenai.

26 BAD MEDICINE

Scenic rating: 8
on Bull Lake in Kootenai National Forest

At 2,350 feet on the southwest corner of 4.5-mile-long Bull Lake, Bad Medicine is the closest campground for hiking the one-mile Ross Creek Cedars interpretive trail. Located four miles from the campground, the 100-acre ancient grove of western red cedar trees—some that were saplings when Columbus landed in the New World—survived the ravages of floods, fires, and insects. Great-grandfather trees span eight feet in diameter and stand over 175 feet tall. The campground

A swinging bridge crosses the Kootenai River below Kootenai Falls.

© BECKY LOMAX

has a boat ramp, dock, and small swimming beach. Waterskiing or paddling the lake early or late in the day yields calmer waters with big views of the surrounding Scotchman Peaks and the Cabinet Mountains. Boating anglers can catch trout, kokanee salmon, and large mouth bass.

A paved road makes two loops through the campground, parts of which are reminiscent of dark, coastal cedar and hemlock rain forests dripping with moss. Dense vegetation and thick trees close off the views from the campsites but also provide seclusion and cool shade for hot days. Sites 3, 4, and 9-12 are especially private. Sites 1 and 2 sit closest to the lake. For views, head to the beach for beautiful reflections of the Cabinet Mountains on calm days. Prepare for mosquitoes, and plan to arrive before 10 p.m. when the security gate is locked.

Campsites, facilities: The campground has 18 RV or tent campsites. RVs are limited to 32 feet. Facilities include picnic tables, fire rings with grills, vault toilets (wheelchair accessible), campground hosts, drinking water, garbage service, a boat launch, and swimming beach. Leashed pets are permitted.

Reservations, fees: Reservations are not accepted. Campsites cost $10. Cash or check. Open year-round, but with limited services and weather-dependent access September-May.

Directions: From Libby, drive 15 miles west, or from Troy, drive three miles east to Highway 56. Turn south and drive 21 miles to Ross Creek Cedars Road (Forest Road 398), between mileposts 16 and 17. From Highway 200, drive 13.5 miles north on Highway 53 to the Ross Creek Cedars turnoff on the left. On Forest Road 398, drive two paved miles to the campground, passing the turnoff to Ross Creek Cedars about halfway.

GPS Coordinates: N 48° 13.254' W 115° 51.521'

Contact: Kootenai National Forest, Three Rivers Ranger District, Troy Ranger Station, 12858 Hwy. 2, Troy, MT 59935-8750, 406/295-4693, www.fs.usda.gov/kootenai.

27 SPAR LAKE

Scenic rating: 7

in Scotchman Peaks in Kootenai National Forest

At 3,300 feet, the 383-acre Spar Lake is so popular with locals that the Forest Service expanded the campground in 2009. The lake with a dirt boat ramp is good for small motorboats, canoes, and kayaks. Fish species include kokanee salmon, brook trout, and lake trout. Two hiking trails in the Scotchman Peaks—a proposed wilderness area—sit about three miles south of the campground, starting from the same trailhead. Gaining 2,300 feet in three miles, the Little Spar Lake Trail (#143) ascends along Spar Creek through lush forest to the small lake, which harbors native westslope cutthroat trout. The Spar Peak Trail (#324) grunts up 3,000 feet on a steep 3.2-mile path along Cub Creek through bear grass meadows to the summit. At 6,585 feet, the above-tree-line peak grants a 360-degree view of Scotchman Peaks and Cabinet Mountains. Mountain bikers ride logging roads and trails in the area.

The ultra-quiet campground is tucked in tall firs above the lake at the head of a west side bay. The expansion added a new toilet and four more campsites, but the campground is so far removed from roads and towns that it guarantees solitude. Campsites are spread out for privacy.

Campsites, facilities: The campground has 13 RV or tent campsites. Sites can fit RVs and trailer combinations up to 28 feet long. Facilities include picnic tables, fire rings with grills, vault toilets, campground hosts, and drinking water. Pack out your trash. Leashed pets are permitted.

Reservations, fees: Reservations are not accepted. Campsites cost $8. Open mid-May-mid-November, but only with full services May-early September.

Directions: From two miles east of Troy on Highway 2, drive 20 miles south on Lake

Creek Road (Forest Road 384). The paved road passes by small ranches for 10 miles before turning to dirt. It crosses Lake Creek, enters the national forest, and climbs to the lake.
GPS Coordinates: N 48° 16.183' W 115° 57.258'
Contact: Kootenai National Forest, Three Rivers Ranger District, Troy Ranger Station, 12858 Hwy. 2, Troy, MT 59935-8750, 406/295-4693, www.fs.usda.gov/kootenai.

28 BIG EDDY

Scenic rating: 7
on Cabinet Gorge Reservoir in Kootenai National Forest

Seven miles east of the Montana-Idaho border, Big Eddy Campground flanks the north shore of 18-mile-long Cabinet Gorge Reservoir near the Cabinet Gorge Dam. The dam's viewing platform (open spring-fall) affords a bird's-eye view of the spillway and is an interpretive site for the new Ice Age Floods National Geologic Trail, created by Congress in 2009. The site marks the location of an ice dam that formed Glacial Lake Missoula 14,000 years ago and repeatedly failed, flooding Idaho, Washington, and Oregon. Across the highway from the campground, the Big Eddy Trail ascends to Star Peak Lookout in 4.5 miles. In Idaho, the Scotchman Peak Trail climbs 3.5 miles in 3,700 feet up bear grass-flanked switchbacks in the proposed Scotchman Peak Wilderness Area for views of the Clark Fork River and Lake Pend Oreille. The boat ramp at the campground accesses the Cabinet Gorge Reservoir for fishing, waterskiing, paddling canoes or kayaks, and bird-watching. Anglers go after bass and pike.

At 2,185 feet, the tiny campground with small campsites rims a narrow dirt road that loops through the old-growth forest of hemlock and cedar admitting filtered sunlight.

An overnight parking area with undesignated campsites provides overflow camping. Noise from trucks and trains seeps into the campground.
Campsites, facilities: The campground has five RV or tent campsites. RVs and trailer combinations are limited to 30 feet. Facilities include picnic tables, fire rings, vault toilet (wheelchair-accessible), and a boat ramp, but no drinking water. Bring water with you, or treat the reservoir water. Leashed pets are permitted.
Reservations, fees: Reservations are not accepted. Campsites are free. Open year-round, but serviced only mid-May-early September. Winter access may be limited because of snow.
Directions: From Noxon, drive eight miles west on Highway 200. From Libby, drive 55 miles, heading west on Highway 2 and then south on Highway 56. Turn west on Highway 200 for three miles. From Sandpoint, Idaho, drive 41 miles east on Highway 200. The campground sits on the south side of the highway at milepost 7.
GPS Coordinates: N 48° 3.997' W 115° 55.282'
Contact: Kootenai National Forest, Cabinet Ranger District, Trout Creek Ranger Station, 2693 Hwy. 200, Trout Creek, MT 59874-9503, 406/827-3533, www.fs.usda.gov/kootenai.

29 BULL RIVER

Scenic rating: 8
on Bull River in Kootenai National Forest

BEST (

Located in the Bull River Recreation Area at 2,214 feet, the campground sits at the confluence of the Bull River and the 18-mile-long Cabinet Gorge Reservoir below the Cabinet Mountains. On the east shore of a narrow bay formed by the Bull River, the campground is one of the most popular in the area because of its diverse activities, including swimming in the sheltered bay. The boat ramp sits at the campground entrance, allowing boaters, water-skiers, anglers, and paddlers to launch on the bay rather than the reservoir. Paddlers can tour the bay to look for wildlife, while anglers head out on the reservoir to fish for bass, trout, and large northern pike. The campground also makes a good base camp for exploring trails on the west side of the Cabinet Mountain Wilderness, and mountain bikers ride the Old Bull River Road.

Set in thick, green Douglas firs and cedars, the campground has three loops with paved roads. Sites 12, 13, and 15-18 overlook the water, but the upper loop campsites have more privacy—especially site 6. From the campsite loops, two sets of stairs drop down the bank to the water. Campsites are spread out for privacy, but you will see neighbors. You can also hear a few commercial trucks on the highway and trains across the water at night. Only two of the campsites are pull-throughs. Claim a site early in high season.

Campsites, facilities: The campground has 26 RV or tent campsites. RVs and trailer combinations are limited to 40 feet. Facilities include picnic tables, fire rings, vault and flush toilets (wheelchair-accessible), drinking water, campground hosts, group campsite, and boat ramp. Firewood is available during the serviced season. Leashed pets are permitted, and group site.

Reservations, fees: Reservations are not accepted. Campsites cost $10. Cash or check. Open May-November, but serviced only late May-early September.

Directions: From Noxon, drive four miles west on Highway 200, or from Libby drive 55 miles, heading west on Highway 2, south on Highway 56, and then east on Highway 200 for 0.5 mile. Turn north into the campground. GPS Coordinates: N 48° 1.748' W 115° 50.530'

Contact: Kootenai National Forest, Cabinet Ranger District, Trout Creek Ranger Station, 2693 Hwy. 200, Trout Creek, MT 59874-9503, 406/827-3533, www.fs.usda.gov/kootenai.

30 MARTEN CREEK

Scenic rating: 5

on Noxon Rapids Reservoir in Kootenai National Forest

At 2,200 feet, Marten Creek Campground is popular with locals when the Noxon Rapids Reservoir is full. The Noxon Rapids Dam backs up the reservoir for 25 miles, making it a playground for swimmers, anglers, boaters, water-skiers, paddlers, and bird-watchers. Anglers drop lines in for a variety of fish, including bass, pike, walleye, and brown trout. Launch boats from the paved ramp and dock. Accessed via long gravel roads, the campground sits on a narrow side bay, which offers a little protection from winds that can crop up on the main reservoir.

Set in a forest of conifers, the campground loops with a gravel road. Three sites sit adjacent to the water. Shelters at most of the sites give this campground appeal and protection from the elements in inclement weather. One shelter includes three picnic tables for a larger group. Because of the campground's location on the reservoir's west side, you'll hear little noise, except for the rumble of a few trains across the water.

Campsites, facilities: The campground has six RV or tent campsites. RVs and trailer combinations are limited to 40 feet. Facilities include picnic tables, fire rings, vault toilets (wheelchair accessible), picnic shelters, large group campsite, and boat ramp. No drinking water is available; bring your own, or treat reservoir water. Pack out your trash. Leashed pets are permitted.

Reservations, fees: Reservations are not accepted. Campsites are free. Open year-round, but with limited services and weather-dependent access September-May.

Directions: From Trout Creek, drive the Marten Lake Road 5.8 miles to a junction. Turn right for Marten Lake Road to continue and drive for another 2.9 miles. Turn right for 0.1 mile to the campground entrance on the right.

GPS Coordinates: N 47° 52.943' W 115° 44.942'

Contact: Kootenai National Forest, Cabinet Ranger District, Trout Creek Ranger Station, 2693 Hwy. 200, Trout Creek, MT 59874-9503, 406/827-3533, www.fs.usda.gov/kootenai.

31 NORTH SHORE

Scenic rating: 5
on Noxon Rapids Reservoir in Kootenai National Forest

Located on the east side of Noxon Rapids Reservoir at 2,200 feet, the North Shore Campground is heavily used by anglers, especially for its ease of access from Highway 200. The Noxon Rapids Dam backs up the reservoir for 25 miles, making it a playground for swimmers, anglers, boaters, water-skiers, paddlers, and bird-watchers. Anglers drop lines in for a variety of fish, including bass, pike, walleye, and brown trout. A paved ramp and dock aid with launching boats, and a boat trailer parking area allows for more room in your campsite. The campground's proximity to Noxon makes for easy resupply.

The campground loops its paved road with paved parking spurs through a loose arid forest on the hillside above the reservoir. Sites have filtered sunlight, shade, and privacy. At night, expect to hear noise from trains across the water and trucks on the adjacent highway. Three of the campsites offer pull-through parking.

Campsites, facilities: The campground has 16 RV or tent campsites. RVs and trailer combinations are limited to 40 feet. Facilities include picnic tables, fire rings, vault toilets (wheelchair accessible), campground hosts, drinking water, and boat launch. Firewood is sometimes for sale. Leashed pets are permitted.

Reservations, fees: Reservations are not accepted. Campsites cost $10. Cash or check. Open May-November, but with full services only late May-early September.

Directions: From Trout Creek, drive Highway 200 north for three miles. Turn left onto North Shore Drive. Drive 0.1 mile to the campground loop entrance.

GPS Coordinates: N 47° 51.694' W 115° 37.896'

Contact: Kootenai National Forest, Cabinet Ranger District, Trout Creek Ranger Station, 2693 Hwy. 200, Trout Creek, MT 59874-9503, 406/827-3533, www.fs.usda.gov/kootenai.

32 WILLOW CREEK

Scenic rating: 5
east of Trout Creek in Kootenai National Forest

Located in the southern trailing peaks from the Cabinet Mountains, Willow Creek Campground requires a bone-rattling, long drive. The access road is rough: bumpy, potholded, washboarded, dusty, and loaded with curves. Cars can handle the road by driving slowly, but high-clearance vehicles will survive better. Even though the campsite size can fit RVs up to 40 feet, smaller RVs will do better on the road. The campground is a favorite with the ATV fans, who have plenty of forest roads to ride in several directions from the campground. Anglers can fish the adjacent Vermillion River.

The campground tucks at 3,789 feet in elevation below heavily-forested mountains. A gravel road loops through the campground with gravel parking spurs. Shaded campsites flank the Vermillion River. The remote location means that night sounds consist of the river or wildlife.

Campsites, facilities: The campground has six RV or tent campsites. Facilities include picnic tables, fire rings, vault toilet, and tent pads. Leashed pets are permitted.

Reservations, fees: Reservations are not accepted. Campsites are free. Open year-round, but with limited services early September-late May. Winter access may be limited because of snow.

Directions: From Trout Creek, drive Highway 200 north past the bridge over Noxon Rapids Reservoir. Turn right onto Vermillion River Road for 4.2 miles to a junction. Continue straight for about 14 bumpy, curvy miles on Forest Road 154. At the four-way junction, go straight to reach the campground entrance. GPS Coordinates: N 47° 52.243' W 115° 18.654'

Contact: Kootenai National Forest, Cabinet Ranger District, Trout Creek Ranger Station, 2693 Hwy. 200, Trout Creek, MT 59874-9503, 406/827-3533, www.fs.usda.gov/kootenai.

33 THOMPSON FALLS STATE PARK

🚶 🚲 🏊 🛶 🚤 🎣 🐕 ♿ 🚐 ⛺

Scenic rating: 8
near Thompson Falls on the Clark Fork River

Located less than five minutes from downtown Thompson Falls or Rivers Bend Golf Course, the 36-acre state park sits under firs and tall ponderosa pines right on the Clark Fork River. The campground overlooks the river, flowing with a few riffles into Noxon Reservoir. The campground's boat ramp is suitable for small boats. For a full-sized boat launch, head 0.5 mile north on Blue Slide Road across the bridge. The river is popular for boating, waterskiing, paddling, and fishing. In the campground, a trail tours the riverbank and loops around a small pond that houses turtles, frogs, and fish. The park also provides good bird-watching: ospreys, hawks, Canada geese, and songbirds.

Thinning at the campground increased the filtered sunlight reaching the grassy campsites, which sit in two loops. Sites 16 and 17 are the most private and closest to the river. Bring earplugs for sleeping, as the trains pass on the railroad tracks across the river all night long.

Campsites, facilities: The campground has 17 RV or tent campsites. Fourteen sites can accommodate RVs up to 30 feet. Facilities include picnic tables, fire rings with grills, vault toilets (wheelchair accessible), drinking water, firewood for sale, boat launch, nature trail, campground hosts, and a group site with covered tables. Leashed pets are permitted.

Reservations, fees: Reservations are accepted online or by phone (855/922-6788). Campsites cost $15 for Montana residents (seniors and disabled get half price) and $23 for nonresidents Memorial Day weekend-Labor Day, or $12 for Montana residents and $20 for nonresidents off-season. Nonresidents with a Non-Resident Entrance Pass ($25) get a $5 discount on camping fees. Cash, check, or credit card. Open April-November.

Directions: From Thompson Falls, drive Highway 200 one mile northwest. At milepost 49.5, turn right onto Blue Slide Road. Drive 1.5 miles to the entrance on the west side of the road. Coming from the west on Highway 200, turn left onto Birdland Bay Road at mile marker 47.5 and drive 0.5 mile to the entrance on the right. GPS Coordinates: N 47° 36.980' W 115° 23.216'

Contact: Montana Fish, Wildlife, and Parks, Region 1, 490 N. Meridian Rd., Kalispell, MT 59901, 406/752-5501, http://stateparks.mt.gov.

34 COPPER KING AND CLARK MEMORIAL

🛶 🚤 🎣 🐕 ♿ 🚐 ⛺

Scenic rating: 7
on the Thompson River in Lolo National Forest

Drive up the Thompson River Road, and you'll find your neck craning upward. Huge rock outcroppings and cliffs frame the steep-walled valley, home to bighorn sheep. Sitting at 2,550 feet, Copper King is the only campground accessible via pavement. The road turns to gravel to access Clark Memorial one mile further. Anglers visit the campgrounds to fish the river for brook, brown, or rainbow trout. Rafters and kayakers also paddle the Class II and III river down to the confluence with the Clark Fork. Clark Memorial Campground sits near a memorial grove of huge western red cedars, which grow only in areas that receive abundant moisture—hence abundant mosquitoes.

Tucked under shady old-growth cedar trees, Copper King encompasses two acres with four of its sites sidling up to the riverfront. The campground's tight corners and short parking pads relegate this campground to truck campers, minibus campers, and tents. The grassy Clark Memorial sits more in the open, with views of the rugged mountains that pinch the river. Half of its sites claim riverfront. Only one thing encroaches on the singing robins and sound of the river—the rumble from logging trucks hidden in the woods across the river. However, they do not drive at night.

Campsites, facilities: Each of the two campgrounds has five RV or tent campsites. RVs are limited to small vehicles. Trailers are not recommended on the Thompson River Road. Facilities include picnic tables, fire rings with grills, and vault toilets (wheelchair-accessible), but no drinking water. Bring your own water, or treat river water. Pack out your trash. Leashed pets are permitted.

Reservations, fees: Reservations are not accepted. Camping is free. Open late May-late September.

Directions: From Thompson Falls, drive five miles northeast on Highway 200. On the west side of the Thompson River, turn north onto the paved Thompson River Road and drive four miles. Turn right into the campground. (Stay off the east side road. It sees logging trucks kicking up dust and turns into a private road.) Drive one mile past Copper King to reach Clark Memorial Campground.

Copper King GPS Coordinates: N 47° 36.997' W 115° 11.306'

Clark Memorial GPS Coordinates: N 47° 37.925' W 115° 10.422'

Contact: Lolo National Forest, Plains/ Thompson Falls Ranger District, P.O. Box 429, Plains, MT 598859, 406/826-3821, www. fs.usda.gov/lolo.

35 FISHTRAP LAKE

Scenic rating: 7

near Fishtrap Lake in Lolo National Forest

Located at 4,000 feet, Fishtrap Lake is for those who love remote long drives to reach quiet and solitude. The campground sits on a bench above the lake. At the lake, a primitive boat ramp helps with launching small watercraft: canoes, kayaks, float tubes, and boats. Anglers go after native westslope cutthroat trout from the shoreline or by boat. An easy hiking trail loops around Fishtrap Lake and connects with Upper Fishtrap Lake.

The sunny campground sits on one loop in a sparse forest of western larch trees and meadows. Pull-through sites are available, tucked around a gravel loop.

Campsites, facilities: The campground has four RV or tent campsites. Trailers are not recommended on the Thompson River Road because of its skinny width and sharp corners, and the campground is suitable only for very small RVs and tents. Facilities include picnic tables, fire rings with grills, and vault toilet (wheelchair-accessible). Drinking water is available late May through late September. Leashed pets are permitted.

Reservations, fees: Reservations are not accepted. Camping is free. Open late May-late September.

Directions: From Thompson Falls, drive six miles northeast on Highway 200. On the west side of the Thompson River, turn north onto the paved Thompson River Road and drive 15 miles. (Stay off the east side road. It sees logging trucks kicking up dust and turns into a private road.) The Thompson River Road turns to dirt and narrows just past Copper King. A few pullouts sit along the road to deal with oncoming vehicles. Turn west on Fishtrap Creek Road (Forest Road 516) and drive for 14 miles. Turn west on Forest Road 7593 for two miles. After passing the lake access, turn into the campground.

GPS Coordinates: N 47° 51.711' W 115° 12.191'

Contact: Lolo National Forest, Plains/ Thompson Falls Ranger District, P.O. Box 429, Plains, MT 598859, 406/826-3821, www. fs.usda.gov/lolo.

36 CASCADE

Scenic rating: 7

on the Clark Fork River in Lolo National Forest

BEST (

Across the road from the Clark Fork River, sitting at 2,900 feet, Cascade is the only designated campground on Highway 135, so it frequently fills up—especially with its close proximity to a hot spring resort. Four miles east of the campground, Quinn's Hot Springs welcomes drop-ins. Sink into the two hot tubs and four soaking pools before hopping in the 65° cold pool or swimming pool. Open daily, the resort refills the pools nightly rather than using chemicals. Five miles west of the campground, a fishing access allows for launching drift boats, rafts, canoes, and kayaks onto the Clark Fork River, which harbors several species of trout. The Cascade National Recreation Trail begins at the campground, and a 1.4-mile nature walk leads to Cascade Falls and views of the Clark Fork River.

Adjacent to the paved highway, the four-acre campground is tucked under a shady canopy of ponderosa pines and larch. The narrow canyon walls shade the campground until filtered sun arrives late in the morning. Both truck and train noise enters the campground, making earplugs advisable. Low brush lends some privacy, but you'll see a few neighboring campers. If the campground fills up, locate free, dispersed, primitive campsites between the campground and the fishing access. As long as no sign is posted banning camping, it is legal to camp at large in the national forest.

Campsites, facilities: The campground has 10 RV or tent campsites. Facilities include picnic tables, fire rings with grills, vault toilets (wheelchair accessible), drinking water, and a large group campsite. Pack out your trash. Leashed pets are permitted.

Reservations, fees: Reservations are not accepted. Campsites cost $10. Cash or check. Open May-September.

Directions: From St. Regis, drive 17 miles northeast on Highway 135, or from Paradise, drive south on Highway 200 across the Clark Fork River and turn west onto Highway 135 for 6.2 miles. Turn south into the campground.

GPS Coordinates: N 47° 18.513' W 114° 50.805'

Contact: Lolo National Forest, Plains/ Thompson Falls Ranger District, P.O. Box 429, Plains, MT 598859, 406/826-3821, www. fs.usda.gov/lolo.

37 LITTLE THERRIAULT LAKE

Scenic rating: 9

in the Whitefish Range in Kootenai National Forest

BEST (

At 5,520 feet after a long, dusty dirt road drive, idyllic trout-filled Little Therriault Lake provides a convenient base camp for exploring Ten Lakes Scenic Area, a proposed alpine wilderness area in the north end of the Whitefish Range. A one-mile graveled trail loops the 28-acre shallow lake. Less than 0.5 mile from the campground, trailhead #83 leads 1.5 miles up to a pair of subalpine lakes. Surrounded by wildflower meadows, Paradise and Bluebird Lakes make the best kid-friendly destinations,

© BECKY LOMAX

Poorman Peak yields panoramic views in Ten Lakes Scenic Area.

but the trail also connects with the longer Galton Range Trail (#88), which runs along the crest of Ten Lakes toward Poorman Peak, the site of an old lookout at 7,832 feet. Starting from the horse camp above the campground, an 11-mile loop trail, with both lakes and ridge walking, links the Wolverine Lakes with the Bluebird Basin on trails #82, 84, 88, and 83. A rough ramp provides for launching smaller boats and canoes; powerboats are not permitted. Snowmobilers ride here in winter.

The small, quiet, secluded three-acre campground sits right on the lake. Bring the bug spray, for the area sometimes breeds voracious mosquitoes. Campsites are spread out for privacy and shaded by evergreens. Because of the proximity of the campsites on the lakeshore, this campground often fills first before those just around the corner at Big Therriault Lake.

Campsites, facilities: The campground has six RV or tent campsites. RVs are limited to 32 feet in length. Facilities include picnic tables, fire rings, a vault toilet (wheelchair-accessible),

and drinking water July-early September from a hand pump. Leashed pets are permitted.

Reservations, fees: No reservations are accepted. A campsite costs $5. Cash or check. Open year-round, but usually snowbound November-mid-June.

Directions: From Highway 93 eight miles south of Eureka, turn east onto Graves Creek Road. Follow the road, which turns from pavement into the dirt Forest Road 114, for 14 miles as it heads east and circles north. Where Trail Creek Road (Forest Road 114) veers east, drive north for 14 miles on Forest Road 319. Turn right onto Bluebird Creek Road (Forest Road 7805) for 0.7 miles to the campground entrance.

GPS Coordinates: N 48° 56.626' W 144° 53.350'

Contact: Kootenai National Forest, Fortine Ranger District, Murphy Lake Ranger Station, P.O. Box 116, 12797 Hwy. 93 S., Fortine, MT 59918-0116, 406/882-4451, www.fs.usda.gov/kootenai.

38 BIG THERRIAULT LAKE

Scenic rating: 9

in the Whitefish Range in Kootenai National Forest

BEST (

On the edge of Ten Lakes Scenic Area at 5,554 feet, Big Therriault Lake provides a popular base camp for exploring the proposed alpine wilderness area in the north end of the Whitefish Range. Departing from the lake, a trail climbs 1.5 miles up to Therriault Pass, which in itself isn't much of a destination in the trees, but it links to several other trails. The Galton Range Trail (#88) walks north across the entire Ten Lakes Scenic Area just under the ridge toward Poorman Peak, the highest mountain in the area. From the pass, a trail also leads 1.75 miles farther to Stahl Lookout at 7,392 feet. The lookout provides views of the northern

Whitefish Range, plus Glacier Park in the distance. A 1.2-mile shoreline trail also loops around the lake. A rough ramp provides for launching boats for fishing or canoeing on the 56-acre lake; no power boating is permitted. The campground is a snowmobile destination in winter.

The dusty dirt-and-gravel drive to get to the campground goes on forever. The campground sprawls its few campsites tucked into five acres of thick Douglas and subalpine firs. Heavy vegetation creates privacy between most of the sites, and the remote location guarantees nighttime quiet.

Campsites, facilities: This campground has 10 RV or tent campsites. RVs are limited to 32 feet in length. Facilities include picnic tables, fire rings, a vault toilet (wheelchair-accessible), food storage boxes, and drinking water July-early September from a hand pump. Leashed pets are permitted.

Reservations, fees: No reservations are accepted. Campsites costs $5. Cash or check. Open year-round, but snowbound November-June.

Directions: From Highway 93 eight miles south of Eureka, turn east onto Grave Creek Road. Follow the road, which turns from pavement into the dirt Forest Road 114, for 14 miles as it heads east and circles north. Where Trail Creek Road (Forest Road 114) veers east, drive north for 14 miles on Forest Road 319. Veer right onto Big Therriault Lake Road (Forest Road 7116) for 0.4 mile to the campground entrance. The lake sits at the end of the road. GPS Coordinates: N 48° 56.185' W 114° 52.621'

Contact: Kootenai National Forest, Fortine Ranger District, Murphy Lake Ranger Station, P.O. Box 116, 12797 Hwy. 93 S., Fortine, MT 59918-0116, 406/882-4451, www.fs.usda.gov/kootenai.

39 TUCHUCK

Scenic rating: 6

in the Whitefish Range in Flathead National Forest

A night or two at Tuchuck lets you explore some of the remote trails at the north end of Flathead National Forest. Thoma Lookout, in particular, is worth the grunt up its 1,900 vertical feet in three miles because of its panoramic view of Glacier's Kintla-Kinnerly peaks. Miles below, on the Flathead Valley floor, the international boundary swath cuts through the forest, and north of it sit the peaks of Canada's Akamina-Kishenena Provincial Park. Locate the trailhead about 6.6 miles east of the campground and up Forest Road 114a, where the road dead-ends. A faint trail also connects to Mount Hefty from the Thoma trail. At 4,632 feet, the campground is near the confluence of the Yakinikak, Tuchuck, and Trail Creeks, all with fishing.

Regardless of the approach road, accessing this two-acre forested campground requires driving long, bumpy, dusty gravel and dirt roads. Its quiet location, miles from highways, gives it appeal. Sites are spread out for privacy in a shaded loop.

Campsites, facilities: The small campground has seven RV or tent campsites. RVs are limited to 22 feet. Facilities include picnic tables, fire rings, a vault toilet (wheelchair-accessible), and stock hitch rails and ramp. Drinking water is not available; bring your own or treat the creeks. Pack out your trash. Leashed pets are permitted.

Reservations, fees: Reservations are not accepted. Campsites are free. Open mid-May-September.

Directions: From Polebridge, drive 15 miles north on the North Fork Road to Trail Creek Road (Forest Road 114) and turn west for nine miles. Turn south into the campground. From Highway 93 eight miles south of Eureka, turn east onto Graves Creek Road for 20 miles to the campground. Note: Graves Creek Road turns from pavement into the dirt Forest Road 114, which becomes Trail Creek Road.

GPS Coordinates: N 48° 55.400' W 114° 36.041'

Contact: Flathead National Forest, Glacier View District, 10 Hungry Horse Dr., Hungry Horse, MT 59919, 406/387-3800, www.fs.usda.gov/flathead/.

40 GRAVE CREEK

Scenic rating: 6

in the Whitefish Range in Kootenai National Forest

At 3,022 feet on the east edge of the Tobacco Valley, Grave Creek Campground provides a base camp for exploring trails in Ten Lakes Scenic Area. A 12-mile drive ends at the south trailhead to Stahl Peak Lookout. A four-mile climb on trail #81 leads to the lookout, which sits at 7,435 feet with views of Therriault Pass, Gibralter Ridge, and peaks of Glacier National Park in the distance. The nearest trailhead, however, departs from two miles away to climb Gibralter Ridge (#335) for views down into the Tobacco Valley. The trail continues to 7,131 feet on Mount Gibralter after a five-mile ascent. With the campground set on Grave Creek at the site of a historical dam, anglers can stream fish.

An open, mixed forest of birches, cottonwoods, and firs dominates the narrow canyon that houses the campground that shows abuse from unconscientious campers. The campsites line up along the creek with the Graves Creek Road visible across the stream. The sites spread out for privacy.

Campsites, facilities: The campground has four RV or tent campsites. The maximum vehicle length is 20 feet, and trailers should be 12 feet or less. Facilities include picnic tables, fire rings, and a vault toilet (wheelchair-accessible). The campground has no water. Bring your own, or treat creek water. Pack out your trash. Leashed pets are permitted.

Reservations, fees: No reservations are accepted, and the campsites are free. Open year-round, but serviced only late May-early September. Winter access may be limited by snow.

Directions: From Highway 93 eight miles south of Eureka, turn east onto Grave Creek Road 114. Drive three miles and turn right onto gravel Stoken Road 7019. Cross the bridge, continue for 0.6 mile, and make a left turn, dropping down the steep, narrow gravel road into the campground.

GPS Coordinates: N 48° 49.150' W 114° 53.177'

Contact: Kootenai National Forest, Fortine Ranger District, Murphy Lake Ranger Station, P.O. Box 116, 12797 Hwy. 93 S., Fortine, MT 59918-0116, 406/882-4451, www.fs.usda.gov/kootenai.

41 NORTH DICKEY LAKE

Scenic rating: 8

in the Whitefish Range in Kootenai National Forest

Located adjacent to Highway 93 at 4,483 feet, North Dickey Lake Campground is a cinch to reach compared to many of the other Kootenai National Forest campgrounds. Its popular day-use area includes a boat ramp, dock, trailer parking, roped-off swimming area, and grassy beach. The 800-acre lake lures anglers going after kokanee salmon and rainbow trout, paddlers, and water-skiers. The Mount Marston Trailhead sits on the east side of Highway 93 just opposite the entrance road. The nine-mile climb slogs up to the lookout, sitting at 7,343 feet, for views of the Whitefish Range. Dickey Lake attracts songbirds, raptors, waterfowl, and loons, which may provide a morning wake-up call in early summer. From the campground, a short wheelchair-accessible trail leads to a platform for viewing the lake, and a footpath drops downhill to the lake. Interpretive programs are offered in summer. Cyclists can tour the bucolic paved roads to Trego.

The shady hillside campground is tucked back from the shoreline in the lodgepole pine and larch forest, with low brush as ground cover, allowing visibility of other campsites. With a paved loop through the trees, the campground has a secluded feel, but you can still hear commercial trucks on the two-lane highway and see the highway from the beach.

Campsites, facilities: The campground has 25 RV or tent campsites. RVs are limited to 32 feet. Facilities include picnic tables, fire rings with grills, vault toilets (wheelchair-accessible), tent pads, garbage service, drinking water, campground host, and a disposal station. Leashed pets are permitted.

Reservations, fees: Reservations are accepted (877/444-6777, www.recreation.gov). Campsites cost $10. Cash or check. Open mid-May-November, but serviced only mid-May-early September.

Directions: On Highway 93, drive 14.8 miles south from Eureka or 35.3 miles north from Whitefish to the signed Trego turnoff. Turn west and drive 0.2 mile to a left turn into the campground.

GPS Coordinates: N 48° 43.195' W 114° 50.063'

Contact: Kootenai National Forest, Fortine Ranger District, Murphy Lake Ranger Station, P.O. Box 116, 12797 Hwy. 93 S., Fortine, MT 59918-0116, 406/882-4451, www.fs.usda.gov/kootenai.

42 RED MEADOW LAKE

Scenic rating: 10
in the Whitefish Range of Flathead National Forest

Red Meadow Lake perches like a jewel at 5,599 feet atop the Whitefish Divide on the bumpy, dusty, jarring midway dirt-road crossover from the Flathead Valley to the North Fork Valley. About 0.5 mile south of the lake, the Ralph Thayer Memorial Trail ascends to the Whitefish Divide crest and traverses 17 miles south to Werner Peak Lookout, with big views of the Whitefish Range and Glacier Park; turn around at Diamond Peak for a 10-mile day. Other trails, within a 10-minute drive from the lake, climb to Chain Lakes (a very steep two miles), Link Lake (1.5 miles), or Nasukoin Mountain (5.8 miles), the highest peak in the Whitefish Range. Mountain bikers tour the road and some of the trails. Small hand-carried boats, canoes, and kayaks can be launched from the shoreline for paddling or fishing. The fish in early summer are ravenous. Snowmobiles can access the campground in winter.

The small campground is quite open with exceptional views, but at the cost of privacy. Winter avalanches keep much of the mature timber pruned out around the lake. A couple of the campsites sit right on the lakeshore only inches off the road; others sit across the road from the lake and in a small loop. Despite the road slicing right through the campground, this is a quiet location.

Campsites, facilities: The campground has six RV or tent campsites. RVs are limited to 32 feet. Facilities include picnic tables, fire rings, and a vault toilet (wheelchair-accessible). Drinking water is not available; bring water, or treat lake water. Pack out your trash. Leashed pets are permitted.

Reservations, fees: No reservations are accepted. Camping is free. Open mid-May-October, and snowbound remainder of year.

Directions: From the North Fork Road five miles north of the Polebridge junction, drive 11 miles west on Red Meadows Road (Forest Road 115). From Highway 93 north of Whitefish, turn east onto the Olney Crossover Road across the highway from Olney and drive 8.5 miles to a signed three-way junction. Turn left and continue another 11 miles on Forest Road

115, staying on the main road and climbing steeply in the last two miles.

GPS Coordinates: N 48° 45.259' W 114° 33.821'

Contact: Flathead National Forest, Glacier View District, 10 Hungry Horse Dr., Hungry Horse, MT 59919, 406/387-3800, www.fs.usda.gov/flathead/.

43 MOOSE LAKE

🚶 🚵 🏊 🛶 🛥 🚣 🎣 🐕 🚐 ⛺

Scenic rating: 7

in the Whitefish Range of Flathead National Forest

Utterly remote, Moose Lake perches at 5,666 feet smack in hefty bear country. It requires about 25 miles of gravel and dirt road driving on washboards, potholes, and dust. But that is precisely the attraction, for you won't run into crowds, and you might see moose, elk, deer, bear, mountain lion, or wolves. The shallow lake is only 0.3 miles long, but works for hand-carried watercraft. Fishing is best from a boat because of heavy brush along the shoreline. Hikers can climb 1,850 feet in three miles up Moose Peak with a scenic ridge walk with views of the Whitefish Range. Mountain biking is available on forest roads. Deer hunters use the campground in fall.

The idyllic tiny campground sits at the southern end of Moose Lake adjacent to the outlet. Campsites are set under conifers for shade. With the miles of rough dirt deterring lots of traffic, the campground yields quiet, privacy, and a sky full of stars.

Campsites, facilities: The campground has three RV or tent campsites. Only smaller RVs are recommended. Facilities include picnic tables, fire rings, and vault toilet. Drinking water is not available; bring your own, or treat lake water. Pack out your trash. Leashed pets are permitted.

Reservations, fees: No reservations are accepted. Camping is free. Open mid-May-October, and snowbound remainder of year.

Directions: From Columbia Falls, drive the North Fork Road 20 miles. Shortly past Big Creek, turn left onto Big Creek Road (Forest Road 316) for eight miles. Veer right onto Forest Road 315 for three miles to another fork. Veer right onto Forest Road 317D for 5.8 miles to the campground entrance on the right.

GPS Coordinates: N 48° 37.708' W 114° 23.343'

Contact: Flathead National Forest, Glacier View District, 10 Hungry Horse Dr., Hungry Horse, MT 59919, 406/387-3800, www.fs.usda.gov/flathead/.

44 UPPER WHITEFISH LAKE

🚶 🚵 🏊 🛶 🛥 🚣 🎣 🐕 ♿ 🚐 ⛺

Scenic rating: 9

in the Whitefish Range in Stillwater State Forest

A favorite with anglers in summer and hunters in fall, the 80-acre Upper Whitefish Lake sits at 4,432 feet below the Whitefish Divide. While fly-fishing and spin-casting can work from shore, a boat launched from the primitive dirt ramp helps to catch the bigger native westslope cutthroat. Paddle the placid lake in morning or evening to see waterfowl, songbirds, and raptors. Most of the hiking trails in the area depart from trailheads in the vicinity of Red Meadows Lake, about six miles up the road. The trail to three destinations—Link Lake (1.5 miles), Lake Mountain (3.5 miles), and Nasukoin Mountain (5.8 miles)—departs off a spur road (Road 589). Look for the Link Lake sign and drive 1.3 miles to the trailhead. Mountain bikers ride forest roads.

Sitting on the southeastern corner of the lake, the six-acre quiet campground splits on both sides of the road north of the outlet stream bridge. A few additional sites are accessed via a spur road just before the bridge. Foliage and mature trees maintain privacy between the shaded sites. Some have views of the surrounding mountains.

Campsites, facilities: The campground has 13 RV or tent campsites. RVs are limited to 32 feet. Facilities include picnic tables, fire rings with grills, vault toilets (wheelchair-accessible), and a boat launch. No drinking water is available; bring your own, or treat lake water. Pack out your trash. Leashed pets are permitted.

Reservations, fees: No reservations are accepted, and campsites are free. The campground is open mid-June-October.

Directions: From Highway 93 north of Whitefish, turn east onto the Olney Crossover Road across the highway from Olney and drive 8.5 miles to a signed three-way junction. Turn left and continue another five miles on Forest Road 115 to the campground, which sits on both sides of the creek and road.

GPS Coordinates: N 48° 41.053' W 114° 34.462'

Contact: Stillwater State Forest, P.O. Box 164, Olney, MT 59919, 406/881-2371, http://dnrc.mt.gov.

45 STILLWATER LAKE

Scenic rating: 7

on Upper Stillwater Lake in Flathead National Forest

Located at 3,250 feet, this tiny ultra-popular campground is favored by anglers year-round. Winter brings ice fishing, and summer stream fishing in the slow-moving Stillwater River nearby can land a 20- to 30-pound pike. Canoeists enjoy the lake but should be wary of logjams when floating the river. A gravel boat ramp works for launching small watercraft (only nonmotorized boats permitted). Mountain bikers hit the forest roads around the lake. For hikers, a nearby 1.5-mile trail tours the LeBeau Natural Area through old-growth larches and ancient Belt Sea formation rocks

to large bluffs above Finger Lake. A spur trail cuts off to Hole-in-the-Wall Lake. Hunters also use the campground in fall.

With three sites right on the lakeshore in sparse tall trees, the campsites may have you waking up to the slap of beavertails on the water. Gravel parking pads rim the gravel loop. For viewing the beaver lodge and wildlife, a bench sits near the boat ramp. Watch for moose, otter, and songbirds.

Campsites, facilities: The campground has five RV or tent campsites. RVs are limited to 25 feet. Facilities include picnic tables, fire rings with grills, vault toilet (wheelchair-accessible), bear food hanging pole, and campground hosts. Drinking water is not available; bring your own or treat lake water. Pack out your own garbage. Leashed pets are permitted.

Reservations, fees: Reservations are not accepted, and camping is free. Open May-November.

Directions: From Whitefish, drive 21 miles north on Highway 93 and turn west at the Stillwater Lake Campground sign at milepost 151.5. Follow the signs two miles to the campground. The dirt road snakes left, then right, before crossing the railroad tracks and turning left to climb over a hill.

GPS Coordinates: N 48° 36.207' W 114° 39.457'

Contact: Flathead National Forest, Talley Lake Ranger District, 650 Wolfpack Way, Kalispell, MT 59901, 406/758-5204, www.fs.usda.gov/flathead/.

46 TALLY LAKE

Scenic rating: 9

in the Salish Mountains in Flathead National Forest

At 492 feet deep, Tally Lake claims the record as Montana's deepest lake. Located at 3,600 feet, the lake attracts weekend campers as well as those out for a day of fishing,

Paddlers enjoy Tally Lake, one of Montana's deepest lakes.

waterskiing, paddling, or swimming on the sandy beach. A cement boat ramp, dock, and trailer parking are available. An interpretive site has a spotting scope for watching bald eagles fishing or migratory waterfowl. Several hiking and mountain-biking trails explore the surrounding forest. The 1.25-mile Tally Lake Overlook trail departs from the campground to climb through mature timber. While the walk through the trees provides a close-up view of old-growth forest, the overlook is fast losing its view to crowding trees. Also departing near the campground, a nine-mile loop trail through old-growth forest and spring fairy slipper orchids climbs 1,955 vertical feet up Tally Mountain, where it connects with the Boney Gulch Trail to drop back to the road two miles south of the trailhead.

The 23-acre, quiet campground sits on the lake's north shore. The campground loops through mature timber that provides filtered shade. Most of the sites are set back from the lakeshore and spread out for privacy. Prime campsites on the northwest loop have lake frontage, plus views of the lake and surrounding mountainside.

Campsites, facilities: The campground has 40 RV or tent campsites. Maximum trailer length for the campground is 40 feet. Facilities include picnic tables, fire rings with grills, vault toilets (wheelchair accessible), drinking water, a disposal station, garbage service, boat launch, swimming beach, volleyball, horseshoe pits, group campsite with large pavilion, campground hosts, and firewood for sale. Leashed pets are permitted.

Reservations, fees: Reservations are only accepted for the large group campsite (877/444-6777, www.recreation.gov). Campsites cost $15. Cash or check. Open mid-May-November.

Directions: From Whitefish, drive Highway 93 west for 10 miles and turn left onto Farm to Market Road for 1.5 miles. Turn right onto Star Meadows Road and drive nine miles. Turn left onto the gravel Forest Road 913 for 3.2 miles to the campground entrance on the left. GPS Coordinates: N 48° 24.883' W 114° 35.209'

Contact: Flathead National Forest, Talley Lake Ranger District, 650 Wolfpack Way, Kalispell, MT 59901, 406/758-5204, www.fs.usda.gov/flathead/.

47 SYLVIA LAKE

🏃 🚴 🏊 🎣 🛶 🚣 💺 🐕 🚐 ⛺

Scenic rating: 7

in the Salish Mountains in Flathead National Forest

Anglers head to Sylvia Lake for its arctic grayling and westslope cutthroat trout. The 23-acre lake, which sits at 5,189 feet, is stocked frequently by the state. Bird-watchers and canoers also enjoy the lake. A rough boat ramp aids in launching smaller watercraft onto the lake (no motors allowed). A trail (#171) across the road climbs 3.5 miles to the summit of Ingalls Mountain, with views of the Salish Mountains. The area attracts mountain bikers for its single-track trail riding and double-track old forest roads. Hunters also use the camp in fall.

Surrounded by silver and burnt conifer remnants from fire, the campground sits on the east shore of the lake where you might hear the haunting call of loons in the morning. Because of its distance from pavement, the ultra-quiet campground is usually a place to garner solitude. Additional primitive campsites with no services are located on a spur road south of the lake.

Campsites, facilities: The campground has three RV or tent campsites. The maximum length for an RV or trailer combinations is 20 feet. Facilities include picnic tables, rock-ring fire pits, and a pit toilet. Drinking water is not available, so bring your own or treat lake water. Pack out your trash. Leashed pets are permitted.

Reservations, fees: Reservations are not accepted, and camping is free. Open mid-May-mid-November.

Directions: From Whitefish, drive Highway 93 northwest to Farm to Market Road. Turn left, and drive 1.5 miles and turn right onto Star Meadows Road (Forest Road 539), which becomes Forest Road 113 when the pavement changes to dirt about 15 miles up. Stay to the left at the next two junctions, following the signs about six miles to Sylvia Lake.

GPS Coordinates: N 48° 20.681' W 114° 49.121'

Contact: Flathead National Forest, Talley Lake Ranger District, 650 Wolfpack Way, Kalispell, MT 59901, 406/758-5204, www.fs.usda.gov/flathead/.

48 WHITEFISH LAKE STATE PARK

🏃 🚴 🏊 🎣 🚤 🚣 🐕 ♿ 🚐 ⛺

Scenic rating: 9

in Whitefish

The state park, which sits at 3,012 feet on the south side of Whitefish Lake, garners views of Big Mountain from the beach. But prepare for numerous trains per day rumbling on the tracks adjacent to the campground. Local anglers, water-skiers, paddlers, and lake sightseers use the boat launch for the day, and the cordoned-off swimming area attracts families from town to cool off in the summer heat. Downtown Whitefish, with shops, restaurants, groceries, gas, and nightlife, is only two miles away. Whitefish Golf Course with 36 holes is only one mile away, as is the Whitefish Trail for hikers and mountain bikers. Whitefish Mountain Resort above the lake runs its chairlift in the summer for sightseeing and mountain biking, and the four-mile Danny On Trail connects the summit of Big Mountain with the resort.

With a paved campground road and parking pads, the campsites tuck under a mature forest with substantial undergrowth foliage. None of the campsites sit right on the shoreline, and campers must walk through the day-use parking lot to reach the beach. Sites 1-12 cluster around a loop separated from the road that day users drive to reach the boat ramp, beach, and parking lot. Sites 13-15 and 22-24 sit just beneath the slope leading up to the railroad tracks; sites 2-9 are the farthest away from the tracks.

Campsites, facilities: The campground has 25 RV or tent campsites. RVs or trailer combinations are limited to 40 feet. Facilities include picnic tables, fire rings with grills, flush toilets, showers, drinking water, bear boxes, firewood for sale, boat ramp with a dock, and a swimming area. Leashed pets are permitted. A wheelchair-accessible toilet and campsite are available.

Reservations, fees: Reservations are not accepted. Campsites cost $15 for Montana residents (seniors and disabled get half price) and $23 for nonresidents Memorial Day weekend-Labor Day, or $12 for Montana residents and $20 for nonresidents September-May. Nonresidents with a Non-Resident Entrance Pass ($25) get a $5 discount on camping fees. Cash or check. Open year-round, but drinking water and showers are only available May-September.

Directions: From downtown Whitefish, drive Highway 93 west for 1.3 miles. Veer right at the state park sign around the golf course. Take the next right onto State Park Road and follow it about one mile until it crosses the railroad tracks. The entrance sits just past the tracks on the left.

GPS Coordinates: N 48° 25.447' W 114° 22.237'

Contact: Montana Fish, Wildlife, and Parks, Region 1, 490 N. Meridian Rd., Kalispell, MT 59901, 406/752-5501, http://stateparks.mt.gov.

49 WHITEFISH KOA

Scenic rating: 7

south of Whitefish

At 3,100 feet, the campground is conveniently near Whitefish or a 35-minute drive from the west entrance to Glacier National Park. Four miles north of the campground, downtown Whitefish clusters shopping, restaurants, and nightlife within a few blocks, along with groceries, gas, and other shops lining the two miles leading into town. Recreation abounds: boating on Whitefish Lake, canoeing the Whitefish River, hiking and mountain biking on the Whitefish Trail and Big Mountain at Whitefish Mountain Resort.

The campground tucks back deep in the woods, surrounded by a fir forest. Campsites sprinkle across 33 acres of mature forest connected by a gravel road. Open pull-through sites for large RVs allow for satellite reception. Deluxe RV sites include wooden decks. Tent sites sit closer to the bathhouse in grassy or forested locations with options including electricity and water.

Campsites, facilities: There are 86 RV sites, pull-throughs for the largest rigs, and seven tents. RV hookups include sewer, water, and electricity up to 50 amps. Facilities include picnic tables, fire rings, flush toilets (wheelchair-accessible), showers, camp store, seasonal restaurant, games center, playground, and indoor/outdoor pool (mid-April-September only), an adults-only hot tub, wireless Internet, free mini-golf, a disposal station, and firewood. Leashed pets are permitted.

Reservations, fees: Reservations are accepted. RV hookups run $40-75; tent sites cost $43-50. Rates are for two people; extra people are charged $8. Cash, check, or credit card. Add on a 7 percent Montana bed tax. Open mid-April-mid-October.

Directions: From Whitefish at the junction of Highways 93 and 40, drive two miles south on Highway 93, or from the junction of Highways 2 and 93 in Kalispell, drive nine miles north on Highway 93. At mile marker 123, turn east into the campground.

GPS Coordinates: N 48° 20.801' W 114° 19.807'

Contact: Whitefish KOA, 5121 Hwy. 93 S., Whitefish, MT 59937, 406/862-4242 or 800/562-8734, www.glacierparkkoa.com.

50 COLUMBIA FALLS RV PARK

🏃 🚵 🏊 🛶 🎣 🏊 🐎 ♿ 🚍 ⛰

Scenic rating: 7

in Columbia Falls

Tucked under Columbia Mountain at 3,100 feet, this RV park works for those who want to drive 20 minutes to Glacier National Park or 15 minutes to Flathead Valley shopping, restaurants, and recreation. The Columbia Falls post office, outdoor community pool, coffee shop, and restaurants sit within a six-block walk. Big Sky Waterslides, one mile east, opens June-Labor Day. A mountain-biking and hiking trail runs six miles up to the summit of Columbia Mountain for broad views of the valley. At the fishing access and boat launch 0.5 mile to the east, you can float the Flathead River in drift boats, kayaks, rafts, and canoes, and anglers fish from the bridge.

Nothing blocks the campground from the highway, so light sleepers should bring ear plugs. Not much privacy exists between sites either; however, the open sites appeal to those requiring satellite reception. Fifty-one sites are gravel pull-throughs adjacent to landscaped grass islands. Extra-large spaces accommodate RVs with double slide-outs. Some seasonal RV residents are here. Most sites garner views of Columbia Mountain or the Whitefish Range. Tent sites sit in a separate large, grassy lawn area.

Campsites, facilities: The campground has 64 RV campsites and 10 tent campsites. Hookups include sewer, water, electricity up to 50 amps, and cable TV, and some of the sites have phone lines. Facilities include picnic tables, flush toilets (wheelchair-accessible), showers, a launderette, wireless Internet, and camp store. Leashed pets are permitted.

Reservations, fees: Reservations are accepted and highly recommended for July and August. Hookups cost $30-37; tent sites cost $26. Rates cover two people per site; each extra person is charged $5. Cash, check, or credit card. Add on 7 percent Montana bed tax. Check website for specials. Open April-mid-October.

Directions: From the intersection of Highway 2 and Nucleus Avenue in Columbia Falls, drive 0.25 mile east. The campground sits on the north side of the highway. For those coming from the east, the campground is 0.5 mile west of the bridge over the Flathead River.

GPS Coordinates: N 48° 22.133' W 114° 10.748'

Contact: Columbia Falls RV Park, 103 Hwy. 2 E., Columbia Falls, MT 59912, 406/892-1122 or 888/401-7268, www.columbiafallsrvpark.com.

51 ROCKY MOUNTAIN HI

🚵 🏊 🛶 🎣 🐎 🏕 🚍 ⛰

Scenic rating: 7

in Kalispell

At 2,950 feet on the east side of Kalispell, Rocky Mountain Hi sits on Spring Creek, almost equidistant from Whitefish, Columbia Falls, and Bigfork. Three golf courses—Northern Pines, Village Greens, and Buffalo Hills—are within six miles. Within five miles of the campground are two fishing access sites on the Flathead River and shopping, box stores, and restaurants in Kalispell. A 25-minute drive connects with the west entrance to Glacier National Park, and 20 minutes leads to Flathead Lake. For kids, the campground has a large playground with a miniature western town and swimming in the creek. A grassy beach lines the creek, and the slow-moving stream works for fishing and canoeing.

The quiet, forested campground sits on the east side of Spring Creek away from the highway noise. Sites 90-98 sit closest to the creek, along with the tent campsites. Many of the pull-through sites sit in a large open area good for clear satellite reception, but with little privacy between sites. Tent sites are separated by wooden privacy fences. The campground has some long-term RVers.

Campsites, facilities: The campground has 98 RV campsites and 10 tent campsites. Pull-through sites can fit the largest RVs. Hookups include sewer, water, electricity up to 50 amps, and cable TV. Facilities include picnic tables, flush toilets, showers, a launderette, swimming area with dock, canoe landing, and camp store. Leashed pets are permitted.

Reservations, fees: Reservations are accepted and recommended for July and August. Hookups run $31-33 for one or two people. For extra people over 12 years old, add $6. Tent sites cost $22. Add on 7 percent Montana bed tax. Cash, check, or credit card. Open year-round.

Directions: From Kalispell, drive Highway 2 north toward Columbia Falls. Turn right on East Reserve Drive and go one mile before turning left onto Helena Flats Road. About 0.8 mile up the road, turn right into the campground.

GPS Coordinates: N 48° 15.106' W 114° 15.125'

Contact: Rocky Mountain Hi RV Park and Campground, 825 Helena Flats Rd, Kalispell, MT 59901, 406/755-9573 or 800/968-5637, www.glaciercamping.com.

52 WEST SHORE STATE PARK

Scenic rating: 9

on Flathead Lake

Located at 2,900 feet, Flathead Lake has 128 miles of shoreline with water as clear as glass. The glacially fed lake, which draws its waters from Glacier Park, Canada, and the Bob Marshall Wilderness, grew from Ice Age glaciers melting 10,000 years ago. Located on the west shore with sunrise views over the Mission and Swan Mountains, the West Shore State Park has the reputation of being the most private state park on the lake. The campground sits on a bluff on Goose Bay with tiny Goose Island about 0.3 mile out in the lake. A concrete boat ramp facilitates launching watercraft for fishing, waterskiing, sailing, kayaking, canoeing, and sightseeing. Walking trails tour the forest.

The quiet 129-acre park spans a forested hillside with a rocky beach. Filtered sunlight hits the campsites through tall larches and pines. Some of the campsites (especially two walk-in sites) have peek-a-boo views across the lake to the mountains rising above the opposite shore about eight miles away. The campground road is paved with two loops.

Campsites, facilities: The campground has 24 RV or tent campsites, plus seven tent-only campsites. RVs are limited to 40 feet. Facilities include picnic tables, fire rings with grills, vault toilets, drinking water, garbage service, a playground, a boat launch, campground hosts, firewood for sale, and electrical hookups. For bicyclists, a bear-resistant food storage locker is available. Leashed pets are permitted. Wheelchair-accessible facilities include a toilet and a campsite with electrical and water hookups.

Reservations, fees: Reservations are accepted online or by phone (855/922-6788). Campsites cost $15 for Montana residents (seniors and campers with disabilites get half price) and $23 for nonresidents Memorial Day weekend-Labor Day, or $12 for Montana residents and $20 for nonresidents off-season. Campsites with electrical hookups cost $17-28, depending on season and residency. Nonresidents with a Non-Resident Entrance Pass ($25) get a $5 discount on camping fees. Cash, check, or credit card. Open all year.

Directions: From Kalispell, drive 20 miles south on Highway 93, or from Polson, drive 32 miles north on Highway 93. Turn east at the signed entrance to drop into the campground. GPS Coordinates: N 47° 56.901' W 114° 11.129'

Contact: Montana Fish, Wildlife, and Parks, Region 1, 490 N. Meridian Rd., Kalispell, MT 59901, 406/752-5501, http://stateparks.mt.gov.

53 LAKE MARY RONAN STATE PARK

Scenic rating: 6

on Lake Mary Ronan in the Salish Mountains

Lake Mary Ronan, which sits seven miles west of Flathead Lake at 3,770 feet, doesn't get nearly the traffic that the Flathead Lake parks see, but the lake draws its share of people. At 1,513 acres, the lake is considerably smaller than Flathead Lake, but it still attracts bird-watchers, swimmers, kayakers, canoers, water-skiers, and mushroom and huckleberry pickers. Anglers go after kokanee, largemouth bass, pumpkinseed, rainbow trout, yellow perch, and westslope cutthroat trout. Trails lead to the beach, which has a concrete boat ramp with an adjacent dock, a small swimming beach, and paved parking for boat trailers.

The quiet, 120-acre park shaded by Douglas firs and western larches tucks its campground back in the shady woods on paved loops with paved back-in spurs. The sites around the outside rim of the loop are more private than those inside the circle. A group campsite is available.

Campsites, facilities: The campground has 27 RV or tent campsites. RVs are limited to 35 feet. Facilities include picnic tables, fire rings with grills, vault toilets (wheelchair accessible), drinking water, electrical hookups, firewood for sale, boat launch, and campground host. Leashed pets are permitted.

Reservations, fees: Reservations are accepted online or by phone (855/922-6788). Campsites cost $15 for Montana residents (seniors and campers with disabilities get half price) and $23 for nonresidents Memorial Day weekend-Labor Day, or $12 for Montana residents and $20 for nonresidents off-season. Campsites with electrical hookups cost $17-28, depending on season and residency. Nonresidents with a Non-Resident Entrance Pass ($25) get a $5 discount on camping fees. Cash, check, or credit card. Open mid-May-September.

Directions: From Highway 93 at Dayton, turn

Big Arm State Park is one of five Montana state parks on Flathead Lake.

north onto the Lake Mary Ronan Road and drive six miles to the park entrance.

GPS Coordinates: N 47° 55.602' W 114° 22.942'

Contact: Montana Fish, Wildlife, and Parks, Region 1, 490 N. Meridian Rd., Kalispell, MT 59901, 406/752-5501, http://stateparks.mt.gov.

54 BIG ARM STATE PARK

Scenic rating: 10

on Flathead Lake

BEST (

Flathead Lake covers 188 square miles, but from the vantage of Big Arm State Park, islands cut off some of the wide-open water and shrink the size of the lake in appearance. Located on the lake's west side on Big Arm Bay at 2,900 feet, the park faces the morning sunrise coming over the Mission Mountains. The campground includes a cement boat ramp, dock, and trailer parking for launching to motor or paddle 5.5 miles to Wild Horse Island—a day-use state park renowned for its wild horses, bighorn sheep, birds, wildflowers, and hiking. Paddlers should watch the weather; winds can whip up whitecaps in minutes. The park also sits on the Flathead Reservation; joint state-tribal fishing permits are required to fish the lake. With a 2.5-mile nature trail through its prairie grasslands and forest, the park is also good for bird-watching—especially with bald eagles and ospreys fishing in the lake.

Large ponderosa pines and junipers bring part shade to the campground. A long swimming beach runs from the boat ramp and dock north to the end of B loop. Campsites are tucked around two narrow, long, paved loops with gravel aprons. Both loops have half of the sites overlooking the lake. Privacy is minimal with multiple campsites sharing large pull-over style parking areas, but that takes second seat when picnic tables sit mere feet from the beach.

Campsites, facilities: The campground has 41 RV and seven tent campsites. RVs are limited to 30 feet. Facilities include picnic tables, fire rings with grills, flush and vault toilets, showers, drinking water, firewood for sale, garbage service, and boat launch. Bicyclists can use the bear resistant food storage lockers. The campground also rents a yurt. Leashed pets are permitted. A wheelchair-accessible toilet and campsite with electricity are available.

Reservations, fees: Reservations are accepted online or by phone (855/922-6788). Campsites cost $15 for Montana residents (seniors and campers with disabilities get half price) and $23 for nonresidents Memorial Day weekend-Labor Day, or $12 for Montana residents and $20 for nonresidents off-season. Campsites with electrical hookups cost $17-28, depending on season and residency. Nonresidents with a Non-Resident Entrance Pass ($25) get a $5 discount on camping fees. Cash, check, or credit card. Open all year.

Directions: From Polson, drive 14 miles north on Highway 93, or from Kalispell, drive about 38 miles south on Highway 35. Turn east at the signed entrance.

GPS Coordinates: N 47° 48.335' W 114° 18.808'

Contact: Montana Fish, Wildlife, and Parks, Region 1, 490 N. Meridian Rd., Kalispell, MT 59901, 406/752-5501, http://stateparks.mt.gov.

55 WAYFARERS STATE PARK

Scenic rating: 9

on Flathead Lake

Sitting at 2,900 feet on the largest natural freshwater lake in the West, Wayfarers State Park hops in high season with fishing, sailing, waterskiing, paddling, and sightseeing. For boaters, a concrete ramp, boat trailer parking, dock, and pump-out service are available. A 1.5-mile hiking trail climbs through the 67-acre forested park with scenic overlooks of the lake. The park is also adjacent to Bigfork, with its summer theater, restaurants, and shopping.

Bigfork is also home to the annual Whitewater Festival in late May, and the dam releases flows one night a week for whitewater kayaking on the Wild Mile of the Swan River. Wayfarers is the closest campground to Jewel Basin, a 15,349-acre hiking area in mountain goat terrain with 50 miles of trails that loop among 27 alpine lakes.

The paved entrance road passes an osprey nest as it drops to the lake, where the boat launch and picnic area sit on the beach, with the campground a five-minute walk away. Most of the campground loops through a shady canopy of mature firs and ponderosa pines. Sites 10-15 have more privacy than sites 19-25, which sit on a big meadow. Sites 1-4 also sit on the meadow, right at the campground entrance with more traffic. Six sites offer pull-through parking pads. Three tent sites are walk-ins.

Campsites, facilities: The campground has 23 RV or tent campsites and seven tent-only campsites. RVs are limited to 50 feet. Facilities include picnic tables, fire rings with grills, vault and flush toilets, showers, drinking water, garbage service, disposal station, firewood for sale, playground, campground hosts, and bear-resistant food storage locker for bikers. Leashed pets are permitted. Wheelchair-accessible facilities include a toilet at one campsite (#23) with 30-amp electrical hookup.

Reservations, fees: Reservations are accepted online or by phone (855/922-6788). Campsites cost $15 for Montana residents (seniors and campers with disabilities get half price) and $23 for nonresidents Memorial Day weekend-Labor Day, or $12 for Montana residents and $20 for nonresidents off-season. Campsites with electrical hookups cost $17-28, depending on season and residency. Nonresidents with a Non-Resident Entrance Pass ($25) get a $5 discount on camping fees. Cash, check, or credit card. Open all year, but serviced only May-September.

Directions: From Bigfork, drive 0.5 mile south on Highway 35. Turn west at the signed entrance into the park.

GPS Coordinates: N 48° 3.217' W 114° 4.856'
Contact: Montana Fish, Wildlife, and Parks, Region 1, 490 N. Meridian Rd., Kalispell, MT 59901, 406/752-5501, http://stateparks.mt.gov.

56 YELLOW BAY STATE PARK

Scenic rating: 8

on Flathead Lake

For those looking for less hectic experience on Flathead Lake, Yellow Bay may be the answer on the flanks of the Mission Mountains in cherry orchard country. In July, look for stands selling freshly picked cherries along Highway 35; on hot days, you can smell the fruit in the air. Located on the lake's east side with a concrete boat ramp for fishing, waterskiing, canoeing, and sightseeing, the park sits across from Wild Horse Island—a day-use state park with bighorn sheep, eagles, and wild horses. With 10 miles of water in between, power boaters go from this eastern side. Paddlers tend to stick to the east shoreline. The park also sits on the Flathead Reservation; joint state-tribal fishing permits are required to fish the lake. Located in sheltered Yellow Bay, the 15-acre park sidles up to the lake with a wide, sandy southeast-facing beach for swimming and Yellow Bay Creek running through the park.

Although the access off the highway is paved, the road is steep and narrow. Picking up traffic noise, the tent sites sit back from the beach, tucked under a thick canopy of trees between the campground and the highway.

Campsites, facilities: The campground has four walk-in tenting sites. Facilities include picnic tables, pedestal grills, flush and vault toilets, drinking water, bear boxes, and garbage service. Wood fires are not permitted; bring your own charcoal. Leashed pets are permitted.

Reservations, fees: Reservations are not accepted. Campsites cost $7 for Montana residents (seniors and campers with disabilities get half price) and $15 for nonresidents Memorial Day weekend-Labor Day, or $4 for Montana residents and $12 for nonresidents off-season. Nonresidents with a Non-Resident Entrance Pass ($25) get a $5 discount on camping fees. Cash or check. Open May-September.

Directions: From Polson, drive 17.5 miles north on Highway 35, or from Bigfork, drive 13.5 miles south on Highway 35. Turn west at the signed entrance to the park.

GPS Coordinates: N 47° 52.532' W 114° 1.728'

Contact: Montana Fish, Wildlife, and Parks, Region 1, 490 N. Meridian Rd., Kalispell, MT 59901, 406/752-5501, http://stateparks.mt.gov.

57 BLUE BAY

Scenic rating: 10

on Flathead Lake

Blue Bay commands a spectacular location on Flathead Lake's east side, with views of Wild Horse Island. The campground, which faces southeast down the lake, sets up the majority of its campsites with prime real estate on the waterfront. Owned and operated by the Confederated Salish and Kootenai Tribes, Blue Bay has three parts: a lodge area reserved for groups, the day-use beach and marina, and the campground. The marina includes 32 boat slips, a concrete ramp and boat docks, a fishing pier, boat trailer parking, and a fish-cleaning station. The day-use swim beach has picnic tables, a dock, and a buoyed-off area to protect swimmers. Personal watercraft are not permitted.

The campground, on the opposite side of the marina from the day-use area, has another buoyed swim area with a dock at the group shelter and another swim dock with no buoy line located between sites 18 and 19. Large ponderosa pines shade some of the grassy area. Sites 1-6, 41, and 51 are farther apart from their neighbors, while the remainder of the

sites line up close to each other. Sites 7-33 line the waterfront. In a row on a bluff behind the waterfront campsites are the sites with hook-ups. No alcohol is permitted in the campground. Most of the campsites are buffered from the highway by the bluff with the lodges.

Campsites, facilities: The campground has 55 campsites. RV hookups are available at 17 sites with hookups for sewer and water, and some have electricity. Facilities include picnic tables, fire rings, drinking water, garbage service, and flush toilets. Leashed pets are permitted.

Reservations, fees: Reservations are not accepted. Day use for the area costs $5 per vehicle. For non-tribal members, tents cost $10-15 and hookups are $20-30. For tribal members, tenting is free and hookups cost $10-20. Cash or check. Open May-September.

Directions: From Polson, drive 13.5 miles north on Highway 35. From Bigfork, drive 17.5 miles south on Highway 35. Turn west at the signed entrance.

GPS Coordinates: N 47° 49.649' W 114° 1.694'

Contact: Confederated Salish and Kootenai Tribes, 51383 Hwy. 93 N., Pablo, MT 59855, 406/675-2700 or 406/982-3123 (campground), www.cskt.org.

58 FINLEY POINT STATE PARK

Scenic rating: 9

on Flathead Lake

Flathead Lake, the largest natural freshwater lake west of the Mississippi, tucks Finley Point State Park at 2,900 feet at its south end below the Mission Mountains. The point is actually a half-mile-wide spit that sticks out into the lake, forming Skidoo Bay to the northeast and Polson Bay to the southeast—both littered with summer homes. The proximity to Polson 15 minutes away brings heavy day use to the park.

Anglers come here to fish for whitefish, rainbow and bull trout, northern pike, and lake trout that grow up to 20 pounds. A joint state-tribal fishing license is required. A boat ramp, marina, boat pump-out, and trailer parking are available. The National Bison Range and Ninepipes National Wildlife Refuge are about 40 minutes south.

The 28-acre campground sits on the shore of Flathead Lake with all of its cramped campsites lined up along the lake facing the sunset. The grassy campground, shaded by mature firs and birches, lacks privacy. From the beach, you'll see summer homes and Polson across the bay. However, the campground's popularity comes from its prime waterfront campsites. Sites 1-4 with tent pads are designated for tents only. Two walk-in tent sites are available, too. Tents are not permitted in the RV sites, which line up in parking-lot fashion in front of their tables and fire rings.

Campsites, facilities: The campground has 12 RV campsites, six tent campsites, and 16 boat slip campsites. RV hookups include electricity, and the maximum RV length is 40 feet. Facilities include picnic tables, fire rings with grills, flush and vault toilets, drinking water, boat facilities, firewood for sale, and a swimming area. Four of the 16 boat slips also have electrical and water hookups. Boats are limited to 25 feet. Leashed pets are permitted. A wheelchair-accessible toilet and campsite with electricity are available.

Reservations, fees: Reservations are accepted online or by phone (855/922-6788). Campsites cost $15 for Montana residents (seniors and campers with disabilities get half price) and $23 for nonresidents Memorial Day weekend-Labor Day, or $12 for Montana residents and $20 for nonresidents off-season. Campsites with electrical hookups cost $17-28, depending on season and residency. Nonresidents with a Non-Resident Entrance Pass ($25) get a $5 discount on camping fees. Cash, check, or credit card. Open May-September.

Directions: From Polson, drive seven miles north on Highway 35. Turn left and follow the signs four miles northwest on narrow Finley Point Road. Turn left into the campground. GPS Coordinates: N 47° 45.299' W 114° 5.092'

Contact: Montana Fish, Wildlife, and Parks, Region 1, 490 N. Meridian Rd., Kalispell, MT 59901, 406/752-5501, http://stateparks.mt.gov.

59 POLSON-FLATHEAD LAKE KOA

Scenic rating: 7

in the Mission Valley

Located just outside the town of Polson on the south end of Flathead Lake, the Polson-Flathead Lake KOA is a prime place to camp for boating, fishing, waterskiing, and paddling on Flathead Lake. Boats can be launched at local marinas. Other nearby activities include rafting on the Lower Flathead River and golf. A short bike ride or 20-minute walk connects with downtown for dining out or shopping. A scenic drive down the Mission Valley leads to wildlife-watching at Ninepipes National Wildlife Refuge and the National Bison Range.

At first glance, the airport adjacent to the campground can be a deterrent. But it's a local airport that only sees small private planes rather than large commercial jets. From the campground, views span the jagged Mission Mountains, which light up with alpenglow at sunset. Surrounded by open fields, sunny sites with sporadic trees for shade allow for satellite reception. With the proximity to the highway, you'll hear some truck noise at night.

Campsites, facilities: The KOA has 41 RV sites. Larger sites can fit trailer combinations up to 71 feet. All of the campsites are pull-throughs. RV hookups include sewer, water, and electricity up to 50 amps. Super premium sites have tables, chairs, and gas barbecue grills. Facilities include picnic tables, decks and patios, flush toilets, showers, camp store,

© BECKY LOMAX

The National Bison Range offers chances to see bison, elk, and birds.

seasonal restaurant, volleyball and basketball courts, playground, horseshoes, launderette, group fire pit area, fenced dog run, outdoor pool (late May-early September only), adult hot tub, wireless Internet, mini-golf, and disposal station. Firewood and propane are for sale. Leashed pets are permitted.

Reservations, fees: Reservations are accepted. RV hookups run $40-75. Rates are for two people; for extra people, add $8. Cash, check, or credit card. Add on a 7 percent Montana bed tax. Open mid-April-mid-October.

Directions: From downtown Polson, drive north on Highway 93. Go 0.5 mile past the bridge over the Flathead River and turn south onto Irvine Flats Road. Drive 0.2 mile and turn right into the campground.

GPS Coordinates: N 47° 41.977' W 114° 11.167'

Contact: Polson-Flathead Lake KOA, 200 Irvine Flats Road, Polson, MT 59860, 888/883-2151 or 800/562-2130, www.flatheadlakekoa.com.

60 EAGLE NEST RV

Scenic rating: 7

in the Mission Valley

Located in the town of Polson on the south end of Flathead Lake, the Eagle Nest RV works for boating, fishing, waterskiing, and paddling on Flathead Lake. Swimming is also available at the lake. Boats can be launched at local marinas. Other nearby activities include rafting on the Lower Flathead River and golf at the adjacent course. A nearby walking and biking path connects with downtown for dining out or shopping. A scenic drive south through the Mission Valley leads to wildlife-watching at Ninepipes National Wildlife Refuge and the National Bison Range.

Surrounded by fields and a golf course, the Eagle Nest yields views of the jagged Mission Mountains, which light up with alpenglow at sunset. Sunny sites with sporadic trees for shade allow for satellite reception. The landscaped grass makes for a neat, clean appearance.

Campsites, facilities: The Eagle Nest has 56 RV sites. Pull-through sites can fit large rigs. RV hookups include sewer, water, electricity up to 50 amps, and cable TV. Facilities include picnic tables, concrete patios, flush toilets, showers, camp store, seasonal restaurant, fitness room, playground, launderette, outdoor pool (late May-early September only), hot tub, wireless Internet, game room, and pickleball court. Leashed pets are permitted.

Reservations, fees: Reservations are accepted. RV hookups run $31-48, depending on the season. Rates are for two people; extra people are charged $3. Cash, check, or credit card. Add on a 7 percent Montana bed tax. Check website for discounts. Open April-October.

Directions: From downtown Polson, drive south on Highway 93 and turn east onto Highway 35. Go 0.3 mile and turn left onto Eagle Nest Drive. The campground flanks the end of the road.

GPS Coordinates: N 47° 41.523' W 114° 7.197'
Contact: Eagle Nest RV, 35800 Eagle Nest Drive, Polson, MT 59860, 406/883-5904, www.eaglenestrv.com.

61 SWAN LAKE

🏃 🚲 ⛵ 🏖 🏊 🎣 🐴 ♿ 🚐 ⛺

Scenic rating: 9

in Swan Valley in Flathead National Forest

BEST (

At 3,100 feet, Swan Lake—a long, skinny cold-water lake located just southeast of Bigfork in the Swan Valley—gets packed with recreational boaters and water-skiers. The lake, with a swimming beach, dock, and boat ramp, is surrounded by the high Swan Mountains. Paddlers head to the lake's south end for bird-watching along the Swan River National Wildlife Refuge—home to moose, deer, and bear, too. Anglers go for the rainbow and westslope cutthroat trout. Local hikes lead to lookouts and lakes: a four-mile climb tops Sixmile Mountain, the site of an old lookout at the north end of the southern Swan Crest Trail (Alpine 7), and a seven-mile trail ascends to Bond and Trinkus Lakes, which cuddle in basins just below the crest.

Shaded by big cedars, the picnic area sits right on the beach of Swan Lake, while the campground tucks its paved loops back into trees on the opposite side of the highway. Underbrush lends a sense of privacy between many of the campsites; those on the outsides of the loops have more privacy than those on the inside. The Forest Service holds campfire programs in the evenings. Catering to cyclists, the campground has bike lanes and one bicycle-only campsite. To get a site on weekends or holidays, you'll need reservations.

Campsites, facilities: The campground has 36 RV or tent campsites. The campground can accommodate RVs and trailer combinations up to 55 feet. Facilities include picnic tables, fire rings with grills, vault toilets (wheelchair

accessible), drinking water, campground hosts, and garbage service. Leashed pets are permitted.

Reservations, fees: Reservations are accepted (877/444-6777, www.recreation.gov). Campsites cost $15. Cash, check, or credit card. Open mid-May-September.

Directions: From two miles north of Bigfork, drive east on Highway 83 and 19.7 miles south to Swan Lake. From Seeley Lake, drive 56.5 miles north on Highway 83. Turn east into the campground.

GPS Coordinates: N 47° 56.149' W 113° 51.134'

Contact: Flathead National Forest, Swan Lake Ranger District, 200 Ranger Station Rd., Bigfork, MT 59911, 406/837-7500, www.fs.usda.gov/flathead.

62 HOLLAND LAKE

🏃 ⛵ 🏖 🏊 🎣 🐴 ♿ 🚐 ⛺

Scenic rating: 10

in Swan Valley in Flathead National Forest

BEST (

At 4,150 feet in the southern Swan Valley, Holland Lake provides a leap-off point into the Bob Marshall Wilderness. Both backpackers and horse-packing trips depart from here. Surrounded by the rugged Swan Mountains, the lake lures boaters for waterskiing, fishing, and paddling. Hiking trails depart right from the Bay Loop campground. A 1.5-mile easy hike hugs the lake to Holland Falls, roaring and spewing mist. A steep 3.5-mile trail climbs to Holland Lookout for dramatic views into the wilderness area, and a stunning 12-mile loop ties together Upper Holland Lake and the smaller Sapphire Lake in an alpine bowl of wildflowers and huckleberry bushes. The historical lodge—which has a restaurant and bar—also rents canoes and kayaks and leads horseback trail rides.

The quiet campground snuggles under a fir forest canopy adjacent to Holland Lake, with trails that run between the campsites and the lake. Two loops comprise the campground: Larch Loop flanks the west end of the lake while Bay Loop sits on the north side close to Holland Lake Lodge. Some of the sites are very private because of thick foliage; others are more open with minimal understory. Owl Creek Packer Camp, with eight additional campsites, two stock ramps, vault toilets, and drinking water, sits about 0.5 mile away.

Campsites, facilities: The campground has 40 RV or tent campsites. RVs are limited to 50 feet. Facilities include picnic tables, fire rings with grills, vault toilets (wheelchair accessible), drinking water, campground hosts, a boat ramp, a disposal station, and garbage service. Leashed pets are permitted.

Reservations, fees: Reservations are accepted (877/444-6777, www.recreation.gov). Campsites cost $15. Cash, check, or credit card. Open mid-May-September.

Directions: From the start of Highway 83 two miles north of Bigfork, drive 35.2 miles south past Condon to Holland Lake Road. From Seeley Lake, drive 19.3 miles north on Highway 83 to Holland Lake Road. Turn east and drive 2.5 miles to the Y, and turn left. Follow the signs to the campground, which has two turnoffs into separate loops.

Larch Loop GPS Coordinates: N 47° 26.898' W 113° 36.959'

Bay Loop GPS Coordinates: N 47° 27.082' W 113° 36.524'

Contact: Flathead National Forest, Swan Lake Ranger District, 200 Ranger Station Rd., Bigfork, MT 59911, 406/837-7500, www.fs.usda.gov/flathead.

63 LINDBERGH LAKE

Scenic rating: 7
in Swan Valley in Flathead National Forest

Four-mile-long Lindbergh Lake draws fewer campers than Holland Lake despite being twice as large. This larger lake has more room for swimmers, water-skiers, anglers, and paddlers to spread out. A boat ramp eases launching onto the lake. Streams from the Mission Mountain Wilderness feed the 815-acre lake, which sits at 4,494 feet and fosters several trout species plus mountain whitefish, kokanee salmon, northern pike minnow, longnose suckers, yellow perch, plus stocked kokanee and westslope cutthroat trout. Mountain bikers can tour the maze of old logging roads in the area. Long dirt-road drives connect to hiking trails to high clear lakes in the Mission Mountain Wilderness. One short trail tours west along the lake.

The campground tucks under a thick forest of spindly conifers, with plenty of shrubs and small trees lending privacy to most of the campsites. The sites are small but spread out. Because of the distance from the highway, the campground is quiet.

Campsites, facilities: The campground has 11 RV or tent campsites. The maximum length for RVs is 20 feet. Facilities include picnic tables, fire rings with grills, and vault toilets (wheelchair accessible). No drinking water is available. Bring your own, or haul it from the lake. Pack out your trash. Leashed pets are permitted.

Reservations, fees: Reservations not accepted. Camping is free. Open May-September.

Directions: From the start of Highway 83 two miles north of Bigfork, drive 36.5 miles south past Condon to Lindbergh Lake Road (Forest Road 79). From Seeley Lake, drive 18 miles north on Highway 83 to Forest Road 79. Turn west and drive three miles, veering right onto the campground road (79C).

GPS Coordinates: N 47° 24.486' W 113° 43.500'

Contact: Flathead National Forest, Swan Lake Ranger District, 200 Ranger Station Rd., Bigfork, MT 59911, 406/837-7500, www.fs.usda.gov/flathead.

64 RAINY LAKE

Scenic rating: 8
between the Swan and Mission Mountains in
Lolo National Forest

Accessed via a short, dirt forest road, Rainy
Lake is a favorite of those who like small,
primitive off-beat campgrounds. The campground sits at 4,100 feet on the divide between
the Swan and Clearwater drainages. The small
lake attracts float tube anglers and visitors who
want to lounge on the grassy shore with the
snow-covered Swan Range reflecting in the
water. The lake is also close enough to the
parking lot to carry lightweight canoes and
kayaks down to the shore.

Recent thinning exposed the campground
to more sunlight, and some campsites show
excessive wear. Three of the walk-in sites sit
back in the mixed forest, two with peek-a-boo
views of the lake. But the one walk-in site on
the peninsula commands a view not only of
most of the lake, but also the Swan Mountains.
The one small, open drive-up site has no views.
The campsites spread out for privacy, but all
are within sight of each other.
Campsites, facilities: The campground has
one campsite suitable only for a small RV or
tenters and four walk-in tent campsites. Facilities include picnic tables, fire rings with grills,
a vault toilet, and bear pole. The walk-in sites
provide large flat areas for tents. No drinking
water is available; bring your own, or treat lake
water. Leashed pets are permitted. Pack out
your trash.
Reservations, fees: Reservations are
not accepted. Camping is free. Open
May-November.
Directions: Turn west off Highway 83 at milepost 27 onto Forest Road 4357. Drive 0.5 mile
on the dirt road to where the road loops in a
dead end.
GPS Coordinates: N 47° 20.203' W 113°
35.545'
Contact: Lolo National Forest, Seeley Lake

Ranger District, HC-31, Box 3200, Seeley Lake, MT 59868, 406/677-2233, www.
fs.usda.gov/lolo.

65 LAKE ALVA

Scenic rating: 7
between the Swan and Mission Mountains in
Lolo National Forest

With two campgrounds, Lake Alva—one of
the string of lakes tied along the upper Clearwater River—attracts boaters, water-skiers, anglers, paddlers, and swimmers. Sitting at 4,198
feet, the 298-acre lake is fed by cold water
from the Mission and Swan Mountains. The
lake yields four species of trout plus redside
shiners, suckers, yellow perch, and kokanee.
It also harbors nesting loons at the head and
on the tiny island. To see the knife-like Swan
Range, paddle or boat to the opposite shore
of the lake. (Wish the campground had those
views!) For hiking or mountain biking, drive
five miles up the Clearwater Loop Road 4370,
following the signs, to hike the Clearwater
Lake Loop trail.

Squeezed between the highway and the lake,
the campgrounds hear road noise through the
trees—towering spruces, larches, and subalpine firs. Lake Alva Campground sprinkles
campsites around three paved loops with paved
parking pads. Because of the thick foliage,
none of the campsites has a view of the lake,
but the sites are private and loaded with clumps
of bear grass. The more rustic Lakeside Campground features campsites overlooking the lake
but also within sight of the highway. Broken
into two sections with three campsites each,
the campground runs along a single-lane, narrow, curvy dirt road with a few pullouts in case
vehicles meet. Trailers are not recommended.
Campsites, facilities: Lake Alva has 39 RV
or tent campsites with RVs limited to 22 feet.
Lakeside has five tent or small RV campsites,
plus one walk-in tent site. Facilities include

© BECKY LOMAX

Morrell Falls sprays mist in June.

picnic tables, fire rings with grills, vault toilets (wheelchair accessible), garbage service, group campsites, and campground hosts. Drinking water is only available at Lake Alva. For Lakeside, bring your own, fill up at Alva, or treat lake water. Leashed pets are permitted.

Reservations, fees: Reservations are not accepted, except for two group campsites (877/444-6777, www.recreation.gov). Campsites cost $10. Each extra vehicle costs $5. Cash or check. Open Memorial Day weekend-September.

Directions: Find both campgrounds north of Seeley Lake on Highway 83. For Lake Alva, turn west at milepost 26.1 onto Forest Road 1098. For Lakeside, turn west at milepost 25.6.
Lake Alva GPS Coordinates: N 47° 19.403' W 113° 35.019'
Lakeside GPS Coordinates: N 47° 18.749' W 113° 34.655'

Contact: Lolo National Forest, Seeley Lake Ranger District, HC-31, Box 3200, Seeley Lake, MT 59868, 406/677-2233, www.fs.usda.gov/lolo.

66 LAKE INEZ

🚶 🚴 🏊 🛶 🛥 🚣 🐕 🚐 ⛺

Scenic rating: 7

between the Swan and Mission Mountains in Lolo National Forest

Two miles south of Lake Alva sits another one of the Clearwater River's chain of lakes. At 4,100 feet, the 288-acre Lake Inez is popular for swimming, fishing, boating, waterskiing, and paddling. Get out on the lake for the views of the southern Swan Mountains. Because of its location, it has the same fishing, mountain-biking, and hiking options as Lake Alva. For those with canoes to paddle its willow-laden north shore, bird-watching is prime. Look for red-necked grebes, bald eagles, rufous hummingbirds, American redstarts, flycatchers, and sparrows. The lakes along this chain make good habitat for loons, too, with suitable nesting areas protected from human disturbance and a substantial supply of fish. Listen in the morning or evening for the haunting call of the loon. About 60 pairs of loons nest in this chain of lakes, but only about 30 offspring survive.

The shady campground sits at the north end of Lake Inez on a dirt road tucked in a thick forest of firs. Find the primitive boat ramp with small grassy parking for boat trailers at the campground's north end as well as the three main campsites. Two other campsites sit farther south on the road with lake views.

Campsites, facilities: The campground has five RV or tent campsites and one group campsite. Facilities include picnic tables, fire rings with grills, and vault toilets. Drinking water is not available. Bring your own, or treat lake water. Pack out your trash. Leashed pets are permitted.

Reservations, fees: Reservations are not accepted. Camping is free. Open May-November.

Directions: From Highway 83 north of Seeley Lake, the campground has two entrances, neither marked by obvious signs on the road. Turn west into the north entrance at milepost

24.1 or into the south entrance at milepost 22.9.

GPS Coordinates: N 47° 17.701' W 113° 34.120'

Contact: Lolo National Forest, Seeley Lake Ranger District, HC-31, Box 3200, Seeley Lake, MT 59868, 406/677-2233, www.fs.usda.gov/lolo.

67 BIG LARCH

Scenic rating: 8

between the Swan and Mission Mountains in Lolo National Forest

On Seeley Lake's east side, Big Larch is a busy campground, thanks to its location one mile from the town of Seeley Lake. At 4,000 feet, it sprawls between the highway and the lake, which offers fishing, boating, waterskiing, paddling, and swimming. Two sandy swimming beaches sprawl along the shoreline. The campground also has a 0.5-mile nature trail. Loaded with bird-watching, the Clearwater Canoe Trail is easy to access from this side of the lake as the put-in and take-out sit 5-10 minutes up the highway. A hiking trail connects the start and finish of the canoe trail with a stop at a wildlife viewing blind. The campground also sits closest to the Morrell Falls National Recreation Trail. Located seven miles up Morrell Creek Drive, the easy-walking 2.5-mile trail (open to mountain bikers and hikers) wanders past a series of small lakes and ponds before finishing at the 90-foot-tall falls.

A paved road wanders through the campground with a mix of dirt, gravel, and paved parking aprons in the three overlapping loops. As the name suggests, huge larch trees along with some equally large Ponderosa pines shade much of the campground. In this type of forest, however, little underbrush survives, so most of the campsites are open beneath the trees, affording very little privacy. Sites 1-30 in the first two loops have shorter but wider

campsites. Sites 34-49 are longer but narrower. Check the bulletin board at the check-in station for evening interpretive programs.

Campsites, facilities: The campground has 48 RV or tent campsites and two large group campsites. Trailers are limited to 32 feet. Facilities include picnic tables, fire rings with grills, vault toilets (wheelchair accessible), drinking water, garbage service, large swimming beach, campground hosts, and a concrete boat launch. Leashed pets are permitted.

Reservations, fees: Reservations are not accepted. Campsites cost $10. Each extra vehicle costs $5. Cash or check. Open Memorial Day weekend-September.

Directions: From Seeley Lake, drive one mile north on Highway 83. Turn west at the signed entrance into the campground.

GPS Coordinates: N 47° 11.173' W 113° 29.718'

Contact: Lolo National Forest, Seeley Lake Ranger District, HC-31, Box 3200, Seeley Lake, MT 59868, 406/677-2233, www.fs.usda.gov/lolo.

68 RIVER POINT

Scenic rating: 9

between the Swan and Mission Mountains in Lolo National Forest

Of the three campgrounds on Seeley Lake, the eight-acre River Point is the smallest. It sits at 4,000 feet at the foot of the lake where the broad, slow-moving Clearwater River exits the lake. With the proximity to the town of Seeley Lake, the campground is within a short bike ride to town for groceries, gift shops, and restaurants. This campground is also the closest to Seeley Lake's golf course south of town. For hikers and mountain bikers, the Morrell Falls National Recreation Trail is within an 11-mile drive. The day-use area of the campground sits on both Seeley Lake and the Clearwater River, with fishing in both.

Views from the beach include the south Swan Peaks. The campground borders the river and the lake, but no boat launch ramp is available. Use the one at Seeley Lake Campground 1.2 miles north. You can launch rafts, canoes, and kayaks from the river campsites, plus the beach in the day-use area.

A paved road leads through the one-loop campground, which has paved parking aprons. Large spruces, larches, and subalpine firs shade most of the roomy campsites, but with little understory and only short brush, the campsites have little privacy. Sites 11, 12, 14, 17, 19, and 20 sit on the river.

Campsites, facilities: The campground has 26 RV or tent campsites. Trailers are limited to 22 feet. Facilities include picnic tables, fire rings with grills, vault toilets (wheelchair accessible), drinking water, garbage service, and a swimming beach. Leashed pets are permitted.

Reservations, fees: Reservations are not accepted. Campsites cost $10. Each extra vehicle costs $5. Cash or check. Open Memorial Day weekend-Labor Day.

Directions: In the town of Seeley Lake at milepost 14 on Highway 83, turn west onto Boys Scout Road on the north side of Pyramid Lumber Company. Drive two miles to the campground, which sits on the north side of the road.

GPS Coordinates: N 47° 11.101' W 113° 30.731'

Contact: Lolo National Forest, Seeley Lake Ranger District, HC-31, Box 3200, Seeley Lake, MT 59868, 406/677-2233, www.fs.usda.gov/lolo.

69 SEELEY LAKE

Scenic rating: 9
between the Swan and Mission Mountains in Lolo National Forest

At 4,000 feet, Seeley Lake is the largest of the upper Clearwater River's lakes. The 1,031-acre lake cranks with the noise of water-skiers, Jet Skiers, and power boaters. The big picnic area spans a long grassy beach that includes a cordoned-off swimming area, cement boat launch, and boat trailer parking. The campground also attracts quiet paddlers because of the Clearwater Canoe Trail, which feeds into the lake from the Clearwater River. The 3.5-mile trail paddles through a dense willow marsh full of the music of songbirds such as ruby crowned kinglets. A hiking trail connects the start and finish of the canoe trail with a stop at a wildlife viewing blind. Located on the west side of the lake just opposite the River Point campground, Seeley Lake campground grabs a bigger view of the south Swan Mountains from the beach than other campgrounds in the area.

A paved road leads up the west side of the lake to the 11-acre campground. The campground's road is narrow and curvy; large trees pinch the corners as it winds through the two loops. The road is paved, but the parking aprons are mostly dirt. Large spruces, monster larches, and subalpine firs shade most of the campground. The sites have little privacy, but they are very roomy. None of the campsites sit right on the lake, but sites 28 and 29 are right across from the beach. Sites 5, 7, and 8 are more private because they're on a side inlet from the lake.

Campsites, facilities: The campground has 29 RV or tent campsites. The maximum recommended trailer length is 32 feet. Facilities include picnic tables, fire rings, flush toilets (wheelchair-accessible), drinking water, garbage service, a swimming beach, campground hosts, and a boat launch. Leashed pets are permitted.

Reservations, fees: Reservations are not accepted. Campsites cost $10. Each extra vehicle costs $5. Cash or check. Open Memorial Day weekend-Labor Day.

Directions: From milepost 14 on Highway 83 in the town of Seeley Lake, turn west onto Boy Scout Road and drive 3.2 miles. Turn right into the campground.

GPS Coordinates: N 47° 11.576' W 113° 31.229'

Contact: Lolo National Forest, Seeley Lake Ranger District, HC-31, Box 3200, Seeley Lake, MT 59868, 406/677-2233, www.fs.usda.gov/lolo.

70 PLACID LAKE STATE PARK

Scenic rating: 8

south of Seeley Lake in Lolo National Forest

At 4,100 feet, Placid Lake State Park sits on one of the smaller pools in the upper Clearwater River's chain of lakes. The 31-acre lake is tiny in comparison to its northern sisters, but still attracts boaters for waterskiing, fishing, sightseeing, paddling, and wildlife-watching. Look for ospreys fishing, but keep your distance from nesting loons. Because private homes surround much of the shoreline, on weekends and hot August days the water hops with Jet Skiers and boat noise (not exactly placid!). A short foot trail tours the shoreline. The boat docks include slips for 12 boats.

The 32-acre campground sits on the shore of Placid Lake, with the campsites tucked on three loops in the trees. A wide, potholed dirt road leads to the campground, but the campground road and parking pads are paved. Sites 1, 2, 3, 5, 6, 10, 11, 16, and 17 sit adjacent to the beach. Large ponderosas and firs partly shade campsites, but the lack of undergrowth yields little privacy.

Campsites, facilities: The campground has 40 RV or tent campsites. RVs are limited to 25 feet. Up to eight people and two camping units (vehicles or tents) are allowed per site. Facilities include picnic tables, fire rings with grills, flush and vault toilets, electrical hookups, pay showers, drinking water, a disposal station, campground hosts, firewood for sale, swimming beach, boat docks, boat trailer parking, and a concrete boat ramp. Leashed pets are permitted. Wheelchair-accessible facilities include toilets and two campsites with electrical hookups.

Reservations, fees: Reservations are accepted online or by phone (855/922-6768). Campsites cost $15 for Montana residents (seniors and campers with disabilities get half price) and $23 for nonresidents Memorial Day weekend-Labor Day, or $12 for Montana residents and $20 for nonresidents off-season. Campsites with electrical hookups cost $17-28, depending on season and residency. Nonresidents with a Non-Resident Entrance Pass ($25) get a $5 discount on camping fees. Cash, check, or credit card. Open May-November.

Directions: From the Clearwater Junction (look for the big cow at the junction of Highways 83 and 200), drive 10 miles north on Highway 83. From Seeley Lake, drive Highway 83 south for three miles. Turn west onto the Placid Lake Road at milepost 10.2, and drive 2.7 miles. At the campground sign, turn left, and then make an immediate right to reach the entrance in 0.3 mile.

GPS Coordinates: N 47° 7.105' W 113° 30.207'

Contact: Montana Fish, Wildlife, and Parks, Region 1, 490 N. Meridian Rd., Kalispell, MT 59901, 406/752-5501, http://stateparks.mt.gov.

71 SALMON LAKE STATE PARK

Scenic rating: 8

south of Seeley Lake in Lolo National Forest

At 3,900 feet, the 631-acre Salmon Lake is the last lake in the chain of the Clearwater lakes. Small steep-walled mountains constrict the valley into a narrow channel that holds the lake, forming a natural impoundment for the Clearwater River. A few islands—some with private homes—also sit in the lake, which is popular for trout fishing, boating, paddling, and waterskiing. The 42-acre long, narrow park has separate entrances for the campground and day-use area, which holds the cement boat ramp, boat trailer parking, 60-foot boat dock, and cordoned-off swimming beach. A foot trail with lupines, arrowleaf balsamroot, and shooting stars in spring connects the campground loop with the day-use area.

North of the day-use area, the campground squeezes between the lake and highway, with most of the campsites in one loop under firs and larch. Sites 1 and 2 sit closest to the lake. Sites 1, 2, 4, 5, and 7 have lake views. Sites 10-15 sit adjacent to the highway, but given how narrow the campground is, no one is far from the lake or the highway noise. The amphitheater hosts evening interpretive programs.

Campsites, facilities: The campground has 20 RV or tent campsites. RVs are limited to 25 feet. Facilities include picnic tables, fire rings with grills, flush and vault toilets, pay showers, drinking water, disposal station, campground hosts, ranger programs, swimming beach, firewood for sale, and boat launch. Leashed pets are permitted. Wheelchair-accessible facilities include toilets and one campsite with electrical hookups.

Reservations, fees: Reservations are accepted online or by phone (855/922-6788). Campsites cost $15 for Montana residents (seniors and campers with disabilities get half price) and $23 for nonresidents Memorial Day weekend-Labor Day, or $12 for Montana residents and $20 for nonresidents off-season. Campsites with electrical hookups cost $17-28, depending on season and residency. Nonresidents with a Non-Resident Entrance Pass ($25) get a $5 discount on camping fees. Cash, check, or credit card. Open May-September.

Directions: From the Clearwater Junction (look for the big cow at the junction of Highways 83 and 200), drive seven miles north on Highway 83. From Seeley Lake, drive Highway 83 south for six miles. At milepost 7, turn west into the campground. The day-use entrance is at milepost 6.5.

GPS Coordinates: N 47° 5.552' W 113° 23.869'

Contact: Montana Fish, Wildlife, and Parks, Region 1, 490 N. Meridian Rd., Kalispell, MT 59901, 406/752-5501, http://stateparks.mt.gov.

72 DORIS CREEK

Scenic rating: 9

on Hungry Horse Reservoir in Flathead National Forest

At 3,600 feet on the west side of Hungry Horse Reservoir, Doris Creek Campground sits one mile past the Doris Boat Launch site. The launch site provides the easiest access to the reservoir for boating, paddling, sailing, waterskiing, or fishing. It includes two cement boat ramps with a dock and loads of parking for boat trailers. A $4 day-use fee is charged. Swimming is also available at the reservoir. North of the inlet, mountain bikers can climb the eight-mile Beta Road, while from its terminus, hikers can ascend three miles to Doris Lake or five miles to Doris Peak for dramatic views of Flathead Valley, the reservoir, and Glacier National Park.

Doris Camp flanks Doris Creek at the head of Doris Bay on the reservoir. One gravel loop comprises the campground with two pull-through sites. The campground is surrounded by forest, but with its new construction, some sites are fairly open with little undergrowth to provide privacy. As water levels drop in the reservoir toward August, the sandy beach grows larger. Because of the paved road access and the proximity to Hungry Horse, this popular campground fills up faster than other campgrounds on the reservoir.

Campsites, facilities: Doris Camp has 10 RV or tent campsites that can accommodate RVs or trailer combinations up to 32 feet. Facilities include picnic tables, fire rings with grills, vault toilets (wheelchair accessible), and boat ramp. Drinking water is not available; bring your own, or treat reservoir water. Pack out your trash. Leashed pets are permitted.

Reservations, fees: No reservations are accepted. The campsites cost $11. Cash or check. Open mid-May-September.

Directions: From the town of Hungry Horse, drive south on the paved West Reservoir Road (Forest Road 895) for nine miles, crossing the dam. Turn left into both campgrounds, located 0.2 mile apart.

GPS Coordinates: N 48° 18.266' W 113° 58.910'

Contact: Flathead National Forest, Hungry Horse Ranger District, 10 Hungry Horse Dr., Hungry Horse, MT 59919, 406/387-3800, www.fs.usda.gov/flathead/.

7 3 LOST JOHNNY

Scenic rating: 9

on Hungry Horse Reservoir in Flathead National Forest

At 3,600 feet on Doris Creek inlet, Lost Johnny Camp and Lost Johnny Point provide a pair of campgrounds 0.2 mile apart. Lost Johnny Point has a cement boat ramp to launch boats for sightseeing, waterskiing, fishing, and paddling, but you can launch hand-carried watercraft from Lost Johnny Campground. North of the inlet, mountain bikers can climb the eight-mile Beta Road, while from its terminus, hikers can ascend three miles to Doris Lake or five miles to Doris Peak for dramatic views of Flathead Valley, the reservoir, and Glacier National Park.

Deep, thick conifers cover both of these quiet campgrounds, providing shade, and underbrush works well as a privacy fence. Lost Johnny Creek runs adjacent to the smaller campground, but Lost Johnny Point Campground, with its paved road and parking pads, tops a bluff on a steep hill with a more open forest and some sites overlooking the reservoir. Because of the paved road access and the proximity to Hungry Horse, the campgrounds fill up faster than other campgrounds on the reservoir.

Campsites, facilities: Lost Johnny Camp has five private RV or tent campsites that can accommodate trailers up to 50 feet, and Lost Johnny Point has 21 RV or tent campsites that can fit trailers up to 40 feet. Facilities include picnic tables, fire rings with grills, drinking water, vault toilets (wheelchair accessible), a boat ramp, and a campground host. Pack out your trash. Leashed pets are permitted. A wheelchair-accessible toilet is available at Lost Johnny Point.

Reservations, fees: No reservations are accepted. The campsites cost $13. Cash or check. Open mid-May-September.

Directions: From the town of Hungry Horse, drive south on the paved West Reservoir Road (Forest Road 895) for nine miles, crossing the dam. Turn left into both campgrounds, located 0.2 mile apart.

Lost Johnny GPS Coordinates: N 48° 18.313' W 113° 58.152'

Lost Johnny Point GPS Coordinates: N 48° 18.561' W 113° 57.854'

Contact: Flathead National Forest, Hungry Horse Ranger District, 10 Hungry Horse Dr., Hungry Horse, MT 59919, 406/387-3800, www.fs.usda.gov/flathead/.

7 4 LID CREEK

Scenic rating: 9

on Hungry Horse Reservoir in Flathead National Forest

At 3,600 feet on the west side of Hungry Horse Reservoir, Lid Creek sits at the end of the paved part of the road. A fishing access permits you to launch small boats, rafts, kayaks, and canoes onto the water. A motor or paddle about one mile across the reservoir reaches Fire Island. The nearest large boat launch is at Lost Johnny Point, five miles to the north. The nearest trail for hiking and mountain biking is at the end of Forest Road 895C, about two miles from the campground entrance and 3.5 miles up the Wounded Buck drainage. The three-mile trail climbs to the top of the Swan Crest, meeting up with the Alpine 7 trail, where you can head south to the summit of Strawberry Mountain or Strawberry Lake. The area is favored by huckleberry pickers and bears.

Known for its quiet and seclusion, the campground sits in thick, mixed conifer forest on a large loop on the slope above the reservoir. Tent spaces are tight, small, or lacking in some campsites; you may need to pitch the tent on the parking pad. The campsites are spaced out for privacy. The upper loop offers more primitive campsites. Views from the beach include the rugged Flathead Range and the knife-edged Great Northern Mountain.

Campsites, facilities: The campground has 23 RV or tent campsites. RVs and trailer combinations longer than 32 feet are not recommended in the campground. Facilities include picnic tables, fire rings with grills, vault toilets, and campground hosts. No drinking water is available; bring your own or treat reservoir water. Pack out your garbage. Leashed pets are permitted.

Reservations, fees: No reservations are accepted. Campsites cost $11. Cash or check. Open mid-May-September.

Directions: From the town of Hungry Horse, take the Hungry Horse Reservoir's West Reservoir Road (Forest Road 895) south for 15 miles. The paved road crosses the reservoir on the dam and traverses south along the shore. Turn left at the signed entrance onto a gravel road for one mile into the campground. GPS Coordinates: N 48° 16.814' W 113° 54.563'

Contact: Flathead National Forest, Hungry Horse Ranger District, 10 Hungry Horse Dr., Hungry Horse, MT 59919, 406/387-3800, www.fs.usda.gov/flathead/.

75 FIRE ISLAND

Scenic rating: 8

on Hungry Horse Reservoir in Flathead National Forest

Fire Island is a boat-in campground. While Hungry Horse Reservoir has several islands for dispersed camping, only two have established designated campgrounds on them—Elk and Fire. At 3,600 feet, Fire Island sits farther north than Elk and requires no dirt road driving to get to its closest launch ramp at Lid Creek Campground. However, the island's location in the reservoir requires paddling or motoring across open water. The reservoir offers fishing for westslope cutthroat trout. Beach boats completely at night in case winds crop up.

Located on the southwest side of the island, the campsites are primitive, with small spaces for tents tucked into an open forest. The campsites are spread out for privacy in the tall brush and blooming bear grass in early summer. Unlike Elk Island's gentle beach, Fire Island requires a steep climb up the bank to the campsites. Nonetheless, it still offers quiet and solitude.

Campsites, facilities: The island has four designated tent campsites. Facilities include picnic tables, fire rings with grills, and a pit toilet. Drinking water is not available; bring your own or treat reservoir water. Pack out your trash. Leashed pets are permitted.

Reservations, fees: Reservations are not accepted. Campsites are free. Open mid-May-September.

Directions: From the town of Hungry Horse, take the Hungry Horse Reservoir's West Reservoir Road (Forest Road 895) south for 15 miles to Lid Creek Campground. The paved but curvy road crosses the reservoir on the dam and traverses the west shoreline. Turn left at the signed entrance onto a gravel road for one mile to reach the boat launch.

GPS Coordinates: N 48° 17.675' W 113° 53.773'
Contact: Flathead National Forest, Hungry Horse Ranger District, 10 Hungry Horse Dr., Hungry Horse, MT 59919, 406/387-3800, www.fs.usda.gov/flathead/.

76 LAKEVIEW

🚶 🏊 🛶 ⛵ 📷 🐕 🚐 ⛺

Scenic rating: 8

on Hungry Horse Reservoir in Flathead National Forest

Lakeview Campground, at 3,600 feet, is one of the less crowded destinations on the west side of Hungry Horse Reservoir. Boating and fishing on the reservoir is only available via hand-carried watercraft. The lake is known for its native westslope cutthroat fishery. To the west on Forest Road 1633, the 2.5-mile trail #420 climbs to Clayton Lake in Jewel Basin Hiking Area. Locate the road about 3.5 miles north of Lakeview and drive 2.5 miles to the trailhead. Hunters use the campground in fall.

The campground sits on a forested slope between the road and the reservoir. The quiet campsites, tucked in a mix of firs and spruce, spread out for privacy and are partly shaded with peek-a-boo views of the lake. Spectacular views greet you at the beach; the knife-like Great Northern and Grant Peak across the lake are snow-covered still in June.

Campsites, facilities: The campground has five RV or tent campsites. Trailers longer than 22 feet are not recommended in the campground. Facilities include picnic tables, fire rings with grills, and a vault toilet. No drinking water is available. Bring your own, or treat creek water. Pack out your garbage. Leashed pets are permitted.

Reservations, fees: Reservations are not accepted. Camping is free. Open June-November.

Directions: From the town of Hungry Horse, drive the Hungry Horse Reservoir's West Reservoir Road (Forest Road 895) south for 24 miles. The road crosses the reservoir on the dam and is paved as far as Lid Creek before turning to dirt for about nine miles. Turn left into the campground.
GPS Coordinates: N 48° 13.131' W 113° 48.381'
Contact: Flathead National Forest, Hungry Horse Ranger District, 10 Hungry Horse Dr., Hungry Horse, MT 59919, 406/387-3800, www.fs.usda.gov/flathead/.

77 HANDKERCHIEF LAKE

🚶 🏊 🛶 ⛵ 📷 🐕 🚐 ⛺

Scenic rating: 7

near Hungry Horse Reservoir in Flathead National Forest

At 3,850 feet, the 30-acre Handkerchief Lake sits only two miles from Graves Bay. The small lake makes for nice canoeing or float tube fishing; no boat launch is available, only trails leading to the shore. Native trout fill the lake. Continue up the road another two miles to reach the Graves Creek Trailhead. The trail climbs in five miles to Black Lake—a native westslope cutthroat fishery—in Jewel Basin Hiking Area, with views of Mount Aeneas and the Great Bear Wilderness across the reservoir. Hunters use the campground in fall.

The primitive campground has a unique layout. You park on a pull-off on the road, but sites are walk-ins spread out all along the shore below the road. Given the walk-in campsites, most people use tents, but some RVers still visit the lake. The campsites sit in a deep forest of thick spruce and firs with privacy between campsites created from abundant underbrush. Only natural sounds fill the campground, making it prized for its quiet.

Campsites, facilities: The campground has three RV or tent campsites. Trailers are limited to 22 feet. Facilities include picnic tables, fire rings, and a vault toilet. No drinking water is available; bring your own, or treat creek water. Pack out your trash. Leashed pets are permitted.

Reservations, fees: Reservations are not accepted. Camping is free. Open June-November.

Directions: From the town of Hungry Horse, take the Hungry Horse Reservoir West Road (Forest Road 895) south for 35 miles. The road crosses the reservoir on the dam and is paved as far as Lid Creek (halfway) before turning to dusty washboards and potholes. At 35 miles, turn right onto Forest Road 9796 and drive two miles to the campground.

GPS Coordinates: N 48° 8.357' W 113° 49.399'

Contact: Flathead National Forest, Hungry Horse Ranger District, 10 Hungry Horse Dr., Hungry Horse, MT 59919, 406/387-3800, www.fs.usda.gov/flathead/.

78 GRAVES BAY

Scenic rating: 8

on Hungry Horse Reservoir in Flathead National Forest

On the west side of Hungry Horse Reservoir at 3,600 feet, Graves Bay Campground (sometimes called Graves Creek) sits on the largest bay—stretching almost three miles long. The primitive boat launch works best for hand-carried small boats, canoes, and kayaks. Smaller trailered boats can launch when the water level is high. Waters tumble from Jewel Basin down to the bay, which increases beach size as the reservoir drops during the summer. The narrow bay's water offers a protected place to paddle and fish. The Graves Creek Trail, which departs from above Handkerchief Lake, climbs to Black Lake into Jewel Basin Hiking Area for views of Mount Aeneas and the Great Bear Wilderness.

The quiet, forested campground sits at the head of Graves Bay on both sides of the road. Several campsites sit along the creek on a spur

road opposite the bay. The Forest Service has plans to remove the campsites on the reservoir side of the road and develop the sites on the west side of the road with a vault toilet and an ADA camping site.

Campsites, facilities: The campground has 10 RV or tent campsites. Trailers longer than 22 feet are not recommended in the campground. Facilities include picnic tables, fire rings with grills, and vault toilets (wheelchair accessible). No drinking water is available. Bring your own, or plan to filter or treat creek water. Pack out your garbage. Leashed pets are permitted.

Reservations, fees: Reservations are not accepted. Camping is free. Open June-September.

Directions: From the town of Hungry Horse, take the Hungry Horse Reservoir's West Reservoir Road (Forest Road 895) south for 35 miles. The road crosses the reservoir on the dam and is paved as far as Lid Creek, about halfway. After that, the curvy dirt road becomes interminable dust and washboards. Turn west into the campground.

GPS Coordinates: N 48° 7.597' W 113° 48.588'

Contact: Flathead National Forest, Hungry Horse Ranger District, 10 Hungry Horse Dr., Hungry Horse, MT 59919, 406/387-3800, www.fs.usda.gov/flathead/.

79 ABBOT BAY

Scenic rating: 8

on Hungry Horse Reservoir in Flathead National Forest

At 3,600 feet on the east side of Hungry Horse Reservoir, Abbot Bay is a secluded inlet that is popular with local paddlers and boaters. A cement boat ramp aids in launching boats for fishing, waterskiing, and sightseeing, but boat launching is only permitted in spring and fall. During summer, boaters must launch from the

FKL site about two miles away. Mountain biking and hiking trails are available three miles north in the Coram Experimental Forest. Six miles northeast of the campground, the Ousel Peak West Trail #331 also leads to the crest of the Flathead Mountains for stunning views into the Great Bear Wilderness and Glacier National Park.

The quiet campground huddles under a conifer forest that provides partly sunny or shaded sites with a few peek-a-boo views of the reservoir. The beach is very popular with locals in summer because of its quick access, so expect busy daytimes. The Forest Service renovated the sites in 2012.

Campsites, facilities: Abbot Bay has four RV or tent campsites that can fit smaller RVs and trailer combinations. Facilities include picnic tables, fire rings with grills, and a vault toilet (wheelchair-accessible). Drinking water is not available; bring your own or treat reservoir water. Pack out your trash. Leashed pets are permitted.

Reservations, fees: Reservations are not accepted. Camping is free. Open May-September.

Directions: From the town of Hungry Horse, drive 0.6 mile to Martin City and turn east, following signs to the Hungry Horse Reservoir East Road (Forest Road 38) for 4.5 miles and veering right at the sign and dropping 0.9 mile to the beach and campground.

GPS Coordinates: N 48° 20.558' W 113° 58.866'

Contact: Flathead National Forest, Hungry Horse Ranger District, 10 Hungry Horse Dr., Hungry Horse, MT 59919, 406/387-3800, www.fs.usda.gov/flathead/.

80 EMERY BAY

Scenic rating: 9
on Hungry Horse Reservoir in Flathead National Forest

At 3,600 feet, Emery Bay has a quickly reached campground on the east side of the reservoir. A cement boat ramp and dock help launch watercraft for boating, fishing, waterskiing, and paddling. Canoes and kayaks can explore the more sheltered inlets rather than venture out onto the open reservoir where winds can crop up. Mountain biking and hiking trails are available four miles north in the Coram Experimental Forest. Five miles northeast of the campground, the Ousel Peak West Trail #331 also leads to the crest of the Flathead Mountains for stunning views into the Great Bear Wilderness and Glacier National Park.

The quiet campground huddles under a conifer forest that provides partly sunny or shaded sites; however, peek-a-boo views of the reservoir do exist from the bluff that overlooks the main reservoir, Emery Bay, and the Flathead and Swan Mountains. The spacious campsites are spread out, with young trees and tall grass lending privacy between sites. Wildflowers bloom in early summer, too. The parking pads are gravel back ins, except for two pull-throughs. The Forest Service renovated some of the facilities here in 2012.

Campsites, facilities: Emery Bay has 26 RV or tent campsites. RVs and trailer combinations are limited to 32 feet. Facilities include picnic tables, fire rings with grills, vault toilets (wheelchair accessible), drinking water, bear boxes, boat ramp, and campground hosts. Pack out your trash. Leashed pets are permitted.

Reservations, fees: Reservations are accepted (www.recreation.gov, 877-444-6777). Campsites cost $13. Cash or check. Open mid-May-September.

Directions: From the town of Hungry Horse, drive 0.6 mile to Martin City and turn east, following signs to the Hungry Horse Reservoir East Road (Forest Road 38) for six miles and veering right at the Y, where the road turns to dusty rough dirt and gravel. Veer right at the campground sign and drop 0.4 mile to the campground.

GPS Coordinates: N 48° 20.053' W 113° 57.162'

Contact: Flathead National Forest, Hungry

Horse Ranger District, 10 Hungry Horse Dr., Hungry Horse, MT 59919, 406/387-3800, www.fs.usda.gov/flathead/.

81 RIVERSIDE AND MURRAY BAY

Scenic rating: 8

on Hungry Horse Reservoir in Flathead National Forest

At 3,600 feet on the east side of Hungry Horse Reservoir, Riverside and Murray Bay provide a pair of adjacent campgrounds for enjoying Hungry Horse Reservoir. Both locations include cement ramps, trailer parking, and mooring posts in the bay for overnighting boats, although the Murray Bay launch only works with high water. For boaters, the reservoir offers fishing, waterskiing, paddling, and sightseeing. You can boat to several nearby islands that have primitive camping without amenities. The islands and adjacent bays offer protected water for swimming, kayaking, and canoeing. From nearby Forest Road 1048, the Great Northern Mountain trail shoots up 4,300 feet in 4.5 miles to the summit for spectacular views of Grant Glacier and Glacier National Park. If snow clings to the upper mountain, the climb can be treacherous and should not be attempted without an ice axe. Mountain bikers ride up to Firefighter Mountain Lookout for panoramic views of the reservoir and knife-like Great Northern Mountain.

Both quiet campgrounds, renovated in 2012, sit in a loose larch and fir forest with partly sunny campsites that bloom with bear grass in July. Some sites have views of the water and the Swan Mountains, and short trails drop to the shoreline. The smaller Riverside Campground sits on one loop separate from the spur road that accesses the boat ramp. The larger 19-acre Murray Bay Campground sits on square peninsula that sticks out toward Kelly Island. When the reservoir water drops low enough, you can swim or wade across the narrow channel to explore the island. Future plans include the restoration of 28 campsites on a larger defunct loop.

Campsites, facilities: Riverside Campground has four RV or tent campsites that can fit smaller RVs. Murray Bay Campground has 21 RV or tent campsites. RVs are limited to 32 feet. Facilities include picnic tables, fire rings with grills, vault toilets (wheelchair accessible), and campground hosts. Pack out your garbage. Riverside has no drinking water. Murray Bay has a hand pump for water and bear boxes. Leashed pets are permitted.

Reservations, fees: No reservations are accepted. Camping is free at Riverside but costs $11 at Murray Bay. Cash or check. Open mid-May-September.

Directions: From the town of Hungry Horse, go east on Highway 2 for 0.6 mile to Martin City and turn eastward, following the signs leading toward the east side of Hungry Horse Reservoir and veering right at the Y, where the road becomes a battle with dust and washboards. Drive 21.2 miles south on Forest Road 38. For Riverside, turn right onto a road that descends to the boat launch and campground. For Murray Bay, drive 0.8 mile further before turning right.

Riverside GPS Coordinates: N 48° 16.363' W 113° 49.030'

Murray Bay GPS Coordinates: N 48° 15.951' W 113° 48.782'

Contact: Flathead National Forest, Hungry Horse Ranger District, 10 Hungry Horse Dr., Hungry Horse, MT 59919, 406/387-3800, www.fs.usda.gov/flathead/.

82 ELK ISLAND

Scenic rating: 10

in Hungry Horse Reservoir in Flathead National Forest

Located on the east side of Hungry Horse

Reservoir, Elk Island is a boat-in campground at 3,600 feet. Paddling to Elk Island in a sea kayak or canoe yields gorgeous views of Great Northern Mountain, Grant Peak, and the Swan Range. Put in at the Riverside Boat Launch, which has a cement ramp. Paddle or motor between the Murray Bay Campground and Kelly Island south to Elk Island, beaching on the north side of the island to reach the campsites. If winds come up, stay near the shoreline. If the waters are calm, add tours around Kelly and Elk Islands. Beach boats completely at night in case winds crop up. On Elk, a 90-minute walk will tour you around the shoreline.

On the north shore of the island, the campsites are primitive with small spaces for tents. With lower water levels, some flat sites appear on the beaches. In June, the island blooms with both bear grass and a good crop of mosquitoes. Pull out the camera for the sunset over the Swan Range and the sunrise from the Great Bear Wilderness. The songs of birds, water lapping the shore, and wind are the only sounds on the island.

Campsites, facilities: The island has seven designated tent campsites, plus several more primitive sites. Facilities include picnic tables, fire rings with grills, and pit toilets. Pack out your trash. Drinking water is not available; bring your own or treat reservoir water. Leashed pets are permitted.

Reservations, fees: Reservations are not accepted. The campsites are free. Open May-November.

Directions: From the town of Hungry Horse, go east on Highway 2 for 0.6 mile to Martin City and turn eastward, following the signs leading toward the east side of Hungry Horse Reservoir and veering right at the Y onto the gravel road. Drive 21 miles south on the dusty washboard of Forest Road 38. Turn right into Riverside boat launch.

GPS Coordinates: N 48° 14.461' W 113° 48.123'

Contact: Flathead National Forest, Hungry Horse Ranger District, 10 Hungry Horse Dr.,

Hungry Horse, MT 59919, 406/387-3800, www.fs.usda.gov/flathead/.

83 DEVIL'S CORKSCREW

Scenic rating: 7

on the east side of Hungry Horse Reservoir in Flathead National Forest

The long dirt road on the east side of the reservoir into Devil's Corkscrew deters many people. Before departing from the town of Hungry Horse, gas up and check the spare tire in preparation for the dust, washboards, and lack of services. Located at 3,600 feet, the campground has a primitive boat launch for small boats, kayaks, and canoes. Larger boats should launch from ramps located 10 miles in either direction. The 35-mile-long Hungry Horse Reservoir is known for its native fishery. Nearby trailheads depart for climbing the six-mile Logan Creek Trail (#62) into the Great Bear Wilderness or the 5.8-mile trail (#63) to Baptiste Lookout for views of the reservoir.

The Forest Service thinned the campground area several years ago, opening up the thick forest for partial sun. The quiet small campground sits back in the trees from the shore with campsites spread out for privacy. This is one prized for its quiet and solitude.

Campsites, facilities: The campground has four RV or tent campsites. Trailers are limited to 32 feet. Facilities include picnic tables, fire rings with grills, and a vault toilet. Drinking water is not available; bring your own. Pack out your trash. Leashed pets are permitted.

Reservations, fees: Reservations are not accepted. The campsites are free. Open mid-May-September.

Directions: From the town of Hungry Horse, go east on Highway 2 for 0.6 mile to Martin City and turn eastward, following the signs leading toward the east side of Hungry Horse Reservoir and veering right at the Y onto the gravel road. Drive 32 miles south on Forest

Road 38. Turn right onto Forest Road 1063
to access the campground.
GPS Coordinates: N 48° 6.609' W 113°
41.666'
Contact: Flathead National Forest, Spotted
Bear Ranger District, 10 Hungry Horse Dr.,
Hungry Horse, MT 59919, 406/387-3800,
www.fs.usda.gov/flathead/.

84 PETER'S CREEK

Scenic rating: 8
on Hungry Horse Reservoir in Flathead
National Forest

The long, dusty road on the east side of the
reservoir into Peter's Creek deters many people.
Gas up, and check the spare tire before you
depart. At 3,600 feet on the east shore of the
35-mile-long reservoir, the campground is
prized for its sheer remoteness. You can launch
hand-carried watercraft from the campground,
but larger boats need to launch from the Crossover boat launch about 4.5 miles south. It has
a cement low-water boat ramp for water-skiers,
sightseers, and anglers fishing for native trout.
Mountain biking is available on a tangle of forest roads on the flanks of the Flathead Mountains. Hunters use the campground in fall.

A thick forest of larch and Douglas fir covers the small two-acre campground, but with
enough openings through the trees for views of
the Swan Range across the reservoir. The quiet,
secluded partly sunny campsites are spaced out
with plenty of underbrush for privacy. Short
trails lead down to the reservoir, where the
beach grows larger throughout the summer
as the dam draws the water down.
Campsites, facilities: The campground has
six RV or tent campsites. Trailers are limited
to 30 feet. Facilities include picnic tables, fire
rings with grills, and a vault toilet (wheelchair-
accessible). Drinking water is not available;
bring your own or treat creek water. Pack out
your trash. Leashed pets are permitted.

Reservations, fees: Reservations are
not accepted. Camping is free. Open
mid-May-November.
Directions: From the town of Hungry Horse,
go east on Highway 2 for 0.6 mile to Martin
City. Turn eastward, following the signs leading toward the east side of Hungry Horse Reservoir and veering right at the Y onto the gravel
road. Drive 37 miles south on Forest Road
38. Turn right to drop into the campground.
GPS Coordinates: N 48° 3.493' W 113°
38.735'
Contact: Flathead National Forest, Spotted
Bear Ranger District, 10 Hungry Horse Dr.,
Hungry Horse, MT 59919, 406/387-3800,
www.fs.usda.gov/flathead/.

85 SPOTTED BEAR

Scenic rating: 9
south of Hungry Horse Reservoir in Flathead
National Forest

BEST (

Gas up the vehicle to drive to Spotted Bear,
and take along emergency tire repair equipment, for no services exist on the long, dusty
access road. Located at 3,700 feet at the confluence of the Spotted Bear River and South
Fork of the Flathead River, the campground
features fishing in both rivers. A Wild and Scenic River, the South Fork also provides Class II
rafting, canoeing, or kayaking. Nearby trails
for hiking, mountain biking, and horseback
riding depart to Spotted Bear Lake (2 miles),
Spotted Bear Lookout (a long 7-mile climb),
and Meadow Creek Gorge (10 miles). The
Spotted Bear Ranger Station, which is staffed
seven days per week, sits across Spotted Bear
River, and the Diamond R Guest Ranch is
across the road. Find the footbridge across the
South Fork River behind the ranger station to
reach the river for fishing and swimming holes.

Located on a bench above the confluence of
the rivers, the campground sits partly shaded
under a loose forest of Douglas firs and western

larch, with underbrush adding to privacy. Because of its distance from pavement, the campground offers the rare commodities of silence and solitude. The campsites, with gravel parking pads, are spread out on both sides of the campground loop, with half of the sites high above Spotted Bear River.

Campsites, facilities: The campground has 13 campsites for RVs or tents. Trailers are limited to 32 feet. Facilities include picnic tables, fire rings with grills, a vault toilet (wheelchair-accessible), drinking water, garbage service, bear boxes, and campground hosts. Leashed pets are permitted.

Reservations, fees: No reservations are accepted. Campsites cost $10. Cash or check. Open mid-May–September.

Directions: From the town of Hungry Horse, go east on Highway 2 for 0.6 mile to Martin City and turn eastward, following the signs leading toward the east side of Hungry Horse Reservoir and veering right at the Y just outside Martin City, where the road becomes an interminable battle with dust and washboards. Drive 54 miles south on Forest Road 38. Turn right into the campground.

GPS Coordinates: N 47° 55.634' W 113° 31.558'

Contact: Flathead National Forest, Spotted Bear Ranger District, 10 Hungry Horse Dr., Hungry Horse, MT 59919, 406/387-3800, www.fs.usda.gov/flathead/.

86 BEAVER CREEK

Scenic rating: 8

south of Hungry Horse Reservoir in Flathead National Forest

At 4,150 feet on Spotted Bear River over 60 miles from pavement, Beaver Creek is the last campground before jumping off into the Bob Marshall Wilderness. Don't go here on a whim: The distance will take you several hours, and no services are available en route. Be sure your spare tire is pumped up and ready for use. Within five miles of the campground are five trailheads—Silvertip, Upper Big Bill, Lower Big Bill, South Creek, and Meadow Creek—with trails winding up long drainages into the heart of the wilderness. The 34-mile-long Spotted Bear River south of the campground supports mountain whitefish, native westslope cutthroat, and the threatened bull trout for fly-fishing. Because of flooding, the riverbed is broad, with braided streams weaving through rocks and sand in late summer. Hunters use the campground in fall.

With its remote location, the tiny campground offers utter quiet, except for the sound of the river. The secluded forested campground spreads out its sites for privacy, and undergrowth adds to it. Should the campground be full, the Forest Service permits dispersed camping in this area. Choose a site that shows previous use rather than starting a new site, and follow Leave No Trace principles.

Campsites, facilities: The campground has four RV or tent campsites. Trailers are limited to 32 feet. Facilities include picnic tables, fire rings with grills, vault toilet, stock ramp, hitch rails, and feed bins. Drinking water is not available; bring your own or treat river water. Pack out your trash. Leashed pets are permitted.

Reservations, fees: Reservations are not accepted. The campsites are free. Open mid-May–November.

Directions: From the town of Hungry Horse, go east on Highway 2 for 0.6 mile to the Martin City turnoff and head eastward, veering right at the Y onto the dusty gravel road that traverses the east side of Hungry Horse Reservoir. Drive 54 miles south on Forest Road 38 and then 9.2 miles east on Forest Road 568. Turn right into the campground.

GPS Coordinates: N 47° 55.441' W 113° 22.295'

Contact: Flathead National Forest, Spotted Bear Ranger District, 10 Hungry Horse Dr., Hungry Horse, MT 59919, 406/387-3800, www.fs.usda.gov/flathead/.

GLACIER NATIONAL PARK

© BECKY LOMAX

The best way to experience the Crown of the Continent's wonders is camping. The park, which is a National Heritage Site and UNESCO Biosphere Reserve, harbors 13 drive-to park service campgrounds within its boundaries. The popular ones fill by noon in midsummer and on holiday weekends. Two of the park's campgrounds sit at trailheads where you can stay for multiple days, hiking to a different place each day without driving. You can also boat to an additional handful of backcountry campgrounds. The surrounding national forests provide less-crowded campgrounds and primitive places to camp with access to trailheads. Three small towns dotting the park's perimeter offer RVers places to hook up to services. There are plenty of places to pitch a tent, so plan to linger here for several days to a week.

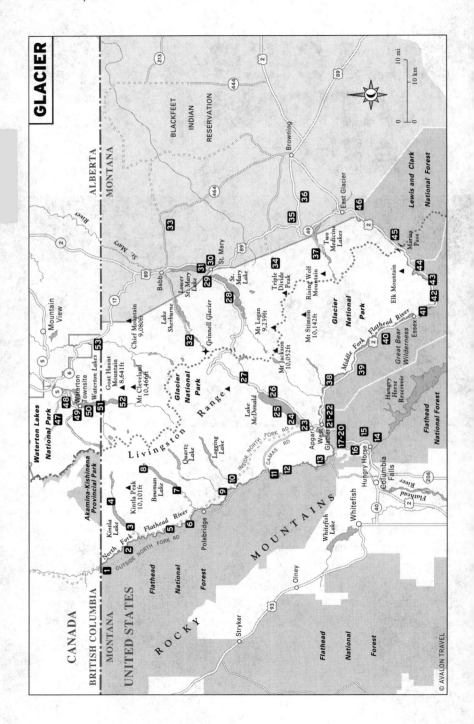

1 NORTH FORK BORDER PRIMITIVE

🏃 🏊 ⛴ 🚣 🦌 ⛺

Scenic rating: 7

on the North Fork of the Flathead River in Flathead National Forest

The North Fork of the Flathead River enters the United States at the northwest corner of Glacier National Park. At the Border River Access for floating the river, a few dispersed tent-only campsites line the river near the parking lot. The campsites make a good base for rafting, canoeing, or fishing the river. The camp is also a 10-mile drive from the trailhead Thoma Lookout on Trail Creek Road. The trail climbs 2,917 feet in five miles to views that stretch across Glacier's entire northern peaks, the North Fork River, the border swath, and into Canada. While the border patrol still uses the station near the river, the crossing into Canada has been closed for almost two decades after a flood washed out the Canadian road.

The primitive, partially shaded tent campsites with views of the river sit south of the parking lot. Since the bumpy, potholed drive to the border takes so long, the campsites are the most remote in the North Fork of the Flathead River Valley, guaranteeing privacy with only the sound of the river and the crackling campfire. Tucked under cottonwoods and firs, the campsites sit in their own cubbyholes, but within earshot of each other. During a mid-summer day, the river access sees traffic, but at night there are only wolf howls.

Campsites, facilities: The river access has three primitive tent campsites. Facilities include rock fire rings and a vault toilet in the parking lot. Bring your own water, or treat river water. Pack out your trash. Camping is limited to three days. Leashed pets are permitted.

Reservations, fees: No reservations are accepted. Camping is free. Open year-round, although the last 0.1 mile is not plowed to the parking lot.

Directions: From Polebridge, drive north on the North Fork Road (Forest Road 486) for 22 miles to the U.S. border station. Turn right for 0.1 mile to the river access parking lot. GPS Coordinates: N 49° 0.031' W 114° 28.561'

Contact: Flathead National Forest, Glacier View District, 10 Hungry Horse Dr., Hungry Horse, MT 59919, 406/387-3800, www.fs.usda.gov/flathead/.

2 NORTH FORK OF THE FLATHEAD RIVER

🏊 ⛴ 🚣 🦌 ⛺

Scenic rating: 9

in Flathead National Forest adjacent to Glacier National Park

With its headwaters in Canada, the North Fork of the Flathead River flows 59 miles from the border along the western boundary of Glacier National Park. Its route through the North Fork Valley flows through one of the most ecologically diverse areas of Montana, home to rare plants, woodpeckers and birds, and wildlife from the pygmy shrew to the wolf. The river, designated as Wild and Scenic, runs with Class II-III rapids with flows peaking in early June. Eight river accesses accommodate those rafting, kayaking, and canoeing: the border, Ford, Polebridge, Coal Creek, Big Creek, Great Northern Flats, Glacier Rim, and Blankenship. The river is best for rafting mid-May-early September.

Accessed only via rafts, canoes, or kayaks, primitive campsites flank the river's west bank. Camping on the east bank in Glacier, including Round Prairie, is only by special permit. Most campsites tuck under cottonwoods and firs within view of the river, and most are not in sight of each other, which guarantees solitude. You'll see moose walking through the water, and at night, fall asleep to the sound of the river.

Campsites, facilities: About 15 primitive tent campsites that can accommodate 4-6 people each line the river. Campers are required to take a groover for human waste and a fire pan to minimize burn scars. Purchase the *Three Forks of the Flathead River Floating Guide* from the Hungry Horse Ranger Station to aid in finding sites and avoiding private land. A permit is not required to camp overnight in the river corridor. Vault toilets are available at the eight river access sites. Pack out your trash. Pets are permitted.

Reservations, fees: No reservations are accepted. Camping is free. Open April-November.

Directions: From Columbia Falls, drive the potholed washboard North Fork Road (Forest Road 486) to the river access site of your choice. The border put-in is the farthest away at 53 miles. The other river access sites require turning east off the North Fork Road and driving less than 0.5 mile to reach launch sites. Each river access site is signed.

Northernmost GPS Coordinates: N 49° 0.031' W 114° 28.561'

Southernmost GPS Coordinates: N 48° 29.592' W 114° 7.585'

Contact: Flathead National Forest, Glacier View District, 10 Hungry Horse Dr., Hungry Horse, MT 59919, 406/387-3800, www.fs.usda.gov/flathead/.

3 KINTLA LAKE

🚶 ⛰ 🚣 🛶 🎣 🐕 🚐 ⛺

Scenic rating: 8

on Kintla Lake in Glacier National Park

BEST (

Located at 4,015 feet in elevation between Starvation and Parke Ridges, Kintla Lake defines remote. Not only do you have to drive miles of bumpy, dusty dirt road to reach the Polebridge entrance station to Glacier, but then you need to drive another hour of dirt road (single-lane in places) to reach the lake. Because of the cantankerous road, which is not recommended for large RVs and trailer combinations, and the distance from pavement, the lake attracts few people; campers who come here find the rewards of solitude, and brave swimmers can enjoy pristine clear water. No motorboats or Jet Skis are permitted on the lake, leaving paddlers to ply its waters in quiet. Anglers—especially those who can get away from shore in a row boat—can catch-and-release native westslope cutthroat trout and bull trout. One trail departs the campground along the north shore and reaches the head of the lake in 6.2 miles. Backpackers continue on to Upper Kintla and over Boulder Pass to end at Goat Haunt at Waterton Lake (32 miles total) or Bowman Lake (37 miles total).

The tiny, quiet campground cuddles under big trees in one loop. Several of the campsites near Kintla Creek have their parking spot on the loop, but their tent sites, tables, and campfires are down an embankment below the road. Sites 10 and 12 sit closest to the lake; sites 1-3 sit the farthest away. Sites 4-10 border Kintla Creek. Little privacy remains between them because of stripped underbrush.

Campsites, facilities: The 13 RV and tent campsites can accommodate small RVs, although the park service discourages RVs or trailer combinations. Facilities include picnic tables, fire rings with grills, hand pumps for potable water, vault toilets, garbage service, and a boat ramp. During primitive camping, bring your own water or treat lake water. Bring firewood; collecting is illegal. Leashed pets are permitted.

Reservations, fees: No reservations are accepted. Campsites cost $15 late May-early September. Cash, check, or credit card. Depending on snow, primitive camping ($10) is available in early May and mid-September-November.

Directions: From the Polebridge entrance station to Glacier National Park, drive 14.3 miles north on the Inside Road. The road terminates in the campground.

GPS Coordinates: N 48° 56.140' W 114° 20.789'

Contact: Glacier National Park, P.O. Box 128, West Glacier, MT 59936, 406/888-7800, www.nps.gov/glac.

CAMPING IN GLACIER NATIONAL PARK

Located a full day's drive north of Yellowstone, Glacier Park is worth a trip by itself. Its one million acres split along a north-south line—the Continental Divide—that runs from the Canadian border to Marias Pass. Clad in thick evergreens, the western mountains tuck campgrounds into thick forests or at the toe of long lakes that feed into the Flathead River's Middle Fork and North Fork, rivers that form the park's western and southwestern boundaries. On the eastern flanks, campgrounds cluster in a mix of grasslands, forests, and aspen groves, as the mountains tumble onto the Blackfeet Reservation's prairie. The border with Canada divides Glacier from its northern sister, Waterton Lakes National Park; together they form the world's first International Peace Park.

Only one road bisects the core of Glacier Park. In a feat of ingenious 1920s engineering, **Going-to-the-Sun Road** slices through cliffs as it crawls on a narrow, precipitous path to Logan Pass. Tunnels, arches, and retaining walls give the road its unique character while leading cars into an alpine wonderland where marmot whistles ride air currents through top-of-the-world scenery. Because only smaller vehicles can cross it, shuttles and historic red tour buses provide ways to see the road. Five campgrounds flank its natural wonders, including a pocket of rain forest harboring huge western red cedars up to 500 years old.

On the west side of the Continental Divide, several long, forested valleys spill from Glacier's peaks. The most accessible houses the park's largest body of water—**Lake McDonald**—and three campgrounds, including two of the park's biggest. Forming the park's southern boundary, the Middle Fork of the Flathead River, which parallels **Highway 2,** runs from a canyon into **West Glacier,** the local capital for white-water rafting, fishing, float trips, and a string of private RV parks and campgrounds. To the north, long dirt roads cut through the bucolic backwoods of the **North Fork** of the Flathead River Valley to primitive river campsites or remote lake campgrounds that provide solitude.

On the east side of the Continental Divide, private campgrounds on the **Blackfeet Reservation** offer hookup services unavailable at the park's five campgrounds. The private campgrounds of **St. Mary** garner views of Red Eagle Mountain's maroon slopes, with peaks rising straight up from the prairie. Of the east-side park service campgrounds, **Two Medicine** on the southeast corner ranks as highest drive-to lake in the park, and **Many Glacier** in the Swiftcurrent Valley is a hub for well-traveled trails that lead to lakes floating with icebergs even in August.

4 HEAD OF KINTLA LAKE

Scenic rating: 9
on Kintla Lake in Glacier National Park

BEST (

Huddling between Starvation and Parke Ridges in Glacier's remote northwest corner, the six-mile-long Kintla Lake sees very few people at its upper end. Those who visit its campground at 4,100 feet in elevation enjoy solitude and watching bald eagles and bears. A 2.7-mile trail from the campground continues on to Upper Kintla Lake, where scenery unfolds with glaciers hanging off Kintla Peak and

Kinnerly Peak rising straight from the lake. Take a brisk swim in the glacial waters before hiking back to the campground.

Reach the campground at the head of the lake by hiking 6.2 miles or paddling up the lake from Kintla Campground at the foot of the lake. At the head of the lake, the remote, quiet campground is built on a hillside with two communal cooking sites in the cedars near the shore and tent sites scattered on shaded terraces in the forest above. There are bears, so bring a rope for hanging food and cooking gear. In spring, high water floods some of the beach, but in summer as the water level drops, the smooth-stoned beach provides an easier place to pull boats out of the water. Tie up all boats at night in case winds arise!

Campsites, facilities: The campground has six designated tent campsites, and each holds up to four people each. Facilities include rock-rimmed fire pits, log benches, a food hanging cable, and a pit toilet. Bring drinking water, or treat lake water. Pack out your trash. Pets are not permitted.

Reservations, fees: Backcountry permits are required. Advance reservations ($30) for three of the campsites are available starting April 15. Get permits for remaining sites in person 24 hours in advance at the Apgar Backcountry Office in Apgar. Permits cost $5 per adult per night and $2.50 for children 8-15. They are free for children seven and under. Cash, check, or credit card. Open June-November. With early snowmelt, the campground may be available by late May.

Directions: From the Polebridge entrance station to Glacier National Park, drive 14.3 miles north on the Inside Road (single-lane in places) to the Kintla Campground.

GPS Coordinates: N 48° 58.557' W 114° 15.152'

Contact: Glacier National Park, P.O. Box 128, West Glacier, MT 59936, 406/888-7800, www.nps.gov/glac.

5 ROUND PRAIRIE

Scenic rating: 7

on the North Fork of the Flathead River in Glacier National Park

At 3,850 feet, Round Prairie is the only designated campground on the North Fork of the Flathead River's east bank in Glacier National Park. It is one of four Palouse prairies in the North Fork Valley, blooming with wheatgrass, fescues, oatgrass, sagebrush, and rare plants. Due a rain shadow from the Whitefish Mountains, Round Prairie sees only 20 inches of annual precipitation. Access the campground by

floating the river or driving the bumpy, dirt Inside Road followed by a walk of 5-10 minutes.

A mixed forest of firs and cottonwoods lines the river around the quiet, remote campground, which sits on the edge of Round Prairie. Bring a rope for hanging food and cooking gear. A large gravel bar allows boats to be beached. In the campground, a communal cooking site is available, and three tent sites are separated for privacy in the trees. The campground faces the sunset over the Whitefish Mountains. Additional undesignated campsites are available by special permit on the national park side of the river.

Campsites, facilities: The walk-in or boat-in campground has three tent campsites, each holding up to four people. Facilities include a rock fire ring, log benches, pit toilet, and food-hanging cable. Bring drinking water, or treat river water. Pack out your trash. Permits for two of the three sites are reserved until 3pm each day for river floaters. No pets are permitted.

Reservations, fees: Backcountry permits are required. Advance reservations ($20) for two of the campsites are available starting April 15. Get permits for other sites in person 24 hours in advance at the Apgar Backcountry Office in Apgar. Permits cost $5 per adult per night and $2.50 for children 8-15. They are free for children seven and under. Cash, check, or credit card. Opens June-November. With early snowmelt, the campground may be available in late May.

Directions: For walking in, drive from the Polebridge park entrance station 7.6 miles north on the skinny Inside Road; turn left to drive 0.5 miles to the parking area. For boating, drive north from the town of Polebridge on the dirt North Fork Road for 21 miles to the border or 10 miles to Ford to launch onto the river.

GPS Coordinates: N 48° 51.465' W 114° 21.984'

Contact: Glacier National Park, P.O. Box 128, West Glacier, MT 59936, 406/888-7800, www.nps.gov/glac.

6 SONDERSON MEADOW

🏃 🏊 🛶 🚣 🦌 🚐 ⛺

Scenic rating: 9
on the North Fork of the Flathead River in
Flathead National Forest

North of the town of Polebridge in the North Fork Valley, Sonderson Meadow sprawls into large open fields surrounded by fir forests and beaver ponds. The North Fork of the Flathead River runs around the perimeter of the meadow, making it popular for camping with those floating the river, but you can also drive to it. A skinny, rough dirt road accesses the meadow, which used to harbor an old airstrip. Unmarked game trails good for morning and evening wildlife-watching hikes wander around the meadow. Call the Forest Service first to be sure the gate on the access road is open.

From campsites along the meadow and river, you get shots of the rugged, remote Livingston Range of Glacier National Park with the sunrise coming over the park. The primitive, quiet campsites sit along the river's bank with wide-open views of the night sky and the music of the river. The campsites are spread far apart for privacy at the north and south ends of the meadows, accessed by two rough jeep trails.

Campsites, facilities: Sonderson Meadow has three primitive RV or tent campsites. The road is suitable for small truck campers—not trailers or large RVs. Facilities are not available. Fire pans are recommended. Bring drinking water, or treat river water. Campers are required to use a self-contained system for solid waste and carry it out to an RV dump station. Pack out your trash. Follow Leave No Trace principles in camping: Erect your tent on ground or rocks rather than sensitive vegetation. Leashed pets are permitted.

Reservations, fees: Reservations are not accepted. Camping is free. Open April-November.

Directions: Drive seven miles north from the town of Polebridge on the North Fork Road.

Turn right at the sign for Schnauss Cabin onto Forest Road 10372 and follow the narrow road as it drops one mile down the steep hill to the river.

GPS Coordinates: N 48° 50.061' W 114° 20.392'

Contact: Flathead National Forest, Glacier View District, 10 Hungry Horse Dr., Hungry Horse, MT 59919, 406/387-3800, www.fs.usda.gov/flathead/.

7 BOWMAN LAKE

🏃 🏊 🛶 🚣 🚐 🛶 🦌 🚐 ⛺

Scenic rating: 10
on Bowman Lake in Glacier National Park

BEST (

Sitting at 4,038 feet in elevation, Bowman Lake is one of two remote drive-to lakes in Glacier's northwest corner. Even though access to the campground requires miles of potholed dirt road driving—on either the Outside North Fork Road or the Inside North

© BECKY LOMAX

Rafters and floaters can camp along the North Fork of the Flathead River.

Fork Road—it is the most popular campground in the North Fork Valley. Sitting on the beach yields gorgeous views up the lake, while swimming in the chilly water will take your breath away. Trailheads lead to Numa Lookout (5.6 miles) for stunning views across to the Rainbow-Carter massif, Quartz Lake Loop (12.4 miles) for fishing, and the Bowman Lake Trail (7.1 miles) along the north shore. Motorboats of 10 horsepower or less are permitted, but not Jet Skiing and waterskiing. Canoeists and kayakers tour the shoreline to watch for bald eagles. The best fishing is from a boat; anglers go after westslope cutthroat and bull trout.

Sitting at the foot of Bowman Lake, the quiet campground winds one large loop through the brushy spruce forest. Filtered sunlight warms most of the campsites. A short road and trails connect to the beach and boat launch. Campsites are spread out for privacy, but you will see a few other campsites through the trees. Sites on the east side of the loop sit closer to the beach, but none border the shoreline. Walk to the lakeshore after dark for a stunning look at the stars.

Campsites, facilities: The campground has 48 RV or tent campsites, which can fit small RVs. The park service does not recommend large RVs or trailer combinations on the rough, narrow access road. Facilities include picnic tables, fire rings with grills, pit toilets, drinking water, and garbage service. During primitive camping, bring drinking water, or treat lake water. Leashed pets are permitted. Bring firewood; collecting is illegal.

Reservations, fees: No reservations are accepted. Campsites cost $15. Cash, check, or credit card. Open late May-mid-September; however, primitive camping ($10) is possible mid-September-November and sometimes in May with early snowmelt.

Directions: From the Polebridge entrance station to Glacier, drive 0.3 mile north to the Bowman Lake Road. Turn right and drive six miles on a single-lane road with minimal turnouts to the campground on the left.

GPS Coordinates: N 48° 49.691' W 114° 12.091'
Contact: Glacier National Park, P.O. Box 128, West Glacier, MT 59936, 406/888-7800, www.nps.gov/glac.

⑧ HEAD OF BOWMAN LAKE
🏃🏊🛶🏊🚤🏕️

Scenic rating: 10
on Bowman Lake in Glacier National Park

BEST (

In Glacier Park's remote northwest corner, six-mile-long Bowman Lake cuts through a steep-walled valley between the hulks of Rainbow and Numa Peaks. Craggy Thunderbird Peak rises out of the lake's head. At an elevation of 4,048 feet near the east end, the backcountry campground is favored by canoeists, kayakers, boaters, and hikers for its rugged remote setting and few people. You can swim, but be prepared for chilly water. Paddling to the campground takes about two hours; hiking the 7.1 miles along the northwest shore takes about three hours. A boat ramp at the foot of the lake assists with launching, and a parking lot is available for overnight parking. Watch for winds; the half-mile-wide lake kicks up big whitecaps fast.

The quiet campground sprawls on both sides of a creek, with tent sites scattered in the trees for privacy and two communal cooking sites. Bring a rope for hanging food and cooking gear. In spring, high water floods some of the beach, but in summer as the water level drops, the smooth-stoned beach provides an easier place to pull boats out of the water. Beach all boats securely at night in case winds arise!

Campsites, facilities: The campground has six tent campsites, each holding up to four people. Facilities include rock fire pits, food hanging cables, and pit toilet. Bring drinking water or treat lake water. Pack out your trash. Pets are not permitted.

Reservations, fees: Backcountry permits are

required. Advance reservations ($30) for three of the campsites are available starting April 15. Get permits for remaining sites in person 24 hours in advance at the Apgar Backcountry Office in Apgar. Plan to be in the office as soon as it opens as the popular campground fills its sites fast. Permits cost $5 per adult per night and $2.50 for children 8-15. They are free for children seven and under. Cash, check, or credit card. Opens mid-June-November. With early snowmelt, the campground may be available as early as late May.

Directions: From the Polebridge entrance station to Glacier, drive 0.3 mile north on the Inside Road to the Bowman Lake Road. Turn right and drive six miles on a single-lane road with minimal turnouts to the foot of Bowman Lake.

GPS Coordinates: N 48° 54.225' W 114° 7.272'

Contact: Glacier National Park, P.O. Box 128, West Glacier, MT 59936, 406/888-7800, www.nps.gov/glac.

9 QUARTZ CREEK

Scenic rating: 6

on the Inside North Fork Road in Glacier National Park

Located on the Inside North Fork Road through Glacier's western forests, tiny Quartz Creek Campground is used by campers looking for quiet and solitude. Its access requires driving miles of dirt road that is as notorious for its jarring potholes and bumpy washboards as it is for its clouds of dust. Adjacent to the campground, an infrequently maintained trail follows Quartz Creek for 6.8 miles to Lower Quartz Lake. Mountain bikers use this camp on North Fork tours, and anglers fish the creek and Quartz Lakes for native westslope cutthroat trout. Some camping supplies are available at the Polebridge Mercantile, 1.5 miles from the Polebridge entrance station;

cookies and cinnamon rolls are freshly baked there daily.

The campground, which is tucked under a mix of large shade-producing firs and sunny brush, rarely fills up because of its remoteness. Sites 4, 5, and 6 border the creek. Bring bug juice as the riparian area tends to breed mosquitoes in droves. The small sites also have tiny dirt parking pads.

Campsites, facilities: The campground has seven RV and tent campsites that can accommodate small RVs. Large RVs and trailer combinations are not recommended on the Inside Road. Facilities include picnic tables, fire rings with grills, and pit toilet. Bring drinking water, or treat creek water. Pack out your trash. Collecting of downed firewood is permitted on the Inside North Fork Road, but not in the campground. Leashed pets are permitted.

Reservations, fees: No reservations are accepted. Campsites cost $10. Cash, check, or credit card. Open July-early November.

Directions: From the Polebridge entrance station to Glacier National Park, drive 5.7 miles south on the Inside North Fork Road (Glacier Route 7). From Fish Creek Campground, drive 21.3 miles north on the Inside Road. The campground sits on the east side of the road.

GPS Coordinates: N 48° 43.286' W 114° 13.474'

Contact: Glacier National Park, P.O. Box 128, West Glacier, MT 59936, 406/888-7800, www.nps.gov/glac.

10 LOGGING CREEK

Scenic rating: 7

on the Inside North Fork Road in Glacier National Park

Located on Glacier's western forest slopes, Logging Creek sits on the Inside North Fork Road a long distance from pavement. Top speeds for driving the potholed, washboarded, curvy road reach about 20 mph. Sullivan Meadows, a few miles south of the campground, was home to the first pack of wolves that migrated from Canada in the 1980s. A nearby trail departs for Logging Lake, a 4.4-mile forested hike. The lake harbors westslope cutthroat trout, but fly-fishing requires wading away from the brushy shore. Many campers—including mountain bikers—use this remote campground for looping on a scenic tour through the North Fork Valley. Pack a birding field guide, for the area around the Logging Ranger Station and Logging Creek provides good bird-watching. Over 196 species of birds have been documented in the North Fork, including at least 112 that nest in the valley.

Logging Creek burbles adjacent to the campground, and across the road the idyllic Logging Ranger Station is staffed intermittently in summer. The quiet campground's one loop swings through large cedars and firs that admit filtered sunlight to the small campsites. Because of its remoteness, the campground rarely fills up. The damp vicinity also is a breeding ground for mosquitoes, so come prepared with repellent. Listen at night for wolf howls.

Campsites, facilities: The campground has seven RV and tent campsites that can accommodate small RVs. Large RVs and trailer combinations are not recommended on the Inside Road. Facilities include picnic tables, fire rings with grills, and pit toilet. Bring drinking water, or treat creek water. Pack out your trash. Collecting of downed firewood is permitted on the Inside North Fork Road, but not in the campground. Leashed pets are permitted.

Reservations, fees: No reservations are accepted. Campsites cost $10. Cash, check, or credit card. Open July-early November.

Directions: From the Polebridge entrance station to Glacier Park, drive 8.3 miles south on the Inside North Fork Road, also called Glacier Route 7 on some maps. Or from the Fish Creek Campground, drive 18 miles north on the Inside Road. The campground sits on the east side of the road.

GPS Coordinates: N 48° 41.902' W 114° 11.520'
Contact: Glacier National Park, P.O. Box 128, West Glacier, MT 59936, 406/888-7800, www.nps.gov/glac.

11 BIG CREEK

Scenic rating: 9
on the North Fork of the Flathead River in Flathead National Forest

BEST (

Located on the North Fork of the Flathead River's west bank across from Glacier National Park, Big Creek nestles below Huckleberry Mountain, which blocks direct sun until late morning. Evidence of the 2001 Moose Fire still surrounds the campground, but the forest is regenerating with lodgepole pines and pink fireweed. The fire bypassed the campground, leaving its trees green. At 2.5 miles north of the campground, the Glacier View Trail climbs the steep 2.3 miles up to a ridgetop meadow that yields panoramic views of Glacier Park. Anglers fish both Big Creek and the North Fork of the Flathead River for westslope cutthroat and rainbow trout. The campground has a boat launch for rafting and kayaking.

Tall lodgepoles and firs shade most of the campsites, with a few cottonwoods sprinkled along the river. More than half of the campsites overlook the river or sit adjacent to it. Backing in to alcoves of trees on a gravel loop and spur road, the spacious campsites spread out for privacy, but you'll see neighboring tents through the trunks with no underbrush. Some of the river campsites capture more sun along the meadows, and you'll only hear the sound of the river.

Campsites, facilities: The campground has 22 RV and tent campsites that can accommodate RVs up to 40 feet. The huge group campsite fits up to 200 people. Facilities include picnic tables, fire rings with grills, drinking water, vault toilets (wheelchair-accessible), boat ramp, firewood for sale, and campground hosts. Pack out your trash. Leashed pets are permitted.

Reservations, fees: Reservations are not accepted, except for the large group campsite (877/444-6777, www.recreation.gov, $25). Campsites cost $13. Cash or check. Open mid-May-mid-October.

Directions: From Apgar, drive 11.5 miles north on the Camas Road. Turn left on the North Fork Road and drive 2.5 miles south to the campground entrance. From Columbia Falls, drive 20 miles north on the North Fork Road. Find the signed entrance road on the road's east side. When you drive in, bypass the road to the river launch site and the group campsite loop to reach the individual campsites.

GPS Coordinates: N 48° 36.100' W 114° 9.817'

Contact: Flathead National Forest, Glacier View District, 10 Hungry Horse Dr., Hungry Horse, MT 59919, 406/387-3800, www.fs.usda.gov/flathead/.

12 GREAT NORTHERN FLATS

Scenic rating: 6

on the North Fork of the Flathead River in Flathead National Forest

Along the North Fork of the Flathead River, Great Northern Flats has been revamped from a park-and-camp-anywhere place to designated campsites. The flats, a large river bar on the west bank opposite Glacier National Park, provide a river access for rafters, kayakers, and anglers. From the flats to Glacier Rim includes the Class II-III Fools Hen Rapids. Only hand-carried watercraft can be launched. From here downriver, motorboats with a 10-horsepower limit are also permitted. The flats huddle under the Apgar Mountains, which rise in steep semi-arid faces across the river. In 2001, the Moose Fire swept through here, part of a

73,000-acre fire that raged for two months. Despite the fire, the Great Northern Flats environs is fast regenerating with lodgepole pines.

Growing with grass and wildflowers, the arid, dusty, sunny flats are wide open with no shade and no privacy. The primitive back-in campsites tuck close together around a small gravel loop near the river. At night, after the daytime river traffic disappears, the campground goes quiet, with only the sound of the wind and the river. Tents are usually set up on the gravel parking pads, as no additional tent space is available.

Campsites, facilities: The campground has three RV or tent campsites that can accommodate small RVs. Facilities include fire rings with grills and a vault toilet (wheelchair-accessible). Bring your own water, or treat river water. Camping is limited to three days. Leashed pets are permitted.

Reservations, fees: No reservations are accepted. Camping is free. Open late April-November.

Directions: From Apgar, drive 11.5 miles north on Camas Road. Turn left on North Fork Road and drive 5.8 miles to the campground. From Columbia Falls, drive 16 miles north on North Fork Road to the campground. Turn east into the river access site, marked only with a small sign saying "1070."

GPS Coordinates: N 48° 34.162' W 114° 7.798'

Contact: Flathead National Forest, Glacier View District, 10 Hungry Horse Dr., Hungry Horse, MT 59919, 406/387-3800, www.fs.usda.gov/flathead/.

13 GLACIER RIM PRIMITIVE

Scenic rating: 7

on the North Fork of the Flathead River in Flathead National Forest

Located on the North Fork of the Flathead River at 3,179 feet in elevation, the Glacier

Rim River Access sits on the west bank opposite Glacier National Park. Close to Columbia Falls (about 15 minutes south), this is a popular place to camp because its access is via pavement instead of dirt road. The area is also popular for local anglers, rafters, kayakers, and canoeists buzzing out for the evening after work to float to Blankenship Bridge. Motorboats with a 10-horsepower limit are also permitted on the river.

The two campsites are strikingly different. The RV site sits on a sloped gravel spur north of the parking lot. The site is sunny, visible from the cars driving in, and requires a five-minute walk to see the river. The idyllic tent site sits on the river adjacent to the boat ramp under heavy shade and filled with the sound of the river. Vehicles for the tent site must park up the hill 50 feet or in the parking lot. Plan to arrive early to claim a spot.

Campsites, facilities: Glacier Rim has two campsites. Facilities include rock fire rings, boat launch, boat trailer parking, and vault toilet (wheelchair-accessible). Bring your own water, or treat river water. A three-day maximum for camping is enforced. Leashed pets are permitted.

Reservations, fees: Reservations are not accepted. Camping is free. Open late April-November.

Directions: From Apgar, drive 11.5 miles north on Camas Road. Turn left on the North Fork Road and drive 11.8 miles to Glacier Rim. From Columbia Falls, drive 10 miles north on North Fork Road to reach Glacier Rim. Look for the river access sign and turn off toward the east.

GPS Coordinates: N 48° 29.592' W 114° 7.585'

Contact: Flathead National Forest, Glacier View District, 10 Hungry Horse Dr., Hungry Horse, MT 59919, 406/387-3800, www.fs.usda.gov/flathead/.

14 TIMBER WOLF RESORT

Scenic rating: 7
between Hungry Horse and West Glacier

Timber Wolf Resort is the farthest west in the string of private RV campgrounds that line Highway 2 between Hungry Horse and West Glacier with its rafting, golf, trail rides, shopping, and restaurants. It sits about 10 minutes from Glacier National Park's west entrance station. The tiny town of Hungry Horse is 0.5 mile west. Less than two miles away, a frontage road parallels the dam-controlled section of the South Fork of the Flathead River, making for easy shoreline access to cast flies for rainbows and cutthroat. The resort's large group campfire serves as a place to meet other campers. A hiking trail loops around part of the campground, and a paved bike trail parallels the highway.

The campground, in 20 wooded acres on a gravel road through a terraced hillside, offers peek-a-boo views of Glacier's Apgar Range. Most of the narrow pull-through RV campsites have a tree for partial shade but garner plenty of traffic views and highway noise. Tucked at the back of the campground, the tent sites enjoy shade and privacy from the road.

Campsites, facilities: The campground has 24 RV campsites that can accommodate RVs up to 40 feet, as well as five tent campsites. Hookups include sewer, water, and electricity up to 50 amps. Facilities include picnic tables, fire rings, pedestal charcoal grills (bring your own charcoal), flush toilets, showers, wireless Internet, camp store, playground, gazebo with gas grills, and firewood for sale. Leashed pets are permitted.

Reservations, fees: Reservations are accepted. Hookups cost $40-45. Tent sites cost $25 for one tent; each additional tent costs $7. Check the resort's website for specials. Rates cover two people. Kids age five and younger camp for free, but additional adults are charged

$5 per night and extra tents cost $5 each. The 7 percent Montana bed tax will be added on. Cash or credit card. Open May-September.
Directions: From Hungry Horse, on Highway 2 drive eastward 0.25 mile past Hungry Horse Dam Road. From West Glacier, drive west on Highway 2 for nine miles. Find the resort entrance on the south side of the highway.
GPS Coordinates: N 48° 23.221' W 114° 2.868'
Contact: Timber Wolf Resort, P.O. Box 190250, 9105 Hwy. 2 E., Hungry Horse, MT 59919, 406/387-9653, www.timberwolfresort.com.

15 MOUNTAIN MEADOWS

Scenic rating: 8
between Hungry Horse and West Glacier

Located nine miles west of Glacier National Park's west entrance, Mountain Meadows is one of the many private campgrounds lining the highway between Hungry Horse and West Glacier with its rafting, golf, trail rides, shopping, and restaurants. A paved walking-bicycle path parallels the highway in front of the campground, connecting the small towns of Coram and Hungry Horse. About two miles east, the Coram Experimental Forest, which houses several 500-year-old larch trees, loops with trails through an area used by the Forest Service for research. You can also fish the campground's private catch-and-release stocked rainbow trout pond (no license needed).

The campground sits on 33 acres in a natural forest with views of Glacier's Apgar Range from its pond. Benches are available to watch the sun set over the peaks. Less railroad and highway noise filters into the campground than in others in the area. On a gravel road, the back-in and pull-through campsites gain partial shade and privacy under a tall forest of mixed trees.

Campsites, facilities: The campground has 52 RV sites that can accommodate RVs up to 45 feet long with slide-outs and awnings. Hookups are available for water, sewer, and electricity up to 50 amps. Facilities include picnic tables, fire rings with grills, flush toilets, showers, a coin-operated launderette, disposal station, camp store, firewood for sale, and wireless Internet. Leashed pets are permitted.
Reservations, fees: Make midsummer reservations in winter to guarantee a spot. Hookups run $39-42. Check for discounts on their website. Rates are based on two-person occupancy per site. For additional adults, add $4, and for children, add $2, with a maximum of six people per site. A 7 percent Montana bed tax will be added on. Cash or credit card. Open May-September.
Directions: From Hungry Horse, drive east on Highway 2 up the hill 0.6 mile. From West Glacier, drive west on Highway 2 for nine miles. Find the park entrance on the highway's east side.
GPS Coordinates: N 48° 23.254' W 114° 2.603'
Contact: Mountain Meadows RV Park, P.O. Box 190442, 9125 Hwy. 2 E., Hungry Horse, MT 59919, 406/387-9125, www.mmrvpark.com.

16 CANYON RV AND CAMPGROUND

Scenic rating: 7
between Hungry Horse and West Glacier

Located in the nine miles of Highway 2 between West Glacier and Hungry Horse, Canyon RV and Campground is the only campground with river access. An eight-mile drive leads to the west entrance to Glacier National Park and West Glacier, with its rafting, golf, trail rides, shopping, and restaurants. The campground neighbors Montana Fur

Traders and sits across the highway from a paved walking-bicycling path that parallels the road. The campground sits on a treed plateau above the Flathead River, but its property runs right down to the river's bank. You can cast a line from the shore for rainbow or cutthroat trout, or just sit to watch rafts float by. A trail through the woods connects to the river.

A few sparse mature trees offer a wee bit of shade in the sunny campground that generally gets good satellite reception. A narrow gravel road loops through the grassy narrow pull-through and back-in campsites, which are lined up in RV parking lot fashion—close to the neighbors. Because of the proximity of the railroad tracks across the river and the highway, noise seeps into the campground.

Campsites, facilities: The campground has 50 RV and tent campsites that can accommodate RVs up to 45 feet and slideouts. Hookups include water, sewer, and electricity up to 50 amps. Facilities include picnic tables, flush toilets, showers, launderette, disposal station, camp store, and wireless Internet. Leashed pets are permitted. A wheelchair-accessible toilet and campsites are available.

Reservations, fees: Reservations are accepted. Hookups cost $39-42, but only $35 in May and September. Tent and unserviced sites cost $27-30. Rates are based on two people; each extra person is charged $3. Sometimes the park offers the seventh night free. A 7 percent Montana bed tax will be added to the bill. Cash, check, or credit card. Open May-September.

Directions: On Highway 2, from Hungry Horse, drive one mile east, or from West Glacier, drive eight miles west. Turn west into the campground entrance.

GPS Coordinates: N 48° 23.827' W 114° 2.519'

Contact: Glacier National Park, P.O. Box 7, 9540 Hwy. 2 E., Hungry Horse, MT 59919, 406/387-9393, www.montanacampground.com.

17 SUNDANCE CAMPGROUND AND RV PARK

Scenic rating: 5
between Hungry Horse and West Glacier

Sundance sits in the middle of the line of private RV parks and campgrounds strung along Highway between West Glacier and Hungry Horse. The entrance to Glacier National Park is 6.5 miles to the east, along with West Glacier's rafting, golf, trail rides, shopping, and restaurants. For those with pets, Sundance offers one amenity that other campgrounds do not: While you tour Glacier for the day, you can kennel Fido at the campground. For hikers, kenneling the dog allows you to explore the national park trails on which pets are not permitted. The neighboring Great Bear Adventure Park—a drive-through habitat with captive black bears—sits over the fence on the campground's east side.

A natural forest surrounds the campground, with little in the way of understory between the tall shade trees. Most campsites are grassy, and a dirt road loops through the campground for access to sites with gravel parking. The north-end sites are farthest from the highway but are closest to the railroad tracks. The east-side sites border the bear park.

Campsites, facilities: The campground has nine tent sites and 22 RV sites that are pull-throughs with hookups for water and electricity up to 50 amps. Facilities include picnic tables, fire rings, flush toilets (wheelchair-accessible), hot showers, disposal station, truck dump service, camp store, wireless Internet, launderette, covered day kennel, fenced pet play area, firewood for sale, and dishwashing station with water for tenters. Leashed pets are permitted.

Reservations, fees: Reservations are accepted. Hookups cost $30; tent sites cost $20. Rates cover two people; for additional campers over 10 years old, add $3 each. Inquire about pet kenneling costs. Add on 7 percent

Montana bed tax. Cash, check, or credit card. Open May–mid-October.

Directions: From West Glacier, drive six miles west on Highway 2. The campground is on the north side of the road between mileposts 147 and 148. Look for a red sign.

GPS Coordinates: N 48° 26.032' W 114° 2.574'

Contact: Sundance Campground and RV Park, 10545 Hwy. 2 E., Coram, MT 59913, 406/387-5016 or 866/782-2677, www.sundancecampground.com.

18 NORTH AMERICAN RV PARK

Scenic rating: 5

between Hungry Horse and West Glacier

North American RV Park sits six miles west of West Glacier with close proximity to rafting, fishing, golf, and horseback riding companies, plus the West Glacier Golf Course. It is also 6.5 miles west from the entrance to Glacier National Park. The gravel roads through the campground use names of famous places in Glacier Park.

Recent growth in the past decade put a fir-tree barrier, cabins, and yurts between the highway and the campground yielding more privacy from highway gawkers. Trees lend shade to some sites. Most of the campsites, however, are sunny with good satellite reception, surrounded by mowed lawn, but crammed tightly together. Big-rig drivers prefer this park because its fewer trees and pull-through sites allow for easier maneuvering. Highway and train noise creeps into the campground. Sites 7-9 sit the farthest from the highway with the most privacy. Sites 43, 45, 47, 49, 51, 53, 54, and 55 also back up toward woods rather than other campers.

Campsites, facilities: The campground has 60 RV sites, which can fit RVs up to 45 feet. Hookups are available for sewer, water, and electricity up to 50 amps. Facilities include picnic tables, fire rings, flush toilets, showers, launderette, wireless Internet, recreation room, playground, camp store, and firewood for sale. Leashed pets are permitted.

Reservations, fees: Reservations are highly recommended in midsummer. Hookups cost $42 ($36 in shoulder seasons). Rates are for two people. Each additional person is charged $5, but kids 12 years old and under camp for free. Check website for discounts. Add on 7 percent Montana bed tax. Cash, check, or credit card. Open mid-April-October.

Directions: From West Glacier, drive 5.5 miles west on Highway 2 to milepost 147.5. Turn south into the campground.

GPS Coordinates: N 48° 26.264' W 114° 2.417'

Contact: North American RV Park, 10640 Hwy. 2 E., Coram, MT 59913, 800/704-4266, www.northamericanrvpark.com.

19 LAKE FIVE RESORT

Scenic rating: 7

between Hungry Horse and West Glacier

Lake Five Resort sets its cabins and campground on a 235-acre lake west of West Glacier. The shallow lake depth causes its waters to be warmer than the chilly glacier-fed Lake McDonald five miles away in Glacier National Park—hence the tiny lake's attraction for waterskiing, canoeing, fishing, and swimming. The lake buzzes with motorboats on hot summer days, but Jet Skis are banned. Bicyclists can ride the local paved and dirt back roads to circle the lake or ride to the confluence of the Middle Fork and the North Fork of the Flathead Rivers.

Unfortunately, most of the cabins claim the front spots on the lake, with the campground lining up most of it its tiny, cramped back-in sites close together behind them in a grassy, wooded setting that offers partial shade. Six campsites have beachfront, and the resort also has two tipis right on the shoreline for those who want the experience of camping in a Native American tradition. Set off Highway 2 on a side road, Lake Five Resort is quieter than some of the other area campgrounds, but it picks up noise from the nearby trains.

Campsites, facilities: The resort has 50 RV campsites that can fit RVs up to 40 feet. Hookups include sewer, water, and electricity up to 50 amps, but only 14 sites include sewer hookups. Facilities include fire rings, flush toilets, showers, wireless Internet, disposal station, boat launch, boat dock, playground, volleyball, canoe rentals, and horseshoes. Tipis sleep up to four people. Leashed pets are permitted.

Reservations, fees: Reservations are highly recommended during midsummer. Campsites cost $50-56. The rate covers two people. Extra campers are charged $5 per night. Tipis rent for $63 per night. For dogs, add $10 per day. Add on 7 percent Montana bed tax. Check website for off-season discounts. Cash or credit card. Open May-October.

Directions: Drive 2.7 miles westward from West Glacier on Highway 2 and turn right onto the Lake Five Road. After driving 0.4 mile to Belton Stage Road, turn left and go 0.5 mile. Turn right into the campground. GPS Coordinates: N 48° 27.734' W 114° 1.084'

Contact: Lake Five Resort, P.O. Box 338, 540 Belton Stage Rd., West Glacier, MT 59936, 406/387-5601, www.lakefiveresort.com.

20 SAN-SUZ-ED RV PARK

Scenic rating: 5

between Hungry Horse and West Glacier

Located on Highway 2, this RV park is one of the closer private campgrounds to Glacier National Park's west entrance three miles to the east with paved shoulders for cycling. It is also 2.5 miles from West Glacier activities: trail rides, white-water rafting, float trips, fishing, golf, and shopping. Instead of individual campfire rings at each site, the campground has one large community campfire every night. Bring your own marshmallows or hot dogs for roasting and glean news from fellow campers: where the fish are biting, where the bears are feeding, and where the huckleberries are ripe. The owners also bake homemade pies and, during the summer, serve a breakfast of Belgian waffles and sourdough hotcakes with homemade syrup.

Set in a mix of forest—with some sites shaded and others sunny—the campground sits between Highway 2 and the railroad tracks, which allows some noise to percolate through the trees. Light sleepers should bring earplugs. Part of the campground is paved, with paved pull-through and back-in parking pads, which eliminates dust. Wide sites allow for RV slide-outs and awnings. Each campsite has a different colored picnic table.

Campsites, facilities: The park contains 21 tent sites and 55 RV sites that can accommodate RVs up to 45 feet. Hookups include sewer, water, and electricity up to 50 amps. Facilities include picnic tables, flush toilets (wheelchair-accessible), showers, wireless Internet, launderette, convenience store, and four enclosed shelters with or without electricity. Leashed pets are permitted.

Reservations, fees: Reservations are appreciated. Hookups cost $41-45. Tents and unserviced sites cost $35. Rates are for two people. Extra campers are charged $5 per person, but kids under 11 years old stay free. The enclosed shelters cost $45-55 for up to four people. Add on the 7 percent Montana bed tax. Cash or credit card. Open May-October.

Directions: On Highway 2, from West Glacier, drive west for 2.5 miles, or from Hungry Horse, drive east for 6.5 miles. The campground sits on the north side of the highway between mileposts 150 and 151. GPS Coordinates: N 48° 27.761' W 114° 0.131'

Contact: San-Suz-Ed RV, P.O. Box 387,

11505 Hwy. 2 W., West Glacier, MT 59936, 406/387-5280 or 800/630-2623, www.sansuzedrvpark.com.

21 WEST GLACIER KOA

Scenic rating: 7

near West Glacier

Located one mile south of the busy Highway 2 to the west of West Glacier, the KOA is 2.5 miles from Glacier National Park's west entrance. It is also two miles—an easy bike ride—to West Glacier's rafting companies, horseback rides, golf, restaurants, and gift shops. The campground boasts the only swimming pool (June–mid-September) on the park's west side with hot tubs steaming all season long. The campground serves breakfast, ice cream, and an evening barbecue during summer months, and features a Tom Ulrich wildlife slide show for evening entertainment twice a week. As of 2013, the owners are looking at expanding the campground.

Set in lodgepole pines, the campsites are separated from the pool area by a large grassy lawn, good for a game of Frisbee. Sites 121-152, which are grassy and more open, do not permit tents or campfires; the other sites have fire rings. Sites 113-125 sit at the back, away from the main camp hubbub but close to one restroom; tent sites 100-112 also gain privacy with larger spaces and picnic tables.

Campsites, facilities: The KOA has 139 RV sites that can accommodate 45-foot RVs. Fifty of the campsites are pull-throughs. Hookups include sewer, water, and electricity up to 50 amps. Facilities include picnic tables, fire rings, flush toilets, showers, coin-operated launderette, swimming pool, hot tubs, playground, game room, wireless Internet, disposal station, super sites, patio sites, and dog-walk area. Leashed pets are permitted. Wheelchair-accessible facilities are available.

Reservations, fees: Reservations are accepted. Hookups run $56-90; no hookups and tent sites cost $38. Rates are based on two people. Extra adults are charged $7.50 each, but kids 17 years old and under stay free. In shoulder seasons (May–early June, mid-September–October 1) campsite rates are discounted. Add on 7 percent Montana bed tax. Cash, traveler's check, or credit card. Open May–September.

Directions: From West Glacier, drive west on Highway 2 for 2.5 miles. Turn south onto paved Half Moon Flats Road and drive one mile.

GPS Coordinates: N 48° 27.869' W 113° 58.862'

Contact: West Glacier KOA, 355 Half Moon Flats Rd., West Glacier, MT 59936, 406/387-5341 or 800/562-3313, www.westglacierkoa.com.

22 GLACIER CAMPGROUND

Scenic rating: 6

near West Glacier

Located one mile from the west entrance to the Glacier National Park, Glacier Campground is the closest private campground to the park in the long string of RV park campgrounds between West Glacier and Hungry Horse. Golf, restaurants, gift shops, an espresso stand, a post office, and the train depot sit 0.5 mile to the east. Four rafting companies that run white-water and float trips on the Middle Fork of the Flathead also have their offices within a five-minute drive. The park's historical red tour buses also will stop by the campground to pick up riders. For evening entertainment, the campground sponsors Forest Service presentations.

The family-owned campground is on 40 timbered acres set back a bit from the highway. The trees not only reduce the highway and railroad noise (you'll still hear it) but grant shade for hot days. Firs, birches, and copious underbrush verging on jungle help to maintain privacy for the campsites. Big rigs can get a few pull-through sites, but otherwise, parking requires a tight squeeze to back into the forest slot. Not all of the campsites have picnic tables and fire rings; ask specifically for these when you arrive or reserve a spot. The campground also has grassy sites for bicyclists and backpackers to share.

Campsites, facilities: The campground has 80 RV sites, with some pull-through sites that can accommodate RVs up to 40 feet, and 80 tent campsites. Hookups include water and electricity up to 30 amps. Facilities include flush toilets, showers, a pumper truck for sewer service ($20), camp store, coin-operated launderette, wood-heated recreation room, playground, and wireless Internet. Leashed pets are permitted.

Reservations, fees: Reservations are accepted. Hookups cost $24-29; no hookup and tent sites cost $19-22. For bikers and hikers, the campground charges $10 per person. Add on 7 percent Montana bed tax. Cash or credit card. Open May-September.

Directions: On Highway 2, from West Glacier, drive 0.5 mile west, or from Hungry Horse, drive 8.5 miles east. Turn south off the highway at the signed entrance. GPS Coordinates: N 48° 28.970' W 113° 59.798'

Contact: Glacier Campground, P.O. Box 447, 12070 Hwy. 2 W., West Glacier, MT 59936, 406/387-5689 or 888/387-5689, www.glaciercampground.com.

23 APGAR

Scenic rating: 9
on Lake McDonald in Glacier National Park

At the foot of Lake McDonald and on Going-to-the-Sun Road, Apgar campground bustles with campers walking to Lake McDonald for a swim, bicycling to the Middle Fork of the Flathead River, or hopping shuttles up Going-to-the-Sun Road to Logan Pass. Adjacent to Apgar Village, the campground connects via paved trails to the Apgar Visitor Center, Eddy's Restaurant, a camp store, ice cream stand, and gift shops. Lake McDonald's only boat ramp sits between the picnic area and the village. You can rent canoes, kayaks, or boats with small horsepower engines. Lower McDonald Creek sees heavy fishing and is a warm-day favorite for floating on kayaks, rafts, or tubes to Quarter Circle Bridge. Nearby, hikers can climb 2.8 miles to Apgar Lookout, which overlooks McDonald Valley and Glacier's jagged peaks. Other trails head to McDonald Creek.

None of the campsites sit right on Lake McDonald; however, the amphitheater where the park service holds evening programs does. Surrounded by birch and hemlocks, the campground is Glacier's largest, with open campsites beneath the trees and some road noise from Going-to-the-Sun Road. Vehicles over 21 feet must access this campground from West Glacier.

Campsites, facilities: The campground has 194 RV or tent campsites, including 25 that can accommodate RVs up to 40 feet and group sites for 9-24 people. Facilities include picnic tables, fire rings with grills, flush toilets (wheelchair-accessible), drinking water, raised gravel tent platforms, shared sites for hikers and bikers, garbage service, interpretive programs, and a disposal station. Bring firewood; collecting it is illegal. During the primitive camping season (April, mid-October-Nov) the campground has only pit toilets and no running water. In winter, camp at the picnic area—a plowed parking lot with a pit toilet. Leashed pets are permitted.

Reservations, fees: Reservations are not accepted. Sites cost $20 per night May-mid-October. Biker and hiker sites cost $5 per person. Primitive camping costs $10; winter camping is free. Cash, check, or credit card. Open year-round.

Directions: From the west entrance of Glacier

National Park, drive northeast on Going-to-the-Sun Road one mile to the Apgar Junction. Turn right, driving for one mile, then turn left at the sign to Apgar Village, and drive 0.3 mile to the campground entrance on the left. GPS Coordinates: N 48° 31.602' W 113° 59.059'

Contact: Glacier National Park, P.O. Box 128, West Glacier, MT 59936, 406/888-7800, www.nps.gov/glac.

24 FISH CREEK

Scenic rating: 9
on Lake McDonald in Glacier National Park

Fish Creek Campground is located on Lake McDonald's north shore three miles from Apgar on Glacier's west side. Fish Creek flows through the campground, but the stream is closed to fishing. Anglers still fish nearby in Lake McDonald, especially where the creek runs into the lake. Built on a hillside in deep cedars, lodgepoles, and larches, the campground and picnic area border the shoreline with its multicolored perfect rock-skipping stones. As the water level drops throughout the summer, the beaches become larger and more appealing for sunbathing, swimming, and sunset-watching. The Lake McDonald Trail departs from loop C for a one-mile jaunt to Rocky Point—a rock bluff with views of Mount Edwards and Mount Brown. Hike farther up the lake to remote beaches, or loop back through the 2003 fire zone, which has interpretive signs. You can launch hand-carried watercraft from the picnic area, but the closest boat launch is in Apgar.

Loops C and D have the best sites for the quickest access to the lake. Some of their southern campsites have peek-a-boo water views, too. If privacy is valued, ask for one of the smaller campsites on the outer, uphill side of loop B. The shaded campground sits far enough away from the Apgar hubbub to be a peaceful, quiet place. Be prepared for mosquitoes.

Campsites, facilities: Fish Creek has 178 RV or tent campsites, including 18 campsites accommodating RVs up to 35 feet long and 62 sites fitting RVs up to 27 feet. Facilities include picnic tables, fire rings with grills, flush toilets (wheelchair-accessible), drinking water, shared hiker and biker campsites, garbage service, token showers in loop C, evening amphitheater ranger talks, and a disposal station. Bring firewood; collecting it is illegal. Leashed pets are permitted.

Reservations, fees: Reservations are available (877/444-6777, www.reservations.gov). Campsites cost $23 per night; shared hiker or biker sites cost $5 per person. Cash, check, or credit card. Open June-early September.

Directions: From Glacier's west entrance, drive one mile northeast to the Apgar Junction. Turn left and drive 1.25 miles north on Camas Road and turn right at the campground sign, dropping one mile down past the picnic area to the staffed campground entrance station.

GPS Coordinates: N 48° 32.877' W 113° 59.127'

Contact: Glacier National Park, P.O. Box 128, West Glacier, MT 59936, 406/888-7800, www.nps.gov/glac.

25 LAKE MCDONALD

Scenic rating: 10
on Lake McDonald in Glacier National Park

At 10 miles long and 1.5 miles wide, Lake McDonald is the largest lake in Glacier National Park. Its southern flank is bordered by Going-to-the-Sun Road, but its north side—where the Lake McDonald backcountry campground sits—is accessed only by hiking the Lake McDonald Trail from Fish Creek Campground or by boating the lake.

© BECKY LOMAX

The Lake McDonald backcountry campsite offers solitude for boaters or hikers.

The Robert Fire in 2003 burned the campground, leaving only a few charred trees. From the camp, you get views of Mount Brown, Edwards, and Jackson Peak—mountains not visible from the Sun Road. The lake harbors kokanee salmon and lake trout. Paddling to the campground takes about 90 minutes from Apgar; traveling with a motorboat takes about 30 minutes. No dock is available; completely beach all boats at night in case winds arise.

The campground sits about halfway up the north side of the lake on a point jutting into the lake. The communal cooking site and sleeping campsites sit back from the shoreline in sparse trees. In June, the rocky beach is minimal, but by August, it increases to a quiet spacious place to relax on the shore in the sun. The campground is prized for its quiet and solitude. Take 30 feet of rope for hanging food and cooking gear.

Campsites, facilities: The campground has two tent campsites; each holds up to four people. Facilities include a rock fire pit,

food-hanging cable, communal cooking site with log benches, and pit toilet. Bring drinking water, or treat lake water. Pack out your trash. Pets are not permitted.

Reservations, fees: Backcountry permits are required. Advance reservations ($30) for one of the campsites is available starting April 15. Get permits for remaining sites in person 24 hours in advance at the Apgar Backcountry Office in Apgar. Permits cost $5 per adult per night and $2.50 for children 8-15. They are free for children seven and under. Cash, check, or credit card. Opens mid-May-November.

Directions: For boating, launch from the Apgar boat ramp. Parking for trailers is available across the street. For hiking, park at the Fish Creek picnic area.

GPS Coordinates: N 48° 35.650' W 113° 55.518'

Contact: Glacier National Park, P.O. Box 128, West Glacier, MT 59936, 406/888-7800, www.nps.gov/glac.

26 SPRAGUE CREEK

Scenic rating: 10
on Lake McDonald in Glacier National Park

BEST (

Sitting at 3,200 feet on Lake McDonald's southeast shore, Sprague Creek is one of five campgrounds lining Going-to-the-Sun Road. It is the smallest drive-in campground on Lake McDonald and the first to fill up. Paths access the lake for launching canoes or kayaks, but large boats must go to Apgar for the boat ramp. Anglers fish the lake for lake trout and kokanee salmon. Squeezed in between Going-to-the-Sun Road and the lake, the campground sits one mile from historical Lake McDonald Lodge, restaurants, boat tours, red bus tours, a camp store, horseback riding, and the Sperry Trailhead. The trail ascends to Snyder Lake (4.4 miles), historical Sperry Chalet (6.4 miles), Sperry Glacier (10.4 miles), and Mount Brown Lookout (5.8 steep miles), with its dizzying view down to Lake McDonald. A shuttle stop at the campground connects with 17 places on Going-to-the-Sun Road, including Logan Pass.

Shaded by large cedars, the campsites cluster tightly in the forest with little to no underbrush between them to add privacy. Strung around a narrow, curvy, paved loop, sites 1, 2, 5, 7, 8, 10, 12, 13, 15, and 16 overlook the lake with more privacy. The backs of sites 17, 20, 21, 22, and 24 flank the busy Going-to-the-Sun Road, but traffic quiets after dark. Considering the campground's popularity, plan on arriving around 11am in midsummer.

Campsites, facilities: The campground has 25 RV or tent campsites that can accommodate small RVs up to 21 feet. No towed units are allowed. Facilities include picnic tables, fire rings with grills, flush toilets (wheelchair-accessible), raised gravel tent platforms, drinking water, and garbage service. Bring firewood; collecting is illegal. Leashed pets are permitted.

Reservations, fees: No reservations are accepted. Campsites cost $20. Shared sites for hikers and bikers cost $5 per person. Cash, check, or credit card. Open mid-May-mid-September.

Directions: From the west entrance to Glacier National Park, drive 9.5 miles east on Going-to-the-Sun Road. From the St. Mary entrance, drive 40.5 miles west over Logan Pass. Find the campground entrance on the lake side of the road.

GPS Coordinates: N 48° 36.370' W 113° 53.099'

Contact: Glacier National Park, P.O. Box 128, West Glacier, MT 59936, 406/888-7800, www.nps.gov/glac.

27 AVALANCHE

Scenic rating: 9
in McDonald Valley in Glacier National Park

Tucked into a narrow canyon between massive peaks, Avalanche Campground sits at 3,550 feet on Going-to-the-Sun Road. This is the closest west-side campground to Logan Pass, 16 miles east. Named for the nearby avalanches that rip down Mount Cannon's slopes, the campground sits in a pocket of rain forest preserved from fire. The 0.7-mile, wheelchair-accessible, paved and boardwalk Trail of the Cedars loops from the campground through ancient cedars and past red-rocked Avalanche Gorge. A spur trail climbs two miles up to Avalanche Lake, where giant waterfalls plummet from a hanging valley. In midsummer, the trail sees a constant stream of foot traffic heading to the lake for swimming, fishing, or gazing at mountain goats on the cliffs. The free Going-to-the-Sun Road shuttles stop at Avalanche. Vehicles over 21 feet are not permitted over Logan Pass.

Driving into the shady campground is akin to driving into a jungle. Grandfather cedar trees and thick underbrush crowd into campsites, and boggy places can produce prodigious numbers of mosquitoes. Avalanche Creek runs adjacent to the campground. You'll be

© BECKY LOMAX

The Hidden Lake Overlook Trail at Logan Pass gets hikers on top of the Continental Divide.

able to see a couple other campsites, but the campground goes silent after dark. Given the campground's popularity, plan on arriving before 3pm during midsummer and before noon on Saturdays. Vehicles over 21 feet must access this campground from West Glacier, not St. Mary.

Campsites, facilities: The campground has 87 RV or tent campsites that can accommodate RVs up to 26 feet. Facilities include picnic tables, fire rings with grills, drinking water, flush toilets (wheelchair-accessible), garbage service, shared hiker and biker campsites, and an amphitheater for evening interpretive programs. Bring firewood; collecting is illegal. Leashed pets are permitted.

Reservations, fees: No reservations are accepted. Campsites cost $20. Shared sites for hikers and bikers cost $5 per person. Cash, check, or credit card. Open early June-early September.

Directions: From the west entrance to Glacier National Park, drive 15.7 miles up

Going-to-the-Sun Road. From the St. Mary entrance, drive 34 miles west over Logan Pass. The entrance is on the south side of the road. GPS Coordinates: N 48° 40.743' W 113° 49.117'

Contact: Glacier National Park, P.O. Box 128, West Glacier, MT 59936, 406/888-7800, www.nps.gov/glac.

28 RISING SUN

Scenic rating: 10

near St. Mary Lake in Glacier National Park

BEST (

Below Otokomi and Goat Mountains off the north shore of St. Mary Lake, Rising Sun is one of two east-side campgrounds on Going-to-the-Sun Road and the closest to Logan Pass. As daylight shifts, streaks of red argillite douse peaks, offset by the lake's turquoise water. The Rising Sun complex includes cabins, a restaurant, a camp store, a boat ramp, boat tours, a picnic area, shuttle stop, and trailhead. Walk across the road to swim in the lake, or hop a boat tour around Wild Goose Island. If boating, windsurfing, or fishing, watch the winds; in minutes, fierce tempests kick up huge white-caps on St. Mary Lake. On Going-to-the-Sun Road a five-minute drive west, photographers will want to shoot Wild Goose Island at sunrise. From the campground, hike five miles up to Otokomi Lake to watch mountain goats climb on the cliffs, or hop a free shuttle up to other popular trailheads around Logan Pass. Vehicles over 21 feet are not permitted over Logan Pass.

Set on a hillside, the campground's two loops feature varied site types. Many hunker under firs and cottonwoods for shade, while grassy sites yield views of Red Eagle, Curly Bear, and Divide, as well as the night sky. Rising Sun bustles during the day, but quiets after dark when traffic diminishes on Going-to-the-Sun Road.

Campsites, facilities: The campground has

83 RV or tent campsites. Only 10 campsites can accommodate RVs or trailer combinations up to 25 feet long. Facilities include picnic tables, fire rings with grills, drinking water, flush toilets (wheelchair-accessible), disposal station, shared hiker and biker campsites, and an amphitheater for interpretive programs. Purchase tokens from the camp store for showers at the adjacent motel. Leashed pets are permitted.

Reservations, fees: No reservations are accepted. Campsites cost $20. Shared sites for hikers and bikers cost $5 per person. Cash, check, or credit card. Open late May-mid-September.

Directions: From the St. Mary entrance to Glacier, drive six miles west up Going-to-the-Sun Road. From the west entrance to Glacier National Park, drive 43.5 miles over Logan Pass. The campground entrance is on the north side of the road.

GPS Coordinates: N 48° 41.637' W 113° 31.272'

Contact: Glacier National Park, P.O. Box 128, West Glacier, MT 59936, 406/888-7800, www.nps.gov/glac.

29 ST. MARY

Scenic rating: 9

near St. Mary Lake in Glacier National Park

St. Mary marks the east entrance to Glacier National Park, in a place where the mountains sweep up right out of the lakes. The campground, which sits just inside the park entrance, requires a half-mile walk to reach the visitors center, where interpretive programs are held and free shuttles depart up Going-to-the-Sun Road for trailheads and Logan Pass. Nearby is the 1913 ranger station and trailhead that departs for Red Eagle Lake, where a state record 16-pound native westslope cutthroat was caught. The 7.5-mile trail to the lake passes through broad, colorful wildflower meadows blooming with lupines and crosses the outlet river twice on Indiana Jones-type suspension bridges. From the campground, a rough game trail with downed trees climbs four miles along the park boundary to the top of Napi Point, named for the creator of Blackfeet legends. A one-mile walk or drive from the campground takes you outside the park to the town of St. Mary, with its restaurants, gift shops, launderette, and gas station. Vehicles over 21 feet are not permitted over Logan Pass.

The campground circles a wide-open prairie comprising grasses, currant bushes, and ground squirrel holes, but with views of Divide and Red Eagle Mountains, particularly in the C loop. Some of the small campsites are tucked into aspen groves that afford some shade, but many are hot, windy, or within sight of each other. Traffic on Going-to-the-Sun Road quiets after dark.

Campsites, facilities: The campground has 148 RV or tent campsites. Only 25 of the sites can accommodate RVs or trailer combinations up to 35 feet long. Facilities include picnic tables, fire rings with grills, flush toilets, drinking water, a disposal station, large group sites, token-operated showers in Loop C, and shared hiker and biker campsites. During winter and primitive camping (April-mid-May, late September-November), there are only pit toilets, and no potable water is available. Leashed pets are permitted.

Reservations, fees: Reservations are accepted (877/444-6777, www.recreation.gov). Campsites cost $23 late May-mid-September. Shared sites for hikers and bikers cost $5 per person. Primitive camping (April-mid-May and late September-November) costs $10. Winter camping is free. Cash, check, or credit card.

Directions: From the St. Mary entrance station to Glacier, drive 0.5 mile on Going-to-the-Sun Road. Turn right into the campground.

GPS Coordinates: N 48° 45.056' W 113° 26.779'

Contact: Glacier National Park, P.O. Box 128, West Glacier, MT 59936, 406/888-7800, www.nps.gov/glac.

30 JOHNSON'S OF ST. MARY

🚶 🚴 🏊 🐕 🚐 ⛺

Scenic rating: 9
in St. Mary on the Blackfeet Reservation

Johnson's of St. Mary is located on a knoll above the tiny seasonal town of St. Mary at the east entrance station to Going-to-the-Sun Road through Glacier National Park. The town, with its restaurants, gift shops, lodges, cabins, and grocery store, packs out with visitors in summer. Since vehicles over 21 feet are not permitted past Sun Point on Going-to-the-Sun Road, those with big RVs can catch park tours from the campground on the historical red jammer buses or Native American Sun Tours. Cyclists on Highway 89 use the campground for its convenience, and a five-minute drive leads to trailheads for a 0.1-mile stroll to the historical ranger station or a 7.5-mile hike to Red Eagle Lake. Fishing is also available at St. Mary Lake and on the St. Mary River.

For many of the RV sites, the knoll affords spectacular views of the St. Mary Valley with Glacier's peaks lighting up red at sunrise and backlit by sunsets. Views include Napi Point to the north, a rocky outcrop named for the creator in Blackfeet legends. The RV sites are notoriously narrow, cramping the use of awnings and slide-outs. A dirt road, which can be dusty in late summer, winds through the campground to get to the tent sites—sitting in grassy open meadows for sun or aspen groves for shade. The tent area has one old tiny cinder-block restroom and shower house, but campers can hike down the hill to use the RV restroom and showers.

Campsites, facilities: Johnson's has 82 RV sites with pull-throughs that can fit large RVs, plus 75 tent sites. Hookups include water, sewer, and electricity up to 30 amps. Facilities include picnic tables, fire rings, flush toilets, showers, coin-operated launderette, wireless Internet in the office, a disposal station, propane, restaurant, campground pavilion with kitchen, and small camp store. Johnson's also has overnight facilities for horses. Leashed pets are permitted.

Reservations, fees: Reservations are accepted. Hookups run $37-46. RVs using no hookups cost $31; tents cost $27. Fees include two adults, two kids, and two vehicles per site. Extra people and vehicles incur a charge of $5 each. Add on 7 percent Montana bed tax. Cash, check, or credit card. Open late April-late September.

Directions: In St. Mary, drive 0.5 mile north of the Going-to-the-Sun and Highway 89 intersection. Turn right up the hill at the sign for the campground.

GPS Coordinates: N 48° 45.008' W 113° 25.557'

Contact: Johnson's of St. Mary, HC 72-10, Star Route, St. Mary, MT 59417-9701, 406/732-4207, www.johnsonsofstmary.com.

31 ST. MARY KOA

🚶 🚴 🏊 🎣 🛶 🐕 🏕 🚐 ⛺

Scenic rating: 9
in St. Mary on the Blackfeet Reservation

Located east of the town of St. Mary, the KOA sits on the west end of Lower St. Mary Lake bordering the St. Mary River. The east entrance to Glacier Park and Going-to-the-Sun Road sits less than two miles away, with restaurants, groceries, and gas in the town one mile away. At the KOA, you can rent a kayak or canoe to paddle the lake, hone golf skills on the campground's putting green, and tour back roads on a mountain bike. Anglers can fish the lake or river (Blackfeet Fishing License required). Elk frequent the campground, and the riparian habitat along the water attracts scads of birds, including eagles. Since vehicles over 21 feet are not permitted past Sun Point on Going-to-the-Sun Road, you can catch the Blackfeet-led Sun Tours from here.

Pull-through RV sites line up parking-lot style on gravel, with dramatic views of

Hikers tour the slopes above Grinnell Glacier.

Singleshot Mountain. Tent sites are scattered in grassy sunny meadows or among the aspens and firs for partial shade. The complex centers around an outdoor pool and a 22-person hot tub, both with views of Glacier's peaks and stars at night. Campground views include Napi Point, named for the creator in Blackfeet legends. Several tent sites in the L and K loops border the river.

Campsites, facilities: The campground has 100 RV sites and 59 tent campsites. Maximum RV length is 75 feet. Hookups include water, sewer, and electricity up to 50 amps. Facilities include picnic tables, fire rings with grills, firewood for sale, flush toilets (wheelchair-accessible), showers, wireless Internet, pool, hot tub, splash park, disposal station, playground, camp store, bike rentals, and a café that serves breakfast and dinner in the summer. Leashed pets are permitted, and pet sitting is available for a fee.

Reservations, fees: Reservations are accepted. Hookups cost $57-62. Tents cost $35-45. Rates cover two people. Additional people are charged $5-7. Kids 12 and under camp free. Add on 7 percent Montana bed tax. Cash, check, or credit card. Open mid-May-September.

Directions: From Babb, drive 8.7 miles south on Highway 89 and turn right heading north on W. Shore Road. From St. Mary Resort gas station, drive 0.4 mile north on Highway 89 and turn left on W. Shore Road. The campground is 0.9 mile north from the turnoff. GPS Coordinates: N 48° 45.486' W 113° 26.137'

Contact: St. Mary KOA, 106 W. Shore, St. Mary, MT 59417, 406/732-4122 or 800/562-1504, www.goglacier.com.

32 MANY GLACIER

Scenic rating: 10

in Swiftcurrent Valley in Glacier National Park

BEST (

Park the car for days at this most coveted campground on the Continental Divide's east side in Glacier National Park! Located below Grinnell Point, the campground sits at a hub of trails. Hike 4.5 miles to Iceberg Lake to swim with icebergs in August. Ascend the 5.5 miles to see Grinnell Glacier melting fast into a turquoise pool. Grunt up the 5.2 miles to the Ptarmigan Tunnel for views of the Belly River drainage. Slog eight miles of switchbacks to the top of the Continental Divide at Swiftcurrent Lookout. Shorter walks lead to waterfalls, wildflowers meadows, and blue lakes with moose feeding. Launch canoes, kayaks, and small motorboats onto Swiftcurrent Lake for paddling or fishing. Boats are also available for rent.

Set in firs and aspens, the small, shaded campsites pack in tight next to the busy Swiftcurrent parking lot and the ranger station. Across the Swiftcurrent parking lot you'll find a restaurant, a camp store, and showers (buy tokens in the store), and often the park service erects telescopes for viewing bighorn sheep and grizzly bears on the surrounding slopes. A few campsites get peek-a-boo views of Grinnell Point, especially those on the south side of the southern loop and the northwest corner of the northwest loop. In view of the campground's extreme popularity, claim a site before 11am during July and August.

Campsites, facilities: The campground has 110 RV or tent campsites. Only 13 sites can accommodate RVs up to 35 feet long. Facilities include picnic tables, fire rings with grills, flush toilets (wheelchair-accessible), drinking water, a disposal station, large group sites, bear boxes, shared hiker and biker campsites, garbage service, and campground hosts. Primitive camping (late September-October) offers only pit toilets and no potable water. Leashed pets are permitted.

Reservations, fees: No reservations are accepted. Campsites cost $20 late May-mid-September. Primitive camping costs $10. Shared sites for hikers and bikers cost $5 per person. Cash, check, or credit card. Open late May-October.

Directions: From Babb, drive 12 miles on Many Glacier Road (Glacier Route 3). Turn left at the ranger station sign and veer right into the campground.

GPS Coordinates: N 48° 47.825' W 113° 40.454'

Contact: Glacier National Park, P.O. Box 128, West Glacier, MT 59936, 406/888-7800, www.nps.gov/glac.

33 DUCK LAKE LODGE

Scenic rating: 7

near Duck Lake on the Blackfeet Reservation

At 4,781 feet, small Duck Lake Lodge sits the Blackfeet Reservation two miles west of Duck Lake. Duck Lake is renowned for fishing, including ice fishing in winter. From Duck Lake, Glacier's peaks spread across the horizon, with Chief Mountain taking prominence to the northwest. The lake harbors rainbow and brown trout averaging 8 pounds, but a few lucky anglers pluck out 15-pounders. Float tubes or boats work best in the lake for fishing, rather than casting from shoreline, and motorized boats are restricted to a 10 mph speed limit. Anglers are required to purchase a tribal fishing license and recreation tags for boats. The lodge sells both. The east entrance to Glacier's Going-to-the-Sun Road sits less than 15 minutes to the west.

Duck Lake Lodge has a small campground tucked in aspen groves. Ponds border the gravel access road leading to the lodge. Tents fit on an open grassy field with no privacy, catching the full sun and wind, and the RV campsites stack very close together along the edge of the aspens. The campground mostly attracts anglers and hunters coming to experience the reservation. The lodge draws on a collection of reliable Blackfeet outfitters for guided fishing or hunting trips on the reservation. It also has a restaurant and bar.

Campsites, facilities: The campground has five RV sites that can fit midsized RVs, plus room for five tents in a grassy meadow.

Hookups include electricity, water, and sewer. Facilities include flush toilets, showers, a launderette, and wireless Internet in the lodge. Leashed pets are permitted.

Reservations, fees: Reservations are recommended. Hookups cost $40. Tent camping costs $10. Cash, check, or credit card. The lodge is open year-round, but camping runs May-October.

Directions: From St. Mary, drive eight miles south on Highway 89 and turn right onto Highway 464. Drive 1.3 miles to milepost 29. At the lodge sign, turn right onto the gravel entrance road.

GPS Coordinates: N 48° 50.270' W 113° 23.553'

Contact: Duck Lake Lodge, P.O. Box 210, 3215 Hwy. 464, Babb, MT 59411, 406/338-5770, http://ducklakelodge.com.

34 CUT BANK

Scenic rating: 7

in Cut Bank Valley in Glacier National Park

At 5,200 feet in a rugged, remote valley on Glacier's east side, Cut Bank sits between East Glacier and St. Mary. Two barriers deter large RVs from going to Cut Bank—the narrow curvy Highway 89 and the five miles of potholed dirt road leading to the campground. The campground is a favorite for tenters, who relish the quiet and the campground's real rusticity. A 7.2-mile trail departs up-valley from here toward Triple Divide Pass, so named for the peak above that feeds water to the Atlantic, Pacific, and Hudson Bay drainages. A less strenuous hike ends in six miles at Medicine Grizzly Lake, a lure for anglers and bears alike because of its 12-inch rainbow trout. Frequently, the lake closes because of lingering bears. Another spur leads to Atlantic Creek Falls at 4.1 miles; add on another 2.5 miles to reach Morning Star Lake, in a small cirque below cliffs that hold mountain goat paths.

Tucked under a deep shaded forest, the ultra-quiet campground stays cool even on hot August days. Atlantic Creek burbles adjacent to the campground. Unfortunately, most of the undergrowth beneath the canopy is gone, leaving little privacy between sites. The sites are small but do have room for tents. Small RVs may have challenges leveling them.

Campsites, facilities: The campground has 14 RV and tent campsites that can fit only small RVs. The park service discourages RVs and trailers from using this campground. Facilities include picnic tables, fire rings with grills, and pit toilets. Bring your own water, or treat creek water. Bring firewood, as gathering even downed limbs is prohibited in the park. Pack out your trash. Leashed pets are permitted.

Reservations, fees: No reservations are accepted. The fee is $10 per night. Cash, check, or credit card. Open early June- early September.

Directions: From St. Mary, drive 14.5 miles south on Highway 89. From East Glacier, drive 13.5 miles north on Highway 49 and 5.5 miles north on Highway 89. At the campground sign on Highway 89, turn west onto the dirt road for five miles. The road terminates at the campground.

GPS Coordinates: N 48° 36.101' W 113° 23.026'

Contact: Glacier National Park, P.O. Box 128, West Glacier, MT 59936, 406/888-7800, www.nps.gov/glac.

35 ASPENWOOD RESORT

Scenic rating: 7

west of Browning on the Blackfeet Reservation

Located west of Browning below Glacier's eastern front range, the campground and resort sit on the Blackfeet Reservation, where just about the only sound is the incessant wind. On the prairie to the east, Browning has a little over 1,000 residents. The small Museum of the Plains Indians provides the best look at the tribe's history, with dioramas and clothing made with phenomenal beadwork. The Blackfeet Heritage Center and Gallery also provides a venue for locals to market their art. Recently, the tribe built the Glacier Peaks Casino, a 33,000-square-foot gaming facility with more than 300 slot machines. For four days each year, the annual North American Indian Days festival brings out dancing, singing, storytelling, and a rodeo during the second weekend in July, at the powwow grounds behind the museum. At the campground, two beaver ponds offer fishing, paddleboating, wildlife-watching, and hiking. The resort also arranges for Native American guided fishing trips, tours, and horseback riding.

The resort includes a small lodge with rooms, a restaurant, and a campground. The resort's restaurant—the Outlaw Grill—serves breakfast, lunch, and dinner, and does takeout orders if you prefer to eat at your campsite. The RV sites are gravel pull-throughs surrounded by grass with no trees; however, the open venue allows for views of Glacier's peaks. Tent sites are tucked in between the aspen groves for shade and wind protection.

Campsites, facilities: The campground has 10 RV campsites and eight tent campsites. The pull-through RV sites can fit large rigs; eight of the RV spaces have hookups, and two have dry camping. Hookups are available for electricity and water. Facilities include picnic tables, fire pits, flush toilets, showers, a disposal station, firewood, a game and exercise room, and paddleboats. Leashed pets are permitted. Horse boarding is also available.

Reservations, fees: Reservations are accepted and are highly recommended for powwow weekends—the second weekends of July and August. Hookups cost $30-35. Tent sites cost $18. Cash, check, or credit card. Open mid-May-mid-October.

Directions: From the junction of Highway 2 and Highway 89 in Browning, drive west on Highway 89 for 9.5 miles. From Kiowa

Junction, drive 2.3 miles east on Highway 89. The resort sits on the north side of the road. GPS Coordinates: N 48° 32.451' W 113° 13.519'
Contact: Aspenwood Resort, HC-72, Box 5150, Hwy. 89, Browning, MT 59417, 406/338-3009, www.aspenwoodresort.com.

36 LODGEPOLE TIPI VILLAGE

Scenic rating: 9
west of Browning on the Blackfeet Reservation

Located on the Blackfeet Reservation below Glacier's eastern front range, the Lodgepole Tipi Village offers a different type of camping—camping in a tipi with cultural insight into the traditional life of the Blackfeet. The tipi village sprawls across 200 acres of wildflower prairie with a spring-fed lake and unobstructed views of Glacier's southern ramparts. A small herd of Spanish mustangs runs wild on the property. The owners can connect visitors with Blackfeet guides for horseback riding trips on the rolling foothills below Glacier's peaks and fly fishing for rainbow trout on the reservation's renowned lakes. The owner also leads cultural history tours to historical buffalo jumps, tipi rings, and medicine lodges.

Camping in the tipi village is expensive, but you're paying for the cultural experience provided by its Blackfeet owner, Darrell Norman. Tour his small gallery, or add on an art workshop to make a drum or parfleche. Breakfast and a Blackfeet wild game dinner are also available by reservation. With a campfire in the tipi, it glows under the night sky. The sun brightens the inside early when the sunrise hits the prairie. Wind and the hooves of the Spanish mustangs are the only sounds you'll hear.

Campsites, facilities: Camping is permitted only in tipis here—not RVs or tents. The seven double-walled lodgepole tipis remain cool in the summer heat but retain warmth in cooler months. Each tipi centers around a rock-ringed fire pit (firewood provided). Facilities include picnic tables, flush toilets, and showers. A large communal campfire is sheltered from wind by a wooden arbor built to resemble a traditional Blackfeet ceremonial lodge. Bring your own sleeping bag and pad as well as a flashlight. Tipis have no floors, so your sleeping pad will go on the ground. Pets are not permitted.

Reservations, fees: Reservations are wise—especially for Browning powwow weekends during the second weekends of July and August. The first person in the tipi is charged $60 per night, and each additional person is charged $15. Children under 12 years old are charged $10. Sleeping bags and pads are available for $12. Check or credit card. Open May-September.

Directions: From Browning, drive 2.5 miles west on Highway 89. Locate the entrance on the south side of the road.

GPS Coordinates: N 48° 33.254' W 113° 4.492'

Contact: Lodgepole Tipi Village, P.O. Box 1832, Browning, MT 59417, 406/338-2787, www.blackfeetculturecamp.com.

37 TWO MEDICINE

🚶 🚵 🏊 🛶 🚤 🎣 🐕 ♿ 🚐 ⛺

Scenic rating: 10
on Pray Lake in Glacier National Park

BEST (

Huddling below the massive hulk of Rising Wolf Mountain, Two Medicine Campground sits on Pray Lake, a small outlet pool for the much larger Two Medicine Lake. Sitting a mile high, the campground offers hikers, sightseers, boaters, and anglers a taste of Glacier's less crowded realm. From the campground, the 18.8-mile Dawson-Pitamakin Trail loops around Rising Wolf, along the Continental Divide. A mile up the road, the Scenic Point Trail climbs 3.1 miles to a bluff overlooking the lakes and staring out onto the plains. The *Sinopah* tours the lake several times daily for sightseers, and rental canoes, kayaks, and motorboats are available near the boat dock. The historical dining hall from the park's early days now houses a camp store, and the staffed ranger station keeps track of bear sightings on a large map.

Set in stunted subalpine firs, the quiet campground curls around Pray Lake, a good fishing and swimming outlet pool from Two Medicine Lake. At least half of the campsites at Two Medicine have stunning views—most of Rising Wolf. You can sit in your campsite with a pair of binoculars and watch mountain goats or grizzly bears crawl around the slopes. Find these sites in loops A and C. Sites 92-100 yield closer views of the slopes. Given the campground's popularity, plan on arriving before noon during July and August.

Campsites, facilities: The campground has 99 RV or tent campsites. Only 13 sites can accommodate RVs or trailer combinations up to 35 feet. Facilities include picnic tables, fire rings with grills, flush toilets (wheelchair-accessible), drinking water, a disposal station, large group campsites, interpretive programs, shared hiker and biker campsites, and campground hosts. Primitive camping (late September-October) offers only pit toilets, and there's no potable water. Leashed pets are permitted.

Reservations, fees: No reservations are accepted. Campsites cost $20 late May-mid-September. Primitive camping costs $10. Hikers and bikers pay $5 per person. Cash, check, or credit card.

Directions: From East Glacier, drive four miles north on Highway 49 and then swing left onto Two Medicine Road for 7.5 miles. Turn right at the ranger station to enter the campground.

GPS Coordinates: N 48° 29.274' W 113° 22.056'

Contact: Glacier National Park, P.O. Box 128, West Glacier, MT 59936, 406/888-7800, www.nps.gov/glac.

38 MIDDLE FORK OF THE FLATHEAD

🏃 🏊 🛶 🚣 ⛷ 🐕 ⛺

Scenic rating: 9
on the Middle Fork of the Flathead River in Flathead National Forest

The Middle Fork of the Flathead River churns with white water for some of its 87 miles. The Wild and Scenic River, which springs from headwaters deep within the Great Bear Wilderness, races through John F. Stevens Canyon en route to its confluence with the North Fork of the Flathead River near Coram. From Bear Creek, the river flows along the southeast boundary of Glacier National Park, where scenic float sections alternate with Class II-IV white water. Rapids such as Jaws, Bonecrusher, and Screaming Right Hand Turn require technical finesse to navigate. Seven river accesses (Bear Creek, Essex, Paola, Cascadilla, Moccasin Creek, West Glacier, and Blankenship) allow boaters to vary the length of the trips. Most overnight trips take 2-3 days and can add on hiking adventures in the park or the national forest. Most of the white water packs into the section between Moccasin Creek and West Glacier, and notorious logjams litter the Cascadilla to Moccasin Creek float. During high water in late May, some rapids can reach Class IV. Life jackets are required.

The campsites all sit on the south shore of the river on rocky river bars, on willow and grass flats, or in cottonwood, cedar, and fir forests. You can hear the highway at some, but views at all of them look across the river to Glacier.

Campsites, facilities: No camping is permitted between Bear Creek and Essex, but below Essex, at least 10 primitive tent campsites flank the shoreline. Campers are required to take a groover for human waste and a fire pan to minimize burn scars. Camping is only permitted on the south shore in Flathead National Forest; no camping is permitted on the Glacier Park side to the north. Get a copy of *Three Forks of the Flathead Floating Guide* from the Forest Service to help with campsite selection; the national forest side also has private property to avoid. The river accesses all have vault toilets. Pets are permitted.

Reservations, fees: Reservations are not available. No permit is needed; camping is free. The rafting and kayaking season runs mid-May-early September.

Directions: From West Glacier, drive east on Highway 2 to reach the various signed river accesses.

GPS Coordinates: N 48° 14.032' W 113° 33.976'

Contact: Flathead National Forest, Hungry Horse District, 10 Hungry Horse Dr., Hungry Horse, MT 59919, 406/387-3800, www.fs.usda.gov/flathead/.

39 STANTON CREEK LODGE

🏃 🚵 🛶 🎣 🐕 ♿ 🚐 ⛺

Scenic rating: 4
on Highway 2 in Flathead National Forest

At 3,550 feet in Flathead National Forest across from the southwestern boundary to Glacier National Park, Stanton Creek Lodge is one of the old fixtures on the Highway 2 corridor. The lodge, campsites, and cabins sit right next to the highway, with the railroad tracks across the street. (Bring earplugs for a good night's sleep.) A one-mile trail climbs to Stanton Lake in the Great Bear Wilderness. Those looking for bigger views of glaciers and ridgetop walking continue climbing the Grant Ridge Loop, which returns to the lodge in 10.2 miles. A half mile west of the lodge at Coal Creek, a primitive 10-minute trail cuts down to the Middle Fork of the Flathead River. Anglers drop lines into the Stanton Lake and the Middle Fork River for native westslope cutthroat trout.

Hailing from 1932, the lodge itself was one of a string of wild bars dotting the Marias Pass route within a day's horse ride of each other. Drunken visitors rode horses through the bar, and bullets flew at passing trains. You can still see bullet holes in the original floor inside the bar. Because of the adjacent highway and railroad tracks, the camping experience here is not quiet wilderness. The tight, small RV campsites sit in the sun between the cabins; tent campsites are shaded under firs. Views are of the forest, highway, and a snippet of Glacier's southern peaks.

Campsites, facilities: The campground has eight RV campsites that can accommodate midsized RVs. Hookups are available for sewer, water, and electricity up to 30 amps. Facilities include picnic tables, a community fire pit, flush toilets, showers, wireless Internet, restaurant, and bar. Pets are permitted.

Reservations, fees: Reservations are accepted. RV hookups cost $30. Prices are for two people. Extra campers pay $5 each. Children camp for free. A 7 percent Montana bed tax will be added on. Cash, check, Canadian currency, or credit card. Open late May-mid-September.

Directions: From West Glacier, drive 16 miles east on Highway 2. From East Glacier, drive 44 miles west on Highway 2. The lodge and campground are at milepost 170 on the south side of the highway.

GPS Coordinates: N 48° 24.136' W 113° 42.970'

Contact: Stanton Creek Lodge, HC 36 Box 2C, Essex, MT 59916, 406/888-5040 or 866/883-5040, www.stantoncreeklodge.com.

40 GLACIER HAVEN RV

Scenic rating: 7

on Highway 2 near Flathead National Forest

Located west of Essex on Highway 2, the Glacier Haven RV and Campground opened in 2009. It sits in the Middle Fork of the Flathead River corridor across from Glacier National Park. A five-minute drive east to Essex or

west to Paola leads to fishing accesses, also places to launch rafts and kayaks to float the Middle Fork of the Flathead River. Within a five-minute drive, Dickey Lake Road turns south to reach trailheads into Great Bear Wilderness. Marion Lake requires an elevation climb of 1,810 feet over 1.7 miles, and 2.4-mile Dickey Lake trail ascends up a steep, brushy headwall to reach into a hanging valley. The campground is five minutes from the historical Izaak Walton Inn, worth a visit for railroad fans.

Glacier Haven is a complex consisting of the campground, a motel, and a home-style café squeezed between the highway and the railroad tracks. Bring earplugs to help with sleeping as trains rumble by at night. A gravel loop swings through the campground with most of the RV spots having gravel back-ins. One open area is available for tents with undesignated sites. Views include the forest, highway, and railroad tracks. The campground does not permit smoking, even outdoors.

Campsites, facilities: The campground has 19 RV campsites, including three that can accommodate large RVs on pull-through gravel parking pads, and room for five tents in a large camping zone. Hookups include water, sewer, and electricity. Facilities include flush toilets, showers, a launderette, and restaurant. Leashed pets are permitted.

Reservations, fees: Reservations are accepted. RV sites cost $38-40. Tent sites cost $25-28. Rates are for two people; additional people are charged $5 each. Children ages nine and under camp for free. Those with pets are charged $2. The Montana 7 percent tax will be added to the bill. Open May-September.

Directions: On Highway 2 west of Essex, look for milepost markers 173 and 174. Turn south into the campground on the gravel road west of the Glacier Haven Inn.

GPS Coordinates: N 48° 21.884' W 113° 39.772'

Contact: Glacier Haven, 14297 Hwy. 2 E., Essex, MT 59916, 406/888-9987 or 406/888-5720, www.glacierhavenrv-campground.com.

41 ESSEX PRIMITIVE

Scenic rating: 6

on the Middle Fork of the Flathead River in
Flathead National Forest

Adjacent to the tiny community of Essex,
Walton picnic area marks the southernmost
tip of Glacier National Park. Essex also houses
the historical Izaak Walton Inn, and the Half-
Way House convenience store and restaurant.
A bridge over the Middle Fork of the Flathead
River connects Essex and the picnic area, while
the Essex River Access Site provides a place to
launch onto the river for floating or fishing
below the bridge. It is also a location where you
can camp riverside. From Walton picnic area, a
trail climbs 4.7 miles to Scalplock Lookout for a
dramatic view of Mount St. Nicholas. From the
Dickey Lake Road (Hwy. 2, milepost 178.7),
you can access two trailheads into the Great
Bear Wilderness. A popular, steep trail climbs
1.7 miles to Marion Lake, and a 2.4-mile trail
leads up to Dickey Lake in a hanging valley.

The Essex River Access Site sits on a sandy
bar, which increases in size as the river level
drops during the season. (Be cautious of getting stuck in soft sand.) Primitive camping is
permitted on the bar, but it is without privacy.
A few cottonwoods provide some shade for the
campsites. The bridge above the site blocks
some of the view of Scalplock Mountain. Considering the road, the river, and the railroad
track above, this is not a place for quiet.

Campsites, facilities: The campground has
three primitive RV or tent campsites, which
can fit midsized RVs. Facilities include a portable toilet June-August. Bring drinking water,
or treat river water. Pack out your trash. Camping is limited to three days. Leashed pets are
permitted.

Reservations, fees: No reservations are accepted. Camping is free. It's open May-November, but during late May and early June
high water can flood the sandbar.

Directions: On Highway 2 between Essex

and Walton, turn north at milepost 180. The
unsigned exit sits on the west side of the bridge
over the river and swings under the bridge to
reach the sandbar.

GPS Coordinates: N 48° 16.455' W 113°
36.318'

Contact: Flathead National Forest, Hungry
Horse District, 10 Hungry Horse Dr., Hungry Horse, MT 59919, 406/387-3800, www.
fs.usda.gov/flathead/.

42 BEAR CREEK PRIMITIVE

Scenic rating: 7

on the Middle Fork of the Flathead River in
Flathead National Forest

At the confluence of Bear Creek and the Middle Fork of the Flathead River, Bear Creek
River Access Site sits where the Middle Fork
of the Flathead River plunges from the Bob
Marshall Wilderness Area to then form Glacier National Park's southern boundary. It is
a large site used for launching onto the river
to float for day or overnight float trips and
for hikers and horse-packers heading into the
Great Bear Wilderness. Day hikers also use the
trail heading up the Middle Fork, which spurs
off up Edna Creek for a 3.5-mile steep grunt
up to scenic Tranquil Basin Overlook, and a
0.5-mile climb farther to summit 7,394-foot
Mount Furlong yields views of Glacier's peaks.

The area roars equally with churning
rapids and noise from the highway and railroad. Those camping here may want to bring
earplugs. The wide-open, giant dusty parking lot yields big views of the surrounding
mountains—the Great Bear Wilderness and
Glacier—but at a cost to privacy. The area is
not designed with designated campsites, but
the big parking lot permits plenty of room for
primitive camping for those needing campsites
while traveling over Marias Pass.

Campsites, facilities: The area has room for
three RVs or tent campsites. Facilities include

Elk Mountain gets hikers to a high vista with panoramic views.

a wheelchair-accessible vault toilet. Bring drinking water, or treat river water. Pack out your trash. Camping is limited to three days. Leashed pets are permitted.

Reservations, fees: No reservations are accepted. Camping is free. Open May-November.

Directions: On Highway 2, between Essex and Marias Pass, find Bear Creek River Access at milepost 185 on the south side of the highway. GPS Coordinates: N 48° 14.041' W 113° 33.942'

Contact: Flathead National Forest, Hungry Horse District, 10 Hungry Horse Dr., Hungry Horse, MT 59919, 406/387-3800, www.fs.usda.gov/flathead/.

43 DEVIL CREEK

Scenic rating: 6

on Highway 2 in Flathead National Forest

At 4,450 feet in elevation along Highway 2, Devil Creek is close to river recreation in Flathead National Forest and hiking trails in the Great Bear Wilderness and Glacier National Park. Across the highway from the campground, Bear Creek harbors brook trout and westslope cutthroat trout. Five miles to the west, the creek collides with the Middle Fork of the Flathead River as it roars out of the Bob Marshall Wilderness Area, and a 3.5-mile trail climbs to Tranquil Basin. At the Bear Creek River Access Site, rafters and anglers launch to float a portion or all of the 44 miles of the Middle Fork River. Hikers drive two miles east to catch the steep trail up Elk Mountain in Glacier National Park. The 3.5-mile trail slogs up 3,355 feet for top-of-the-world views. From the campground, a trail also leads to Elk Lake (5.9 miles) and Moose Lake (8.2 miles).

The small campground tucks into the forest adjacent to Devil Creek. One loop holds all the campsites, with those at the top of the loop being farthest from the highway. Campsites used to be set in deep shade from the thick forest, but logging of the adjacent parcel and thinning of the campground in 2013 opened it up to more sunlight and the highway. The small sites are spread out, but you can still see neighboring campers. You'll hear both highway and railroad noise in the campground. Considering the limited campgrounds along Highway 2, plan on arriving before 3pm during midsummer.

Campsites, facilities: The campground has 14 RV or tent campsites that can fit RVs up to 40 feet. Facilities include picnic tables, fire rings with grills, drinking water, vault toilets (wheelchair-accessible), and campground hosts. Pack out your trash. Firewood is not provided, but you're free to scour the surrounding forest for downed limbs. Leashed pets are permitted.

Reservations, fees: No reservations are accepted. Campsites cost $10. Cash or check. Open late May-mid-September.

Directions: On Highway 2 between Essex and Marias Pass, turn south at milepost 190 into the campground.

GPS Coordinates: N 48° 15.090' W 113° 27.916'

Contact: Flathead National Forest, Hungry Horse District, 10 Hungry Horse Dr., Hungry Horse, MT 59919, 406/387-3800, www.fs.usda.gov/flathead/.

44 GLACIER MEADOW RV PARK

🏃 🛶 🐕 ⛹ ♿ 🚐 ⛺

Scenic rating: 7
on Highway 2 in Flathead National Forest

Located at 4,450 feet in elevation on Highway 2, Glacier Meadow RV Park has Flathead National Forest on its south boundary and Glacier National Park a mile to the north. From the campground, river rafters and anglers head seven miles to the west to the Middle Fork of the Flathead River. Hikers drive less than 0.5 mile to reach the Elk Mountain Trailhead and its strenuous 3,355-foot, 3.5-mile climb to an old lookout

site with big views in Glacier National Park. For those traveling with RVs over 21 feet long that are not permitted over Going-to-the-Sun Road, the red buses stop at Glacier Meadow to pick up riders for the 8.5-hour tour that loops over Logan Pass. Nearby Skyland Road is also available for ATV riding.

The campground, which sits on 58 acres, adjoins a large meadow that attracts elk in May and June. A gravel road connects the campsites, and for large RVs, the campground's wide-open large grassy field makes for easy parking. Sites in the open have full views of the surrounding peaks. Some sites along the campground's east side receive morning shade from a mixed forest of firs and lodgepoles. The 25 pull-through sites have electric and water hookups; 16 sites along the woods have electricity only. Only some of the sites have picnic tables.

Campsites, facilities: The campground has 41 RV campsites, which can fit RVs up to 40 feet, and 16 tent campsites. Facilities include picnic tables, drinking water, flush toilets (wheelchair-accessible), showers, a launderette, a shuffleboard floor, horseshoe pits, wireless Internet, a playground, and a disposal station. The management can also provide horse boarding. Leashed pets are permitted.

Reservations, fees: Reservations are accepted. Hookups cost $38. Tent sites cost $25. Rates include two people; each additional person is charged $5. Kids 10 years old and under camp for free. The Montana bed tax of 7 percent will be added to the bill. Cash or credit card. Open mid-May-mid-September.

Directions: From East Glacier, drive 16 miles west on Highway 2. From West Glacier, drive 44 miles east on Highway 2. Turn south between mileposts 191 and 192.

GPS Coordinates: N 48° 15.976' W 113° 26.607'

Contact: Glacier Meadow RV Park, P.O. Box 124, East Glacier, MT 59936, 406/226-4479, www.glaciermeadowrvpark.com.

45 SUMMIT

🚶 🛶 🏕 ♿ 🚐 ⛺

Scenic rating: 8

at Marias Pass in Lewis and Clark National Forest

Of all the passes crossing the Rocky Mountains, Marias Pass is the lowest at 5,220 feet. It sits in Lewis and Clark National Forest across from Glacier National Park. Ironically, the pass eluded Lewis and Clark. John F. Stevens discovered it in 1889 while looking for a route for the Great Northern Railway to cut through the mountains. The pass also marks the Continental Divide, the split where waters flow to the Atlantic and Pacific, and the place where geologists first discovered the Lewis Overthrust Fault, where 1.6 billion-year-old rocks buried younger layers from the dinosaur age. Departing across the highway, the Continental Divide Trail enters Glacier Park and passes Three Bears Lake in 0.6 mile—a good place to fish, spot moose, and go bird-watching. At 1.1 miles, the trail intersects with Autumn Creek Trail, which parallels the front range of peaks.

The small forested campground tucks into the lodgepole pines for partial shade on the east side of the Marias Pass rest area. Both the highway and the railroad tracks pass in front of the campground, creating noise all night long. Bring earplugs for a good night's sleep. A few sites on the north side of the loop have peek-a-boo views of Glacier's peaks. Because campgrounds are limited along Highway 2, plan on arriving before 3pm during midsummer to claim a campsite.

Campsites, facilities: The campground has 17 RV or tent campsites that can fit midsized RVs. Facilities include picnic tables, fire rings with grills, vault toilets, disposal station, and potable water. Pack out your trash. Firewood is not provided, but you're free to scour the surrounding national forest for downed limbs. Leashed pets are permitted. A wheelchair-accessible toilet and two campsites are available.

Reservations, fees: No reservations are accepted. Camping costs $10. Cash or check. Open early June-mid-September.

Directions: From East Glacier, drive Highway 2 west for 11.3 miles to Marias Pass at milepost 198. From West Glacier, drive 48.9 miles east. On the south side of the highway, locate the campground entrance just east of the Marias Pass rest area.

GPS Coordinates: N 48° 19.112' W 113° 21.082'

Contact: Lewis and Clark National Forest, Rocky Mountain Ranger District, 1102 N. Main Ave., P.O. Box 340, Choteau, MT 59422, 406/466-5341, www.fs.usda.gov/lewisclark.

46 Y LAZY R RV PARK

🚶 🏕 🚲 🚐 ⛺

Scenic rating: 7

in East Glacier on the Blackfeet Reservation

Located in the town of East Glacier, this campground appears at first to be little more than a large grassy field, but the views of Glacier's peaks, from the Calf Robe to Dancing Lady—especially at sunset—make up for the setting. From the campground, a quick two-block walk puts you in tiny East Glacier, where you'll find groceries, a few gift shops, restaurants, and a post office. Walk under the railroad overpass to see the historical East Glacier Park Hotel, with its monstrous Douglas firs in the lobby. The lodge's golf course (its nine holes are named for former Blackfeet chiefs) has the oldest grass greens in Montana. Drive 12 miles north to Two Medicine Lake for picnicking, hiking, fishing, boating, and sightseeing. Two hiking trails depart from the north side of town, one that heads seven miles to Scenic Point and the other that joins up with Autumn Creek or Firebrand Pass. Pick up Blackfeet Tribal recreation licenses at Bear Tracks Travel Center gas station before hiking these.

The campground covers three acres, most of which is mowed grass with only a couple of trees for shade. The campsites with the trees tend to get snagged early. Sites on the south end at the edge of the bluff overlook Midvale Creek and grab views of the mountains, too. A gravel road accesses the tight sites, and while the overall campground is level, the individual sites can present a challenge for leveling an RV. You can hear both the highway and the railroad tracks from the campground.

Campsites, facilities: The campground has 30 RV campsites that can fit large RVs, plus 10 tent sites. Hookups are available for sewer, water, and electricity. Facilities include picnic tables, flush toilets, coin-operated showers, playground, disposal station, and a huge coin-operated launderette with commercial washers.

Reservations, fees: Reservations are accepted. Hookups cost $23-25. Tent sites cost $20. Cash or check. Open June-mid-September.

Directions: Coming from the east on Highway 2, turn left in East Glacier at the fourth street. Coming from the west on Highway 2, take the first right in town. Then, drive two blocks south to Washington Street and turn right to reach Lindhe Avenue. Turn left for 1.5 blocks. The campground sits west of the junction of Lindhe Avenue and Meade Street. GPS Coordinates: N 48° 26.382' W 113° 12.965'

Contact: Lazy R RV Park, P.O. Box 146, East Glacier, MT 59936, 406/226-5505.

47 CRANDELL MOUNTAIN

🚶🚴🛶🎣♿🚐⛰️

Scenic rating: 9
on Blakiston Creek in Waterton Lakes National Park, Canada

On the opposite side of Crandell Mountain from the Waterton Townsite, this campground tucks into a red-rock valley with outstanding wildlife-watching opportunities in Waterton Lakes National Park, part of the Glacier-Waterton International Peace Park. Wildlife

frequents its narrow paved access road—the Red Rocks Parkway. The campground nestles in the woods along Blakiston Creek, where you can see bears and moose. Bighorn sheep also graze on the slopes across the creek. An easy 3.1-mile round-trip walk to Crandell Lake departs from the campground, and a 10-minute drive leads to the end of Red Rocks Parkway, where trailheads depart to Blakiston Falls (0.6 mile), Goat Lake (3.9 miles), and Avion Ridge (14 miles). You can also mountain bike five miles to Snowshoe Cabin or around Crandell Mountain. Fishing is available in Blakiston Creek; Waterton Park and Alberta fishing licenses are both required.

With many campsites tucked deep in mixed forest, the campground's eight loops have a remote feel, with trees and brush providing some privacy between sites. Campsites A, B, C, and D loops sit in thicker trees; E, F, G, and H loops are more open with views of surrounding peaks. Tight loops and back-ins can cramp some RVs. Plan on arriving at the campsite office by noon in July and August to get a campsite.

Campsites, facilities: Crandell has 129 RV or tent campsites; some can accommodate midsized RVs. Five tipis are also available. Facilities include picnic tables, fire rings, flush toilets (wheelchair-accessible), drinking water, kitchen shelters, firewood, a disposal station, interpretive programs, and bear-resistant food storage lockers. Leashed pets are permitted.

Reservations, fees: Reservations are not accepted for campsites, but are for the tipis (403-859-5133, $11, summer only). Campsites cost CAN$22; tipis cost CAN$55. Add on CAN$9 for a burning permit for fires. Cash or credit card. Open mid-May-early September.

Directions: Drive the 30-mile Chief Mountain International Highway across the border (open mid-May-September), turn west for 0.7 mile to the park entrance, then go 2.8 miles south on the park entrance road, and turn west onto Red Rocks Parkway. Find the campground entrance on the left 3.8 miles up the parkway.

GPS Coordinates: N 49° 5.931' W 113° 56.780'

Contact: Waterton Lakes National Park, Box 200, 215 Mount View Rd., Waterton Park, AB T0K 2M0, Canada, 403/859-2224, www.pc.gc.ca/eng/pn-np/ab/waterton/index.aspx.

48 PASS CREEK

Scenic rating: 8

on Blakiston Creek in Waterton Lakes National Park, Canada

Located 3.1 miles north of the Waterton Townsite, the Pass Creek Campground is a picnic area that converts to a campground in winter, when the town dwindles to a few hundred residents and offers only a few services. It sits in Waterton Lakes National Park, part of the Glacier-Waterton International Peace Park. All of the park's campgrounds close by mid-October, except for Pass Creek. The campground is convenient for ducking in to town for a dinner at Waterton Lakes Lodge—especially if the weather turns brutal. Heated washrooms and running water are available at the fire hall. The campground also provides excellent wildlife-watching in the shoulder seasons as animals, such as elk, move to lower ground. In spring, nearby Lower Waterton Lake and Maskinonge Lake attract scads of migrating birds. In winter, the cross-country skiers hit the two designated trails on the upper Akamina Parkway. Bertha Falls also provides a popular four-mile round-trip snowshoe destination. For those with avalanche gear, the park also has ski touring routes and ice climbing.

Located just south of Red Rocks Parkway and right on the Blakiston River, where you can fish, the campground has big views of the Waterton Valley. Be prepared, however, for winds, as the campground also hovers on the edge of the open prairie. Cottonwood trees provide windbreaks, but wind still whips

through them, and some campsites are visible from the entrance road to the park.

Campsites, facilities: The campground has eight RV or tent campsites that can accommodate midsized RVs. Facilities include picnic tables, kitchen shelter with a wood stove, and pit toilet. Bring your own water, or treat creek water. Leashed pets are permitted.

Reservations, fees: No reservations are accepted. Camping is free. Open mid-October-mid-April.

Directions: From Highway 3 at Pincher Creek, drive 30 miles south on Highway 6 (Chief Mountain International Highway) to the entrance to Waterton Lakes National Park. Turn south and drive 2.8 miles to the campground on the right. (Chief Mountain International Highway is closed October-May.) GPS Coordinates: N 49° 4.645' W 113° 52.860'

Contact: Waterton Lakes National Park, Box 200, 215 Mount View Rd., Waterton Park, AB T0K 2M0, Canada, 403/859-2224, www.pc.gc.ca/eng/pn-np/ab/waterton/index.aspx.

49 WATERTON TOWNSITE

Scenic rating: 10

on Waterton Lake in Waterton National Park, Canada

Located in Waterton Townsite, the campground garners spectacular views and wildlife in Waterton Lakes National Park, part of the Glacier-Waterton International Peace Park. It borders Waterton Lake, with large peaks rising to the north and east of town. Paved walking paths circle the campground, linking to restaurants in town, Cameron Falls, the beach for swimming, and the boat tours on the lake. Do not bicycle on the walking paths, only on the town roads or the several mountain-bike trails in the area. From the campground, the Waterton Lake hiking trail departs to roaring Bertha Falls (2 miles),

© BECKY LOMAX

The Waterton Townsite Campground sits on the north end of Waterton Lake.

Bertha Lake (3.5 miles), or Goat Haunt, U.S.A. (8.7 miles).

A paved road with paved parking pads circles through the mowed lawn campground, which is divided by Cameron Creek. The RV hookup sites line up in the open. A few trees shade some sites but offer no privacy. For lake views, go for unserviced spots in the G loop (sites 26-46), but be prepared for strong winds off the lake. For more sheltered scenery, go for the Cameron Creek E loop sites (even numbers 2-16). In July and August, arrive by noon to claim a site, or make reservations. In shoulder seasons without reservations, you'll have your pick of sites.

Campsites, facilities: The campground has 95 hookup campsites that can accommodate large RVs and 143 unserviced RV or tent campsites. Hookups include sewer, water, and electricity. Facilities include flush toilets (wheelchair-accessible), showers, a disposal station, drinking water, kitchen shelters, bear-resistant food storage lockers, and firewood.

Fires are permitted only in kitchen shelters. Leashed pets are permitted.

Reservations, fees: Reservations are available (877/737-3783, www.pccamping.ca). Hookups cost CAN$33-39. Unserviced sites cost CAN$23-28. A burning permit for fires costs CAN$9. Cash or credit card. Opens May-mid-October.

Directions: Drive the 30-mile Chief Mountain International Highway across the border (open mid-May-September), go west for 0.7 mile to the Waterton entrance, and then go five miles south to the Waterton Townsite. At the townsite, turn left on Mount View Drive for two blocks and right on Windflower Avenue for three blocks to the campground entrance.

GPS Coordinates: N 49° 2.917' W 113° 54.560'

Contact: Waterton Lakes National Park, Box 200, 215 Mount View Rd., Waterton Park, AB T0K 2M0, Canada, 403/859-2224, www.pc.gc.ca/eng/pn-np/ab/waterton/index.aspx.

50 BERTHA BAY

🚶🏊🚣🏊🚤⛺

Scenic rating: 9

on Waterton Lake in Waterton National Park, Canada

On the western shore of Upper Waterton Lake, Bertha Bay is accessible only by a 1.5-mile hike or by boat. It sits in Waterton Lakes National Park, part of the Glacier-Waterton International Peace Park. Boaters must scope the weather out carefully before launching trips because winds kick up fast on the lake, churning up monstrous whitecaps. The backcountry campsite does not have a boat ramp or dock; boats should be completely beached overnight. Views from the beach span the rugged peaks of Waterton and Glacier, and swimmers can enjoy the clear water, albeit chilly. From the campground, a trail ascends 1.3 miles to Bertha

Falls and then switchbacks up another 1.7 miles to Bertha Lake.

For protection from the wind, the campsites are set in the woods back from the rock and pebble shore. A designated cooking site separates food handling, storing, and eating from the tent platforms for sleeping. Keep all food in the cooking area to avoid attracting wildlife into the sleeping zone. Bring a gas stove for cooking and 30 feet of rope for hanging food at night.

Campsites, facilities: Bertha Bay has four tent platforms, which each can hold one tent. The campground can accommodate a total of 12 people, but only six are allowed per party. Facilities include a bear pole for hanging food and garbage, a pit toilet, and a fire pit. Bring your own drinking water, or treat lake or stream water. Pack out your trash. Pets are not permitted.

Reservations, fees: Reservations for required wilderness passes are available by phone 90 days in advance beginning April 1 of each year. The park charges a nonrefundable CAN$12 reservation fee, plus a modification fee for any additional changes. April-mid-May, call the warden's office (403/859-5140); after then, call the visitors center (403/859-5133). Wilderness passes can also be picked up in person no sooner than 24 hours in advance of the starting date. Backcountry camping costs CAN$10 per person per night. Children 16 years old and under camp for free. Cash or credit card. Open May-November.

Directions: Hikers can locate the trailhead at the end of Evergreen Avenue on the west end of the Waterton Townsite. Kayakers and canoeists should launch from the Cameron Bay picnic area. Boat ramps for larger boats are available at Linnet Lake picnic area and the marina in the Townsite.

GPS Coordinates: N 49° 1.710' W 113° 54.636'

Contact: Waterton Lakes National Park, Box 200, 215 Mount View Rd., Waterton Park, AB T0K 2M0, Canada, 403/859-2224, www.pc.gc.ca/eng/pn-np/ab/waterton/index.aspx.

51 BOUNDARY BAY

Scenic rating: 10

on Waterton Lake in Waterton National Park, Canada

BEST (

Boundary Bay sits on the international border between Canada and the United States on the western shore of Upper Waterton Lake. It sits in Waterton Lakes National Park, part of the Glacier-Waterton International Peace Park. The main attraction is the lake, stunning views of Mt. Cleveland, and the two international boundary markers. The camp sits literally on the international boundary swath between Canada and the United States. If you can stand the cold water, you can swim back and forth across the boundary. Reach the campground by hiking a 3.7-mile rolling trail or by boating. Boaters should check the weather forecast before departing because winds kick up fast into whitecaps. The campground does have a seasonal dock, but you can also beach boats securely for overnighting. From the campground, the trail continues another 4.3 miles on to Goat Haunt. Bring your passport to go through customs at Goat Haunt.

Boundary Bay campground is set in a mixed forest of firs and cottonwoods back from the shore for protection from winds. A designated communal cooking site is separated from the tent platforms for sleeping. Keep all food in the cooking area to avoid attracting wildlife into the sleeping zone. Bring a gas stove for cooking and 30 feet of rope for hanging food.

Campsites, facilities: The campground has three tent sites, which allow one tent each. While the campground can accommodate nine campers total, only six are allowed per group. Facilities include a bear pole for hanging food and garbage, a pit toilet, and a fire pit. Bring your own drinking water, or treat lake or stream water. Pack out your trash. Pets are not permitted.

Reservations, fees: Reservations for required wilderness passes are available by phone 90 days in advance beginning April 1 for a non-refundable CAN$12 reservation fee, plus a modification fee for any additional changes. April-mid-May, call the warden's office (403/859-5140); after then, call the visitors center (403/859-5133). Wilderness passes can also be picked up in person no sooner than 24 hours in advance of the starting date. Backcountry camping costs CAN$10 per person per night. Kids 16 years old and under camp for free. Cash or credit card. Open May-November.

Directions: Hikers can locate the trailhead at the end of Evergreen Avenue on the west end of Waterton Townsite. Kayakers and canoeists should launch from the Cameron Bay picnic area. Boat ramps for larger boats are available at Linnet Lake picnic area and the marina in the Townsite.

GPS Coordinates: N 48° 59.927' W 113° 54.401'

Contact: Waterton Lakes National Park, 215 Mount View Rd., Waterton Park, AB T0K 2M0, Canada, 403/859-2224, www.pc.gc.ca.

52 GOAT HAUNT

Scenic rating: 10

on Waterton Lake in Glacier National Park, USA

No roads reach Goat Haunt, which sits at the south end of Waterton Lake. Visitors must hike or boat. Backpackers hike to Goat Haunt in three- to five-day trips that start at six trailheads in Glacier. An 8.7-mile trail also leads from the Waterton Townsite to Goat Haunt. All others must travel through Canada via the tour cruise or a private boat from Waterton Townsite to reach Goat Haunt. When hiking or boating south on Waterton Lake, you cross the international boundary into Montana. Passports are required for those overnighting in Goat Haunt or hiking past the

International Peace Park Pavilion. The beach yields gorgeous views and provides a cooling swim on a hot day.

Sitting above the boat dock and the open-air visitors center, the campground is unique. It is made up of two small shelters with roofs and cement floors—each split with walls for privacy from other campers. No tent is required, but bring a thick pad for your back. During the day, the area throngs with people when the tour boat disgorges tourists, but nighttime brings quiet on your own private beach. Day hikes lead from Goat Haunt to Rainbow Falls (0.7 mile), an overlook (1 steep mile), and Kootenai Lakes (2.8 miles) to spot moose.

Campsites, facilities: The campground has seven designated campsites; each holds up to four people. A community cooking site sits behind the shelters with a bear pole for hanging food. Facilities include flush toilets and drinking water from the sinks. Campfires are permitted; you'll need to gather your own wood. Pets are not permitted.

Reservations, fees: Backcountry permits are required. Advance reservations ($30) for four of the campsites are available starting April 15. Get permits for other sites in person 24 hours in advance at the Apgar Backcountry Office or St. Mary Visitor Center. Permits cost $5 per adult per night and $2.50 for children 8-15. They are free for children seven and under. Cash, check, or credit card. Open mid-June-November, although the tour boat runs only through mid-September.

Directions: From Waterton, Alberta, take a private boat or the tour cruise boat across the lake to reach Goat Haunt, Montana. Contact Waterton Shoreline Cruises (403/859-2362, www.watertoncruise.com) for tour boat prices and departure times.

GPS Coordinates: N 48° 57.574' W 113° 53.269'

Contact: Glacier National Park, P.O. Box 128, West Glacier, MT 59936, 406/888-7800, www.nps.gov/glac.

53 BELLY RIVER

Scenic rating: 6
on Chief Mountain International Highway in
Waterton Lakes National Park, Canada

For those who want to shoot back across the border from Canada first thing in the morning, the Belly River Campground sits five minutes north of Chief Mountain Customs. It sits in Waterton Lakes National Park, part of the Glacier-Waterton International Peace Park. Trout anglers looking to fish here will need a Waterton Lakes National Park fishing license as well as an Alberta fishing license; you can get both at the visitors center in Waterton. A short trail, mostly used by anglers, leads up the Belly River but fizzles before the international boundary or any real destination. Some floaters also launch at the Belly River Campground to paddle the Class II river.

A mixed forest surrounds the campground, but the quaking aspen groves give it character. When breezes blow, the leaves chatter. That and the burbling of the Belly River are about the only noises you'll hear. The campsites are located in a mix of shady sites and open sites. Those that are open have forest views. The campground is also a good site for wildlife-watching and birding, particularly along the river. Look for moose, bears, and foxes.

Campsites, facilities: The campground has 24 RV or tent campsites that can accommodate midsized RVs. Facilities include picnic tables, fire rings, pit and flush toilets, kitchen shelters, group camping sites, firewood, a campground host, and bear-resistant food storage lockers. Bring your own drinking water, or treat river water. Leashed pets are permitted.

Reservations, fees: Reservations are not accepted. Campsites cost CAN$16. Burning permits for fires cost CAN$9. Group campsites are available by reservation only, with a minimum of 25 people; call the park for reservations. Cash or check. Open mid-May-mid-September.

Directions: Drive 19 miles up Chief Mountain International Highway, crossing the border (open mid-May-September). The campground is on the left about five minutes north of the border before the Belly River Bridge. Coming from the north, look for the signed turnoff on the right as soon as you cross the Belly River Bridge.

GPS Coordinates: N 49° 1.576' W 113° 41.057'

Contact: Waterton Lakes National Park, Box 200, 215 Mount View Rd., Waterton Park, AB T0K 2M0, Canada, 403/859-2224, www.pc.gc.ca/eng/pn-np/ab/waterton/index.aspx.

ROCKY MOUNTAIN FRONT

© BECKY LOMAX

The Rocky Mountain Front yields a wondrous combination of campgrounds where the flat prairie collides with the rugged peaks of the Continental Divide. The open prairie, dotted with cow towns, offers windblown places to camp along reservoirs, while long river valleys snake into the mountains with shaded, more-protected campgrounds. The Front attracts campers for fishing, boating, hiking, horseback riding, hunting, and mountain biking and reservoirs hold shoreline campgrounds that fill on hot summer days. Canyon Ferry Lake, the largest, sees the most use of any lake in the state. For more remote places to camp, wrestle the bumpy dirt roads into the Lewis and Clark or Helena National Forests, which form doorways to the Bob Marshall Wilderness Complex and where Forest Service campgrounds are the norm.

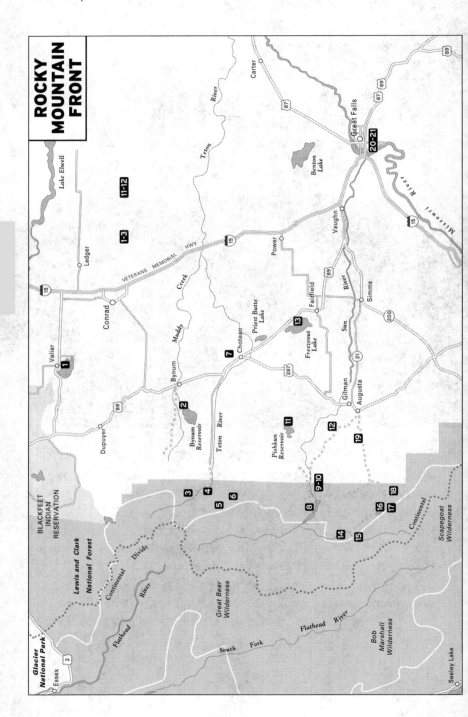

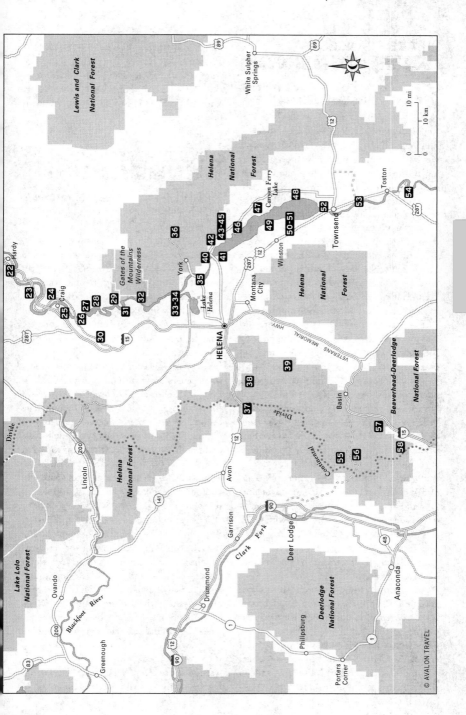

1 LAKE FRANCES

Scenic rating: 7

in Valier on the Blackfeet Indian Reservation

At 3,800 feet on the Blackfeet Indian Reservation prairie, Lake Frances attracts campers for water recreation. In summer, swimming, fishing, boating, waterskiing, sailing, windsurfing, and Jet Skiing are favored. In winter, ice fishing and snowmobiling are popular. The lake has two boat ramps and docks, including one adjacent to the campground, but as water levels drop in late summer, sometimes launching is difficult. An island in the lake harbors a great blue heron rookery. Anglers go after walleye, northern pike, and yellow perch. From the hiking and biking trail along the lakeshore, you get a view of the Rocky Mountains in the distance.

The campground is composed of three interconnected loops, all with back-in parking pads. Eleven sites sit right on the shoreline, but others also have lake views. Perimeter trees provide spots of shade in the sunny campground. Sites pack close together, offering little privacy, but with the campground's location across the little-used airstrip from town and away from the highway, it is quiet. An additional overflow primitive campground with only a pit toilet is at the southeast end of the lake.

Campsites, facilities: The campground has 50 RV campsites that can accommodate large RVs and 10 primitive tent campsites. Facilities include picnic tables, fire rings with grills, flush toilets, drinking water, electrical hookups, disposal station, garbage service, boat ramp, fish-cleaning station, and playground. Leashed pets are permitted.

Reservations, fees: Reservations are not accepted. Campsites cost $15 for electrical hookups; tent sites cost $10. Cash or check. Open year-round.

Directions: From Highway 44 on the west end of Valier, turn south onto Teton Avenue, which becomes Lake Road. Drive 0.9 mile to the campground entrance on the right.

GPS Coordinates: N 48° 18.046' W 112° 15.591'

Contact: Valier Area Development Corporation, P.O. Box 568, 505 Lake Shore Drive, Valier, MT 59486, 406/279-3361, www.valier.org.

2 BYNUM RESERVOIR

Scenic rating: 7

northwest of Choteau

The 3,205-acre Bynum Reservoir is one of the myriad of small lakes dotting the prairie of the Rocky Mountain Front. Sitting at 4,198 feet west of the small village of Bynum, the lake draws anglers for its stocked rainbow trout and walleye. But a fish-consumption advisory is in effect because of mercury buildup. A concrete boat ramp is available, but it is unusable during low water. Contact the Region 4 office for the reservoir's current water levels. Find a small general store, post office, and the educational Two Medicine Dinosaur Center (www.timescale.org, 406/469-2211) in Bynum. The center displays bones from the world's longest dinosaur, a model skeleton of a seismosaurus, and the first baby dinosaur remains found in North America. The Blackleaf Wildlife Management Area—home to mountain goats, elk, and golden eagles—is about 25 minutes to the west.

The campground is primitive and part of the fishing access site run by the state. The sites line up along the shore of the reservoir in a hot, sunny, treeless, grassy area along the dirt campground road. The campground and lake yield expansive views of the Front range peaks in the distance, but when winds crop up, no trees are available as windbreaks. The campground is far enough away from the highway that the only sounds you'll hear are the wind, the waterfowl, and sometimes the western chorus frog. When water levels drop low in August, the rim becomes dusty.

CAMPING ON THE FRONT

Prepare for **weather extremes** while camping and recreating on the Front. High winds contort ridgeline trees into avant-garde sculptures, blow trains off their tracks in winter, and cause white-knuckled driving in RVs. The Front also fluctuates wildly in temperatures, having set records for swinging up to 100 degrees in 24 hours, and Rogers Pass claims fame as one of the top 10 coldest spots in the world.

How ironic that such a harsh environment produces quirks that sustain abundant wildlife. The Front's winds turn it into one of the largest golden eagle migratory flyways in North America. The national forests, game preserves, and wildlife refuges burgeon with elk, bighorn sheep, deer, grizzly bears, mountain lions, coyotes, pronghorn antelope, and birds.

Campers exploring the Rocky Mountain Front will also find themselves confined to **minimal roads.** Only one freeway, I-15, runs north to south through the prairie, linking up Great Falls with Helena. The narrow, more-scenic two-lane **Highway 89** that requires several hours to drive parallels the freeway farther west, connecting the tiny towns closer to the Front mountain ranges. Routes over the Continental Divide dwindle to two: **Highway 200** squeezes over Rogers Pass north of Helena, and **Highway 12** scoots even higher over MacDonald Pass west of Helena. Beyond that, the more-common paved, skinny two-laners and the more-pervasive washboard gravel or potholed dirt routes comprise the web of the Front's roadways to reach campgrounds.

Campsites, facilities: The campground has four RV and tent campsites that can accommodate only smaller RVs. Facilities include picnic tables, fire rings with grills, vault toilets (wheelchair-accessible), and boat ramp. Pack out your trash. Leashed pets are permitted.

Reservations, fees: Reservations are not accepted. Campsites cost $7 with a Montana fishing license and $12 without a Montana fishing license. Cash or check. Open year-round.

Directions: From Bynum at the signed turnoff, drive west on the dirt county road for 4.2 miles. Veer left at the signed fork for 0.6 mile, and turn left for 1.2 miles to reach the reservoir. Follow the road 0.6 mile eastward to reach the fishing access site and campground. GPS Coordinates: N 47° 57.593' W 112° 24.382'

Contact: Montana Fish, Wildlife, and Parks, Region 4, 4600 Giant Springs Rd., Great Falls, MT 59405, 406/454-5840, http://fwp.mt.gov.

3 ELKO

Scenic rating: 7

on the West Fork of the Teton River in Lewis and Clark National Forest

At 5,300 feet, Elko Campground sits in the Lewis and Clark National Forest about five air miles east of the boundary of the Bob Marshall Wilderness. The campground isn't necessarily a destination in itself, except in fall for hunting season, but works as a good overflow site should Cave Mountain fill up. Across the road from the campground, the exceptionally clear waters of the West Fork of the Teton River contain rainbow, brown, and brook trout. The North Fork Teton River Trail (#107) departs nearby and heads four miles through Box Canyon—a cool trail for hot days since it requires fording the river several times.

The heavily-forested campground sits very close to the dusty road, although road traffic abates into silence after dark. Two of the sites are well-used, with broad spaces for tents. The third, less-used site is overgrown with

© BECKY LOMAX

The West Fork of the Teton River flows past Cave Mountain Campground.

thimbleberry and thistle. Tall firs partially shade the campsites, which sit very close together. The site on the right as you drive in sits near a seasonal stream.

Campsites, facilities: The campground has three RV or tent campsites. With the uneven, rocky, short parking pads and little turnaround room, only small RVs can squeeze in here. Facilities include picnic tables, fire rings with grills, and a pit toilet. No water is available; bring your own, or treat river water. Pack out your trash. Leashed pets are permitted.

Reservations, fees: No reservations are accepted. Camping is free. Open late May-November.

Directions: From Choteau, drive about four miles north on Highway 89 to milepost 46.5. Turn west onto Teton River Road (Forest Road 144) and drive 27 miles. The pavement will turn to gravel and dirt with copious washboards around milepost 18. The campground is unsigned on the east side of the road. GPS Coordinates: N 47° 55.449' W 112° 45.817'

Contact: Lewis and Clark National Forest, Rocky Mountain Ranger District, 1102 N. Main Ave., Choteau, MT 59422, 406/466-5341, www.fs.usda.gov/lcnf.

4 CAVE MOUNTAIN
🚶‍♂️🛶🎣🐎♿🚐⛺

Scenic rating: 8
on the West Fork of the Teton River in Lewis and Clark National Forest

BEST (

At 5,200 feet, Cave Mountain Campground sits at the confluence of the Middle Fork with the West Fork of Teton River—both trout fisheries in exceptionally clear waters after spring runoff. The Bob Marshall Wilderness is accessed via the Route Creek Trail (#108) over a high pass six miles up the Middle Fork. The trailhead, which is equipped for stock (hitch rails, feeding trough, loading ramp) is a five-minute drive up the road. The same trail also connects with the Lonesome Ridge Trail (#154), which crosses into the South Fork of the Teton River drainage. The campground is popular with hunters in fall.

The quiet campground rebuilt in 2012 is surrounded by a rail fence to keep out cattle grazing under permit in the area. Aspens, pines, and firs shade many of the campsites, with low vegetation between them. Sites are spread out to offer privacy with about half overlooking the river and half backing up into the hillside. Some sites include views of the area's dramatic cliffs while others have large flat spaces for tents.

Campsites, facilities: The campground has 14 RV or tent campsites, including one double site. The gravel back-in parking pads can fit RVs up to 50 feet. Facilities include picnic tables, fire rings with grills, vault toilets (wheelchair-accessible), and drinking water. Pack out your trash. Leashed pets are permitted.

Reservations, fees: No reservations are accepted. Campsites cost $6 for a single unit

(RV, trailer, or tent). Cash or check. Open late May-November.

Directions: From Choteau, drive four miles north on Highway 89 to milepost 46.5. Turn west onto Teton River Road (Forest Road 144) and drive 22.6 miles. The pavement will turn to gravel and dirt with copious washboards around milepost 18. At the sign for the campground, turn left and drive for 0.4 mile. The entrance road crosses a one-lane bridge, swings right, crosses a second short bridge, and continues straight past the next junction to the campground entrance on the right.

GPS Coordinates: N 47° 53.399' W 112° 43.595'

Contact: Lewis and Clark National Forest, Rocky Mountain Ranger District, 1102 N. Main Ave., Choteau, MT 59422, 406/466-5341, www.fs.usda.gov/lcnf.

5 MILL FALLS

Scenic rating: 8

on the South Fork of the Teton River in Lewis and Clark National Forest

BEST (

Mill Falls Campground sits near the South Fork of the Teton River, a trout fishery. From the campground, you can hike 0.1 mile to its namesake waterfall. A popular trailhead departs 1.5 miles farther up the road for the small scenic alpine Our Lake (2.5 miles) and Headquarters Pass (3 miles), which marks the entrance to the Bob Marshall Wilderness. The Headquarters Pass Trail is also used to scramble up the Class 4 slopes to the summit of Rocky Mountain, one of the highest peaks in the region. The area also is popular for fall hunting.

The tiny, shaded, quiet campground is tucked back off the road with an entrance that looks like a jeep trail. The narrow, rocky, potholed, rutted road with overhanging branches and the uneven, rocky parking pads can only accommodate smaller RVs. Trailers will not have room to turn around. Sites 3 and 4 pair

up close together on the right as you drive in. Also close together, sites 1 and 2 sit at the back of the campground, with large tent spaces adjacent to a small creek.

Campsites, facilities: The campground has four RV or tent campsites. Small RVs only. Facilities include picnic tables, fire rings with grills, and a pit toilet. No drinking water is provided; bring your own. Pack out your trash. Leashed pets are permitted.

Reservations, fees: No reservations are accepted. Camping is free. Open late May-November.

Directions: From Choteau, drive four miles north on Highway 89 to milepost 46.5. Turn west onto Teton River Road (Forest Road 144) and drive 16.9 miles to the Ear Mountain Outstanding Area sign. Turn left onto the gravel road and cross the single-lane bridge. Immediately after the bridge, turn right onto South Fork Road. Drive 3.1 miles, veering right at the Nature Conservancy Pine Butte Guest Ranch sign. Follow the bumpy, washboard Forest Road 109 for 5.4 miles to the signed campground entrance on the right.

GPS Coordinates: N 47° 51.530' W 112° 46.368'

Contact: Lewis and Clark National Forest, Rocky Mountain Ranger District, 1102 N. Main Ave., Choteau, MT 59422, 406/466-5341, www.fs.usda.gov/lcnf.

6 GREEN GULCH

Scenic rating: 7

on the South Fork of the Teton River in Lewis and Clark National Forest

Tiny Green Gulch primitive campground sits at 5,560 feet near the South Fork of the Teton River. The river is a trout fishery with rainbow, brook, and brown trout. The 12-mile-long Green Gulch Trail (#127) tours a deeply wooded valley after fording the river and reaches a pass at 7,232 feet, where it drops into Sheep

Gulch. The area is popular for fall hunting. It also has quick access within a 10-minute drive to the trailhead for Our Lake (2.5 miles) and Headquarters Pass (3 miles)—both much more scenic trails than the Green Gulch trail.

The shaded, quiet, primitive campground is tucked back on the Green Gulch side road. Both sites offer ample room for tents, and with only two sites, you get privacy.

Campsites, facilities: The campground has two RV or tent campsites. The small parking pads, however, can only fit smaller RVs and trailers. Facilities include picnic tables, fire rings with grills, and a pit toilet. No drinking water is provided; bring your own. Pack out your trash. Leashed pets are permitted.

Reservations, fees: No reservations are accepted. Camping is free. Open late May-November.

Directions: From Choteau, drive four miles north on Highway 89 to milepost 46.5. Turn west onto Teton River Road (Forest Road 144) and drive 16.9 miles to the Ear Mountain Outstanding Area sign. Turn left onto the gravel road and cross the single-lane bridge. Immediately after the bridge, turn right onto South Fork Road. Drive 3.1 miles, veering right at the Nature Conservancy Pine Butte Guest Ranch sign. Follow the bumpy, washboard Forest Road 109 for 4.4 miles to Green Gulch Road and veer left onto it for 0.5 mile to the campground.

GPS Coordinates: N 47° 51.557' W 112° 45.423'

Contact: Lewis and Clark National Forest, Rocky Mountain Ranger District, 1102 N. Main Ave., Choteau, MT 59422, 406/466-5341, www.fs.usda.gov/lcnf.

🔟 CHOTEAU CITY PARK

Scenic rating: 4
in Choteau

The city park campground is one block off the downtown main strip in Choteau, an easy option for those bicycling the Rocky Mountain Front. A two-block walk leads to restaurants downtown and the community swimming pool. The nine-hole golf course is less than one mile away. Open daily in summer, the Old Trail Museum on the north end of town includes fossils, Native American artifacts, pioneer history, and wildlife exhibits. Choteau's Rodeo Grounds host rodeo events and music concerts. Eureka Reservoir, eight miles northwest on Teton Canyon Road, provides fishing and boating. Four miles south of town, Freezeout Lake draws bird-watchers in March, when the lake crowds with 300,000 snow geese and 10,000 tundra swans on their migration north, but also offers birding in the fall.

The campground is part of Choteau's city park. Nine of the campsites sit on the hot west side, with views of a warehouse and grain silos and a few perimeter willow and cottonwood trees for shade. The other five campsites are more secluded, tucked on the east side under bigger, thicker trees next to a tiny creek. These shaded sites usually have green grass while the others are brown dry grass. A gravel walking path runs through the park. You may want to bring earplugs because of the adjacent railroad tracks. The campground road is a combination of gravel and pavement, with level sites for tents or RVs.

Campsites, facilities: There are 14 RV and tent campsites. The west-side campsites can accommodate any length of RV. Facilities include picnic tables, a few fire pits or rock fire rings, drinking water, flush toilets, dump station, and garbage service. Leashed pets are permitted.

Reservations, fees: No reservations are accepted. Campsites cost $8 per night. Cash or check. Open May-September.

Directions: In downtown Choteau, turn east off Highway 89 at the campground sign onto 1st Street NE and drive one block. Turn right at the park sign, drive 0.1 mile, and turn left into the campground. You can also get to the campground entrance via 1st Street SE.

© BECKY LOMAX

From Mortimer Gulch Campground, hikers can walk the trail along Gibson Reservoir.

GPS Coordinates: N 47° 48.695' W 112° 10.719'

Contact: Choteau Park and Campground, City of Choteau, P.O. Box 619, Choteau, MT 59422, 406/466-2510.

8 MORTIMER GULCH

Scenic rating: 9

on Gibson Reservoir in Lewis and Clark National Forest

Located at 5,000 feet, Mortimer Gulch is the only designated campground on the 1,289-acre Gibson Reservoir. Dramatically steep upthrust ridges—a mark of the Rocky Mountain Front—surround the reservoir. A steep cement boat ramp, dock, and trailer parking aid in launching boats for fishing, sightseeing, waterskiing, kayaking, and canoeing. Anglers fish for rainbow, brook, and westslope cutthroat trout, and arctic grayling. The campground is popular in early summer when the reserve water levels are higher; in fall, hunters flock to the campground because a seven-mile hike leads into the Sun River Game Preserve. A hiking trail drops from the campground to the boat launch area and connects with the North Fork of the Sun River Trail (#201), which heads along the reservoir's shore. You can mountain bike the trail up to the wilderness boundary (7 miles) and continue on to climb Sun Butte (9.5 miles) for a panoramic view of the area. The Mortimer Gulch National Recreation Trail (7 miles) offers views of Sawtooth Ridge and the reservoir.

The quiet campground's two loops feature partially shaded, partially private campsites. Some are tucked under aspens, others under large Douglas firs. Most of the campsites have back-in parking aprons.

Campsites, facilities: The campground has 27 RV or tent campsites that can accommodate vehicles up to 48 feet. Five are double sites. Facilities include picnic tables, fire rings with grills, vault toilets, and drinking water. Pack out your trash. Leashed pets are permitted.

Wheelchair-accessible facilities include toilets and campsites.

Reservations, fees: No reservations are accepted. Campsites cost $8 for one unit (RV, trailer, or tent). Cash or check. Open late May-November; however, water is turned off after Labor Day.

Directions: In Augusta, drive out of town on Manix Street, which becomes the Sun River Road (Forest Road 108). Drive 3.7 miles to a signed intersection. Turn right and drive 15 miles on dirt, where the road turns to pavement again. Continue driving 6.8 miles on the pavement, which climbs up above the dam. Turn left into the campground at the sign. GPS Coordinates: N 47° 36.586' W 112° 46.279'

Contact: Lewis and Clark National Forest, Rocky Mountain Ranger District, 1102 N. Main Ave., Choteau, MT 59422, 406/466-5341, www.fs.usda.gov/lcnf.

9 SUN CANYON LODGE

Scenic rating: 7
on Sun River in Lewis and Clark National Forest

At 4,600 feet on Sun River, the rustic Sun Canyon Lodge is a bucolic Montana outfitter with trophy antlers on the wall of the octagon 1920s log lodge. The lodge nestles below the towering cliffs one mile south of the North Fork of the Sun River below the Gibson Reservoir dam. The river contains rainbow, brook, and cutthroat trout that can be caught by wade fishing. Within a 10-minute drive to the west, Gibson Reservoir offers lake fishing, hiking and mountain-biking trails, boating, and swimming. Departing from Sun Canyon Lodge, the Home Gulch-Lime Trail (#267, 15 miles) offers spring wildlife-watching opportunities, but more scenic trails depart from the reservoir area.

The campground is part of the Sun Canyon

Lodge complex of restaurant, cabins, and corrals, with campsites lined up along the perimeter of a grassy meadow against aspen trees. Its location off the Sun Canyon Road yields quiet, but the campsites are visible from the restaurant and the parking area.

Campsites, facilities: The campground has 10 RV or tent campsites that can accommodate large RVs. Facilities include picnic tables, drinking water, flush toilets (wheelchair-accessible), showers, disposal station, garbage service, launderette, restaurant, bar, trail rides, playground, boat tours, horse corrals, and outfitting services for fishing and hunting. Leashed pets are permitted.

Reservations, fees: Reservations are accepted. Tent camping costs $10, and RV camping with electrical hookups costs $25. Using the disposal station costs $10, and showers cost $3 per person. Horse boarding costs $5-10 per day. Cash, check, or credit card. Open May-November.

Directions: From Augusta, follow the signs to Gibson Reservoir. Drive out of town on Manix Street, which becomes Sun River Road (Forest Road 108). Drive 3.7 miles to a signed intersection. Turn right and drive 15 miles on dirt to where the road turns to pavement again. Continue three more miles to the Sun Canyon Lodge sign and turn left, traveling for one more mile. GPS Coordinates: N 47° 36.303' W 112° 43.296'

Contact: Sun Canyon Lodge, P.O. Box 327, Sun River Rd., Augusta, MT 59410, 406/562-3654 or 888/749-3654, www.suncanyonlodge.com.

10 HOME GULCH

Scenic rating: 7
on Sun River in Lewis and Clark National Forest

Located at 4,580 feet, Home Gulch nestles below the towering cliffs along the North Fork of the Sun River below the Gibson Reservoir dam. Within a five-minute drive, funky Sun Canyon Lodge offers camper amenities, trail rides, and a cafe. The campground is popular with hunters in the fall, and the North Fork of the Sun River contains rainbow, brook, and cutthroat trout that can be caught by wade fishing. Gibson Reservoir, with fishing, hiking and mountain-biking trails, boating, and swimming is a 10-minute drive to the west. Departing from Sun Canyon Lodge, the Home Gulch-Lime Trail (#267, 15 miles) offers spring wildlife-watching opportunities, but more scenic trails depart from the reservoir area.

The campground squeezes between the Sun Canyon Road and the North Fork of the Sun River. Aspen and alder trees lend partial shade to the campsites. The campground is quiet but does get a fair amount of weekend traffic during the day on the adjacent road, but not at night when the sound of the river is pervasive. A narrow dirt road winds through the campground, which has gravel parking pads; one is a pull-through and the rest are back-ins. Most of the campsites overlook the river.

Campsites, facilities: The campground has 15 RV or tent campsites that can accommodate vehicles up to 45 feet long. Two are double sites. Facilities include picnic tables, fire rings with grills, vault toilets (wheelchair-accessible), and hand pumps for drinking water. Pack out your trash. Leashed pets are permitted.

Reservations, fees: No reservations are accepted. Campsites cost $6 per unit (RV, trailer, or tent). Cash or check. Open late May-November, but the water is shut off after Labor Day.

Directions: From Augusta, follow the signs to Gibson Reservoir. Drive out of town on Manix Street, which becomes Sun River Road (Forest Road 108). Drive 3.7 miles to a signed intersection. Turn right and drive 15 miles on dirt to where the road turns to pavement again. Continue 1.8 miles farther on the pavement and turn right at the sign into the campground. GPS Coordinates: N 47° 36.981' W 112° 43.605'

Contact: Lewis and Clark National Forest, Rocky Mountain Ranger District, 1102 N. Main Ave., Choteau, MT 59422, 406/466-5341, www.fs.usda.gov/lcnf.

11 PISHKUN RESERVOIR

Scenic rating: 8

north of Augusta

The 1,518-acre Pishkun Reservoir is a prairie lake below the Rocky Mountain Front. Long, rough, gravel and dirt access roads lead to it from Choteau or Augusta. Sitting at 4,370 feet, the lake draws anglers for its northern pike, rainbow trout, and yellow perch. Used also in winter for ice fishing, it is stocked regularly with rainbow trout and sometimes kokanee. The concrete boat ramp for motorized and nonmotorized watercraft is unusable during low water. Contact the Region 4 office for current water levels. Also a wildlife management area, the reservoir is a good place for watching waterfowl, loons, and peregrine falcons.

The primitive campground is part of the fishing access site run by the state. Its campsites line up along the shore in a hot, sunny, windy, treeless, grassy area along the dirt campground road facing the dramatic, expansive views of the Rocky Mountain Front peaks. The campground is so distant from any highway that wind is the only sound. The state discourages trailers and RVs from using the campground because of the rough condition of the access road, but smaller RVs and truck-campers often visit the campground anyway. Despite how spread out the campsites are, you'll still see your neighbors.

Campsites, facilities: The campground has five RV and tent campsites that can accommodate only smaller RVs. Facilities include picnic tables with shelters, fire rings with grills, vault toilets, and a boat ramp. Pack out your trash. Leashed pets are permitted.

Reservations, fees: Reservations are not

accepted. Campsites cost $7 with a Montana fishing license and $12 without a Montana fishing license. Cash or check. Open year-round.

Directions: From Choteau, drive 0.5 mile south on Highway 287 and turn southwest for 19 miles on the Pishkun Road. Turn left at the signed entrance to the fishing access site to reach the campground. From Augusta, drive 11.3 miles north on Highway 287 and turn left onto West Spring Valley Road for 7.3 miles as it jogs north and west again. Turn right onto the Pishkun Access Road for 4.8 miles and then turn left onto Pishkun Road for 0.8 mile to the campground entrance on the left.

GPS Coordinates: N 47° 41.666' W 112° 28.650'

Contact: Montana Fish, Wildlife, and Parks, Region 4, 4600 Giant Springs Rd., Great Falls, MT 59405, 406/454-5840, http://fwp.mt.gov.

12 WILLOW CREEK RESERVOIR

Scenic rating: 8

north of Augusta

The 1,314-acre Willow Creek Reservoir is a prairie lake below the Rocky Mountain Front accessible via a rough gravel road. At 4,150 feet, the lake draws anglers for its rainbow and brook trout. Used also in winter for ice fishing, it is stocked regularly with rainbow trout. The concrete boat ramp for motorized and nonmotorized watercraft is unusable during low water levels; contact the Region 4 office for current water levels. Also a wildlife management area, the reservoir is a good place for watching waterfowl and loons, and it attracts hunters in fall.

The primitive campground is part of the fishing access site run by the state. Its spread-out campsites line up along the shore in a hot, sunny, windy, treeless, grassy area along the

dirt campground road. Some of the campsites face east toward the lake's island, but the Front peaks are also in view to the west. Other campsites can nab reflections of the Front peaks in the water on calm days. The campground is so distant from any highway that wind is the only sound. The state discourages trailers and RVs from using the campground because of the rough condition of the access road, but smaller RVs and truck-campers often visit the campground anyway.

Campsites, facilities: The campground has six RV and tent campsites that can accommodate smaller RVs. Facilities include picnic tables, fire rings with grills, vault toilets, and a concrete boat ramp. Pack out your trash. Leashed pets are permitted.

Reservations, fees: Reservations are not accepted. Campsites cost $7 with a Montana fishing license and $12 without a Montana fishing license. Cash or check. Open year-round.

Directions: From Augusta, drive out of town on Manix Street, which becomes the Sun River Road (Forest Road 108). Drive 3.7 miles to a signed intersection. Turn right for 1.6 miles and turn right again at the fishing access site sign onto Willow Creek Road for 1.2 miles. Turn left for 0.1 mile to reach the campground.

GPS Coordinates: N 47° 32.842' W 112° 26.358'

Contact: Montana Fish, Wildlife, and Parks, Region 4, 4600 Giant Springs Rd., Great Falls, MT 59405, 406/454-5840, http://fwp.mt.gov.

13 FREEZEOUT LAKE

Scenic rating: 8

south of Choteau

BEST (

Freezeout Lake sits on a 11,466-acre wildlife state management area at 3,770 feet south of Choteau. The lake—actually one lake and six ponds—provides outstanding wildlife-watching. In late March and early April, as many as 300,000 snow geese and 10,000 tundra swans congregate on the lake amid a cacophony of squawks on their migration northward. For the best experience, watch in early morning as thousands of birds lift off the lake to go feed in nearby grain fields to prepare for their flight to Saskatchewan and then the arctic. Over 200 species of birds use the Freezeout area—either for migration or nesting. Winter brings upland game birds and raptors, spring and fall have waterfowl migrations, and summer includes ducks, herons, shorebirds, sandhill cranes, swans, and raptors. You can call 406/467-2646 for an automated waterfowl update. Perimeter roads are open year-round. Interior roads are closed during hunting season (October-mid-January) for upland game birds and waterfowl. Dike roads are closed to motorized vehicles but open for hiking. A paved walking path leads to a waterfowl blind. Only nonmotorized boats are permitted on the lake.

The primitive campground squeezes between the highway and Pond 5 in an open field divided by hedgerows of brush into back-in grassy campsites. The campground is sunny and windy, and receives noise from commercial trucks at night. But that doesn't compare with the deafening noise of thousands of snow geese at once.

Campsites, facilities: The campground has 12 RV and tent campsites that can accommodate small RVs. Facilities include picnic tables, vault toilets, and primitive boat ramps. Pack out your trash. Leashed pets are permitted. Wheelchair-accessible facilities include a toilet, campsite, and paved trail to a viewing blind.

Reservations, fees: Reservations are not accepted. Camping is free. Open year-round; however, motorized vehicles are restricted October-mid-January when internal roads are closed.

Directions: From Choteau, drive Highway 89 southeast for 12.3 miles. Turn west at the headquarters office. Drive 0.3 mile to a

Freezeout Lake attracts thousands of snow geese during spring migration.

four-way junction. Turn right, continuing for 0.3 mile. Turn right and go 0.1 mile to the campground entrance.
GPS Coordinates: N 47° 40.180' W 112° 0.947'

Contact: Montana Fish, Wildlife, and Parks, Region 4, 4600 Giant Springs Rd., Great Falls, MT 59405, 406/454-5840, http://fwp.mt.gov.

14 SOUTH FORK SUN RIVER

Scenic rating: 7

on the South Fork of the Sun River in Lewis and Clark National Forest

At 5,300 feet, the South Fork of the Sun River Campground sits at one of the most popular trailheads to access the wilderness for backpacking, horse packing, fishing, hunting, and mountain climbing. The 22-mile-long Chinese Wall can be reached via trail in about 18 miles. The Sun River attracts anglers for brown trout, mountain whitefish, and rainbow trout. The South Fork of the Sun Trail (#202), which is part of the Continental Divide Trail, parallels the South Fork of the Sun River to access the Scapegoat Wilderness to the south and the Bob Marshall Wilderness to the north.

This campground is busy and dusty because of the trailhead. The campground loop is adjacent to parking for hikers and stock trailers, which can be packed with up to 20 trucks and trailers that are visible from every campsite. Even though the campground sits on the river, none of the campsites have private river frontage, although you can walk the 100 feet to it. Lodgepole pines lend partial shade to the campground, with campsites surrounded by tall grass. While Benchmark offers much more privacy and camping ambiance, some hikers prefer camping here for the convenience to the trailhead.

Campsites, facilities: The campground has seven RV or tent campsites that can accommodate smaller RVs. Facilities include picnic tables, fire rings, hand pumps for drinking water, and vault toilets. Pack out your trash. Leashed pets are permitted. Wheelchair-accessible facilities include a toilet and campsite.

Reservations, fees: No reservations are accepted. Camping costs $6 per unit (RV, trailer, or tent). Cash or check. Open late May-November.

Directions: From Augusta, follow County Road 435 for 0.3 mile to the Nilan Reservoir sign. Turn right onto Eberl Street. Follow the road as it swings south and then west again, where the road turns to gravel, becoming Forest Road 235. Drive 14.2 miles to an intersection and continue straight for 16.2 miles until the road dead-ends in the campground. GPS Coordinates: N 47° 30.108' W 112° 53.283'

Contact: Lewis and Clark National Forest, Rocky Mountain Ranger District, 1102 N. Main Ave., Choteau, MT 59422, 406/466-5341, www.fs.usda.gov/lcnf.

15 BENCHMARK

Scenic rating: 7

on Straight Creek in Lewis and Clark National Forest

Located at 5,300 feet, Benchmark is a remote Forest Service station with an airstrip and a popular access for those entering the wilderness for hiking, backpacking, horse packing, fishing, and hunting. The 22-mile-long Chinese Wall can be reached via trail in about 18 miles. The campground sits between Straight and Wood Creeks, both tributaries to the South Fork of the Sun River that harbor mottled sculpin and rainbow trout. The 15.2-mile Straight Creek Trail (#212) departs 0.2 mile from the campground, and one mile north the South Fork of the Sun Trail (#202), which is part of the Continental Divide Trail, parallels the river to access the Scapegoat Wilderness to the south and the Bob Marshall Wilderness to the north.

A mixed aspen and conifer forest shades the campground, which is suited for those with stock. The two loops on the right have feeding troughs for horses, plus hitching rails and loading ramps are available. To accommodate stock trailers, the parking pads are large, triple-wide back-ins. The loop to the left is not set up for horses. Low grass covers the forest floor, while lodgepole pines lend partial shade. The spaced-out sites are private as shorter pine trees grow between sites. Sites 18, 19, 20, 24, and 25 have views but also look across the airstrip. Site 16 has a bear pole for hanging food. Most of the campsites have large, flat tent spaces.

Campsites, facilities: The campground has 25 RV or tent campsites that can accommodate RVs up to 35 feet. Facilities include picnic tables, fire rings, hand pumps for drinking water, stock equipment, and pit and vault toilets (wheelchair-accessible). Pack out your trash. Leashed pets are permitted.

Reservations, fees: No reservations are accepted. Campsites cost $6 per unit (RV, trailer, or tent). Cash or check. Open late May-November.

Directions: From Augusta, follow County Road 435 for 0.3 mile to the Nilan Reservoir sign. Turn right onto Eberl Street. Follow the road as it swings south and then west again, where the road turns to gravel, becoming Forest Road 235. Drive 14.2 miles to an intersection and turn left for another 15.2 miles on the Benchmark Road. At the campground sign, turn left, driving across the single-lane bridge, and swing left for another 0.2 mile.

GPS Coordinates: N 47° 29.207' W 112° 52.942'

Contact: Lewis and Clark National Forest, Rocky Mountain Ranger District, 1102 N. Main Ave., Choteau, MT 59422, 406/466-5341, www.fs.usda.gov/lcnf.

16 WOOD LAKE

Scenic rating: 9

at Wood Lake in Lewis and Clark National Forest

At 5,799 feet, Wood Lake is a small, shallow lake on Benchmark Road just east of the Scapegoat Wilderness Area. The lake is popular with anglers for its westslope cutthroat trout; you can often see six or more people fly-fishing along its shore. A primitive boat ramp is available for nonmotorized rowboats, kayaks, and canoes.

Sitting across the road from the lake, the aspen, lodgepole, and fir campground is enclosed with a rail fence to keep cattle grazing under permit in the area from entering. It sits very close to Benchmark Road, where every vehicle kicks up dust, which filters into the campsites adjacent to the road. Sites 2, 3, and 5 are more open, with views of the forested slopes. In July, cow parsnips, black-eyed susans, and cinquefoil bloom around the campsites, which are close together and lacking foliage. Site 7 is a small, private site with a

view of a small rocky gorge; a rough trail cuts through the fence and tours it. Sites 11 and 12 sit in a second area to the left when you drive in. These sites are open, with views of Wood Lake across the road, and with extra parking pads for trailers or additional vehicles.

Campsites, facilities: The campground has nine RV or tent campsites that can accommodate a maximum RV length of 22 feet. Facilities include picnic tables, fire rings with grills, vault toilets, and hand pumps for drinking water. Leashed pets are permitted. Wheelchair-accessible facilities include toilets and campsites.

Reservations, fees: No reservations are accepted. Camping costs $6 per unit (RV, trailer, or tent). Cash or check. Open late May-November.

Directions: From Augusta, follow County Road 435 for 0.3 mile to the Nilan Reservoir sign. Turn right onto Eberl Street. Follow the road as it swings south and then west again, where the road turns to gravel, becoming Forest Road 235. Drive 14.2 miles to an intersection and turn left onto Benchmark Road. Drive nine miles to Wood Lake. The campground entrance is on the right just before the lake.

GPS Coordinates: N 47° 25.706' W 112° 47.697'

Contact: Lewis and Clark National Forest, Rocky Mountain Ranger District, 1102 N. Main Ave., Choteau, MT 59422, 406/466-5341, www.fs.usda.gov/lcnf.

17 BENCHMARK ROAD PRIMITIVE

Scenic rating: 7

on the Benchmark Road in Lewis and Clark National Forest

At 5,600 feet, the Benchmark Road parallels Ford and Wood Creeks, two Rocky Mountain Front trout streams. Dispersed primitive campsites flank both sides of the road, some on the creeks and others in pine forest settings on the opposite side of the road. A few are open and visible from the road. Located on dirt spurs, some are marked with numbered tent icon signs; others are unmarked. Scout the roads first before driving in blind—especially if you are pulling a small trailer or driving an RV. Not all of the sites have turnaround room. Trailheads depart from the end of Benchmark Road.

The primitive campsites are attractive for their solitude and privacy broken only by the sounds of nature. Some are forested while others sit in partly sunny aspen groves. Follow Leave No Trace principles when camping at these dispersed sites, using only pre-existing fire rings and driving only on jeep trails.

Campsites, facilities: The Benchmark Road has 13 dispersed campsites for small RVs or tents. Facilities include rock fire rings. No drinking water is available. Bring your own, or treat creek water. Pack out your trash. Leashed pets are permitted.

Reservations, fees: No reservations are accepted. Camping is free. Open May-November.

Directions: From Augusta, follow County Road 435 for 0.3 mile to the Nilan Reservoir sign. Turn right onto Eberl Street. Follow the road as it swings south and then west again, where the road turns to gravel becoming Forest Road 235. Drive 14.2 miles to an intersection and turn left onto the Benchmark Road. Find dispersed campsites on both sides of the road between MP 4.5 and the Benchmark airstrip.

Contact: Lewis and Clark National Forest, Rocky Mountain Ranger District, 1102 N. Main Ave., Choteau, MT 59422, 406/466-5341, www.fs.usda.gov/lcnf.

18 DOUBLE FALLS

🏃 🛶 🐎 🚐 ⛺

Scenic rating: 7

on Wood Creek in Lewis and Clark National Forest

At 5,500 feet near the confluence of Wood and Ford Creeks, Double Falls Campground sits on the road to Benchmark—one of the most popular entrances to the Scapegoat and Bob Marshall Wildernesses. It is named for the falls just east of the campground. A 0.1-mile trail follows the north side of the creek to the falls. The campground is also the trailhead for Petty Ford Creek Trail (#244). With views of Crown and Steamboat Mountains, the 3.5-mile trail climbs out of Ford Creek and drops to Petty Creek. Ford Creek harbors brook trout.

This small, primitive campground is reached via a steep, narrow, rocky dirt road. The road can be muddy in wet weather. While high-clearance vehicles are not mandatory, they will manage the rocks better. Both campsites sit right on the river, hence the campground's appeal despite its primitive status. One campsite is open with views across the meadow (full of pink sticky geraniums in July) and of the mountainsides. The other campsite on the east end tucks behind tall firs for more privacy. Both have large, flat spaces for tents and rough dirt parking pads.

Campsites, facilities: The campground has two RV or tent campsites that can accommodate small RVs and trailers. Facilities include picnic tables, fire rings with grills, and a vault toilet. No drinking water is available. Bring your own, or treat creek water. Pack out your trash. Leashed pets are permitted.

Reservations, fees: No reservations are accepted. Camping is free. Open May-November.

Directions: From Augusta, follow County Road 435 for 0.3 mile to the Fishing Access for Nilan Reservoir sign. Turn right onto Eberl Street. Follow the road as it swings south and then west again, where the road turns to gravel, becoming Forest Road 235. Drive 14.2 miles to an intersection and turn left onto the Benchmark Road. Continue on 4.5 miles to the campground entrance on the left.

GPS Coordinates: N 47° 24.443' W 112° 43.329'

Contact: Lewis and Clark National Forest, Rocky Mountain Ranger District, 1102 N.

Main Ave., Choteau, MT 59422, 406/466-5341, www.fs.usda.gov/lcnf.

19 NILAN RESERVOIR

Scenic rating: 9

west of Augusta

At 4,440 feet, west of Augusta on the road to Benchmark, Nilan Reservoir is one of the most scenic of the Rocky Mountain Front reservoirs because of its surrounding prairie and the looming peaks. The 520-acre reservoir offers boating for motorized craft as well as canoes and kayaks. For anglers, the reservoir houses rainbow and brown trout. It is also a popular ice-fishing location in winter. Bird-watchers can see a variety of birds, from raptors to American pelicans.

The campground sprawls along the south shore of Nilan Reservoir, with open gravel, rock, and dry grass campsites in pairs. The lack of trees makes them sunny and affords outstanding views of the Rocky Mountain Front peaks, but winds whip right through them. Mornings tend to be calm, with the water often reflecting the peaks, but breezes pick up in the afternoon. Sites 1-6, which are large gravel pull-throughs, have the best views but get dusted by passing vehicles because of the road; sites 7 and 8 sit adjacent to the dusty road away from the water on the boat ramp spur. Sites 3 and 4 each have their own small jetty; site 2 has a small windbreak from cottonwood trees. Given the rough road access, the state does not recommend the campground for trailers or RVs, but plenty of people drive in with both.

Campsites, facilities: The campground has eight RV or tent campsites that can accommodate midsized RVs. Facilities include picnic tables, fire rings with grills, vault toilets, and a boat ramp. No drinking water is available. Bring your own, or treat reservoir water. Pack out your trash. Leashed pets are permitted.

Reservations, fees: No reservations are accepted. Camping costs $7 if you have a Montana fishing license or $12 without. Cash or check. Open year-round.

Directions: From Augusta, follow County Road 435 for 0.3 mile to Fishing Access for Nilan Reservoir sign. Turn right onto Eberl Street. Follow the road as it swings south and then west again, where the road turns to gravel, becoming Forest Road 235. Drive seven miles to the campground. Sites are on the right side of the road over the next 0.3 mile.

GPS Coordinates: N 47° 28.387' W 112° 31.074'

Contact: Montana Fish, Wildlife, and Parks, Region 4 Office, 4600 Giant Springs Rd., Great Falls, MT 59405, 406/454-5840, http://fwp.mt.gov.

20 DICK'S RV PARK

Scenic rating: 5

in Great Falls

At 3,505 feet, Dick's RV Park is convenient for exploring the C.M. Russell Museum, which celebrates the work of the famous western artist, and the Lewis and Clark Interpretive Center, with displays about the Corps of Discovery, as well as hiking trails and bicycling paths. Although the campground sits along the Sun River, the confluence of the Sun River with the Missouri River is less than a five-minute drive away. The campground is also a five-minute drive from two golf courses and fishing, boating, and floating on the Missouri River, along with hiking and biking trails at Giant Springs State Park, one of the largest freshwater springs in the country. First People's Buffalo Jump State Park containing one of the largest bison cliff jump archeological sites, interpretive trails, and a new visitors center sits 10 miles west.

The older campground squeezes between the Sun River and a four-lane freeway with

© BECKY LOMAX

Chilly, clear water bubbles up at Giant Springs State Park in Great Falls.

trucking traffic, and it picks up noise from the nearby railroad. Both pull-through and back-in sites are available, with small plots of grass between sites. Sites cram close together with no privacy. The sunny campground has only a few trees. Some long-term residents live here.

Campsites, facilities: The campground has 141 RV sites that can fit large RVs, 20 tent campsites, and 30 unserviced overflow sites. Hookups include water, sewer, electricity, and cable TV. Facilities include picnic tables, flush toilets, showers, launderette, drinking water, store, wireless Internet, cable TV, dog walk, propane, and recreation hall. Leashed pets are permitted.

Reservations, fees: Reservations are accepted. Hookups cost $26-41. Tent sites cost $22. Rates are for two people; each extra person is charged $5. Cash, check, or credit card. Open year-round.

Directions: From I-15 at Great Falls, take Exit 278 (10th Avenue S.) onto Highway 87/89/200 heading east. Take Exit 0, turning north onto 14th Street. Turn right at 13th Avenue SW

and drive two blocks, going under the railroad bridge, to the campground entrance on the right.

GPS Coordinates: N 47° 29.459' W 111° 19.981'

Contact: Dick's RV Park, 1403 11th St. SW, Great Falls, MT 59404, 406/452-0333, www. dicksrvpark.com.

21 GREAT FALLS KOA

Scenic rating: 5

in Great Falls

At 3,505 feet, the Great Falls KOA is convenient for exploring three of the town's main attractions: the C.M. Russell Museum Complex, the Lewis and Clark Interpretive Center, and Giant Springs State Park, home to one of the largest freshwater springs in the country. Great Falls also boasts the River's Edge Trail system, miles of walking and bicycle trails that run along both sides of the Missouri River. Great Falls also has three golf courses and fishing, boating, and floating on the Missouri River. Outside Ulm, First People's Buffalo Jump State Park containing one of the largest bison cliff jump archeological sites, interpretive trails, and a new visitors center sits about 10 miles west of town.

This manicured grassy campground provides partial shade from the cottonwood trees, and some of the sites have privacy from bushes. Sites include full hookups, partial hookups, dry camping, and tent villages with partial shade and fenced grass. The quiet location on the edge of town still picks up a little noise from commercial trucks on the highway. Shower facilities include family rooms, and a covered outdoor kitchen is available. Mornings start with an all-you-can-eat pancake breakfast with chokecherry syrup. On summer evenings, entertainment includes live bluegrass music and cowpoke poetry.

Campsites, facilities: The campground has

120 RV and tent campsites that can fit RVs up to 60 feet. Hookups include water, sewer, and electricity up to 50 amps. The tent village includes hookups for water and electricity. Facilities include picnic tables, pedestal grills, flush toilets, showers, launderette, drinking water, playground, swimming pool (late May-early September), water slides, water park, hot tub, game room, movie nights, catering, basketball and volleyball courts, dog walk, bike rentals, wireless Internet, cable TV, café, camp store, firewood, propane, and dump station. Leashed pets are permitted.

Reservations, fees: Reservations are accepted. Hookups cost $53-63. Tent sites cost $36-54. Rates cover two people. Add on $8-10 for each extra person. Children five years old and under stay free. Six people maximum are permitted per campsite. Cash, check, or credit card. Open year-round.

Directions: From I-15 in Great Falls, take Exit 278 and drive five miles east on Highway 87/89/200 (also called 10th Ave. S.) to the east edge of the city. Turn south onto 51st Street South and drive 0.3 mile to the campground entrance on the corner.

GPS Coordinates: N 47° 29.269' W 111° 13.304'

Contact: Great Falls KOA, 1500 51st St. S, Great Falls, MT 59405, 406/727-3191 or 800/562-6584, www.greatfallskoa.com.

22 PREWETT CREEK

Scenic rating: 8
on the Missouri River in the Big Belt Mountains

On the Missouri River at 3,430 feet in a dramatic canyon cut through the Big Belt Mountains, Prewett Creek RV offers campsites on its complex that includes a restaurant, casino, and a full-service fly shop. Guide services are available through the shop, and boaters can also use their river shuttle services. A rustic state-run fishing access site with a gravel ramp

sits across the road for launching drift boats, rafts, and kayaks to float the Missouri River. Anglers go after a variety of game fish: black crappie, brown trout, burbot, channel catfish, northern pike, paddlefish, rainbow trout, shovelnose sturgeon, and smallmouth bass. About 1.5 mile north, Tower Rock State Park features a 424-foot-high rock formation that served as a landmark for Native Americans, Lewis and Clark, and early fur trappers. A trail climbs to the saddle, but most of it is not maintained.

Sunny back-in sites make up this campground set behind the restaurant and inn. The complex is located across the old highway from the river rather than occupying river frontage. Views from the campground take in the surrounding arid canyon with rock outcroppings.

Campsites, facilities: The campground has 19 RV campsites, but they also will accept tenters, too. RVs are limited to 45 feet. Hookups are available for sewer, water, and electricity up to 50 amps. Facilities include barbecue pavilion with picnic tables, flush toilets, showers,

A path tours tipis and a historic Native American site at First Peoples Buffalo Jump State Park.

launderette, boat trailer parking, and dog kennel. Leashed pets are permitted.

Reservations, fees: Reservations are accepted. Campsites costs $35. Cash or check. Open April-October.

Directions: From I-15 between Helena and Great Falls, take Exit 247 at Hardy Creek. Drive 1.6-mile south on Old Highway 91 and turn right into the complex.

GPS Coordinates: N 47° 10.334' W 111° 49.504'

Contact: Prewett Creek RV Park, 2474 Old Highway 91, Cascade, MT 59421, 406/468-9244, http://prewettcreekrv.com.

accepted. Camping costs $7 if you have a Montana fishing license or $12 without. Cash or check. Open year round, but call as sometimes seasonal restrictions limit access.

Directions: From I-15 between Helena and Great Falls, take Exit 240 at Dearborn. Drive 0.5-mile south on Bald Eagle Drive and turn left onto Golden Eagle Drive. Turn right at the T and drive 0.3 miles to the fishing access site. GPS Coordinates: N 47° 7.480' W 111° 53.075'

Contact: Montana Fish, Wildlife, and Parks, Region 4 Office, 4600 Giant Springs Rd., Great Falls, MT 59405, 406/454-5840, http://fwp.mt.gov.

23 MID CANON

Scenic rating: 7
on the Missouri River in the Big Belt Mountains

On the Missouri River, Mid Canon is a fishing access site located at 3,425 feet in the Big Belt Mountains. The fishing and boating access launches drift boats, rafts, and kayaks onto the Missouri River at Mile 2,187 to float through the spectacular canyon cut through the Big Belts. A gravel boat ramp and trailer parking aids launching onto the river. Anglers go after a variety of game fish: black crappie, brown trout, burbot, channel catfish, northern pike, paddlefish, rainbow trout, shovelnose sturgeon, and smallmouth bass.

The nine-acre campground spread grassy sites around the fringes of the gravel fishing access. When drivers come through, they can kick up dust. Choose between sites in full sun or shaded by cottonwoods or willows.

Campsites, facilities: The campground has six RV or tent campsites. Midsized RVs are okay. Facilities include picnic tables, fire rings with grills, vault toilets, and a boat ramp. No drinking water is available; bring your own. Pack out your trash. Leashed pets are permitted.

Reservations, fees: No reservations are

24 CRAIG

Scenic rating: 7
on the Missouri River in the Big Belt Mountains

On the Missouri River, Craig is a small fishing access site located at 3,451 feet adjacent to the Big Belt Mountains. The popular fishing and boating access launches drift boats, rafts, and kayaks onto the Missouri River at Mile 2,194 to float through the spectacular canyon cut through the Big Belts. A cement boat ramp and trailer parking aids launching onto the river. The river is tame enough for inner tube floating to the next river access four miles downstream. Anglers go after a variety of game fish: black crappie, brown trout, burbot, channel catfish, northern pike, paddlefish, rainbow trout, shovelnose sturgeon, and smallmouth bass.

On the riverfront in the town of Craig, the three-acre campground has one paved loop with paved parking spurs. Five back-in sites sidle up to the river while two pull-through sites sit on the back side of the loop. Three of the river sites have large shade trees while the other campsites sit in open sun.

Campsites, facilities: The campground has seven RV or tent campsites. Larger RVs can fit in the pull-through sites. Facilities include picnic tables, fire rings with grills, vault toilets, and a boat ramp. No drinking water is available; bring your own. Pack out your trash. Leashed pets are permitted.

Reservations, fees: No reservations are accepted. Camping costs $7 if you have a Montana fishing license or $12 without. Cash or check. Open May-October.

Directions: From I-15 between Helena and Great Falls, take Exit 234 at Craig. Follow Bridge Street for about three blocks toward the river, but before crossing the bridge, turn right into the fishing access site and campground. GPS Coordinates: N 47° 4.394' W 111° 57.784'

Contact: Montana Fish, Wildlife, and Parks, Region 4 Office, 4600 Giant Springs Rd., Great Falls, MT 59405, 406/454-5840, http://fwp.mt.gov.

25 WOLF BRIDGE

Scenic rating: 4
on the Missouri River north of Helena

On the Missouri River north of Holter Dam, Wolf Bridge, at 3,500 feet, is a popular fishing and boating access, but not a prime camping location. You can launch upriver at Holter Dam Campground and float two miles back to the camp, or you can float from Wolf Bridge eight miles north to Craig. Anglers go after a variety of game fish: black crappie, brown trout, burbot, channel catfish, northern pike, paddlefish, rainbow trout, shovelnose sturgeon, and smallmouth bass.

Squeezed up against the road and bridge, the campground is really a strip of dry grass along the edge of a large gravel parking lot and boat launch—a fishing access site run by the state. It's a place to camp for convenience rather than ambiance. Two of the sites have flat spaces for tents. The campground has no trees for shade or to block wind. The area does have a bench along the river for watching the passing boats. Campsite 1 is the closest to the

river. Individual parking pads do not exist; just pull up next to a picnic table.

Campsites, facilities: The campground has five RV or tent campsites; however, small RVs fit better with the parking situation. Facilities include picnic tables, fire rings with grills, vault toilets (wheelchair-accessible), and a boat ramp. No drinking water is available. Bring your own, or treat river water. Pack out your trash. Leashed pets are permitted.

Reservations, fees: No reservations are accepted. Camping costs $7 if you have a Montana fishing license or $12 without. Cash or check. Open year-round.

Directions: From I-15 north of Helena, take Exit 226 at Wolf Creek. From Wolf Creek on the south side of the freeway, drive Recreation Road for 3.3 miles and turn left after crossing the bridge over the Missouri River. GPS Coordinates: N 47° 1.198' W 112° 0.612'

Contact: Montana Fish, Wildlife, and Parks, Region 4 Office, 4600 Giant Springs Rd., Great Falls, MT 59405, 406/454-5840, http://fwp.mt.gov.

26 HOLTER DAM

Scenic rating: 6
on the Missouri River north of Helena

Below Holter Dam on the west bank of the Missouri River, at 3,550 feet, Holter Dam Campground drones with the constant noise of the dam, and views are of the dam as well as the surrounding arid mountain slopes. Yet it attracts many anglers, who fish from shore or hop on rafts or drift boats to float the Missouri River for its game fish. During high water, the dam may need to release water; a siren and lights alert those in the river channel to move up into the campground.

The campground is in two parts, adjacent to the gravel boat launch area. The first part (sites 1-11) centers around a large gravel parking lot with picnic tables with shade covers. Sites 1 and 11 sit on the water, but the remainder line up on the grass on the opposite side of the parking lot from the river. Only a couple of large willow trees provide shade. Sites 13-17 line up with double-wide back-in gravel parking pads and no covers on the tables. Neither of the sections affords privacy given the lack of trees and close quarters.

Campsites, facilities: There are 33 RV or tent campsites that can accommodate midsized RVs. Facilities include picnic tables, fire rings with grills, vault toilets, drinking water, boat launch, boat trailer parking, dock, garbage service, firewood for sale, and a campground manager on site. Leashed pets are permitted. Site 7 and toilets are wheelchair-accessible.

Reservations, fees: No reservations are accepted. Campsites cost $6 per unit (RV, trailer, or tent). Cash or check. Open early May-October.

Directions: From I-15 north of Helena, take Exit 226 at Wolf Creek. From Wolf Creek on the south side of the freeway, drive Recreation Road for 3.3 miles and turn right just before the bridge over the Missouri River. Drive two miles. The road has large washboards and potholes that make driving the two miles a challenge.

GPS Coordinates: N 46° 59.705' W 112° 00.682'

Contact: Bureau of Land Management, Butte Field Office, 106 N. Parkmont, Butte, MT 59702, 406/533-7600, www.blm.gov/mt/st/en.html.

27 HOLTER LAKE

🏊 🎣 🛶 🚤 🐎 ♿ 🚐 ⛺

Scenic rating: 8

on Holter Lake on the Missouri River

Located at 3,600 feet on the east shore of Holter Lake north of Helena, this campground sits on the Missouri River in a lake created by Holter Dam. From the campground, you can boat south into Gates of the Mountains

Wilderness for sightseeing along the route that Lewis and Clark traveled. The lake is popular for waterskiing, kayaking, canoeing, and game fishing and accessed via a paved multilane boat launch with boat trailer parking, docks, boat slips, and fish-cleaning stations. A marina with boat rentals and gas sits 0.5 mile south on Beartooth Road.

Sitting on a bluff above the lake, the campground appears as a green, mowed-lawn oasis amid the surrounding dry grassland and pine hills. Two interconnected paved loops waltz through the cramped, crowded open campground, which has no privacy between sites. Only a few short cottonwoods offer shade for hot days, causing most campers to cower in the cool shadow of their trailer or RV. Paved walkways connect the campground to the beach, boat launch, and fishing jetty. Sites 3, 5, 6, 7, 8, 10, 12, 13, 15, and 18 overlook the lake. A separate walk-in tent area is available.

Campsites, facilities: There are 33 RV or tent campsites, plus an additional open walk-in tenting area without assigned sites. The gravel parking pads can accommodate midsized RVs. Facilities include picnic tables, fire rings with grills, vault toilets, drinking water, garbage service, swimming area, and campground manager on-site. Leashed pets are permitted. Toilets are wheelchair-accessible.

Reservations, fees: No reservations are accepted. Campsites cost $10 per unit (RV, trailer, or tent). Cash or check. Open early May-October.

Directions: From I-15 north of Helena, take Exit 226 at Wolf Creek. From Wolf Creek on the south side of the freeway, drive Recreation Road for 3.3 miles until you cross the Missouri River on a bridge; turn right onto paved Beartooth Road for 2.3 miles to the campground on the right.

GPS Coordinates: N 46° 59.640' W 111° 59.436'

Contact: Bureau of Land Management, Butte Field Office, 106 N. Parkmont, Butte, MT 59702, 406/533-7600, www.blm.gov/mt/st/en.html.

28 LOG GULCH

Scenic rating: 9
on Holter Lake on the Missouri River

Log Gulch, at 3,600 feet on the east shore of Holter Lake (a reservoir on the Missouri River), provides access for fishing and a sandy swimming beach. You can launch for boating up the Oxbow to Gates of the Mountains Wilderness. Once at the Gates, you can hike one hour into Mann Gulch, a National Historic Landmark that marks the site of a tragic wildfire in 1949 that killed 13 firefighters. Crosses up the steep hillside mark where each firefighter died. A paved multilane boat launch includes boat trailer parking, docks, boat slips, and fish-cleaning stations.

The campground flanks a hillside with three different options for camping—none with privacy. The main campground circles in several paved loops upslope in the gulch. A few of these lawn campsites have pull-through gravel parking pads, a cottonwood or pine tree for partial shade, and views of the lake (from the sites at the top of the loop). A second area—Little Log—climbs a steep hill with staggered terraced campsites, some with peek-a-boo views of the lake. A third area—a large, flat, treeless, gravel parking lot for RVs to back into—offers prime views of spiny Sleeping Giant Mountain and the lake. Watch for rattlesnakes around the campground.

Campsites, facilities: There are 70 RV or tent campsites; some can accommodate the largest RVs. Facilities include picnic tables, fire rings with grills, vault toilets, drinking water, garbage service, swimming area, and campground manager on-site. Leashed pets are permitted. Toilets are wheelchair-accessible.

Reservations, fees: No reservations are accepted. Campsites cost $10 per unit (RV, trailer, or tent). Cash or check. Open early May-October.

Directions: From I-15 north of Helena, take Exit 226 at Wolf Creek. From Wolf Creek on the south side of the freeway, drive Recreation Road for 3.3 miles until you cross the bridge over the Missouri River; turn right onto Beartooth Road for 6.5 miles. After passing Holter Lake campground, the paved road turns to bumpy oiled dirt and narrows with sharp, blind corners, but pavement resumes just before the campground.

GPS Coordinates: N 46° 57.683' W 111° 56.601'

Contact: Bureau of Land Management, Butte Field Office, 106 N. Parkmont, Butte, MT 59702, 406/533-7600, www.blm.gov/mt/st/en.html.

29 DEPARTURE POINT

Scenic rating: 8
on Holter Lake on the Missouri River

BEST (

At 3,600 feet on Holter Lake's east shore, Departure Point is a tiny campground one bay south of Log Gulch. A narrow paved road connects it with the larger campground, but be prepared for its sharp, blind corners. The campground is as far as you can drive along the shoreline of Holter Lake's east side, and it sits at the northern entrance to the Beartooth Wildlife Management Area, where you can see elk, deer, bighorn sheep, and a variety of raptors and birds. Go for wildlife drives either in early morning or evening when sightings are usually best. A double boat launch with a dock and boat slips offers the last place to start boating up the lake. Canoes and kayaks can reach the Oxbow. Another beach and picnic area sits 0.3 mile south on the Beartooth Road.

With only a handful of trees for shade, the expanded campground loops through the gulch above the day-use area and beach with one loop on the lower south end of the beach. Rattlesnakes are in the area; caution is advised. Paved loops access gravel parking pads, a few of which are pull-throughs.

Campsites, facilities: The campground has

57 RV or tent campsites. RVs are limited to midsized. Facilities include picnic tables, fire rings with grills, vault toilets, drinking water, garbage service, and a buoyed swimming area. Leashed pets are permitted. Toilets are wheelchair-accessible.

Reservations, fees: No reservations are accepted. Campsites cost $10 per unit (RV, trailer, or tent). Cash or check. Open early May-October.

Directions: From I-15 north of Helena, take Exit 226 at Wolf Creek. From Wolf Creek on the south side of the freeway, drive Recreation Road for 3.3 miles until you cross the bridge over the Missouri River; turn right onto paved Beartooth Road for seven miles. The paved surface will change to a rough, oiled dirt road about a lane and a half wide for a couple of miles. Drive slowly—it is narrow with blind corners. GPS Coordinates: N 46°57.391' W 111° 56.418'

Contact: Bureau of Land Management, Butte Field Office, 106 N. Parkmont, Butte, MT 59702, 406/533-7600, www.blm.gov/mt/st/en.html.

30 PRICKLY PEAR RIVER

Scenic rating: 6
on the Prickly Pear River north of Helena

On the Prickly Pear River, a tributary of the Missouri River, three state-run fishing access campsites dot this stream, which attracts anglers with its brown and rainbow trout. At 3,760 feet, the camps snuggle into Prickly Pear Canyon—a dramatic geological slice through layered pink rock. The campsites are divided into two locations—the Lichen Cliff on the north and Prickly Pear to the south.

Despite the side road locations, both primitive campgrounds fill with noise from the paralleling I-15 and railroad tracks. The Prickly Pear campsite sits 20 feet from the tracks. The two Lichen Cliff campsites are pull-overs off the road located right on the stream. The Prickly Pear campsite, tucked down a short spur, offers a better tent area secluded from the road, but you must walk across the railroad tracks to several two-minute trails to reach the creek.

Campsites, facilities: The campgrounds have three RV or tent campsites. Lichen Cliff can accommodate larger RVs, but the Prickly Pear spot is suitable only for smaller RVs or trailers with minimal turnaround space. The state does not recommend trailers or RVs. Facilities include picnic tables, fire rings with grills, and vault toilets. No drinking water is available. Bring your own, or treat river water. Pack out your trash. Leashed pets are permitted.

Reservations, fees: No reservations are accepted. Camping costs $7 if you have a Montana fishing license or $12 without. Cash or check. Open year-round.

Directions: From I-15 north of Helena, take Exit 226 at Wolf Creek and drive south on Recreation Road, or take Exit 219 and drive north on Spring Creek Road. The milepost numbering starts at the south and begins renumbering again at Lyons Creek Road around milepost 3. Find Prickly Pear at milepost 0.8 between Exit 219 and Lyons Creek Road. Find Lichen Cliff at milepost 1.6 between Lyons Creek Road and Wolf Creek.

GPS coordinates for Lichen Cliff: N 46° 56.316' W 112° 7.300'

GPS coordinates for Prickly Pear: N 46° 55.004' W 112° 7.371'

Contact: Montana Fish, Wildlife, and Parks, Region 4 Office, 4600 Giant Springs Rd., Great Falls, MT 59405, 406/454-5840, http://fwp.mt.gov.

31 BEARTOOTH LANDING

Scenic rating: 8
on Holter Lake on the Missouri River

On west shore of the Missouri River on Holter Lake, at 3,600 feet, Beartooth Landing is a small boat-in only campground below the Sleeping Giant. It sits just downstream from the 2,225-mile mark on the Missouri, across from Ming Bar, which has shallow water over a sandy swimming basin. Boating from the north requires navigating 10.2 river miles through the convoluted Oxbow from Log Gulch, roughly double the air miles. You can also boat in 6.8 miles from the south through the steep-walled canyon of Gate of the Mountains. The campground sits 1.8 miles upstream from Mann Gulch National Historic Site and the north entrance to Gates of the Mountains and across the river from the Beartooth Wildlife Management Area, with pronghorns, deer, elk, bighorn sheep, raptors, and songbirds.

The tiny, north-facing, partially shaded campsites sit along the shore, with views of Beartooth Mountain. A dock is available. During the day, the area bustles with motorboats—water-skiers, sightseers, and anglers—but in the evening, quiet pervades the river. Rattlesnakes are in the area; caution is advised.

Campsites, facilities: The campground has four tent sites. Facilities include picnic tables, fire rings, and a vault toilet. No drinking water is available. Pack out your trash. Leashed pets are permitted.

Reservations, fees: No reservations are accepted. Camping is free. Open early May-October.

Directions: To launch from the north on Holter Lake, drive I-15 north of Helena to Exit 226 at Wolf Creek. From Wolf Creek on the south side of the freeway, drive Recreation Road for 3.3 miles until you cross the bridge over the Missouri River; turn right onto Beartooth Road for 6.5 miles. The paved road turns to bumpy oiled dirt and narrows with sharp, blind corners, but pavement resumes just before the Log Gulch Campground, where you can launch a boat. Kayaks and canoes can also launch 0.6 mile farther south at Departure Point Recreation Area. To launch from the south, drive 20 miles north of Helena on I-15 to Exit 209 and then east on Gates of the

Mountains Road for 2.7 miles to Gates of the Mountains Marina.

GPS Coordinates: N 46° 53.121' W 111° 56.484'

Contact: Bureau of Land Management, Butte Field Office, 106 N. Parkmont, Butte, MT 59702, 406/533-7600, www.blm.gov/mt/st/en.html.

32 COULTER

Scenic rating: 10

in Gates of the Mountains in Helena National Forest

BEST (

Located on the Missouri River at 3,610 feet, Coulter is a boat-in only campground in the Gates of the Mountains, a steep-walled narrow gorge named by Lewis and Clark. The campground sits about midway through the canyon on the east shore. You can launch from Gates of the Mountains Marina ($5 for boats from

© BECKY LOMAX

Coulter Campground is only accessible by boat.

trailers; $3 for kayaks and canoes) and motor or paddle 3.3 miles downstream. Be prepared for winds. The campground sits about 1.5 miles south of the entrance to Mann Gulch, a National Historic Landmark honoring 13 firefighters who lost their lives in 1949 (their crosses still stand on the hillside), and 0.8 mile south of the Meriwether picnic area, which has trails, interpretive displays, and a boat dock. Trails also go upstream from the campground to several overlooks. Watch for ospreys and bald eagles fishing for trout.

The campground sits on a grassy hillside with campsites in the open sun or tucked back in more secluded pines and junipers that offer partial shade. After the day boaters and the tour boat disappear, a quiet descends on the canyon.

Campsites, facilities: The campground has seven tent sites. Facilities include picnic tables, fire rings, vault toilet, and boat docks. Pack out your trash. Leashed pets are permitted.

Reservations, fees: No reservations are accepted. Camping is free. Open late May-September.

Directions: To launch boats from the south, drive 20 miles north of Helena on I-15 to Exit 209 and then east on Gates of the Mountains Road for 2.7 miles to Gates of the Mountains Marina to launch boats.

GPS Coordinates: N 46° 51.568' W 111° 54.482'

Contact: Helena National Forest, Helena Ranger District, 2001 Poplar, Helena, MT 59601, 406/449-5490, www.fs.usda.gov/helena.

33 BLACK SANDY

Scenic rating: 8
on Hauser Lake on the Missouri River

On the west side of Hauser Lake, south of Hauser Dam at 3,835 feet, the popular 43-acre campground, which sits just north of White Sandy Campground, has the benefit of both a lake and canyon scenery as the walls rise straight from the water. Hauser Lake is a reservoir on the Missouri River, and the campground sits on the Lewis and Clark Trail. A hiking trail leads one mile along the lake, which is popular for water-skiing, swimming, boating, paddling, and fishing for kokanee salmon, trout, and other game fish.

Most of the campsites cram along the river frontage with no privacy and nearly on top of each other. Picnic tables sit on cement pads surrounded by grass. The campground bakes on hot days; only one-third of the sites have willows to offer some shade, but the sun drops behind the canyon walls early to begin cooling off the campground for evening. Dry, dusty, and lacking trees, three of the walk-in tent sites have river frontage; the other two overlook the lake from a flat bench.

Campsites, facilities: The campground has 29 RV sites with electricity, five walk-in tent sites, and 16 boat slips. Parking pads can accommodate trailers up to 35 feet. Facilities include picnic tables, fire rings with grills, vault and flush toilets, boat ramp, dock, boat slips, drinking water, garbage service, dump station, campfire programs, and campground host. Leashed pets are permitted. Wheelchair-accessible facilities include toilets and two campsites.

Reservations, fees: Reservations are highly recommended online or by phone (855/922-6788). Reservations are accepted online or by phone (855-922-6768). Campsites cost $15 for Montana residents (seniors and disabled get half price) and $23 for nonresidents Memorial Weekend-Labor Day, or $12 for Montana residents and $20 for nonresidents September-May. Campsites with electrical hookups cost $17-28, depending on season and residency. Nonresidents with a Non-Resident Entrance Pass ($25) get a $5 discount on camping fees. Cash, check, or credit card. Open year-round.

Directions: From I-15 north of Helena, take Exit 200 and drive west on Lincoln Road for

5.1 miles. Turn left at the signed junction onto Hauser Dam Road for three miles, which turns to a wide gravel boulevard. At the fork where the pavement resumes, swing left, following the sign to Black Sandy State Park. The campground entrance sits on the right after the dump station and sign.

GPS Coordinates: N 46° 44.733' W 111° 53.199'

Contact: Montana Fish, Wildlife, and Parks, Region 4 Office, 4600 Giant Springs Rd., Great Falls, MT 59405, 406/454-5840, http://stateparks.mt.gov.

34 WHITE SANDY

Scenic rating: 8

on Hauser Lake on the Missouri River

Located on the west side of Hauser Lake south of Hauser Dam, the campground sits at 3,835 feet adjacent to Black Sandy Campground. Hauser Lake is on the Missouri River where it narrows into a canyon with steep cliff walls. The campground sits on the Lewis and Clark Trail. Hauser Lake is popular for fishing, swimming, boating, paddling, and waterskiing. The lake houses kokanee salmon, walleye, yellow perch, mountain whitefish, and several species of trout.

White Sandy opened in 2007. As such, its trees are small, affording little shade or windbreak yet. The sites, however, are bigger and more spacious than in the adjacent Black Sandy, gaining more privacy by distance, even though you can see the neighbors. The grassy campground has two separate areas for campsites. The upper spur has five sites that back in against a hill with a turnaround loop at the end; these have views of the lower bluff and lake. The lower bluff area is more popular for its 14 lakefront sites. Most of the gravel back-in parking pads are double-wide.

Campsites, facilities: The campground has 34 RV or tent campsites that can accommodate larger RVs. Facilities include picnic tables, fire rings with grills, vault toilets, concrete boat ramp, dock, fish-cleaning station, drinking water, garbage service, firewood for sale, and campground hosts. Leashed pets are permitted. Site 14 and toilets are wheelchair-accessible.

Reservations, fees: No reservations are accepted. Camping costs $10. Cash or check. Open mid-May-September.

Directions: From I-15 north of Helena, take Exit 200 and drive west on Lincoln Road for 5.1 miles. Turn left at the signed junction onto Hauser Dam Road for three miles, which turns to a wide gravel boulevard in 0.2 mile. At the fork where the pavement resumes, swing right, following the sign to Black Sandy State Park. The road climbs over a bluff and drops. Veer right before the state park to reach the campground in 0.2 mile.

GPS Coordinates: N 46° 44.503' W 111° 53.251'

Contact: Bureau of Land Management, Butte Field Office, 106 N. Parkmont, Butte, MT 59702, 406/533-7600, www.blm.gov/mt/st/en.html.

35 DEVIL'S ELBOW

Scenic rating: 9

on Hauser Lake on the Missouri River

BEST (

At 3,700 feet on the west side of Hauser Lake on the Missouri River, the Devil's Elbow campground sits where the river makes a sharp oxbow around a peninsula before entering a steep-walled slot canyon. The campground sits on that peninsula about one mile north of the York Bridge, the access to the Gates of the Mountains Wilderness and Helena National Forest. The scenic drive through the narrow rocky canyon across the bridge is worth the time. The campground sits below the Two Camps Vista, which affords a dramatic view of the area as well as interpretive information on the Lewis and Clark expedition. Hiking trails connect to Clark's Bay picnic area and the vista. Hauser Lake is popular for swimming, boating, waterskiing, and fishing for kokanee salmon, trout, and other game fish.

The spacious, sunny campground has three grassy loops on a sagebrush bluff above the lake. Young trees scatter throughout the open camp's double-wide gravel parking pads. Some areas are fenced above steep cliffs. Sites are spread out to feel private, but you can see the neighbors. In loop A, sites 1, 3, 5, 6, and 7 overlook the water. In loop B, sites 18, 20, 21, 22, and 24 have water views. Loop C sits farther back from the edge of the bluffs, but with expansive views across the water to distant mountains.

Campsites, facilities: The campground has 42 RV or tent campsites that can accommodate larger RVs on their double-wide parking pads. Facilities include picnic tables, fire rings with grills, vault toilets, concrete boat ramp, docks, boat slips, boat trailer parking, a fish-cleaning station, drinking water, garbage service, firewood for sale, and campground hosts. Leashed pets are permitted. Toilets are wheelchair-accessible.

Reservations, fees: No reservations are accepted. Camping costs $10. Cash or check. Open mid-May-mid-October.

Directions: From I-15 in Helena, take Exit 193 to the east side of the freeway and go north on Washington Street for 0.8 mile. Turn east onto Canyon Ferry Road for 0.7 mile. Turn north onto York Road and drive 11.6 miles to the signed campground entrance on the right. Drop 0.5 mile down into the campground. GPS Coordinates: N 46° 42.021' W 111° 48.272'

Contact: Bureau of Land Management, Butte Field Office, 106 N. Parkmont, Butte, MT 59702, 406/533-7600, www.blm.gov/mt/st/en.html.

36 VIGILANTE

Scenic rating: 8

in the Big Belt Mountains of Helena National Forest

Tucked at 4,400 feet at the west end of the deep Trout Creek Canyon in the Big Belt Mountains, Vigilante Campground is the only designated campground for exploring this area of Helena National Forest. The Vigilante Trail (#247)—a National Recreation Trail—begins at the campground and climbs six miles into a hanging valley with an overlook into Trout Creek Canyon. The last 300-foot section requires climbing through steep crevasses in the rocks. The Trout Creek Canyon Trail (#270), which begins with a one-mile wheelchair-accessible paved section, traverses up the canyon for three miles, with clear views of its limestone walls. Shaded areas of the canyon stay cool in the heat of summer, and an interpretive brochure identifies features along the trail, including the original road, which was washed out in a 1981 flood. The canyon is also good for bird- and wildlife-watching.

The quiet, secluded campground snuggles at the bottom of a canyon, with choices of shady or sunny campsites. Some campsites have a forest duff floor; others are grassy. The campground is small, so you will see the neighbors, but enough undergrowth is present in places to make you feel private. Prepare for an onslaught of mosquitoes in early summer.

Campsites, facilities: The campground has 14 RV or tent campsites, including two double sites. RVs are limited to 16 feet. Facilities include picnic tables, fire rings, drinking water, and vault toilets (wheelchair-accessible). Pack out your trash. Leashed pets are permitted.

Reservations, fees: No reservations are accepted. Campsites cost $5 per unit (RV, trailer, or tent). Cash or check. Open late May-September.

Directions: From I-15 in Helena, take Exit 193 to the east side of the freeway and go north on

Washington Street for 0.8 mile. Turn east onto Canyon Ferry Road for 0.7 mile. Turn north onto York Road and drive 12.6 miles to the York Bridge. After crossing the bridge, drive 10 miles on the York-Trout Creek Road to the campground entrance on the right.
GPS Coordinates: N 46° 46.024' W 111° 39.030'
Contact: Helena National Forest, Helena Ranger District, 2001 Poplar, Helena, MT 59601, 406/449-5490, www.fs.usda.gov/helena.

37 CROMWELL DIXON

Scenic rating: 6
on MacDonald Pass in Helena National Forest

At 6,260 feet at the top of MacDonald Pass west of Helena, Cromwell Dixon Campground sits on the Continental Divide. Hikers can explore routes north or south on the nearby Continental Divide Trail. Bicyclists use the campground while doing long-distance rides. The campground is more one for convenience when traveling west from Helena rather than a destination in itself.

With the campground's proximity to Highway 12—a trucking route—noise pervades the area even at night. The paved campground road loops around a hillside of mature Douglas fir and lodgepole pines. Fireweed and cow parsnip meadows also flank the campground, offering a mix of choices for campsites. Open to the wind, grassy sites 6 and 8 have sunny expansive views across meadows; other sites tuck protected under big trees with a forest duff floor. Some sites include large, shapely granitic boulders that kids find fun for climbing. Most of the gravel parking pads are back-ins. Because of the hillside, only some of the sites have level tent spaces. The sites at the end of the loop are closer together than those that are further spaced out at the beginning of the loop.

Campsites, facilities: The campground has 15 RV or tent campsites. Some of the sites can fit midsized RVs, and site 9 offers a big pull-through. Facilities include picnic tables, fire rings, vault toilets (wheelchair-accessible), and drinking water. Pack out your trash. Leashed pets are permitted.
Reservations, fees: No reservations are accepted. Campsites cost $8 per unit (RV, trailer, or tent). Cash or check. Open late May-September.
Directions: From Helena, go 15 miles west on Highway 12. At milepost 27.8, turn south off the highway at the campground sign and immediately turn right over the cattle grate for 0.2 mile to the campground entrance.
GPS Coordinates: N 46° 33.455' W 112° 18.879'
Contact: Helena National Forest, Helena Ranger District, 2100 Poplar, Helena, MT 59601, 406/449-5490, www.fs.usda.gov/helena.

38 MOOSE CREEK

Scenic rating: 7
in the Boulder Mountains in Helena National Forest

At 4,870 feet, Moose Creek Campground sits just east of the Continental Divide. Hikers can climb the Switchback Ridge Trail #348 to the top of the Continental Divide in a heavily-timbered lower elevation north end of the Boulder Mountains. Tenmile Creek runs between the campground and Rimini Road, giving a place for anglers to fish for trout. Moose Creek also provides for fishing. Wildlife watchers may spot elk or deer.

A sunny location, the campground offers a place for solitude and quiet once nightfall comes. Sitting below a rocky slope, the campground is divided from the access road by the stream. Campsites spread out along a 0.3-mile gravel road with a turnaround at the end. All of the campsites have back-in gravel and dirt parking aprons.

Campsites, facilities: The campground has nine RV or tent campsites. Only small RVs are recommended. Facilities include picnic tables, fire rings, vault toilets (wheelchair-accessible), and drinking water. Pack out your trash. Leashed pets are permitted.

Reservations, fees: No reservations are accepted. Campsites cost $5 per unit (RV, trailer, or tent). Cash or check. Open late May-September.

Directions: From Helena, go about eight miles west on Highway 12 and turn south onto Rimini Road (Forest Road 695). Drive 3.9 miles south to the campground entrance on the right.

GPS Coordinates: N 46° 31.739' W 112° 15.207'

Contact: Helena National Forest, Helena Ranger District, 2100 Poplar, Helena, MT 59601, 406/449-5490, www.fs.usda.gov/helena.

39 PARK LAKE

Scenic rating: 7

in the Boulder Mountains in Helena National Forest

At 6,400 feet, Park Lake Campground tucks into the Boulder Mountains on the small 0.4-mile-long Park Lake, an idyllic pond for quiet water enjoyment. For anglers, the lake holds trout and arctic grayling. From a primitive boat ramp, you can launch small nonmotorized, hand-carried watercraft such as rowboats, canoes, and float tubes. Campers can cool off in the lake with a swim.

Even though the access requires dirt road driving, the campground road is paved with paved parking spurs. The single campground loop tours around the open flat bench, where the sunny campsites are spotted with only a couple trees and views include neighboring

campers. Small boulders in the campground provide fun places for kids to climb. Enjoy the quiet at this remote lake surrounded by dense lodgepole forest.

Campsites, facilities: The campground has 22 RV or tent campsites. RVs are limited to 20 feet. Facilities include picnic tables, fire rings, vault toilets (wheelchair-accessible), and drinking water from a hand pump. Pack out your trash. Leashed pets are permitted.

Reservations, fees: No reservations are accepted. Campsites cost $8 per unit (RV, trailer, or tent). Cash or check. Open late May-November.

Directions: From Helena, drive south on I-15 for eight miles to the Clancy exit (182). Drive the Lump Gulch Road eight miles west; then turn right onto Coral Gulch Road (Forest Road 4009) for six miles where the road dead-ends at the campground.

GPS Coordinates: N 46° 26.601' W 112° 10.111'

Contact: Helena National Forest, Helena Ranger District, 2100 Poplar, Helena, MT 59601, 406/449-5490, www.fs.usda.gov/helena.

40 RIVERSIDE

Scenic rating: 7

on the Missouri River below Canyon Ferry Dam

Most people who visit Riverside Campground, which sits at 3,700 feet, head onto the Missouri River. You can launch from here to float, motor, or paddle downstream as far as Hauser Dam 15 river miles north. Campers stay here rather than up on Canyon Ferry Reservoir because they prefer the feel of the slow-moving river to the lake. A primitive, dirt boat ramp and dock aid in launching small motorboats, rafts, drift boats, kayaks, and canoes. Boat trailer parking is available. A wheelchair-accessible fishing platform is also available.

Surrounded by dry sagebrush and juniper

hillsides, the wide-open, breezy, and sunny campground sits just below the Canyon Ferry Dam, which is visible and emits a constant audible drone. Four interconnected loops make up most of the campground, and the bulk of the campsites circle two of them. Sites 1-4, 6-9, and 20 have river frontage, with their picnic tables a few feet from the shoreline. The lack of trees equals no privacy, shade, or windbreaks, but the flat grassy sites afford plenty of room for setting up large tents. Site 21 sits off by itself overlooking the boat launch.

Campsites, facilities: The campground has 33 RV or tent campsites. Facilities include picnic tables (three are covered), fire rings with grills, vault toilets, garbage service, drinking water, boat ramp, and campground hosts. Leashed pets are permitted. Wheelchair-accessible facilities include toilets and four campsites.

Reservations, fees: No reservations are accepted. Campsites cost $15. Cash or check. Open May-September.

Directions: From I-15 in Helena, take Exit 193 to the east side of the freeway and go north on Washington Street for 0.8 mile. Turn east onto Canyon Ferry Road for 14.3 miles to the Canyon Ferry Dam. Cross the dam, driving 1.2 miles. Turn north onto Jimtown Road for one mile, veering left at both junctions, until you reach the campground entrance on the right. GPS Coordinates: N 46° 39.372' W 111° 44.107'

Contact: Bureau of Reclamation, Montana Area Office, Canyon Ferry Field Office, 7661 Canyon Ferry Rd., Helena, MT 59602, 406/475-3921, www.usbr.gov/gp/mtao/canyonferry/.

41 FISH HAWK

Scenic rating: 8

on the northwest shore of Canyon Ferry Reservoir

On bluffs at 3,850 feet, Fishhawk Campground is a treat for tent campers overlooking the 25-mile-long Canyon Ferry Reservoir loaded with water recreation. While Fish Hawk does not have lake access for boating, it does provide views of the intricate web of islands, peninsulas, and coves at the north end of the lake, and you can climb down to the rocky lakeshore to swim or fish. The campsites face the sunrise, with views of the Big Belt Mountains flanking the lake's east side.

The unnumbered walk-in campsites are divided by rocky outcrops and tall ponderosa pines that offer a bit of shade and privacy, but most of the campsites are quite sunny. Many campers bring tarps for shade as well as rain protection. Sagebrush and junipers also grow on the hillside, casting a scent into the air after rains. Each of the sites has flat spaces for tents, and some can fit more than one tent. Even from the vantage point of the bluffs, you can hear motorboats on the lake during the day, but the noise disappears at night. Bring binoculars for watching bald eagles and ospreys fishing. The gravel entry road is narrow and curves sharply around the loop that contains the parking areas. Bear in mind that you must hike uphill to the toilet from most of the campsites.

Campsites, facilities: The campground has six walk-in tent campsites. Facilities include picnic tables, fire rings with grills, and vault toilet. Bring your own water. Pack out your trash. Leashed pets are permitted. Wheelchair-accessible facilities include toilets and one campsite.

Reservations, fees: No reservations are accepted. Camping is free. Open year-round.

Directions: From I-15 in Helena, take Exit 193 to the east side of the freeway and go north on Washington Street for 0.8 mile. Turn east onto Canyon Ferry Road for 13.4 miles to West Shore Drive. Turn south and drive 0.5 mile on the narrow, paved, hilly single-lane road to the campground entrance on the left. GPS Coordinates: N 46° 37.992' W 111° 43.035'

Contact: Bureau of Reclamation, Montana

© BECKY LOMAX

Court Sheriff Campground offers waterfront camping and boating on Canyon Ferry Reservoir.

Area Office, Canyon Ferry Field Office, 7661 Canyon Ferry Rd., Helena, MT 59602, 406/475-3921, www.usbr.gov/gp/mtao/canyonferry/.

42 COURT SHERIFF

Scenic rating: 7

on the northeast shore of Canyon Ferry Reservoir

At 3,800 feet on the rugged north end of the 25-mile-long Canyon Ferry Reservoir, Court Sheriff is the closest campground to the Canyon Ferry Visitor Center, 0.7 mile to the west. The reservoir serves for all types of water recreation. While Court Sheriff doesn't have a boat ramp, it has plenty of easy-access shoreline for launching hand-carried watercraft. (You can launch larger boats at Chinamen's Gulch, 0.3 mile south, or at Kim's Marina about 0.5 mile south.) A few islands sit offshore, and

lagoons divide parts of the campground, giving the landscape a playful look. The islands also grant destinations for exploration. Much of the shoreline is muddy and willowy, but open areas are available for beaching boats. Anglers go after walleye, rainbow trout, brown trout, ling, and perch in the lake and ice fish in winter.

Almost half of the campsites have waterfront—on either the lake or one of the lagoons. The grassy, open, sunny campground affords little privacy or shade, but a few sites have large pines for partial shade. Large flat tent spaces are available, and several campsites have paved, double-wide, back-in parking to accommodate trailers. A few pull-through sites are also available. This is a busy end of the lake, humming with the noise of Jet skis and motorboats until the sun goes down. The campground faces the sunset.

Campsites, facilities: The campground has 47 RV or tent campsites that can accommodate midsized RVs. Facilities include picnic tables, fire rings with grills, vault toilets, drinking water, garbage service, boat trailer parking, and campground hosts. Leashed pets are permitted. Wheelchair-accessible facilities include toilets and three campsites.

Reservations, fees: No reservations are accepted. Campsites cost $15. Cash or check. Open year-round; however, services are available only May-September.

Directions: From I-15 in Helena, take Exit 193 to the east side of the freeway and go north on Washington Street for 0.8 mile. Turn east onto Canyon Ferry Road for 14.3 miles to the Canyon Ferry Dam. Continue 1.7 miles past the dam to milepost 10.8 and turn right.

GPS Coordinates: N 46° 39.461' W 111° 42.504'

Contact: Bureau of Reclamation, Montana Area Office, Canyon Ferry Field Office, 7661 Canyon Ferry Rd., Helena, MT 59602, 406/475-3921, www.usbr.gov/gp/mtao/canyonferry/.

43 CHINAMEN'S GULCH

Scenic rating: 7
on the east shore of Canyon Ferry Reservoir

Located at 3,800 feet on the east shore at the north end of the 25-mile-long Canyon Ferry Reservoir, Chinamen's Gulch sits in a small, narrow canyon that descends to the lakeshore. The reservoir features all types of water recreation. Contrary to other campgrounds that spread out along the shore, this campground has a tiny beach area. But it includes a shallow area for swimming, primitive gravel boat launch, and a small dock. The beach flanks a small bay, which offers canoeing out of the wind, game fishing in summer, and ice fishing in winter.

Chinamen's Gulch Campground is a slice of a hot, dry, dusty narrow canyon that faces the sunset. Large ponderosa pines cover some of the upper sites, offering shade, but some of these are dying because of pine beetles. The upper campsites are more spread out, with large boulders and big trees dividing some of the sites for a little privacy. The lower 12 campsites are small and terraced with views of the water and each other. Most sit west-facing in full sun. Most of the sites have dirt floors with little surrounding ground cover. Even though the campground is on the busy north end of the lake, it quiets at night.

Campsites, facilities: The campground has 38 RV or tent campsites that can accommodate smaller RVs and trailers. Facilities include picnic tables, fire rings with grills, vault toilets, drinking water, garbage service, boat ramp, dock, and campground hosts. Leashed pets are permitted. Wheelchair-accessible facilities include toilets and two campsites.

Reservations, fees: No reservations are accepted. Campsites cost $10. Cash or check. Open year-round; however, services are available only May-September.

Directions: From I-15 in Helena, take Exit 193 to the east side of the freeway and go north on Washington Street for 0.8 mile. Turn east onto Canyon Ferry Road for 14.3 miles to the Canyon Ferry Dam. Continue two miles past the dam to milepost 11.1 and turn right, descending on a dirt washboard road down into the campground.

GPS Coordinates: N 46° 39.058' W 111° 42.551'

Contact: Bureau of Reclamation, Montana Area Office, Canyon Ferry Field Office, 7661 Canyon Ferry Rd., Helena, MT 59602, 406/475-3921, www.usbr.gov/gp/mtao/canyonferry/.

44 KIM'S MARINA AND RV RESORT

Scenic rating: 6
on the east shore of Canyon Ferry Lake

Kim's Marina is one of three marinas on the 33,500-acre Canyon Ferry Lake, a haven for water recreationists. Located at 3,800 feet, the marina and RV resort sit on the northeast corner of the lake in a sheltered bay. The resort services boaters, water-skiers, and anglers going after the walleye, rainbow trout, brown trout, ling, and perch that inhabit the reservoir.

The campground is cramped wall-to-wall with RVs. Premium sites on the water for dry camping and electrical-only hookups cost more than those off the waterfront. Full hookup sites are set back in the campground, some on a large, dry, gravel hillside. A paved road loops through the grassy campground, but the parking pads—all back-ins—are gravel. A few big willows dot the shoreline along the waterfront sites for partial shade, but most of the sites are sunny. The campground rents long-term RV sites, and the bay is busy with motorboats during the day as the marina houses around 165 boats.

Campsites, facilities: The campground maintains 105 RV sites. Facilities include picnic tables, pedestal grills, flush toilets, showers, drinking water, launderette, store with fishing tackle, disposal station, horseshoe pits, tennis courts, boat rentals, docks, boat trailer parking, boat slips, buoyed swimming beach, and hookups for sewer, water, and electricity. Leashed pets are permitted.

Reservations, fees: Reservations are accepted. Hookups cost $25-30. Dry camping costs $15-17. Fees are based on four people per site; each additional person is charged $2. A 7 percent Montana bed tax will be added. Showers cost $5. Use of the RV and boat disposal station costs $7. Boat ramp use costs $5. Open year-round; however, services are available only April-September.

Directions: From I-15 in Helena, take Exit 193 to the east side of the freeway and go north on Washington Street for 0.8 mile. Turn east onto Canyon Ferry Road for 14.3 miles to the Canyon Ferry Dam. Cross the dam, driving another 2.5 miles around the head of the lake. The marina is on the right at milepost 11.5. GPS Coordinates: N 46° 39.144' W 111° 42.070'

Contact: Kim's Marina and RV Resort, 8015 Canyon Ferry Rd., Helena, MT 59602, 406/475-3723, http://kimsmarina.com.

45 JO BONNER

Scenic rating: 6

on the east shore of Canyon Ferry Reservoir

Located at 3,800 feet on the east shore of 25-mile-long Canyon Ferry Reservoir, Jo Bonner Campground sits at the head of a long bay that is flanked with summer homes. It is the farthest south of the busy north-end campgrounds, which attract water-skiers, sailors, Jet Skiers, windsurfers, paddlers, and anglers. Game fish opportunities include brook trout, brown trout, burbot, rainbow trout, walleye, and yellow perch. In winter, the lake is popular for ice fishing. Opposite the campground turnoff, the Magpie Creek Road leads to a back route (trail #248) that connects with the Hanging Valley National Recreation Trail, which climbs and then drops through a narrow rocky chasm to an overlook above Trout Creek Canyon.

The campground sits on an open grassy slope speckled with a few cottonwoods and junipers with large trees and willows along the lakeshore. The gravel campground loop connects the sloped, uneven parking pads. Most of the campsites are sunny and open with no privacy; the four campsites on the shore gain partial afternoon shade from the trees. The shoreline camps are muddy and overused; one even floods in high water. The remainder of the campground doesn't see much use, so you can feel like you have the place to yourself. At nighttime, the campground and bay quiet.

Campsites, facilities: The campground has 18 RV or tent campsites that can accommodate smaller RVs. Facilities include picnic tables, fire rings with grills, vault toilets, drinking water, garbage service, boat ramp, boat dock, and campground hosts. Leashed pets are permitted. Wheelchair-accessible facilities include toilet and one campsite.

Reservations, fees: No reservations are accepted. Campsites cost $10. Cash or check. Open year-round; however, services are available only May–September.

Directions: From I-15 in Helena, take Exit 193 to the east side of the freeway and go north on Washington Street for 0.8 mile. Turn east onto Canyon Ferry Road for 14.3 miles to the Canyon Ferry Dam. Cross the dam, driving another 3.7 miles around the head of the lake. At milepost 12.7 at the campground sign, turn right for 0.1 mile. The campground entrance sits at the junction between East Shore Drive and East Shore Drive North.

GPS Coordinates: N 46° 38.664' W 111° 41.022'

Contact: Bureau of Reclamation, Montana Area Office, Canyon Ferry Field Office, 7661 Canyon Ferry Rd., Helena, MT 59602, 406/475-3921, www.usbr.gov/gp/mtao/canyonferry/.

46 HELLGATE

Scenic rating: 6
on the east shore of Canyon Ferry Reservoir

Hellgate sits along the south shore of a long, narrow bay at 3,800 feet on the east side of Canyon Ferry Reservoir. The 25-mile-long reservoir features water recreation: swimming, boating, waterskiing, canoeing, kayaking, and year-round fishing. While the bay is somewhat protected, this section of the lake is known for wind, and the nearly treeless peninsula housing the campground offers little protection from breezes. The bay lacks summers homes, making it a much more wild location than some of the campgrounds farther north.

The 1.2-mile-long campground offers a variety of terrain for camping. The first section flanks a creek with large cottonwoods and lush grass. Even though the sites here are south-facing, they are separated from each other by undergrowth (you can still see the campground road, though). On the bay, three loops with back-in gravel parking pads have waterfront sites. These vary between partial shade, with willows and cottonwoods along the shore where you can beach a boat, to full sun, with overlooks of the water. Many have a little privacy with neighboring campers visible. A last loop curves around the barren bluff at the end of the peninsula. The sites here garner grand views of the lake but are very windy and have zero privacy.

Campsites, facilities: The campground has 69 RV or tent campsites that can accommodate large RVs. Facilities include picnic tables, fire rings with grills, vault toilets, one flush toilet, drinking water, garbage service, boat ramps, boat docks, a life jacket loan station, and campground hosts. Leashed pets are permitted. Wheelchair-accessible facilities include toilets and three campsites.

Reservations, fees: No reservations are accepted. Campsites cost $10. Cash or check. Open year-round; however, services are available only May–September.

Directions: From I-15 in Helena, take Exit 193 to the east side of the freeway and go north on Washington Street for 0.8 mile. Turn east onto Canyon Ferry Road for 14.3 miles to the Canyon Ferry Dam. Continue driving for eight miles. At the campground sign at milepost 17.1, turn west onto the gravel road for 0.7 mile. The gravel soon gives way to rutted dirt with potholes and bumpy washboards as it descends to the campground.

GPS Coordinates: N 46° 37.060' W 111° 38.438'

Contact: Bureau of Reclamation, Montana Area Office, Canyon Ferry Field Office, 7661 Canyon Ferry Rd., Helena, MT 59602, 406/475-3921, www.usbr.gov/gp/mtao/canyonferry/.

47 GOOSE BAY MARINA

Scenic rating: 6
on the east shore of Canyon Ferry Reservoir

At 3,800 feet on the east shore of Canyon Ferry Reservoir, Goose Bay—one of the largest deepwater finger inlets, sits midway down the 25-mile-long lake in a remote high desert area. The bay and reservoir draw boaters for fishing, waterskiing, and canoeing. Contrary Canyon Ferry's rugged and semiforested north end, Goose Bay is surrounded by low, arid sagebrush, sparse grassland, and rare shade. The campground will be closed in 2014 for reconstruction, but will re-open in July 2015 with a new concessionaire. Scheduled renovations include removing the permanent mobile homes, adding trees for shade, building trails, improving roads, and upgrading facilities, including restrooms and showers.

The campground sits adjacent to the marina overlooking Goose Bay. The location can be hot, frigid, or windy, depending on the season. Additional primitive undesignated free campsites scatter adjacent to the developed campground; find these located around the two peninsulas and two small bays to the north.

Campsites, facilities: RV hookups will include water, sewer, and electricity up to 50 amps at 45 sites, and electrical service only at 30 sites. Twenty nonserviced RV sites and six walk-in tent sites will be available. Large RVs are okay. Facilities include flush and vault toilets, showers, drinking water, garbage service, disposal station, boat ramp, docks with boat slips, boat trailer parking, convenience store, propane and gas for sale, launderette, group campsites, and campground hosts. Wheelchair-accessible facilities will include two tent campsites, docks, and restrooms. Leashed pets are permitted.

Reservations, fees: Reservations are accepted. Call to check on rates, status and season. Cash, check, or credit card.

Directions: From I-15 in Helena, take Exit 193 to the east side of the freeway and go north on Washington Street for 0.8 mile. Turn east onto Canyon Ferry Road for 26.5 miles, circling around the north end of the lake and down the east side to the Goose Bay sign. Turn right onto the rough gravel road and drive 2.8 miles. The road tours around one bay before reaching Goose Bay Marina. From Townsend at the lake's south end, drive east on Highway 12 for 3.3 miles and then north on Highway 284 for 20.3 miles to the Goose Bay turnoff. GPS Coordinates: N 46° 32.513' W 111° 34.269'

Contact: Goose Bay Marina, 300 Goose Bay Lane, Townsend, MT 59644, 406/266-3645; Canyon Ferry Field Office, 7700 Canyon Ferry Road, Helena, MT 59602, 406/475-3921, http://www.usbr.gov/gp/mtao/canyonferry/goosebay/.

48 CONFEDERATE

Scenic rating: 6
on the east shore of Canyon Ferry Reservoir

Located at 3,800 feet on the east shore of the 25-mile-long Canyon Ferry Reservoir, the campground flanks the north and south sand and pebble beaches of Confederate Bay. This remote area draws only a few people because of the rough condition of the access road, which waffles between ruts, washboards, jarring cattle grates, large potholes, and rocky sections. The road narrows to one lane and can be a mudhole when wet. Even though the campground doesn't have a boat ramp, you can launch from your campsite any hand-carried watercraft for fishing, sightseeing, or windsurfing. In winter, the bay draws ice anglers. The beaches grow larger as the lake level drops throughout the summer.

The primitive campsites string along two sandy beaches. The south beach offers more trees and willows for a bit of shade and wind protection, but the north beach has only one cottonwood tree. While you won't have privacy from neighboring campers, the campground as a whole offers solitude, quiet, and privacy from the hubbub at the north end of the lake. Both beaches are sunny, hot in midsummer, and windy, but you can have your tent door a few feet from the water.

Campsites, facilities: The campground has 16 undesignated RV or tent campsites that can accommodate midsized RVs. Facilities include rock fire rings at some sites and two wheelchair-accessible vault toilets, one at each beach. Leashed pets are permitted.

Reservations, fees: No reservations are accepted. Camping is free. Open year-round.

Directions: From Townsend on Highway 12/287, drive east on Highway 12 for 3.3 miles and then north on Highway 284 for 16.8 miles to the Confederate turnoff. At milepost 25, turn west onto the gravel Lower Confederate Lane and drive 4.2 miles. Turn right to reach the north beach or continue 0.5 mile around the bay to reach the south beach. From I-15 in Helena, take Exit 193 to the east side of the freeway and go north on Washington Street for 0.8 mile. Turn east onto Canyon Ferry Road for 30 miles, circling around the lake's north end and down the east side to the Confederate sign.

GPS Coordinates: N 46° 29.324' W 111° 31.516'

Contact: Bureau of Reclamation, Montana Area Office, Canyon Ferry Field Office, 7661 Canyon Ferry Rd., Helena, MT 59602, 406/475-3921, www.usbr.gov/gp/mtao/canyonferry/.

49 WHITE EARTH

Scenic rating: 6
on the west shore of Canyon Ferry Reservoir

At an elevation of 3,800 feet on the west shore of Canyon Ferry Reservoir, White Earth is named for its white sand and pebble beaches, although the sand is more like silty clay. As the 25-mile-long reservoir level drops during the summer, the beaches get bigger. Call the Canyon Ferry Field Office for current water levels. The cement boat ramp, dock, and trailer parking aid those launching boats onto the lake for waterskiing, sightseeing, canoeing, and fishing. In winter, anglers turn to ice fishing. The 29-mile-long lake is a trout fishery and also has ling, walleye, and perch.

The campground is open, treeless, windy, hot, and sunny. Many of the campsites line up along the north shore of a bay while others flank the main lakeshore. A few also rim a small lagoon. With no shrubs and trees, the grassy campground offers no privacy, protection from the afternoon winds, or shade. The campground does, however, gain good views of the sunrise over the Big Belt Mountains on the east side of the lake.

Campsites, facilities: The campground has 38 RV or tent campsites that can accommodate larger RVs. Facilities include picnic tables, fire rings with grills, vault toilets, drinking water, garbage service, boat ramp, boat dock, and campground hosts. Leashed pets are permitted. Wheelchair-accessible facilities include toilets and three campsites.

Reservations, fees: No reservations are accepted. Campsites cost $10. Cash or check. Open year-round; however, services are available only May-September.

Directions: From Winston on Highway 12/287 between Townsend and Helena, drive 5.3 miles northeast on dirt Beaver Creek Road (turning right at 2.3 miles) to reach the campground.

GPS Coordinates: N 46° 31.292' W 111° 35.253'

Contact: Bureau of Reclamation, Montana Area Office, Canyon Ferry Field Office, 7661 Canyon Ferry Rd., Helena, MT 59602, 406/475-3921, www.usbr.gov/gp/mtao/canyonferry.

50 CANYON FERRY LAKE KOA

Scenic rating: 6
on the west shore of Canyon Ferry Reservoir

At 3,850 feet on the west slopes of the 25-mile-long Canyon Ferry Reservoir, the KOA provides access to the lake even though it doesn't have waterfront. A Bureau of Reclamation boat ramp sits 0.2 mile to the east, and slip rental is available at The Silos Marina on Broadwater Bay. Designated swimming areas are also available near the marina. The campground is about five miles north of the 5,000-acre Canyon Ferry Wildlife Management Area, where birders and wildlife watchers can access trails to wildlife-viewing spots.

The KOA sits on an arid hillside above Canyon Ferry Lake, with views across to the Big Belt Mountains. Small pines and firs lend partial shade and windbreaks, but overall the site is very sunny and hot in midsummer. The campground road is gravel, along with the parking pads, which are stacked close together with no privacy. The upper part of the campground is more open, drier, and dustier than the lower portion, which is built around patches of lawn. The KOA also runs the on-site Flamingo Grill, which is open for breakfast, lunch, and dinner.

Campsites, facilities: The campground has 47 RV campsites with a maximum pull-through length of 75 feet and 12 tent campsites. Facilities include picnic tables, fire rings, flush toilets, showers, drinking water, garbage service, disposal station, launderette, wireless Internet, convenience store, café, playground, dog walk, propane, recreation room, and horseshoe pits. Hookups include sewer, water, and electricity for up to 50 amps. Leashed pets are permitted. Wheelchair-accessible toilets are available.

Reservations, fees: Reservations are accepted. Hookups cost $27-50. Tent campsites cost $17-27 for one tent and $10 for a second tent.

Tipis cost $27. Rates are for two adults and two children under 16 years old. A 7 percent Montana bed tax will be added on. Use of the disposal station costs $5. Cash, check, or credit card. Open year-round.

Directions: From Townsend, drive Highway 12/287 north for 7.5 miles to milepost 70. Turn east onto Silos Road. (You'll see the two big, red brick silos.) Drive 0.8 mile east to the campground entrance on the left.
GPS Coordinates: N 46° 24.852' W 111° 34.839'

Contact: Townsend-Canyon Ferry Lake KOA, 81 Silos Rd., Townsend, MT 59644, 406/266-3100, www.canyonferrylakekoa.com.

51 SILOS

Scenic rating: 6
on the west shore of Canyon Ferry Reservoir

At 3,800 feet on the west shore of the 25-mile-long Canyon Ferry Reservoir, Silos is popular for its ease of access off the highway. You only have to drive one mile of the dusty washboard, gravel road. Despite its popularity, this end of the lake is less congested than the more popular north end. The lake attracts boaters, water-skiers, windsurfers, anglers, paddlers, Jet Skiers, and, in winter, ice anglers. The campground inlets contain beaches that grow larger throughout the summer as the reservoir levels drop. These work for swimming and beaching boats for the night. The boat launch includes cement ramps and docks. In the evening, the post-boating crowd heads to the Silos Bar and Restaurant, located at the highway turnoff to the campground. The campground is about five miles north of the Canyon Ferry Wildlife Management Area, which has trails for accessing wildlife-viewing spots to see waterfowl, songbirds, raptors, moose, and deer.

Located on large, flat, treeless, grassy plateaus, the campground has four main loops that kick up dust, each divided by a small,

Silos Campground on Canyon Ferry Reservoir is popular with boaters.

narrow inlet. Two additional small loops on the southern peninsulas contain undesignated campsites. Baking in sun, the campsites offer a semblance of privacy because they are spread out, but since there is no vegetation taller than grass, you will still see neighbors. Some small willows flank a few of the more popular campsites along the inlets. Even from a mile away, you can hear some of the trucking noise at night along the highway.

Campsites, facilities: The campground has 84 RV or tent campsites that can fit larger RVs. Facilities include picnic tables, fire rings with grills, vault toilets, drinking water, garbage service, boat ramp, and campground hosts. Leashed pets are permitted. Wheelchair-accessible facilities include toilets and four campsites.

Reservations, fees: No reservations are accepted. Campsites cost $10. Cash or check. Open year-round.

Directions: From Townsend, drive Highway 12/287 north for 7.5 miles to milepost 70. Turn east onto Silos Road. (You'll see the two big, red brick silos.) Drive one mile east to the boat launch area. Turn right to access the campground loops.

GPS Coordinates: N 46° 24.687' W 111° 34.574'

Contact: Bureau of Reclamation, Montana Area Office, Canyon Ferry Field Office, 7661 Canyon Ferry Rd., Helena, MT 59602, 406/475-3921 or 406/266-3100, www.usbr.gov/gp/mtao/canyonferry/.

52 INDIAN ROAD

Scenic rating: 6

on the Missouri River south of Canyon Ferry Reservoir

At 3,850 feet, Indian Road Campground, as its name implies, sits on an ancient Native American route that the Lewis and Clark expedition also followed. The campground, with its interpretive displays, is on the Missouri River just before it enters Canyon Ferry Reservoir. A lush oasis amid the arid surrounding hills, the park includes a children's fishing pond, which is ringed by a gravel walking trail and crossed by a bridge. Swimming is not permitted in the pond. Several breaks through the willows afford access to the Missouri River for fishing and wading. A paved bicycling and walking path parallels the highway into Townsend. North of the Missouri River, the Canyon Ferry Wildlife Management Area also offers short trails to wildlife-viewing spots. It's an excellent place for bird-watching and good moose habitat.

A gravel campground road circles the park, with a couple pull-through gravel parking pads. The remainder of the parking pads are short back-ins. A few cottonwood trees and shorter willows provide some shade, but the mowed-lawn campground affords no privacy between the close sites. You can, however, have views of the surrounding mountains. At night, the trucks on the highway are loud.

Campsites, facilities: The campground has 12 RV or tent campsites that can accommodate midsized RVs. Facilities include picnic tables, fire rings with grills, pedestal grills, vault toilets, drinking water, and garbage service. Leashed pets are permitted. Wheelchair-accessible facilities include toilets, two campsites, paved walkways, and a fishing platform.

Reservations, fees: No reservations are accepted. Camping is free. Open year-round.

Directions: From the north end of Townsend, drive Highway 12/287 north for 0.5 mile. Before the bridge over the Missouri River, turn east onto Centerville Road and drive 0.1 mile. Turn north into the campground.

GPS Coordinates: N 46° 19.988' W 111° 31.734'

Contact: Bureau of Reclamation, Montana Area Office, Canyon Ferry Field Office, 7661 Canyon Ferry Rd., Helena, MT 59602, 406/475-3921, www.usbr.gov/gp/mtao/canyonferry/.

53 YORK'S ISLANDS

Scenic rating: 6
south of Townsend on the Missouri River

Compared to the surrounding arid countryside, York's Islands is a lush oasis along the Missouri River, at 3,838 feet. The area is named for York, Captain William Clark's servant who accompanied him on the Corps of Discovery expedition, and it is a place where the Missouri River fragments into different channels around eight islands, the result of beaver dams shifting the water flows. The campground is primitive, part of the fishing access site run by the state. Rafters, kayakers, anglers, and river floaters can launch eight river miles upstream at Tosten and float back to camp. A downstream float leads to Townsend and farther into the Canyon Ferry Wildlife Management Area, but no watercraft are permitted March-August to protect nesting waterfowl.

The grassy sites, which are crammed together and small, are partially shaded under tall cottonwoods. Junipers, willows, and lots of brush provide some privacy between sites, especially those ringing the outside of the loop. You can hear the railroad and the highway at night as the river here is slow moving and quiet. Flat spaces on the grass provide for pitching tents.

Campsites, facilities: The campground has 10 RV or tent campsites that can accommodate trailers up to 30 feet. Facilities include picnic tables, fire rings with grills, vault toilets (wheelchair-accessible), and concrete boat ramp. Pack out your trash. Leashed pets are permitted.

Reservations, fees: Reservations are not accepted. Campsites cost $7 with a Montana fishing license and $12 without a Montana fishing license. Cash or check. Open year-round.

Directions: From Townsend, drive south on Highway 287 for four miles to milepost 81.5.

Turn west and cross the railroad tracks, driving one mile on the potholed gravel road. (Watch for cows on the road.) The road dead-ends at the campground.

GPS Coordinates: N 46° 15.995' W 111° 29.529'

Contact: Montana Fish, Wildlife, and Parks, Region 3, 1400 S. 19th Ave., Bozeman, MT 59718, 406/994-4042, http://fwp.mt.gov.

54 LOWER TOSTEN DAM RECREATION AREA

Scenic rating: 6

south of Townsend on the Missouri River

Lower Tosten Dam Recreation Area sits at 4,000 feet in a small canyon cut through dramatic sedimentary layers of orange and white stone amid surrounding sagebrush and juniper hillsides. Below the dam, the Missouri River rolls at a slow pace. Rafters, kayakers, and anglers launch boats from here to float down to Tosten fishing access site or farther to York's Islands. Above the dam, a small reservoir affords fishing, swimming, and boating. You can motor around a broad oxbow and islands in the river. Both sides of the dam are good for watching American pelicans.

The recreation area is divided into two campgrounds—one below the dam and one above. The lower area has two grassy, unshaded campsites adjacent to the cement boat ramp and squeezed between the road and the river. Large willow brush blocks the view of the river. The upper area has three grassy campsites on the shore of the lake formed by the dam. The picnic tables are covered, and small trees lend minimal shade. A cement boat ramp and dock are available. All five campsites are small, close together, and open. The humming from the dam is audible in both areas. The road to access the dam is rough dirt with potholes, but the campground roads are gravel.

Campsites, facilities: The campground has five RV or tent campsites that can accommodate midsized RVs. Facilities include picnic tables, fire rings with grills, vault toilets (wheelchair-accessible), boat dock, and boat ramps. Leashed pets are permitted.

Reservations, fees: No reservations are accepted. Camping is free. Open year-round.

Directions: From Townsend, drive Highway 287 south for 12.6 miles, passing Tosten and crossing the Missouri River. Turn east at the BLM sign onto Tosten Dam Road and drive 4.3 miles to the lower campground or 5.2 miles to the upper campground. The rough dirt road has a one-lane bridge. Watch for cattle on the road.

GPS Coordinates: N 46° 20.065' W 111° 31.763'

Contact: Bureau of Land Management, Butte Field Office, 106 N. Parkmont, Butte, MT 59702, 406/533-7600, www.blm.gov/mt/st/en.html.

55 WHITEHOUSE

Scenic rating: 7

in the Boulder Mountains in Beaverhead-Deerlodge National Forest

At 6,000 feet, Whitehouse sits along the Boulder River in the Boulder Mountains, a mecca for ATV riders. The river houses mountain whitefish along with brook, brown, and rainbow trout, although the stream shores are quite willowy. The 2.5-mile Cottonwood Lake Trailhead (#65) sits about three miles from the campground. From the lake, trails also climb farther to Thunderbolt Mountain and Electric Peak. Be prepared for a rough, potholed, rutted road into the campground.

Of the three campgrounds on the Boulder River, Whitehouse is the most popular. The campground, which sits on the Boulder River, surrounds large meadows with a perimeter of aspens and a few lodgepole pines that are dying from beetle attacks. The sites with large flat tent spaces are spread out for privacy, but with the open, sunny meadow, you'll have views of neighboring campers. Some sites also command views of forested slopes as well as views of a few power lines. The meadows bloom in midsummer with harebells, yarrow, and purple asters. Should the campground be full, you can find an additional five dispersed primitive campsites, also on the Boulder River, 0.5 mile east just opposite the junction the Red Rock Road. Other than the ATV noise, the campground is quiet.

Campsites, facilities: The campground has five RV or tent campsites. RVs are limited to 22 feet. Facilities include picnic tables, fire rings with grills, drinking water, and a wheelchair-accessible vault toilet. Pack out your trash. Leashed pets are permitted.

Reservations, fees: No reservations are accepted. Camping is free. Open late June-November.

Directions: From I-15 between Helena and Butte, take Exit 151 (4.6 miles south of Basin). Cross to the west side onto Boulder River Road (Forest Road 82). Drive 3.25 miles, turning right at the fork and crossing the Boulder River. Continue for 3.9 miles. Turn left at the signed entrance to the campground. GPS Coordinates: N 46° 15.520' W 112° 28.703'

Contact: Beaverhead-Deerlodge National Forest, Jefferson Ranger District, 3 Whitetail Rd., Whitehall, MT 59759, 406/287-3223, www. fs.usda.gov/bdnf.

56 LADYSMITH

Scenic rating: 4

in the Boulder Mountains in Beaverhead-Deerlodge National Forest

Ladysmith, at 5,800 feet, is a small, little-used forest campground. The Boulder River near the campground is on private land, so you must drive three or so miles to public land, where you can fish for trout. The surrounding forest has seen severe thinning, from pine-beetle-killed trees.

A rough-paved, potholed narrow road loops through the campground, which sits on a meadow and open forest slope. Buffalo berries, sticky pink geraniums, and yellow cinquefoil dot the slope. The dirt back-in parking pads are small, bumpy, and sloped. Because of pine beetle infestations, the trees were removed from this campground, leaving it sunny and open with views of neighboring campers. While the access road has some noise during the day from forest travelers and ATVs, the night brings quiet.

Campsites, facilities: The campground has six RV or tent campsites that can accommodate small RVs. Facilities include picnic tables, fire rings with grills, a large group fire ring with three benches, and vault toilet. No water is available; bring your own. Pack out your trash. Leashed pets are permitted.

Reservations, fees: No reservations are accepted. Camping is free. Open late June-September.

Directions: From I-15 between Helena and Butte, take Exit 151 (4.6 miles south of Basin). Cross to the west side onto the Boulder River Road (Forest Road 82). Drive 3.2 miles, turning left at the signed entrance to the campground, driving over the cattle grate. GPS Coordinates: N 46° 15.121' W 112° 24.224'

Contact: Beaverhead-Deerlodge National Forest, Jefferson Ranger District, 3 Whitetail Rd., Whitehall, MT 59759, 406/287-3223, www. fs.usda.gov/bdnf.

57 MORMON CREEK

Scenic rating: 4

in the Boulder Mountains in Beaverhead-Deerlodge National Forest

Mormon Creek—also called Mormon

Gulch—is a small, forest campground at an elevation of 5,800 feet with a tiny creek trickling through the campground. With its quick access off the freeway, the campground makes for an convenient overnight for travelers. The Boulder River near the campground is on private land, so you must drive four or so miles to public land, where you can fish for trout. Because of pine beetle infestations killing trees, the campground has been logged.

Campsites are set close together in a grassy area blooming with wild roses, penstemon, cow parsnip, and bedstraw. The flat spaces available in some sites will fit only smaller tents. One result of the logging is the sites no longer have privacy but garner full sun. Even though the freeway is a mile away, you can hear a bit of commercial trucking noise at night.

Campsites, facilities: The campground has nine RV or tent campsites that can hold trailers up to 16 feet. Facilities include picnic tables, fire rings with grills, and vault toilets. No water is available; bring your own. Pack out your trash. Leashed pets are permitted.

Reservations, fees: No reservations are accepted. Camping is free. Open late June-September.

Directions: From I-15 between Helena and Butte, take Exit 151 (4.6 miles south of Basin). Cross to the west side onto Boulder River Road (Forest Road 82). Drive one mile and turn left at the campground sign. Climb on the single-lane, rough pavement over the cattle grate and dodge chuckholes 0.1 mile to the campground. GPS Coordinates: N 46° 15.418' W 112° 21.747'

Contact: Beaverhead-Deerlodge National Forest, Jefferson Ranger District, 3 Whitetail Rd., Whitehall, MT 59759, 406/287-3223, www.fs.usda.gov/bdnf.

58 LOWLAND

Scenic rating: 6

in the Boulder Mountains in Beaverhead-Deerlodge National Forest

At 6,600 feet in the Boulder Mountains, Lowland Campground sits a few miles from the Sheepshead Mountain Recreation Area, a day-use picnic area that includes streams and a small lake for paddling or fishing with a wheelchair-accessible fishing dock. A wheelchair-accessible interpretive trail is available, and trails for hiking and mountain biking. Children enjoy the playground, and larger groups can play softball, horseshoes, or volleyball. The area also attracts birdwatchers.

Located in a thinned forest on a hillside, this quiet campground offers sunny and partially shaded sites. A gravel road loops through the campground with mostly back-in sites that are spread out for privacy.

Campsites, facilities: The campground has 11 RV or tent campsites. RVs are limited to 22 feet. Facilities include picnic tables, fire rings with grills, vault toilets (wheelchair-accessible), and drinking water. The Sheepshead host monitors the campground. Leashed pets are permitted.

Reservations, fees: Reservations are not accepted. Campsites cost $5. Cash or check. Open mid-June-September.

Directions: From Butte, drive north on I-15 for about eight miles. Take the Elk Park Exit (138), and drive west on Forest Road 442 for 4.9 miles. Turn left onto Forest Road 9485 for 1.6 miles and turn left for 0.3 miles to the campground entrance on the right. GPS Coordinates: N 46° 8.192' W 112° 30.372'

Contact: Beaverhead-Deerlodge National Forest, Butte Ranger District, 1820 Meadowlark, Butte, MT 59701, 406/494-2147, www.fs.usda.gov/bdnf.

WESTERN MONTANA

© BECKY LOMAX

The extremes that baffled Lewis and Clark on their travels across the Continental Divide yield a variety of camping opportunities along blue-ribbon trout streams and mountain lakes. This region, known for its rich history, also sports white-water rafting, wilderness areas and hiking trails, and a wealth of wildlife. Lake camping is best at three large dammed reservoirs: Georgetown Lake, Lake Como, and Clark Canyon Reservoir offer the best options, with multiple campgrounds rimming the shorelines of each. Many campgrounds offer trails to stunning vistas. The Pioneer Mountains, sliced by the campground-loaded Pioneer Scenic Byway, top out at 11,000 feet, with trails wrapping around several of its peaks. The Bitterroot Mountains yield well-traveled trails with campgrounds at many trailheads. In addition, many campgrounds include interpretive information about local species.

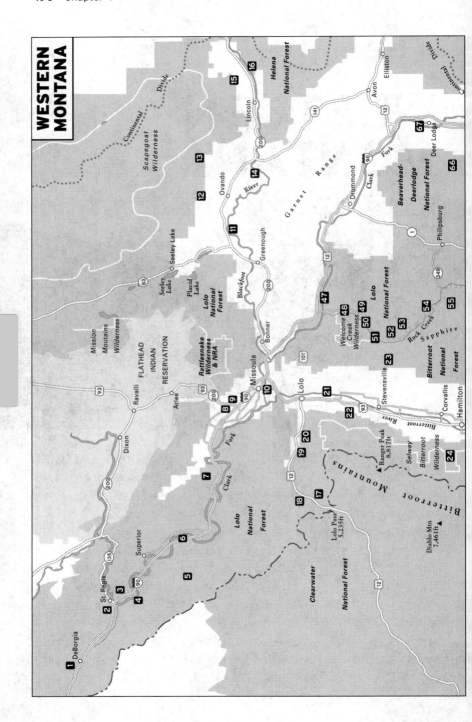

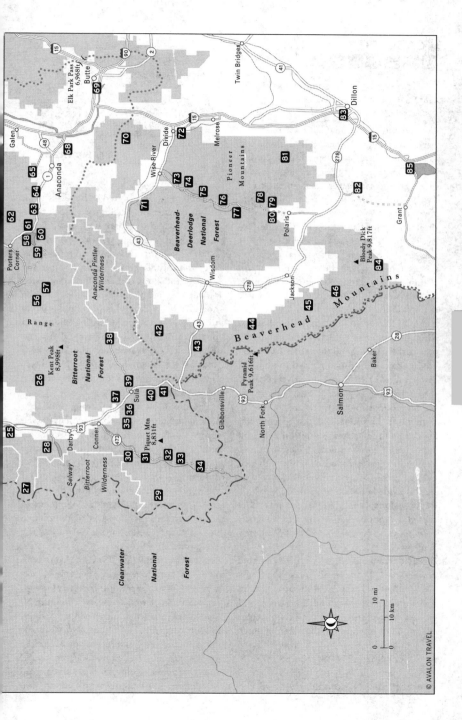

© AVALON TRAVEL

1 CABIN CITY

Scenic rating: 6

near St. Regis in Lolo National Forest

Contrary to the name, Cabin City is not a town; it is a quiet forest campground adjacent to a community of vacation cabin properties. Walkers can enjoy the 0.7-mile self-guided nature trail and see beaver dams on the creek. Twelve-mile Creek holds trout for fishing. The campground sits about 10 miles east of the Trail of the Hiawatha, a 15-mile interpretive mountain bike trail that includes tunnels and trestles from the original train route. A fee is charged to ride the trail, and you can also ride one-way (downhill) and catch a bus back up to the top. Bike rentals are available at Lookout Pass.

At 3,180 feet, the campground loops through a forest of fir, larch, and ponderosa pine that lends shade to the campsites, which are spread out for privacy. Even though the campground's two loops sit relatively close to the freeway, the location is quiet, making you feel far more remote than you are.

Campsites, facilities: The campground has 24 RV or tent campsites. RVs are limited to 50 feet. Facilities include picnic tables, fire rings, drinking water, campground hosts, and vault toilets (wheelchair-accessible). Pack out your trash. Leashed pets are permitted.

Reservations, fees: Reservations are not accepted. Camping costs $7. An extra vehicle costs $3. Cash or check. Open late May-early September.

Directions: From I-90, take Exit 22 and head northeast on 12 Mile Road (Forest Road 353). Go 1.5 miles and veer left at the campground sign for 0.2 miles. Turn left into the campground. You can also exit at DeBorgia (Exit 18) and drive 2.7 miles on Camel Hump Road to reach 12 Mile Road.

GPS Coordinates: N 47° 22.488' W 115° 15.818'

Contact: Lolo National Forest, Superior Ranger District, 209 West Riverside Rd., Superior, MT 59872, 406/822-4233, www.fs.usda.gov/lolo.

2 CAMPGROUND ST. REGIS

Scenic rating: 6

on I-90 in St. Regis

At 2,800 feet, Campground St. Regis sits about two miles west of the tiny two-block town of St. Regis and the Clark Fork River. Local outfitters guide fishing and floating trips on the river. In town, a conservation trail weaves through the St. Regis Community Park. The campground also sits about 30 minutes from the west entrance of the Route of the Hiawatha mountain bike trail, a 15-mile rail trail with 10 tunnels and seven trestles. (Bring a headlamp for the tunnels!) Class II rafting, canoeing, and kayaking is available on the Clark Fork River from St. Regis downstream. Drift boats cart anglers downstream for trout fishing. Two golf courses are nearby.

Paved roads lead to the campground, but past the entrance, the road becomes gravel. Open grassy sites with little privacy compose most of the campground, with large ponderosa pines for shade on the loop to the right of the office. The largest loop circles the playground, tiny swimming pool, and lawn. The campground has a separate broad grassy site for tents. With its proximity to the freeway, trucking noise permeates the campground.

Campsites, facilities: The campground has 47 RV sites and 28 tent sites. Some sites accommodate 75-foot-long pull-throughs. Hookups include water, sewer, and electricity up to 50 amps. Facilities include picnic tables, fire rings, flush toilets, drinking water, a small swimming pool, wireless Internet, disposal station, propane, camp store, game room, dog walk, firewood for sale, playground, and coin-op launderette. Leashed pets are permitted.

Reservations, fees: Reservations are accepted. Hookup campsites with water and electricity cost $23-26. Add on a sewer connection for $2. Tent sites cost $24. Rates are for two people; additional people for $4 each. Add a 7 percent bed tax. Cash, check, Visa, or Mastercard. Open all year.

Directions: From I-90, take Exit 33 at St. Regis. Head to the north side of the freeway to the four-way stoplight. Turn left onto Old Highway 10 for 0.7 mile. Turn left onto Little Joe Road and drive 0.5 mile. Turn right onto Frontage Road W. and drive 0.6 mile. Then, turn right into the campground.

GPS Coordinates: N 47° 18.063' W 115° 8.006'

Contact: Campground St. Regis, Drawer A, 44 Frontage Rd. W., St. Regis, MT 59866, 406/247-8734 or 888/247-8734, www.campgroundstregis.com.

❸ NUGGET RV PARK

Scenic rating: 7

on I-90 in St. Regis

At 2,800 feet east of St. Regis above the Clark Fork River, this RV park is convenient for golfing, fishing, rafting, hiking, or mountain biking. The nine-hole Trestle Creek Golf Course sits across the road. The Clark Fork River offers fishing and floating with guides in St. Regis. Class II rafting, canoeing, and kayaking is available on the Clark Fork River from St. Regis downstream. In town, a conservation trail weaves through the St. Regis Community Park, and walking paths wander around the 30-acre campground. Mountain bikers can ride the Hiawatha trail—a 15-mile rail path with trestles and long tunnels.

A miniature mining camp—log cabin, blacksmith shop, and hotel—sits at the paved campground entrance, and the historical theme continues with a small fort in the playground. Interior gravel roads connect

gravel parking pads. RV sites 1-4 sit up on a bluff with views overlooking the valley and forested mountains. The big-rig RV sites (mostly pull-throughs) sit in an open terraced area. Tent campsites rim the border of the campground, separated from the RV areas. No fires are permitted in the campground. Up on its high knoll, the campground is removed from freeway noise.

Campsites, facilities: The campground has 66 RV campsites and 21 tent sites. All sites, including tent sites, have hookups for water and electricity up to 50 amps. RV sites add sewer hookups, too. Facilities include picnic tables, flush toilets (wheelchair-accessible), showers, drinking water, wireless Internet, a swimming pool, basketball court, playground, launderette, propane, and a disposal station. A central kitchen includes microwave, tables, and grills. Leashed pets are permitted.

Reservations, fees: Reservations are accepted. Full hookups cost $34. Tent sites cost $27. Rates include two people; any additional people over five years old are charged $3 each. Montana also adds on a 7 percent bed tax. Cash, check, or credit card. Open April-October.

Directions: From I-90, take Exit 33 at St. Regis. Go to the north side of the freeway and turn east at the four-way stop onto Old Highway 10. Drive one mile, crossing the Clark Fork River and climbing a hill. Look for the entrance on the left.

GPS Coordinates: N 47° 17.365' W 115° 4.970'

Contact: Nugget RV Park, 105 Old Hwy. 10 E., St. Regis, MT 59866, 406/649-2122 or 888/800-0125, www.nuggetrvpark.com.

❹ SLOWEY

Scenic rating: 7

on the Clark Fork River in Lolo National Forest

At 2,664 feet, Slowey is located adjacent to the freeway. It is a campground for convenience, not a place to get away from it all. However, it sits right on the Clark Fork River, Montana's largest river by water volume, and a favorite for trout fishing. A primitive boat ramp allows for launching hand-carried rafts, canoes, and kayaks. The campground also caters to traveling equestrians with a corral, feeders, and hitch rails in one site. Upstream, the Alberton Gorge offers white-water rafting and kayaking. Commercial rafting trips are available from several local outfitters. For launching larger rafts on the river, river access points are east or north on the river.

An arid ponderosa pine forest shades the campground. One loop contains RV campsites that snuggle close together with little privacy; the other loop has more spread out campsites divided by undergrowth. To get a good night's sleep, bring earplugs as freeway trucking traffic runs all night, drowning out the river. Pull-through sites and paved parking spurs are available.

Campsites, facilities: The campground has 12 RV sites that will fit the largest RVs and 15 RV or tent campsites. Facilities include picnic tables, fire rings, vault toilets (wheelchair-accessible), drinking water, campground hosts, volleyball court, horseshoes, sandbox, boat launch, horse hitch rail, and corral with feeders. Leashed pets are permitted.

Reservations, fees: Reservations are not accepted. Camping costs $10. An extra vehicle costs $5. Cash or check. Open late May-early September.

Directions: From I-90 between St. Regis and Superior, take Exit 43 and drive the old highway (Hwy. 10) paralleling the freeway west for 3.2 miles, or take Exit 37 and drive the old highway 2.8 miles east. The campground sits on the south side of the road.

GPS Coordinates: N 47° 14.023' W 115° 1.590'

Contact: Lolo National Forest, Superior Ranger District, 209 West Riverside Road, Superior, MT 59872, 406/822-4233, www.fs.usda.gov/lolo.

5 TROUT CREEK

Scenic rating: 7

in the Bitterroot Mountains in Lolo National Forest

At 2,950 feet, Trout Creek offers a quick place to get away from the I-90 corridor without much effort. The campground tucks in a forested side valley of the Bitterroot Mountains along a tributary of the Clark Fork River. Trout Creek, known for fly-fishing, has brook, rainbow, brown, and westslope cutthroat trout. The Trout Creek Road serves for a scenic drive to the Great Burn, a proposed wilderness area that derived its name from the immense 1910 fires. The road also accesses a few small alpine lakes.

The campground tucks into a ponderosa pine and larch forest that shades the campsites. Privacy is enhanced by a thick understory of brush and grasses. The quiet campground provides relaxation with the sound of Trout Creek nearby. Some sites overlook the creek.

Campsites, facilities: The campground has 12 RV or tent campsites. RVs and trailer combinations are limited to 30 feet. Facilities include picnic tables, fire rings, vault toilets (wheelchair-accessible), drinking water, and campground hosts. Leashed pets are permitted.

Reservations, fees: Reservations are not accepted. Camping costs $6. An extra vehicle costs $3. Cash or check. Open all year, but only serviced late May-early September.

Directions: From I-90 near Superior, take Exit 46 and go south of the freeway. (If you were driving westbound on the Interstate, at the end of the exit ramp, turn left and then take the first left to cross under the freeway.) At the T intersection, turn east onto Diamond Road for five miles. At mile five, the road becomes the gravel Trout Creek Road (Forest Road 250). Drive two miles and turn left into the campground.

GPS Coordinates: N 47° 7.035' W 114° 52.139'

Contact: Lolo National Forest, Superior Ranger District, 209 West Riverside Road, Superior, MT 59872, 406/822-4233, www.fs.usda.gov/lolo.

6 QUARTZ FLAT

Scenic rating: 6
on the Clark Fork River in Lolo National Forest

At 2,871 feet, Quartz Flat offers a convenient place to camp adjacent to the freeway, but without the silence of the backwoods. A 0.5-mile self-guided nature trail leads to the Clark Fork River, Montana's largest river by water volume and a favorite for trout fishing. A parade of rafts, kayaks, canoes, and drift boats float downstream. Upstream, commercial outfitters guide white-water raft trips through the Alberton Gorge. The campground does not have a river launch site; river access points sit east or north on the river.

The campground loops through a ponderosa pine forest that lends shade to the campsites, which are spread out for privacy. To get a good night's sleep, bring earplugs as freeway traffic runs all night. Regular campsites sit on the west side of the freeway while the group campsite is on the east side. Pull-through sites and paved parking spurs are available.

Campsites, facilities: The campground has 77 RV or tent campsites, including group camping. The largest RV combinations can fit in some sites. Facilities include picnic tables, fire rings, vault and flush toilets (wheelchair-accessible), drinking water, campground hosts, and disposal station. Leashed pets are permitted.

Reservations, fees: Reservations are not accepted. Camping costs $10. An extra vehicle costs $5. Cash or check. Open late May-early September.

Directions: From I-90 about 10 miles east of Superior, go to the rest area on either side of the freeway. Follow the signs to access the campground. A tunnel under the freeway connects both sections of the campground.

GPS Coordinates: N 47° 4.566' W 114° 46.092'

Contact: Lolo National Forest, Superior Ranger District, 209 West Riverside Road, Superior, MT 59872, 406/822-4233, www.fs.usda.gov/lolo.

7 KREIS POND

Scenic rating: 7
northwest of Ninemile in Lolo National Forest

Kreis Pond has recently become popular with mountain bikers. Surrounding the pond, mountain bikers can ride 35 miles of trails. Beginners should start on the 2.3-mile Yellow Trail Loop. Riders with more advanced skills to handle steep, narrow single-track can tackle the longer Blue, Green, Orange, and Red trails. Pick up a brochure and map of the bike trails from Ninemile Ranger Station on your way to the campground. The pond also attracts anglers going after trout and bass in its shallow waters. While fishing from shore is possible, you may have more luck from a canoe, rowboat, or float tube. The lake is only accessible for hand-carried watercraft.

The campground loops around Kreis Pond in a sunny forest of lodgepole and ponderosa pines. Campsites are spread out for privacy. Because of the distance from pavement, this campground is quiet.

Campsites, facilities: The campground has seven RV or tent campsites. RVs are limited to 30 feet. Facilities include picnic tables, fire rings, and vault toilets (wheelchair-accessible). No drinking water is available; bring your own or treat lake water. Pack out your trash. Leashed pets are permitted.

Reservations, fees: Reservations are not accepted. Camping is free. Open May-September.

Directions: From I-90 at Ninemile, turn off at

Exit 82. Go west on the Frontage Road (Hwy. 10) for 1.3 miles to Remount Road. Drive 2.6 miles north to the Ninemile Ranger Station. Continue north on Edith Peak Road (Forest Road 476) for 1.3 miles, veering right onto Butler Creek Loop. Stay on Butler Creek Road (Forest Road 456) for 2.1 miles and turn left onto the campground road (Forest Road 2176) for 1.5 miles to Kreis Pond.

GPS Coordinates: N 47° 5.997' W 114° 25.595'

Contact: Lolo National Forest, Ninemile Ranger District, 20325 Remount Road, Huson, MT 59846, 406/626-5201, www. fs.usda.gov/lolo.

8 JELLYSTONE PARK

Scenic rating: 6
on the outskirts of Missoula

At 3,300 feet at the intersection of I-90 and Highway 93, Jellystone Park is convenient for those heading north to the National Bison Range, Ninepipes National Wildlife Refuge, and Glacier National Park. The Rocky Mountain Elk Museum and Smoke Jumper Center are within a five-minute drive. A 15-minute drive leads to downtown Missoula and the University of Montana to hike the 1.75 miles passing the M to Mount Sentinel's summit. A trail used by runners, walkers, and bicyclers, the two-mile Clark Fork Riverfront Trail runs through town from the Van Buren Street Footbridge to Caras Park, where a hand-carved carousel spins year-round. The Clark Fork River provides kayaking, canoeing, and rafting. Of Missoula's four golf courses, the Ranch Club is a 10-minute drive away. The new Milltown State Park sits on the Clark Fork River superfund site.

Sitting in the open for easy satellite reception, the sunny campsites with small trees pack close together, with views of surrounding sagebrush hills. Paved roads loop through the campground, with gravel parking pads

surrounded by mowed lawns. Yogi Bear shows up nightly in summer, starting about July 4. Trucking noise is audible.

Campsites, facilities: The campground has 110 RV campsites and seven tent campsites. For big RVs, 81 pull-through sites fit rigs up to 70 feet. Hookups include water, sewer, electricity up to 50 amps, and cable TV. Facilities include picnic tables, flush toilets (wheelchair-accessible), showers, drinking water, wireless Internet, an outdoor heated swimming pool, mini-golf, a basketball court, horseshoes, playground, TV and game room, launderette, camp store, propane, disposal station, and pet walk. Leashed pets are permitted.

Reservations, fees: Reservations are highly recommended for July and August. Hookups cost $40-42. Tent sites cost $33. All rates are for two people; additional people over five years old are charged $3-4 per person. Check website for discounts and ask about off-season rates. Add on a 7 percent bed tax. Cash, check, or credit card. Open year-round.

Directions: From I-90, take Exit 96 on the west side of Missoula. Go north on Highway 93 to milepost 1. Turn left onto Jellystone Avenue to enter the park.

GPS Coordinates: N 46° 57.660' W 114° 8.103'

Contact: Yogi Bear's Jellystone Park, 9900 Jellystone Ave., Missoula, MT 59808, 406/543-9400 or 800/318-9644, www. campjellystonemt.com.

9 JIM AND MARY'S RV PARK

Scenic rating: 6
on the outskirts of Missoula

Just north of the I-90 and Highway 93 junction at 3,300 feet, this RV park works as a stopover for those heading north to the National Bison Range, Ninepipes National Wildlife Refuge, Flathead Valley, and Glacier National Park. A 10-minute drive leads to downtown Missoula, which offers art galleries, shopping, restaurants, farmers markets, breweries, theaters, museums, the University of Montana, and city parks. The campground is also convenient for touring the Smoke Jumper Center or the Rocky Mountain Elk Foundation, both within a five-minute drive. Outdoor activities—hiking, mountain biking, cycling, golf, kayaking, and river rafting—are all in the area, too, along with the new Milltown State Park built on a superfund site on the Clark Fork River.

You'll be greeted by colorful flowers grown in the owner's greenhouse. Surrounded partially by shade-producing fir trees, the lawn campground has a park feel with southern sites getting more sunshine. A paved road loops through the campground with gravel parking pads, about 75 percent pull-throughs. Permanent residents live in some sites. Freeway noise is audible.

Campsites, facilities: The campground has 68 RV sites that can fit large RVs. Hookups include sewer, water, electricity up to 50 amps, and cable TV. Facilities include picnic tables, flush toilets (wheelchair-accessible), showers, drinking water, wireless Internet, and a coin-op launderette. Leashed pets are permitted.

Reservations, fees: Reservations are highly recommended. Campsites cost $42. The 7 percent state bed tax is included. Cash, check, or credit card. Open year-round.

Directions: From I-90, take Exit 96 on the west side of Missoula. Go north on Highway 93 to milepost 1.2. Turn right onto Lady Slipper Lane and right again to enter the RV park. GPS Coordinates: N 46° 57.868' W 114° 7.835'

Contact: Jim and Mary's RV Park, 9800 Hwy. 93 N., Missoula, MT 59808, 406/549-4416, www.jimandmarys.com.

10 MISSOULA KOA

Scenic rating: 4

in downtown Missoula

At 3,500 feet in Missoula, surrounded by

Bicycle trails in Missoula flank the Clark Fork River.

© BECKY LOMAX

residential and commercial property, the KOA is Missoula's largest campground. It's a five-minute drive from Missoula's hand-built carousel—Dragon Hollow— a monster-sized playground shaped like a three-headed dragon, and Caras Park, which holds a kayak play wave (an artificial wave for river kayakers to practice skills) on the Clark Fork River. Caras also hosts weekly summer music festivals and farmers markets. Boating, floating, fishing, walking, and biking are available on or along the Clark Fork River, which runs through town. You can also visit Milltown State Park, a new park built on a superfund site that reclaimed the Clark Fork River.

All RV campsites are pull-throughs, and premium sites include a patio, log swing, fire ring, and two sewer hookups. Tent sites—some with electricity and water—sit in a separate grassy area. Campsites are packed in close together with little privacy, and traffic noise from the busy Reserve Street is audible. The campground has rental bikes for the paved

TROUT FISHING AND WHITE-WATER RAFTING

Those looking for trout streams will find them in western Montana. A third of the state's 12 renowned blue-ribbon trout streams flow through the region. The **Big Hole,** which runs 155 miles from the Beaverhead Mountains to the prairies, winds through the idyllic Big Hole River Valley, with its postcard Montana views and prime trout fishery. Hopping with brown and rainbow trout, the **Beaverhead River** runs 69 miles from Clark Canyon Reservoir to meet up with the Big Hole. The 127-mile **Blackfoot River** is seeing a restoration of native trout species--especially westslope cutthroat--as its waters plummet from the Continental Divide westward. **Rock Creek,** another west-slope cutthroat trout fishery, flows 52 miles through a canyon dotted with campgrounds. Other top fisheries include the **Clark Fork** and **Bitterroot Rivers.** All six of these rivers offer a combination of Forest Service, Bureau of Land Management, and state-run river access campgrounds.

Campers seeking serene pools and frothing whitewater for rafting, canoeing, and kayaking will find floating stretches on these rivers. Most of western Montana's rivers run with Class II water, broken by boulder-strewn patches of Class III rapids. The one exception is the **Clark Fork River,** which adds the ferocity of challenging Class III-IV white water through Alberton Gorge.

trail looping the campground, community bonfires, and ice cream socials.

Campsites, facilities: The campground has 180 RV campsites and 43 tent sites. RV combinations are limited to 70 feet. Hookups include sewer, water, electricity up to 50 amps, and cable TV. Facilities include picnic tables, flush toilets, showers, launderette, disposal station, wireless Internet, heated outdoor swimming pool, two outdoor hot tubs, firewood for sale, game center, mini-golf, basketball, volleyball, badminton, playground, camp store, café, and three fenced dog walks. Tent sites have fire pits, but RV sites do not. Leashed pets are permitted. A wheelchair-accessible toilet and campsite are available.

Reservations, fees: Reservations are accepted by phone or online. RV sites cost $35-75. Tent sites cost $28-35. Rates are for two people; for additional campers, add $5. Kids nine years old and under stay free. Add on 7 percent bed tax. Cash, check, or credit card. Open year-round.

Directions: From I-90, take Exit 101 and drive south for 1.5 miles on Reserve Street. Turn right at the light onto England Boulevard. Turn right onto Tina Avenue. Coming from south of Missoula, go to the junction of Highway 93 and Highway 12. Turn north onto Reserve Street and drive four miles. Turn left at the light onto England Boulevard and right onto Tina Avenue.

GPS Coordinates: N 46° 53.731' W 114° 2.612'

Contact: Missoula KOA, 3450 Tina Ave., Missoula, MT 59808, 406/549-0881 or 800/562-5366, www.missoulakoa.com.

11 RUSSELL GATES MEMORIAL

Scenic rating: 7

on the Blackfoot River

BEST (

Located at 3,865 feet on the Blackfoot River, Russell Gates Memorial Campground tucks into a narrow river canyon in the Blackfoot-Clearwater Wildlife Management Area. The river—one of Montana's blue-ribbon trout streams—harbors brown, rainbow, and westslope cutthroat trout. Anglers fish by wading or floating the river. A primitive boat launch allows for launching rafts, kayaks, and canoes. Put in at Harry Morgan to float the Class II section to the campground, or launch at the campground to float to Clearwater Junction. Boulder-crammed rapids clog the river below Clearwater Junction.

Hiking trails and mountain biking roads loop through the wildlife management area across the highway.

The south-facing campground swelters in midsummer, but the water cools off the campers. Partly shaded by large ponderosas, the grassy campsites sit in the open with views of neighboring campers, the river, and the canyon. Seven of the campsites enjoy river frontage, with sites 10 and 11 the most private at the end but also the closest to the highway. While the sound of rushing water fills the campground, so does commercial trucking highway noise.

Campsites, facilities: The campground has 11 campsites. Trailer length is limited to 25 feet. Facilities include picnic tables, fire rings with grills, vault toilets (wheelchair-accessible), drinking water, and garbage service. Leashed pets are permitted.

Reservations, fees: Reservations are not accepted. Campsites cost $12 for those without Montana fishing licenses and $7 for those who have licenses. Open year-round.

Directions: On Highway 200, drive 3.7 miles east of Clearwater Junction or 20 miles west of the Highway 141 junction to the signed turnoff at milepost 35.5. Turn south into the campground.

GPS Coordinates: N 47° 1.374' W 113° 18.431'

Contact: Montana Fish, Wildlife, and Parks, Region 2 Headquarters, 3201 Spurgin Rd., Missoula, MT 59804, 406/542-5500, http://fwp.mt.gov.

12 MONTURE CREEK

Scenic rating: 6

near the Bob Marshall Wilderness in Lolo National Forest

At 4,182 feet, Monture Creek Trailhead leaps into two of the wildernesses in the Bob Marshall Wilderness Complex. Long hiking or horseback riding trails lead 11 miles to the

Scapegoat Wilderness and 16 miles to the Bob Marshall Wilderness. Sitting adjacent to the trailhead, the campground has stock facilities: loading ramp, hitching rails, watering tank, and corrals. Anglers can fish Monture Creek, a classic fly-fishing stream containing brook, brown, rainbow, and westslope cutthroat trout. Wade-fishing works best.

A combination of open grassy meadows flanked by shade-producing ponderosa pines gives this campground appeal. Considering its distance from paved roads, you won't hear vehicle noise at night. The campsites spread out around one gravel road loop with short paths leading to Monture Creek.

Campsites, facilities: The campground has five RV or tent campsites. Midsized RVs can fit in some sites. Facilities include picnic tables, fire rings, vault toilets (wheelchair-accessible), and horse amenities. No drinking water is available; bring your own or treat creek water. Pack out your trash. Leashed pets are permitted.

Reservations, fees: Reservations are not accepted. Camping is free. Open May-November.

Directions: On Highway 200 from Clearwater Junction (junction with Hwy. 83), drive 12.5 miles east. Turn north onto the gravel Monture Road (Forest Road 89) and drive seven miles. Turn right into the campground just before the bridge crosses Monture Creek.

GPS Coordinates: N 47° 7.503' W 113° 8.718'

Contact: Lolo National Forest, Seeley Lake Ranger District, 3583 Highway 83, Seeley Lake, MT 59868, 406/677-2233, www.fs.usda.gov/lolo.

13 BIG NELSON

Scenic rating: 7

near the Bob Marshall Wilderness in Lolo National Forest

At 4,500 feet, Big Nelson flanks Cooper

Lake—a small remote lake with some private cabins tucked south of the Scapegoat Wilderness Area. The 1.3-mile-long lake attracts boaters, but only hand-carried canoes, kayaks, and rowboats can be launched from the campground. Anglers can fish for several species of trout. With trailheads within a few miles of the campground, hikers and horseback riders can reach the Scapegoat and Bob Marshall Wildernesses. Most of the trails require a long hiking to reach a destination.

This shoreline campground caters to tent campers with all campsites using one common parking lot. Stairs and short trails access the walk-in sites on the steep hillside above the lake. Tree thinning in 2010 opened up the campground to more sunlight, with remaining large trees lending shade.

Campsites, facilities: The campground has four tent campsites. Facilities include picnic tables, fire rings, and vault toilet. No drinking water is available; bring your own or treat lake water. Pack out your trash. Leashed pets are permitted.

Reservations, fees: Reservations are not accepted. Camping is free. Open May-October.

Directions: On Highway 200 from Clearwater Junction (junction with Hwy. 83), drive 19.5 miles east. Turn north onto the gravel North Fork Blackfoot Road (Forest Road 5550, called Cooper Lake Road on some maps) and drive 12 miles. The road will take several 90-degree turns around ranch properties before climbing a switchback and dropping to the campground entrance on the right. GPS Coordinates: N 47° 4.209' W 112° 55.328'

Contact: Lolo National Forest, Seeley Lake Ranger District, 3583 Highway 83, Seeley Lake, MT 59868, 406/677-2233, www.fs.usda.gov/lolo.

14 BROWN'S LAKE

Scenic rating: 7

in the Blackfoot River Valley

BEST (

At 4,308 feet, Brown's Lake is a large, 516-acre lake between Ovando and Lincoln. With marshy wetlands, Brown's Lake is a favorite spot for bird-watchers in spring, with nesting areas adjacent to the Blackfoot Waterfowl Production Area—open only to foot traffic. Watch for bald eagles, ospreys, great blue herons, American white pelicans, American avocets, and sandhill cranes. Boaters can use the concrete boat ramp and boat trailer parking. A portion of the lake, marked by barrel booms, is closed to all boats April-mid-July. Anglers fish for stocked rainbow trout that can get up to 20 inches. Windsurfers cruise the lake on summer afternoons, and ice fishing is popular in winter.

The campground sits on a treeless spit of land protruding out into the lake's south end. The shadeless campsites get strong afternoon winds. While views from the campsites include other campers, they also swing to the panorama of the Scapegoat Wilderness peaks. Outside of the developed campground, primitive campsites surround the lake.

Campsites, facilities: The campground has 10 tent campsites. RVs and trailers are not recommended, but plenty still camp here. Facilities include picnic tables, fire rings with grills, vault toilets (wheelchair-accessible), and boat ramp, but no drinking water. Bring your own water, or treat lake water. Pack out your trash. Leashed pets are permitted.

Reservations, fees: Reservations are not accepted. Campsites cost $12 for those without Montana fishing licenses and $7 for those who have licenses. Open year-round.

Directions: From Highway 200, locate the Brown's Lake turnoff seven miles east of Ovando or 2.7 miles west of the Highway 141 junction. Turn south onto County Road 112. Follow it around the east side of the lake for 3.5 miles and then north onto the spit into the campground.

GPS Coordinates: N 46° 57.044' W 113° 0.678'

Contact: Montana Fish, Wildlife, and Parks, Region 2 Headquarters, 3201 Spurgin Rd., Missoula, MT 59804, 406/542-5500, http://fwp.mt.gov.

15 COPPER CREEK

Scenic rating: 7

on Copper Creek in Helena National Forest

Located at 5,300 feet west of the Continental Divide, Copper Creek Campground flanks Copper Creek above the nearby five-acre Snowbank Lake. The lake works for trout fishing, swimming, and canoeing. A 10-mile hiking and mountain biking trail departs from the Snowbank picnic area, and a trailhead two miles from the campground leads into the Scapegoat Wilderness Area and Heart Lakes.

A dirt road accesses the campground, which has gravel back-in sites. Set in one loop on a knoll, the sunny campground gains views of the surrounding mountainsides, denuded of trees from a forest fire. Lodgepoles, spruce and Douglas fir remained at the campground to yield shade.

Campsites, facilities: The campground has 17 RV or tent campsites. RVs are limited to 20 feet. Facilities include concrete picnic tables, fire rings, drinking water from a hand pump, garbage service, and vault toilets (wheelchair-accessible). Leashed pets are permitted.

Reservations, fees: Reservations are not accepted. Campsites cost $8 per unit (RV, trailer, or tent). Open late May-early September.

Directions: From Lincoln, drive east on Highway 200 for six miles and turn north onto Copper Creek Road (Forest Road 330). Drive 8.5 miles to the campground on the right.

GPS Coordinates: N 47° 4.632' W 112° 37.104'

Contact: Helena National Forest, Lincoln Ranger District, 1569 Hwy. 200, Lincoln, MT 59639, 406/362-7000, www.fs.usda.gov/helena.

16 ASPEN GROVE

Scenic rating: 7

on the Blackfoot River in Helena National Forest

On the west side of the Continental Divide, Aspen Grove, elevation 4,800 feet, is the only quick-access Forest Service campground between Missoula and Great Falls along Highway 200. It sits about 11.5 miles from Rogers Pass on the Continental Divide, where you can climb up 1.5 miles on the Continental Divide Trail for expansive views of the mountains and the prairie. The campground attracts anglers for the famed Blackfoot River, which harbors several species of trout: brown, westslope cutthroat, brook, and rainbow.

Contrary to the name, the quiet eight-acre campground sprawls in a large grove of shady cottonwood trees. There are some aspens, but they're not the dominant trees. Some more open sites are grassy with a mix of sagebrush. Two gravel loops with gravel parking aprons have sites that border the Blackfoot River, which fills the campground with the sound of flowing water.

Campsites, facilities: The campground has 20 RV or tent campsites. Most of the parking pads are 20 feet long, but a couple can handle RVs up to 50 feet long. Facilities include picnic tables, fire rings with grills, drinking water, vault toilets (wheelchair-accessible), garbage service, and campground hosts. Leashed pets are permitted.

Reservations, fees: Reservations are accepted (877/444-6777, www.recreation.gov). Campsites cost $8. Open late May-early September.

Directions: From Lincoln, drive 6.5 miles east on Highway 200. Turn south at the Aspen

HISTORIC STEPS

With campgrounds speckling historic paths, campers can trace the 1805 footsteps of Lewis and Clark down the **Bitterroot River.** In the Bitterroot Mountains, the expedition suffered the worst fatigue of their journey, compounded by cold and hunger.

Following much of the same route in 1877, Chief Joseph and the Nez Perce ran from the U.S. Army trying to force them onto a reservation. Their route down the **Lolo River to Fort Fizzle** culminated in the Battle of the Big Hole; the site, west of Wisdom, is now a national battlefield with a visitors center, interpretive displays, and encampments.

Montana's Wild West mining heritage also left a swath of ghost towns--vacated as inhabitants disappeared to another gold-frenzied town. **Bannack State Park,** west of Dillon, offers both camping and a look at life in the 1860s through the 60 buildings left standing.

Grove Campground sign. Drive 0.5 mile on the gravel road to the campground.
GPS Coordinates: N 46° 58.696' W 112° 31.968'
Contact: Helena National Forest, Lincoln Ranger District, 1569 Hwy. 200, Lincoln, MT 59639, 406/362-7000, www.fs.usda.gov/helena.

17 LEE CREEK

Scenic rating: 7
in the Bitterroot Mountains in Lolo National Forest

Of the Highway 12 campgrounds between Lolo and Lolo Pass, Lee Creek sits the closest to the pass at 4,200 feet. A portion of the historic Lolo Trail, once used by the Nez Perce, Salish, and Kootenai tribes and explored by Lewis and Clark, parallels the opposite side of the highway, accessed 0.5 mile away at Fish Creek Road, a mountain-biking road. Lolo Hot Springs Resort, with its outdoor hot pool, sits one mile to the east, and the Lolo Pass Visitor Center is six miles to the west. You can hike to the hot springs or the visitors center via the Lolo Trail. For anglers, Lolo Creek contains brook, brown, westslope cutthroat, and rainbow trout as well as mountain whitefish. A one-mile trail also leads up Lee Ridge.

The campground has two loops, serviced by paved roads and connected to paved parking pads. Six of the campsites have pull-through parking. In the lower loop, sites 1-5 spread out between lodgepoles and wild roses for more privacy. In the upper loop, remaining sites cram together on a hillside of scrawny lodgepole pines with little undergrowth to lend privacy from the neighbors. A stairway connects the two loops.

Campsites, facilities: The campground has 22 RV or tent campsites. RVs are limited to 45 feet. Facilities include picnic tables, fire rings with grills, vault toilets (wheelchair-accessible), drinking water, campground hosts, and garbage service. During September, the drinking water may be turned off and garbage service ended. If so, pack out your trash. Site 22 has a bear box for bicyclists. Leashed pets are permitted.

Reservations, fees: Reservations are not accepted. Campsites cost $10. Additional vehicles cost $4. Cash or check only. Open late May-September.

Directions: From Lolo, drive 26 miles west on Highway 12. From Lolo Pass, drive six miles east. Turn south onto Lee Creek Road and cross a small bridge over Lolo Creek.
GPS Coordinates: N 46° 42.329' W 114° 32.157'

Contact: Lolo National Forest, Missoula Ranger District, Bldg. 24A, Fort Missoula, Missoula, MT 59804, 406/329-3814, www.fs.usda.gov/lolo.

18 LOLO HOT SPRINGS RESORT

🚶 🚴 ⛵ 🏊 ❄️ ♨️ 🦌 ♿ 🚐 ⛺

Scenic rating: 7

in the Bitterroot Mountains in Lolo National Forest

BEST (

Sitting at 4,000 feet, Lolo Hot Springs Resort has two natural year-round pools—one hot pool indoors and another cooler outdoor pool, both open daily (10am-10pm summers; pools close at 8pm winters, $7 for adults, $5 for kids 12 and under). The 32-mile Lewis and Clark National Historic Trail, also called the Lolo Trail, parallels the north side of the highway. Hike either direction to follow in the 1805 footsteps of the Corps of Discovery and later the Nez Perce in their flight from the U.S. Army. The trail is for hikers only, but Fish Creek Road north allows mountain biking. For anglers, Lolo Creek contains trout. In winter, the resort is a base for snowmobiling in the national forest and cross-country skiing at Lee Creek and Lolo Pass.

Located in an open grassy sunny area, the campground sits across the highway and Lolo Creek from the hot pools, restaurant, bar, and casino. The sites cram close together, and some of the tent sites snuggle up against the forest. Privacy is minimal, and highway noise from commercial hauling trucks is audible.

Campsites, facilities: The campground has 70 RV campsites with hookups for water, sewer, and electricity; 60 tent and RV dry campsites are also available. Parking pads can accommodate large RVs. Facilities include picnic tables, fire rings, flush toilets (wheelchair-accessible), showers, horseshoe pits, volleyball

Northern harriers can be seen frequently in the Bitterroot Valley.

© BECKY LOMAX

nets, tipis for rent, and a disposal station. Wireless Internet is available in the bar and restaurant across the street. Leashed pets are permitted.

Reservations, fees: Reservations are accepted. Full hookups cost $24. Seniors camp at a discounted rate of $20. Tent sites cost $16. A $15 nonrefundable deposit is charged per pet. Add on 7 percent bed tax. Cash, check, or credit card. Open year-round.

Directions: From Lolo, drive 25 miles west on Highway 12, or from Lolo Pass, drive seven miles east. Locate the resort on both sides of the road at milepost 7. The campground sits south of the highway and the pools are on the north side.

GPS Coordinates: N 46° 43.496' W 114° 31.864'

Contact: Lolo Hot Springs Resort, 38500 Hwy. 12, Lolo, MT 59847, 406/273-2294 or 800/273-2290, www.lolohotsprings.com.

19 EARL TENANT
🚶🚴🛶🐕♿🚐⛺

Scenic rating: 6
in the Bitterroot Mountains in Lolo National
Forest

Between Missoula and Lolo Pass, Earl Tenant
Campground flanks Lolo Creek at 3,900 feet.
Across the highway, the historic Lolo Trail—
also called the Lewis and Clark National Historic Trail—parallels the highway for over 32
miles. Hop onto the hiking-only trail at the
Howard Creek Trailhead and walk where the
Nez Perce, Salish, and Kootenai tribes once
traveled. The Corps of Discovery passed
through here in fall of 1805. For anglers,
Lolo Creek houses trout. The campground
is named in honor of the first ranger at Lolo
Ranger Station. Lolo Hot Springs sits seven
miles to the west.

Surrounded by wild grasses and a few tall
ponderosa pines, the campground, looping
on a gravel road, waxes dry and dusty in late
August. The partly sunny campsites, with
graveled, wide parking pads, have views of
each other and the highway.

Campsites, facilities: The campground has
six RV or tent campsites. RVs are limited to 40
feet. Facilities include picnic tables, fire rings
with grills, vault toilets (wheelchair-accessible),
and garbage service, but no drinking water.
You can get drinking water two miles west at
Lolo Creek Campground. Leashed pets are
permitted.

Reservations, fees: Reservations are not
accepted. Campsites cost $8. A second ve-
hicle costs $4. Cash or check. Open late
May-September.

Directions: From Lolo, drive 16 miles west on
Highway 12, or from Lolo Pass, drive 14 miles
east. Locate the campground at milepost 14.3.
The campground sits south of the highway
across a small bridge over Lolo Creek.

GPS Coordinates: N 46° 46.417' W 114°
26.135'

Contact: Lolo National Forest, Missoula

Ranger District, Bldg. 24A, Fort Missoula,
Missoula, MT 59804, 406/329-3814, www.
fs.usda.gov/lolo.

20 LOLO CREEK
🚶🚴🛶🐕♿🚐⛺

Scenic rating: 7
in the Bitterroot Mountains in Lolo National
Forest

Midway between Lolo and Lolo Pass at 3,800
feet, this campground enjoys Lolo Creek. Still
called Lewis and Clark Campground on some
maps, Lolo Creek Campground is about 11
miles west from Fort Fizzle Historic Site, where
the U.S. Army erected a wooden barricade to
stop the advance of Chief Joseph during the
Nez Perce war. The Nez Perce dodged the barricade and climbed a ravine with their horses
and possessions to evade the soldiers. For hikers, the 32-mile Lewis and Clark National Historic Trail parallels the highway. For anglers,
Lolo Creek houses brook, brown, westslope
cutthroat, and rainbow trout. Of the Forest
Service campgrounds on Highway 12, this one
is the closest to services in Lolo—gas, groceries, shopping, and restaurants.

A paved road loops through the campground with paved parking pads on a hillside
of mixed open forest. Several campsites have
tiny pull-through parking. Although several
of the campsites are small, tenters can find
some large flat spaces. Sites 1 and 2, on a spur
road nearest the creek, do not have turnaround
room for trailers. The campground picks up
noise from highway trucks.

Campsites, facilities: The campground has
15 RV or tent campsites, plus two tent-only
sites. RVs are limited to 30 feet. Facilities
include picnic tables, fire rings with grills,
vault toilets (wheelchair-accessible), garbage
service, and drinking water. Leashed pets are
permitted.

Reservations, fees: Reservations are not accepted. Campsites cost $10. A second vehicle

costs $4. Cash or check. Open mid-May-September.

Directions: From Lolo, drive 15 miles west on Highway 12. From Lolo Pass, drive 17 miles east. Locate the campground at milepost 17. Turn south off the highway and immediately right again to cross the bridge over Lolo Creek into the campground.

GPS Coordinates: N 46° 46.541' W 114° 22.965'

Contact: Lolo National Forest, Missoula Ranger District, Bldg. 24A, Fort Missoula, Missoula, MT 59804, 406/329-3814, www.fs.usda.gov/lolo.

21 CHIEF LOOKING GLASS FISHING ACCESS

Scenic rating: 6

on the Bitterroot River

Located 21 miles upstream from the mouth of the Bitterroot River and just south of the town of Lolo and the junction with Highway 12, Chief Looking Glass is a 13-acre fishing access site at 3,182 feet. The Bitterroot River divides into several channels with broad sand and rock beaches that open up as water levels drop during summer. Chief Looking Glass is one of a dozen fishing access sites on the Bitterroot River, but one of the few with a campground. The river, which runs deep, quiet, and slow-moving without rapids in this stretch, harbors brown trout, rainbow trout, mountain whitefish, and swimming holes. The area is also rich with nesting birds in June. The campground has several sites where you can launch hand-carried rafts and canoes (only nonmotorized craft are allowed). You can also launch at the Florence Bridge, about five miles upstream, and float back to camp.

While pavement reaches the entrance, the campground road and parking aprons are gravel. The quiet, sunlit campground has a mix of tall ponderosas, short aspens, and open meadows. Sites 1, 2, 4, 5, 6, and 7 border the

river. Site 4 is very private, surrounded by brush. The others are open with little privacy. The sounds of nature—birds and water—fill the campground.

Campsites, facilities: The campground has 19 RV or tent campsites. RVs are limited to 28 feet. Facilities include picnic tables, fire rings, drinking water, vault toilets (wheelchair-accessible), campground hosts, and garbage service. Leashed pets are permitted.

Reservations, fees: Reservations are not accepted. Campsites cost $12 for those without Montana fishing licenses and $7 for those with licenses. Cash or check. Open May-November.

Directions: From Lolo, go six miles south on Highway 93 to milepost 77. Turn east onto Chief Looking Glass Road and drive one mile to the campground entrance on the left.

GPS Coordinates: N 46° 39.658' W 114° 3.254'

Contact: Montana Fish, Wildlife, and Parks, 3201 Spurgin Rd., Missoula, MT 59804, 406/542-5500, http://fwp.mt.gov.

22 CHARLES WATERS

Scenic rating: 7

in the Bitterroot Mountains in Bitterroot National Forest

Charles Waters Campground huddles at 3,520 feet under the east slopes of the Bitterroot Mountains. Since a paved bike trail parallels the highway, the campground reserves one campsite for bicyclists. It is near the Bass Creek Trailhead and Bass Creek Overlook. From the campground, a half-mile nature trail tours a dry ponderosa pine forest and a moist old-growth forest adjacent to Bass Creek. Trail #4 also follows Bass Creek for 9.1 miles to Bass Lake. For views of the Bitterroot Valley, you can drive to an overlook at 6,100 feet. Five miles east is the Lee Metcalf National Wildlife Refuge, with nature trails (including a 0.5-mile wheelchair-accessible path), bird-watching, hunting, and fishing.

Paved access and the paved campground road eliminated much of the dust at this quiet campground, where most of the campsites sit under large ponderosa pines. Campsites 9-11 border a large meadow with views of the base of the mountains. Campsites on the south side of the loop—13, 15, 16, 17, 18, 20, 22, and 25—have privacy in the woods adjacent to Bass Creek. Four sites have pull-through parking pads.

Campsites, facilities: The campground has 27 RV or tent campsites, one of which is a double site. The maximum length for RVs and trailer combinations is 70 feet. Facilities include picnic tables, fire rings with grills, drinking water, vault toilets, garbage service, and a camp host. Leashed pets are permitted. A wheelchair-accessible toilet and campsite are available.

Reservations, fees: Reservations are not accepted. Campsites cost $10. An extra vehicle costs $5. Cash or check. Open May-October.

Directions: From Florence, drive Highway 93 south for 3.1 miles to milepost 71.5 or from Stevensville, drive about four miles north. Watch for the Bass Creek Recreation Site sign and turn west onto Bass Creek Road. Drive two miles to the entrance. (You'll see the campground sign about 0.3 mile before you actually reach the entrance.)

GPS Coordinates: N 46° 34.504' W 114° 8.480'

Contact: Bitterroot National Forest, Stevensville Ranger District, 88 Main St., Stevensville, MT 59870, 406/777-5461, www.fs.usda.gov/bitterroot.

23 GOLD CREEK

Scenic rating: 6

in the Sapphire Mountains in Bitterroot National Forest

At 4,830 feet, Gold Creek Campground hides in the rounded Sapphire Mountains at the confluence of Gold Creek and the Burnt

Fork Bitterroot River, which both end in wild country. Anglers go for the stream fly-fishing; hunters go for elk and mule deer hunting seasons in the fall. Nearby trails are popular with motorcycle and horseback riders, although a few hikers and mountain bikers tackle them, too. The eight-mile Gold Creek Ridge Trail launches right from the campground. The nine-mile Burnt Fork Trail departs about one mile beyond the campground. Both connect to other trails rather than ending scenic destinations.

Located around a grassy meadow in the forest, the small campground abounds with quiet. Sites are shaded from summer heat and protected from off-season storms.

Campsites, facilities: The campground has five RV or tent campsites, one of which is a double site. RVs are limited to 25 feet. Facilities include picnic tables, fire rings with grills, and a vault toilet (wheelchair-accessible). No drinking water is available; bring your own. Pack out your trash. Leashed pets are permitted.

Reservations, fees: Reservations are not accepted. Camping is free. Open year-round, but snowbound usually December-April.

Directions: From Stevensville, head south on the East Side Highway for 0.5 miles. Turn east onto Burnt Fork Road (County Road 372) and drive for 14 miles. In the first few miles, the road will turn south and become South Burnt Fork Road (Forest Road 312).

GPS Coordinates: N 46° 23.861' W 113° 54.169'

Contact: Bitterroot National Forest, Stevensville Ranger District, 88 Main St., Stevensville, MT 59870, 406/777-5461, www.fs.usda.gov/bitterroot.

24 BLODGETT CANYON

Scenic rating: 9

in the Bitterroot Mountains in Bitterroot National Forest

At 4,300 feet, Blodgett Canyon is one of the

Bitterroot Mountain's hidden treats, offering dramatic spires and cliff faces. Surrounded by the Selway-Bitterroot Wilderness, the canyon houses huge 500-foot walls that attract rock climbers. Departing from the campground, the Blodgett Canyon Trail looks up to the rugged canyon walls above Blodgett Creek. Destinations include a 20-foot waterfall (3.6 miles), High Lake (8 miles), and Blodgett Lake (12.5 miles) in the Selway-Bitterroot Wilderness. A second interpretive trail—departing 4.5 miles from the campground—climbs a fire-ravaged slope to overlook the canyon.

The small campground nestles on the canyon bottom next to roaring Blodgett Creek. Even though a potholed dirt road leads up to the campground, the campground loop is paved and so are the parking pads. Mature trees shade the campsites, and thick underbrush lends privacy, while above on the hillside charred remnants stand as a testament to fire. Large boulders litter the campground—fun bouldering for kids and climbers.

Campsites, facilities: The campground has six RV or tent campsites, plus two walk-in tent campsites. RVs are limited to 45 feet. Facilities include picnic tables, fire rings with grills, vault toilets, campground hosts, and drinking water. Pack out your trash. Because of its popularity, the campground has a five-day stay limit; arrive early to claim a campsite. Leashed pets are permitted. A wheelchair-accessible toilet and two campsites are available.

Reservations, fees: Reservations are not accepted. Camping is free. Open year-round, but snowbound usually December-April.

Directions: Just north of Hamilton on Highway 93 at milepost 50.2 on the north side of the bridge over the Bitterroot River, turn west onto Bowman Road. Drive 0.7 mile and then swing left onto Richetts Road for two miles to a stop sign. (During that two miles, at 1.7 miles, it will turn 90 degrees to head straight for the Bitterroot Mountains and reach the stop sign 0.3 mile later.) Go straight through the stop sign onto Blodgett Camp Road. Follow it 1.9 miles until the pavement ends. In 0.6

Blodgett Canyon is rimmed with spires and vertical cliffs.

© BECKY LOMAX

mile into the gravel road, the road to Blodgett Canyon Overlook Trailhead turns west, but continue straight for 1.4 miles to the road's terminus at the campground.

GPS Coordinates: N 46° 16.155' W 114° 14.632'

Contact: Bitterroot National Forest, Stevensville Ranger District, 88 Main St., Stevensville, MT 59870, 406/777-5461, www.fs.usda.gov/bitterroot.

25 ANGLER'S ROOST
🥾 🚴 ♨ 🛶 🛷 🎣 🐎 🚗 ♿ 🚐 ⛺

Scenic rating: 5

on the Bitterroot River

At 3,750 feet about four miles south of Hamilton, Angler's Roost is a combination state-run fishing access site and private campground. The cement boat ramp accommodates launching onto the river for floating and fishing. You can also launch at Wally Crawford fishing access site about 10 miles upstream to float back to Angler's Roost, or launch at the campground to float half that distance to Demmons in Hamilton. The river is known for its long fishing season and multiple species of trout. Only nonmotorized boats are allowed on the river throughout most of the year, but October-January, you can use motorized craft of 15 horsepower or less. Fishing equipment (rafts, waders, and rods) is for rent. A bicycle/pedestrian path connects with downtown Hamilton. As of 2014, the campground property was for sale.

The campground squeezes in between the highway and the river, with most of the RV sites lined up in a large grassy open meadow in parking-lot fashion within sight and sound of the highway. Sites along the river have cottonwood trees for shade. The treed tenting area sits on the river at the campground's north end.

Campsites, facilities: The campground has nine tent campsites and 59 RV campsites, 14 that can fit RVs up to 65 feet. Hookups include sewer, water, and electricity up to 50 amps. Facilities include picnic tables, fire rings with grills, flush and vault toilets (wheelchair-accessible), showers, launderette, store, firewood for sale, dog exercise area, gas, propane, and disposal station. Leashed pets are permitted.

Reservations, fees: Reservations are accepted, especially for the busy May-September season. Hookups cost $23-30. Tent campsites cost $18. A 7 percent bed tax is added on. Cash, check, or credit card. Open year-round.

Directions: From Hamilton on Highway 93, drive four miles south to the campground. The entrance is on the right just before the bridge crosses the Bitterroot River.

GPS Coordinates: N 46° 11.977' W 114° 10.008'

Contact: Angler's Roost, 815 Hwy. 93 S., Hamilton, MT 59840, 406/363-1268, www.anglersroost-montana.com.

26 BLACK BEAR

Scenic rating: 6
in the Sapphire Mountains in Bitterroot National Forest

The Skalkaho Highway climbs to Skalkaho Pass at 7,260 feet in the Sapphire Mountains via a route once used by Native Americans. The scenic drive appeals to those who like exploring primitive, seasonal forest roads. Because the narrow gravel road twists with curves and has minimal pullouts near the pass, it is not recommended for trailers. Skalkaho Falls and the 23,000-acre Skalkaho Game Preserve with wildlife-watching are attractions on the road. In fall, you may hear elk bugle. Black Bear is the only campground on the west side of Skalkaho Pass. Near the campground, the Centennial Grove interpretive trail loops 0.3-mile near Skalkaho Creek. You can hike, mountain bike, or motorcycle ride on trails near the pass, or fish the creek.

Distance from civilization guarantees quiet to enjoy the creek sounds at this remote valley-bottom campground. A loose forest yields campsites that mix sunlight and shade with views of the arid mountainsides.

Campsites, facilities: The campground has six RV or tent campsites. The parking pads can handle a maximum RV length of 50 feet. Facilities include picnic tables, fire rings with grills, and vault toilets (wheelchair-accessible). No drinking water is available; bring your own or treat creek water. Pack out your trash. Leashed pets are permitted.

Reservations, fees: Reservations are not accepted. Camping is free. Open June-September.

Directions: From Hamilton, drive two miles south on Highway 93. Turn east onto Skalkaho Highway 38. Drive 13 miles and turn right into the campground.

GPS Coordinates: N 46° 9.977' W 113° 55.286'

Contact: Bitterroot National Forest,

Stevensville Ranger District, 88 Main St., Stevensville, MT 59870, 406/777-5461, www.fs.usda.gov/bitterroot.

27 SCHUMAKER

Scenic rating: 9

in the Bitterroot Mountains in Bitterroot National Forest

Perched at 6,500 feet, Schumaker Campground is one of the highest elevation campgrounds in the Bitterroots. Some years, heavy snow precludes campground access until mid-July. Snow feeds adjacent Twin Lakes, which provides irrigation for the Bitterroot Valley and a cold dip for swimmers. Water levels usually drop in August. Nonmotorized boating is permitted on the lakes, as is fishing. A hiking trail at the second lake heads into the Selway-Bitterroot Wilderness, where the path divides to cross two different scenic passes.

The remote location guarantees ultra-quiet at this high subalpine campground, which sits at the south end of Twin Lakes. The combination of elevation and forest for shade keeps the campground cool. Campsites are spread out for privacy.

Campsites, facilities: The campground has 16 RV or tent campsites. The parking pads can handle a maximum RV length of 55 feet. Facilities include picnic tables, fire rings with grills, vault toilets, and campground hosts. No drinking water is available; bring your own, or treat lake water. Pack out your trash. Leashed pets are permitted. Wheelchair-accessible facilities include a toilet and two campsites.

Reservations, fees: Reservations are not accepted. Camping is free. Open July-September.

Directions: From Darby, drive seven miles heading north on Highway 93. Turn west onto Lost Horse Road (Forest Road 429) and drive 18 miles. High-clearance vehicles are best for handling the rocky, potholed steep road. At Lost Horse Cabin, turn right onto Forest Road 5605 for two miles. Turn right into the campground.

© BECKY LOMAX

Lake Como offers fishing and boating in the Bitterroot Mountains.

GPS Coordinates: N 46° 9.077' W 114° 29.849'

Contact: Bitterroot National Forest, Stevensville Ranger District, 88 Main St., Stevensville, MT 59870, 406/777-5461, www.fs.usda.gov/bitterroot.

28 LAKE COMO

🏃🚴🏊🛶🚤🛥🐕♿🚐⛺

Scenic rating: 9

in the Bitterroot Mountains in Bitterroot National Forest

Tucked at 4,250 feet into the eastern slopes of the Bitterroot Mountains, Lake Como sits right at the base of the Selway-Bitterroot Wilderness flanked by three popular campgrounds. Popular for boating and fishing, the lake, which was formed by a dam built in 1905, stays at full pool through mid-July. Boating usually goes until mid-August, before water levels drop too low, shrinking the head of the lake to mud and a small stream and stranding the buoyed swimming area high and dry. South of the dam, a boat launch includes a concrete ramp, dock, and trailer parking. A day-use area has a buoyed sandy swimming beach, changing shelters, vault toilets, and picnic tables. The Rock Creek Trail and the Lake Como National Recreation Trail form mountain-biking and hiking routes on the south and north shores of the lake, meeting a half mile before the wilderness boundary. Hikers and equestrians can continue into the wilderness, but not mountain bikers. Stock facilities include hitch rails, feed bunks, and ramps. North of the lake, the Lick Creek Auto Tour—a one-hour interpretive drive through a research forest—departs for seven miles to Lost Horse Creek Road. The three campgrounds crowd on weekends; plan to stake out your campsite early in the day.

In ponderosa pines and Douglas firs, Lake Como's three campgrounds appeal to different types of campers. Above the north shore adjacent to the swimming beach, the ultra-quiet Three Frogs Campground loops around Kramis Pond, with spacious shaded sites set far apart for privacy on a mixed forest hillside. The Forest Service spruced up the campground with reconstruction in 2011, adding tent platforms in some campsites and improving the gravel parking pads. Located below the dam along the creek, the Lower Lake Como Campground, which is designed for RVs, has a paved road and paved parking pads, mostly pull-throughs. The shaded campsites spread out in the woods, but with other campers visible. Nearest the boat launch and south shore trailhead, the Rock Creek Horse Camp tucks several gravel loops under hefty shade with an open understory and stock facilities. Open to campers without horses, it serves as overflow when the other two campgrounds are full.

Campsites, facilities: Three Frogs Campground has 16 RV or tent campsites plus four walk-in tent sites; RVs are limited to 30 feet. Lower Lake Como Campground has 12 RV campsites with electrical and water hookups; RVs are limited to 125 feet. Rock Creek Horse Camp has 11 RV or tent campsites, including a large group site; RVs are limited to 40 feet. Facilities include picnic tables, fire rings with grills, a few pedestal grills, vault toilets, garbage service, and campground hosts. Drinking water is available at Three Frogs and Lower Lake Como Campgrounds, but not at Rock Creek. Leashed pets are permitted. Wheelchair-accessible toilets and campsites are available.

Reservations, fees: Reservations are not accepted. RV hookup campsites cost $16. Other sites cost $8. Fees include day use. Cash or check. Open late May-early September.

Directions: About four miles north of Darby, look for milepost 35.1 on Highway 93. Turn west onto Lake Como Road and drive for three miles. Turn right at the signed junction for Three Frogs and Lower Lake Como Campgrounds and left for Rock Creek and the boat launch.

Three Frogs GPS Coordinates: N 46° 3.817'
W 114° 13.871'
Lower Lake Como GPS Coordinates: N 46°
4.099' W 114° 14.240'
Rock Creek GPS Coordinates: N 46° 3.847'
W 114° 13.910'
Contact: Bitterroot National Forest, Stevensville Ranger District, 88 Main St., Stevensville, MT 59870, 406/777-5461, www.fs.usda.gov/bitterroot.

29 FALES FLAT

Scenic rating: 7

in the Bitterroot Mountains in Bitterroot
National Forest

At 5,125 feet in the southern Bitterroot Mountains, Fales Flat is the only campground east of the 6,598-foot-high Nez Perce Pass on the 101-mile primitive Magruder Road Corridor that crosses into Idaho's Selway-Bitterroot Wilderness. The campground sits on the east ascent to the pass, a scenic drive and mountain-biking destination. It affords views into the Selway-Bitterroot and Frank Church River of No Return Wildernesses. Erratic pavement—the remnant of thwarted timber sales—starts one mile before the campground and continues the seven miles to the pass. Watch for falling rocks, downed trees, and large sinkholes on the unmaintained and unplowed road. At 1.5 miles south of the campground, the Watchtower Creek Trailhead (#669) departs.

The ultra-quiet campground sprawls across a large, open, grassy meadow bordered by mixed forest. If the group campsite is not reserved, you may use it. Most of the campsites snuggle into the edge of the trees for shade and weather protection, with the exception of primitive sites in the meadow.

Campsites, facilities: The campground has one large group campsite for RVs or tents and three primitive campsites. The campsites can fit midsized RVs, but the condition of the road may dissuade interest. Facilities include picnic tables, fire rings with grills or rock fire rings, vault toilets (wheelchair-accessible), and a fenced stock area, but no drinking water. Bring your own, or treat creek water. Pack out your trash. Leashed pets are permitted.

Reservations, fees: Reservations are not accepted except for the group site (877/444-6777, www.recreation.gov, $15). Camping is free for individual primitive sites. Open year-round, but buried in snow December-April.

Directions: From Highway 93 four miles south of Darby, drive south on the West Fork Road. At 0.3 mile past milepost 14, turn right onto the Nez Perce Road, which is also known as the Magruder Road Corridor and Forest Road 468. At 3.7 miles up the road at Little West Fork Creek, the pavement ends, and large potholes and bumpy washboards litter the dirt road for the next six miles before rough pavement resumes. Reach the campground on the left at 10.6 miles. Enter the campground at the group sign.
GPS Coordinates: N 45° 44.743' W 114° 26.605'
Contact: Bitterroot National Forest, West Fork Ranger District, 6735 West Fork Rd., Darby, MT 59829, 406/821-3269, www.fs.usda.gov/bitterroot.

30 SAM BILLINGS MEMORIAL

Scenic rating: 6

in the Bitterroot Mountains in Bitterroot
National Forest

Located at 4,500 feet in the southern Bitterroot Mountains, Sam Billings Campground is the first developed campground reached on the long drive south along the West Fork of the Bitterroot River, shortened by locals to the West Fork River. A canoe, kayak, and raft launch for floating or fishing the West Fork sits 0.2 mile past the turnoff from the West Fork Road. One mile of potholed dirt road leads

Backroads drivers can tour over Nez Perce Pass in the Bitterroot Mountains.

from the West Fork Road to the campground, which sits on Boulder Creek, a West Fork River tributary. Further up the road, the Boulder Creek Trail leads in 4.5 miles to Boulder Creek Falls in the Selway-Bitterroot Wilderness and further into the Boulder Lakes Basin.

Sprawled out under ponderosa pines, the large campsites hug the gravel campground loop, but far enough apart to gain privacy. Several of the campsites have decent gravel parking pads, and thinning cleaned up scraggly small-growth trees, making more room for tents. A trail cuts down to the creek between sites 7 and 8. Enjoy the sound of tumbling Boulder Creek.

Campsites, facilities: The campground has 12 RV or tent campsites, including one large group site. The maximum length for RVs is 30 feet. Facilities include picnic tables, fire rings with grills, a few pedestal grills, and vault toilets. No drinking water is available. Bring your own, or treat creek water. Pack out your trash. Leashed pets are permitted. Wheelchair-accessible facilities include a toilet and three campsites.

Reservations, fees: Reservations are not accepted. Camping is free. Open year-round, but usually closed by snow December-April.
Directions: From Highway 93 four miles south of Darby, drive south on the West Fork Road for 13.1 miles. Turn right onto Forest Road 5631 and drive 0.9 mile. After you cross a single-lane bridge, the campground entrance will be on the left.
GPS Coordinates: N 45° 49.478' W 114° 14.903'
Contact: Bitterroot National Forest, West Fork Ranger District, 6735 West Fork Rd., Darby, MT 59829, 406/821-3269, www.fs.usda.gov/bitterroot.

31 ROMBO

Scenic rating: 6
in the Bitterroot Mountains in Bitterroot National Forest

On the the West Fork of the Bitterroot River

at 4,500 feet, Rombo is a campground for those who want to fish or float the river. The campground, however, does not permit launching boats, but a primitive launch sits upstream 0.2 mile across the bridge on the opposite side of the river. The campground has plenty of fishing access along the river. The 42-mile river is a favorite of fly-casters going after brown, rainbow, bull, brook, and westslope cutthroat trout.

Shaded by mature ponderosa pines, the campground loops with a gravel road with gravel back-in parking pads. Some of the campsites (13 and 14, in particular) have views of the surrounding forested hills. Sites 1, 2, 5, 6, 8, and 13 border the river, with short trails through the brush connecting to it. Sites are spread out for privacy, but neighboring camps are visible.

Campsites, facilities: The campground has 15 RV or tent campsites. With the short parking pads, the maximum RV length is 30 feet. Facilities include picnic tables, fire rings with grills, a few pedestal grills, vault toilets, drinking water, garbage service, and campground hosts. Leashed pets are permitted. Wheelchair-accessible facilities include toilets and four campsites.

Reservations, fees: Reservations are accepted (877/444-6777, www.recreation.gov). Campsites cost $8 per night. Cash or check. Open late May-mid-October.

Directions: From Darby, go four miles south on Highway 93 to the West Fork Road. Drive south past milepost 17 for 0.9 mile and take a sharp right-hand turn to enter the campground.

GPS Coordinates: N 45° 45.806' W 114° 16.923'

Contact: Bitterroot National Forest, West Fork Ranger District, 6735 West Fork Rd., Darby, MT 59829, 406/821-3269, www.fs.usda.gov/bitterroot.

32 SLATE CREEK

Scenic rating: 7

in the Bitterroot Mountains in Bitterroot National Forest

Slate Creek Campground sits on the east side of Painted Rocks Lake at 4,875 feet. From its position in a narrow side gorge, the campground has no views of the stunning orange lichen-covered rocks or the lake. You can drive or mountain bike across the lake's 800-foot-long dam on a narrow, single-lane dirt road to reach remote trailheads such as Castle Rock and the natural undeveloped hot springs on Forest Road 362. The 143-foot-high dam, built in 1939 for irrigation, created the lake, but boating is best before August, when water demand reduces the lake level significantly. The lake harbors mountain whitefish and five species of trout. A primitive boat launch, beach, and fishing access sit near the campground, but the developed boat launch with paved trailer parking and a concrete ramp is near the dam.

Along a narrow, gravel road loop, the tiny quiet, shaded campground lines up along Slate Creek, which flows into the lake. With room for small tents, the sites each have access to the creek. The entrance road looks down on the campground, affording little privacy from passing motorists.

Campsites, facilities: The campground has four RV or tent campsites. The parking pads can fit RVs up to 25 feet in length. Facilities include picnic tables, fire rings with grills, and a vault toilet, but no drinking water. Bring your own, or treat creek water. Pack out your trash. Leashed pets are permitted.

Reservations, fees: Reservations are not accepted. Camping is free. The campground is open year-round but usually snowbound December-April.

Directions: From Darby, go four miles south on Highway 93 to the West Fork Road. Drive south to milepost 23 and continue another 0.5

mile up the east side of Painted Rocks Lake. Turn left onto a narrow gravel road and drive 0.1 mile to the entrance on the right.
GPS Coordinates: N 45° 41.849' W 114° 16.923'
Contact: Bitterroot National Forest, West Fork Ranger District, 6735 West Fork Rd., Darby, MT 59829, 406/821-3269, www.fs.usda.gov/bitterroot.

33 PAINTED ROCK STATE PARK

Scenic rating: 8

in the Bitterroot Mountains in Bitterroot National Forest

On the south end of Painted Rocks Lake, the 23-acre state park, elevation 4,750 feet, is the only campground that sits right on the lake. It is named for the dramatic orange, black, green, and tan colors that smear across rocky outcrops above the lake. The colors are a result of lichens growing on the granitic and rhyolite cliffs, which are 70-90 million years old. The lake is a trout fishery. The campground's boat launch includes a cement ramp, dock, and trailer parking. By August, water levels drop in the reservoir, leaving a long bare beach below the campground.

While the road is paved to the entrance, the campground loop is dirt with mostly back-in parking pads—muddy when wet and dusty when dry—and big flat spaces for tents. The quiet campground squeezes together campsites under lodgepoles and firs with minimal privacy from the lack of undergrowth. Both loops have a few lake frontage sites with views. One sits in the open next to the boat launch, if you don't mind the commotion.
Campsites, facilities: The campground is a primitive state park with 25 RV or tent campsites. Facilities include picnic tables, fire rings with grills, and vault toilets (wheelchair-accessible), but no drinking water. Bring your own,

or treat lake water. You can also get water four miles up the road at Alta Campground. Pack out your trash. Leashed pets are permitted.
Reservations, fees: Reservations are not accepted. Campsites cost $20 for Montana residents (seniors and disabled get half price) and $23 for nonresidents or $12 for Montana residents. Nonresidents with a Non-Resident Entrance Pass ($25) get a $5 discount on camping fees. Cash or check. Open year-round, but covered in snow in winter.
Directions: From Darby, go four miles south on Highway 93 to the West Fork Road. Drive south to milepost 25 on the east side of Painted Rocks Lake and continue another 0.2 mile. Turn right into the campground.
GPS Coordinates: N 45° 40.879' W 114° 18.069'
Contact: Montana Fish, Wildlife, and Parks, 3201 Spurgin Rd., Missoula, MT 59804, 406/542-5500, http://stateparks.mt.gov.

34 ALTA

Scenic rating: 6

in the Bitterroot Mountains in Bitterroot National Forest

Located the farthest south of the developed campgrounds on the West Fork of the Bitterroot River, Alta Campground gives access to the river for fishing. At this end of the river at 5,000 feet, only small, hand-carried rafts, canoes, and kayaks work for floating. Painted Rocks Reservoir sits less than five miles to the north—another option for fishing and boating. Multiple hiking trails depart up valley with peak top destinations. The surrounding Bitterroot Mountains zigzag with myriad forest roads popular with ATV riders and mountain bikers. You can often spot bighorn sheep, moose, and elk in the area.

Large ponderosa pines shade the campground, which is surrounded by a small community of cabins and homes. The tiny day-use area includes a long bench for sitting by the river, bird-watching, or soaking up the sounds of the forest. The quiet campsites are a mix of sizes, with varying degrees of privacy. Some have room for large tents; others only fit small, two-person tents. Four sites border the river.

Campsites, facilities: The campground has 15 RV or tent campsites. The parking pads can accommodate RVs up to 30 feet in length. Facilities include picnic tables, fire rings with grills, a few pedestal grills, vault toilets, drinking water, overflow parking, campground hosts, and garbage service. Leashed pets are permitted. Wheelchair-accessible facilities include toilets and three campsites.

Reservations, fees: Reservations are accepted (877/444-6777, www.recreation.gov). Campsites cost $8. Cash, check, or credit card. Open year-round, but the campground is usually buried by snow December-April.

Directions: From Darby, go four miles south on Highway 93 to the West Fork Road. Drive south to milepost 29.5 miles, passing Painted Rocks Lake, to reach the campground entrance on the left.

GPS Coordinates: N 45° 37.445' W 114° 18.115'

Contact: Bitterroot National Forest, West Fork Ranger District, 6735 West Fork Rd., Darby, MT 59829, 406/821-3269, www.fs.usda.gov/bitterroot.

35 CRAZY CREEK

🚶 🚴 ⛴ 🐕 ♿ 🚐 ⛺

Scenic rating: 8

in the Bitterroot Mountains in Bitterroot National Forest

At the confluence of Warm Spring Creek and Crazy Creek at 4,800 feet, a pair of adjacent campgrounds squeezes into a narrow canyon. The upper campground services tent and RV campers with sites along the river or with views up the valley. The lower campground

is equipped with a watering trough, hitch rails, and stock ramps for horse-packers. Trails for hikers, equestrians, and mountain bikers depart from here both up-valley and down—to Warm Springs (#103), Porcupine Creek (#205), and Shields Creek (#673)—via a footbridge that crosses Warm Springs in the upper campground. Crazy Creek contains several species of trout, but mostly rainbow trout.

Both of the ultra-quiet campgrounds sit along Warm Springs Creek in a mixed forest with shaded sites. Crazy Creek tumbles through the upper campground. Sites 1 and 2 have views of the rocky cliffs of the canyon. Sites 3, 6, and 7 look up-valley with mountain views. Because of the hillside placement of the campsites, many can only accommodate small tents.

Campsites, facilities: The upper campground has seven RV or tent campsites, and the horse camp has five sites. Both have a maximum RV length of 26 feet. Facilities include picnic tables, fire rings with grills, and vault toilets (wheelchair-accessible). Drinking water is available in the upper campground but not the lower. Pack out your trash. Leashed pets are permitted.

Reservations, fees: Reservations are not accepted. Campsites cost $8 in the upper campground while the lower campground is free. Cash or check. The campgrounds are open year-round but usually snowbound December-April.

Directions: From Highway 93 between Darby and Sula 0.1 mile north of Spring Gulch Campground, turn west onto the rough pavement of Medicine Springs Road (Forest Road 370). Drive 0.8 mile to the campground sign for Warm Springs, where the pavement ends, and continue driving for three more miles to reach both campground entrances—the horse camp downhill to the left and the individual campsites uphill to the right.

GPS Coordinates: N 45° 48.727' W 114° 4.135'

Contact: Bitterroot National Forest, Sula Ranger District, 7338 Hwy. 93 S., Sula, MT

59871, 406/821-3201, www.fs.usda.gov/bitterroot.

36 WARM SPRINGS

Scenic rating: 6

in the Bitterroot Mountains in Bitterroot National Forest

Located at 4,500 feet on Warm Springs Creek, a tributary of the East Fork of the Bitterroot River, the campground is an alternative if Crazy Creek and Spring Gulch are full. It doesn't have the things to commend it that the other two campgrounds do and is in need of some TLC, but it works if you need a campground in this general location and want the quiet of being away from highway trucking noise. It sits one mile off the highway from Spring Gulch Campground and three miles below Crazy Creek Campground. On the way to the campground, you'll pass the Warm Springs Trailhead (#166) for hikers, equestrians, and mountain bikers. The trail follows the drainage upstream. The stream contains rainbow trout.

Tall grass and out-of-control brush are taking over the campground, which makes claiming tent space difficult amid the mix of open meadow and shaded tree sites. Although the narrow campground road is paved, the pavement is old with cracks and bumps. Surrounding the meadow, sites 1, 2, 3, and 14 sit in the open with views of the rocky hillsides. Sites 4-13 are in the trees.

Campsites, facilities: The campground has 14 RV or tent campsites, including one group site. No RVs larger than 26 feet should try to camp here. Facilities include picnic tables, fire rings with grills, vault toilets (wheelchair-accessible), drinking water, and garbage service. Leashed pets are permitted.

Reservations, fees: Reservations are not accepted. Campsites cost $10. Cash or check. Open late May-September.

Directions: From Highway 93 between Darby and Sula 0.1 mile north of Spring Gulch Campground, turn west onto the rough pavement of Medicine Springs Road (#370). Drive 1.2 miles to the campground sign and turn left, going up the hill past a few cabins to the campground entrance. (The pavement ends just past the sign.)
GPS Coordinates: N 45° 50.570' W 114° 2.380'
Contact: Bitterroot National Forest, Sula Ranger District, 7338 Hwy. 93 S., Sula, MT 59871, 406/821-3201, www.fs.usda.gov/bitterroot.

37 SPRING GULCH

Scenic rating: 7

in the Bitterroot Mountains in Bitterroot National Forest

On the climb up to Lost Trail Pass, Spring Gulch is conveniently right on the highway just north of Sula at 4,500 feet. Of course, the trade-off for convenience is road noise. Since it sits right on the East Fork of the Bitterroot River, you can launch rafts, kayaks, and canoes from the campground. A small parking area fits boat trailers. Striking rock outcroppings loom above the river. A very short paved trail connects with the river, where a large fishing deck allows you to soak up the views and the sounds of the water. Hiking and mountain biking are available on Medicine Springs Road across the highway.

Tucked under large ponderosa pines, the grass and brush campground picks up some shade where it squeezes in between the river and the highway. Campsites 2, 4, 5, and 8 sit close to the river. Site 6 and 8 garner mountain views. Sites 2, 6, 11, and 12 have room for tents. The campground loop and back-in parking aprons are paved. Watch for rattlesnakes.
Campsites, facilities: The campground has 11 RV or tent campsites, including one large

group site and four double sites. Only a couple of parking pads can handle RVs and trailer combinations up to 50 feet. Facilities include picnic tables, fire rings with grills, vault toilets, drinking water, a campground host, and garbage service. Leashed pets are permitted. Wheelchair-accessible facilities include toilets and one campsite.

Reservations, fees: Reservations are accepted (877/444-6777, www.recreation.gov). Campsites cost $12. Extra vehicles cost $3. Cash, check, or credit card. Open late May-September.

Directions: From Highway 93 between Darby and Sula 0.1 mile south of the Medicine Creek Road, turn east into the campground.

GPS Coordinates: N 45° 51.510' W 114° 1.415'

Contact: Bitterroot National Forest, Sula Ranger District, 7338 Hwy. 93 S., Sula, MT 59871, 406/821-3201, www.fs.usda.gov/bitterroot.

38 MARTIN CREEK

Scenic rating: 6

in the Sapphire Mountains in Bitterroot National Forest

Located at 5,300 feet on a remote hillside in the Bitterroot National Forest, Martin Creek Campground sits just above the confluence of Martin Creek and Moose Creek. Both streams can be fished, but they have a reputation for marginal luck. Nearby trails launch from the ends of Forest Roads 5771 and 724, popular entries into the Anaconda-Pintler Wilderness. Mountain bikers can tour trails in the area only up to the wilderness boundary, but plenty of forest roads offer biking opportunities, too.

Flanking the southern slope of a mountain with a gravel loop and gravel parking pads, the campground picks up plenty of sunshine. Smaller trees provide privacy between campsites. Miles away from pavement, nights here are utterly quiet. If the campground is full,

backtrack six miles to the more primitive Jennings Campground for small RVs or tents.

Campsites, facilities: The campground has seven RV or tent campsites. It can fit RVs up to 50 feet. Facilities include picnic tables, fire rings with grills, vault toilets (wheelchair-accessible), and drinking water. Pack out your trash. Leashed pets are permitted.

Reservations, fees: Reservations are not accepted. Campsites cost $10. Extra vehicles cost $3. Cash or check. Open late May-September.

Directions: From Highway 93 at Sula, drive 0.2 mile north and turn right onto East Fork Road (County Road 472) for 16.5 miles. At the Moose Creek and Martin Creek junction, turn left onto Forest Road 726 for 0.1 mile to the campground entrance on the right.

GPS Coordinates: N 45° 55.893' W 113° 43.361'

Contact: Bitterroot National Forest, Sula Ranger District, 7338 Hwy. 93 S., Sula, MT 59871, 406/821-3201, www.fs.usda.gov/bitterroot.

39 SULA COUNTRY STORE AND RESORT

Scenic rating: 6

in the Bitterroot Mountains

Squeezed in between the southern ranges of the Bitterroot and Sapphire Mountains at 4,450 feet, the Sula Country Store is an icon of Montana. The roadside store and restaurant that serves home-style meals (the breakfast specialty is homemade country sausage gravy with biscuits) are favorite stops in winter en route to Lost Trail for downhill skiing, Chief Joseph Pass for cross-country skiing, or forest roads for snowmobiling. In summer, the resort serves as a base for fishing the Bitterroot forks, hiking, rafting, and mountain biking. In fall, the area attracts hunters. The East Fork of the Bitterroot River flows behind the campground, and a short path leads to the Lewis and Clark

Discovery Trail interpretive site. Lost Trail Hot Springs is seven miles south.

The 16-acre campground is right on Highway 93, behind the store, surrounded by cabins, large ponderosas, and mowed lawns. The gravel road and parking pads weave around a kids' fishing pond. Most of the sites are back-ins, but at least seven are pull-throughs. Expect highway noise and minimal privacy with tight campsites.

Campsites, facilities: The campground has 19 RV sites and 10 tent campsites. Hookups are available for sewer, water, and electricity up to 50 amps. Five pull-through sites can fit RV combinations up to 68 feet. Facilities include picnic tables, fire rings or pedestal grills, flush toilets (wheelchair-accessible), showers, coin-op launderette, gas, diesel, propane, store, disposal station, cabins, mini-golf, kids' fishing pond, and hot tub. Leashed pets are permitted.

Reservations, fees: Reservations are accepted. Hookups cost $20-25. Tent sites cost $15. Rates are for one or two people. Add $4-5 for each additional person. Cash, check, or credit card. Open year-round.

Directions: Locate the resort on the north side of Highway 93. It sits 13 miles north of the Idaho-Montana border.

GPS Coordinates: N 45° 50.184' W 113° 58.935'

Contact: Sula Country Store, Campground, and RV Park, 7060 Hwy. 93 S., Sula, MT 59871, 406/821-3364, http://bitterroot-montana.com.

40 INDIAN TREES

Scenic rating: 7

in the Bitterroot Mountains in Bitterroot National Forest

In the southern Bitteroots at 5,200 feet, Indian Trees Campground is named for the scarring left on its huge ponderosa pines when the Salish people in the 1800s fed on cambium layers. Located nearby, the Nee-Me-Poo Trail—the four-state Nez Perce National Historic Trail—traces the flight of the Nez Perce from the U.S. Army over Gibbons Pass to Trail Creek. The gravel auto and mountain-biking route connects to Highway 43 and Big Hole National Battlefield. The Porcupine Saddle Trailhead is within a 10-minute drive. After hiking, you can soak in Lost Trail Hot Springs, a five-minute drive south.

Large ponderosas provide a semi-open forest, where some brush between campsites helps create privacy. Most of the sites are grassy with good tent spaces. One large loop swings through the campground, which has a paved road and paved parking pads. Campsite 2 is reserved for bicyclists. Even though the campground sits back from the highway, you'll still hear trucks gearing up and down.

Campsites, facilities: The campground has 15 RV or tent campsites. RVs are limited to 50 feet. Facilities include picnic tables, fire rings with grills, vault toilets, drinking water, garbage service, and campground hosts. Leashed pets are permitted. Wheelchair-accessible facilities include toilets and one campsite.

Reservations, fees: Reservations are accepted (877/444-6777, www.recreation.gov). Campsites cost $10 per night. An extra vehicle costs $3. Cash, check, or credit card. Open late May-September.

Directions: From Sula, go six miles south on Highway 93. Turn west on Forest Road 729 for 0.5 mile past a right turn. Follow the dirt road for 0.2 mile over a cattle guard, veering right to where the road turns back to pavement. Turn left at the entrance sign.

GPS Coordinates: N 45° 45.387' W 113° 57.215'

Contact: Bitterroot National Forest, Sula Ranger District, 7338 Hwy. 93 S., Sula, MT 59871, 406/821-3201, www.fs.usda.gov/bitterroot.

41 LOST TRAIL HOT SPRINGS RESORT

🥾 🚴 🏊 ⛵ 🎣 🎿 ❄️ 🦌 ♿ 🚐 ⛺

Scenic rating: 7

in the Bitterroot Mountains in Bitterroot National Forest

BEST (

Just north of Lost Trail Pass and the Idaho-Montana border at 5,200 feet, Lost Trail Hot Springs Resort features a natural hot springs pool with water temperatures that hang around 93°F year-round and no chemicals added. Covered by a dome in winter, the pool plunges deep on one end with the other end for wading. The resort, which also includes cabins and a restaurant, provides a base for those downhill skiing at Lost Trail, cross-country skiing at Chief Joseph Pass, and snowmobiling in the national forest. In summer, the resort attracts hikers, mountain bikers, sightseers, and anglers. In fall, it's a hunting destination. The resort can help arrange white-water rafting and connect you with fishing or hunting outfitters.

Surrounded by thick forest, the resort cowers in treed ravine within earshot of highway trucking. A gravel road loops through the campground with gravel parking pads. Campsites are shaded, tucked close together, and have minimal privacy. Generators are not permitted.

Campsites, facilities: The resort has 18 RV and four tent campsites. Eight have full hookups with sewer, water, and electricity. Facilities include flush toilets (wheelchair-accessible), showers, a restaurant, casino, lounge, and lodge. Leashed pets are permitted.

Reservations, fees: Reservations are accepted. Hookups cost $32-43. Dry camping sites (RV or tent) cost $16 per night. Admission to the hot pool is extra: $2-7 per person depending on age. Cash, check, or credit card (discounts given for cash). Open year-round.

Directions: From Highway 93 between Sula and Lost Trail Pass six miles north of the Idaho-Montana border, turn west off the highway at the signed entrance. Drive 0.25 mile.

GPS Coordinates: N 45° 45.243' W 113° 56.745'

Contact: Lost Trail Hot Springs Resort, 8321 Hwy. 93 S., Sula, MT 59871, 406/821-3574 or 800/825-3574, www.losttrailhotsprings.com.

42 MUSSIGBROD LAKE

🏕️ ⛵ 🚐 🏊 🎣 🦌 ♿ 🚐 ⛺

Scenic rating: 7

in the Beaverhead Mountains in Beaverhead-Deerlodge National Forest

At 6,200 feet, the 102-acre Mussigbrod Lake attracts anglers for trout fishing and arctic grayling. No boat launch site is available, but you can carry boats (rowboats, rafts, kayaks, canoes, and float tubes) to the lake. Powerboats must have electric motors. From the campground, the Mussigbrod Lake Trail (#372) runs up the north side of the lake to enter the Anaconda-Pintlar Wilderness. Huge swaths of forest at the head of the lake burned in 2000 in a fire that totaled around 60,000 acres. Hikers and horseback riders can see the natural regeneration in young trees and rampant wildflowers.

Because of its remoteness, the campground guarantees quiet. A few sites overlook the lake, and most tuck into the shady lodgepole forest. A few pull-through gravel parking pads are available. An additional four campsites with pull-through parking sit just outside the campground entrance with hitch rails for stock.

Campsites, facilities: The campground has 10 RV or tent campsites. RV are limited to 30 feet. Facilities include picnic tables, fire rings, vault toilets, and drinking water from a hand pump. Pack out your trash. Leashed pets are permitted. A wheelchair-accessible toilet is available in the adjacent horse camp.

Reservations, fees: Reservations are not accepted. Campsites cost $7. An extra vehicle costs $3. Cash or check. Open mid-June-early September.

Directions: From Wisdom, go one mile west

on Highway 43. Turn north onto the Lower North Fork Road for 7.5 miles. Turn left onto the single-lane (with pullouts), rough gravel Mussigbrod Road (Forest Road 573) for 10 miles to the campground.

GPS Coordinates: N 45° 47.433' W 113° 36.632'

Contact: Beaverhead-Deerlodge National Forest, Wisdom Ranger District, P.O. Box 238, Wisdom, MT 59761, 406/689-3243, www.fs.usda.gov/bdnf.

43 MAY CREEK

Scenic rating: 7

in the Beaverhead Mountains in Beaverhead-Deerlodge National Forest

At 6,300 feet, May Creek is the only designated campground on the highway between Chief Joseph Pass and Wisdom. Miles of willow bogs line the streams—good habitat for moose. The nearby Nee-Me-Poo Trail, a gravel driving or mountain-biking route from Highway 93 over Gibbons Pass, follows the path of the Nez Perce fleeing after the seizure of their lands. The route is part of the four-state Nez Perce National Historic Trail. East of the campground in the Big Hole Valley is the Big Hole National Battlefield. Adjacent to May Creek, the campground attracts anglers and those looking to hike May Creek Trail (#103), which follows the creek up two miles to a cabin. The campground's west side has a horse corral, stock ramp, and pasture.

The quiet campground is surrounded by log fences to keep grazing cattle out. Campsites 4, 6, 7, 9, and 10 border the meadow and willows along the perimeter of the lodgepole-shaded campground. While the sites spread out for privacy, neighboring campers are visible.

Campsites, facilities: The campground has 21 RV or tent campsites. Parking pads can fit a maximum RV length of 30 feet. Facilities include picnic tables, fire rings with grills, some pedestal grills, vault toilets (wheelchair-accessible), and drinking water. Pack out your trash. Leashed pets are permitted.

Reservations, fees: Reservations are not accepted. Campsites cost $7. An extra vehicle costs $3. Cash or check. Open mid-June-early September.

Directions: From Wisdom, go 17 miles west on Highway 43 to the campground. From Highway 93 at Lost Trail Pass, drive 9.7 miles west on Highway 43. Turn south to enter the campground via a rough, potholed dirt road that crosses a cattle guard.

GPS Coordinates: N 45° 39.224' W 113° 46.815'

Contact: Beaverhead-Deerlodge National Forest, Wisdom Ranger District, P.O. Box 238, Wisdom, MT 59761, 406/689-3243, www.fs.usda.gov/bdnf.

44 TWIN LAKES

Scenic rating: 9

in the Beaverhead Mountains in Beaverhead-Deerlodge National Forest

At 7,200 feet, Twin Lakes is a scenic pair of subalpine lakes set just below the 10,000-foot-high peaks of the Continental Divide between Squaw and Jumbo Mountains. Boat ramps allow for launching motorboats, rowboats, kayaks, and canoes on both lakes. Nearby hiking trails, including the Big Lake Creek Trail, give places to hike, mountain bike, and ride horses, and you can cool off with a swim in Twin Lakes when finished. Twin Lakes harbors lake trout and burbot.

Set on the north shore of the smaller lake, the campground tucks under lodgepoles. Several sites border the lake, and most have views of the lakes. The location so far from civilization guarantees quiet. Keep binoculars handy for watching birds and moose.

Campsites, facilities: The campground has 21 RV or tent campsites. RVs are limited to

25 feet. Facilities include picnic tables, fire rings, vault toilets (wheelchair-accessible), and drinking water. Pack out your trash. Leashed pets are permitted.

Reservations, fees: Reservations are not accepted. Campsites cost $7. An extra vehicle costs $3. Cash or check. Open mid-June-early September.

Directions: From Wisdom, go south on Highway 278 for seven miles and turn west onto the gravel Twin Lakes Road for 4.1 miles with several 90-degree turns and jogs around ranch properties. Turn left, staying on Twin Lakes Road (Forest Road 183) for nine miles and turn right for six miles to the campground entrance.

GPS Coordinates: N 45° 24.658' W 113° 41.271'

Contact: Beaverhead-Deerlodge National Forest, Wisdom Ranger District, P.O. Box 238, Wisdom, MT 59761, 406/689-3243, www.fs.usda.gov/bdnf.

45 MINER LAKE

Scenic rating: 7

in the Beaverhead Mountains in Beaverhead-Deerlodge National Forest

At 7,000 feet, the half-mile-long shallow Miner Lake is more like a broad pool on May Creek, but it makes excellent bird and wildlife habitat. Water plants and algae are beginning to clog portions of the lake, which offers mediocre fishing. A primitive boat ramp allows for launching nonmotorized crafts such as canoes, kayaks, and rowboats. A trailhead located three miles further up the road accesses the Continental Divide Trail on the Beaverhead crest and multiple alpine lakes, including Upper Miner Lake. Anglers go for the trout in the upper lakes; hikers go for views of the stunning Sacajawea Peaks. Surrounding forest roads attract mountain bikers.

The campground flanks the west shore of Miner Lake with many of the campsites bordering the lakeshore. A mix of meadow and forest makes campsites vary between partly sunny and full shade, but the location guarantees ultra-quiet broken only by the sound of birds, waterfowl, and wildlife.

Campsites, facilities: The campground has 18 RV or tent campsites. RVs are limited to 20 feet. Facilities include picnic tables, fire rings, vault toilets (wheelchair-accessible), and drinking water. Pack out your trash. Leashed pets are permitted.

Reservations, fees: Reservations are not accepted. Campsites cost $7. An extra vehicle costs $3. Cash or check. Open mid-June-early September.

Directions: From Jackson, go south on Highway 278 for 0.5 mile and turn west onto Miner Lake Road (County Road 182) for 10 miles. It will take two 90-degree turns around ranch property and turn into the rutted gravel Forest Road 182 before reaching the campground.

GPS Coordinates: N 45° 19.371' W 113° 34.702'

Contact: Beaverhead-Deerlodge National Forest, Wisdom Ranger District, P.O. Box 238, Wisdom, MT 59761, 406/689-3243, www.fs.usda.gov/bdnf.

46 VAN HOUTEN LAKE

Scenic rating: 7

in the Beaverhead Mountains in Beaverhead-Deerlodge National Forest

At 6,700 feet, tiny Van Houten Lake offers a place to swim on a hot day or fish. But its 11 acres only allow for small rowboats, canoes, or float tubes. A primitive ramp is available for launching on the north side of the lake. Van Houten Lake feeds into the headwaters of Big Hole River, one of Montana's blue ribbon trout fisheries and a rare home to arctic grayling. Hiking and mountain biking trails depart west of the campground with long hauls to reach high alpine destinations around the Continental Divide.

The quiet campground splits between the north and south shores of the lake with three campsites on each side. The campsites rim meadows but tuck into a lodgepole pine forest, garnering a mix of sun and shade.

Campsites, facilities: The lake has six RV or tent campsites. RVs are limited to 20 feet in the north campsites and 30 feet in the south campsites. Facilities include picnic tables, fire rings, and vault toilets (wheelchair-accessible). No drinking water is available; bring your own or treat lake water. Pack out your trash. Leashed pets are permitted.

Reservations, fees: Reservations are not accepted. Camping is free. Open mid-June-September.

Directions: From Jackson, go south on Highway 278 for one mile and turn west onto the dirt Forest Road 181 for 10.5 miles to the lake. GPS Coordinates: N 45° 14.704' W 113° 28.670'

Contact: Beaverhead-Deerlodge National Forest, Wisdom Ranger District, P.O. Box 238, Wisdom, MT 59761, 406/689-3243, www.fs.usda.gov/bdnf.

47 BEAVERTAIL HILL STATE PARK

Scenic rating: 6

on the Clark Fork River

At 3,615 feet, east of Missoula, Beavertail Hill State Park is named for a large hill to the west that resembles a beavertail. Unfortunately, I-90 sliced the beavertail in half. The 65-acre park has a half-mile of river frontage: Gates from the campground access the shoreline for fishing and launching hand-carried boats—rafts, canoes, and kayaks. The next take-out downstream is Schwartz Creek about seven miles west. The campground is the closest to Garnet Ghost Town—home in 1898 to 1,000 people digging for gold. Locate the road to Garnet eight miles east on I-90. Hiking and mountain-biking trails are available around Garnet. A one-mile interpretive trail circles the campground—a good place to watch for nighthawks and great horned owls at dusk.

Reconstructed in 2012, the campground tucks grassy sites under large cottonwoods and pines. Sites 7, 9, 11, 12, 19, 20, 21, and 22 have river frontage. A fence with gated access divides the river and the campground to protect children from running into the flowing water. Be prepared for trucking noise at night.

Campsites, facilities: The campground has 28 RV or tent campsites. Most of the gravel parking pads can fit trailers up to 28 feet in length. Facilities include picnic tables, fire rings with grills, flush and vault toilets, electrical hookups, drinking water, campground hosts, garbage service, interpretive amphitheater programs, firewood for sale, and two tipis for rent. Leashed pets are permitted. Wheelchair-accessible facilities include toilet, campsites, and tipis.

Reservations, fees: Reservations are accepted online or by phone (855/922-6768). Campsites cost $15 for Montana residents (seniors and disabled get half price) and $23 for nonresidents Memorial Day weekend-Labor Day, or $12 for Montana residents and $20 for nonresidents September-May. Campsites with electrical hookups cost $17-28, depending on season and residency. Tipi rental is $22-35 per night. Nonresidents with a Non-Resident Entrance Pass ($25) get a $5 discount on camping fees. Cash, check, or credit card. Open May-October.

Directions: From I-90 between Missoula and Drummond, take Exit 130. Head south following the signs for 0.3 mile and turn left into the campground.

GPS Coordinates: N 46° 43.228' W 113° 34.577'

Contact: Montana Fish, Wildlife, and Parks, 3201 Spurgin Rd., Missoula, MT 59804, 406/542-5500, http://stateparks.mt.gov.

48 NORTON

Scenic rating: 8
on Rock Creek in Lolo National Forest

West of Missoula beneath the Sapphire Mountains, Rock Creek spills into the Clark Fork River in the I-90 corridor. Of the campgrounds lining Rock Creek's 41-mile road, Norton Campground sits the farthest north—the only one accessible by pavement and the lowest at 3,900 feet. A 10-minute drive north, the Valley of the Moon 0.5-mile interpretive boardwalk trail tours the riparian corridor. The river is popular for rafting and kayaking, and it's one of Montana's blue ribbon trout fishing streams. Rock Creek Road works for easy mountain biking, and a trail connects the campground to the river.

South of a string of cabins, the quiet campground jumbles campsites willy-nilly on the inside of a dirt loop under firs and lodgepoles. Park around the ring in pullover spaces and walk in to the picnic tables, which are quite close together and have zero privacy. Flat spaces for tents are small.

Campsites, facilities: The campground has 13 RV or tent campsites. RVs are limited to small rigs. Facilities include picnic tables, fire rings with grills, vault toilets (wheelchair-accessible), and campground hosts. From mid-May-September, drinking water and garbage service are available. When the water is turned off, treat creek water. Pack out your trash when the garbage service closes down. Leashed pets are permitted.

Reservations, fees: Reservations are not accepted. Campsites cost $6 mid-May-September but are otherwise free. Cash or check. Open year-round, but covered in snow in winter.

Directions: From I-90, locate Rock Creek at Exit 126 halfway between Missoula and Drummond. Drive south on the paved part of Rock Creek Road (Forest Road 102) to milepost 10.6. The campground sits between the road and the river. Coming from Philipsburg, drive 14 miles on Highway 348 to reach Forest Road 102. Turn right at the bridge over Rock Creek and drive 30.4 miles north on the bumpy dirt road. Between mileposts 30 and 25, the skinny road shrinks to one lane with turnouts and steep cliff sections—unsuitable for large RVs and trailers.

GPS Coordinates: N 46° 35.364' W 113° 40.203'

Contact: Lolo National Forest, Missoula Ranger District, Bldg. 24A, Fort Missoula, Missoula, MT 59804, 406/329-3814, www.fs.usda.gov/lolo.

49 GRIZZLY

Scenic rating: 7
near Rock Creek in Lolo National Forest

Located on a tributary of Rock Creek, Grizzly Campground sits at 4,200 feet. Hikers and mountain bikers climb the Grizzly Trail up the creek to Grizzly Point. Find the trailhead on Rock Creek Road 0.25 mile north of the campground turnoff. Fishing the Ranch Creek that flows past the campground provides challenges because of the brushy banks.

With well-spread-out sites under a mix of ponderosa and fir, the ultra-quiet campground tucks in between a large black talus slope and Ranch Creek. The dirt road makes two loops through the campground. The loop to the right houses only two sites—both very private. The loop to the left contains sites with peek-a-boo views of surrounding slopes. Sites 2-5 back up to the talus slope, and sites 7-9 border the creek.

Campsites, facilities: The campground has nine RV or tent campsites. RVs are limited to small rigs, and trailers are discouraged because of the road. Facilities include picnic tables, fire rings with grills, pit toilets, horseshoe pits, and a volleyball court (bring your own net). From mid-May-September, drinking water and garbage service are available. When the water is turned off, treat creek water. Pack out your trash when the garbage service closes down. Leashed pets are permitted.

Reservations, fees: Reservations are not accepted. Campsites cost $6 May-September but are otherwise free. Cash or check. Open year-round, but covered in snow in winter.

Directions: From I-90, take the Rock Creek Exit 126 halfway between Missoula and Drummond. Drive south on the paved part of Rock Creek Road (Forest Road 102) to milepost 11.2. Turn east onto the dirt Forest Road 4296 for 0.7 mile and then turn right, driving over Ranch Creek to enter the campground. Coming from Philipsburg, drive 14 miles on Highway 348 to reach Forest Road 102. Turn right at the bridge over Rock Creek and drive 29.8 miles north on the bumpy dirt road. Between mileposts 30 and 25, the skinny road shrinks to one lane with turnouts and steep cliff sections—unsuitable for large RVs and trailers.

GPS Coordinates: N 46° 34.410' W 113° 39.670'

Contact: Lolo National Forest, Missoula Ranger District, Bldg. 24A, Fort Missoula, Missoula, MT 59804, 406/329-3814, www.fs.usda.gov/lolo.

50 DALLES

🚶 🚴 🛶 🎣 🚣 🐕 🚐 ⛺

Scenic rating: 7

on Rock Creek in Lolo National Forest

BEST (

Rock Creek borders tiny Welcome Creek Wilderness, a pocket nine miles long and seven miles wide in the Sapphire Mountains west of Missoula. At 4,200 feet, Dalles Campground provides a major entrance to the wilderness with the Welcome Creek Trailhead located 0.4 mile north of the campground. A swinging bridge crosses Rock Creek into the wilderness, where the trail climbs 7.5 miles to the steep, rocky Sapphire divide. Mountain bikers are not allowed in the wilderness but can bike the road. From the campground, paths lead down to the riverbank for fishing on the blue-ribbon trout stream that is also popular for rafting, kayaking, and canoeing. Only small RVs should attempt to come from the south.

Sitting on a bluff overlooking the river, Dalles Campground provides large, spread-out campsites good for tenting. Sites 4, 6, and 8 overlook the river. A mature forest lends partial shade to the campsites, which are quiet enough to hear the river.

Campsites, facilities: The campground has 10 RV or tent campsites. Some parking pads can accommodate midsized RVs. Facilities include picnic tables, fire rings with grills, and pit toilets. From mid-May-September, drinking water and garbage service are available. When the water is turned off, treat river water. Pack out your trash when the garbage service closes down. Leashed pets are permitted.

Reservations, fees: Reservations are not accepted. Campsites cost $6 May-September; otherwise they're free. Cash or check. Open year-round, but covered in snow in winter.

Directions: From I-90, take Rock Creek Exit 126 halfway between Missoula and Drummond. Drive south on Rock Creek Road (Forest Road 102) to milepost 14.1 to the campground entrance on the river side. (The pavement ends after 11.5 miles.) Coming from Philipsburg, drive 14 miles on Highway 348 to reach Forest Road 102. Turn right at the bridge over Rock Creek and drive 26.9 miles north on the bumpy dirt road. Between mileposts 30 and 25, the skinny road shrinks to one lane with turnouts and steep cliff sections—unsuitable for large RVs and trailers.

GPS Coordinates: N 46° 33.465' W 113° 42.610'

Contact: Lolo National Forest, Missoula Ranger District, Bldg. 24A, Fort Missoula, Missoula, MT 59804, 406/329-3814, www.fs.usda.gov/lolo.

51 HARRY'S FLAT

Scenic rating: 5

on Rock Creek in Lolo National Forest

Rock Creek, which flows through a canyon hanging east of the Sapphire Mountains, is home to bighorn sheep and mountain goats. Harry's Flat Campground, at 4,200 feet, perches in the narrow canyon's lower end, where steep talus slopes tumble into the river. Across the river is the Welcome Creek Wilderness. The blue-ribbon trout stream attracts rafters, kayakers, and anglers. Mountain bikers ride the road, and hikers can find trailheads south of the campground.

The quiet campground spreads out around two loops under large ponderosa pines. The loop housing sites 10-19 has a pit toilet; the loop with sites 1-9 has a vault toilet, plus more private sites. Most of the campsites have large flat spaces for tents. Sites 1, 2, 3, and 5 claim riverfront.

Campsites, facilities: The campground has 15 RV or tent campsites. The configuration of the dirt loops and the size of the parking pads can accommodate larger RVs. However, be aware that the drive requires more than five miles on a rough narrow dirt road from the north; only small RVs should attempt access from the south. Facilities include picnic tables, fire rings with grills, and vault toilets (wheelchair-accessible). From mid-May-September, drinking water and garbage service are available. When the water is turned off, treat river water. Pack out your trash when the garbage service closes down. Leashed pets are permitted.

Reservations, fees: Reservations are not accepted. Campsites cost $6 May-September. Cash or check. Open year-round, but covered in snow in winter.

Directions: From I-90, take Rock Creek Exit 126 halfway between Missoula and Drummond and drive south on Rock Creek Road (Forest Road 102) to milepost 16.5 with the campground entrance on the river side. (The pavement ends after 11.5 miles.) Coming from Philipsburg, drive 14 miles on Highway 348 to reach Forest Road 102. Turn right at the bridge over Rock Creek and drive 24.5 miles north on the bumpy dirt road. Between mileposts 30 and 25, the skinny road shrinks to one lane with turnouts and steep cliff sections—unsuitable for large RVs and trailers.

GPS Coordinates: N 46° 32.222' W 113° 44.004'

Contact: Lolo National Forest, Missoula Ranger District, Bldg. 24A, Fort Missoula, Missoula, MT 59804, 406/329-3814, www.fs.usda.gov/lolo.

52 ROCK CREEK PRIMITIVE

Scenic rating: 7

on Rock Creek in Lolo National Forest

Rock Creek—a 52-mile blue-ribbon trout river draining the Sapphire Mountains southwest of Missoula—flows north into the Clark Fork River with Rock Creek Road paralleling most of its distance. Camping in dispersed sites is not permitted in this area of Lolo National Forest except for 15 designated primitive sites between mileposts 12 and 33. Most may be accessed from the river for those who want to overnight while rafting or kayaking; all may be accessed via the rugged 41-mile dirt Forest Road 102, which parallels the river.

Each signed primitive campsite is different and identified by number. These forested locations are attractive for the quiet and solitude they provide. Two sit in the woods on the east side of the road, but the others command river frontage. Primitive sites 4, 7, 8, and 11 are walk-in sites for tenting.

Campsites, facilities: Fifteen primitive camps line the Rock Creek Road between milepost 12 and 33. Most have one campsite; camp 14 has three sites. Eleven camps accommodate small RVs or tents; four camps are tents only.

Facilities include pit toilets at two camps and metal or rock fire rings. Those with no toilets require campers to follow Leave No Trace ethics for human waste. No drinking water is available; bring your own or treat river water. (You can get water at Norton, Dalles, Harry's Flat, and Bitterroot Flat campgrounds, also on Rock Creek Road.) Pack out your trash. Leashed pets are permitted.

Reservations, fees: Reservations are not accepted. Camping is free. Open year-round, but snow covers sites in winter.

Directions: From I-90, take Rock Creek Exit 126 halfway between Missoula and Drummond and drive south on Rock Creek Road (Forest Road 102) about 12 miles to where the pavement ends to reach the first primitive campsite. From the Philipsburg direction, drive west on Highway 348 to access Forest Road 102 to reach primitive campsite 15 eight miles north of the bridge crossing Rock Creek. The remaining primitive campsites sprinkle along Rock Creek Road every one to three miles. Five of the single-lane, steep miles from milepost 25 to 30 have very few turnouts and are only suitable for small RVs. Trailers are not recommended.

GPS Coordinates: between N 46° 34.411' W 113° 41.091' and N 46° 22.591' W 113° 38.866'

Contact: Lolo National Forest, Missoula Ranger District, Bldg. 24A, Fort Missoula, Missoula, MT 59804, 406/329-3814, www.fs.usda.gov/lolo.

53 BITTERROOT FLAT

Scenic rating: 6

on Rock Creek in Lolo National Forest

Popular for rafting and kayaking, Rock Creek—a blue-ribbon trout-fishing tributary of the Clark Fork River—squeezes in between the Sapphire and Long John Mountains east of Missoula. At 4,450 feet, Bitterroot Flat is almost equidistant from either end of the rugged forest road along the creek, but coming from the north gains the advantage of 11.5 miles of pavement. Heading into the Sapphires, the Wahlquist Trailhead is three miles to the north.

The grassy campground with low brush sits under a canopy of firs. A group fire pit with benches is available. Sites 1, 2, 3, 5, 8, 10, 11, 13, and 14 have river frontage—some right on the bank staring across the river at the huge talus slope. Since most campers head for these, the sites on the inside of the loop are more overgrown from less use. Site 14 is large enough for two big tents, and several sites have double-wide parking.

Campsites, facilities: The campground has 15 RV or tent campsites that can fit midsized RVs. Facilities include picnic tables, fire rings with grills, bear box (Site 2), and three vault toilets (wheelchair-accessible). From mid-May-September, drinking water and garbage service are available. When the water is turned off, treat river water. Pack out your trash when the garbage service closes down. Leashed pets are permitted.

Reservations, fees: Reservations are not accepted. Campsites cost $6 May-September. Cash or check. Open year-round, but snowbound in winter.

Directions: From I-90, take Rock Creek Exit 126 halfway between Missoula and Drummond and drive south on Rock Creek Road (Forest Road 102) to milepost 22.5 with the campground entrance on the river side. (The pavement ends after 11.5 miles.) Coming from Philipsburg, drive 14 miles on Highway 348 to reach Forest Road 102. Turn right at the bridge over Rock Creek and drive 18.5 miles north on the bumpy dirt road. Between mileposts 30 and 25, the skinny road shrinks to one lane with turnouts and steep cliff sections—unsuitable for large RVs and trailers.

GPS Coordinates: N 46° 28.106' W 113° 46.645'

Contact: Lolo National Forest, Missoula Ranger District, Bldg. 24A, Fort Missoula,

Missoula, MT 59804, 406/329-3814, www.
fs.usda.gov/lolo.

54 SIRIA

🏃 🚵 🛶 🎣 🚤 🐎 🚐 🏕

Scenic rating: 6
on Rock Creek in Lolo National Forest

Only those with a hankering for driving the
long, slow miles of bumpy, potholed dirt road
of Rock Creek should head to Siria Campground, located at 4,600 feet. The campground
grants utter solitude, quiet, and remoteness,
but it is a chore to reach. The last few miles on
either side of the campground squeeze down to
one lane, with a few turnouts, plus steep cliff
sections. A fishing access for launching rafts
and kayaks sits 0.6 mile north of the campground. The river is known for its blue-ribbon
trout fishery. Trailheads are within two miles
of north and south of the campground, and
mountain bikers ride the road. At milepost
25.1, an interpretive site explains the impressive
destruction from a microburst across the river.

With paths leading to the river, the campground sits opposite the historical ranger station. Large, tall ponderosa pines shade the
ultra-quiet campground nearly overgrown with
grass and brush, a testament to its lack of use.
Campsites, facilities: The campground has
four RV or tent campsites. The campground
is only suitable for small RVs; trailers are not
recommended. Facilities include picnic tables,
fire rings with grills, and a vault toilet, but no
drinking water. Bring your own, treat river
water. Pack out your trash. Leashed pets are
permitted.
Reservations, fees: Reservations are not accepted. Camping costs $6 May-September.
Open year-round, but snowbound in winter.
Directions: From I-90, take Rock Creek Exit
126 halfway between Missoula and Drummond and drive south on Rock Creek Road
(Forest Road 102) to milepost 27.9. The pavement ends after 11.5 miles. Starting at milepost

25, the already narrow road shrinks to one
lane with turnouts and a steep cliff section.
North of the ranger station, turn west into
Siria Campground. Coming from Philipsburg,
drive 14 miles on Highway 348 to reach Forest Road 102. Turn right at the bridge over
Rock Creek and drive 13.1 miles north on the
bumpy dirt road. At milepost 30, the skinny
road narrows to a single-lane to traverse around
a steep bluff—unsuitable for large RVs and
trailers.
GPS Coordinates: N 46° 25.359' W 113°
43.066'
Contact: Lolo National Forest, Missoula
Ranger District, Bldg. 24A, Fort Missoula,
Missoula, MT 59804, 406/329-3814, www.
fs.usda.gov/lolo.

55 STONY

🏃 🚵 🎣 🛶 🚤 🐎 ♿ 🚐 🏕

Scenic rating: 8
near Rock Creek in Beaverhead-Deerlodge
National Forest

At 4,800 feet, northwest of Philipsburg, Stony
Campground is the most southern of the
campgrounds lining Rock Creek. The river
maintains a high reputation for fly-fishing
for rainbow, cutthroat, brown, and bull trout.
Hatches of mayflies and caddis flies last all
season long. Accesses for launching drift boats,
rafts, and kayaks sit north and south of the
campground at the bridges at mileposts 41 and
35.5. At the end of Forest Road 241, trail #2
follows Stony Creek up to Stony Lake in the
Sapphire Mountains, a destination for hikers
and mountain bikers. The campground sits
in the upper end of the canyon across from
huge orange and rust cliffs that light up with
the setting sun.

The long, narrow campground parallels
Stony Creek. Most of the sites, some with
weed-covered parking pads, tuck under firs,
but three sites (8, 9, and 10) command prime
views of the cliffs from an open meadow. (Too

bad houses and phone lines are in the view, too.) Sites 3 and 6 have creek frontage.

Campsites, facilities: The campground has 10 RV or tent campsites. Parking pads can fit RVs up to 32 feet in length. Facilities include picnic tables, fire rings with grills, vault toilets (wheelchair-accessible), and drinking water. Pack out your trash. Leashed pets are permitted.

Reservations, fees: Reservations are not accepted. Camping is free. Open mid-May-late September.

Directions: From I-90, take Rock Creek Exit 126 halfway between Missoula and Drummond and drive south on the mostly gravel Rock Creek Road (Forest Road 102) to milepost 36.6. Those coming from the north will encounter five miles (mileposts 25-30) of steep, skinny road suitable only for small RVs (trailers not recommended). The easier drive enters from Philipsburg via Highway 348 to the bridge crossing Rock Creek. Turn right onto the dirt Forest Road 102 for 4.4 miles. At the campground sign, turn west onto Forest Road 241 and drive 0.1 mile to turn left into the campground over the cattle guard.
GPS Coordinates: N 46° 20.936' W 113° 36.537'

Contact: Beaverhead-Deerlodge National Forest, Pintler Ranger District, 88 Business Loop, Philipsburg, MT 59858, 406/859-3211, www.fs.usda.gov/bdnf.

56 COPPER CREEK

Scenic rating: 7

near the Anaconda Mountains in Beaverhead-Deerlodge National Forest

Located northwest of the Anaconda Mountains, Copper Creek Campground is mostly used by hikers and anglers accessing the Anaconda-Pintler Wilderness and the Continental Divide Trail that bisects it. Anglers can find plenty of trout fishing in the Middle Fork of

Rock Creek, Copper Creek, and Moose Lake about one mile south of the campground. Hikers can pick from several trails in the area, including destinations in the lake-filled basins below Warren Peak in the wilderness. The drive requires miles of dirt and gravel road travel.

In one loop, the quiet campground circles an arid meadow adjacent to the Middle Fork of Rock Creek. Campsites tuck under pines for shade. Copper Creek runs past the campground with several sites adjacent to it.

Campsites, facilities: The campground has seven RV or tent campsites. RVs are limited to 22 feet long. Facilities include picnic tables, fire rings, vault toilets (wheelchair-accessible), and drinking water. Pack out your trash. Leashed pets are permitted.

Reservations, fees: Reservations are not accepted. Camping is free. Open June-September.

Directions: From Philipsburg, drive south for 6.5 miles on Highway 1. Turn west onto Skalkaho Highway (Hwy. 38) for 10.8 miles. Turn south on the Middle Fork Road (Forest Rd. 5106) for 10 miles. Turn right and drive 0.2 miles to the campground entrance on the right.
GPS Coordinates: N 46° 3.965' W 113° 32.511'

Contact: Beaverhead-Deerlodge National Forest, Pintler Ranger District, 88 Business Loop, Philipsburg, MT 59858, 406/859-3211, www.fs.usda.gov/bdnf.

57 SPILLWAY

Scenic rating: 7

near the Anaconda Mountains in Beaverhead-Deerlodge National Forest

Located northwest of the Anaconda Mountains, Spillway Campground is mostly used by hikers and anglers accessing the Anaconda-Pintler Wilderness and the Continental Divide Trail that bisects it. The campground sits on the East Fork Reservoir, a 1.7-mile-long lake at 6,000 feet. A primitive boat ramp aids in launching boats and canoes. Anglers go after brook, bull, rainbow, and westslope cutthroat trout in the reservoir. Hikers can take a long drive to the end of the East Fork Road to access a 10-mile loop trail in the Anaconda-Pintler Wilderness. The trail leads to the pair of Carpp Lakes and links with Warren Pass for views of the rugged 10,463-foot Warren Peak. Swimmers can cool off in the East Fork Reservoir.

The quiet campground circles one loop in a forest of pines on the west side of the East Fork Reservoir. A few sites overlook the reservoir, and trails connect with the water. Go in early summer for the lake to be at its highest level.

Campsites, facilities: The campground has 13 RV or tent campsites. RVs are limited to 22 feet long. Facilities include picnic tables, fire rings, vault toilets (wheelchair-accessible), and drinking water. Pack out your trash. Leashed pets are permitted.

Reservations, fees: Reservations are not accepted. Camping is free. Open June-September.

Directions: From Philipsburg, drive south for 6.5 miles on Highway 1. Turn west onto Skalkaho Highway (Hwy. 38) for six miles. Turn south on the East Fork Road (Forest Road 672) for 6.4 miles. Turn right at the East Fork Reservoir and drive 0.3 miles to the campground entrance on the left.

GPS Coordinates: N 46° 7.669' W 113° 23.035'

Contact: Beaverhead-Deerlodge National Forest, Pintler Ranger District, 88 Business Loop, Philipsburg, MT 59858, 406/859-3211, www.fs.usda.gov/bdnf.

58 FLINT CREEK

Scenic rating: 5

near Georgetown Lake in Beaverhead-Deerlodge National Forest

Located on the Pintler Scenic Byway, Flint

Creek Campground suffers repeated flooding during high water releases from the dam at Georgetown Lake. Flint Creek flows north from the lake, cuts through the bedrock, and then tumbles through a chiseled steep gorge to the valley floor, where the campground sits at 5,650 feet. The scenic byway in this section is equally dramatic, as it climbs the steep grade to reach Georgetown Lake's elevation. Much of the area is sandy because of the flooding. In June, it is muddy and wet, with some of the upper campsites containing small lakes. During high-water season (May-June), be prepared to evacuate if an alarm sounds, indicating a release from the dam. Flint Creek and the small pond early summer pond in the campground provide fishing.

A potholed sandy road leads into the campground, where all of the campsites line up along the creek. To access the campground's upper end, the road crosses a small dam. Campsites are spread out, affording privacy, but the road overhead adds noise from trucks.

Campsites, facilities: The campground has 16 RV or tent campsites. RVs are limited to 22 feet. Facilities include picnic tables, fire rings, and vault toilets (wheelchair-accessible). Leashed pets are permitted.

Reservations, fees: Reservations are not accepted. Camping is free. Open early May-late September.

Directions: From Philipsburg, drive eight miles south on the Pintler Scenic Byway (Highway 1) to reach the campground at milepost 30.3. Turn south to enter the campground. From Georgetown Lake, drive north on the highway, descending through the gorge.

GPS Coordinates: N 46° 14.015' W 113° 18.028'

Contact: Beaverhead-Deerlodge National Forest, Pintler Ranger District, 88 Business Loop, Philipsburg, MT 59858, 406/859-3211, www.fs.usda.gov/bdnf.

59 PINEY AND PHILIPSBURG BAY

🚶 🚵 ⛵ 🛶 🏊 🚣 🐎 ♿ 🚐 ⛺

Scenic rating: 9

on Georgetown Lake in Beaverhead-Deerlodge National Forest

Located at 6,400 feet between Philipsburg and Anaconda on the Pintler Scenic Byway, Piney and Philipsburg Bay Campgrounds offer popular lakeside locations one mile apart. On Georgetown Lake's western shore, the campgrounds have concrete boat ramps, docks, and trailer parking for launching onto the lake for waterskiing, fishing, kayaking, and canoeing. The lake splays out at the base of the Pintler Mountains—a gorgeous view in June with snow on the peaks. Trails run through the campgrounds to swimming beaches, and other trails flank the nearby slopes, including an overlook above Phillipsburg Bay. Bicyclists can tour the lake loop, but use caution on the narrow road.

Tall lodgepole pines used to shade the campgrounds, but many of the trees have been removed because of beetle kill. Both campgrounds sit in bays off the main lake with paved loops and paved parking aprons. Short whortleberry provides groundcover (taste the red berries), but at only a few inches tall, it does not contribute to privacy. Many sites are roomy with spaces for large tents. At Piney, a handful of sites have prime lake frontage: 7, 9, 37, 44, and 46. Remaining campsites stack up the hillside. At Philipsburg Bay, all of the sites flank the hillside; none have lake frontage. Both campgrounds are locked nightly between 10pm and 6am for security.

Campsites, facilities: Piney has 48 RV or tent campsites, and Philipsburg Bay has 69 RV or tent campsites. RVs are limited to 32 feet. Facilities include picnic tables, fire rings with grills, vault toilets (wheelchair-accessible), drinking water, garbage service, and campground hosts. Leashed pets are permitted.

Reservations, fees: Reservations are accepted for Philipsburg Bay (877/444-6777, www.recreation.gov), but not Piney. Campsites cost $14. Extra camping units (tent, RV, trailer) cost an additional $14. Cash or check. Open mid-May-late September.

Directions: From the Pintler Scenic Byway (Hwy. 1), take the northern Georgetown Lake Road west along the lakeshore. Drive 1.5 miles to reach Philipsburg Bay and 2.4 miles to Piney. (Note: Georgetown Lake Road loops completely around the lake. For the shortest route, take the north end of the loop at the dam rather than the one at the southeast corner of the lake.)
Piney GPS Coordinates: N 46° 11.859' W 113° 18.297'
Phillipsburg Bay GPS Coordinates: N 46° 12.359' W 113° 17.184'

Contact: Beaverhead-Deerlodge National Forest, Pintler Ranger District, 88 Business Loop, Philipsburg, MT 59858, 406/859-3211, www.fs.usda.gov/bdnf.

60 STUART MILL BAY

🚵 ⛵ 🛶 🏊 🚣 🐎 ♿ 🚐 ⛺

Scenic rating: 8

on Georgetown Lake

Off the Pintler Scenic Byway on Georgetown Lake's south side, Stuart Mill Bay is a 363-acre state fishing access park that contains wetlands, grasslands, and forest. The area houses moose, deer, ospreys, bald eagles, coots, red-necked grebes, and great blue herons. Georgetown Lake harbors brook trout, rainbow trout, and kokanee salmon. The campground, at 6,400 feet, has two boat launches—a primitive ramp to accommodate smaller hand-carried crafts such as canoes, kayaks, and rafts and a concrete ramp with a dock to launch power boats for waterskiing or fishing. Trailer parking is also available.

Nearly every campsite in the park has waterfront or water views of the Anaconda Mountains dominated by Mount Haggin.

Large gravel parking pads are surrounded by grass, and some willows break up the shoreline. Only a few trees shade a couple of the sites; most are wide open, allowing winds to whip through them. Sites 1-11 sit in pods of three or four campsites; the remaining campsites (12-16) line up along the water. Some of the campsites have double-wide parking pads; a few are pull-throughs.

Campsites, facilities: The campground has 16 RV or tent campsites. RVs are limited to 30 feet. Facilities include picnic tables, fire rings with grills, a few pedestal grills, and vault toilets (wheelchair-accessible). No drinking water is available. Bring your own, or treat lake water. Pack out your trash. Leashed pets are permitted.

Reservations, fees: Reservations are not accepted. Campsites cost $12 for those without Montana fishing licenses and $7 for those with licenses. Cash or check. Open year-round.

Directions: From the Pintler Scenic Byway (Hwy. 1), take the southern Georgetown Lake Road west along the lakeshore for 1.4 miles. Turn right into the park. You'll come to the primitive launch first, then to a sign for the large boat launch and two campground loops. (Note: Georgetown Lake Road loops completely around the lake. For the shortest route in, do not take the north end of the loop at the dam but the one at the southeast corner of the lake.)

GPS Coordinates: N 46° 10.424' W 113° 16.456'

Contact: Montana Fish, Wildlife, and Parks, 3201 Spurgin Rd., Missoula, MT 59804, 406/542-5500, http://fwp.mt.gov.

61 LODGEPOLE

Scenic rating: 7

near Georgetown Lake in Beaverhead-Deerlodge National Forest

At 6,400 feet, Lodgepole Campground is the easiest campground to reach on Georgetown Lake, as it is located right on the Pintler Scenic Byway between Anaconda and Philipsburg. However, it is not as popular as the Piney and Philipsburg Bay Campgrounds because it is older, sits on the two-lane highway, and requires crossing the highway to reach the Red Bridge boat launch. The boat launch has a cement boat ramp, dock, and boat trailer parking. Anglers go after kokanee salmon and trout in the lake. At the back of the campground unmarked trails climb into the forest for hiking, mountain biking, and walking dogs.

The two loops of the shady hillside campground have old, rough pavement that connects to dirt parking pads, some of which are very narrow. While the campsites are spaced out, you can still see other campers through the lodgepole forest. Some of the sites accommodate tents; others do not. Those on the upper sides of the loops tend to be built into steep hills and very sloped.

Campsites, facilities: The campground has 31 RV or tent campsites. RVs are limited to 32 feet. Facilities include picnic tables, fire rings with grills, drinking water, pit and vault toilets (wheelchair-accessible), garbage service, and campground hosts. Leashed pets are permitted.

Reservations, fees: Reservations are accepted (877/444-6777, www.recreation.gov). Campsites cost $12 for one camping unit (RV, tent, or trailer). Each additional camping unit costs $12, too. Cash or check. Open late May-late September.

Directions: On the Pintler Scenic Byway (Hwy. 1) at Georgetown Lake halfway between Anaconda and Philipsburg, turn east at milepost 26.9 opposite the Red Bridge boat launch. GPS Coordinates: N 46° 12.676' W 113° 16.442'

Contact: Beaverhead-Deerlodge National Forest, Pintler Ranger District, 88 Business Loop, Philipsburg, MT 59858, 406/859-3211, www.fs.usda.gov/bdnf.

62 CABLE MOUNTAIN

Scenic rating: 5

near Georgetown Lake in Beaverhead-
Deerlodge National Forest

Halfway between Anaconda and Philipsburg east of the Pintler Scenic Byway, Cable Mountain Campground, elevation 6,700 feet, sits south of Discovery Basin Ski Area. In winter, the area provides parking for snowmobiles taking off to explore the Flint Creek Range. In summer, the campground is popular with anglers, mountain bikers, and ATV enthusiasts. Echo Lake boat launch and fishing access sits 2.4 miles away on a rugged, bumpy dirt road unsuitable for trailers. The North Fork of Flint Creek runs adjacent to several campsites. It is closed to fishing until July 1 to protect spawning rainbow trout.

Just before you cross North Flint Creek into the campground, you'll hit the first campsite. It sits right on the creek and right on the entrance road with no privacy. Under lodgepoles, the other campsites line up along the opposite creek bank and sprawl into the woods, spread out with roomy flat areas for tents. The campground road is dirt, as are the parking pads. The campground is quiet unless ATVs are driving around the area.

Campsites, facilities: The campground has 11 RV or tent campsites. RVs are limited to 22 feet. Facilities include picnic tables, fire rings with grills, pit and vault toilets (wheelchair-accessible), and drinking water. Pack out your trash. Leashed pets are permitted.

Reservations, fees: Reservations are not accepted. Campsites cost $10 for the first camping unit (tent, RV, trailer) and $10 for each additional unit. Cash or check. Open late June–mid-September.

Directions: From the Pintler Scenic Byway (Hwy. 1) at Georgetown Lake, halfway between Philipsburg and Anaconda, turn east onto the road with the ski area sign at milepost 25.2. At the three-way split, continue left and follow the route to the ski area. At 2.8 miles from the highway, turn right onto the dirt Forest Road 242 and drive 0.2 mile. Turn right over the narrow bridge into the campground. GPS Coordinates: N 46° 13.345' W 113° 14.818'

Contact: Beaverhead-Deerlodge National Forest, Pintler Ranger District, 88 Business Loop, Philipsburg, MT 59858, 406/859-3211, www.fs.usda.gov/bdnf.

63 SPRING HILL

Scenic rating: 5

in the Flint Creek Mountains of Beaverhead-
Deerlodge National Forest

Located on the Pintler Scenic Byway at 6,500 feet, Spring Hill has sheer convenience to the highway, but that translates into some highway noise in the campground. Warm Spring Creek runs adjacent to the campground; the creek harbors a variety of trout. Within four miles west of the campground, Silver Lake is a favorite haunt for bird-watchers, but the lake's clarity, coldness, and changing water depth means it lacks fish. Georgetown Lake, eight miles west, offers fishing, boating, waterskiing, canoeing, and kayaking.

One gravel loop circles the campground, with shaded roomy campsites under thick lodgepole pines. A second loop circles an open meadow with sunnier sites. A few sites have raised, gravel tent pads, but most of the other campsites can accommodate large tents, too. Site 5 is a walk-in campsite.

Campsites, facilities: The campground has 13 RV or tent campsites, plus two tent-only sites. Trailers are limited to 22 feet. Facilities include picnic tables, fire rings with grills, a few pedestal grills, vault toilets, garbage service, and drinking water. Pack out your trash. Leashed pets are permitted.

Reservations, fees: Reservations are accepted (877/444-6777, www.recreation.gov). Campsites cost $12. An extra camping unit (trailer, tent, or RV) costs $12. Cash or check. Open late June–mid-September.

Directions: At milepost 19.4 on the Pintler Scenic Byway (Hwy. 1), turn north into the campground.

GPS Coordinates: N 46° 10.235' W 113° 9.902'

Contact: Beaverhead-Deerlodge National Forest, Pintler Ranger District, Philipsburg Office, 88 Business Loop, Philipsburg, MT 59858, 406/859-3211, www.fs.usda.gov/bdnf.

64 WARM SPRINGS

Scenic rating: 4

in the Flint Creek Mountains of Beaverhead-Deerlodge National Forest

Just north of the Pintler Scenic Byway at 6,500 feet, Warm Springs is an older campground that attracts ATVers and anglers. It is one of two campgrounds that access the south Flint Creek Range, a lower elevation range of peaks. The jarring Forest Service road passing bucolic farms packs in the potholes, and you'll notice the number of beetle-killed lodgepole pines compared to the healthy aspens. Warm Springs Creek harbors trout (brook, bull, brown, rainbow, westslope cutthroat, and hybrids) plus longnose suckers, mountain whitefish, and sculpin. Mountain bikers can explore the forest roads north of the campground.

After crossing a cattle guard and Warm Springs Creek on a skimpy bridge, the narrow campground road weaves between lodgepoles with barely enough room to breathe. The small shaded campsites are packed in close together, making you immediate buddies with the neighbors. Parking pads are quite small. Campsites on the north end of the loop have good views up the Warm Springs Creek drainage. With its location back from the highway, the campground is quiet.

Campsites, facilities: The campground has six RV or tent campsites. The maximum length for trailers is 16 feet. Facilities include picnic tables, fire rings with grills, vault toilet, and

drinking water. Pack out your trash. Leashed pets are permitted.

Reservations, fees: Reservations are not accepted. Camping is free. Open late June–mid-September.

Directions: At milepost 19.2 on the Pintler Scenic Byway (Hwy. 1), turn north onto Forest Road 170. Dodge the copious potholes on the dirt road for 2.4 miles and turn left into the campground.

GPS Coordinates: N 46° 11.967' W 113° 10.006'

Contact: Beaverhead Deerlodge National Forest, Pintler Ranger District, Philipsburg Office, 88 Business Loop, Philipsburg, MT 59858, 406/859-3211, www.fs.usda.gov/bdnf.

65 LOST CREEK STATE PARK

Scenic rating: 8

in the Flint Creek Mountains

North of Anaconda, 502-acre Lost Creek State Park hides at 6,250 feet in a narrow canyon. The 1,200-foot-tall granite and limestone cliffs dance with an array of colors: gray, pink, beige, orange, and rust. Large granite dikes cut stripes of igneous intrusions through the 1.3-billion-year-old rock. Rock climbers navigate various routes on cliff faces and spires, as do the mountain goats and bighorn sheep. A short paved interpretive trail leads to Lost Creek Falls, which tumbles 50 vertical feet in its descent through the canyon. A Forest Service trail for hiking or mountain biking follows the fishable Lost Creek west for several miles into the canyon in Beaverhead-Deerlodge National Forest.

The sunny campground with minimal privacy has lower and upper sections, both serviced by gravel roads and small gravel parking pads. While both have views of the cliffs and sit along Lost Creek, the upper is the more scenic campground. At night, the campground is quiet.

Campsites, facilities: The campground has

25 RV or tent campsites. RVs are limited to 23 feet. Facilities include picnic tables, fire rings with grills, vault toilets (wheelchair-accessible), drinking water in the upper campground only, and campground hosts. Pack out your trash. Leashed pets are permitted.

Reservations, fees: Reservations are not accepted. Campsites cost $15 for Montana residents (seniors and disabled get half price) and $23 for nonresidents Memorial Day weekend-Labor Day, or $12 for Montana residents and $20 for nonresidents September-May. Nonresidents with a Non-Resident Entrance Pass ($25) get a $5 discount on camping fees. Cash or check. Open May-November.

Directions: From east of Anaconda, head northwest on road 273. After 1.8 miles, turn left. Follow the road for 5.8 miles to the state park entrance. Continue on the paved road, which turns to dirt in 0.4 mile. You'll reach the lower campground first and the upper campground one mile later.

GPS Coordinates: N 46° 11.868' W 112° 58.957'

Contact: Montana Fish, Wildlife, and Parks, 3201 Spurgin Rd., Missoula, MT 59804, 406/542-5500, http://stateparks.mt.gov.

66 RACETRACK

Scenic rating: 6

in the Flint Creek Mountains in Beaverhead-Deerlodge National Forest

Located at 5,400 feet, Racetrack Campground is the closest Forest Service campground to Deer Lodge. The Flint Creek Mountains descend east with pine forests giving way to grass and sagebrush meadows that are stunningly green in spring, but crisp and dry by August. Fishing is available in Racetrack Creek, a native trout fishery. The campground is also the nearest public campground to stay in while visiting the Grant-Kohrs Ranch National Historic Site near Deer Lodge.

Frequented by locals, the campground spreads out along Racetrack Creek with about half of the sites having creek frontage and trails to the stream. Some sites tuck on the edge of the forest while others sit out on the sagebrush meadow hillside. Far from pavement, the campground is quiet.

Campsites, facilities: The campground has 13 RV or tent campsites. RVs are limited to 22 feet long. Facilities include picnic tables, fire rings, vault toilets (wheelchair-accessible), and drinking water. Pack out your trash. Leashed pets are permitted.

Reservations, fees: Reservations are not accepted. Camping is free. Open June-September.

Directions: From I-90, take the Racetrack Exit 195 south of Deerlodge. Drive west for 0.9 mile on Racetrack Road, then south for 0.8 mile on Yellowstone Trail, and then west on Forest Road 169 (Bowman Road) for 5.3 miles. Veer right for four miles to the campground entrance on the left.

GPS Coordinates: N 46° 16.945' W 112° 56.071'

Contact: Beaverhead-Deerlodge National Forest, Pintler Ranger District, 88 Business Loop, Philipsburg, MT 59858, 406/859-3211, www.fs.usda.gov/bdnf.

67 DEER LODGE KOA

Scenic rating: 6

on the Clark Fork River in Deer Lodge

In Deer Lodge, the KOA sits within walking distance of restaurants in town. From the campground, you can fish for rainbow trout in the river. But the main reason to stay here is to visit the Grant-Kohrs Ranch National Historic Site about 1.5 miles northwest. The 1,600-acre ranch with 80 historical buildings is a working cattle ranch that preserves the cowboy life of the American West. The ranch (open daily; free admission) offers guided tours, children's activities, walking trails, and special events. Wagon tours run several times daily throughout the summer.

The sunny, open campground sits between the railroad tracks and the river, so be prepared for noise. Tent sites (some with electrical hookups) cuddle in a big grassy area shaded by a few mature trees. The RV sites have gravel parking pads lined up in parking lot fashion, half of which are pull-throughs with room for slide-outs. Several line up along the riverfront, and some sites can see the Flint Creek Mountains.

Campsites, facilities: The campground has 40 RV campsites and 25 tent campsites. RVs are limited to 75 feet, and hookups are available for water, sewer, and electricity up to 50 amps. Facilities include picnic tables, fire rings with grills, flush toilets, showers, drinking water, garbage service, wireless Internet, camping kitchen, playground, firewood for sale, and camp store. Leashed pets are permitted.

Reservations, fees: Reservations are accepted. Hookups cost $35-41; tent sites cost $23-28. Rates include two people. Cost is $5 per additional adult, $3 per additional child ages 13-17, free for children under 13 years old. Add on 7 percent Montana bed tax. Open April-late October.

Directions: From I-90 at Deer Lodge, take Exit 184 or 187 onto Main Street. Drive north or south to the stoplight at Milwaukee Avenue and turn west. Drive three blocks and turn right at the sign.

GPS Coordinates: N 46° 23.932' W 112° 44.454'

Contact: Deer Lodge KOA, 330 Park St., Deer Lodge, MT 59722, 406/846-1629 or 800/562-1629, www.koa.com.

68 FAIRMONT RV PARK

Scenic rating: 5

near Anaconda

BEST (

Fairmont RV Park neighbors Fairmont Hot

Springs Resort (406/797-3337 or 800/332-3272, www.fairmontmontana.com), with two Olympic-sized swimming pools, two mineral soaking pools, a 350-foot enclosed five-story-tall water slide, and an 18-hole golf course. The pools are open to the public, usually 8am to 10pm, with lifeguards on duty. Admission to the pools costs $5-9, depending on age. Add on $6-7 for the waterslide. The par-72 golf course is known for its mile-high, mile-long fifth hole and five ponds adding to the difficulty. The last hole finishes with a fountain pond.

Surrounded by sagebrush and fields, the mowed-lawn campground has very few shade trees. Most of the sunny sites cram close together. RV camping choices consist of 36 pull-through sites, 49 back-in sites, 28 big rig back-ins, 52 partial hookups, and 11 dry sites. The campground is quiet, but you can hear trucks on the freeway in the distance unless the wind drowns them out.

Campsites, facilities: The campground has 133 RV campsites and 13 tent sites. Hookups are available for sewer, water, and electricity up to 50 amps; the park accommodates RVs up to 75 feet. Facilities include picnic tables, barbecue stands, flush toilets (wheelchair-accessible), showers, launderette, wireless Internet, three rental tipis that sleep four people each, camp store, gas, diesel, movie rentals, horseshoe pits, disposal station, dog walk, and recreation center. Leashed pets are permitted.

Reservations, fees: Reservations are accepted. Hookups cost $34-43. Dry camping and tent sites cost $22. Tipi rentals cost $32. A 7 percent Montana bed tax will be added on. Rates are for two people. Extra people cost more: children $2.50 and adults $5. Cash, check, or credit card. Open mid-April-mid-October.

Directions: On I-90, drive west for 15 miles from Butte or east for 108 miles from Missoula to Exit 211. Follow the signs southwest for four miles to Fairmont RV Park on the left.

GPS Coordinates: N 45° 2.531' W 112° 48.311'

Contact: Fairmont RV Park, 1700 Fairmont

Rd., Fairmont, MT 59711, 866/797-3505 or 406/797-3505, www.fairmontrvresort.com.

69 BUTTE KOA

🧍🚴🚣🛶🏕️🛻♿🚐⛺

Scenic rating: 4

in downtown Butte

At 5,462 feet, the Butte KOA is one for convenience. But you can also explore the town: its copper mining boomtown heritage, the monstrous open Berkeley Pit, the 90-foot-tall Our Lady of the Rockies statue, underground mine tours, museums, and historical mansions. The campground abuts the Blacktail Creek Trail, a paved walking and biking trail that reaches a city park in two miles and connects with other paved trails. Fishing is available in a stream behind the campground.

Set adjacent to the freeway, the Butte KOA offers convenience more than a getaway. Gravel roads weave through the sunny campground with lots of pull-through parking for RVs. Small patches of grass separate sites, which are very close together. Only a handful of trees offer sporadic shade. Tent campsites line up along the edge of the campground.

Campsites, facilities: The campground has 90 RV campsites and 20 tent sites. RV combinations are limited to 80 feet. Hookups include sewer, water, and electricity up to 50 amps. Facilities include picnic tables, fire rings, flush toilets (wheelchair-accessible), showers, launderette, disposal station, wireless Internet, heated outdoor swimming pool (June-early September), propane, firewood for sale, playground, and camp store. Leashed pets are permitted.

Reservations, fees: Reservations are accepted by phone or online. RV sites cost $30-42. Tent sites cost $22-33. Rates are for two people; the cost for additional campers is $5. Kids seven years old and under stay free. Add on 7 percent bed tax. Cash, check, or credit card. Open mid-April-October.

Directions: From I-90 in Butte, exit at Montana Street. Drive one block north and turn right on George Street. Go two blocks and turn right on Kaw Avenue with the campground entrance on the right.
GPS Coordinates: N 45° 59.639' W 112° 31.824'
Contact: Butte KOA, 1601 Kaw Avenue, Butte, MT 59701, 406/782-8080 or 800/562-8089, www.missoulakoa.com.

70 BEAVER DAM

🧍🚴🛶🏕️♿🚐⛺

Scenic rating: 7

in the Anaconda-Pintler Mountains in Beaverhead-Deerlodge National Forest

At 6,485 feet, Beaver Dam Campground flanks the Continental Divide. Several trails that climb to the Continental Divide offer opportunities for mountain biking and hiking. North Fork Divide Creek tumbles from the Continental Divide and offers fishing for westslope cutthroat trout. The campground gets its name from the number of beaver dams along the creek.

Tucked into the trees, this campground offers a mix of partial shade and full-shade sites in a lodgepole pine forest. A gravel road through the campground makes two small loops with a couple pull-through campsites.

Campsites, facilities: The campground has 15 RV or tent campsites. RVs are limited to 50 feet. Facilities include picnic tables, fire rings with grills, vault toilets (wheelchair-accessible), and drinking water. Leashed pets are permitted.

Reservations, fees: Reservations are not accepted. Campsites cost $5. Cash or check. Open mid-June-September.

Directions: From the junction of I-15 and I-90 west of Butte, drive 12 miles south and take Exit 111. Drive west on Divide Creek Road for six miles and turn left into the campground.
GPS Coordinates: N 45° 53.090' W 113° 3.650'

Contact: Beaverhead-Deerlodge National Forest, Butte Ranger District, 1820 Meadowlark, Butte, MT 59701, 406/494-2147, www.fs.usda.gov/bdnf.

71 DICKIE BRIDGE

Scenic rating: 7
on the Big Hole River near the Pioneer Mountains

Northwest of Dillon, the Divide Bridge Campground, at 5,700 feet, is one of the river access points for the famous Big Hole River. The 153-mile-long free-flowing river gathers its headwaters in southwest Montana's Beaverhead Mountains and joins the Beaverhead River at Twin Bridges northeast of Dillon. Its fishery—arctic grayling, mountain whitefish, and trout—is considered blue ribbon. One mile west at East Bank, a boat ramp with a large parking area for trailers allows for launching rafts, drift boats, canoes, and kayaks. The Big Hole, closed to motorboats, works rafting or paddling mid-May-mid-July. Floaters can take out at Divide Bridge.

The 26-acre campground with gravel parking pads features back-in campsites tucked into a shaded forest canopy. You can walk to a primitive river access adjacent to Dickie Bridge to enjoy the water or fish.

Campsites, facilities: The campground has 10 RV or tent campsites. RVs are limited to 24 feet. Facilities include picnic tables, fire rings with grills, vault toilets (wheelchair-accessible), and campground hosts. No drinking water is available; bring your own or treat river water. Pack out your trash. Leashed pets are permitted.

Reservations, fees: Reservations are not accepted. Camping is free. Open year-round.

Directions: From I-15 north of Dillon, take Highway 43 west for 19 miles. Turn left on Bryant Creek Road and immediately left again to the campground.

GPS Coordinates: N 45° 50.992' W 112° 4.257'

Contact: Bureau of Land Management, Butte Field Office, 106 N. Parkmont, Butte, MT 59701, 406/533-7600.

72 DIVIDE BRIDGE

Scenic rating: 7
on the Big Hole River near the Pioneer Mountains

BEST

Near I-15 northwest of Dillon, the Divide Bridge Campground, at 5,500 feet, offers river access for the famous Big Hole River. The 153-mile-long free-flowing river gathers its headwaters in southwest Montana's Beaverhead Mountains and joins the Beaverhead River at Twin Bridges northeast of Dillon. Its fishery—arctic grayling, mountain whitefish, and trout—is considered blue ribbon. Between the bridge and campground, a large boat ramp with trailer parking allows for launching rafts, drift boats, kayaks, and canoes. Hand-carried watercrafts can launch from the primitive ramp in the campground. The Big Hole, closed to motorboats, is good for floating mid-May-mid-July. From the campground, a three-mile destination-less trail departs for Sawmill Gulch for exploring the arid high desert environment. Five miles northeast, a trailhead launches hikers and rock climbers into the Humbug Spires, a wilderness study area containing about 50 granite spires.

Accessed via a potholed dirt road, the campground with gravel parking pads divides into two sections, both with back-in sites. One section has mowed lawns on a loop (sites 1-13); the other is a spur surrounded by rugged sagebrush and high desert grasses (sites 14-21) with parking pads wide enough for two vehicles. Both areas are wide open with no shade—except for the few sites along the river (sites 10-13) tucked into the cottonwoods and aspens. Views include the hillsides of Sawmill Gulch.

Campsites, facilities: The campground has 21 RV or tent campsites. Facilities include picnic tables, fire rings with grills, vault toilets (wheelchair-accessible), drinking water, and a campground host. Pack out your trash. Leashed pets are permitted.

Reservations, fees: Reservations are not accepted. Campsites cost $6 mid-May-September. Cash or check. Open year-round.

Directions: From I-15 north of Dillon, take Highway 43 west toward Divide. After crossing the Big Hole River, turn left at milepost 75 and drive 0.4 mile to the campground. Coming from the west on Highway 43, drive 2.5 miles past the town of Divide.

GPS Coordinates: N 45° 45.224' W 112° 46.561'

Contact: Bureau of Land Management, Butte Field Office, 106 N. Parkmont, Butte, MT 59701, 406/533-7600.

73 PETTINGILL

Scenic rating: 7

in the Pioneer Mountains in Beaverhead-Deerlodge National Forest

At 6,200 feet on the 44-mile Pioneer Mountains Scenic Byway, Pettingill Campground is the first campground reached from the north. It is the tiniest of the campgrounds along the byway and often fills up because of its location and size. The campground is less than a mile from Pattengail Road, which heads into the western Pioneer Mountains. The road accesses the trailhead for Grouse Lakes (4 miles), stock camp areas, and the Pattengail Jeep Trail, which is open to ATVs, mountain bikes, and motorcycles. The campground sits at the confluence of the Wise River and Pettingill Creek, harboring mountain whitefish.

Squeezed between the Wise River and the byway on a paved road with paved parking pads, the tiny campground with nighttime quiet spreads its three sites on a hillside just south of a large day-use parking lot, where you can grab views up to surrounding hillsides.

Lodgepole pines shade the campsites, and all three sites border the river.

Campsites, facilities: The campground has three RV or tent campsites. Parking pads can fit RVs up to 24 feet in length. Facilities include picnic tables, fire rings with grills, vault toilets (wheelchair-accessible), and garbage service. The campground has no drinking water. Bring your own, or treat river water. You can also get drinking water 1.2 miles south at Fourth of July Campground. Leashed pets are permitted.

Reservations, fees: Reservations are not accepted. Campsites cost $6. An extra vehicle costs $3. Cash or check. Open mid-June-September.

Directions: From the junction of Highway 43 and the Pioneer Mountains Scenic Byway, drive 10 miles south. Turn east off the byway into the campground. From the junction of Highway 278 and the scenic byway, drive 35.1 miles north.

GPS Coordinates: N 45° 40.863' W 113° 3.650'

Contact: Beaverhead-Deerlodge National Forest, Wise River Ranger District, P.O. Box 100, Wise River, MT 59762, 406/832-3178, www.fs.usda.gov/bdnf.

74 FOURTH OF JULY

Scenic rating: 7

in the Pioneer Mountains in Beaverhead-Deerlodge National Forest

At 6,400 feet on the 44-mile Pioneer Scenic Byway, Fourth of July Campground offers a paved wheelchair-accessible trail that loops around the entire campground—including along the Wise River. Access for fishing the Wise River is easy from the trail, too. The 26-mile river harbors several species of trout, including brook, brown, rainbow, Yellowstone cutthroat, and westslope cutthroat. Pattengail Road, departing west from the byway two miles north of the campground, leads to the Grouse

The Pioneer Mountains stretch over 11,000 feet in elevation.

Lakes Trailhead (#219). The steep trail climbs four miles to Grouse Lakes, which sit in granite basins, and the Pattengail Jeep Trail is open to mountain bikes, motorcycles, and ATVs.

With a paved road and paved parking pads, the narrow quiet campground squeezes between the byway and the river, but contrary to other forested campsites along the byway, this one is an open lodgepole forest broken by large sagebrush and wildflower meadows that offer views of the timbered hillsides surrounding the campground and varying degrees of shade or privacy. In June, the meadows bloom with purple larkspur.

Campsites, facilities: The campground has five RV or tent campsites. Parking pads can accommodate RVs up to 30 feet. Facilities include picnic tables, fire rings with grills, vault toilets (wheelchair-accessible), drinking water, and garbage service. Leashed pets are permitted.

Reservations, fees: Reservations are not accepted. Campsites cost $8. An extra vehicle costs $3. Cash or check. Open mid-June-September.

Directions: From the junction of Highway 43 and the Pioneer Mountains Scenic Byway,

drive 11.2 miles south. Turn east into the campground. From the junction of Highway 278 and the scenic byway, drive 33.9 miles north.

GPS Coordinates: N 45° 39.818' W 113° 3.872'

Contact: Beaverhead-Deerlodge National Forest, Wise River Ranger District, P.O. Box 100, Wise River, MT 59762, 406/832-3178, www.fs.usda.gov/bdnf.

7 5 LODGEPOLE AND BOULDER CREEK

Scenic rating: 7

in the Pioneer Mountains in Beaverhead-Deerlodge National Forest

At 6,550 feet on the 44-mile Pioneer Mountains Scenic Byway, Lodgepole and Boulder Campgrounds flank both sides of the highway along the Wise River. The narrow canyon prevents seeing the 10,000-foot-high peaks of the Pioneer Mountains and forces the river to pick up speed compared to the meandering slower segments near the summit. You can fish the Wise River from Lodgepole Campground and Boulder Creek, which runs behind Boulder Campground. The nearby Boulder Trail links in with the Sheep Creek and Gold Creek drainage trails, used mostly by hikers, anglers, and horse-packers, but it is also open to mountain bikers.

Both campgrounds sit shaded under lodgepoles with paved roads, paved parking pads, and large tent spaces. Lodgepole Campground lines up campsites right along the river, enjoying the sound of rushing water and garnering territorial views because of adjacent large meadows. Five campsites have double-wide parking spaces. In Boulder Campground, more than half of the campsites overlook the river from a high bench, with the other campsites relishing privacy. At the back of the campground, a single-lane dirt road leads to a few extra primitive campsites.

Campsites, facilities: Lodgepole has 10 RV or tent campsites. Boulder Creek has 13 RV or tent campsites. RVs are limited to 30 feet. Facilities include picnic tables, fire rings with grills, a few pedestal grills, vault toilets (wheelchair-accessible), drinking water, garbage service, and campground hosts. Leashed pets are permitted.

Reservations, fees: Reservations are not accepted. Campsites cost $8. Extra vehicles cost $3. Cash or check. Open mid-June-September.

Directions: From the junction of Highway 43 and the Pioneer Mountains Scenic Byway, drive 12.2 miles south. Or from the junction of Highway 278 and the scenic byway, drive 32.9 miles north. Turn west into Lodgepole or east into Boulder Creek.

Lodgepole GPS Coordinates: N 45° 38.910' W 113° 4.256'

Boulder Creek GPS Coordinates: N 45° 38.985' W 113° 4.095'

Contact: Beaverhead-Deerlodge National Forest, Wise River Ranger District, P.O. Box 100, Wise River, MT 59762, 406/832-3178, www.fs.usda.gov/bdnf.

76 WILLOW

Scenic rating: 7

in the Pioneer Mountains in Beaverhead-Deerlodge National Forest

On the 44-mile Pioneer Mountains Scenic Byway, Willow Campground sits at 6,600 feet right on the 26-mile Wise River, where it begins to drop in elevation as the canyon narrows. The river tumbles and froths white in June's high water in contrast to the slow-moving willow bottoms upstream. Anglers go after trout: brook, brown, rainbow, westslope cutthroat, and Yellowstone cutthroat. Nearby trails offer hiking and mountains biking. The Lacy Creek Trail (#259), part of the Pioneer Loop National Scenic Recreation Trail, leads in 5.5 miles to Lake of the Woods and Odell Lake. The Bobcat Trail (#50) heads 8 miles up to Bobcat Lakes, located in glacial cirques.

With paved parking aprons, one small paved loop forms the tiny campground, with campsite 5 sitting right in the middle of the loop. Sites 1, 2, and 3 have river frontage, with site 3's picnic table just a few feet from the water. Sites 4 and 5 have gravel tent platforms. The sound of the river fills the campground.

Campsites, facilities: The campground has five RV or tent campsites. The parking aprons can accommodate RVs up to 26 feet. Facilities include picnic tables, fire rings with grills, vault toilet (wheelchair-accessible), drinking water, and garbage service. Leashed pets are permitted.

Reservations, fees: Reservations are not accepted. Campsites cost $8. Extra vehicles cost $3. Cash or check. Open mid-June-September.

Directions: From the junction of Highway 43 and the Pioneer Mountains Scenic Byway, drive 13.1 miles south. Turn east into the campground. From the junction of Highway 278 and the scenic byway, drive 32 miles north.

GPS Coordinates: N 45° 38.460' W 113° 4.234'

Contact: Beaverhead-Deerlodge National Forest, Wise River Ranger District, P.O. Box 100, Wise River, MT 59762, 406/832-3178, www.fs.usda.gov/bdnf.

77 LITTLE JOE

Scenic rating: 8

in the Pioneer Mountains in Beaverhead Deerlodge National Forest

On the 44-mile Pioneer Mountains Scenic Byway, Little Joe Campground offers a quiet place to camp at 6,800 feet along the Wise River. The river meanders through large willow meadows—good places for spotting moose. Anglers go after brook, brown, and rainbow trout plus mountain whitefish, but must battle brushy willow along the riverbanks. Just north of the campground, the Grand Vista Viewpoint overlooks the Wise River and the 10,000-foot summits of the Pioneer Mountains. A paved wheelchair-accessible interpretive nature trail drops to the river willow bottom. Hiking and mountain biking are available out of the Mono Creek area, 0.5 mile south.

Although the tiny quiet campground crams its sites close together on a very small paved loop with paved parking pads (sites 3 and 4 almost sit on top of each other), its tiny size lends an intimate feel. Sites 2 and 5 have large spaces for tents, and site 2 includes peek-a-boo views of the river.

Campsites, facilities: The campground has five RV or tent campsites. Trailers are limited to 28 feet. Facilities include picnic tables, fire rings with grills, vault toilets (wheelchair-accessible), drinking water, and garbage service. Leashed pets are permitted.

Reservations, fees: Reservations are not accepted. Campsites cost $8. Extra vehicles cost $3. Cash or check. Open mid-June-September.

Directions: From the junction of Highway 43 and the Pioneer Mountains Scenic Byway, drive 20.5 miles south. Turn west into the campground. From the junction of Highway 278 and the scenic byway, drive 25 miles north. GPS Coordinates: N 45° 33.400' W 113° 5.454'

Contact: Beaverhead-Deerlodge National Forest, Wise River Ranger District, P.O. Box 100, Wise River, MT 59762, 406/832-3178, www.fs.usda.gov/bdnf.

78 MONO CREEK

Scenic rating: 8

in the Pioneer Mountains in Beaverhead-Deerlodge National Forest

At 7,000 feet, about halfway on the 44-mile Pioneer Mountains Scenic Byway in the Pioneer Mountains, Mono Creek is convenient for those intending to explore Coolidge Ghost Town. The relic from mining days is reached by driving four miles past the campground on a single-lane dirt road with pullouts. After a Montana politician bought up mining claims, the town sprang up in 1919 to support the Tunnel Silver Mine, but within 20 years most residents left. Mono Creek is also in the summit area of the byway, where miles of high meadows attract wildlife in the evening for feeding. Look for elk, deer, and moose. From a trailhead adjacent to the campground, hikers, mountain bikers, horses, and motorcycles climb through Jacobson Meadows to the David Creek Trail (#56, eight miles) and Brownes Lake Trail (#2, six miles)—both with multiple lake destinations.

Tucked under lodgepoles, the tiny, quiet Mono Creek Campground sits back off the byway. The grassy campsites are roomy and spaced out enough to afford some privacy among the thinned trees. Two sites have raised tent platforms. Tiny Mono Creek runs through the campground.

Campsites, facilities: The campground has three RV or tent campsites plus two sites for tents only. RVs are limited to 18 feet. Facilities include picnic tables, fire rings with grills, a few pedestal grills, vault toilets (wheelchair-accessible), drinking water, and garbage service. Leashed pets are permitted.

Reservations, fees: Reservations are not accepted. Campsites cost $8. Extra vehicles cost $3. Cash or check. Open mid-June-September.

Directions: From the junction of Highway 43 and the Pioneer Mountains Scenic Byway, drive 21 miles south. Turn east off the byway onto Forest Road 484 and drive 0.8 mile to the campground. From the junction of Highway 278 and the scenic byway, drive 24.1 miles north. GPS Coordinates: N 45° 32.091' W 113° 4.790'

Contact: Beaverhead-Deerlodge National Forest, Wise River Ranger District, P.O. Box 100, Wise River, MT 59762, 406/832-3178, www.fs.usda.gov/bdnf.

79 PRICE CREEK

Scenic rating: 9

in the Pioneer Mountains in Beaverhead-Deerlodge National Forest

On the 44-mile Pioneer Mountains Scenic Byway, Price Creek sits at 7,600 feet near the summit, where miles of high meadows allow wildlife-watching for elk, moose, and bears. The 10,212-foot Saddleback Mountain looms to the east, but you only get snippets of views through the trees. One mile north of the campground, Crystal Park attracts rock hounds, who dig for amethyst, smoky quartz, and clear quartz crystals. The day-use area charges $5 for parking, but digging for crystals is free. Multiuse trails, which are open to hikers, mountain climbers, mountain bikers, equestrians, and motorcyclists, lead into the highest peaks of the Pioneer Mountains and connect with the trails from Mono Creek.

The largest of the byway campgrounds, quiet Price Creek has several paved loops that wander through firs and lodgepoles. Most of the large campsites have back-in paved parking aprons, but five sites have pull-throughs. Lining

the edge of one loop, sites 14, 15, and 16 are more private. For views and possible evening wildlife-watching, walk to the large meadow adjacent to the campground along the fence. In fall, listen for elk bugling in the night.

Campsites, facilities: The campground has 28 RV or tent campsites. RVs are limited to 30 feet. Facilities include picnic tables, fire rings with grills, log benches, vault toilets (wheelchair-accessible), drinking water, garbage service, and campground hosts. Leashed pets are permitted.

Reservations, fees: Reservations are not accepted, except for the group campsite (call the ranger station). Campsites cost $8. Extra vehicles cost $3. Cash or check. Open June-September.

Directions: From the junction of Highway 43 and the Pioneer Mountains Scenic Byway, drive 28.3 miles south. Turn east off the byway and drive 0.5 mile to the campground entrance. From the junction of Highway 278 and the scenic byway, drive 16.8 miles north. GPS Coordinates: N 45° 28.788' W 113° 5.002'

Contact: Beaverhead-Deerlodge National Forest, Dillon Ranger District, 420 Barrett St., Dillon, MT 59725, 406/683-3900, www.fs.usda.gov/bdnf.

80 GRASSHOPPER

Scenic rating: 7

in the Pioneer Mountains in Beaverhead-Deerlodge National Forest

Located at 7,000 feet on the southern end of the 44-mile Pioneer Mountains Scenic Byway, Grasshopper attracts campers for campsites along the creek, plus nearby Elkhorn Hot Springs (406/834-3434). The hot springs (open year-round) have two outdoor pools, showers, flush toilets, and an indoor sauna. The pool water is high in mineral content but without sulfur. The large pool's temperature ranges 95-100°F and the smaller pool ranges 102-106°F. Hikers, equestrians, and mountain bikers can tour the Blue Creek Trail for fishing and wildlife-watching, with the trailhead located 0.3 mile south of the campground.

The grassy campground spreads out in an aspen and lodgepole forest on the hillside along Grasshopper Creek. Eleven of the campsites have creek frontage, with sites 9-12 and 14-17 being the farthest from the campground entrance. Trails climb the hillside behind the campground to explore the rocky outcrop. At night, you'll fall sleep to the sound of aspen leaves clicking in the breeze.

Campsites, facilities: The campground has 24 RV or tent campsites, plus a large group campsite. RVs are limited to 25 feet. Facilities include picnic tables, fire rings with grills, a few pedestal grills, vault toilets (wheelchair-accessible), drinking water, garbage service, and campground hosts. Leashed pets are permitted.

Reservations, fees: Reservations are not accepted except for the group campsite. (Call the ranger station.) Campsites cost $8. An extra vehicle costs $3. Cash or check. Open mid-June-mid-September.

Directions: From the junction of Highway 43 and the Pioneer Mountains Scenic Byway, drive 32.5 miles south. Turn northwest off the byway at the signed campground entrance. From the junction of Highway 278 and the scenic byway, drive 12.6 miles north.

GPS Coordinates: N 45° 27.054' W 113° 7.123'

Contact: Beaverhead-Deerlodge National Forest, Dillon Ranger District, 420 Barrett St., Dillon, MT 59725, 406/683-3900, www. fs.usda.gov/bdnf.

81 DINNER STATION

Scenic rating: 6

in the Pioneer Mountains in Beaverhead-Deerlodge National Forest

Located at 7,147 feet on the eastern side of the Pioneer Mountains, Dinner Station lures hikers and anglers. Fishing is available in Birch Creek, which runs adjacent to the campground, and the trailhead to Deerhead Lake sits 300 feet from the campground entrance. A 1.5-mile hike, Deerhead Lake offers trout fishing and a relatively easy hiking destination. The last part of the hike is on road.

The quiet campground, which used to be shaded under thick evergreens, has changed. Because of pine beetles, all of the trees were removed in 2010, leaving a barren open meadow. You'll see other campers, but also garner views of the Pioneer Mountains.

Campsites, facilities: The campground has eight RV or tent campsites. RVs are limited to 16 feet. Facilities include picnic tables, fire rings with grills, vault toilets (wheelchair-accessible), and drinking water. Pack out your trash. Leashed pets are permitted.

Reservations, fees: Reservations are not accepted. Camping is free. Open mid-June-September.

Directions: From I-15, drive 12 miles north of Dillon. Take Exit 74 and drive west on Birch Creek Road for 11.5 miles.

GPS Coordinates: N 45° 25.735' W 112° 54.216'

Contact: Beaverhead-Deerlodge National Forest, Dillon Ranger District, 420 Barrett St., Dillon, MT 59725, 406/683-3900, www. fs.usda.gov/bdnf.

82 BANNACK STATE PARK

Scenic rating: 5

south of the Pioneer Mountains

At 5,800 feet between Wisdom and Dillon, Bannack is a ghost town on Grasshopper Creek—the site of Montana's first major gold discovery in 1862 and Montana's first territorial capital in 1864. Striking gold catapulted Bannack's population to 3,000 residents in one year, but other gold rushes lured residents away. Over 50 historical log and frame

© BECKY LOMAX

Bannack State Park preserves a ghost town that once served as Montana's capital.

structures still stand in Bannack. You can look out the jail bars, sit in the schoolroom, and even sidle up to the dusty bar. Short hiking trails lead to the gallows, cemetery, and mines, and mountain biking is available. Grasshopper Creek also has fishing. Flooding in 2013 destroyed some of the town's historical buildings; call for updates.

The state park has two campgrounds adjacent to each other on Grasshopper Creek 0.2 mile west of the ghost town. Road Agent camp sits across the creek to the left, and Vigilante camp sits to the right. Both have dirt roads that loop through the campgrounds, with unnumbered grassy sites tucked under cottonwoods. The open sunny sites are very close to each other, with no boundaries between many of them. Vigilante has several open walk-in sites on the grass along the creek and a tipi for rent.

Campsites, facilities: The campgrounds have 25 RV or tent campsites plus three walk-in sites for tenters. RVs are limited to 35 feet. Facilities include picnic tables, fire rings with grills, vault toilets (wheelchair-accessible), drinking water, garbage service, tipi rental, and firewood

for sale. Pack out your trash if the garbage bins are not present. Leashed pets are permitted.

Reservations, fees: Reservations are accepted online or by phone (855/922-6768). Campsites cost $15 for Montana residents (seniors and disabled get half price) and $23 for nonresidents Memorial Day weekend-Labor Day, or $12 for Montana residents and $20 for nonresidents September-May. Campsites with electrical hookups cost $17-28, depending on season and residency. Nonresidents with a Non-Resident Entrance Pass ($25) get a $5 discount on camping fees. Tipi rental costs $22-35. Cash, check, or credit card. Entry fee for the ghost town costs $5, but it's free for Montana residents. Open year-round.

Directions: From Dillon, drive south on I-15 to Exit 59 and drive west on Highway 278 for 17 miles. Turn south onto the paved Bannack Bench Road for three miles. Turn left onto the dirt Bannack Road and go 0.6 mile to the campgrounds, which are on the south side of the road.

GPS Coordinates: N 45° 9.819' W 113° 0.137'

Contact: Montana Fish, Wildlife, and Parks,

4200 Bannack Rd., Dillon, MT 59725, 406/834-3413, http://stateparks.mt.gov.

83 DILLON KOA

Scenic rating: 6

in Dillon

At 5,101 feet in Dillon, surrounded by small farms, the Dillon KOA is a campground of convenience when traveling I-15. Montanans stop in Dillon to visit the Patagonia outlet store downtown, hit the pro rodeo on Labor Day weekend, or golf. The campground sits on the Beaverhead River, one of Montana's blue ribbon trout fisheries, and it makes a good base camp for exploring the Pioneer Mountains, Bannack State Park ghost town, Beaverhead Rock State Park, and Clark's Lookout State Park.

From the campsites, surrounding mountains are visible, which are luscious green in spring and brown by August. Expect to hear trucking noise from the freeway. The grassy campground has pull-through and back-in sites with sporadic trees for shade. Campsites are packed in close together with little privacy.

Campsites, facilities: The campground has 68 RV campsites and 30 tent sites. RV combinations are limited to 100 feet. Hookups include sewer, water, electricity up to 50 amps, and cable TV. Facilities include picnic tables, fire rings (tent sites only), flush toilets (wheelchair-accessible), showers, launderette, disposal station, wireless Internet, heated outdoor swimming pool (mid-June–early September), propane, firewood for sale, bike rentals, playground, ice cream socials, and camp store. Leashed pets are permitted.

Reservations, fees: Reservations are accepted. RV sites cost $35-45. Tent sites cost $25. Rates are for two people; additional campers are charged $3-5 each. Kids six years old and under stay free. Add on 7 percent bed tax. Cash, check, or credit card. Open year-round.

Directions: When heading south on I-15, take Exit 63 at Dillon and turn right onto Montana Street followed by a right onto Reeder Street. When heading north on I-15, take Exit 62 and turn right onto Atlantic Street followed by a left onto Reeder Street. From the north end of Reeder Street, turn left on West Park Street and cross under the freeway to the KOA entrance on the right.

GPS Coordinates: N 45° 13.127' W 112° 39.040'

Contact: Dillon KOA, 735 West Park Street, Dillon, MT 59725, 406/683-2749 or 800/562-2751, http://koa.com/campgrounds/dillon/.

84 RESERVOIR LAKE

Scenic rating: 6

in the Beaverhead Mountains in Beaverhead-Deerlodge National Forest

Located at 7,000 feet on the eastern side of the Beaverhead Mountains, Reservoir Lake requires a long drive on a dirt road that can be rough in spots. It attracts mostly anglers going after brook and cutthroat trout. However, the reservoir is small—only 11 acres and less than 0.5-mile in length. Considering its size, only electric motors are permitted. A primitive boat ramp is available to aid in launching canoes, boats, and float tubes. Swimmers can cool off in the lake.

The campground flanks the foot of the reservoir. A portion of the campground sits in a mature pine forest while the other portion is in sage meadows that are green in spring and crispy dry much of the late summer. A few sites sit adjacent to the lake.

Campsites, facilities: The campground has 16 RV or tent campsites. The Forest Service recommends a limit of 16 feet for RVs and trailers, but many of the parking aprons can accommodate rigs double that size. Facilities include picnic tables, fire rings with grills, vault toilets (wheelchair-accessible), and drinking water. Pack out your trash. Leashed pets are permitted.

Reservations, fees: Reservations are not accepted. Camping costs $8. An extra vehicle costs $3. Open mid-June-September.

Directions: From I-15 south of Dillon, take Exit 44 and drive west on Highway 324 for 20 miles. Follow signs to the campground, turning right onto the gravel road that becomes Bloody Dick Road (Forest Road 181). Drive 21 miles and turn right into the campground. GPS Coordinates: N 45° 7.242' W 113° 27.286'

Contact: Beaverhead-Deerlodge National Forest, Dillon Ranger District, 420 Barrett St., Dillon, MT 59725, 406/683-3900, www.fs.usda.gov/bdnf.

85 CLARK CANYON RESERVOIR

🏃 🛶 � 🚤 ❄ 🐴 ♿ 🚐 ⛺

Scenic rating: 7

on Clark Canyon Reservoir

Located south of Dillon at 5,600 feet at the base of the Beaverhead Mountains, Clark Canyon Reservoir is the site of Camp Fortunate, where the Lewis and Clark expedition met the Lemhi Shoshoni Tribe, Sacagawea reunited with her brother, and the expedition cached their supplies and boats for the return trip. The 4,935-acre reservoir with small islands is ringed by 17 miles of shoreline with four cement boat launch ramps for waterskiing, sightseeing, kayaking, canoeing, and fishing. The reservoir harbors rainbow and brown trout. Fishing goes year-round, including on ice in winter, and the reservoir is stocked heavily with rainbow trout. The Cattail Marsh Nature Trail, below Clark Canyon Dam, offers wildlife-watching opportunities for waterfowl, birds, pronghorn antelope, and yellow-bellied marmots.

A complex of developed campgrounds plus dispersed primitive camping sites rim the reservoir. Be prepared for wind at all locations! Most of the campsites sit on treeless broad, arid sagebrush slopes, accompanied by expansive views of the reservoir. On the north shore, the Lewis and Clark Campground has RV hookups. Seven other small campgrounds contain less than 20 sites each. On the east side with the easiest access, Beaverhead Campground squeezes between the interstate and the water with a few shade-producing cottonwoods and willows. Nearby, the Beaverhead River Campground borders the river below the dam. Both pick up road noise. Four quieter campgrounds—Horse Prairie, Cameahwait, West Cameahwait, and Hap Hawkins—flank the north and southwest shore. On the southwest shore, Lone Tree Campground requires the longest access.

Campsites, facilities: The RV park has 55 sites with hookups for water, sewer, and electricity. The other campgrounds contain 41 campsites for RVs or tents without hookups. Many of the campsites can accommodate large RVs. Facilities include picnic tables with shelters, fire rings with grills, vault toilets (wheelchair-accessible), hand pumps for drinking water, garbage service, and campground hosts. Leashed pets are permitted.

Reservations, fees: Reservations are not accepted. Camping is free, except for the RV campsite with hookups that costs $30. Cash or check. Open year-round, although winter snow can close the roads and cover the campgrounds.

Directions: From I-15, take Exit 44 at Clark Canyon Reservoir. Drive east on Highway 324 across the dam to access the north and southwest shore campgrounds, or drive south before the dam to reach the east shore. GPS Coordinates: N 44° 59.943' W 112° 51.326'

Contact: Bureau of Reclamation, 1200 Hwy. 41, Dillon, MT 59725, 406/683-6472.

NORTHERN YELLOWSTONE GATEWAYS

© BECKY LOMAX

The Gallatin, Madison, Yellowstone, and Clarks Fork of the Yellowstone River valleys provide the four main corridors to reach Yellowstone National Park's northern gateways of West Yellowstone, Gardiner, and Cooke City. Most of the campgrounds along these three rivers are easily accessible via pavement with only a few dirt-road driving miles. The Gallatin River draws the most crowds, due to its proximity to Bozeman. These campgrounds also lure campers for outstanding hiking, climbing, rafting, and mountain biking in Gallatin National Forest. Campgrounds are much more frequent on the Madison than on the Yellowstone River, which flows through more private land in Paradise Valley. The Beartooth Highway climbs over a two-mile-high pass en route to Yellowstone; six developed campgrounds sit within a few miles of one another, accessible for the three months it is snow-free.

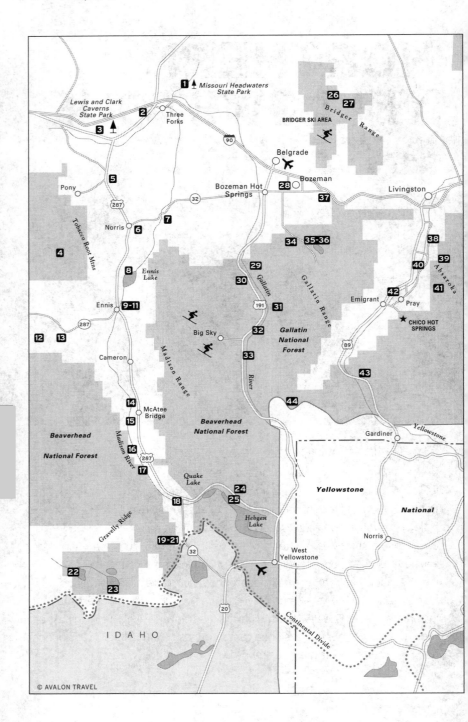

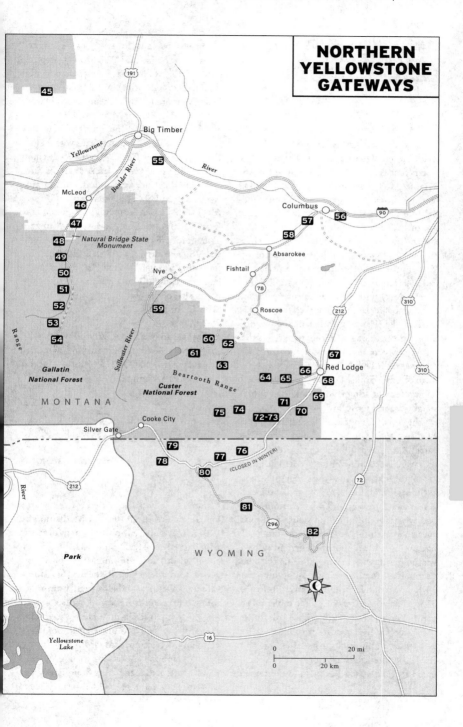

NORTHERN
YELLOWSTONE
GATEWAYS

1 MISSOURI HEADWATERS STATE PARK

🚶 🚴 ⛵ 🛶 🏊 🎣 🐕 ♿ 🚐 ⛺

Scenic rating: 7

on the Missouri River near Three Forks

BEST (

Located at the confluence of the Gallatin, Madison, and Jefferson Rivers, Missouri Headwaters State Park marks the beginning of the Mighty Mo's 2,565-mile journey. At 4,045 feet, the 506-acre state park provides outstanding interpretive sites about Native American use of the area, Lewis and Clark's passage, and the river ecosystems. For anyone who lives along the Missouri, families with school-age kids, or history buffs, this is a "must do" educational stop. Four miles of hiking trails (some permit dogs) tour the park. A concrete ramp launches boaters, rafters, kayakers, and anglers to float the first eight miles of the nation's longest river. Along with the three rivers that form the Missouri, the big waters harbor trout. A paved six-mile bike trail connects with the town of Three Forks. The park provides superb habitat for watching wildlife: moose, raptors, songbirds, and waterfowl.

The small campground sits adjacent to the Madison River, but the thick jungle of willows, cattails, and brush block campsite views of the river. Short trails connect to it. The grassy campground packs sites close together; those at the front are wide open, but sites at the back garner a little privacy. A few large cottonwoods and willows lend morning shade, but most sites bake with hot afternoon sun, especially midsummer. Owls hoot at night, and catbirds fill the marsh with mimicry during the day.

Campsites, facilities: The campground has 17 RV or tent campsites. RVs are limited to 35 feet. Facilities include picnic tables on cement pads, fire rings with grills, vault toilets, drinking water, campfire programs, rental tipi, and campground hosts. Pack out your trash. Leashed pets are permitted. Wheelchair-accessible facilities include a toilet and campsite.

Reservations, fees: Reservations are accepted online or by phone (855/922-6768). Campsites cost $15 for Montana residents (seniors and disabled get half price) and $23 for nonresidents Memorial Day weekend-Labor Day, or campsites cost $12 for Montana residents and $20 for nonresidents September and May. Tipi rental costs $22-50. Nonresidents with a Non-Resident Entrance Pass ($25) get a $5 discount on camping fees. Cash, check, or credit card.

The park is open year-round, but camping is available only May-September.

Directions: From I-90 at Three Forks, take Exit 278 and head on Highway 205 toward Trident for 1.8 miles. Turn north onto Highway 286 and drive 1.6 miles to the park's information plaza on the right. Pay for campsites here; the campground entrance is on the opposite side of the road.

GPS Coordinates: N 45° 55.214' W 111° 29.927'

Contact: Montana Fish, Wildlife, and Parks, Missouri Headwaters State Park, 1400 S. 19th St., Bozeman, MT 59718, 406/994-4042, http://stateparks.mt.gov.

2 CAMP THREE FORKS

🚶 🚴 ⛵ 🛶 🎣 🏊 🐕 🎣 🚐 ⛺

Scenic rating: 6

west of Three Forks

Camp Three Forks is named for the nearby confluence of the Jefferson, Madison, and Gallatin Rivers, which together form the Missouri River. The Drouillard fishing access site is within a five-minute drive, providing access to the Jefferson River for fly-fishing, rafting, kayaking, and floating. Within four miles, Three Forks has a golf course, groceries, gas, the paved six-mile Headwaters Trail system for hikers and bikers, and ponds for canoeing, kayaking, and children's fishing. The campground also sits less than seven miles from Missouri Headwaters State Park. The Wheat Montana store and deli—the place to buy Montana flour—is 1.3 miles to the north. The campground conveniently lies at the junction of I-90 and the Madison and Jefferson River Valleys.

Flanked by flower beds, the landscaped campground has loops of gravel roads with gravel parking pads. A variety of leafy trees lend partial shade. This ex-KOA campground has sites close together, and truck noise from the highway floats in at night. Some of the campsites have southeast-facing views of the Gallatin Mountains.

Campsites, facilities: The campground has 65 pull-through RV sites and 21 tent campsites. RVs are limited to 63 feet. Facilities include picnic tables, fire rings, vault toilets, drinking water, garbage service, launderette, playground, wireless Internet, swimming pool, and firewood for sale. Leashed pets are permitted.

Reservations, fees: Reservations are accepted. Hookups cost $26-38. Tent sites cost $24. Cash or check. Open late May-mid-September.

Directions: From I-90 west of Three Forks, take Exit 274 and drive south on Highway 287 for 1.1 miles. Turn right onto KOA Road for 0.1 mile and turn left into the campground. GPS Coordinates: N 45° 54.174' W111° 36.134'

Contact: Camp Three Forks, 15 KOA Rd., Three Forks, MT 59752, 406/285-3611 or 866/523-1773, campthreeforks.com.

❸ LEWIS AND CLARK CAVERNS STATE PARK

🚶 🚴 ⛴ 🏕 🐕 ⛹ ♿ 🚐 ⛺

Scenic rating: 7

on the Jefferson River

`BEST (`

On the Jefferson River, Lewis and Clark Caverns State Park offers a tour through the limestone caves with fantastical stalactites, columns, dripstones, ribbons, and cave popcorn. Guided two-hour tours ($5-10) of the caverns are available May-September. You'll descend

The Lewis and Clark Caverns hold otherworldly limestone formations.

© BECKY LOMAX

600 steps and see utter darkness when the guide flips off the lights. The caverns are 1,400 vertical feet above the campground on a road not suitable for trailers. It's a 3.2-mile drive from the campground. Across the highway, an access site allows for shore or wade fishing on the Jefferson River. Nine miles of hiking trails, including a 0.25-mile nature trail, tour the 2,920-acre park. Mountain bikes are allowed of some of these. The park also provides good wildlife-watching.

The campground, which sits at river level in the dramatic canyon, is good for tenters, with oodles of flat spaces. The grassy campground, which turns brown by the end of summer, offers no privacy, and only a couple of trees provide partial shade to a few sites. With the highway and the railroad tracks in the canyon, the campground is noisy at night. Watch for rattlesnakes.

Campsites, facilities: The campground has 40 RV or tent campsites. RVs are limited to 60 feet long. Facilities include picnic tables, fire rings with grills, flush toilets

YELLOWSTONE GATEWAY RIVERS

Yellowstone National Park feeds some of the nation's most well-known blue-ribbon trout streams—waters that rush northward, forming its northern gateways. In Montana, these rivers wended their way into the history books, literature, and movies. From the Lewis and Clark expedition to the movie *A River Runs Through It*, the iconic image of wading thigh-deep in a river while casting a fly on its surface has sunk deep into the psyche of every angler.

For those who camp, the dream of lunker trout can become a reality in this region of rivers. Many of Yellowstone's northern gateway trout streams sit so far from towns brimming with hotels that tents and RVs become the way to travel if you want to savor days on the river. Campgrounds are much more frequent than lodges.

The northern Yellowstone gateway rivers flow south to north, lining up in parallel valleys with roads running alongside. You'll be lucky to find yourself alone in midsummer fly-fishing on a stretch of the famous **Madison, Gallatin,** or **Yellowstone Rivers.** The 140 miles of the Madison River may be the most famous Montana blue-ribbon trout stream, hopping with rainbow and brown trout, but its canyon and sagebrush banks are largely public. In addition, the Madison, Jefferson, and Gallatin Rivers feed the Mighty Mo, the **Missouri River.** The longest river in the U.S. has its birthplace in **Missouri Headwaters State Park.**

U.S. Forest Service and Bureau of Land Management campgrounds make up the largest camping options on the rivers. But

(wheelchair-accessible), electrical hookups, showers, drinking water, garbage service, amphitheater programs, disposal station, playground, and campground host. Leashed pets are permitted.

Reservations, fees: Reservations are accepted online or by phone (855/922-6768). Campsites cost $15 for Montana residents (seniors and disabled get half price) and $23 for nonresidents Memorial Day weekend-Labor Day, or $12 for Montana residents and $20 for nonresidents September-May. Campsites with electrical hookups cost $17-28, depending on season and residency. Nonresidents with a Non-Resident Entrance Pass ($25) get a $5 discount on camping fees. Cash, check, or credit card. Open year-round.

Directions: From I-90 east of Whitehall, take Exit 256. On the south side of the freeway, drive east on Highway 2 for 7.3 miles. From I-90 near Three Forks, take Exit 274 and go south on Highway 2/287 for 11.2 miles. Stay on Highway 2 as it splits off from 287 and head west for five miles. The signed park entrance is on the north side of the road.

Drive 0.2 mile up and turn left to enter the campground.
GPS Coordinates: N 45° 49.422' W 111° 51.324'

Contact: Montana Fish, Wildlife, and Parks, Lewis and Clark Caverns, P.O. Box 489, Whitehall, MT 59759, 406/287-3541, http://stateparks.mt.gov.

4 BRANHAM LAKES

Scenic rating: 9

in the Tobacco Root Mountains in Beaverhead-Deerlodge National Forest

At 8,800 feet in the Tobacco Root Mountains, Branham Lakes offer an idyllic pair of high subalpine lakes cradled in a basin below the 10,367-foot Mount Bradley. The tiny lakes make great swimming holes on hot days, but be prepared for chilly water. Trout fishing is best from a float tube, and a primitive boat ramp allows for launching small hand-carried watercraft such as in a testament to the popularity of fishing, rafting, floating, and kayaking, the state of Montana operates a horde of small, primitive campgrounds at fishing access sites. The rare RV park sidles up to the riverbank with hookups.

To escape the crowds of the three big-name rivers, head to the gaggle of smaller streams that plunge from the high peaks of the Absaroka-Beartooth Mountains. The **Stillwater, Big Timber, Rosebud,** and **Rock Creek Rivers** each offer something different for campers, hikers, mountain bikers, anglers, and rafters. However, routes into Montana's highest mountains along these rivers are mostly via long, dirt roads with wall-to-wall washboards and potholes sometimes large enough to swallow truck wheels. The smaller, more-primitive campgrounds along these rivers

fill with tenters and only small to mid-size RVs due to the difficulty of the access.

These smaller rivers plummet from glaciers in the Absaroka-Beartooth Wilderness. As Rock Creek tumbles eastward, its valley also forms the eastern ascent from Red Lodge for the Beartooth Highway. The Beartooth Highway—touted by Charles Kuralt as "America's most beautiful highway"—lives up to its nickname and outclasses other Yellowstone gateways with its high alpine plateaus framed by snowcapped peaks. Outside of its six developed campgrounds, you can find solitude in the ream of primitive dispersed campsites along **Rock Creek.**

Although Montana's gateways to Yellowstone are all rivers bouncing with trout, the state's highest mountains also provide unparalleled hiking and mountain biking. Camping is the way to see them best.

rowboats and canoes. A 1.5-mile, steep hiking trail departs from the campground for the ridge at 9,700 feet in high in alpine mountain goat terrain with panoramic views.

The campground loop snuggles under trees adjacent to the upper lake. The two sites at the north end of the loop sit nearest the lake. Utter quiet, privacy, and scenery abound with this campground. Be prepared for mosquitoes in July!

Campsites, facilities: The campground has six RV or tent campsites that can accommodate small RVs. Facilities include picnic tables, fire rings, and vault toilets (wheelchair-accessible). Drinking water is not available; bring your own or treat lake water. Pack out your trash. Leashed pets are permitted.

Reservations, fees: Reservations are not accepted. Camping is free. Open mid-May-September.

Directions: From Sheridan on Montana Highway 287, drive east on Mill Creek Road for 13 miles until it ends in the campground loop. The road becomes dirt, narrow, rough, slow-going, and not recommended for trailers, but it

is accessible by two-wheel-drive vehicles. Call to check on road conditions before driving. GPS Coordinates: N 45° 30.962' W 111° 59.469'

Contact: Beaverhead-Deerlodge National Forest, Madison Ranger District, 5 Forest Service Rd., Ennis, MT 59729, 406/682-4253, www.fs.usda.gov/bdnf.

5 HARRISON LAKE

Scenic rating: 6

on Willow Creek Reservoir

Harrison Lake, elevation 4,741 feet, is a primitive fishing access site run by the state. Its real name is Willow Creek Reservoir, but it carries the Harrison name after the nearby town. The 713-acre lake contains brown and westslope cutthroat trout and is stocked regularly with rainbow trout. True to its name, the lake is surrounded by willow brush, making the best fishing via boat. The access road to get to the campground is rough, rutted, and bumpy. It turns to gumbo when wet and is dusty when dry. A concrete boat ramp and a primitive boat ramp aid launching onto the lake in two different locations of the campground. The lake is a locals' hangout for waterskiing, boating, canoeing, and fishing.

The primitive campground spreads out in three different locations around a large peninsula with low mountain views in the distance. The weedy sites are rough, uneven, and dusty or muddy. Most of the sites are open, sunny, and visited by black flies. The campground sees more use on weekends and holidays, while weekdays have sparser visitation. After boats pull off the lake in the evening, the area is exceptionally quiet, with only a songbird or two in the early morning.

Campsites, facilities: The campground has 12 RV or tent campsites that can accommodate midsize RVs. Facilities include picnic tables, fire rings with grills, and vault toilets (wheelchair-accessible). Leashed pets are permitted.

Reservations, fees: Reservations are not accepted. Campsites cost $7 with a Montana fishing license and $12 without a Montana fishing license. Cash or check. Open year-round.

Directions: From Highway 287 in Harrison, turn east onto Harrison Lake Road for four dirt-road miles.

GPS Coordinates: N 45° 41.982' W 111° 42.582'

Contact: Montana Fish, Wildlife, and Parks, Region 3, 1400 S. 19th Ave., Bozeman, MT 59718, 406/994-4042, http://fwp.mt.gov.

6 NORRIS HOT SPRINGS

Scenic rating: 6

near Norris

BEST (

Norris Hot Springs, elevation 4,834 feet, is a true Montana relic with a cult-type following. The 30- by 40-foot wooden hot pool fills with hot mineral water every morning. Temperatures vary seasonally between 100°F and 106°F. The hot springs are open year-round, Wednesdays through Sundays, but closed two days per week for cleaning and letting the wood dry. Live music comes to the hot springs on Friday through Sunday nights. The All Local Foods Grill serves up organic, locally sourced Montana meats and fresh veggies, some grown in the hot springs greenhouse. An onsite saloon serves up Montana microbrews along with wine.

The small sunny campground lines up RV sites close together in a row, but separates the sites with privacy fences. The tent sites, located furthest from the hot springs pool, sit in a shared grassy area. Views from the campsites span the surrounding low arid hills and the highway. No shade trees are in the campground.

Campsites, facilities: The campground has nine RV sites and three tent campsites. RVs are limited to midsized rigs. Hookups include water, sewer, and electricity. Facilities include flush toilets, showers, wireless Internet, and discounts on unlimited soaking in the hot springs ($3 per day). Leashed pets are permitted. No generators are allowed.

Reservations, fees: Reservations are not accepted. Campsites cost $30 for hookups and $20 for tents. Cash or check. Open May-September.

Directions: From Highway 287 in Norris, turn east onto Highway 84 for 0.25-miles to the entrance on the right.

GPS Coordinates: N 45° 34.460' W 111° 41.074'

Contact: Norris Hot Springs, 1400 S. 19th Ave., Bozeman, MT 59718, 406/685-3303, www.norrishotsprings.com.

7 RED MOUNTAIN

Scenic rating: 8

on the Madison River

BEST (

On the banks of the lower Madison River,

Red Mountain Campground sits at the bottom of Bear Trap Canyon, a narrow slice through 1,500-foot-tall red cliffs on the Madison River. Upriver in the Lee Metcalf Wilderness, waters plunge through the canyon with the Class IV Kitchen Sink rapid. Paralleling the rapids, the nine-mile Bear Trap Canyon National Recreation Trail departs from Warm Springs Recreation Area, which also serves as the take-out for rafting the canyon about two miles south of the campground. A new boat launch now sits across the bridge from the campground, offering another option for launching or taking out. The river harbors 18-inch rainbow and brown trout, but the wade fishing is best before mid-July when the water warms up. It is also close to Norris Hot Springs, Montana's only wooden hot springs pool, eight miles west.

Recent additions have enlarged the camping opportunities here. Red Mountain, the original campground, rims with a few junipers and willow brush that survived the recent fire. Although surrounding slopes contain the burnt remnants of sparse trees, green grass and wildflowers have returned. The new Trapper Springs loop, located across the highway from Red Mountain, is rougher with mostly sagebrush. Two spur roads on both sides of the river (Beartrap and County Roads) lead to more primitive sites that vary with grass and willow brush, but line up along the riverfront. Sun is pervasive and hot in August. Given the lack of trees, none of the sites offer privacy. Even though you'll hear some trucking noise from the adjacent highway at night, catbirds will wake you in the morning. Watch for rattlesnakes.

Campsites, facilities: The zone has four camping areas for RVs or tents: Red Mountain has 17 sites, Trapper Springs has 15 sites, Beartrap Road has 7 sites, and County Road has 8 sites. Many can accommodate large RVs. Facilities at Red Mountain and Trapper Springs include picnic tables, fire rings with grills, vault toilets, drinking water, firewood for sale, and campground hosts. Facilities at the Beartrap and County Road sites include picnic tables and fire rings. Pack out your trash. Leashed pets are permitted. Wheelchair-accessible toilets are available.

Reservations, fees: Reservations are not accepted. Campsites in the Red Mountain loops or Trapper Springs loop cost $8. An extra vehicle costs $5. Campsites on the Beartrap or County Roads cost $5 per vehicle. Cash or check. Open May-November.

Directions: From Highway 287 at Norris, drive 8.1 miles to the campground. The entrance is on the north side of the road after crossing the Madison River.

GPS Coordinates: N 45° 36.666' W 111° 34.144'

Contact: Bureau of Land Management, Dillon Field Office, 1005 Selway Dr., Dillon, MT 59725, 406/683-8000, www.blm.gov.

8 MEADOW LAKE

Scenic rating: 8

on Ennis Lake

At 4,815 feet in elevation, Ennis Lake sits in the middle of the Madison River Valley surrounded by the Madison and Tobacco Root mountain ranges. The lake—a fishery known for its brown and rainbow trout—is also a haven for waterskiing, sailing, canoeing, and boating. Kobayashi Bay, with its buoyed swimming area and boat ramp, sits one mile east. From the campground, you can launch hand-carried boats, but no ramp is available. Because of the lake's shallowness, it warms in summer but kicks up with whitecaps in afternoon winds. The lake's outlet launches the Madison River through Bear Trap Canyon through a 1,500-foot-deep gorge and the Class IV Kitchen Sink rapid.

The sunny, treeless primitive campground—a fishing access run by the state—spreads out along the shore of the lake near the inlet for the mosquito-breeding haven Meadow Creek. Five of the campsites back in on gravel parking pads to waterfront with a brushy shoreline. Views look south to the Madison Range, which on a calm day reflects in the water. Ennis Lake Road garners substantial traffic during the summer from those heading to raft in the canyon or visit Kobayashi Bay, but the traffic dwindles at night.

Campsites, facilities: The campground has nine RV or tent campsites. RVs are limited to 25 feet. Facilities include picnic tables, fire rings with grills, and vault toilets. No water is available; bring your own or treat lake water. Leashed pets are permitted. Wheelchair-accessible facilities include toilet and campsite.

Reservations, fees: Reservations are not accepted. Camping is free. Open year-round.

Directions: From Highway 287 six miles north of Ennis, turn east at milepost 55 onto North Ennis Lake Road and drive 1.4 miles to the fishing access sign and campground on the right.

GPS Coordinates: N 45° 26.596' W 111° 42.414'

Contact: Montana Fish, Wildlife, and Parks, Region 3, 1400 S. 19th Ave., Bozeman, MT 59718, 406/994-4042, http://fwp.mt.gov.

9 ENNIS RV VILLAGE

Scenic rating: 7

in Ennis

One mile north of Ennis, this campground is convenient for shopping in the town's art galleries and western stores as well as for eating out in its restaurants. The town is best known for its Fourth of July parade and rodeo as well as fly-fishing. A small park in town has a kids-only fishing pond to get little ones started. Ennis Lake, good for swimming, fishing, boating, and water-skiing, sits five miles to the north, and the Kobayashi day-use area for swimming is less than seven miles north. Madison River fishing access sites are within two miles, and white-water rafting companies are available for guided trips through Bear Trap Canyon and its Class IV Kitchen Sink rapid. Madison Meadows Golf Course is also in Ennis, and the surrounding Gallatin and Beaverhead-Deerlodge National Forests offer hiking and mountain-biking trails.

The campground lines up its RV campsites in parking-lot fashion along small patches of lawn in the sunny Madison River Valley. Views from the campground span the Madison Mountains to the east and the Tobacco Root Mountains to the northwest. In June, they are still covered by snow; in August, they are bare. You can hear some trucks along Highway 287 at night.

Campsites, facilities: The campground has 90 RV and 11 tent campsites. RVs are limited to 80 feet. Facilities include picnic tables, pedestal grills, flush toilets (wheelchair-accessible), showers, drinking water, garbage service, disposal station, wireless Internet, convenience store, launderette, and hookups for sewer, water, and electricity up to 50 amps. Leashed pets are permitted.

Reservations, fees: Reservations are not accepted. Hookups cost $27-38. Tent sites and dry camping for small RVs costs $19-25. Rates are based on two people per site. Additional campers are charged $2 each. Children under 12 years old camp for free. Use of the disposal station costs $6. The 7 percent Montana bed tax will be added on. Cash, check, or credit card. Open mid-April-mid-November.

Directions: Drive 1.2 miles north of Ennis on Highway 287. Turn east and drive 300 feet to the campground entrance, which is straight ahead.

GPS Coordinates: N 45° 22.053' W 111° 43.700'

Contact: Ennis RV Village, 15 Geyser Street, Ennis, MT 59729, 406/682-5272 or 866/682-5272, www.ennisrv.com.

10 VALLEY GARDEN

Scenic rating: 7

on the Madison River

Valley Garden, elevation 4,885 feet, is a state-run fishing access site on the Madison River. It is a popular location, as the town of Ennis, with its restaurants, shops, art galleries, and fishing outfitters, is less than a 10-minute drive away. The campground has a primitive gravel boat ramp where you can launch onto the river to float or paddle down to Ennis Lake. The Madison River gains worldwide fame for its blue-ribbon trout fishing, which is catch-and-release only for rainbow trout.

A narrow, potholed dirt road accesses the campground, where an osprey nest sits on a platform above the pay station. Views from the campsites span the Tobacco Root Mountains to the northwest and the Madison Mountains to the east. Two sunny loops through the tall grass offer flat spaces mowed out for tents. Four sites overlook the river; other sites can access the river through the brushy willows. The sites are spaced out for privacy, but the openness means you can see other campers. The myriad songbirds and the river fill the air with sound. The tall grass is green into July but fades to gold by August.

Campsites, facilities: The campground has nine RV or tent campsites. RVs are limited to 25 feet. Facilities include picnic tables, fire rings with grills, boat ramp, and vault toilets (wheelchair-accessible). Drinking water is not available; bring your own or treat river water. Leashed pets are permitted.

Reservations, fees: Reservations are not accepted. Camping costs $12 without a Montana fishing license or $7 with a fishing license. Open year-round.

Directions: From Ennis, drive south on Highway 287 about 1.5 miles to milepost 48. Turn north just after crossing Jeffers Creek and drive 1.9 miles. Turn left at the fishing access sign and drive over the cattle grate to reach the campground.

GPS Coordinates: N 45° 21.895' W 111° 42.319'

Contact: Montana Fish, Wildlife, and Parks, Region 3, 1400 S. 19th Ave., Bozeman, MT 59718, 406/994-4042, http://fwp.mt.gov.

11 ENNIS

Scenic rating: 4

on the Madison River

At 4,938 feet, Ennis is a state-run fishing access site on the Madison River. It is a popular location, as you can walk five minutes into the town of Ennis, which offers restaurants, shops, art galleries, and fishing outfitters. A primitive gravel boat ramp allows a place to launch onto the river to float down to Valley Garden or Ennis Lake, but you can also go catch-and-release wade-fishing for trout. The river harbors brown, rainbow, brook, Yellowstone cutthroat trout, and mountain whitefish. Bicyclists also use this campground while cycling Highway 287. A kid's fishing pond sits across the bridge in a community park.

A narrow, potholed dirt road accesses the campground's one big loop, which seems more like a maze because of the high brush. Campsites tuck into the brush under several large willow trees that provide partial shade and privacy from the 15-foot-high willow jungle, but a few are in sight of other campers. The three campsites on the river are open with views across the river to houses. The campsites, which are a mix of grass, dirt, and gravel, collect a combination of sounds, from the highway to songbirds. Locate the mowed path to the hand pump for drinking water by site 13. Some years the campground closes in late May and early June with high water flooding.

Campsites, facilities: The campground has 17 RV or tent campsites. RVs are limited to 25 feet. Facilities include picnic tables, rock fire rings, a boat ramp, drinking water, and vault toilets. Leashed pets are permitted.

Reservations, fees: Reservations are not accepted. Camping costs $12 without a Montana fishing license or $7 with a fishing license. Open May-November.

Directions: From Ennis, drive south on Highway 287 about 0.1 mile. Turn right at the fishing access sign as soon as you cross the Madison River.

GPS Coordinates: N 45° 20.665' W 111° 43.449'

Contact: Montana Fish, Wildlife, and Parks, Region 3, 1400 S. 19th Ave., Bozeman, MT 59718, 406/994-4042, http://fwp.mt.gov.

12 RUBY RESERVOIR

Scenic rating: 6

on the Madison River

Located at 5,409 feet, the Ruby Reservoir is a 2.5-mile-long lake set between the Ruby and Greenhorn Mountains. Because it was created to supply irrigation water for agriculture, water levels drop significantly in late summer. In early summer, the lake attracts anglers, boaters, and paddlers. Rainbow trout are stocked in the reservoir, and hand-carried watercraft can easily be launched from multiple locations. Rock hounds can find garnets along the shore.

Located on an arid dusty bench on the southeast shore of Ruby Reservoir, the campground offers very primitive camping in unmaintained sites. The area garners full sun and wind. A handful of campsites sidle up to a few trees for protection. More campsites are available along pullouts between the campground and Ruby Dam.

Campsites, facilities: The campground has seven primitive RV or tent campsites that can accommodate large RVs. Facilities include fire pits in some locations and vault toilets. Drinking water is not available; bring your own. Pack

out your trash. Leashed pets are permitted. Two wheelchair-accessible toilets are available.

Reservations, fees: Reservations are not accepted. Camping is free. Open year-round.

Directions: From State Highway 287 west of Virginia City (not to be confused with Highway 287), take Judy Lane west for 0.5 mile. (The road sits just south of Alder.) Turn south onto the paved Upper Ruby Road (Forest Road 357) and drive eight miles south to the campground entrance on the right.

GPS Coordinates: N 45° 13.589' W 112° 7.124'

Contact: Bureau of Land Management, Dillon Field Office, 1005 Selway Dr., Dillon, MT 59725, 406/683-8000, www.blm.gov.

13 VIRGINIA CITY RV PARK

Scenic rating: 4

in Virginia City

Surrounded by arid juniper and sagebrush hills, the campground is within a 10-minute walk to Virginia City's main street, where the town has preserved more than 100 historical buildings from its 1860s gold rush days, when it was the largest town in the inland Northwest. Shopping, restaurants, living history and frontier museums, galleries, and live theaters operate out of the ghost town buildings connected by boardwalks at this National Historic Landmark. You can also take rides in a 1910 refurbished steam locomotive, a stagecoach, or a 1941 fire engine. Kids can fish in the Virginia City ponds. Horseback riding and garnet or gold panning are also possibilities. Nevada City, a second ghost town, is 1.5 miles west of Virginia City.

The small, cramped campground is sunny and hot with only a few trees that shade a couple of sites. Most campers are here to see the ghost towns rather than spend time in their campsites, though, as this is the only campground within 13 miles of Virginia City. Some of the campsites overlook the graveyard, and full-time residents also live in the park. Even though sites can accommodate longer RVs on the paved parking pads, spaces between sites are dry and dusty.

Campsites, facilities: The campground has 50 RV campsites and four tent campsites. RVs are limited to 52 feet. Facilities include picnic tables, pedestal grills, flush toilets, showers, drinking water, garbage service, disposal station, wireless Internet, and hookups for sewer, water, and electricity up to 30 amps. Leashed pets are permitted.

Reservations, fees: Reservations are highly recommended. Hookups cost $33-39. Tent sites cost $25. Rates are based on four people per site. Additional campers are charged $3 each. Children under four years old camp for free. Extra vehicles are $5. A 10 percent tax will be added. Cash or credit card. Open mid-May-late September.

Directions: On State Route 287 (not to be confused with Highway 287), from Ennis drive southwest for 13.1 miles, or from Virginia City drive 0.5 mile east. Turn south for 0.1 mile to enter the campground.

GPS Coordinates: N 45° 17.670' W 111° 55.660'

Contact: Virginia City RV Park, P.O. Box 235, Virginia City, MT 59755, 406/843-5493 or 888/833-5493, www.virginiacityrvpark.com.

14 RUBY CREEK

Scenic rating: 8

on the Madison River

Located at 5,500 feet on the west bank of the Madison River south of Ennis, Ruby Creek Campground attracts mostly anglers looking to hook trout. Sometimes, this upper Madison catch-and-release-only area fills with anglers at every river bend. The campground also backs against the Wall Creek Wildlife Management Area, a wintering range for elk but also home

to pronghorn antelope, moose, deer, black bears, and raptors. Designated roads, open May-November, allow touring for wildlife-watching, hiking, or hunting. The boat launch sits south of the campground, accessed quicker by walking than driving. By vehicle, drive out of the campground, turn left, and wrap 0.4 mile around to the boat launch, from which you can float or paddle the river north to McAtee Bridge.

Surrounded by sagebrush bench lands, the campground sits on an arid, bunchgrass prairie with large rocky outcroppings to the west and the Madison Mountains looming to the east. Unfortunately, you can also see a few houses up on the plateau, but the highway disappears—along with its noise—behind the plateau. Two gravel loops swing through the sunny campground, one on each side of Ruby Creek. The campground houses only a handful of 20-foot-high willows—not enough for shade or windbreaks. Both loops have four sites adjacent to the river. Three sites have pull-over parking, which can accommodate those with trailers.

Campsites, facilities: The campground has 22 RV or tent campsites that can accommodate midsized RVs. Facilities include picnic tables, fire rings with grills, vault toilets (wheelchair-accessible), drinking water, and campground hosts. Pack out your trash. Leashed pets are permitted.

Reservations, fees: Reservations are not accepted. Campsites cost $8. An extra vehicle costs $5. Only three vehicles are allowed per site. Cash or check. Open year-round; fees collected May-November.

Directions: From Highway 287 south of Ennis, turn west at the campground sign at milepost 30.9 onto a wide gravel road and cross the Madison River. Turn left just past the McAtee Bridge fishing access site and drive 2.6 miles south to the campground entrance on the left.

GPS Coordinates: N 45° 3.593' W 111° 39.929'

Contact: Bureau of Land Management, Dillon Field Office, 1005 Selway Dr., Dillon, MT

59725, 406/683-8000, www.blm.gov/mt/st/en.html.

15 PALISADES (MADISON RIVER)

🛶 🚐 ⚓ 🐎 ♿ 🚻 ⛺

Scenic rating: 7

on the Madison River

BEST (

On the east bank of the Madison River at 5,662 feet, Palisades Campground is named for the several-mile-long cliff band that runs along the hillside on the opposite side of the river. The cliffs light up in the morning sun. The paved boat ramp for launching rafts, drift boats, canoes, and kayaks onto the Madison River is in the Palisades picnic area, 0.9 mile south of the campground. You can float from here 8.5 miles to McAtee Bridge. Catch-and-release anglers can go wade fishing in the river, which has a blue-ribbon reputation for its brown and rainbow trout. This area of the river can sometimes fill with anglers in every stretch.

Surrounded by sagebrush bench lands, the campground's sites are on a wide-open, arid, treeless bunchgrass prairie with views of the Madison Mountains. Unfortunately, those views also include a few homes up on the bluff, but the highway is hidden behind. Half of the sites sit on the river. You can see pronghorn antelope and deer from the campground as well as wake up to songbirds. All of the sites are sunny gravel back-ins with neighboring campers in sight.

Campsites, facilities: The campground has 10 RV or tent campsites that can accommodate midsized RVs. Facilities include picnic tables, fire rings with grills, vault toilets (wheelchair-accessible), drinking water, and campground hosts. Pack out your trash. Leashed pets are permitted.

Reservations, fees: Reservations are not accepted. Campsites cost $8. An extra vehicle costs $5. Three vehicles are permitted per site.

Cash or check. Open year-round; fees are collected May-December.

Directions: From Highway 287 south of Ennis, turn west at milepost 22.9 onto the gravel road. Drive a bumpy 0.4 mile to a junction and veer right for the campground, which you'll reach 0.6 mile later.

GPS Coordinates: N 44° 59.775' W 111° 39.562'

Contact: Bureau of Land Management, Dillon Field Office, 1005 Selway Dr., Dillon, MT 59725, 406/683-8000, www.blm.gov/mt/st/en.html.

16 WEST FORK CABINS AND RV

🛶 🚐 ⚓ 🐎 🚐 ⛺

Scenic rating: 7

on the Madison River

Located at 5,880 feet along the Madison River, West Fork Cabins Camp offers fishing adjacent to the campground in the catch-and-release section of the Madison River. This upper section of the Madison River often is packed in summer with wading anglers at every bend in the river—it has a blue-ribbon reputation for wild trout. The company also offers guided fishing and float trips, plus rents rafts with trailers and personal kick boats. The campground is surrounded by Beaverhead-Deerlodge National Forest and the Madison Mountains. Horses are also available for riding.

The campground has two loops surrounding a grassy lawn. While some trees surround the campground, they are not in locations to provide shade. But those looking for satellite reception will have a clear shot at the sky. The campsites are all visible from each other, but each has its own cement patio. You can hear the highway across the river in the campground.

Campsites, facilities: The campground has 24 RV campsites that can accommodate large RVs, and 20 tent sites. Facilities include picnic tables, flush toilets, showers, drinking water, garbage service, launderette, tackle shop, and hookups for sewer, water, and electricity. Leashed pets are permitted.

Reservations, fees: Reservations are accepted. Hookups cost $30. Tent spaces cost $15. A 7 percent Montana bed tax is added. Cash, check, or credit card. Open April-November.

Directions: From Ennis, drive 35 miles south on Highway 287. (From West Yellowstone, the drive is also 35 miles.) Exit Highway 287 to the west and cross the Madison River, turning left onto Sundance Bench Road.

GPS Coordinates: N 44° 53.246' W 111° 34.831'

Contact: West Fork Cabins and RV, 24 Sundance Bench Rd., Cameron, MT 59720, 406/682-4802 or 866/343-8267, http://wfork.com.

17 WEST FORK MADISON

Scenic rating: 7

on the Madison River in Beaverhead-Deerlodge National Forest

At 5,950 feet, the campground squeezes in between the West Fork of the Madison River and the main stem of the Madison River. The Madison River—one of Montana's blue ribbon trout fisheries—attracts anglers, who wade fish or use drift boats. Canoes also float the river. River access sites for launching are located north and south of the campground.

This reconstructed campground now sits in two separated loops on open sagebrush terrain overlooking the river and homes on the other side. Sites are sunny with little privacy. With the road between the loops and the Madison River, the north loop sits on a gentle hillside above the river while the south loop parallels the river.

Campsites, facilities: The campground has 27 RV or tent campsites that can accommodate midsized RVs. Facilities include picnic tables,

fire rings with grills, drinking water, vault toilets (wheelchair-accessible), and campground hosts. Pack out your trash. Leashed pets are permitted.

Reservations, fees: Reservations are not accepted. Campsites cost $10. Open year-round, but services are available only May-September.

Directions: From Highway 287 at milepost 15.9, exit west and cross the Madison River. Turn left onto Sundance Bench Road for 0.4 mile to the campground entrance on the right. The second loops sits 0.3 mile further south. GPS Coordinates: N 44° 52.916' W 111° 34.598'

Contact: Beaverhead-Deerlodge National Forest, Madison Ranger District, 5 Forest Service Rd., Ennis, MT 59729, 406/682-4253, www.fs.usda.gov/bdnf.

18 RAYNOLD'S PASS

Scenic rating: 6

on the Madison River

At 6,140 feet, Raynold's Pass Campground is a state-run fishing access site on the Madison River, the main attraction. The Madison River is known for its wild trout fishery—particularly brown, rainbow, and Yellowstone cutthroat trout. This is a catch-and-release only section. You can go wade fishing in the river or launch a drift boat, kayak, canoe, or raft from the revamped gravel boat ramp. From here, you can float three river miles west to Three Dollar Bridge or continue for a 10-mile float to Lyons Bridge. A geological site of the 1959 earthquake slide that killed 28 people and dammed up the Madison River, the Earthquake Lake Visitor Center (open daily Memorial Day-mid-September) sits 3.2 miles to the east.

The arid, dusty campground loop sits in the open sagebrush and dry grass prairie with views of the Madison Mountains. No trees are available for shade or windbreaks, and the sites lack privacy because of the openness and the small loop. The proximity to the two highways adds noise from large trucks, even at night.

Campsites, facilities: The campground has six RV or tent campsites. RVs are limited to 25 feet. Facilities include picnic tables, rock fire rings, boat ramp, and vault toilets (wheelchair-accessible). Drinking water is not available; bring your own or treat river water. Leashed pets are permitted.

Reservations, fees: Reservations are not accepted. Camping is free. Open year-round.

Directions: From Ennis, drive south on Highway 287 to the junction with Highway 87. Turn south onto Highway 87 and drive 0.4 mile. Turn right into the fishing access site. GPS Coordinates: N 44° 49.622' W 111° 29.214'

Contact: Montana Fish, Wildlife, and Parks, Region 3, 1400 S. 19th Ave., Bozeman, MT 59718, 406/994-4042, http://fwp.mt.gov.

19 WADE LAKE

Scenic rating: 8

in the Gravelly Mountains in Beaverhead-Deerlodge National Forest

BEST (

At 6,200 feet steep mountains, skinny Wade Lake sinks into a deep forest trough. The lake is popular, especially with kids, for its sandy beach and turquoise water in the shallows. Lake water warms a bit by August. Anglers have caught record-breaking brown trout, and you can often see bald eagles and ospreys fishing, plus river otters. Canoes and kayaks are available to rent from the adjacent Wade Lake Resort. Only nonmotorized watercraft are permitted. The surrounding forested slopes contain hiking trails, one of which is a nature trail that climbs one mile to the Hilltop Campground.

The quiet, shady campground stacks on a steep hillside above the boat ramp and swimming area with steep access trails. Sites 3-6 have outstanding water views but also garner campground traffic on the way to the boat launch. Several sites in the upper loop have peek-a-boo views plummeting down to the lake. The upper loop sites offer more privacy because people aren't tromping by all day. Douglas firs shade most of the campground, and hollyhocks, pink sticky geraniums, and wild roses grow in sunny spots.

Campsites, facilities: The campground has 30 RV or tent campsites. RVs are limited to 32 feet. Facilities include picnic tables, fire rings with grills, vault toilets (wheelchair-accessible), drinking water, and campground hosts. Leashed pets are permitted.

Reservations, fees: Reservations are not accepted. Campsites cost $12. Open mid-May-September.

Directions: From Highway 287 south of Ennis, turn off south at milepost 9.6 at the Cliff and Wade Lake sign onto Wade Lake Road (Forest Road 241). Drive over the Madison River and pass the Three Dollar Bridge fishing access site. Be prepared for a long, bumpy drive with large rocks in the road. At 3.4 miles, turn right at the fork and climb steeply over the ridge for 1.7 miles. Watch for cattle on the road. At the signed fork in the road, turn right and drive 0.7 mile to the campground entrance. GPS Coordinates: N 44° 48.400' W 111° 33.971'

Contact: Beaverhead-Deerlodge National Forest, Madison Ranger District, 5 Forest Service Rd., Ennis, MT 59729, 406/682-4253, www.fs.usda.gov/bdnf.

20 HILLTOP

Scenic rating: 7

in the Gravelly Mountains in Beaverhead-Deerlodge National Forest

At 6,800 feet up a short, steep mountain, Hilltop is aptly named, for it sits on the spine of a ridge in between Wade and Cliff Lakes. A one-mile trail drops from the campground to Wade Lake, where you can swim, fish, and rent canoes or kayaks from Wade Lake Resort. The climb back up the hill requires more than 500 feet of ascent.

Hilltop is an older campground with smaller, back-in dirt parking pads, overhanging branches on the campground road, and trees that make for narrow turns. But it also has sites with spacious flat tent spaces. Douglas firs and lodgepole pines filter the sunlight and lend partial shade. More open campsites are rimmed with cow parsnip and lupine. Sites 11-14 and 16-18 overlook the canyon and opposite cliff wall, with a rail fence marking the end lip of the cliff. A few campsites offer peek-a-boo views of the Madison Mountains. Its remote location makes the campground quiet. Also, it is less crowded than Wade or Cliff Lake; you can often gain privacy just because of vacant neighboring campsites.

Campsites, facilities: The campground has 18 RV or tent campsites that can accommodate RVs up to 22 feet. Facilities include picnic tables, fire rings with grills, vault toilets (wheelchair-accessible), drinking water, and campground host. Leashed pets are permitted.

Reservations, fees: Reservations are not accepted. Campsites cost $12. Open mid-May-September.

Directions: From Highway 287 south of Ennis, turn off south at milepost 9.6 at the Cliff and Wade Lake sign onto Wade Lake Road (Forest Road 241). Drive over the Madison River and pass the Three Dollar Bridge fishing access site. Be prepared for a long, bumpy drive with large rocks in the road. At 3.4 miles, turn right at the fork and climb steeply over the ridge down for 1.7 miles. Watch for cattle on the road. At the signed fork in the road, turn left for 0.1 mile and turn right to climb steeply for 0.8 mile to the campground.

GPS Coordinates: N 44° 47.769' W 111° 33.682'

Contact: Beaverhead-Deerlodge National Forest, Madison Ranger District, 5 Forest Service

Rd., Ennis, MT 59729, 406/682-4253, www.fs.usda.gov/bdnf.

21 CLIFF POINT

Scenic rating: 8

in the Gravelly Mountains in Beaverhead-Deerlodge National Forest

BEST (

At 6,335 feet on the shore of Cliff Lake, the tiny Cliff Point Campground clusters around a small peninsula with popular campsites. Surrounded by steep forested slopes, the narrow lake is actually twice as big as Wade Lake, but more serene. The one-mile Fault Trail (#430) departs from the campground, touring through the canyon and connecting with the Wade Lake nature trail. As at Wade Lake, Cliff Lake's shallower bays shine turquoise because of the sandy bottom. Only nonmotorized boating is permitted, making it a quiet place for canoeing or kayaking. The lake's clear waters produce rainbow trout and cutthroat trout, and you can often watch bald eagles fish, plus see beaver.

These campsites are coveted for their locations on the point. Sites 3 and 4 claim the prime spots with big lake views and waterfront. Most of the sites have flat spaces for big tents. Small in size and filled with pink sticky geraniums and a few large Douglas fir trees for partial shade, this campground is one where you will see the neighbors, but you'll also get to wake up to the call of loons.

Campsites, facilities: The campground has six RV or tent campsites. RVs are limited to 16 feet. Facilities include picnic tables, fire rings with grills, vault toilets (wheelchair-accessible), drinking water, bear boxes, and garbage service. Leashed pets are permitted.

Reservations, fees: Reservations are not accepted. Campsites cost $12. Open mid-May-September.

Directions: From Highway 287 south of Ennis, turn off south at milepost 9.6 at the Cliff and Wade Lake sign onto Wade Lake

Road (Forest Road 241). Drive over the Madison River and pass the Three Dollar Bridge fishing access site. Be prepared for a long, bumpy drive with large rocks in the road. At 3.4 miles, turn right at the fork and climb steeply over the ridge down for 1.7 miles. Watch for cattle on the road. At the signed fork in the road, turn left for 0.4 mile to the boat ramp and continue another 0.6 mile to the campground. The road narrows to a single lane with curvy, blind corners.

GPS Coordinates: N 44° 47.600' W 111° 33.703'

Contact: Beaverhead-Deerlodge National Forest, Madison Ranger District, 5 Forest Service Rd., Ennis, MT 59729, 406/682-4253, www.fs.usda.gov/bdnf.

22 RIVER MARSH

Scenic rating: 6
in Red Rock Lakes National Wildlife Refuge

At the outlet of Lower Red Rock Lake's west shore, this campground sits in the 45,000-acre Red Rock Lakes National Wildlife Refuge—an essential nesting area for trumpeter swans, with more than 2,000 using the lakes during the fall migration. The refuge is also an outstanding wildlife-watching area with 232 species of birds. The lakes are open for nonmechanized boats (except sailing) from mid-July to freeze out, and you can paddle between the two lakes. Fishing is permitted on Odell Creek east of the lower lake. Mountain bikers ride the refuge roads to Red Rock Pass, and around the lower lake the Idlewild and Odell trails lead to wildlife-watching areas from the refuge headquarters area about five miles from the campground. The refuge also permits antelope, elk, deer, and waterfowl hunting. Reaching the refuge requires miles of rough dirt road driving without any services; call the refuge to check road conditions, and gas up.

The primitive sunny campground sits in mixed prairie grass and sagebrush. With no trees, the campsites claim big views of the Centennial Mountains and the Continental Divide, but the marsh area produces voluminous summer mosquitoes, which abate as long as the wind blows. Very few people camp here, almost guaranteeing privacy, and you'll wake up to the sounds of birds.

Campsites, facilities: The primitive campground has four RV or tent campsites that can accommodate small RVs. Facilities include fire pits and pit toilets. Water is available at refuge headquarters in Lakeview between the two lakes. Pack out your trash. Leashed pets are permitted.

Reservations, fees: Reservations are not accepted. Camping is free. Open year-round, although snow can close the roads and cover the campgrounds.

Directions: From Monida on I-15, take Exit 0 and drive north on the gravel Southside Centennial Road (MT Hwy. 509) for 24.8 miles. Turn north and drive 2.6 miles; then turn right. From Highway 87/287 in Idaho at the north end of Henry's Lake, you can also drive over Red Rock Pass to reach the campground in 29 miles.

GPS Coordinates: N 44° 38.790' W 111° 52.806'

Contact: Red Rocks Lake National Wildlife Refuge, 27820 Southside Centennial Rd., Lima, MT 59739, 406/276-3536, www.fws.gov/redrocks/.

23 UPPER RED ROCK LAKE

Scenic rating: 8
in Red Rock Lakes National Wildlife Refuge

BEST (

On the south shore of Upper Red Rock Lake, the campground sits in the middle of the 45,000-acre Red Rock Lakes National Wildlife Refuge. The refuge is an essential nesting area for trumpeter swans, with more than 2,000 using the lakes during the fall migration. The lakes are open for nonmechanized boats (except sailing) from mid-July to freeze out, and you can paddle between the two lakes. Fishing is permitted in Red Rock and Elk Springs Creeks, plus three ponds east of the upper lake. Mountain bikers ride the refuge roads to Red Rock Pass, and two hiking trails connect to wildlife-watching areas around the lower lake. The refuge also permits antelope, elk, deer, and waterfowl hunting. Reaching the refuge requires miles of rough dirt-road driving without any services; call the refuge to check road conditions, and gas up.

Of the two campgrounds in the refuge, Upper Red Rock Lake is visited more, but more often than not, you'll have the place to yourself. It fills with summer mosquitoes but offers views of the upper lake and Centennial Mountains, and sits on a lush hillside with aspens, chokecherries, willows, nettles, and sticky pink geraniums. Most of the sites garner full sun; a few tuck under the aspens for partial shade. At night, you won't hear a sound until the sandhill cranes call in the morning.

Campsites, facilities: The primitive campground has seven RV or tent campsites that can accommodate small RVs. Facilities include picnic tables, fire pits, pit toilets, and drinking water from a spring. Pack out your trash. Leashed pets are permitted. A gravel-path wheelchair-accessible toilet and campsite are available.

Reservations, fees: Reservations are not accepted. Camping is free. Open year-round, although snow can close the roads and cover the campgrounds.

Directions: From Monida on I-15, take Exit 0 and drive north on gravel Southside Centennial Road (MT Hwy. 509) for 31.8 miles. The campground is on the north side of the road. From Highway 87/287 in Idaho at the north end of Henry's Lake, you can also drive over Red Rock Pass to reach the campground in 22 miles.

GPS Coordinates: N 44° 35.590' W 111° 43.736'

Contact: Red Rocks Lake National Wildlife Refuge, 27820 Southside Centennial Rd., Lima, MT 59739, 406/276-3536, www.fws.gov/redrocks/.

24 CABIN CREEK

Scenic rating: 7

in the Madison Mountains in Gallatin National Forest

Cabin Creek Campground sits at 6,400 feet in the Madison Range. The Earthquake Scarp Interpretive Area is adjacent to the campground. At the beginning of the Cabin Creek Scarp Trailhead, you'll pass a fault scarp, a 20-foot-high dirt bank where the ground dropped down and the earth rose up, trapping some campers during the 1959 earthquake. The trailhead for the Cabin Creek Scarp-Red Canyon complex of trails is across the creek from the campground. Many of the trails are open to hikers, mountain bikers, motorcycles, and ATVs. To the west, Quake Lake's boat launch is 2.3 miles away, followed by the Earthquake Center Visitor Area eight miles away. Fishing and boating are available on Quake Lake.

The campground rests alongside the busy highway. Sites are very close together, and many have views of the road. A canopy of Douglas firs shades the campground, but with only low ground cover and cow parsnips, you can see the entire campground from almost every site. Double-wide dirt parking pads allow for two vehicles or a trailer separated from its vehicle. Four sites line up along Cabin Creek.

Campsites, facilities: The campground has 15 RV or tent campsites. RVs are limited to 30 feet. Facilities include picnic tables, fire rings with grills, vault toilets, drinking water, bear boxes, garbage service, firewood for sale, and campground host. Leashed pets are permitted. Wheelchair-accessible facilities include toilet and one campsite.

Reservations, fees: Reservations are

accepted (877/444-6777, www.recreation. gov). Campsites cost $14. An extra vehicle costs $6. Cash, check, or credit card. Open mid-May-mid-September.

Directions: On Highway 287 east of Quake Lake Visitor Center and west of Hebgen Lake, turn north off the highway at milepost 8.6 into the campground.

GPS Coordinates: N 44° 52.273' W 111° 20.691'

Contact: Gallatin National Forest, Hebgen Lake Ranger Station, 330 Gallatin Rd., West Yellowstone, MT 59758, 406/823-6961, www. fs.usda.gov/gallatin.

25 BEAVER CREEK

Scenic rating: 9

in the Madison Mountains in Gallatin National Forest

BEST (

Located on the slopes of a small mountain at 6,600 feet at the foot of Quake Lake, Beaver Creek is the closest campground to the Earthquake Lake Visitor Center (open daily Memorial Day-mid-September) 4.6 miles to the west. The center marks the site of a 1959 earthquake landslide that killed 28 people and dammed the Madison River, forming Quake Lake. Short walks lead to Memorial Rock and overlooks of the landslide path. Expert kayakers run the 1.5 miles of Class IV-V river from Quake Lake's outlet. From the campground, two short hiking trails descend to the six-mile-long Quake Lake, and a boat launch 0.5 mile to the west allows access for boating, canoeing, and fishing for brown and rainbow trout. Mountain bikers, hikers, and ATVers can use many of the Cabin Creek trails 1.7 miles to the east.

Situated in three loops on meadow hilltops, the campground blooms prolifically in July with paintbrush, lupines, and harebells. Loose groves of aspens and thin lodgepoles provide partial shade; other sites draw full sun. Three sites on A loop flank the beaver ponds,

The dead trees in Quake Lake are a testament to the landslide that formed the lake.

© BECKY LOMAX

where lily pads bloom with yellow flowers. Sites spread out for privacy, and thanks to the open forest, you get views of the surrounding peaks or Quake Lake but also can see other campers. The quiet campground rings with the sounds of songbirds or the light chatter of aspen leaves clacking in the breeze.

Campsites, facilities: The campground has 64 RV or tent campsites. RVs are limited to 50 feet. Facilities include picnic tables, fire rings with grills, vault toilets, drinking water, garbage service, firewood for sale, and campground hosts. Leashed pets are permitted. Wheelchair-accessible facilities include toilets and two campsites.

Reservations, fees: Reservations are accepted (877/444-6777, www.recreation.gov). Campsites cost $14. An extra vehicle costs $6. Cash, check, or credit card. Open early June-mid-September.

Directions: On Highway 287, east of Quake Lake Visitor Center and west of Hebgen Lake, turn south off the highway at milepost 7 onto the paved narrow road. Climb 0.6 mile to the campground entrance junction, with loop A to the left and loops B and C to the right.

GPS Coordinates: N 44° 51.390' W 111° 22.384'

Contact: Gallatin National Forest, Hebgen Lake Ranger Station, 330 Gallatin Rd., West Yellowstone, MT 59758, 406/823-6961, www.fs.usda.gov/gallatin.

26 FAIRY LAKE

Scenic rating: 9

in the Bridger Mountains in Gallatin National Forest

Plan to arrive early at this popular campground at 7,640 feet in the Bridger Mountains. Tucked below the rugged 9,665-foot ramparts of Sacagawea Peak, the campground sits near picturesque Fairy Lake—a place to swim on a hot day, but at this elevation and with late snowmelt, be ready for frigid water. A 2.5-mile trail (#534) climbs the peak—the highest in the Bridger Range—for spectacular views and encounters with mountain goats. A 0.1-mile path leads to Fairy Lake, which you can circumnavigate in less than an hour. The lake trail is short enough that you can carry a canoe or inflatable raft, although the lake is only 0.2-mile long. A mountain biking option, the Shafthouse Trail (#540) runs along Fairy Lake and traverses the northeast side of the Bridger Mountains below the crest. Anglers can fish the lake and Fairy Creek.

Reconstruction in 2012 improved this campground dramatically. Some trees were removed, opening up the thick forest to more sunlight, and the campground road, parking spurs, campsites, and facilities were rebuilt. Considering the campground's popularity, plan to arrive by early afternoon to claim a site.

Campsites, facilities: The campground has nine RV or tent campsites. Parking spurs can accommodate RVs to 32 feet; however, they are not recommended on the access road. Facilities include picnic tables, fire rings with grills, vault toilets (wheelchair-accessible), and drinking water. Pack out your trash. Leashed pets are permitted.

Reservations, fees: Reservations are not accepted. Camping is free. Open July-mid-September.

Directions: From Bozeman, travel north on Bridger Canyon Road (Hwy. 86) for 22.5 miles. Turn left onto the steep, gravel Fairy Lake Road for five miles, continuing straight past Cache Creek Road. The road is not recommended for RVs or trailers. Call for access road status.

GPS Coordinates: N 45° 54.409' W 110° 57.635'

Contact: Gallatin National Forest, Bozeman Ranger District, 3710 Fallon St., Bozeman, MT 59718, 406/522-2520, www.fs.usda.gov/gallatin.

27 BATTLE RIDGE

🧍 🚴 🐕 🚙 ⛺

Scenic rating: 8

in the Bridger Mountains in Gallatin National
Forest

At 6,391 feet, Battle Ridge Campground
cowers on the valley floor below the Bridger
Mountains, where their height casts an early
twilight on the camp. The campground attracts off-road motorists, mountain bikers, and
hikers who want to explore the Bridger Range,
and it is the only designated campground
available in early summer. For hiking, visitors pulling trailers can leave the RV to drive
up the rough road to Fairy Lake Recreation
Area, located 5.5 miles west. Intermediate-
skilled mountain bikers will want to ride the
26-mile Bangtail Ridge singletrack (31 miles
for full loop without shuttling) for views of
the Bridger and Crazy Mountains. South of
the campground, Bohart Ranch opens their
cross-country ski trails in summer for mountain biking.

Broad meadows that are lush green in
June, but dry brown in August weave around
the pine forest that shades some campsites
sprinkled on a gentle slope above the road.
Many of the campsites have views of the
Bridger Mountains to the west. After dark,
the road tends to see minimal traffic, quiet-
ing the area.

Campsites, facilities: The campground has
13 RV or tent campsites. RVs are limited to 30
feet. Facilities include picnic tables, fire rings,
pit toilets, and drinking water. Leashed pets
are permitted.

Reservations, fees: Reservations are
not accepted. Camping is free. Open
mid-May-mid-September.

Directions: From Bozeman, travel north on
Bridger Canyon Road (Hwy. 86) for 22 miles.
Turn right to the campground entrance.
GPS Coordinates: N 45° 52.922' W 110°
52.800'

Contact: Gallatin National Forest, Bozeman
Ranger District, 3710 Fallon St., Bozeman,
MT 59718, 406/522-2520, www.fs.usda.gov/
gallatin.

28 BOZEMAN KOA

🏊 🚣 🌊 🐕 🚶 🚐 ⛺

Scenic rating: 6

in the Gallatin Valley

BEST (

At 4,741 feet, about 10 minutes south of I-90,
the Bozeman KOA has two creeks running
through the campground, which offer fishing. But its big attraction is the neighboring
Bozeman Hot Springs and Spa (open daily,
406/586-6492, www.bozemanhotsprings.
com). It has nine pools between 59°F and
106°F for dips ranging from icy to steaming.
Cascading waterfalls plunge into two pools,
and a large pool accommodates lap swimming.
One pool is outdoors. Dry and wet saunas, a
fitness facility, and spa services are available.
The campground sits 0.5 mile from 27 holes
of golf and 20 minutes from the Museum of
the Rockies. Its location at the head of the
Gallatin Valley makes an easy 40-minute drive
to Yellowstone National Park.

The campground sits on a busy highway—
the main road heading down the Gallatin
River Valley to Yellowstone National Park.
Vehicle traffic is nonstop in summer and
during rush hours. The KOA has partially
shaded campsites on mowed lawn with sites
very close together. The KOA's swimming
pool, hot tub, and splash park closed in 2013;
call for updates.

Campsites, facilities: The campground has
126 campsites: Hookups at 86 sites, 27 non-
hookup sites for smaller RVs or tents, plus 13
overflow sites with water and electrical hookups or no hookups. RVs are limited to 90 feet.
Hookups are available for water, sewer, and
electricity up to 50 amps. Facilities include
flush toilets, showers, picnic tables, fire rings
with grills, garbage service, cable TV, wireless Internet, playground, disposal station, pet

walk, mini-golf, camp store, firewood for sale, electrical hookups at tent sites, and camping kitchen. Leashed pets are permitted.

Reservations, fees: Reservations are accepted. Hookups cost $40-51. Tent sites cost $30-34. Rates cover two people. Extra campers are charged $5-6. Children 14 and under stay free. Add on 7 percent tax. Cash, check, or credit card. Open mid-April-October.

Directions: On the west side of Bozeman at Belgrade on I-90, take Exit 298 and turn south on Jackrabbit Lane (Hwy. 85) for 7.7 miles. The road becomes Highway 191. Turn right on Lower Rainbow Road for one-half block to the campground entrance on the right.

GPS Coordinates: N 45° 39.584' W 111° 11.360'

Contact: Bozeman KOA, 81123 Gallatin Rd. (Hwy. 191), Bozeman, MT 59718, 406/587-3030 or 800/562-3036, www.koa.com.

29 SPIRE ROCK

Scenic rating: 7

in the Gallatin Mountains in Gallatin National Forest

Spire Rock Campground nestles at 5,500 feet in a narrow canyon just south of Storm Castle Mountain in Gallatin National Forest. The canyon is home to several trailheads for hikers and mountain bikers. You can summit the 7,165-foot Storm Castle Mountain or 8,202-foot Garnet Mountain Lookout for views of the Spanish Peaks or head to Rat Lake. Just south of Storm Castle in the Gallatin Canyon, the Scorched Earth area offers sport climbing ranging in grade from 5.8 to 5.13. To the north in the canyon, rock climbers will find traditional routes on Gallatin Towers. The forested canyon yields a color drama in the evening with the limestone outcroppings lighting up.

Along a very skinny dirt road, the campground sprawls for one mile up the canyon with the campsites clumped together in twos

and threes with 0.1 mile or so in between the clusters. That creates a feeling of camping in a tiny campground with only a couple campsites. Many of the campsites sit along the creek, with large, flat tent spaces. Lush undergrowth of thimbleberries, wild roses, and vine maples lends privacy between sites, many of which are partially shaded by Douglas firs. The only sound you'll hear is the creek.

Campsites, facilities: The campground has 19 RV or tent campsites. RVs are limited to 50 feet. Facilities include picnic tables, fire rings with grills, pit toilets (wheelchair-accessible), bear boxes, garbage service, and firewood for sale. Drinking water is not available; bring your own or treat creek water. Leashed pets are permitted.

Reservations, fees: Reservations are accepted (877/444-6777, www.recreation.gov). Campsites cost $10. An extra vehicle costs $6. Cash, check, or credit card. Open mid-May-late September.

Directions: West of Bozeman, travel south on Highway 191 to milepost 65.2. Turn east and cross the river. Turn immediately south onto the dirt road and drive past the heli-base. The gravel road narrows along the river, with an abrupt drop-off and potholes for 1.6 miles, and then turns east for one mile, passing the trailhead for Storm Castle Mountain before reaching the campground. Turn right into the campground.

GPS Coordinates: N 45° 26.477' W 111° 12.398'

Contact: Gallatin National Forest, Bozeman Ranger District, 3710 Fallon St., Bozeman, MT 59718, 406/522-2520, www.fs.usda.gov/gallatin.

30 GREEK CREEK

Scenic rating: 7

in Gallatin Canyon in Gallatin National Forest

Located at 5,800 feet in elevation, Greek Creek

Campground splits on both sides of the highway cutting through the Gallatin Canyon in Gallatin National Forest. The loops on the west side flank the river; those on the east side tuck into the forest up against a mountainside. For guided raft trips on the Class II-III river, Montana Whitewater Rafting Company is six miles north. Kayaker, rafters, and anglers going after brown and rainbow trout use the river. The Lava Lake Trailhead is 3.2 miles north at Cascade Creek. The trail, for hikers only past the wilderness boundary, climbs into the Spanish Peaks of the Lee Metcalf Wilderness, reaching the lake in 3.5 miles after a 1,600-foot elevation gain. The trail is one of the most popular in the area, so you won't find solitude here—especially on weekends. Bicyclists riding to Yellowstone use this campground.

In the narrow canyon, the campground squeezes around the highway, making the sound of passing vehicles ubiquitous in the campground. Not even the river can drown out the larger trucks. Unfortunately, some campsites have views of the road, too. The Douglas fir forest admits filtered sunlight to the mountainside loops, which are more private, separated from each other by low brush, wild roses, and tall grass. The river loops, which are roomier with larger flat spaces for tents, are more open. On the left river loop, sites 14 and 15 overlook the river. The hot midsummer sun leaves the canyon early, cooling off the campground.

Campsites, facilities: The campground has 14 RV or tent campsites. RVs are limited to 60 feet. Facilities include picnic tables, fire rings with grills, vault toilets, drinking water, bear boxes, garbage service, and firewood for sale. Leashed pets are permitted. Wheelchair-accessible toilets and seven sites are available.

Reservations, fees: Reservations are accepted (877/444-6777, www.recreation.gov). Campsites cost $13. An extra vehicle costs $8. Cash or check. Open mid-May-late September.

Directions: West of Bozeman, travel south on Highway 191 to milepost 58.2. The campground splits on both sides of the highway, so turn right or left, depending on whether you want a site near the river or not.

GPS Coordinates: N 45° 22.818' W 111° 10.945'

Contact: Gallatin National Forest, Bozeman Ranger District, 3710 Fallon St., Suite C, Bozeman, MT 59718, 406/522-2520, www.fs.usda.gov/gallatin.

31 SWAN CREEK

Scenic rating: 7

in the Gallatin Mountains in Gallatin National Forest

At 5,800 feet, Swan Creek Campground sits in a quiet side canyon east of Gallatin Canyon in Gallatin National Forest. The forested, steep-walled canyon pinches the narrow access road with overhanging branches, precluding many larger RVs from access. At the end of Swan Creek Canyon, a steep trail, #186, leads about 12 miles to Hyalite Peak. It is open to hikers, mountain bikers, and motorcycles. More hiking and mountain-biking trails are available from the Moose Creek area about 1.5 miles south on the highway. The nearby Gallatin River provides rafting, kayaking, and fishing.

Swan Creek Campground's two loops offers respite from the busy Gallatin Canyon campgrounds right on the highway. All of the campsites, which have back-in gravel parking spurs, line Swan Creek, where the burbling water is the sound you'll hear, rather than traffic. Douglas firs, spruces, and lodgepole pines lend partial to heavy shade to the campsites, and sunnier spots bloom with paintbrush, pink fireweed, and white yarrow. Several campsites have large, flat gravel spaces for tents.

Campsites, facilities: The campground has 14 RV or tent campsites. RVs are limited to 45 feet. Facilities include picnic tables, fire rings with grills, pit and vault toilets, hand

Gallatin National Forest offers camping, hiking, and rafting.

pumps for drinking water, bear boxes, garbage service, and firewood for sale. Leashed pets are permitted. Wheelchair-accessible facilities include toilets and seven sites.

Reservations, fees: Reservations are accepted (877/444-6777, www.recreation.gov). Campsites cost $14. An extra vehicle costs $6. Cash, check, or credit card. Open mid-May–late September.

Directions: West of Bozeman, travel south on Highway 191 to milepost 57.4. Turn east onto Swan Creek Road (Forest Road 481), a single-lane road with turnouts (trailers should be able to back up), and drive 0.5 mile. Use caution on turning off from the curvy highway as locals drive fast. Both loops sit on the right side of the road about 0.6 mile apart.

GPS Coordinates: N 45° 22.399' W 111° 9.287'

Contact: Gallatin National Forest, Bozeman Ranger District, 3710 Fallon St., Suite C, Bozeman, MT 59718, 406/522-2520, www.fs.usda.gov/gallatin.

32 MOOSE CREEK FLATS

Scenic rating: 7

in Gallatin Canyon in Gallatin National Forest

At 5,700 feet, Moose Creek Flats Campground squeezes into an open meadow between the Gallatin River and the highway. The Class II-III river is popular for white-water rafting, kayaking, and wade-fishing. The campground works as both a take-out and put-in. For hikers and mountain bikers, the Moose Creek Trail (#187) departs on a spur road across the highway, leading eventually to the Gallatin Crest and Windy Pass Cabin. Other nearby trails for hikers access the Spanish Peaks of the Lee Metcalf Wilderness. The campground is the closest one to the north of Big Sky Resort, which offers summer scenic chair rides, mountain biking, ziplining, and hiking.

A paved road with gravel back-in parking spurs and three pull-throughs weaves through the campground. Surrounded by a wide-open flat grassy meadow, all of the sunny campsites have views of the forested canyon walls as well as views of other campsites plus the highway, with its accompanying noise. A few Douglas firs are sprinkled along the river. Within the narrow Gallatin Canyon, the hot midsummer sun sinks out of sight earlier, which cools the campground. Sites 1-9 overlook the river.

Campsites, facilities: The campground has 13 RV or tent campsites. RVs are limited to 60 feet. One of the sites is for small groups. Facilities include picnic tables, fire rings with grills, vault toilets, drinking water, bear boxes, garbage service, and firewood for sale. Leashed pets are permitted. Toilets, four campsites, and a fishing access are wheelchair-accessible.

Reservations, fees: Reservations are accepted (877/444-6777, www.recreation. gov). Campsites cost $14. An extra vehicle costs $6. Cash, check, or credit card. Open mid-May-mid-September.

Directions: West of Bozeman, travel south on Highway 191 to milepost 56.3. Be cautious about turning into the campground as locals drive fast in the canyon. The campground sits on the west side of the highway.

GPS Coordinates: N 45° 21.363' W 111° 10.318'

Contact: Gallatin National Forest, Bozeman Ranger District, 3710 Fallon St., Suite C, Bozeman, MT 59718, 406/522-2520, www. fs.usda.gov/gallatin.

33 RED CLIFF

Scenic rating: 8

in Gallatin Canyon in Gallatin National Forest

At 6,250 feet, Red Cliff Campground is the only Forest Service campground in the upper Gallatin Canyon between Big Sky and Yellowstone National Park. The campground, which is named for the orange cliffs in the area, has places to carry rafts and kayaks to the Gallatin River for launching. The river houses rainbow, brown, brook, and Yellowstone cutthroat trout, plus mountain whitefish and arctic grayling. At the end of the south loop, the 4.8-mile Elkhorn Trail (#165) is open to hiking and horse-packing only, in a significant wildlife area. The campground is the closest one to the south of Big Sky Resort, which offers summer scenic chair rides, mountain biking, ziplining, and hiking.

When you enter the campground on the gravel road, loops head off in both directions. The north loop contains the campsites without hookups; the south loop has those with electrical hookups. Although the campground is on the opposite side of the river from the highway, the water doesn't drown out the motor sounds. A young Douglas fir forest covers most of the campground, with both shady and partly sunny campsites available. The south loop ends in a meadow blooming with pink sticky geraniums, and five north loop sites have views of the treed canyon. Several riverside sites have large flat spaces for tents where the door can sit right on the bank.

Campsites, facilities: The campground has 65 RV or tent campsites. RVs are limited to 50 feet. One of the sites is for small groups. Electrical hookups are available at 27 sites. Facilities include picnic tables, fire rings with grills, vault toilets, drinking water, bear boxes, garbage service, campground hosts, and firewood for sale. Leashed pets are permitted. Wheelchair-accessible toilets, tables, and water are available.

Reservations, fees: Reservations are accepted (877/444-6777, www.recreation.gov). No-hookup campsites cost $14; electrical hookup campsites cost $16. An extra vehicle costs $6. Cash, check, or credit card. Open mid-May-late September.

Directions: West of Bozeman, travel south on Highway 191 to milepost 41.5. Be cautious about turning into the campground—locals drive fast in the canyon. Turn east off the highway and cross the Gallatin River.

GPS Coordinates: N 45° 10.603' W 111° 14.490'

Contact: Gallatin National Forest, Bozeman

Ranger District, 3710 Fallon St., Suite C, Bozeman, MT 59718, 406/522-2520, www.fs.usda.gov/gallatin.

34 LANGOHR

Scenic rating: 8
in Hyalite Canyon in Gallatin National Forest

At 6,100 feet in Hyalite Canyon, Langohr Campground sits on the site of the first ranger station for the national forest. A short interpretive trail crosses the creek in the campground, and Hyalite Canyon is packed with hiking and mountain-biking trails, but the most popular trails depart from the no-wake Hyalite Reservoir area five miles farther up the road. The Blackmore picnic area and boat launch sits at the northwest corner of the reservoir. Hyalite Creek, which flows through the campground, harbors rainbow and Yellowstone cutthroat trout. Class IV-V stretches of white water in the canyon north of the campground draw expert kayakers.

The campground has two paved loops with paved campsite spurs lining up along Hyalite Creek. Most of the campsites enjoy creek frontage. The campground sits in a wild garden of midsummer color with yarrow, sticky pink geraniums, cow parsnips, and bladder campions surrounded by a Douglas fir forest. The lush surroundings make up for the fact that you can see neighboring campers, despite the spread-out sites. After dark, a few late hikers still race back down the canyon to Bozeman on the adjacent road (which you can see above), but then only the sound of the stream remains. Most of the campsites have views of meadow hillsides and mixed forest slopes.

Campsites, facilities: The campground has 19 RV or tent campsites. RVs are limited to 32 feet. Facilities include picnic tables, fire rings with grills, vault toilets, drinking water, garbage service, bear boxes, firewood for sale, and campground host. Leashed pets are permitted.

Wheelchair-accessible facilities include toilets, a trail, and two campsites.

Reservations, fees: Reservations are accepted (877/444-6777, www.recreation.gov). Campsites cost $14. An extra vehicle costs $6. Cash, check, or credit card. Open mid-May-mid-September.

Directions: From downtown Bozeman, drive west on Highway 191 to Cottonwood Road. Turn south and drive 5.5 miles. Turn east onto South 19th Avenue and go one mile. Turn south onto Hyalite Canyon Road, which turns into Forest Road 62. Climb 5.9 miles to the campground entrance on the right.

GPS Coordinates: N 45° 31.970' W 111° 0.908'

Contact: Gallatin National Forest, Bozeman Ranger District, 3710 Fallon St., Suite C, Bozeman, MT 59718, 406/522-2520, www.fs.usda.gov/gallatin.

35 HOOD CREEK

Scenic rating: 10
in Hyalite Canyon in Gallatin National Forest

At 6,730 feet, Hood Creek Campground sits on Hyalite Reservoir's northeast shore in Gallatin National Forest, with views up the canyon to Hyalite Peak. The lake is a no-wake zone, best for canoes, kayaks, and small sailboats, which can be launched from the boat ramp in the campground; motorboats can launch from the Blackmore picnic area less than a mile away. For anglers, the lake harbors Yellowstone cutthroat trout, brook trout, and arctic grayling. Across the road from the campground, Mystic Lake Trail (#436) leads 5.5 miles up to the lake. The trail is open to hikers, mountain bikers, and motorbikes.

The quiet, idyllic campsites at Hood Creek are prized for their location right on the reservoir shore with big views of Hyalite Peak. The close proximity of the picnic tables and tent sites to the water is rare because of concerns over water quality. The reconstructed campground now features level campsites, new facilities, and a smoother gravel road. Large conifers lend shade to some campsites, while others campsites enjoy sunny meadows bursting with wildflowers.

Campsites, facilities: The campground has 25 RV or tent campsites and one group site. RVs are limited to 50 feet. Facilities include picnic tables, fire rings with grills, vault toilets, drinking water, bear boxes, garbage service, firewood for sale, tent pads, and campground host. Leashed pets are permitted. Wheelchair-accessible facilities include toilets and two campsites.

Reservations, fees: Reservations are highly recommended (877/444-6777, www.recreation.gov). Campsites cost $14. An extra vehicle costs $6. Cash, check, or credit card. Open mid-May-late September.

Directions: From downtown Bozeman, drive west on Highway 191 to Cottonwood Road. Turn south and drive 5.5 miles. Turn east onto South 19th Avenue and go one mile. Turn south onto Hyalite Canyon Road, which turns into Forest Road 62. Drive 10.5 miles to the campground entrance on the right. (You'll cross over Hyalite Dam.)
GPS Coordinates: N 45° 29.101' W 110° 58.136'

Contact: Gallatin National Forest, Bozeman Ranger District, 3710 Fallon St., Suite C, Bozeman, MT 59718, 406/522-2520, www.fs.usda.gov/gallatin.

36 CHISHOLM

🚶 🚲 🏊 🛶 🚐 🚤 🐕 ♿ 🚗 ⛺

Scenic rating: 9

in Hyalite Canyon in Gallatin National Forest

Chisholm Campground, elevation 6,740 feet, sits on the west side of Hyalite Reservoir. But contrary to Hood Creek waterfront campsites, this campground offers only peek-a-boo water views through the trees and trails to the reservoir. However, its location lends easy access to several trails, including wheelchair-accessible trails. The paved 0.5-mile Palisades Falls trail, littered with 50-million-year-old basalt from volcanoes, departs one mile from the campground and leads to the 80-foot waterfall. Trail #434 leads 5.5 miles to Emerald and Heather Lakes, and #427 saunters past 11 waterfalls en route to Hyalite Lake and the 10,299-foot summit of Hyalite Peak. You can launch boats at the Blackmore picnic area about 1.5 miles away. The lake, which harbors Yellowstone cutthroat trout and arctic grayling, is a no-wake zone. With the campground's location on the reservoir's upper end, late summer can leave this end dry when water levels drop.

The campground has one loop with all back-in parking spurs. Sites are spread out for privacy; some have a thick forest of pines and firs between them, but others are more open, with neighboring campers in view. Most of the campsites sit under heavy shade or filtered sunlight. A creek runs along the northwest side of the campground, with three sites along it. Besides the creek, you'll hear only songbirds in the morning.

Campsites, facilities: The campground has 10 RV or tent campsites. RVs are limited to 60 feet. Facilities include picnic tables, fire rings with grills, vault toilets (wheelchair-accessible), drinking water, bear boxes, garbage service, firewood for sale, and campground hosts. Leashed pets are permitted.

Reservations, fees: Reservations are accepted (877/444-6777, www.recreation.gov). Campsites cost $14. An extra vehicle costs $6. Cash or, check, or credit card. Open mid-May-late September.

Directions: From downtown Bozeman, drive west on Highway 191 to Cottonwood Road. Turn south and drive 5.5 miles. Turn east onto South 19th Avenue and go one mile. Turn south onto Hyalite Canyon Road, which turns into Forest Road 62. Drive 11.7 miles to the campground entrance on the right. (You'll cross over Hyalite Dam.)
GPS Coordinates: N 45° 28.491' W 110° 57.325'

Contact: Gallatin National Forest, Bozeman Ranger District, 3710 Fallon St., Suite C, Bozeman, MT 59718, 406/522-2520, www.fs.usda.gov/gallatin.

37 BEAR CANYON

Scenic rating: 6

east of Bozeman

Located five minutes from downtown Bozeman, Bear Canyon Campground is convenient for shopping, nightlife, galleries, and restaurants along the main street as well as concerts in the Emerson Center. Bozeman is also home to golf courses, the Bozeman Hot Springs, and the Museum of the Rockies, with its celebrated dinosaur exhibits. A five-minute drive on the freeway also puts you at the entrance to Bridger Canyon, where the Bridger Bowl Ski Area hosts the annual Raptor Festival in early October. The free event takes place during the largest golden eagle migration in the United States, and you can hike to the ridge for a better view of the birds flying overhead. Hiking and mountain-biking trails are also in Bridger Canyon.

Bear Canyon Campground sits on a bluff above the freeway, but despite the proximity, some of the sites are surprisingly quiet. The campground commands views of the valley and surrounding mountains. Campsites are close together lined up in parking-lot fashion with some shorter trees providing partial shade. The campground has both pull-through and back-in gravel sites for RVs.

Campsites, facilities: The campground has 80 RV sites that can fit large RVs and 14 tent sites. Hookups are available for water, sewer, and electricity up to 50 amps. Facilities include flush toilets, showers, picnic tables, garbage service, wireless Internet, outdoor swimming pool, playground, launderette, disposal station, and camp store. Leashed pets are permitted.

Reservations, fees: Reservations are accepted. Hookups cost $28-35. Tent sites cost $20. Rates are for two people and one vehicle (includes trailer). Additional campers are charged $5 per person. Children age three or younger stay free. An extra vehicle costs $2. For each pet, add $1. A 7 percent Montana bed tax will be added on. Cash or credit card. Open May-mid-October.

Directions: From Bozeman, drive east on I-90 about 3.5 miles. Take Exit 313 and drive to the southwest side of the freeway, turning left into the campground in 400 feet.

GPS Coordinates: N 45° 39.080' W 110° 56.780'

Contact: Bear Canyon Campground, 4000 Bozeman Trail Road, Bozeman, MT 59718, 406/587-1575 or 800/438-1575, www.bearcanyoncampground.com.

38 PARADISE VALLEY KOA

Scenic rating: 8

on the Yellowstone River

At 4,700 feet in the Paradise Valley, the KOA flanks the Yellowstone River with 500 feet of waterfront. Flowing between the Gallatin and Absaroka Mountains, the Yellowstone River is favored by anglers as an iconic blue-ribbon trout stream. Anglers fish from drift boats, canoes, and rafts in addition to wading. A wheelchair-accessible 1.5-mile trail to Pine Creek Falls departs less than three miles away, and Pine Creek Road offers pleasant bicycle touring.

Large cottonwood trees shade the grassy campground, but a few sunny sites in the open garner views of the rugged Absaroka Mountains. Located on the opposite side of the river from the highway, the campground is quiet. Sites pack close together, with back-in and pull-through parking. Summer features pancake breakfasts and ice cream socials.

Campsites, facilities: The campground has 52 RV campsites with a maximum length pull-through of 95 feet. Hookups include water, sewer, and electricity up to 50 amps. The campground also has 27 tent campsites, some with electricity. Facilities include picnic tables, fire rings, flush toilets, showers, outdoor swimming pools (late May-early October), launderette, drinking water, playground, dog walk, wireless Internet, camp store, firewood and propane for sale, and bicycle rentals. Leashed pets are permitted.

Reservations, fees: Reservations are accepted. Hookups cost $43-50. Tent sites cost $28-35. Rates cover two adults. Extra campers are charged $4. Kids under 12 years old stay free. A 7 percent Montana bed tax will be added on. Open May-early October.

Directions: From Livingston, drive 10 miles south on Highway 89 toward Yellowstone Park to around milepost 42.8. Turn east on Pine Creek Road and drive 1.25 miles across the river to the campground entrance on the left. GPS Coordinates: N 45° 30.718' W 110° 34.731'

Contact: Livingston/Paradise Valley KOA, 163 Pine Creek Rd., Livingston, MT 59047, 406/222-0992 or 800/562-2805, www.koa.com.

39 PINE CREEK

Scenic rating: 8

in the Absaroka Mountains in Gallatin National Forest

Pine Creek Recreation Area, located at 5,600 feet just up from the floor of Paradise Valley, tucks in the northwest foothills of the Absaroka Mountains. Anglers can fish in Pine Creek for rainbow trout and mountain whitefish. A 0.5-mile nature trail explores the creek, and the Pine Creek Trail has two worthy destinations: Pine Creek Falls roars one flat mile up the trail, spraying mist onto the bridge, and hikers can reach Pine Creek Lake in five uphill miles with switchbacks. The 32-acre idyllic alpine lake cuddles in a cirque below massive rock walls and is stocked for fishing.

A loose forest of Douglas fir and spruce provides mixed sun and shade for the quiet campground. A lush understory between most of the sites lends a sense of privacy, but a few have neighbors in view. Trails lead to Pine Creek, which runs adjacent to Loop B.

Campsites, facilities: The campground has 23 RV or tent campsites, including one group site, and two tent-only sites (one is a walk-in). RVs are limited to 50 feet. Facilities include picnic tables, fire rings, vault toilets, drinking water (Memorial Day-Labor Day), garbage service, firewood for sale, and campground hosts. Leashed pets are permitted. Wheelchair-accessible facilities include toilets, nature trail, fishing dock, and 17 campsites.

Reservations, fees: Reservations are accepted (877/444-6777, www.recreation.gov). Campsites cost $14. An extra vehicle costs $6. Cash or, check, or credit card. Open mid-May-October.

Directions: From Livingston, drive nine miles south on Highway 89. Turn east onto Pine Creek Road for 2.4 miles, crossing the Yellowstone River. At State Route 540, turn right for 0.7 miles. Turn left onto Forest Road 202 for 2.75 miles of narrow, winding road to the Pine Creek Recreation Area. GPS Coordinates: N 45° 29.901' W 110° 31.415'

Contact: Gallatin National Forest, Yellowstone Ranger District/Livingston Office, 5242 Hwy. 89, Livingston, MT 59047, 406/222-1892, www.fs.usda.gov/gallatin.

40 MALLARD'S REST

Scenic rating: 6

on the Yellowstone River

At 4,731 feet south of Livingston, Mallard's Rest is a state-run fishing access on the Yellowstone River in Paradise Valley. A cement boat ramp with trailer parking is available for launching rafts, drift boats, canoes, and kayaks, and the river garners fame as a blue-ribbon trout fishery. Located between Loch Leven and Pine Creek fishing access sites, Mallard's Rest is one of nine fishing access sites with boat ramps in the 56 river miles of the Yellowstone River between Livingston and Gardiner.

With reconstructed campsites and road, the state revamped this campground that sits on a tall grass and juniper river bar—green in early summer, but gold by the end of July. Willow brush flanks part of the riverbank, and a handful of big willow trees offer partial shade to a few campsites. All of the sunny campsites have big views across the river of the Absaroka Mountains. Some traffic noise filters down into the campground.

Campsites, facilities: The campground has 12 RV or tent campsites that can accommodate RVs up to 30 feet. Facilities include picnic tables, fire rings with grills, drinking water, vault toilets (wheelchair-accessible), and concrete boat ramp. Leashed pets are permitted.

Reservations, fees: Reservations are not accepted. Campsites cost $7 with a Montana fishing license and $12 without a Montana fishing license. Cash or check. Open year-round.

Directions: From Livingston, drive south on Highway 89 for approximately nine miles to milepost 41.5. Turn east onto the 0.2-mile steep gravel road, which swings around a sharp hairpin down to the river level and the campground.

GPS Coordinates: N 45° 28.975' W 110° 37.235'

Contact: Montana Fish, Wildlife, and Parks, Region 3, 1400 S. 19th Ave., Bozeman, MT 59718, 406/994-4042, http://fwp.mt.gov.

41 SNOWBANK

Scenic rating: 8

in the Absaroka Mountains in Gallatin National Forest

Located at 5,750 feet at the western edge of the Absaroka-Beartooth Wilderness, Snowbank Campground is a place to go for solitude, fishing, and hiking. The only interruption to the quiet can be motors from off-road vehicles on some trails and roads outside the wilderness area. Mill Creek harbors several species of trout and mountain whitefish. Near the campground entrance, the 6.3-mile Wicked Ridge Trail (#78) for hikers or mountain bikers climbs past logging roads to some views, but better hiking trails into the wilderness launch within a few miles up further up the road. An easy two-mile trail (#58) leads to scenic Passage Falls.

A thick fir and spruce forest broken by grassy meadows lends a mix of shade and sun to the quiet campground. Between a lush understory of wild berry bushes screening sites and spacious distribution along the campground road, most campsites are private. You'll wake to the sounds of birds and the stream. Eight sites spread along the creek while two campsites sit on a hillside spur.

Campsites, facilities: The campground has 10 RV or tent campsites, including one group site. RVs are limited to 35 feet. Facilities include picnic tables, fire rings, vault toilets, drinking water (Memorial Day-Labor Day), garbage service, firewood for sale, and campground hosts. Leashed pets are permitted.

Reservations, fees: Reservations are accepted (877/444-6777, www.recreation.gov). Campsites cost $14. An extra vehicle costs $6. Cash or, check, or credit card. Open mid-May-October.

Directions: From Livingston, drive 15 miles south on Highway 89. Turn east onto Mill Creek Road for 12 miles, crossing the

Yellowstone River. Drive the gravel forest road to the campground entrance on the right.

GPS Coordinates: N 45° 17.281' W 110° 32.508'

Contact: Gallatin National Forest, Yellowstone Ranger District/Livingston Office, 5242 Hwy. 89, Livingston, MT 59047, 406/222-1892, www.fs.usda.gov/gallatin.

42 YELLOWSTONE'S EDGE RV PARK

Scenic rating: 6

on the Yellowstone River

At 4,850 feet, the Yellowstone's Edge RV Park sits on the west bank of the Yellowstone River south of Livingston in the Paradise Valley. From the campground, you can launch hand-carried canoes, kayaks, or rafts and fish for brown and rainbow trout from the river's bank. A state-run fishing access site with a boat ramp and a fishing guide service is five miles south at Emigrant. Scenic floats are also available on the river. Chico Hot Springs is seven miles south.

The campground sits on a sunny, flat bar with 3,000 feet of river frontage. More than one-third of the campsites line up along the river, but all sites have views of the surrounding Gallatin and Absaroka Mountains. At such a proximity to the highway, vehicle noise is prevalent. The campground has evening campfires for socializing. Both back-in and pull-through sites—some with concrete patios—line up very close together with mowed lawn in between.

Campsites, facilities: The campground has 80 RV campsites. RVs are limited to 90 feet. Hookups are available for sewer, water, and electricity up to 50 amps. Facilities include picnic tables, flush toilets, showers, garbage service, convenience store, wireless Internet, launderette, game room, horseshoe pits, and dog walk. Leashed pets are permitted. A wheelchair-accessible toilet and shower are available.

Reservations, fees: Reservations are recommended. Campsites cost $48-53. Rates are based on two people. Additional adults are charged $4.50; for additional children ages 4-17, add $2.50. A 7 percent Montana bed tax will be added on. Cash, check, or credit card. Open May-early October.

Directions: On Highway 89 between Livingston and Yellowstone National Park, find the campground on the east side of the road at milepost 35. It is 18 miles south of Livingston and 35 miles north of the park.

GPS Coordinates: N 45° 24.998' W 110° 41.077'

Contact: Yellowstone's Edge RV Park, 3502 Hwy. 89 S., Livingston, MT 59047, 406/333-4036 or 800/865-7322, www.mtrv.com.

43 CANYON

Scenic rating: 7

in Yankee Jim Canyon in Gallatin National Forest

At 5,073 feet, Canyon Campground nestles in Yankee Jim Canyon below Dome Mountain, 15 miles from the northwest entrance to Yellowstone National Park. The canyon is home to bighorn sheep, the famed cutthroat trout fishery of the Yellowstone River, and white-water rafting and kayaking. The campground sits across the highway from the river, which drops about 25 feet per mile in the five miles of Class III rapids through the canyon. You can launch rafts and kayaks at Joe Brown Creek and take out at Carbella on either side of the campground. Guided raft trips are available in Gardiner. History buffs and hikers can walk the Yankee Jim interpretive trail on the opposite side of the river, accessed at the Tom Miner Bridge.

© BECKY LOMAX

rafting on the Yellowstone River in Paradise Valley

The Joe Brown trailhead also sits east of the campground. The trail originally served as the access to Yellowstone and even earlier a Native American route. Because of the easy access, the campground works for cyclists touring Paradise Valley. Hunters use the camp in fall.

Sitting at the base of a massive talus slope, the campground is a cluster of open junipers, Douglas firs, and giant granitic boulders, some bigger than vehicles. Between the trees and boulders, some of the arid campsites are partly shaded; others are sunny. With the highway running adjacent to the campground, you can hear passing vehicles. Sites 3, 4, and 6 tuck back in mini-canyons in the boulders and trees, with minimal views of the road. Of the campground's two loops, the right one features more open sites; the left one has more private sites that offer better protection when winds howl through the canyon. Watch for rattlesnakes. Larger RVs may have difficulty squeezing on the narrow road through the boulders.

Campsites, facilities: The campground has 17 RV or tent campsites. RVs are limited to 48 feet. Facilities include picnic tables, fire rings with grills, vault toilets, and bear boxes. Drinking water is not available; bring your own. Pack out your trash. Leashed pets are permitted. Wheelchair-accessible toilets and tables are available.

Reservations, fees: Reservations are not accepted. Campsites cost $7. An extra vehicle costs $3. Cash or check. Open year-round.

Directions: From Livingston, travel south on Highway 89 to milepost 14.9. Turn north off the highway into the campground immediately after entering Gallatin National Forest. You can also reach the campground about 15 minutes northwest of Gardiner. GPS Coordinates: N 45° 10.964' W 110° 53.285'

Contact: Gallatin National Forest, Gardiner Ranger District, 805 Scott Street, Gardiner, MT 59030, 406/848-7375, www.fs.usda.gov/gallatin.

44 TOM MINER

Scenic rating: 8

in the Gallatin Mountains in Gallatin National Forest

At 7,000 feet, Tom Miner Campground hides far off the beaten path at the tail end of a long dirt road in the Gallatin Mountains. From the back of the campground, a trail heads to the Petrified Forest, a geological wonder 35-55 million years old where trees were petrified in upright positions as well as horizontal. A 0.5-mile steep interpretive trail teaches visitors what to look for in the rock cliffs to identify specimens. Another trail leads through alpine meadows and pine forests in 2.5 miles to Buffalo Horn Pass or five miles to the impressive summit views from 10,296-foot Ramshorn Peak—both on the crest of the Gallatin Range.

The shady campground clusters under pines and aspens with wildflower meadows flanking the hillsides in July. Views look up the steep arid southern slope of the southeast Ramshorn ridge. The sheer distance from the highway guarantees quiet at night.

Campsites, facilities: The campground has 16 RV or tent campsites. RVs are limited to 42 feet. Facilities include picnic tables, fire rings, vault toilets (wheelchair-accessible), hand pump for drinking water, and bear boxes. Pack out your trash. Leashed pets are permitted.

Reservations, fees: Reservations are not accepted. Campsites cost $7. An extra vehicle costs $3. Cash or check. Open June-October.

Directions: From Gardiner, travel northwest on Highway 89 for 16 miles or from Livingston, go 37 miles south. Turn sharply off the west side of the highway to head south on Tom Miner Road for 12 miles, following signs at junctions to campground.

GPS Coordinates: N 45° 7.750' W 111° 3.781'

Contact: Gallatin National Forest, Gardiner Ranger District, 805 Scott Street, Gardiner, MT 59030, 406/848-7375, www.fs.usda.gov/gallatin.

45 HALFMOON

Scenic rating: 8

in the Crazy Mountains in Gallatin National Forest

Fifty million years ago, the Crazy Mountains rose to 11,000 feet from magma cutting through the muddy bottom of an inland sea, leaving an island of mountains shooting up from the prairie. Glaciers sculpted the rock into dramatic alpine basins, many containing lakes. Halfmoon Campground is the only designated vehicle-accessible campground in the Crazies, hence its popularity. You might even see skiers hiking in July to make turns down snowfields. From the campground, the Big Timber Creek Trail #119 (hikers and horses only) ascends into terrain inhabited by mountain goats, elk, and a patchwork of private landowners. Big Timber Creek Falls sits about 0.25 miles up the trail; look for an unmarked path on the left. The double gems of Twin Lakes sit three miles up the trail, with abundant mosquitoes and fishing. Spur trails lead to Granite and Blue Lakes, and a 2,000-foot ascent tops out on a pass at the divide with big views down the drainage.

Despite the popularity of the area, the remoteness of this campground guarantees after dark quiet and solitude—something you will earn on the long gravel access road. A mix of meadows and pine forest give campsites views of the Crazy Mountains. The campground loop sits adjacent to Big Timber Creek, with sites 1, 2, and 7 in audible distance. Two trails access the stream for fishing and wading.

Campsites, facilities: The campground has 12 RV or tent campsites. Some parking spurs can fit 60-foot RVs, but the Forest Service recommends RVs be 32 feet or shorter because of the access road. Facilities include picnic tables, fire rings, drinking water (Memorial Day-Labor Day), and vault toilets. Pack out your trash. Leashed pets are permitted.

Wheelchair-accessible facilities include toilets and six campsites.

Reservations, fees: Reservations are not accepted. Camping costs $5. Cash or check. Open year-round, but snowbound in winter.

Directions: From Big Timber, travel north on Highway 191 for 11.5 miles. Turn west onto the gravel Big Timber Canyon Road (Wormser Rd. on some maps) for two miles. Turn right onto Big Timber Canyon Road for 10 miles until its terminus at the campground.

GPS Coordinates: N 46° 2.508' W 110° 14.429'

Contact: Gallatin National Forest, Yellowstone Ranger District/Big Timber Office, 225 Big Timber Loop Road, Big Timber, MT 59011, 406/932-5155, www.fs.usda.gov/gallatin.

46 WEST BOULDER

Scenic rating: 8

in the Absaroka Mountains in Gallatin National Forest

At 5,550 feet in Gallatin National Forest, West Boulder Campground requires a long gravel and dirt road drive with rough curvy stretches in its final miles. As the only designated campground on the West Boulder River, it serves to access the canyon and 10,000-foot-high peaks of the Absaroka Mountains. The river provides a fly-fishing haven for wild trout, especially for hikers heading three miles up to the West Boulder Meadows where the river slows into giant pools. The Davis Creek Trail (#38) departs via a bridge across the river to climb for 10 miles to Deep Creek Divide for views of the Paradise Valley and Absaroka Mountains.

Surrounded by private ranches, the ultra-quiet campground offers choices of sunny campsites with big views of the canyon and mountains or campsites partially shaded by pines and aspens. Most campsites sit back from the river, but trails connect to the riverbank.

Sites spread out for privacy; the one at the end of the turnaround loop has the most spacious setting.

Campsites, facilities: The campground has 10 RV and tent campsites. Although a couple parking pads can fit rigs up to 60 feet, the Forest Service recommends an RV limit of 20 feet because of the access road. Facilities include picnic tables, fire rings, pit toilet, drinking water (Memorial Day-Labor Day), and bear boxes. Pack out your trash. Leashed pets are permitted.

Reservations, fees: Reservations are not accepted. Camping costs $5. Open year-round, but snowbound in winter.

Directions: From Big Timber, travel south on Highway 298 for 16 miles. After passing McLeod, turn right onto the gravel County Road 30 for 7.5 miles. Turn left onto the West Boulder Road for six miles to the campground entrance on the right.

GPS Coordinates: N 45° 32.826' W 110° 18.444'

Contact: Gallatin National Forest, Yellowstone Ranger District/Big Timber Office, 225 Big Timber Loop Road, Big Timber, MT 59011, 406/932-5155, www.fs.usda.gov/gallatin.

47 BOULDER FORKS

Scenic rating: 6

on the Boulder River

At 4,780 feet south of Big Timber, Boulder Forks is a state-run fishing access on the Upper Boulder River at the confluence of the west, main, and east forks. The Boulder is a tributary of the Yellowstone River, drawing its water from the high reaches of the Absaroka-Beartooth Wilderness to the south—Montana's tallest peaks. You can launch rafts and kayaks (boats you can carry) from the primitive ramp to float 4.5 miles north to the highway bridge in Class III white water. The blue-ribbon trout stream that anglers wade-fish houses brown trout and rainbow trout, plus mountain whitefish. Littered periodically with boulders, the river is aptly named.

On the perimeter of a sunny pasture with big views of the Absaroka Mountains, the campground spreads the campsites within sight of each other around a small loop. Mature cottonwood trees line the river, but unfortunately, they produce little shade for the south-facing campground. The only sounds you'll hear are the river, the songbirds, and the wind. This is a popular fishing access; the sites frequently fill.

Campsites, facilities: The campground has three primitive RV or tent campsites that can accommodate midsized RVs. Facilities include rock fire rings and a vault toilet. No water is available; bring your own or treat creek water. Pack out your trash. Leashed pets are permitted. The toilet is wheelchair-accessible.

Reservations, fees: Reservations are not accepted. Camping is free. Open year-round.

Directions: From Big Timber, drive south on McLeod Street, which turns into Highway 298. Go 16 miles to just past McLeod. At milepost 16.4, turn east onto the single-lane gravel road 0.3 mile and drive over the cattle grate. GPS Coordinates: N 45° 39.445' W 110° 6.566'

Contact: Montana Fish, Wildlife, and Parks, Region 5, 2300 Lake Elmo Dr., Billings, MT 59105, 406/247-2940, http://fwp.mt.gov.

48 FALLS CREEK

Scenic rating: 7

in the Absaroka Mountains in Gallatin National Forest

At 5,227 feet, Falls Creek sits on the Boulder River's west bank, surrounded by 10,000-foot-high peaks of the Absaroka Mountains. It is 4.9 miles south of Natural Bridge Falls, an interpretive site with a wheelchair-accessible trail where the river flows over a 100-foot

Bridges and trails tour Natural Bridge Interpretive Area along the Boulder River.

drop in high water; in low water, it disappears into an underground channel. The 5.5-mile Green Mountain Trail (#14), a route with less elevation gain than many of the other trails in the area, also departs from the falls. Summer homes and small ranches populate some of the private land around the campground. The fast plummet of the Boulder River slows here to riffles alternating with deep pools, coughing up 20-inch trout to expert fly-fishers. Kayakers and rafters tackle some of the river's Class II-III boulder-strewn white water above Natural Bridge through early summer.

Each campsite has a large, flat tent space along the creek with aspens, pines, and Douglas firs lending partial shade to some of the sites. The sites are spread out and some tuck under trees for privacy, but you can see the neighboring campsites. The sunnier campsites also have views of the canyon and forest. The nearby road is busy in midsummer but quiets at night, so you only hear the river. No RV turnaround is available.

Campsites, facilities: The campground has eight tent campsites. Facilities include picnic tables, fire rings, vault toilet (wheelchair-accessible), drinking water (Memorial Day-Labor Day), and bear boxes. Pack out your trash. Leashed pets are permitted.

Reservations, fees: Reservations are not accepted. Camping is free. Open year-round, but snowbound in winter.

Directions: From Big Timber, travel south on Highway 298 for 25.6 miles to the Gallatin National Forest boundary, where the road (Forest Road 6639) turns to bumpy dirt and gravel. (Locals call it the Boulder Road.) Drive to milepost 5.1 past the forest boundary and turn left onto the narrow campground road. GPS Coordinates: N 45° 29.409' W 110° 13.149'

Contact: Gallatin National Forest, Yellowstone Ranger District/Big Timber Office, 225 Big Timber Loop Road, Big Timber, MT 59011, 406/932-5155, www.fs.usda.gov/gallatin.

49 BOULDER RIVER PRIMITIVE

Scenic rating: 8

in the Absaroka Mountains in Gallatin National Forest

Along the Boulder River, dispersed primitive campsites are sprinkled down the entire glaciated canyon length. These campsites, prized for their seclusion and privacy, sit between 5,350 and 6,700 feet in elevation on both the east and west banks of the river, flanked by the Absaroka Mountains and the Absaroka-Beartooth Wilderness. The river—a blue-ribbon trout stream—works best for wade fishing, but its boulders require care. From Fourmile to Boulder Falls, rafters and kayakers navigate the river's technical Class II-IV rapids. The floating season usually ends after early summer when water levels drop too low and expose too many boulders. Long hiking trails—requiring 3,000 feet or more of ascent—access the high summits in the wilderness. Mountain bikers and ATV riders tour the Boulder Road.

Most of the dispersed primitive campsites along the Boulder River sit right on the river. You'll find sites shaded under Douglas firs, in filtered sunlight in aspens, and in full sun in grassy fields with big open views of the mountains. Find most of the sites by a small sign with a tent icon; a few are unmarked. Scout their dirt roads and turnaround space before you drive in blind. Etiquette dictates one site per party. Respect private property along the river.

Campsites, facilities: More than 30 dispersed, primitive RV or tent campsites sit along the Boulder River. The Forest Service recommends only RVs up to 32 feet in length on the Boulder Road. Facilities include rock fire rings. Use pre-existing fire rings rather than constructing new ones. Treat river water before drinking. Follow Leave No Trace principles for human waste. Pack out your trash. Leashed pets are permitted.

Reservations, fees: Reservations are not accepted. Camping is free. Open year-round, but snowbound in winter.

Directions: From Big Timber, travel south on Highway 298 for 25.6 miles to the Gallatin National Forest boundary, where the road (Forest Road 6639) turns to bumpy dirt and gravel that alternates between rocky washboards and large potholes. (Locals call it the Boulder Road.) After Falls Creek Campground at 5.1 miles past the forest boundary, it's 20 miles farther to the end of the road at Box Canyon.

GPS Coordinates: N 45° 28.691' W 110° 12.469' (first primitive site)

Contact: Gallatin National Forest, Yellowstone Ranger District/Big Timber Office, 225 Big Timber Loop Road, Big Timber, MT 59011, 406/932-5155, www.fs.usda.gov/gallatin.

50 BIG BEAVER

Scenic rating: 7

in the Absaroka Mountains in Gallatin National Forest

At 5,336 feet, Big Beaver Campground sits on the east bank of the Boulder River surrounded by the 10,000-foot-high peaks of the West and East Boulder Plateaus in the Absaroka Mountains. The Absaroka-Beartooth Wilderness is across the river. One mile to the north, the Graham Creek Trail grinds up countless switchbacks to gain 4,500 feet in elevation and reach the flanks of Chrome Mountain in 11.8 miles. This stretch of rocky river services the expert trout angler who can wade-fish as well as Class II-III white-water rafters and kayakers through early summer. Floaters put in at Chippy Park, about two miles upstream.

The campground squeezes between the road and the river, with flat tent spaces 10 feet from the water. The partly shaded sites, tucked under Douglas firs, line up left and right of the entrance, with views of the canyon walls and talus slopes to the east, plus the road. This stretch of the river and road is quite populated, despite the road's deplorable condition, as a church camp borders the campground. The road kicks up dust all day long with traffic in midsummer, but quiets at night to where you'll just hear the sound of the river.

Campsites, facilities: The campground has five RV or tent campsites. The largest parking pad can accommodate an RV up to 42 feet, but the Forest Service warns the road is not suitable for vehicles longer than 32 feet. Facilities include picnic tables, fire rings, and vault toilet (wheelchair-accessible). No drinking water is available; bring your own or treat creek water. Pack out your trash. Leashed pets are permitted.

Reservations, fees: Reservations are not accepted. Camping is free. Open year-round, but snowbound in winter.

Directions: From Big Timber, travel south on Highway 298 for 25.6 miles to the Gallatin National Forest boundary, where the road (Forest Road 6639) turns to bumpy dirt and gravel that alternates between rocky washboards and large potholes. (Locals call it the Boulder Road.) Drive to milepost 7.3 past the forest boundary, crossing to the east side of the river, and turn right into the campground.

GPS Coordinates: N 45° 27.857' W 110° 11.910'

Contact: Gallatin National Forest, Yellowstone Ranger District/Big Timber Office, 225 Big Timber Loop Road, Big Timber, MT 59011, 406/932-5155, www.fs.usda.gov/gallatin.

51 ASPEN

Scenic rating: 7

in the Absaroka Mountains in Gallatin National Forest

At 5,386 feet, Aspen Campground sits on the Boulder River's east bank, tucked under the 10,000-foot-high summits of the Absaroka Mountains and the Absaroka-Beartooth Wilderness across the river. About 1.5 miles north, Graham Creek Trail grunts up 4,500 feet in elevation through innumerable switchbacks for 11.8 miles to Chrome Mountain. The boney Boulder River in this stretch services both the expert trout angler who can wade-fish as well as white-water rafters and kayakers with its Class II-III froth. Only through early summer, floaters launch at Chippy Park about 1.5 miles upstream. The campground is adjacent to an elk wintering range.

With campsites divided into two loops, the campground sits in a thick grove of aspens and willows blooming with wild roses and bee balm. Unlike the other Boulder campgrounds, most campsites do not flank the river but short trails cut through the brush to reach it. The partly sunny, private sites hear the sound of the river and some passing traffic, but the undergrowth blocks the view of the road. Several campsites grab views of the surrounding mountains.

Campsites, facilities: The campground has eight RV or tent campsites. RVs are limited to 42 feet, but the Forest Service recommends 32 feet or less on the road. Facilities include picnic tables, fire rings, drinking water (Memorial Day-Labor Day), bear boxes, and pit and vault toilets (wheelchair-accessible). Pack out your trash. Leashed pets are permitted.

Reservations, fees: Reservations are not accepted. Camping costs $5. Cash or check. Open year-round, but snowbound in winter.

Directions: From Big Timber, travel south on Highway 298 for 25.6 miles to the Gallatin National Forest boundary, where the road (Forest Road 6639) turns to bumpy dirt and gravel that alternates between rocky washboards and large potholes. (Locals call it the Boulder Road.) Drive to milepost 8 past the forest boundary, crossing to the east side of the river, and turn right down the skinny road into the campground.

GPS Coordinates: N 45° 27.386' W 110° 11.829'

Contact: Gallatin National Forest, Yellowstone Ranger District/Big Timber Office, 225 Big Timber Loop Road, Big Timber, MT 59011, 406/932-5155, www.fs.usda.gov/gallatin.

52 CHIPPY PARK

Scenic rating: 8

in the Absaroka Mountains in Gallatin National Forest

At 5,452 feet, Chippy Park Campground sits on the Boulder River's east bank, tucked under the 10,000-foot-high summits of the Absaroka Mountains. The Absaroka-Beartooth Wilderness flanks both sides of the river. About 2.5 miles south, Speculator Creek Trail climbs 4,500 feet in elevation for 7.3 miles to the West Boulder Plateau north of Boulder Mountain. Chippy Park serves as a starting point for rafters and kayakers to descend the river's Class II-III white water to Boulder Falls. The river from Speculator Creek to Chippy Park contains Class IV rapids. Both boulder-strewn sections are floatable only through early summer. The blue-ribbon trout stream is best fished by wading.

A forest of aspens and Douglas firs provides partial shade for the campground sunk in tall grass. The campsites, which all (except site 5) line up along the riverbank, offer some sunny locations with views of the surrounding mountains. Back-in sites that can accommodate RVs sit to the left; two walk-in tent sites are to the right. Site 3 has spaciousness; site 4 garners more privacy at the loop's end.

Campsites, facilities: The campground has seven RV or tent campsites. RV parking is limited to 42 feet, but the Forest Service advises that only vehicles under 32 feet drive the access road. Facilities include picnic tables, fire rings, drinking water (Memorial Day-Labor Day), bear boxes, and pit and vault toilets. Pack out your trash. Leashed pets are permitted. Wheelchair-accessible facilities include toilets and two campsites.

Reservations, fees: Reservations are not accepted. Camping costs $5. Cash or check. Open year-round, but snowbound in winter.

Directions: From Big Timber, travel south on Highway 298 for 25.6 miles to the Gallatin National Forest boundary, where the road (Forest Road 6639) turns to bumpy dirt and gravel that alternates between rocky washboards and large potholes. (Locals call it the Boulder Road.) Drive to milepost 9.5 past the forest boundary, crossing to the east side of the river, climbing a steep hill, and dropping to the campground road on the right.
GPS Coordinates: N 45° 26.234' W 110° 11.369'

Contact: Gallatin National Forest, Yellowstone Ranger District/Big Timber Office, 225 Big Timber Loop Road, Big Timber, MT 59011, 406/932-5155, www.fs.usda.gov/gallatin.

53 HELLS CANYON

Scenic rating: 8

in the Absaroka Mountains in Gallatin National Forest

At 6,100 feet, Hells Canyon Campground sits on the Boulder River's west side, flanked by the Absaroka-Beartooth Wilderness and 10,000-foot-high pinnacles of The Needles to the west. The constriction of the forested

slopes doesn't allow you to see the summits of the Absaroka Mountains unless you slog up 4,500 feet in elevation. Trailheads are located about one mile to the north and south of the campground. The Hawley Creek Trail climbs six miles to Breakneck Plateau, and the Fourmile Creek Trail ascends 7.8 miles to Silver Lake. The mountain slopes constrict to form Hells Canyon, running with four miles of Class III-IV rapids between Fourmile to the south and Speculator Creek to the north, floatable only in early summer. The river is best fished by wading. Be prepared for tedious, slow-driving miles on the ragged Boulder Road.

Contrary to other area campgrounds, this site sits back from the river under the thick shade of conifers, with some campsites having snippets of views of the surrounding mountains. Sites seem spacious because of little underbrush. Owing to the rough road, traffic drops off considerably in this upper section, making this campground ultra-quiet and private.

Campsites, facilities: The campground has 11 RV or tent campsites. While parking can accommodate vehicles up to 48 feet, the Forest Service recommends that RVs limit length to 20 feet on the campground road. Facilities include picnic tables, fire rings, bear boxes, and pit toilets. Pack out your trash. Leashed pets are permitted.

Reservations, fees: Reservations are not accepted. Camping is free. Open year-round, but snowbound in winter.

Directions: From Big Timber, travel south on Highway 298 for 25.6 miles to the Gallatin National Forest boundary, where the road (Forest Road 6639) turns to bumpy dirt and gravel that alternates between rocky washboards and large potholes. (Locals call it the Boulder Road.) Drive to milepost 15.5 past the forest boundary, crossing the river twice, and turn left into the campground.
GPS Coordinates: N 45° 21.756' W 110° 12.935'

Contact: Gallatin National Forest,

Yellowstone Ranger District/Big Timber Office, 225 Big Timber Loop Road, Big Timber, MT 59011, 406/932-5155, www.fs.usda.gov/gallatin.

54 HICKS PARK

Scenic rating: 8

in the Absaroka Mountains in Gallatin National Forest

At 6,350 feet, Hicks Park Campground sits on the Boulder River's east side, flanked by the Absaroka-Beartooth Wilderness and 10,000-foot-high pinnacles of Carbonate Mountain and Hicks Peak. Requiring climbs of over 3,000 feet in elevation in less than eight miles, Upsidedown Creek Trail departs from the campground to switchback up to Horseshoe Lake, and Bridge Creek Trail climbs to Bridge Lake. Be prepared for long, slow-driving miles on the rough Boulder Road. Hicks Park, the last designated campground, makes a base camp for exploring the road's terminus at Box Canyon and continuing farther on the boulder-filled, curvy trail via mountain bike or ATV to the mining ghost town of Independence. The road ends on Independence Peak, with a short trail to Blue Lake set in an alpine cirque. The Boulder River is best when wade fishing.

Grassy campsites line up overlooking the river, with a loose forest of conifers lending partial shade. The open forest also permits views of the surrounding steep mountain slopes. The campsites are spread out for privacy, but you can see neighboring campers through the trees. With fewer people traveling the upper Boulder Road, the river is the pervasive sound.

Campsites, facilities: The campground has 16 RV or tent campsites. The largest parking pad can accommodate vehicles up to 51 feet, but the Forest Service recommends that RVs driving Boulder Road be no longer than

32 feet. Facilities include picnic tables, fire rings, bear boxes, drinking water (Memorial Day-Labor Day), and pit and vault toilets (wheelchair-accessible). Pack out your trash. Leashed pets are permitted.

Reservations, fees: Reservations are not accepted. Campsites cost $5. Cash or check. Open year-round, but snowbound in winter.

Directions: From Big Timber, travel south on Highway 298 for 25.6 miles to the Gallatin National Forest boundary, where the road (Forest Road 6639) turns to bumpy dirt and gravel that alternates between rocky washboards and large potholes. (Locals call it the Boulder Road.) Drive to milepost 21 past the forest boundary, crossing the river three times, and turn right into the campground.

GPS Coordinates: N 45° 18.014' W 110° 14.431'

Contact: Gallatin National Forest, Yellowstone Ranger District/Big Timber Office, 225 Big Timber Loop Road, Big Timber, MT 59011, 406/932-5155, www.fs.usda.gov/gallatin.

55 BIG TIMBER KOA

Scenic rating: 4

east of Big Timber

Big Timber KOA is convenient for those road-tripping along I-90. At 3,948 feet, it's about a five-minute drive from Greycliff Prairie Dog Town State Park (nonresidents $5 per vehicle, Montana residents free), an interpretive site where you can watch the black-tailed prairie dogs skitter about their natural habitat. The 9-hole Overland Golf Course also is five minutes away. Adjacent to the campground, Big Timber Waterslide Park has an outdoor pool and big slides for older kids and adults as well as small slides for children. The Yellowstone River parallels the freeway's north side, offering fishing and floating in rafts and kayaks.

Being right next to the freeway, you'll hear

trucking noise at night. The grassy campground offers partly shaded campsites under large trees or sunny campsites tucked close to each other in parking-lot fashion on gravel parking pads connected by a gravel road. For kids, the campground has a 68-foot-long jumping air pillow, playground, and swimming pool.

Campsites, facilities: The campground has 17 RV campsites with several that can accommodate big rigs up to 100 feet. Hookups include water, sewer, cable TV, and electricity up to 50 amps. The campground also includes eight tent sites. Facilities include picnic tables, pedestal grills, flush toilets, showers, launderette, drinking water, private hot tub room, game room, horseshoe pits, wireless Internet, café camp store, firewood for sale, and disposal station. Leashed pets are permitted.

Reservations, fees: Reservations are accepted. Hookups cost $42-48. Tent campsites cost $31. Rates are for two people. Extra adults are charged $5 each; for extra children, add $2.50 each. Cash, travelers checks, or credit card. Open mid-May-early September.

Directions: From I-90 nine miles east of Big Timber, take Exit 377. Drive to the south side of the freeway to Frontage Road (Hwy. 10) and turn west for 0.25 mile to the campground entrance on the right.

GPS Coordinates: N 45° 46.405' W 109° 47.984'

Contact: Big Timber KOA, 693 Hwy. 10 E., Big Timber, MT 59011, 406/932-6569 or 800/562-5869, www.bigtimberkoa.com.

56 ITCH-KEP-PE PARK

Scenic rating: 5

on the Yellowstone River

Located at 3,350 feet, Itch-Kep-Pe Park, a city park, sits between the railroad tracks, downtown Columbus, and the Yellowstone River. You can walk or bicycle the half-mile

to town for restaurants, shops, and bars—including the first bar to be licensed in Montana. With a boat ramp at the park's east end, the Yellowstone River offers fishing and floating in drift boats, rafts, kayaks, and canoes. Floaters and anglers also launch on the Stillwater River south of Columbus to float back to the park. The river diverts south of the campground around a few islands, making good places to swim before the water level drops too low. Children can bicycle the park roads, and free wood is sometimes delivered to the campground from a local timber company. The campground, which is popular because of its price, is maintained by the city and patrolled regularly by the city police.

The potholed campground road makes several loops under huge cottonwood trees that provide shade to cool the grassy campground. Although no campsites command water frontage, many sit within sight of the river, and the long shoreline allows plenty of space for campers to spread out to enjoy the water. Campsites are a mix of shade, partial shade, and sunny, depending on location. Some tuck back in between trees for privacy, but most of the campsites are open, with views of neighbors. You'll hear the river, railroad, and trucks on the highway at night. Some sites are pull-throughs, but most are back-ins on gravel spurs.

Campsites, facilities: The campground has 30 RV or tent campsites that can accommodate RVs up to 55 feet long. Facilities include picnic tables, fire rings, flush and pit toilets, drinking water, and a concrete boat ramp. Leashed pets are permitted.

Reservations, fees: Reservations are not accepted. Camping is free, but donations are appreciated. Open April-October.

Directions: From Columbus, drive south on Highway 78 for 0.5 mile. Before the bridge over the Yellowstone River, turn left to enter the campground.

GPS Coordinates: N 45° 37.735' W 109° 15.187'

Contact: City of Columbus, P.O. Box 549, Columbus, MT 59019, 406/322-5313.

57 SWINGING BRIDGE

Scenic rating: 5

on the Stillwater River

At 3,740 feet, Swinging Bridge is a state-run fishing access site on the east bank of the Stillwater River. The river divides around islands creating places to swim, but in high water the Swinging Bridge Rapid and the Beartooth Drop—both at the campground—require caution. The Stillwater runs past the campground with Class II-III rapids. Rafters and kayakers usually put-in farther upstream at Whitebird and float past Swinging Bridge Campground to Fireman's Point, two miles south of Columbus, or Itch-Kep-Pe Park, after the Stillwater pours into the Yellowstone River. As the water level drops throughout the summer, large rocky bars extend as beaches along the shore. The Stillwater contains brook, rainbow, and Yellowstone cutthroat trout.

The campground shows wear from overuse at some sites, three of which sit right on the river. Junipers, large cottonwoods, and willows lend partial shade to the campground, and several sites have room for small tents. The gravel campground road kicks up dust when vehicles drive through, but the area is quiet at night.

Campsites, facilities: The campground has four primitive RV or tent campsites that can accommodate small RVs. Facilities include rock fire rings, vault toilet, and a ramp for hand-carried watercrafts. Treat river water before use. Leashed pets are permitted. The toilet is wheelchair-accessible.

Reservations, fees: Reservations are not accepted. Camping is free. Open year-round.

Directions: From Columbus, drive 5.3 miles south on Highway 78. Turn west at milepost 40.6 onto the one-lane gravel road. The 0.7-mile road jogs right, then left through private property before reaching the campground. Be ready to back up if you meet oncoming vehicles. The road has only a couple of narrow turnouts.

GPS Coordinates: N 45° 35.104' W 109° 19.875'

Contact: Montana Fish, Wildlife, and Parks, Region 5, 2300 Lake Elmo Dr., Billings, MT 59105, 406/247-2940, http://fwp.mt.gov.

58 WHITEBIRD

Scenic rating: 5

on the Stillwater River

At 3,780 feet, Whitebird is a state-run fishing access site on the east bank of the Stillwater River. Here, the lower river curves through arid juniper hillsides, flanks with farms and small ranches, and runs past the campground with Class II-III rapids. Rafters, kayakers, and white-water canoeists usually put-in here to float past Swinging Bridge Campground to Fireman's Point, two miles south of Columbus, or to Itch-Kep-Pe Park, after the Stillwater pours into the Yellowstone River. As the water level drops throughout the summer, large rocky bars extend as beaches along the shore. The Stillwater contains brook, rainbow, and Yellowstone cutthroat trout. The site offers archery and shotgun hunting in season.

None of the campsites have river frontage. Back-in grassy campsites tuck under tall cottonwoods, with a mix of willows providing partial shade. The location is still close enough to the highway to hear a little truck traffic at night.

Campsites, facilities: The campground has seven primitive RV or tent campsites that can accommodate small RVs. Facilities include picnic tables, fire rings with grills, vault toilet, and a ramp for hand-carried watercrafts. Treat river water before use. Leashed pets are permitted. The toilet is wheelchair-accessible.

Reservations, fees: Reservations are not accepted. Campsites cost $7 with a Montana fishing license and $12 without a Montana fishing license. Cash or check. Open year-round.

Directions: From Columbus, drive about seven miles south on Highway 78. Turn west at milepost 39.8 onto the gravel Whitebird Creek Road, crossing the creek on a one-lane bridge. Drive 0.5 mile to the campground entrance. GPS Coordinates: N 45° 34.504' W 109° 20.192'

Contact: Montana Fish, Wildlife, and Parks, Region 5, 2300 Lake Elmo Dr., Billings, MT 59105, 406/247-2940, http://fwp.mt.gov.

59 WOODBINE

Scenic rating: 8

in the Beartooth Mountains in Custer National Forest

At 5,200 feet, Woodbine Campground is the only national forest campground on the Stillwater River. Sitting at the north edge of the Absaroka-Beartooth Wilderness, the campground provides access to very remote country that few people visit. Cathedral Peak and the Granite Range make up the 10,000-foot Absaroka and Beartooth peaks south of the campground. From the campground, the 0.75-mile Woodbine Falls Trail (#93) departs for viewing the waterfall. While horses (hitch rails and loading ramps available) and backpackers use the entire 25-mile-long Stillwater Trail (#29), day hikers climb it 3.1 miles to the marshy Sioux Charley Lake. Small Yellowstone cutthroat trout inhabit Woodbine Creek, and the swift-flowing Stillwater River that you cross when entering the campground harbors small rainbow and brook trout.

Plan to arrive early at this popular campground where many of the campsites command views of the Beartooth Mountains. The two loops of the campground flank a mixed meadow and forest hillside where you have a choice of sunny or partly shaded sites. Despite the miles of dirt road driving, the campground road and parking aprons are paved, and your long drive is rewarded with natural sounds of the wind or the creek.

Campsites, facilities: The campground has 44 RV or tent campsites. RVs are limited to 32 feet. Facilities include picnic tables, fire rings with grills, vault toilets, drinking water, bear boxes, garbage service, and campground hosts. Leashed pets are permitted. Wheelchair-accessible facilities include toilets and campsites.

Reservations, fees: Reservations are accepted (877/444-6777, www.recreation.gov). Campsites cost $16. An extra vehicle costs $9. Cash or check. Open late May-mid-September.

Directions: From Absarokee, drive west on County Road 420 (locals call it the Stillwater River Road) for 20.4 miles and left for one mile as the road swings south to Nye. The road is paved to Nye but potholed. Turn right onto County Road 419 and drive 7.8 miles southwest on the gravel road. The road becomes Forest Road 4200 at the boundary to the national forest. At the signed junction, turn east for 0.2 mile to reach the campground entrance. GPS Coordinates: N 45° 21.189' W 109° 53.872'

Contact: Custer National Forest, Beartooth Ranger District, 6811 Hwy. 212 S., Red Lodge, MT 406/446-2103, www.fs.usda.gov/custer.

60 PINE GROVE

Scenic rating: 8

in the Beartooth Mountains in Custer National Forest

Located at 5,895 feet, Pine Grove is one of two Forest Service campgrounds in the West Rosebud Creek valley on the northeast corner of the Absaroka-Beartooth Wilderness. The river attracts expert kayakers for its three miles of Class III-V white water from Emerald Lake to the campground. Anglers go after brook, brown, rainbow, and Yellowstone cutthroat trout as well as mountain whitefish. Five miles south at the road's terminus at the power plant, trails depart for Mystic Lake (3.1 miles) and Island Lake (5 miles). For huge views, you can also climb scads of switchbacks up to the edge of Froze to Death Plateau (6.6 miles), on the flanks of the 11,765-foot Froze to Death Mountain. These three hikes are in the wilderness area.

Sitting at the base of a long, deep, glacier-carved valley, the quiet campground flanks both sides of the river in a forested setting. Sites are partly shaded, but some garner outstanding views of the surrounding Beartooth Mountains. Pull-through sites are in the section across the river.

Campsites, facilities: The campground has 27 RV or tent campsites that can accommodate RVs up to 30 feet. Another 19 campsites are for tents only. Facilities include picnic tables, fire rings with grills, vault toilets (wheelchair-accessible), drinking water, bear boxes, garbage service, and campground hosts. Leashed pets are permitted.

Reservations, fees: Reservations are not accepted. Campsites cost $9. Extra vehicles cost $5. Cash or check. Open late May–early September.

Directions: From Highway 78 south of Absarokee, take Highway 419 southwest to Fishtail. At a T intersection 0.5 mile south of Fishtail, turn left onto West Rosebud Road (Hwy. 425) for 6.5 miles to where the road turns to bumpy washboard and potholed gravel. Continue 8.8 miles farther to the campground, which sits about 1.2 miles south of the Custer National Forest boundary. The campground has four entrances on the east side of the road, the first leading to the tent campsites and the last connecting across the river with sites best for RVs. GPS Coordinates: N 45° 16.551' W 109° 38.732'

Contact: Custer National Forest, Beartooth Ranger District, 6811 Hwy. 212 S., Red Lodge, MT 406/446-2103, www.fs.usda.gov/custer.

61 EMERALD LAKE

Scenic rating: 10

in the Beartooth Mountains in Custer National Forest

At 6,180 feet, Emerald Lake nestles in West Rosebud Creek valley below the immense Beartooth Mountains. Despite its name, the campground does not flank the lake's shore, but instead parallels the West Rosebud River between Emerald and West Rosebud Lakes. From Emerald Lake to Pine Grove Campground, the river attracts expert kayakers for its three miles of Class III-V white water. Flat-water paddlers and anglers also tour small Emerald Lake (no motors allowed), which you can also reach via a five-minute walk from the campground. The river harbors brook, brown, rainbow, and Yellowstone cutthroat trout as well as mountain whitefish. One mile south, the road terminates at the power plant, where trails depart into Absaroka-Beartooth Wilderness. Scenic hikes include Mystic Lake (3.1 miles), Island Lake (5 miles), and Froze to Death Plateau (6.6 miles), which are also accesses for rock climbing and mountaineering.

The quiet campground splits into two roads, both with gravel back-in parking. The left spur has no RV turnaround, but the right one does. Set on the edge of a heavily forested slope, the campsites vary between partly shaded to more open, garnering superb views of the snowy Beartooth Mountains in early summer.

Campsites, facilities: The campground has 19 RV or tent campsites that can accommodate RVs up to 30 feet. Another 12 campsites are for tents only. Facilities include picnic tables, fire rings with grills, vault toilets (wheelchair-accessible), drinking water, bear boxes, garbage service, and campground hosts. Leashed pets are permitted.

Reservations, fees: Reservations are not accepted. Campsites cost $9. Extra vehicles cost $5. Cash or check. Open late May–November, but services end in early September.

Directions: From Highway 78 south of Absarokee, take Highway 419 southwest to Fishtail. At a T intersection 0.5 mile south of Fishtail, turn left onto West Rosebud Road (Hwy. 425) for 6.5 miles to where the road turns to gravel. Continue 13 miles farther, entering Custer National Forest about halfway, where the road turns to bumpy washboards and potholes. After passing Emerald Lake, turn east into the campground.

GPS Coordinates: N 45° 15.225' W 109° 41.936'

Contact: Custer National Forest, Beartooth Ranger District, 6811 Hwy. 212 S., Red Lodge, MT 406/446-2103, www.fs.usda.gov/custer.

62 JIMMY JOE

Scenic rating: 9

in the Beartooth Mountains in Custer National Forest

At 5,600 feet, Jimmy Joe Campground tucks into the northeast corner of the high Beartooth Mountains along East Rosebud Creek. Summer homes and small farms dot the prairie valley en route to the campground, which is flanked on both canyon walls by the Absaroka-Beartooth Wilderness. Anglers can wade-fish the stream for brown, rainbow, and Yellowstone cutthroat trout. Trailheads for hiking are located four miles farther south around East Rosebud Lake. Trail #17—the nearest one—ascends Phantom Creek up to Froze to Death Plateau, one of two access routes to climbing 12,799-foot Granite Peak, Montana's highest mountain. A stiff 3.5-mile day hike gains 3,900 feet to the saddle between Prairieview Mountain and Froze to Death Mountain.

Set at the bottom of the scooped-out glacier valley, the campground commands big views of the surrounding Beartooth Mountains. A forest fire in 1995 swept through the area, which now blooms with cow parsnips, fireweed, and red paintbrush amid the new-growth lodgepole pines. A few surviving lodgepoles and cottonwoods partially shade a handful of the campsites, but full sun hits most of them. Eight of

© BECKY LOMAX

Jimmy Joe Campground in the Beartooth Mountains

the campsites flank the river. The wind and the river are the only sounds you'll hear at night. Hand pumps have been installed for drinking water, but were not functional in 2013.

Campsites, facilities: The campground has 10 RV or tent campsites. RVs are limited to 30 feet. Facilities include picnic tables, fire rings with grills, and vault toilets. Drinking water is not available; bring your own or plan to treat river water. Pack out your trash. Leashed pets are permitted.

Reservations, fees: Reservations are not accepted. Camping is free. Open late May-early September.

Directions: From Highway 78 at Roscoe south of Absarokee, take East Rosebud Road south for 2.6 miles, where the rough pavement ends and the dusty, potholed, rutted dirt road begins. Go 1.2 miles farther and turn right, staying on East Rosebud Road for 6.5 miles to the campground entrance on the right. The campground is 10.3 miles south of Roscoe. GPS Coordinates: N 45° 13.921' W 109° 36.187'

Contact: Custer National Forest, Beartooth Ranger District, 6811 Hwy. 212 S., Red Lodge, MT 406/446-2103, www.fs.usda.gov/custer.

63 EAST ROSEBUD

Scenic rating: 10

in the Beartooth Mountains in Custer National Forest

BEST (

At 6,400 feet, East Rosebud Campground sits above East Rosebud Lake in the Beartooth Mountains, where rugged cliffs and scooped-out cirques demonstrate the power of glaciers on the landscape. Unfortunately, private property and summer homes surround the lake, but the community provides a primitive boat launch and parking area (relock the gate after entering) for canoes, kayaks, and rafts. The lake is stocked regularly with rainbow trout. Two trails departing from the campground enter the Absaroka-Beartooth Wilderness. One climbs 5.9 steep miles to Sylvan Lake at the timberline. The other tours the lake's southeast rim on a more gentle 5.8-mile ascent to Elk Lake, the first in a long string of backpacking lakes along East Rosebud Creek.

The one campground loop—a narrow, steep, rocky road—circles a hillside on the mixed fir and pine forest fringe. Most of the back-in sites tuck under trees for protection from the sun and wind; the others sit in the sunny north-facing meadows, with big views of the lake and surrounding mountains. Buckwheat, bee balm, and harebells bloom in the meadows. The quiet campground packs its small sites close enough that you'll see neighbors; some in the trees are more private.

Campsites, facilities: The campground has 14 RV or tent campsites. RVs are limited to 20 feet. Another 12 campsites are for tents only. Facilities include picnic tables, fire rings with grills, vault toilets (wheelchair-accessible), drinking water, bear boxes, and garbage service. Leashed pets are permitted.

Reservations, fees: Reservations are not accepted. Campsites cost $9. A second vehicle costs $5. Cash or check. Open late May-early September.

Directions: From Highway 78 at Roscoe south of Absarokee, take the East Rosebud Road south for 2.6 miles, where the rough pavement ends and the dusty, bumpy, potholed, dirt road begins. Go 1.2 miles farther and turn right, staying on East Rosebud Road for 9.9 miles to a junction. Veer left for 0.6 mile over the single-lane bridge and left at the next junction, too. The campground entrance is on the left just past the campground exit. GPS Coordinates: N 45° 11.923' W 109° 38.087'

Contact: Custer National Forest, Beartooth Ranger District, 6811 Hwy. 212 S., Red Lodge, MT 406/446-2103, www.fs.usda.gov/custer.

64 CASCADE

Scenic rating: 8

in the Beartooth Mountains in Custer National
Forest

At 7,550 feet, Cascade Campground sits on
West Fork Rock Creek, known for its trout
fishing, wedged in a high mountain valley on
the eastern rim of the Beartooth Mountains.
Within 1.5 miles west of the campground,
trails depart into the Absaroka-Beartooth
Wilderness. Climb 4.6 miles up to Timberline
Lake, a glacial cirque below the 12,500-foot
Timberline Peak. A 4.3-mile trail grunts up to
the Red Lodge Creek Plateau, where the views
fly endlessly out onto the prairie. A shorter,
gentler trail of less than two miles leads to
Calamity Falls and Sentinel Falls. Backpackers
continue farther to loop over the 11,037-foot
Sundance Pass, also a mountaineering access
for several peaks. Mountain bikers go for the
15-mile loop trail on the Silver Run Plateau.

Although a 2008 fire burned the west tip
of the quiet campground, the fast re-emerging
vegetation blooms with wildflowers and young
lodgepole pines. The campground has two
loops, and most sites still tuck under the partial
shade of green lodgepole pines. On the smaller
left loop, site 30 is a very private site at the
end with a large, flat tent space. Twelve sites
overlook the creek. Sites 11, 13, and 14 have
been cleared hazardous trees, which opened
up the views to the rocky peaks of the East
Rosebud Plateau.

Campsites, facilities: The campground has
30 RV or tent campsites. RVs are limited to
30 feet. Facilities include picnic tables, fire
rings with grills, vault toilets, drinking water,
garbage service, firewood for sale, bear boxes,
and campground hosts. Leashed pets are permitted. A wheelchair-accessible toilet and two
campsites are available.

Reservations, fees: Reservations are accepted (877/444-6777, www.recreation.gov).
Campsites cost $10. An extra vehicle costs $8.

Cash, check, or credit card. Open late May-
early September.

Directions: From Red Lodge on Highway 212
at the sign for the ski area, drive west on Ski
Run Road for 2.8 miles and turn left onto
West Fork Rock Creek Road (Forest Road
2071). Drive 7.7 miles to the campground
entrance on the left. The last 3.3-mile stretch
is on a single-lane potholed road with turnouts.
GPS Coordinates: N 45° 10.378' W 109°
27.052'

Contact: Custer National Forest, Beartooth
Ranger District, 6811 Hwy. 212 S., Red Lodge,
MT 406/446-2103, www.fs.usda.gov/custer.

65 BASIN

Scenic rating: 7

in the Beartooth Mountains in Custer National
Forest

At 6,900 feet, Basin Campground sits on West
Fork Rock Creek, a brook trout fishery, in a
high mountain valley in the eastern Beartooth
Mountains. Three national recreation trails
depart nearby for hikers and mountain bikers.
Across the road, the 3.8-mile Basin Lakes Trail
climbs to a small glacial cirque. One mile east
of the campground, the Silver Run Trail provides a 7.7-mile loop, and a 15-minute nature
trail circles Wild Bill Lake. Wild Bill Lake also
has wheelchair-accessible ramps and docks for
fishing, and you can paddle the small lake,
too. Basin is the most popular campground
in the West Fork drainage because the access
and campground road are paved. Plan to arrive
early in the day to claim a campsite or make
reservations.

The quiet campground sprinkles its campsites under the partial shade of a lodgepole
forest. Unfortunately, because there's no undergrowth, you can see other campers or cars
passing on the road. Pine needles and cones
cover the forest floor of the campsites, which
have plenty of big, level spaces for tents. Sites

3, 5, 7, 9, and 10 overlook the creek. Some sites are more open, with views onto hillsides burned in the 2008 fire. All of the gravel parking aprons are back-ins, but several are double-wide.

Campsites, facilities: The campground has 30 RV or tent campsites. RVs are limited to 30 feet. Facilities include picnic tables, fire rings with grills, vault toilets, drinking water, garbage service, bear boxes, firewood for sale, and campground hosts. Leashed pets are permitted. Wheelchair-accessible facilities include toilets and three campsites.

Reservations, fees: Reservations are accepted (877/444-6777, www.recreation.gov). Campsites cost $15. An extra vehicle costs $8. Cash, check, or credit card. Open mid May-September.

Directions: From Red Lodge on Highway 212 at the sign for the ski area, drive west on Ski Run Road for 2.8 miles and turn left onto West Fork Rock Creek Road (Forest Road 2071). Drive 4.4 miles to the campground entrance on the right.

GPS Coordinates: N 45° 9.618' W 109° 23.232'

Contact: Custer National Forest, Beartooth Ranger District, 6811 Hwy. 212 S., Red Lodge, MT 406/446-2103, www.fs.usda.gov/custer.

66 PALISADES (CUSTER NATIONAL FOREST)

Scenic rating: 6

in the Beartooth Mountains in Custer National Forest

At 6,350 feet, Palisades Campground is named for the swath of limestone spires that poke up from a forested ridge on the eastern lip of the Beartooth Mountains. The campground tucks into the Willow Creek drainage tumbling from Red Lodge Ski Area. For hikers and mountain bikers, the Willow Creek Trail (#105) departs from the top of the campground to follow the

creek upstream to the ski area. Bikers can continue to loop back on the road from the ski area. The Forest Service is planning to build a new 2.5-mile trail from the campground to Fox Lane.

The campground tucks into a draw along the creek that's forested with cottonwoods, aspens, and Douglas firs as well as lush meadows of sticky geraniums, fireweed, and tall grass. Half of the campsites sit along the creek, with the lowest one and the highest one having the most privacy and biggest tent spaces. Two sunny, open sites across the road from each other have views of the Palisades. The campground is also far enough from town to provide quiet, but close enough to run back in for supplies.

Campsites, facilities: The campground has six RV or tent campsites. RVs are limited to 22 feet. Facilities include picnic tables, fire rings with grills, and vault toilet. Pack out your trash. Leashed pets are permitted.

Reservations, fees: Reservations are not accepted. Camping is free. Open late May-early September.

Directions: From Red Lodge on Highway 212, at the sign for the ski area, drive west on Ski Run Road for one mile and veer right onto the rough but paved Palisades Campground Road for 1.2 miles to the top of the hill. Turn right and then left on the road, which narrows and gets rougher with big potholes, before reaching the campground in 0.6 mile.

GPS Coordinates: N 45° 10.294' W 109° 18.547'

Contact: Custer National Forest, Beartooth Ranger District, 6811 Hwy. 212 S., Red Lodge, MT 406/446-2103, www.fs.usda.gov/custer.

67 RED LODGE KOA

Scenic rating: 5

near Red Lodge

At 5,148 feet, the Red Lodge KOA is a

five-minute drive north of downtown Red Lodge, with its restaurants, art galleries, shops, and funky western bars. The Red Lodge Mountain Golf Course sits about 10 minutes south of the campground, and the town is home to several fishing and rafting outfitters. Red Lodge is also the eastern portal to the Beartooth Highway, worth the scenic drive. At the campground, a small children's fishing pond and banana bike rentals are also available.

The grassy campground, ringed by cottonwoods and aspens, offers mostly sunny campsites that pack in tight to each other. Partly shaded tent sites, which are a bit wider than the RV sites, ring the perimeter farthest from the highway. The campground's location right on the highway means you'll hear commercial trucks at night, and vehicle traffic starts up in the early morning. The campground permits after-hours self-registration.

Campsites, facilities: The campground has 68 RV campsites and 19 tent campsites. RVs are limited to 90 feet. Hookups include water, sewer, and electricity up to 50 amps. Facilities include picnic tables, rock fire rings, pedestal grills, flush toilets, showers, launderette, drinking water, playground, swimming pool (late May-early September), dog walk, wireless Internet, camp store, firewood for sale, and disposal station. Leashed pets are permitted.

Reservations, fees: Reservations are accepted. Hookups cost $34-40. Tent sites cost $26-34. Rates cover two adults. Additional adults are charged $4 each; for kids ages 7-17, add $3. Children under six years old stay free. Add on 7 percent Montana bed tax. Cash, check, or credit card. Open early May-September.

Directions: From Red Lodge, drive four miles north on Highway 212 to the campground entrance on the east side of the road.
GPS Coordinates: N 45° 15.407' W 109° 13.698'

Contact: Red Lodge KOA, 7464 Hwy. 212, Red Lodge, MT 59068, 406/446-2364 or 800/562-7540, www.koa.com.

68 PERRY'S RV PARK AND CAMPGROUND

Scenic rating: 6

in Red Lodge

At 5,840 feet, Perry's RV Park and Campground is a three-minute drive or a 10-minute walk from downtown Red Lodge, with its restaurants, art galleries, shops, and funky western bars. The Red Lodge Mountain Golf Course sits about seven minutes north of the campground, and the town is home to several fishing and rafting outfitters. Red Lodge is also the eastern portal to the Beartooth Highway, worth the scenic drive. Fishing is available for brook and brown trout on Rock Creek, which flanks the back of the campground.

The campground has two gravel loops. A large, open, sunny parking-lot-type area houses bigger RVs and borders the highway. Other campsites, including the tent sites, tuck back under cottonwood trees, which offer partial shade. Several campsites line up on the bank of Rock Creek. Campsites are close together, and the highway noise is audible at night. The campground does not permit after-hours self-registration.

Campsites, facilities: The campground has 30 RV campsites and 13 tent sites. RVs are limited to 45 feet. Hookups include water and electricity. Facilities include picnic tables, flush toilets, showers, drinking water, camp store, and disposal station. Leashed pets are permitted.

Reservations, fees: Reservations are accepted. Hookups cost $35. Tent sites cost $20. Rates cover two people. Additional campers are charged $10 each. Add on 7 percent Montana bed tax. Cash or check only. Open late May-September.

Directions: From Red Lodge, drive two miles south on Highway 212. Find the campground entrance on the east side of the road.
GPS Coordinates: N 45° 9.082' W 109° 16.383'

Contact: Perry's RV Park and Campground, 6664 S. Hwy. 212, Red Lodge, MT 59068, 406/446-2722, www.perrysrv.us.

69 SHERIDAN

🚶 🚴 🐟 🛶 ⛵ 🐕 ⚓ ♿ 🚐 ⛺

Scenic rating: 7

in the Beartooth Mountains in Custer National Forest

At 6,282 feet, Sheridan Campground is one of two Forest Service campgrounds at the eastern portal to the Beartooth Highway. Set in a narrow canyon on Rock Creek where you can fish for trout, the two campgrounds provide quick access to Red Lodge for supplies and a good jumping-off point for exploring the scenic highway. Departing 1.1 miles south of the campground, Corral Creek Trail (#9) climbs over 3,000 feet in 4.1 miles up to Line Creek Plateau, for views of the snowcapped Beartooth Mountains. You can also turn the route into a 12.7-mile loop with a waltz along the scenic plateau for views of Wyoming and the prairie before dropping down Maurice Creek. The loop ends about one mile north of the campground. Starting the loop at Maurice Creek lets you face the peaks as you hike. For expert kayakers and rafters, Rock Creek provides Class III-IV white water. Families can mountain bike the road between Sheridan and Ratine campgrounds.

In a forest of cottonwoods, aspens, and Douglas fir, the campground offers a mix of partly shaded (sites 4-8) or sunny campsites with views of mountain slopes (sites 1-3) that are also open to those driving in on the gravel campground road. Lyall's angelica, wild roses, and harebells bloom in the small meadows surrounding some of the sites. Light highway noise can be heard above the burbling creek, but it diminishes at night. Four campsites flank Rock Creek, with short paths through brush to the water.

Campsites, facilities: The campground has nine RV or tent campsites. RVs are limited to 30 feet. Facilities include picnic tables, fire rings with grills, vault toilets, drinking water, garbage service, and firewood for sale. The campground hosts stay one mile west at Rattin. Leashed pets are permitted. A toilet and one campsite are wheelchair-accessible.

Reservations, fees: Reservations are accepted (877/444-6777, www.recreation.gov). Campsites cost $14. An extra vehicle costs $8. Cash or check. Open late May-early September.

Directions: From Red Lodge, drive 7.5 miles southwest on Highway 212 to milepost 61.8. Turn east onto the narrow, potholed, dirt East Side Road and cross the single-lane bridge. The campground entrance is on the left side of the road in 1.3 miles.

GPS Coordinates: N 45° 6.013 W 109° 18.491'

Contact: Custer National Forest, Beartooth Ranger District, 6811 Hwy. 212 S., Red Lodge, MT 406/446-2103, www.fs.usda.gov/custer.

70 RATINE

🚶 🚴 🐟 🛶 ⛵ 🐕 ♿ 🚐 ⛺

Scenic rating: 7

in the Beartooth Mountains in Custer National Forest

At 6,380 feet, Ratine Campground is one of two Forest Service campgrounds at the eastern portal to the Beartooth Highway. In a narrow canyon on Rock Creek where you can fish for trout, the campgrounds provide quick access to Red Lodge for supplies and a good jumping-off point for exploring the scenic highway. Departing 0.1 mile south of the campground, Corral Creek Trail (#9) climbs over 3,000 feet in 4.1 miles up to Line Creek Plateau for views of the snowcapped Beartooth Mountains. You can also turn the route into a 12.7-mile loop with an open walk along the crest of the scenic plateau for views of Wyoming and the prairie before dropping down Maurice Creek, which ends about two miles north of the campground. Starting the loop at Maurice Creek lets you face the peaks as you hike. For expert kayakers and rafters, Rock Creek provides Class III-IV white water. Families can mountain bike the road between Sheridan and Ratine campgrounds.

In a forest of cottonwoods, aspens, pines, and Douglas fir, the campground flanks Rock Creek but doesn't have views of the water. You can hear it, though, along with vehicles on the highway, but the traffic dies down at night. Short paths cut through the brush to the creek. Some of the campsites have partial views of the mountains plus a bit of shade. Foliage limits visibility of other campsites to just a neighbor or two. The skinny, dusty campground road has no turnaround loop at the end.

Campsites, facilities: The campground has six RV or tent campsites. RVs are limited to 30 feet. Facilities include picnic tables, fire rings with grills, vault toilets (wheelchair-accessible), drinking water, garbage service, firewood for sale, and campground hosts. Leashed pets are permitted.

Reservations, fees: Reservations are accepted (877/444-6777, www.recreation.gov). Campsites cost $14. An extra vehicle costs $8. Cash or check. Open mid-May-late September.

Directions: From Red Lodge, drive 7.5 miles southwest on Highway 212 to milepost 61.8. Turn east onto the narrow, potholed, dirt East Side Road and cross the single-lane bridge. The campground entrance is on the left side of the road in 0.3 mile.

GPS Coordinates: N 45° 5.245' W 109° 19.498'

Contact: Custer National Forest, Beartooth Ranger District, 6811 Hwy. 212 S., Red Lodge, MT 406/446-2103, www.fs.usda.gov/custer.

71 PARKSIDE

Scenic rating: 9

in the Beartooth Mountains in Custer National Forest

At 7,150 feet, Parkside is one of three campgrounds clustered within 0.6 mile on Rock Creek Road at the eastern base of the Beartooth Highway, where the scenic highway begins its five-switchback climb to the Beartooth Plateau. From Vista Point at 9,100 feet, you can spot the campground on the valley floor. Cyclists on the Beartooth Highway opt to stay at Parkside to start the 4,000-foot climb up to Beartooth Pass first thing in the morning before the sun hits the switchbacks. The campground also sits adjacent to the Wyoming Creek Trailhead, a two-mile-long, hiking-only Parkside National Recreation Trail that links up four campgrounds along Rock Creek and tiny Greenough Lake. For anglers, Rock Creek harbors rainbow, brook, and Yellowstone cutthroat trout. Because of the campground's popularity in midsummer and on holidays, reservations are highly recommended.

Parkside Campground straddles Rock Creek on a paved road with a single-lane bridge. On the creek's west side, paved back-in parking pads line up sites closer together and visible from each other in the pine forest, which has an open understory with some peek-a-boo views of the peak. Sites 1, 2, 4, and 7-10 overlook Rock Creek. The loop on the creek's east side offers more private, shaded campsites under Douglas firs, aspens, and cottonwoods, with sites 17-19 overlooking the creek. Despite the proximity to the highway, the campground is quiet at night.

Campsites, facilities: The campground has 28 RV or tent campsites. RVs are limited to 40 feet. Facilities include picnic tables, fire rings with grills, vault toilets, drinking water, garbage service, firewood for sale, bear boxes, and campground hosts. Leashed pets are permitted. A toilet and two campsites are wheelchair-accessible.

Reservations, fees: Reservations are accepted (877/444-6777, www.recreation.gov). Campsites cost $15. An extra vehicle costs $8. Cash or check. Open mid-May-September.

Directions: From Red Lodge, drive 11.5 miles southwest on Highway 212 to milepost 57.2.

Turn right onto the paved Rock Creek Road for 0.3 mile to the campground entrance on the right.

GPS Coordinates: N 45° 3.633' W 109° 24.285'

Contact: Custer National Forest, Beartooth Ranger District, 6811 Hwy. 212 S., Red Lodge, MT 406/446-2103, www.fs.usda.gov/custer.

72 GREENOUGH LAKE

🏃 🚴 🛶 🐾 ♿ 🚐 ⛺

Scenic rating: 9

in the Beartooth Mountains in Custer National Forest

At 7,200 feet, Greenough Lake is one of three campgrounds clustered within 0.6 mile of each other on the Rock Creek Road at the eastern base of the Beartooth Highway with a scenic five-switchback climb to the alpine Beartooth Plateau. The campground, on Rock Creek's east bank, lies at the base of a glacier-carved valley flanked by the above-tree-line rocky plateaus of the Beartooth Mountains. At the north end of the campground, the two-mile hiking-only Parkside National Recreation Trail, which links up four campgrounds along Rock Creek, leads 0.25 mile to tiny Greenough Lake, a shallow mosquito pond that is stocked with rainbow trout. Campers often use mountain bikes and ATVs to tour two dirt roads—the continuation of Rock Creek Road and Forest Road 2004, which climbs to Hellroaring Plateau.

With paved internal roads, parking pads, and proximity to the Beartooth Highway, Greenough Lake is a popular campground that requires reservations to get a site on weekends and holidays. Despite the nearness of the highway, the campground is quiet at night, with only the sound of the creek. Sites 1, 2, 3, 5, 7, 9, and 10 overlook Rock Creek and some of the Limber Pine campsites across the creek. A mixed forest of aspens, pines, and short willows lends partial shade and partial privacy to the campsites, some with views to mountain slopes. Site 13 houses a giant glacial erratic, a boulder dropped by receding ice.

Campsites, facilities: The campground has 18 RV or tent campsites. RVs are limited to 45 feet. Facilities include picnic tables, fire rings with grills, vault toilets, drinking water, garbage service, firewood for sale, and bear boxes. The campground hosts stay at adjacent Parkside Campground. Leashed pets are permitted. A wheelchair-accessible toilet and two campsites are available.

Reservations, fees: Reservations are accepted (877/444-6777, www.recreation.gov). Campsites cost $15. An extra vehicle costs $8. Cash or check. Open mid-May-September.

Directions: From Red Lodge, drive 11.5 miles southwest on Highway 212 to milepost 57.2. Turn right onto paved Rock Creek Road for 0.8 mile to the campground entrance on the left.

GPS Coordinates: N 45° 3.375' W 109° 24.738'

Contact: Custer National Forest, Beartooth Ranger District, 6811 Hwy. 212 S., Red Lodge, MT, 406/446-2103, www.fs.usda.gov/custer.

73 LIMBER PINE

🏃 🚴 🛶 🐾 ♿ 🚐 ⛺

Scenic rating: 9

in the Beartooth Mountains in Custer National Forest

At 7,200 feet, Limber Pine is one of three campgrounds clustered within 0.6 mile on the Rock Creek Road at the eastern base of the Beartooth Highway below the five scenic switchbacks that climb to the Beartooth Plateau. Flanked by the immense above-tree-line meadow plateaus of the snowcapped Beartooth Mountains, the campgrounds are dwarfed on the valley floor, where Limber Pine sits on the west bank of Rock Creek. The two-mile-long, hiking-only Parkside National Recreation Trail links up the four campgrounds along Rock Creek and leads 0.5 mile to Greenough Lake. Trout fishing is available at the lake and along Rock Creek. The dirt Forest Road 2004 (some use ATVs or mountain bikes on the road) departs Rock Creek Road near the campgrounds to climb onto the Hellroaring Plateau to the edge of the Absaroka-Beartooth Wilderness, where you can continue hiking on a trail for another 2.5 miles or farther cross-country with big views of alpine meadows and snowcapped peaks.

Limber Pine is a popular campground that requires reservations to get a site on weekends or holidays. Its one paved loop connects campsites that vary from full shade to partial mountain views. Black-eyed susans, sagebrush, harebells, and yellow arrowleaf balsamroot bloom between stands of limber pine. Sites 1, 2, and 10 overlook the creek and campsites in Greenough Lake Campground across the creek. Despite sitting between the highway and Rock Creek Road, the campground quiets at night.

Campsites, facilities: The campground has 10 RV or tent campsites, plus three walk-in tent-only sites (6, 7, and 11). RVs are limited to 45 feet. Facilities include picnic tables, fire rings with grills, vault toilets, drinking water, garbage service, firewood for sale, and bear boxes. The campground hosts stay at adjacent Parkside Campground. Leashed pets are permitted. A wheelchair-accessible toilet and two campsites are available.

Reservations, fees: Reservations are accepted (877/444-6777, www.recreation.gov). Campsites cost $15. An extra vehicle costs $8. Cash or check. Open mid-May-early September.

Directions: From Red Lodge, drive 11.5 miles southwest on Highway 212 to milepost 57.2. Turn right onto paved Rock Creek Road for 0.9 mile to the campground entrance on the left.

GPS Coordinates: N 45° 3.504' W 109° 24.743'

Contact: Custer National Forest, Beartooth Ranger District, 6811 Hwy. 212 S., Red Lodge, MT, 406/446-2103, www.fs.usda.gov/custer.

74 ROCK CREEK PRIMITIVE

Scenic rating: 8

in the Beartooth Mountains in Custer National Forest

Located between 7,500 feet and 8,650 feet, Rock Creek tumbles along a forest road sprinkled on both sides with short spur roads and jeep trails. These offer campers privacy and solitude, accompanied by only the sound of the creek. The U-shaped, glacier-carved valley littered with large boulders left from receding ice sweeps up several thousand feet on both sides to the high alpine plateaus of the east Beartooth Mountains. Rock Creek Road crosses into Wyoming and back before terminating at a popular trailhead. A two-mile trail climbs into a scoured rocky cirque containing Glacier Lake. Anglers go after rainbow, brook, and Yellowstone cutthroat trout in the lake as well as in Rock Creek. Rock Creek Road is a favorite of ATV riders. Mountain bikers use it, too.

Most of the dispersed primitive campsites along Rock Creek sit right on the river. You'll find sites shaded under cottonwoods and pines, in filtered sunlight in aspens, and in full sun in grassy fields with big open views of the mountains. Find most of the sites by a small sign with a tent icon; some are unmarked. Scout the dirt access roads and turnaround space before you drive in blind. Etiquette dictates one site per party.

Campsites, facilities: More than 25 primitive RV or tent campsites that can accommodate small RVs flank Rock Creek Road. Dispersed camping is permitted 300 feet on either side of the road from the centerline. The only facilities are rock fire rings. Use existing rings rather than constructing new ones. Treat river water for use. Pack out your trash. Follow Leave No

Trace principles for human waste. Leashed pets are permitted.

Reservations, fees: Reservations are not accepted. Camping is free. Open year-round, but snowbound in winter.

Directions: From Red Lodge, drive 11.5 miles southwest on Highway 212 to milepost 57.2. Turn right onto paved Rock Creek Road (Forest Road 2421). After passing Limber Pine Campground at 0.9 mile, the pavement disappears, and the road disintegrates into potholes and washboards, which require slow driving. Between Limber Pine and the road's terminus in 7.5 miles, look for spur roads and small posts with tent icons.

GPS Coordinates: N 45° 3.336' W 109° 25.018' (first primitive site)

Contact: Custer National Forest, Beartooth Ranger District, 6811 Hwy. 212 S., Red Lodge, MT, 406/446-2103, www.fs.usda.gov/custer.

A two-mile trail climbs to Glacier Lake in the Beartooth Mountains.

75 M-K

Scenic rating: 8

in the Beartooth Mountains in Custer National Forest

At 7,450 feet, M-K works as an overflow campground if Parkside, Greenough Lake, and Limber Pine are full. However, the two miles of dirt road between them is rough. Flanked by the immense above-tree-line meadow plateaus of the snowcapped Beartooth Mountains, the campground sits on the east bank of Rock Creek. At the end of Rock Creek Road (after five more miles of rough dirt road crossing into Wyoming and back), a popular two-mile trail climbs into a scoured rocky cirque containing Glacier Lake. Anglers also go after rainbow, brook, and Yellowstone cutthroat trout in the lake as well as in Rock Creek. Rock Creek Road is a favorite of ATVers; mountain bikers also use it, but they must suck the dust of passing vehicles. M-K also sits at the south end of the two-mile, hiker-only Parkside National Recreation Trail, which leads to Greenough Lake.

M-K, favored by tenters, is a quiet, partly shaded campground with an open understory between a pine tree canopy and a pine needle and cone floor. Thanks to the lack of foliage, you can see neighbors; however, campsites are spread out for some privacy. The narrow, rough dirt road loops through the campground and connects the unnumbered sites. Those at the upper end overlook the creek, and most have huge flat spaces for multiple tents. A couple of unappealing sites flank Rock Creek Road. The sound of the creek filters through the whole campground.

Campsites, facilities: The campground has 10 RV or tent campsites. RVs are limited to 20 feet. Facilities include picnic tables, fire rings with grills, and vault toilets. Pack out your trash. Treat creek water for use. Leashed pets are permitted.

Reservations, fees: Reservations are not accepted. Camping is free. Open year-round, but snowbound in winter.

Directions: From Red Lodge, drive 11.5 miles southwest on Highway 212 to milepost 57.2. Turn right onto paved Rock Creek Road (Forest Road 2421) for 2.7 miles to the campground entrance on the right. The pavement disappears after one mile and the road disintegrates into potholes and washboards, which require slow driving.

GPS Coordinates: N 45° 2.305' W 109° 25.747'

Contact: Custer National Forest, Beartooth Ranger District, 6811 Hwy. 212 S., Red Lodge, MT, 406/446-2103, www.fs.usda. gov/custer.

76 ISLAND LAKE

Scenic rating: 10

in the Beartooth Highway in Shoshone National Forest

BEST

At 9,600 feet on top of the Beartooth Plateau in Wyoming, Island Lake is the highest campground along the Beartooth Highway as well as the highest drive-to campground in the entire Northern Rocky Mountains. In midsummer, huge alpine meadows overflowing with fuchsia paintbrush and bluebells sprawl between wind-blown pines and firs. The wildflower-rimmed lake containing a tiny island provides boating for small watercraft and fishing for small trout that can't grow big in the short ice-free season. (Fishing requires a Wyoming fishing license available one mile west at Top of the World store.) Canoeists and float tubers portage 100 feet from Island Lake to Night Lake. A trail for hiking and horse-packing departs from the campground, touring the west shore and passing four more lakes within an hour of hiking. In 2.7 miles, it connects with the Beauty Lake Trail from Beartooth Lake. The trail also continues northeast into the Absaroka-Beartooth

Wilderness, linking up lakes, backpacking and mountaineering routes, and rugged, remote granite summits, but mountain bikers may ride only six miles, to the wilderness boundary. Bring DEET for the voracious mosquitoes bred in the boggy alpine meadows, prepare to be winded walking to the outhouse because of the altitude, and be ready for the regular afternoon thunderstorms that can pelt rain, hail, or snow—even in August. Set in loose-knit pine and fir clusters laced with large boulders, the campground has only a handful of campsites that can see the lake (on loop C), but trailers are not recommended on the narrow, steep loop.

Campsites, facilities: The campground has 21 RV or tent campsites. RVs are limited to 32 feet. Facilities include picnic tables, fire rings with grills, vault toilets, drinking water, garbage service, bear boxes, boat ramp, and campground hosts. Leashed pets are permitted.

Reservations, fees: Reservations are not accepted. Campsites cost $15 per unit (RV, trailer, or tent). Cash or check. Open late June-mid-September, snow permitting.

Directions: On Highway 212, drive 29 miles southwest from Red Lodge, or from Yellowstone's northeast entrance drive 33 miles east. Turn north into the campground entrance.

GPS Coordinates: N 44° 56.451' W 109° 32.311'

Contact: Shoshone National Forest, Clarks Fork Ranger District, 203A Yellowstone Ave., Cody, WY 82414, 307/527-6921, www. fs.usda.gov/shoshone.

77 BEARTOOTH LAKE

Scenic rating: 10

in the Beartooth Mountains in Shoshone National Forest

BEST

At 9,000 feet on top of the Beartooth Plateau in Wyoming, Beartooth Lake sits below orange-streaked Beartooth Butte, a sedimentary

© BECKY LOMAX

Hiking trails lead from Island Lake into the Absaroka Wilderness.

anomaly amid the granite Beartooth Mountains. In midsummer, huge alpine bluebell meadows flank the butte's lower slopes across Beartooth Lake, a forest- and bog-rimmed lake with a boat ramp on its south end for launching small watercraft and fishing for small trout that can't grow big in the short ice-free season. A Wyoming fishing license is required, available at the Top of the World store one mile east. From the campground, two trails angle north; one waltzes past Beauty Lake, connecting with the Island Lake trails in 2.4 miles and making a 7.9-mile loop. The loop also aims north into the Absaroka-Beartooth Wilderness, linking up lakes and backpacking and mountaineering routes, but mountain bikers may ride only five miles, to the wilderness boundary. One loop connects to Clay Butte Lookout (you can also drive to it), a 1942 fire lookout that commands a 360-degree panoramic view from 9,811 feet.

Mosquitoes breed armies here in the boggy alpine meadows: bring jumbo-sized bug juice. The air is thin; prepare to be winded walking from the lake to your campsite. Afternoon thunderstorms roll in like clockwork; be ready for August rains, hail, or snow. The quiet-at-night campground packs its three forested, partly shaded loops tight with a few sites on the A loop having peek-a-boo lake views through the trees. Step outside at night to see brilliant stars light up the sky.

Campsites, facilities: The campground has 21 RV or tent campsites. RVs are limited to 32 feet. Facilities include picnic tables, fire rings with grills, vault toilets, drinking water, garbage service, bear boxes, and campground hosts. Leashed pets are permitted.

Reservations, fees: Reservations are not accepted. Campsites cost $15 per unit (RV, trailer, or tent). Cash or check. Open late June-mid-September, snow permitting.

Directions: On Highway 212, drive 31 miles southwest from Red Lodge, or from Yellowstone's northeast entrance drive 31 miles east. Turn north into the campground entrance. GPS Coordinates: N 44° 56.614' W 109° 35.427'

Contact: Shoshone National Forest, Clarks Fork Ranger District, 203A Yellowstone

Ave., Cody, WY 82414, 307/527-6921, www.fs.usda.gov/shoshone.

78 CRAZY CREEK

🚶 🚲 🛶 🐕 🚐 ⛺

Scenic rating: 7

in the Absaroka Mountains in Shoshone National Forest

At 6,900 feet, Crazy Creek Campground snuggles into the lower western slopes of the Beartooth Highway in the Absaroka Mountains in Wyoming. The campground sits at the confluence of Crazy Creek with the Clarks Fork Yellowstone River, where anglers go after trout and mountain whitefish (Wyoming license needed for fishing). Across the highway, the Crazy Lakes Trail (#612) climbs to a series of lakes in the Absaroka-Beartooth Wilderness. Crossing back into Montana in 4.5 miles, the trail splits to various lakes—destinations for day hikers, backpackers, horse-packers, and anglers. (You'll need a Montana fishing license.) A five-minute walk on the trail leads to a waterfall. Cyclists going west to east over the Beartooth Highway stay here before the climb over Beartooth Pass.

Sitting in a spruce and lodgepole pine forest, Crazy Creek offers campsites that vary between sunny and shady. Recent hazardous tree removal work thinned out some of the beetle-killed trees, opening up the forest more around the grassy sites and making it visually greener. The sunny open sites also have views of the cliffs on Jim Smith Peak. Unfortunately, the tree removal also made sites less private; however, sites 10 and 12, which work for smaller tents, have more privacy than the other campsites. Site 14 garners spectacular views of Pilot and Index Peaks. You'll hear road noise in the campground, but the highway does not permit commercial hauling through Yellowstone National Park, so noise dissipates at night.

Campsites, facilities: The campground has 16 RV or tent campsites. RVs are limited to 32 feet. Facilities include picnic tables, fire rings with grills, vault toilets, garbage service, bear boxes, and campground hosts. Bring your own drinking water, or treat creek water. Leashed pets are permitted.

Reservations, fees: Reservations are not accepted. Campsites cost $10 per unit (RV, trailer, or tent). Cash or check. Open late May-early September.

Directions: On Highway 212, drive 47 miles southwest from Red Lodge, or from the northeast entrance to Yellowstone National Park drive 15 miles east. Turn south into the campground entrance.

GPS Coordinates: N 44° 56.518' W 109° 46.429'

Contact: Shoshone National Forest, Clarks Fork Ranger District, 203A Yellowstone Ave., Cody, WY 82414, 307/527-6921, www.fs.usda.gov/shoshone.

79 FOX CREEK

🛶 🐕 🚐 ⛺

Scenic rating: 8

in the Absaroka Mountains in Shoshone National Forest

At 7,100 feet, Fox Creek Campground sits on the western slopes of the Beartooth Mountains on the southern descent from the Beartooth Highway in Wyoming. While you're driving down the west side of the highway, Index and Pilot Peaks, both over 11,000 feet in elevation, jut up as prominent spires. The campground's two loops sit between the Clarks Fork Yellowstone River and the highway. You can wade-fish for trout and mountain whitefish in the nationally designated Wild and Scenic River, but you need a Wyoming fishing license.

The loose mixed forest of spruce, lodgepole pine, grand fir, and Douglas fir lends a bit of shade to the sunny campsites surrounded by grassy wildflower meadows. You'll hear some highway noise; however, the route into

Yellowstone National Park does not permit commercial trucking, so the noise quiets at night. The forest provides a thick screen, so you don't see the highway, but more open sites command views of Index and Pilot Peaks. Sites on the northeast ends of the loops sit nearest the river, but none have river views through the trees. The renovated campground now includes two extra large campsites with electrical hookups can accommodate three RVs each.

Campsites, facilities: The campground has 33 RV or tent campsites. RVs are limited to 32 feet. Facilities include picnic tables, fire rings with grills, electrical hookups, drinking water, vault toilets, garbage service, bear boxes, and campground hosts. Leashed pets are permitted.

Reservations, fees: Reservations are not accepted. Campsites cost $20 for electrical sites and $15 for other sites. Triple sites with electricity cost $60. Cash or check. Open mid-June-early September.

Directions: On Highway 212, drive 51 miles southwest from Red Lodge, or from the northeast entrance to Yellowstone National Park drive 11 miles east. Turn north into the campground entrance.

GPS Coordinates: N 44° 58.545' W 109° 50.023'

Contact: Shoshone National Forest, Clarks Fork Ranger District, 203A Yellowstone Ave., Cody, WY 82414, 307/527-6921, www.fs.usda.gov/shoshone.

80 LAKE CREEK

Scenic rating: 6
on Chief Joseph Highway in Shoshone National Forest

About 20 miles east of Yellowstone National Park, Lake Creek sits at the base of the Beartooth Mountains at 7,000 feet in Wyoming. The campground isn't a destination, but rather convenient for accessing two outstanding scenic drives with distinctly different scenery, the Beartooth Highway and Chief Joseph Highway. The Beartooth Highway climbs through rugged lake-strewn alpine plateaus while the Chief Joseph Highway winds through an arid canyon up to Dead Indian Pass. Cross-country cyclists use this campground before beginning the steep climb 3,000 feet in elevation over Beartooth Pass. Anglers can fish for brook, rainbow, and Yellowstone cutthroat trout in the Wild and Scenic-designated Clarks Fork of the Yellowstone River, which parallels Chief Joseph Highway. The Clarks Fork upstream of the campground offers experts-only Class IV-V+ white water.

Some campers prefer staying at this lower elevation campground than high on the Beartooth Plateau, as it stays warmer and drier, plus some people sleep better at lower elevations. Lake Creek fills the campground with its burbling, but not enough to drown out passing cars on the close highway. Commercial trucking noise, however, is sparse, as trucks do not climb over the Beartooth Highway or travel through Yellowstone National Park. In midsummer, the campground meadows bloom with sticky pink geraniums, wild roses, and grasses. Lodgepole pines provide partial shade. Sites 4 and 5 are tucked into more private locations under the trees, but more open sites garner mountain views.

Campsites, facilities: The campground has six RV or tent campsites. RVs are limited to 22 feet. Facilities include picnic tables, fire rings with grills, vault toilets, and bear boxes. No drinking water is available. Bring your own, or treat creek water. Pack out your trash. Leashed pets are permitted.

Reservations, fees: Reservations are not accepted. Campsites cost $10 per unit (RV, trailer, or tent). Cash or check. Open late June-early September.

Directions: From the junction of the Beartooth Highway (Hwy. 212) and Chief Joseph Highway (Hwy. 296), drive south on Highway 296 for 1.5 miles. From Cody, drive north on State Highway 120 for 16 miles and then west on Chief Joseph Highway

(Hwy. 296) for 44 miles. Turn north into the campground.

GPS Coordinates: N 44° 55.269' W 109° 42.430'

Contact: Shoshone National Forest, Clarks Fork Ranger District, 203A Yellowstone Ave., Cody, WY 82414-9313, 307/527-6921, www.fs.usda.gov/shoshone.

81 HUNTER PEAK

Scenic rating: 7

on Chief Joseph Highway in Shoshone National Forest

At 6,500 feet about 24 miles east of Yellowstone National Park, Hunter Peak Campground squeezes in between the scenic Chief Joseph Highway and the Wild and Scenic-designated Clarks Fork of the Yellowstone River in Wyoming. It sits at the base of the 9,034-foot Hunter Peak, where it attracts elk hunters in the fall. Anglers can fish the river for trout (artificial flies and lures only) from several campsites. Across the highway from the campground, the Clark's Fork Trailhead departs for a 17-mile trek along the rugged canyons of the river as it heads downstream. A 300-foot waterfall awaits about 90 minutes down the trail. The trail, a popular horse-packing route, is also open to mountain bikes and ATVs. North Crandell Trail, which departs three miles south of the campground, climbs 16 miles up North Crandell Creek into Yellowstone National Park.

Most of the campsites ring a loop on the left with the campground hosts on the right spur. The campground tucks under tall lodgepole pines and spruces on a flat grassy plateau on the river. Views from several campsites include large boulders across the river. Meadows bloom throughout the campground with penstemon, buckwheat, and pink sticky geranium. Sites 4, 5, and 6 claim river frontage, but all remaining campsites have access via trails. The sound of the river helps you forget the road passes right above the campground, and sites vary between partly shaded and sunny.

Campsites, facilities: The campground has 10 RV or tent campsites. RVs are limited to 32 feet. Facilities include picnic tables, fire rings with grills, vault toilets, drinking water, bear boxes, garbage service, and campground hosts. Leashed pets are permitted.

Reservations, fees: Reservations are accepted (977/444-6777, www.recreation.gov). Campsites cost $15 per unit (RV, trailer, or tent). Cash or check. Open late May-mid-September; sometimes open longer, but without services.

Directions: From the junction of the Beartooth Highway (Hwy. 212) and Chief Joseph Highway (Hwy. 296), drive southeast for 4.7 miles. From Cody, drive north on State Highway 120 for 16 miles and then turn west onto Chief Joseph Highway (Hwy. 296) for 41 miles. Turn south, descending into the campground.

GPS Coordinates: N 44° 53.118' W 109° 39.306'

Contact: Shoshone National Forest, Clarks Fork Ranger District, 203A Yellowstone Ave., Cody, WY 82414-9313, 307/527-6921, www.fs.usda.gov/shoshone.

82 DEAD INDIAN CREEK

Scenic rating: 7

on Chief Joseph Highway in Shoshone National Forest

At 6,100 feet, surrounded by sagebrush hills broken by orange and white sandstones, Dead Indian Creek Campground, named for the creek and the 8,000-foot-high pass above the campground, sits on the scenic Chief Joseph Highway in between Dead Indian Pass and Sunlight Bridge in Wyoming. The Dead Indian Pass Overlook includes interpretive stories about the escape of Chief Joseph from the army and the trek of the Nez Perce across

Wyoming. The panoramic view spans the rugged country of the Beartooth Mountains to the Absaroka Range. West of the campground, the Sunlight Bridge, the highest bridge in Wyoming, crosses a deep gorge. Road cyclists pedal the switchbacking grade of the highway up to the pass. The Dead Indian Creek Trail walks a portion of the Nez Perce National Historic Trail, reaching the Clarks Fork of the Yellowstone River in less than five miles. Across the highway from the campground, a trail climbs along the creek to the summit of Dead Indian Peak.

The arid campground is divided in two parts by the creek, with five campsites on each side. Most of the campsites sit very near the creek but out of its view thanks to the thick brush. Short paths cut through the brush to the creek. Bits of shade come from cottonwoods, alder, and junipers, but most of the campsites are blazing hot in midsummer. The highway completely circles the campground; every campsite hears vehicles, but the road is not a heavy trucking route, and traffic dwindles at night. The campsites are spread out for privacy.

Campsites, facilities: The campground has 10 RV or tent campsites. RVs are limited to 32 feet. Facilities include picnic tables, fire rings with grills, vault toilets, garbage service, and campground hosts. Drinking water is not available; bring your own or treat creek water. Leashed pets are permitted.

Reservations, fees: Reservations are not accepted. Campsites cost $10 per unit (RV, trailer, or tent). Cash or check. Open late May-mid-September.

Directions: From the junction of the Beartooth Highway (Hwy. 212) and Chief Joseph Highway (Hwy. 296), drive southeast for 25 miles. From Cody, drive north on Highway 120 for 16 miles and then west on Chief Joseph Highway (Hwy. 296) for 21 miles. The campground has two entrances, both on the north side of the road and set on each side of the creek.

GPS Coordinates: N 44° 45.194' W 109° 25.132'

Contact: Shoshone National Forest, Clarks Fork Ranger District, 203A Yellowstone Ave., Cody, WY 82414-9313, 307/527-6921, www.fs.usda.gov/shoshone.

YELLOWSTONE AND GRAND TETON

© BECKY LOMAX

Located a full day's drive south of Glacier National
Park, Yellowstone and Teton National Parks attract about three million visitors
a year—most packed into a short summer season when sightseeing and hik-
ing bring you face to face with bison, pronghorn antelope, and grizzly bears.
Yellowstone and Grand Teton National Parks are prime wildlife watching areas.
Bring the binoculars for enhanced viewing. Yellowstone holds 12 drive-up campgrounds. To the south, Grand Teton offers six large campgrounds. Surrounding
Yellowstone, three small towns neighbor northern entrances: West Yellowstone,
Gardiner, and Cooke City. While RV parks and national forest campgrounds
ring the park's perimeters, camping inside the parks lets you smell the fuming
caldera and hear the howl of wolves at night.

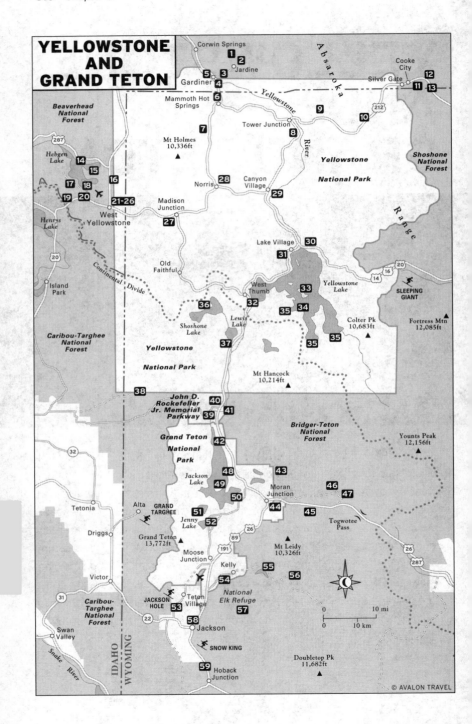

YELLOWSTONE AND GRAND TETON

1 BEAR CREEK

Scenic rating: 5

in the Absaroka Mountains in Gallatin National Forest

In Montana's Absaroka Mountains, Bear Creek Campground, elevation 7,200 feet, sits on the edge of the Absaroka-Beartooth Wilderness. The narrow, forested Bear Creek Valley climbs up to peaks topping out above 10,000 feet. Mountain bikes and ATVs can tour the Forest Service roads on the slopes of Ash Mountain east of the campground, but not into the wilderness. Bear Creek Trail, which departs from a trailhead 0.3 mile north of the campground, follows the creek 2.4 miles to trail #620, which accesses Knox and Fish Lake as well as the ridgeline north of Ash Mountain.

In a scrappy mixed fir and pine forest, the remote campground is for those seeking absolute solitude with only the sounds of nature—jays squawking, squirrels chattering, and a burbling creek. The campsites line up along the creek with flat spaces for tents. The first two sites are well-used, but the more difficult to reach sites are overgrown. Small lupine and paintbrush meadows weave through the campground.

Campsites, facilities: The campground has four primitive RV or tent campsites. RVs are limited to 21 feet. With large potholes and no turnaround space on the campground road, trailers are not recommended, and a high-clearance vehicle will help. Scout all campground roads before driving them. Facilities include rock fire rings and a pit toilet. No drinking water is available. Bring your own, or treat creek water. Pack out your trash. Pets are permitted.

Reservations, fees: Reservations are not accepted. Camping is free. Open mid-June-October, depending on snow.

Directions: From Gardiner, drive northeast on Jardine Road for 5.4 miles. (The pavement ends quickly.) In Jardine, turn right over the worn wooden bridge onto Bear Creek Road (Forest Road 493) and climb on the potholed, single-lane road with turnouts for five miles to a Y. Take the left fork for 0.2 mile and turn left into the campground. Warning: The campground road is extremely narrow.
GPS Coordinates: N 45° 6.661' W 110° 36.016'
Contact: Gallatin National Forest, Gardiner Ranger Station, P.O. Box 5, Hwy. 89 S., Gardiner, MT 59030, 406/848-7375, www.fs.usda.gov/gallatin.

2 TIMBER CAMP

Scenic rating: 7

in the Absaroka Mountains in Gallatin National Forest

At 7,182 feet Montana's Absaroka Mountains, Timber Camp enjoys a high subalpine meadow on the slopes of Ash Mountain, which tops out over 10,000 feet. Because of the forest and the steep terrain, the peak is not visible from the campground. Across the road from the campground, a Forest Service spur road climbs up the west slope, a road explored by mountain bikers and ATVers. Within three miles in both directions on the road, hikers can access trails into the Absaroka-Beartooth Wilderness. Bear Creek Trailhead sits to the north, Pine Creek Trailhead to the south.

Ultra-quiet campsites tuck under mature Douglas firs for protection from weather and partial shade. The campsites surround a large open meadow bursting with July wildflowers—cow parsnips, lupines, sticky geraniums. Rough, unnumbered sites with forest duff spaces for tents are spread out for privacy, but they are in sight of each other because of the open meadow. A creek runs along the camp's north side. Prepare for copious mosquitoes.

Campsites, facilities: The primitive campground has five RV or tent campsites. RVs are limited to 21 feet. Facilities include picnic tables and fire rings with grills at three sites, rock fire rings at two sites, and a pit toilet. No drinking water is available. Bring your own, or treat creek water. Pack out your trash. Pets are permitted.

Reservations, fees: Reservations are not accepted. Camping is free. Open mid-June-October, depending on snow.

Directions: From Gardiner, drive northeast on Jardine Road for 5.4 miles (the pavement ends quickly). In Jardine, turn right over the worn wooden bridge onto Bear Creek Road (Forest Road 493) and climb for 4.2 miles. The road narrows to a potholed single lane with turnouts. Turn left into the campground. Scout out the spur roads into the campsites—some have deep muddy holes.

GPS Coordinates: N 45° 5.743' W 110° 36.323'

Contact: Gallatin National Forest, Gardiner Ranger Station, P.O. Box 5, Hwy. 89 S., Gardiner, MT 59030, 406/848-7375, www.fs.usda.gov/gallatin.

3 EAGLE CREEK

Scenic rating: 8
in the Absaroka Mountains in Gallatin National Forest

Within three miles of Yellowstone National Park, Eagle Creek offers an inexpensive place to camp in Montana with expansive views of the park's north slopes. Eagle Creek is the closest Forest Service campground to the park's north entrance. Surrounded by an arid sagebrush slope, the habitat often draws wildlife, such as elk. Bring binoculars! Hiking is available north of Jardine at Bear Creek, from Gardiner along the Yellowstone River, and in Yellowstone at Mammoth Hot Springs. Gardiner is also the local headquarters for rafting and fishing outfitters, and the Yellowstone River, which flows through town, provides white water for rafting and kayaking.

The campground sits on an open hillside, providing little shade and no privacy between most of the campsites. Site 7 is the exception, tucked into aspens. Eagle Creek runs along the west side of the campground, surrounded by brush, aspens, and willows. The grassy campground—green in July, brown by August—is roomy enough for tents, but many of the sites are sloped. Stock corrals sit adjacent to the main campground road; two campsites ring the dusty parking lot. Views from the campground extend across the valley to Mammoth Hot Springs and Yellowstone National Park's rugged northern peaks.

Campsites, facilities: The campground has 16 RV or tent campsites. RVs are limited to 40 feet. Facilities include picnic tables, fire rings with grills, bear boxes, stock facilities, and vault toilet (wheelchair-accessible). No drinking water is available. Bring your own; to treat creek water. Pack out your trash. Leashed pets are permitted.

Reservations, fees: Reservations are not accepted. Campsites cost $7. An extra vehicle costs $3. Cash or check. Open year-round.

Directions: From Gardiner, climb the hairpins northeast on Jardine Road for 2.1 miles. (The pavement ends in 0.3 mile.) Turn left into the campground.

GPS Coordinates: N 45° 2.581' W 110° 40.840'

Contact: Gallatin National Forest, Gardiner Ranger Station, P.O. Box 5, Hwy. 89 S., Gardiner, MT 59030, 406/848-7375, www.fs.usda.gov/gallatin.

4 ROCKY MOUNTAIN CAMPGROUND

Scenic rating: 8
in downtown Gardiner

Located at 5,357 feet in elevation, Rocky Mountain Campground sits in downtown Gardiner, Montana within walking distance to shopping, restaurants, ranger station, visitors centers, art galleries, and groceries. The campground is four blocks from the Roosevelt Arch, the north entrance to Yellowstone National Park. Gardiner is a hub for guided fishing, rafting, kayaking, zipline, and horseback-riding outfitters. Four raft companies guide trips on the Yellowstone River, which slices through town. Several fly shops can provide advice on the best places to fish the river and what flies to use when. From town, a trail traverses east along the Yellowstone River. Mountain bikers head to the five-mile abandoned railroad bed paralleling the Yellowstone River between Gardiner and the park boundary at Reese Creek.

On a bluff in Gardiner, the sunny campground commands views of the town, Yellowstone River, and north slopes of Yellowstone National Park. The park has two types of campsites: standard and deluxe. Many of the sites rim the edge of the bluff, with the views, and a few tuck under the shade of large trees. The campsites, which are stacked up in parking-lot fashion lacking in privacy, are grassy with gravel parking pads. Traffic noise is audible. Toilet and shower facilities were renovated in 2011.

Campsites, facilities: The campground has 71 RV campsites. RVs are limited to 45 feet. The campground has 28 pull-through campsites, 50 sites that accommodate rigs with four slide-outs, and full hookups for water, sewer, and electricity up to 50 amps. Facilities include flush toilets (wheelchair-accessible), showers, launderette, picnic tables, community campfire area, drinking water, wireless Internet, cable TV, propane, miniature golf, and disposal station. Leashed pets are permitted, but only two per campsite.

Reservations, fees: Reservations are accepted. Campsites cost $52-58. Rates are for two people; $3 for each additional person. Seniors can get a discount, and rates in shoulder seasons are cheaper. Add on 7 percent Montana bed tax. Cash, check, or credit card. Open mid-April-mid-October.

Directions: In Gardiner on Highway 89, turn northeast onto Jardine Road. Drive 0.1 mile up the hill and turn right.
GPS Coordinates: N 45° 1.975' W 110° 42.167'
Contact: Rocky Mountain Campground, 14 Jardine Rd., Gardiner, MT 59030, 406/848-7251 or 877/534-6931, www.rockymountain-campground.com.

5 YELLOWSTONE RV PARK

Scenic rating: 7

in Gardiner

At 5,200 feet, Yellowstone RV Park overlooks the Yellowstone River just outside downtown Gardiner, Montana. Views across the canyon sometimes lend sightings of wildlife—moose, antelope, bighorns, elk, deer, ospreys, and bald eagles. The campground is 1.3 miles from the Roosevelt Arch, the north entrance to Yellowstone National Park. Gardiner is a hub for fishing, rafting, kayaking, zipline, and horseback-riding outfitters. Four raft companies guide trips on the Yellowstone River. Several fly shops can provide advice on the best places to fish the river and what flies to use when. From town, a trail traverses east along the Yellowstone River. Mountain bikers head to the five-mile abandoned railroad bed paralleling the Yellowstone River between Gardiner and the park boundary at Reese Creek.

The campground has two rows of RV sites—one overlooks the river and the other lines up like a parking lot. The campsites are open, sunny, and speckled with a few low trees. A rail fence runs along the river canyon to mark where the slope drops to the water. A dirt road with gravel parking pads loops through the lawn sites but kicks up dust. Views span the brown, barren sagebrush canyon sweeping up from the river. With the campground squeezed between the river and the highway, the sounds of both permeate the campsites. Winds frequently blow through the canyon.

CAMPING IN YELLOWSTONE

Yellowstone, the nation's first national park, spills from mountains to high plateaus, covering more land than Delaware and Rhode Island combined. Its forests and prairies hold 12 drive-up campgrounds. Inside Yellowstone National Park, the Grand Loop Road forms a figure-eight through the caldera, where shaggy brown bison graze next to steam billowing from hot pools. Small campgrounds cluster in the north, while large campgrounds verging on the size of small towns populate the Old Faithful, canyon, and lake areas. For those looking to escape crowds, remote boat-in campsites rim the arms of Yellowstone and Shoshone Lakes.

- **To camp closest to geysers, hot pools, and mud pots:** Head to Mammoth, Norris, Madison, or Canyon Campgrounds.
- **To camp near the famed wildlife watching of Lamar Valley:** Aim for Tower, Slough Creek, or Pebble Creek Campgrounds in the northeast corner.

- **To explore the park's lakes:** Go to Grant, Fishing Bridge, Bridge Bay, or Lewis Lake in the southeast corner. (Fishing Bridge offers hookups for RVs.) Better yet, hit the backcountry office in Bridge Bay for permits for remote, quiet boat-in campsites flanking Yellowstone Lake's 110 miles of shoreline, or kayak or canoe into Shoshone Lake. On both lakes, be ready for afternoon winds.
- **To cast into blue-ribbon trout streams:** Anglers should camp at Madison Junction to fish the Madison River or at Fishing Bridge, Canyon, or Tower Fall to fish the Yellowstone River.

Yellowstone's northern entrances harbor three small towns, West Yellowstone, Gardiner, and Cooke City, that provide RV parks, nearby national forest campgrounds, and services for campers, plus outfitters for rafting, horseback riding, and fishing.

Campsites, facilities: This campground has 46 RV campsites and can accommodate tents in 10 of them. RV pull-throughs can fit rigs up to 70 feet. Hookups are available for water, sewer, and electricity up to 50 amps. Facilities include picnic tables, flush toilets (wheelchair-accessible), showers, drinking water, cable TV, launderette, and wireless Internet. Leashed pets are permitted.

Reservations, fees: Reservations are accepted. Campsites cost $40-45. Rates are based on a maximum of six people per site. Add on 7 percent Montana bed tax. Cash, check, or credit card. Open May-October.

Directions: From downtown Gardiner where the bridge crosses the Yellowstone River, drive northwest on Highway 89 for one mile to the campground entrance to the south.

GPS Coordinates: N 45° 2.324' W 110° 43.438'

Contact: Yellowstone RV Park and Campground, 117 Hwy. 89 S., Gardiner, MT 59030,

406/848-7496, www.ventureswestinc.com/YellowstoneRVPark.htm.

6 MAMMOTH

Scenic rating: 8
on the upper Grand Loop in Yellowstone National Park

BEST (

Located on an arid slope at 6,039 feet at Mammoth Hot Springs, Mammoth Campground offers a sweeping view of the dry, sagebrush canyon and Mount Everts. With elk hanging around the lawns, the town—historical Fort Yellowstone—contains restaurants, gift shops, Albright Visitor Center, medical clinic, horseback trail rides, showers at Mammoth Hotel, gas, post office, and Yellowstone's park headquarters. More services are available about 10 miles north in Gardiner, including guided rafting, kayaking, fishing, and ziplines. Boardwalks, stairs, and trails loop through steaming Mammoth Hot Springs travertine terraces. The narrow, curvy Upper Terrace Drive (no buses, RVs, or trailers) arcs through more mineral terraces. Other trails lead to the Beaver Ponds, Sepulcher Mountain, and Lava Creek. Mountain bikers can ride the six-mile Bunsen Peak Road looping around 8,564-foot Bunsen Peak. The Gardner River offers trout fishing and is a good river for beginning and young anglers. For soaking in a natural hot springs, visit Boiling River after high water recedes in July. Located off the entrance road north of the campground, a 0.5-mile hike leads to the volunteer-maintained hot pools.

If Mammoth Campground were any other place, most people would bypass it. The sagebrush and grass campsites with gravel parking pads have little privacy, little shade, and are exposed to winds and weather. Views include other campsites. Because the campground is tucked in a hairpin on the highway, you'll hear and see vehicles both above and below the campground. Nevertheless, it is a popular campground for exploring the park's northwest corner; in summer, plan to arrive early to claim a campsite. RVs have the advantage of pull-through at most sites.

Campsites, facilities: Mammoth Campground has 85 RV or tent campsites. RVs are limited to 75 feet. Fifty-one campsites have tent platforms. Facilities include picnic tables, fire rings with grills, flush toilets, drinking water, amphitheater for interpretive programs, and garbage service. Leashed pets are permitted. Wheelchair-accessible facilities include toilets and five campsites.

Reservations, fees: Reservations are not accepted. Campsites cost $20. Shared hiker and biker campsites cost $5 per person. Cash or check. Open year-round.

Directions: From the north entrance to Yellowstone National Park, drive south for five miles on the north entrance road, or from park headquarters in Mammoth, drive 0.7

Trails lead through travertine terraces at Mammoth Hot Springs.

mile toward Gardiner. Turn west into the campground.

GPS Coordinates: N 44° 58.377' W 110° 41.600'

Contact: Yellowstone National Park, P.O. Box 168, Yellowstone, WY 82190-0168, 307/344-7381, www.nps.gov/yell.

7 INDIAN CREEK

Scenic rating: 8

on the upper Grand Loop in Yellowstone National Park

BEST (

Sitting at 7,298 feet in elevation, Indian Creek perches at the confluence of the Gardner River, Obsidian Creek, and Indian Creek in Yellowstone's northwest corner. North of the campground, the Grand Loop Road passes the marshy meadows of Gardners Hole and Swan Lake, which offers excellent wildlife-watching opportunities for elk and bears.

Anglers can fish for small brook trout in the Gardner River and the two creeks. Mountain bikers can ride the six-mile Bunsen Peak Road looping around 8,564-foot Bunsen Peak. A separate hiking trail goes to its summit. From the campground, a trail runs 12.8 miles west to Bighorn Pass. Several miles south on the road, other trailheads depart for Grizzly Lake (2.9 miles), Trilobite Lake (7.9 miles), and Mt. Holmes (10 miles).

Indian Creek sat in the midst of the 1988 wildfire that ripped through Yellowstone. While silvered trunks litter hillsides, fast-growing lodgepoles have converted the slopes to green again. A loose lodgepole forest lends partial shade to the campground as grassy meadows add sunny spots. Views of the surrounding peaks include the 10,023-foot Antler Peak to the west. Indian Creek is smaller in size and located away from Yellowstone's big hubs, so this campground is quieter and more relaxing than the park's larger campgrounds. The campsites are also spaced out a little more for privacy, and those adjacent to larger meadows can offer evening and morning wildlife-watching.

Campsites, facilities: The campground has 75 RV or tent campsites. Ten campsites can accommodate RVs up to 40 feet; 35 campsites can fit RVs up to 30 feet. Generators are not permitted. Facilities include picnic tables, fire rings with grills, vault toilets, drinking water, firewood and ice for sale, bear boxes, and garbage service. Leashed pets are permitted. Wheelchair-accessible toilets and campsites are available.

Reservations, fees: Reservations are not accepted. Campsites cost $15. Shared hiker and biker campsites cost $5 per person. Cash or check. Open mid-June-early September.

Directions: From Mammoth, drive 8.5 miles south on the Grand Loop Road, or from Norris Junction, drive 12.5 miles north. Turn west and drive 0.3 mile to the campground. GPS Coordinates: N 44° 53.200' W 110° 44.093'

Contact: Yellowstone National Park, P.O. Box 168, Yellowstone, WY 82190-0168, 307/344-7381, www.nps.gov/yell.

8 TOWER FALL

Scenic rating: 7

on the upper Grand Loop in Yellowstone National Park

Located at 6,535 feet on the east side of the Grand Loop, Tower Fall Campground sits above the Tower Falls Complex in Yellowstone National Park. The area buzzes in summer with visitors stopping at the popular attraction, which includes a general store, picnic tables, and a one-mile trail to view the 132-foot falls and the Yellowstone River. Fishing is available in the river. A trail also tours up Tower Creek. Roosevelt Lodge, 2.5 miles north, offers horseback trail rides, stagecoach rides, nightly western cookout dinners, gas, convenience store, restaurant, and showers. To the south, mountain bikers can climb three miles on a dirt road up Mt. Washburn, at 10,243 feet the tallest mountain in Yellowstone. Hikers can also ascend to the lookout at the summit via the south side trail.

On a bluff above the Grand Loop Road, the campground sits on an arid north-facing hillside in a sparse, mixed forest of firs and pines that only shade some of the campsites. Dry grasses, dust, and forest duff make up the campsite floors, which are surrounded by green wild grasses in early July but brown in August. The open campground permits views of neighboring campers; sites around the outside of the loop have more privacy. Sites at the lower end of the campground overlook employee housing. Most of the campsites include views of forested and sagebrush slopes. Evening ranger programs may be offered in summer. Plan to arrive by 11am to claim a spot.

Campsites, facilities: The campground has 31 RV or tent campsites. RVs are limited to 30 feet, but parking pads work better for smaller RVs, such as truck campers, minivans, and trailer popups. Facilities include picnic tables, fire rings with grills, vault toilets (wheelchair-accessible), drinking water, bear boxes, and garbage service. Generators are not allowed. Leashed pets are permitted.

Reservations, fees: Reservations are not accepted. Campsites cost $12. Shared hiker and biker campsites cost $5 per person. Cash or check. Open late May-September.

Directions: From Tower-Roosevelt Junction, drive three miles south on the Grand Loop Road, or from Canyon Village, drive 16 miles north. Turn west and drive 0.3 mile up the hill to the campground. The campground road has one hairpin turn.

GPS Coordinates: N 44° 53.403' W 110° 23.381'

Contact: Yellowstone National Park, P.O. Box 168, Yellowstone, WY 82190-0168, 307/344-7381, www.nps.gov/yell.

9 SLOUGH CREEK

Scenic rating: 8

in the Absaroka Mountains in Yellowstone National Park

BEST (

At 6,249 feet, Slough Creek is prized for its small size, quiet creekside ambiance, and wildlife watching. The campground sits in the foothills of the Absaroka Mountains at the confluence of Slough Creek and Buffalo Creek. Fly-fishing anglers go after Yellowstone cutthroat trout in the creeks. Trails run up both creek drainages in the Absaroka Mountains, although they travel above the creeks rather than adjacent to them. A few miles west of the entrance road, a trail ascends Specimen Ridge overlooking the Lamar Valley. For wildlife watching, the entrance road to the campground provides several pullover spots to set up scopes to survey the wide-open sagebrush meadow hillsides littered with glacial

erratics. You can often see bison, pronghorn, bears, bighorn sheep, and sometimes wolves. Nearby, a convenience store, gas, showers, restaurant, cowboy cookout, horseback trail rides, and stagecoach rides are at Tower-Roosevelt Junction.

This campground is for those who enjoy solitude away from crowds, so plan to arrive early to claim a site. Its remote location off the main park roads guarantees silence so that you can hear wolves howl and owls hoot at night. Various sunny and shaded campsites are available, most lining up along the creeks. Sites 16 and above are better suited for tents but not limited to them. The campground rims a huge sagebrush and wildflower meadow that can be good for spotting elk, bison, and foxes. Some sites are more private than others, tucked behind trees or brush, but from most, you'll see other campers. The park service spruced up the campground landscaping in 2013.

Campsites, facilities: The campground has 23 RV or tent campsites. RVs are limited to 30 feet, but check the site first before pulling in. Generators are not permitted. Facilities include picnic tables, fire rings with grills, vault toilets (wheelchair-accessible), bear boxes, drinking water, garbage service, and campground host. Leashed pets are permitted.

Reservations, fees: Reservations are not accepted. Sites cost $15. Cash or check. Open mid-June-October.

Directions: From Tower-Roosevelt Junction, drive 5.8 miles east on the northeast entrance road, or from the northeast entrance station, drive 23.2 miles west. Turn north onto the dirt road and drive 2.3 miles to the campground. GPS Coordinates: N 44° 56.915' W 110° 18.410'

Contact: Yellowstone National Park, P.O. Box 168, Yellowstone, WY 82190-0168, 307/344-7381, www.nps.gov/yell.

10 PEBBLE CREEK

Scenic rating: 8

in the Absaroka Mountains in Yellowstone National Park

BEST (

At 6,900 feet, Pebble Creek Campground cuddles under high mountains, in contrast to Yellowstone's other campgrounds. The Absaroka Mountains—snowcapped well into June—rise to 10,000 feet around the Soda Butte Valley that descends from the campground. In summer, Soda Butte Creek lines with anglers casting flies because of its reputation for prime trout fishing. Pebble Creek has fishing, too. Soda Butte Valley and the adjacent Lamar Valley offer outstanding wildlife watching for bears, bison, elk, pronghorn, bighorn sheep, coyote, and wolves. Guides often refer to the area as the Serengeti of the West. Yellowstone Association Institute (406/848-2400, www.yellowstoneassociation.org), headquartered in the Lamar Valley, offers educational programs for all ages. For hikers, the 12-mile Pebble Creek Trail loops northeast to the Warm Creek Trailhead near the northeast park entrance. Nearby, a short 0.6-mile trail tours around Trout Lake and the Thunderer Cutoff Trail ascends 3.7 miles to Chaw Pass before dropping 15-miles down Cache Creek and the Lamar River to the Soda Butte Trailhead.

Pebble Creek squeezes its sunny campsites close together in two loops in a sparse aspen and lodgepole forest mixed with a wildflower meadow that blooms in July with cow parsnips, pink sticky geraniums, and yarrow. While views include neighboring campers, they also sweep up to the rugged, glacier-carved high peaks surrounding the campground. Even though the campground is removed from the more hectic areas of the park, vehicles stream by during the day. But at night, it quiets. The park service spruced up the campground's landscaping in 2013.

Campsites, facilities: The campground has 30 RV or tent campsites. RVs are limited to midsized rigs. Facilities include picnic tables, fire rings with grills, vault toilets (wheelchair-accessible), drinking water, garbage service, bear boxes, and campground hosts. Generators are not allowed. Leashed pets are permitted.

Reservations, fees: Reservations are not accepted. Sites cost $15. Shared hiker and biker campsites cost $5 per person. Cash or check. Open mid-June-September.

Directions: From Tower-Roosevelt Junction, drive 20 miles east on the northeast entrance road, or from the northeast entrance station, drive nine miles west. Turn north onto the dirt road and drive 0.1 mile to the campground. GPS Coordinates: N 44° 55.004' W 110° 6.839'

Contact: Yellowstone National Park, P.O. Box 168, Yellowstone, WY 82190-0168, 307/344-7381, www.nps.gov/yell.

11 SODA BUTTE

Scenic rating: 8

in the Absaroka-Beartooth Mountains in Gallatin National Forest

Sitting at 7,791 feet, Soda Butte Campground is the last Forest Service campground for those heading west into Yellowstone National Park, 4.5 miles from the northeastern entrance. Located one mile east of Cooke City, Montana with 10,000-foot-high Sheep Mountain to the north, the campground is convenient for hooking up with local outfitters for fly-fishing, hunting, or horse-packing trips into the Absaroka-Beartooth Wilderness about two miles north. Several nearby trails head into the wilderness, but mountain bikes are permitted only to the border. A 3.5-mile trail leads to Lady of the Lake. Other nearby trails climb to several strings of lakes in the wilderness. Rafters and kayakers head to the Clarks Fork of the Yellowstone for whitewater, and you can drive the scenic Beartooth Highway over and back in a day. A four-mile scenic drive also leads up a Forest Service road to Daisy Pass.

Thinning of beetle-killed trees has opened up much of this campground to sunlight and views. Cow parsnip, sticky pink geranium, lupine, and grass meadows cover most of the campground, interspersed with a few lodgepole pines and spruces that lend privacy to a few sites. The busy highway runs above the campground, but quiets at night, and you can hear Soda Butte Creek burbling. Neighboring campers are visible. Unfortunately, this campground was the site of a tragic bear attack on tenters in 2010, so it no longer permits tents or tent trailers.

Campsites, facilities: This campground has 27 RV and tent campsites. RVs are limited to 48 feet. Facilities include picnic tables, fire rings with grills, vault toilets (wheelchair-accessible), drinking water, bear boxes, garbage service, and campground hosts. Bring your own firewood. Leashed pets are permitted.

Reservations, fees: Reservations are not accepted. Campsites cost $9. An extra vehicle costs $3. Cash or check. Open July-September, depending on snow.

Directions: From Cooke City, drive the Beartooth Highway (Hwy. 212) about one mile east, or from the Chief Joseph Highway (Hwy. 296) junction drive 14 miles west. Turn south at milepost 4.5 into the campground. GPS Coordinates: N 45° 1.388' W 109° 54.947'

Contact: Gallatin National Forest, Gardiner Ranger Station, P.O. Box 5, Hwy. 89 S., Gardiner, MT 59030, 406/848-7375, www.fs.usda.gov/gallatin.

12 COLTER

Scenic rating: 9

in the Absaroka-Beartooth Mountains in Gallatin National Forest

At an elevation of 8,044 feet, Colter Campground sits two miles east of Cooke City, Montana, and six miles from the northeast entrance to Yellowstone National Park. Surrounding peaks climb over 10,000 feet high, and the 900,000-acre Absaroka-Beartooth Wilderness is two miles to the north. Hiking and mountain-biking trails depart 0.2 mile west. The route heads 3.5 miles to Lady of the Lake, and farther to other lakes in the wilderness area. Other nearby trails ascend into the wilderness to pass reams of lakes. Mountain bikers can only travel as far as the wilderness boundary. Rafters and kayakers head to the Clarks Fork of the Yellowstone River for whitewater, and you can drive the scenic Beartooth Highway over and back in a day. Outfitters for horseback riding, fishing, and hunting are available nearby.

Campsites are spread out in this sunny campground in a loose forest of lodgepoles, spruces, and subalpine firs surrounded by wildflower meadows and new growth forest. Sites in the open garner broad views of the meadows and mountains while others tuck into the shade and privacy of trees. Sites on the spur have more privacy than the loop. Noise from the road seeps into the campground, but the route is not a major trucking thoroughfare, so it quiets at night. Reconstruction following logging spruced up the campground with gravel parking pads, gravel campsites, and new facilities. Due a bear attack on tenters in 2010 in the neighboring campground, tents and tent trailers are no longer permitted.

Campsites, facilities: The campground has 18 RV or tent campsites. The largest gravel parking pad can fit RVs up to 66 feet, but the Forest Service recommends RV combinations less than 48 feet because of the access road. Facilities include picnic tables, fire rings with grills, bear boxes, vault toilets (wheelchair-accessible), drinking water, garbage service, and campground hosts. No firewood is available; bring your own. Leashed pets are permitted.

Reservations, fees: Reservations are not accepted. Campsites cost $9. An extra vehicle costs $3. Cash or check. Open July-September, depending on snow.

Directions: From Cooke City, drive the Beartooth Highway (Hwy. 212), about two miles east, or from the Chief Joseph Highway (Hwy. 296) junction, drive 13 miles west. Turn north at milepost 5.6 into the campground. (The sign is off the highway and difficult to see.) GPS Coordinates: N 45° 1.685' W 109° 53.645'

Contact: Gallatin National Forest, Gardiner Ranger Station, P.O. Box 5, Hwy. 89 S., Gardiner, MT 59030, 406/848-7375, www.fs.usda.gov/gallatin.

13 CHIEF JOSEPH

Scenic rating: 7

in the Absaroka-Beartooth Mountains in Gallatin National Forest

On the west end of the Beartooth Scenic Byway, Chief Joseph Campground, elevation 8,037 feet, sits four miles east of Cooke City, Montana, and seven miles from the northeast entrance to Yellowstone National Park. The campground is named after the Nez Perce chief who led his people across Idaho, Wyoming, and Montana while being chased by the U.S. Army. Across the road from the campground are interpretive sites for the Nez Perce National Historic Trail, wildlife nature trail, and Flume Interpretive Trail and Picnic Area. The latter also has a fishing pier, wheelchair-accessible trail, giant rushing waterfall, historical mining artifacts, view of Granite Peak (Montana's highest peak) and access to the Russell Creek Trail that enters the 900,000-acre Absaroka-Beartooth Wilderness. Nearby, a two-mile trail also leads to Curl Lake. Other short hikes lead to Rock Island Lake and Vernon Lake. Mountain bikers can access the local forest roads and trails only up to the wilderness boundary. Fishing, rafting, and kayaking is available in the Clarks Fork of the Yellowstone River, also across the highway from the campground, and you can drive the scenic Beartooth Highway over and back in a

The Flume Trail near Chief Joseph Campground leads to historic power generation sites.

© BECKY LOMAX

day. Outfitters for horseback riding, fishing, and hunting are available nearby.

Tucked into a mature lodgepole pine and spruce forest, Chief Joseph has more large trees than neighboring Soda Butte or Colter Campgrounds. Its one small loop sits close to the highway, so road noise is pervasive; however, it dwindles substantially at night. Reconstruction spruced up the campground with gravel parking pads and campsites plus new facilities, and hazard tree removal in 2013 allowed more sunlight into the shady campground. Tents and tent trailers are not permitted.

Campsites, facilities: The campground has six RV or tent campsites. The largest gravel parking pad can fit RVs up to 60 feet, but the Forest Service advises a limit of 42 feet because of the access road. Facilities include picnic tables, fire rings with grills, vault toilet (wheelchair-accessible), drinking water, bear boxes, garbage service, and campground hosts. No firewood is available; bring your own. Leashed pets are permitted.

Reservations, fees: Reservations are not accepted. Campsites cost $9. An extra vehicle costs $3. Cash or check. Open July-September.

Directions: From the Beartooth Scenic Byway (Highway 212), about four miles east of Cooke City or 11 miles west of the Chief Joseph Highway 296 junction, turn south at milepost 7 into the campground.

GPS Coordinates: N 45° 1.047' W 109° 52.247'

Contact: Gallatin National Forest, Gardiner Ranger Station, P.O. Box 5, Hwy. 89 S., Gardiner, MT 59030, 406/848-7375, www.fs.usda.gov/gallatin.

14 YELLOWSTONE HOLIDAY RV

Scenic rating: 8

on Hebgen Lake

Located on the north shore of Hebgen Lake at 6,555 feet, Yellowstone Holiday RV Campground sits a 15-minute drive from West Yellowstone and the west entrance to Yellowstone National Park. Flanked by the Madison Mountains, Montana's Hebgen Lake is popular for boating, paddling, waterskiing, sailing, and fishing. The campground includes a marina that has a cement boat ramp, boat slips, fuel, trailer parking, and a fish-cleaning station. The marina also rents fishing boats, kayaks, canoes, and paddleboats and sells fishing licenses.

The campground sits on a low open plateau on the lake, within view of the highway, lake, and mountains, which are snowcapped in June. Mowed lawn surrounds the sunny campsites with little shade or protection from afternoon winds. What you give up in privacy, you get back in a broad panorama of views. Most of the sites are back-ins near the water; pull-through sites are behind a set of cabins near the highway. Sites 6, 8, 9, and 11 claim prime waterfront.

Campsites, facilities: The campground has 36 RV campsites. Eight pull-through sites can accommodate big rigs. Hookups include water, sewer, and electricity up to 50 amps. Facilities include picnic tables, fire rings, flush toilets, showers, launderette, general store, propane, marina, horseshoes, volleyball, swimming beach, and camper kitchen. Leashed dogs are permitted.

Reservations, fees: Reservations are accepted. RV sites cost $43-60. Rates less during shoulder seasons. Add on 7 percent Montana bed tax. Cash, check, or credit card. Open mid-May-early September.

Directions: From West Yellowstone, drive north on Highway 191 for eight miles and then turn west onto Highway 287 for five miles. The entrance sits on the south side of the road.

GPS Coordinates: N 44° 48.202' W 111° 12.950'

Contact: Yellowstone Holiday, 16990 Hebgen Lake Rd., West Yellowstone, MT 59758, 406/646-4242 or 877/646-4242, www.yellowstoneholiday.com.

15 RAINBOW POINT

🏊 ⛵ 🚲 🎣 🐕 ♿ 🚐 ⛺

Scenic rating: 8

on Hebgen Lake in Gallatin National Forest

Located at 6,550 feet, Rainbow Point Campground sits on Rainbow Bay, an east arm of Montana's Hebgen Lake, the site of Montana's largest earthquake in 1959. From the beach at the campground, views look northwest to the Madison Range. The campground, about 10 miles north of West Yellowstone and 11 miles from the west entrance to Yellowstone National Park, has a boat launch, which includes a cement ramp, docks, and trailer parking. The lake is popular for swimming, paddling, waterskiing, boating, and fishing—known for its dry fly trout fishing (Montana fishing license needed). Rainbow Bay is more sheltered from winds than the main lake, making it more appealing for canoeing and kayaking. The 16-mile-long lake is also surrounded by summer homes.

Four loops of of the quiet campsites tuck into a thick shady forest of tall lodgepole pines that admit only filtered sunlight. Tree trunks act as privacy fences between the close campsites because little understory can grow beneath the trees. The loops are set back from the lake with only a few sites at the front of loops A and B catching glimpses of blue water across the road and between the trees. Paths lead from the loops to the beach. Big, flat spaces for tents are available.

Campsites, facilities: The campground has 85 RV and tent campsites. RVs are limited to 40 feet. Facilities include picnic tables, fire rings with grills, vault and pit toilets, drinking water, garbage service, electrical hookups at 15 campsites in Loop C, bear boxes, boat launch, firewood for sale, and campground hosts. Leashed pets are permitted. A wheelchair-accessible toilet and one campsite are available.

Reservations, fees: Reservations are accepted (877/444-6777, www.recreation.gov).

Campsites cost $16, plus $6 more for those with electrical hookups. An extra vehicle costs $6. Cash or check. Open mid-May-mid-September.

Directions: From West Yellowstone, drive north on Highway 191 for five miles and turn west onto the two-lane paved Rainbow Point Road (Forest Road 6954) for 3.2 miles. Then turn north onto the gravel Rainbow Point Road (Forest Road 6952) for 1.7 miles. The road veers right to the boat launch, but continue straight to reach the campground. GPS Coordinates: N 44° 46.725' W 111° 10.466'

Contact: Gallatin National Forest, Hebgen Lake District Office, P.O. Box 520, West Yellowstone, MT 59758, 406/823-6961.

16 BAKER'S HOLE

🥾 🚲 ⛵ 🎣 🐕 ♿ 🚐 ⛺

Scenic rating: 7

on the Madison River in Gallatin National Forest

Baker's Hole Campground, which sits at 6,600 feet, is three miles north of West Yellowstone, Montana and four miles from the west entrance to Yellowstone National Park. The campground is strung along a narrow strip of forest in between the highway and the Madison River. In this stretch, the river slows to a crawl as it winds in convoluted oxbows through willow wetlands that provide habitat for moose and birds, plus churn out hordes of mosquitoes. The Madison River is famed for its trout fishing, and West Yellowstone is the headquarters for fishing outfitters. The 1.4-mile Riverside Trail for mountain bikers and hikers tours the river from West Yellowstone.

Located adjacent to the highway, the campground picks up vehicle noise—especially from commercial trucks. Across the road is the Yellowstone Airport, which sees three commercial flights arrive and depart daily in the summer. A paved road loops through the campground, which is forested with short lodgepole pines and blooming with fireweed. Some campsites have views of the mountains, and several campsites overlook the river. Sites, which vary from shady to sunny, are spread out for privacy, but the lack of undergrowth means you'll see a neighboring campsite or two.

Campsites, facilities: The campground has 73 RV and tent campsites. RVs are limited to 75 feet. Facilities include picnic tables, fire rings with grills, electrical hookups at 33 campsites, vault and pit toilets (wheelchair-accessible), drinking water, garbage service, bear boxes, firewood for sale, campground hosts, and a fishing platform. Leashed pets are permitted.

Reservations, fees: Reservations are not accepted. Campsites cost $14, plus $6 for those sites with electricity. An extra vehicle costs $6. Cash or check. Open mid-May-mid-September.

Directions: From West Yellowstone, drive north on Highway 191 for almost three miles. At milepost 2.9, turn east onto the paved road into the campground.

GPS Coordinates: N 44° 42.249' W 111° 6.083'

Contact: Gallatin National Forest, Hebgen Lake District Office, P.O. Box 520, West Yellowstone, MT 59758, 406/823-6961.

17 MADISON ARM RESORT

Scenic rating: 7

on Hebgen Lake

Madison Arm Resort sits on the south shore of the Madison Arm of Montana's Hebgen Lake at 6,557 feet in elevation. Its sandy beach and marina tuck into a small bay protected by islands of sand that grow larger as the water level in the lake drops throughout the summer. The lake is popular for boating, paddling, fishing, waterskiing, sailing, and swimming. Anglers go after rainbow and brown trout (Montana fishing license needed), and the resort rents out 14-foot aluminum boats with eight horsepower motors, canoes, paddleboats, kayaks, and water-bikes. A buoyed swimming area is available, along with a cement boat ramp and boat slips. The store sells fishing licenses. Bicyclists ride the dirt forest roads in the area. The resort sits 8.5 miles from West Yellowstone and 9.5 miles from the west entrance to Yellowstone National Park.

A forest of tall lodgepole pines surrounds the campground. Tent campsites are along the waterfront between trees, and RV campsites sit back in the trees and open areas. The quiet campground packs its campsites close together; privacy is available only inside the tent or RV. Also, back-in sites can pose difficulties for some RVs squeezing in. The resort tends to get families returning year after year.

Campsites, facilities: The resort has 22 tent campsites and 52 RV campsites with hookups for water, sewer, and up to 30-amp electricity. Pull-through sites can fit large RVs. Facilities include picnic tables, fire rings, flush toilets, showers, launderette, convenience store, propane, firewood for sale, boat rentals, and wireless Internet. Leashed pets are permitted.

Reservations, fees: Reservations are accepted. RV hookups cost $39-42. Tent campsites cost $29. Rates are for two people. Each additional person incurs $5. Add on the 7 percent Montana bed tax. Cash, check, or credit card. Open mid-May-September.

Directions: From West Yellowstone, drive north on Highway 191 for three miles. Turn west onto the dusty gravel Madison Arm Road (Forest Road 291) for 5.3 miles to the resort entrance on the right.

GPS Coordinates: N 44° 44.142' W 111° 11.159'

Contact: Madison Arm Resort, 5475 Madison Arm Rd., West Yellowstone, MT 59758, 406/646-9328, www.madisonarmresort.com.

18 LONESOMEHURST

Scenic rating: 8

on Hebgen Lake in Gallatin National Forest

Located at 6,550 feet, Lonesomehurst Campground sits on the South Fork Arm, a narrow bay on the southern end of Montana's Hebgen Lake. The long beach offers plenty of places to swim and beach boats. The boat launch includes a cement ramp, docks, and trailer parking. The lake is popular for swimming, paddling, waterskiing, boating, and fishing, and known for its dry fly trout fishing (Montana fishing license needed). South Fork Arm is more sheltered from winds than the main lake, making it more appealing for canoeing and kayaking. The campground sits about 10 miles from of West Yellowstone and 11 miles from the west entrance to Yellowstone National Park.

Scatter conifers dot the sunny, quiet campground surrounded by arid grass and sagebrush meadows. Campsites along the east side of the one campground loop overlook the lake, and all campsites have territorial views, which include the Madison Range across the lake. The open terrain means that you'll see neighboring campers.

Campsites, facilities: The campground has 27 RV and tent campsites. Five sites have electrical hookups. RVs are limited to 45 feet. Facilities include picnic tables, fire rings with grills, vault and pit toilets (wheelchair-accessible), drinking water, garbage service, bear boxes, boat launch, firewood for sale, and campground hosts. Leashed pets are permitted.

Reservations, fees: Reservations are accepted (877/444-6777, www.recreation.gov). Campsites cost $16, plus $6 more for those with electrical hookups. An extra vehicle costs $6. Cash or check. Open mid-May-mid-September.

Directions: From West Yellowstone, drive Highway 20 for seven miles west and turn north onto Denny Creek Road. Drive 3.5 miles, jogging right and left around farms to the campground entrance on the right.

GPS Coordinates: N 44° 44.063' W 111° 13.903'
Contact: Gallatin National Forest, Hebgen Lake District Office, P.O. Box 520, West Yellowstone, MT 59758, 406/823-6961.

19 LIONSHEAD RV PARK

Scenic rating: 7

outside West Yellowstone

At 6,718 feet in Montana, Lionshead RV Park is seven miles west of West Yellowstone and eight miles from the west entrance to Yellowstone National Park. For those looking for the convenience of being near town with its activities, but who want a place less crowded and noisy, this campground provides an alternative to the West Yellowstone hubbub. The campground is behind a motel and restaurant. Denny Creek flows past the back of the campground, with two bridges allowing access to a trail and constructed fishing ponds. Other fishing is available within 10 miles at Hebgen Lake or the Madison River. Horseback rides are nearby, too.

Most of the RV area is open without trees, but the tent sites rim the perimeter shaded in pines. A gravel road loops through the campground, which has mowed-lawn campsites set very close together with little privacy and pull-through sites available. The proximity to the highway means vehicle noise enters the campground.

Campsites, facilities: This campground has 175 RV campsites and 20 tent campsites. RVs are limited to 80 feet. Hookups include water, sewer, and electricity up to 50 amps. Facilities include picnic tables, fire rings, grills, flush toilets (wheelchair-accessible), showers, drinking water, launderette, convenience store, propane, playground, pizza café, and camping kitchen. Leashed pets are permitted.

Reservations, fees: Reservations are accepted. RV hookups cost $35-70. Tent campsites

cost $25-35. Rates are for four people. For additional adults, add $6 each, and for kids add $4 each. Additional vehicles cost $15. Add on 7 percent Montana bed tax. Cash, check, or credit card. Open late May-mid-September.
Directions: From West Yellowstone, drive seven miles west on Highway 20 to the campground, on the north side of the road.
GPS Coordinates: N 44° 41.242' W 111° 15.124'
Contact: Lionshead RV Resort, 1545 Targhee Pass Hwy., West Yellowstone, MT 59758, 406/646-7662 or 877/935-5690, www.lionsheadrv.com.

20 YELLOWSTONE KOA

Scenic rating: 7

outside West Yellowstone

Sitting at 6,590 feet outside West Yellowstone, Montana, the Yellowstone KOA offers a place to camp away from the crowded West Yellowstone streets but convenient for exploring the town and Yellowstone National Park. The west entrance to the park sits seven miles east of the campground. Horseback rides and weekend rodeos are available nearby, along with fishing at Hebgen Lake or the Madison River.

The campground fills every niche of the property with close-set campsites. With its location outside of town and surroundings of open prairie, views encompass the mountains of the Madison Range. Pines near almost every campsite provide shade for the sunny, mowed-lawn campground, and tent sites are divided with split rail fences and pines. You can hear vehicles passing on the two-lane highway, but traffic dwindles at night. A paved road loops through the campground, but the parking pads are gravel.
Campsites, facilities: This KOA has 168 RV campsites and 84 tent campsites. Some of the campsites can accommodate big rigs, and

hookups include sewer, water, and electricity up to 50 amps. Thirteen tent sites also have water and electricity. Facilities include picnic tables, fire rings, flush toilets (wheelchair-accessible), showers, drinking water, launderette, convenience store, indoor pool, hot tub, camping kitchen, pancake breakfasts, nightly barbecue dinners, espresso kiosk, mini-golf, playground, basketball, dog walk, game room, surrey bike rentals, propane, and wireless Internet. Leashed pets are permitted.
Reservations, fees: Reservations are accepted. RV hookups cost $32-74. Tent campsites cost $22-41. Rates cover two people. Each extra person incurs $5. Kids under five stay for free. Add on 7 percent Montana bed tax. Cash, check, or credit card. Open late May-September.
Directions: From West Yellowstone, drive Highway 20 west for six miles to the campground entrance to the north.
GPS Coordinates: N 44° 41.204' W 111° 13.008'
Contact: Yellowstone Park KOA, 3305 Targhee Pass Hwy., West Yellowstone, MT 59758, 406/646-7606 or 800/562-7591, www.yellowstonekoa.com.

21 RUSTIC WAGON RV CAMPGROUND

Scenic rating: 4

in West Yellowstone

In West Yellowstone, Montana, the Rustic Wagon RV Campground sits on the opposite side of town from the busy shopping, restaurant, and tourist district. Yet, with town being only seven blocks wide, it still offers the convenience of walking to the visitors center, Yellowstone IMAX Theatre, Grizzly and Wolf Discovery Center, and Museum of the Yellowstone. The town is also headquarters for outfitters for horseback riding, white-water rafting, and fishing. The west entrance gate to Yellowstone National Park is one mile to the east. Hiking four miles or mountain biking 1.4 miles is available on the Riverside Trail, which tours along the Madison River about 1.5 miles east of the campground. Trout fishing is also available in the Madison River.

With its location on the west end of town, the campground is removed from the busy crowds downtown and quieter than the town's east side. The narrow campsites are close together. Spruce and pine trees help give it seclusion from the surrounding residential and commercial properties. Vehicle noise from the highway seeps in, but its side street is not busy. Tent campsites are in a grassy area.

Campsites, facilities: The campground has 45 RV campsites and 10 tent campsites. RV combinations are limited to 70 feet, and hookups have sewer, water, and electricity up to 50 amps. Facilities include picnic tables, flush toilets, showers, launderette, cable TV, patios, wireless Internet, horseshoes, playground, and basketball. Leashed pets are allowed in RV sites, but not in tent sites.

Reservations, fees: Reservations are accepted. RV hookup sites cost $46-50. Tent sites cost $39. Rates cover two people. For each additional person older than three, add $4. Add on 10 percent tax. Cash, check, or credit card. Open year-round with pull-through sites plowed in winter.

Directions: In West Yellowstone at the junction of Highways 20 and 191, drive west on Highway 20 (Firehole Avenue) and then angle north, staying on Highway 20 as it departs Firehole Avenue. Drive three blocks, turn north onto Iris Street, and immediately turn right onto Gibbon Street. The campground entrance is on the left.
GPS Coordinates: N 44° 39.856' W 111° 6.721'

Contact: Rustic Wagon RV Campground and Cabins, 637 Hwy. 20, West Yellowstone, MT 59758, 406/646-7387, www.rusticwagonrv. com.

22 WAGON WHEEL RV

Scenic rating: 4

in West Yellowstone

At 6,663 feet in elevation, the Wagon Wheel RV Campground sits in downtown West Yellowstone, Montana surrounded by residential and commercial properties. The campground spans the length of one block. It is three blocks from the center of town and shopping, restaurants, groceries, and gas. The only reason for staying in town is for the convenience of walking to the visitors center, Yellowstone IMAX Theatre, Grizzly and Wolf Discovery Center, and Museum of the Yellowstone. The campground also sits less than one mile from the west entrance to Yellowstone National Park. Hiking four miles or mountain biking 1.4 miles is available on the Riverside Trail, which tours along the Madison River less than a mile east of the campground. Anglers head to the Madison River for trout fishing. The town is headquarters for outfitters for horseback riding, white-water rafting, and fishing.

The location in downtown West Yellowstone means the campground comes with traffic noise and crowds—although its location off the main drags gives it some seclusion and quiet. The campsites are narrow and squeezed close together. Tall spruces and pines grant shade and a semblance of privacy to the RV sites, which have gravel pull-through or back-in parking pads and patios. Grassy tent sites are in a private area.

Campsites, facilities: The campground has 36 RV campsites and 15 tent campsites. RV combinations are limited to 60 feet. Hookups are available for water, sewer, and electricity up to 30 amps. Facilities include picnic tables, flush toilets, showers, drinking water, launderette, recreation room, cable TV, and wireless Internet. Leashed pets are allowed in the RV sites, but not in the tent sites.

Reservations, fees: Reservations are accepted. RV hookup sites cost $46-50. Tent sites cost $39. Rates cover two people. For each additional person older than three, add $4. Add on 10 percent tax. Cash, check, or credit card. Open mid-May-September.

Directions: In the center of West Yellowstone at the junction of Highway 20 and Highway 191, drive west on Highway 20 (Firehole Avenue) for three blocks. Turn right (north) onto Faithful Street and drive two blocks to Gibbon Avenue. Turn left and immediately left again into the campground.

GPS Coordinates: N 44° 39.829' W 111° 6.408'

Contact: Wagon Wheel RV Campground and Cabins, 408 Gibbon Ave., West Yellowstone, MT 59758, 406/646-7872, www.wagonwheelrv.com.

23 HIDEAWAY RV PARK

Scenic rating: 7

in West Yellowstone

Located 10 blocks from the west entrance to Yellowstone National Park, Hideaway RV Park, at 6,664 feet, allows convenient access to the park and the town of West Yellowstone, Montana. Shopping, restaurants, the visitors center, the Yellowstone IMAX Theatre, the Grizzly and Wolf Discovery Center, and the Museum of the Yellowstone are within three to seven blocks. The town is also headquarters for outfitters for horseback riding, white-water rafting, and fishing. The Riverside Trail along the Madison River offers hiking (four miles) and mountain biking (1.4 miles) about one mile east of the campground. Trout fishing is available in the Madison River. The campground is one block from a city park with a children's playground and a half block from a launderette.

Hideaway is West Yellowstone's smallest campground, and its location on the north edge of town in a residential area removes it from the busy tourist blocks. A gravel road loops through the campground, which has gravel pull-through or back-in parking pads. Tall conifers lend partial shade to many of the campsites, which are close together.

Campsites, facilities: The campground has 14 RV campsites and one tent campsite. RVs are limited to 45 feet, and hookups include water, sewer, and electricity up to 50 amps. Facilities include picnic tables, flush toilets, showers, patios, cable TV, and wireless Internet. Leashed pets are permitted.

Reservations, fees: Reservations are accepted. RV sites cost $32-37. The tent site costs $24. Rates cover two people. Extra people over six years old incur $3 each. Add on 10 percent tax. Cash, check, or credit card. Open mid-May-September.

Directions: From downtown West Yellowstone at the intersection of Highways 20 and 191, drive west on Highway 20 (Firehole Avenue) for two blocks. Turn north onto Electric Street and drive 2.5 blocks to the entrance on the left.

GPS Coordinates: N 44° 39.862' W 111° 6.263'

Contact: Hideaway RV Park, 320 Electric St., West Yellowstone, MT 59758, 406/646-9049, www.hideawayrv.com.

24 PONY EXPRESS RV PARK

Scenic rating: 4

in West Yellowstone

The Pony Express RV Park, at 6,668 feet, sits literally on the edge of West Yellowstone, Montana across the street from Yellowstone National Park. The west entrance gate to the park is five blocks away, along with the visitors center, Yellowstone IMAX Theatre, Grizzly and Wolf Discovery Center, and Museum of the Yellowstone. Shopping, restaurants, gas, and groceries are also within five blocks. The town is headquarters for outfitters for horseback riding, white-water rafting, and fishing.

The Riverside Trail along the Madison River offers hiking (four miles) and mountain biking (1.4 miles) less than 0.5 mile east of the campground. Trout fishing is also available in the Madison River.

Located at a motel, this small campground squeezes campsites close together in an open lot. Some of the campsites look across Boundary Street into the park, but the view is of a forest—no geysers, mountains, or rivers. The territory comes with a certain amount of noise because of its location in downtown, but perched on the edge of town off the main drags, it is quieter than other locations. A handful of trees dot the campground with minimal shade.

Campsites, facilities: The campground has 16 RV campsites. RVs are limited to 38 feet. Hookups include sewer, water, and electricity up to 50 amps. Facilities include picnic tables, flush toilets, showers, launderette, wireless Internet, cable TV, and pull-through sites. Leashed pets are permitted.

Reservations, fees: Reservations are accepted. Campsites cost $40 ($30 in winter). Add on 10 percent tax. Open April-November with full hookups and during winter for dry camping.

Directions: In downtown West Yellowstone, from the intersection of Highway 20 and Highway 191, turn east on Firehole Avenue and drive 1.5 blocks. The entrance is on the left.

GPS Coordinates: N 44° 39.742' W 111° 5.916'

Contact: Pony Express Motel and RV Park, 4 Firehole Ave., West Yellowstone, MT 59758, 406/646-9411 or 800/217-4613, www.yellowstonevacations.com.

25 YELLOWSTONE CABINS AND RV PARK

Scenic rating: 4

in West Yellowstone

At 6,669 feet, Yellowstone Cabins and RV Park offer the conveniences of being right in the middle of West Yellowstone, Montana. The west entrance gate to the Yellowstone National Park is less than one mile west, and you can walk to the visitors center, Yellowstone IMAX Theatre, Grizzly and Wolf Discovery Center, and Museum of the Yellowstone. Shopping, restaurants, gas, and groceries are also within five blocks. The town is headquarters for outfitters for horseback riding, white-water rafting, and fishing. The Riverside Trail along the Madison River offers hiking (four miles) and mountain biking (1.4 miles) less than 0.5 mile east of the campground. Trout fishing is also available in the Madison River.

Conifers shade this campground that is connected with a small cabin and motel complex. The campsites are gravel and grass. Given its location on the highway, traffic is a constant sound.

Campsites, facilities: The campground has eight RV campsites. RVs are limited to 38 feet. Hookups include sewer, water, able TV, and electricity up to 50 amps. Facilities include flush toilets and showers. Leashed pets are permitted.

Reservations, fees: Reservations are accepted. Campsites cost $35. Add on 10 percent tax. Open May-mid-October.

Directions: In downtown West Yellowstone, from the intersection of Highway 20 and Highway 191, drive west on Highway 20 (Firehole Avenue) for four blocks and turn south into the campground right after Geyser Street.

GPS Coordinates: N 44° 39.762' W 111° 6.537'

Contact: Yellowstone Cabins and RV Park, 504 Highway 20, West Yellowstone, MT 59758, 406/646-9350 or 866/646-9350, www.yellowstonecabinsandandrv.com

26 YELLOWSTONE GRIZZLY RV PARK

Scenic rating: 4

in West Yellowstone

Located on West Yellowstone's southern

edge away from the crowded tourist streets, Yellowstone Grizzly RV—the area's newest campground—is bordered on two sides by Montana's Gallatin National Forest. The west entrance to Yellowstone National Park, shopping, restaurants, visitors center, the Yellowstone IMAX Theatre, the Grizzly and Wolf Discovery Center, Museum of the Yellowstone, and all outfitters for rafting, horseback riding, and fishing are within five blocks. The Riverside Trail along the Madison River offers hiking (four miles) and mountain biking (1.4 miles) about one mile east of the campground. Trout fishing is available in the Madison River.

The campground—West Yellowstone's largest—was expanded in 2006. Landscaped gardens, lawns, aspens, and lodgepole pines cover the campground, but the trees are still young and provide only partial shade. The RV sites, with paved back-in or pull-through parking pads, cement walkways, and patios, are positioned right next to each other, but they are roomy enough for slide-outs and awnings. The tent campsites ring a grassy area across from the playground and clubhouse, which has outdoor kitchen sinks.

Campsites, facilities: The campground has 261 RV campsites and 16 tent campsites. RVs are limited to 80 feet, and hookups include for water, sewer, and electricity up to 100 amps. Facilities include picnic tables, barbecue grills (bring your own charcoal), flush toilets (wheelchair-accessible), showers, drinking water, patios, cable TV, wireless Internet, dog walk, game room, playground, convenience store, launderette, and horseshoes. Leashed pets are permitted.

Reservations, fees: Reservations are accepted. RV campsites cost $55-65 for up to six people with each extra person costing $5. Tent campsites cost $40 for four people with each extra person costing $10. A 10 percent tax is added on. Cash, check, or credit card. Off-season rates are lower in May and October. Open May-late October.

Directions: In downtown West Yellowstone from the junction of Highway 20 and Highway 191, drive west on Highway 20 for two

blocks to Electric Street. Turn south and drive 0.5 mile. The campground entrance sits on the west side of the road opposite Gray Wolf Avenue.

GPS Coordinates: N 44° 39.330' W 111° 6.271'

Contact: Yellowstone Grizzly RV Park, 210 S. Electric St., West Yellowstone, MT 59758, 406/646-4466, www.grizzlyrv.com.

27 MADISON

Scenic rating: 9

on the lower Grand Loop in Yellowstone National Park

BEST (

Centrally located in Yellowstone National Park, Madison Campground offers the quickest access to the big geyser basins, including Old Faithful 16 miles south. Between the campground and Old Faithful, basins line up with geysers, mud pots, hot springs, and fumaroles. Firehole Lake Drive tours past the Great Fountain Geyser, which spurts 200 feet high, and Fountain Paint Pots contain multicolored blurping mud. Upper, Lower, and Biscuit Geyser Basins link by boardwalks to colorful, steaming hot pools. The Old Faithful basin contains the most geysers and volcanic features, including the famous Old Faithful Geyser and the Old Faithful Visitor Education Center. Mountain bikers can ride several trails connecting geyser basins, including Fountain Flat Drive to Fairy Falls Trailhead and the Daisy Geyser cut-off to Biscuit Basin. The campground sits at 6,806 feet near the confluence of the Gibbon and Firehole Rivers, where they become the Madison River, each with superb fly-fishing. Near the campground, bison or elk usually hang out in the meadows along the river, accessed via a network of trails from the campground. In fall, the male elk bugle as they round up their harems. Hikers can climb three miles up Purple Mountain for a view of the Firehole and lower Gibbon Valleys.

The Madison River attracts anglers for trout fishing.

Madison Campground has ten loops, in a loose forest of tall pine trees for partial shade. With no understory—only tree trunks—campsites are visible to each other. At the campground's west end, the tenting G and H loops are more open and sunny, but also garner peek-a-boo views of National Park Mountain. Paved roads with paved parking pads (back-in and pull-through) weave through the campground. Although the campground picks up daytime traffic noise from the busy west entrance road, it quiets after dark.

Campsites, facilities: Madison has 278 campsites—213 for RVs or tents and 65 for tents only. RVs are limited to 40 feet. Facilities include picnic tables, fire rings with grills, flush toilets, drinking water, sporadic tent pads, bear boxes, garbage services, disposal station, firewood and ice for sale, amphitheater and ranger station for interpretive programs, and campground hosts. Leashed pets are permitted. A wheelchair-accessible toilet and one campsite are available.

Reservations, fees: Reservations are recommended (307/344-7901 same day, 307/344-7311 or 866/439-7375 advance, www.YellowstoneNationalParkLodges.com). Sites cost $23, plus sales tax and utility fee. Shared hiker and biker campsites cost $5 per person. Cash, check, or credit card. Open May-late October.

Directions: From the west entrance to Yellowstone National Park, drive 14 miles east on the west entrance road to the campground entrance is on the south side of the road. GPS Coordinates: N 44° 38.738' W 110° 51.672'

Contact: Yellowstone National Park, P.O. Box 168, Yellowstone, WY 82190-0168, 307/344-7381, www.nps.gov/yell.

28 NORRIS

Scenic rating: 8

on the lower Grand Loop in Yellowstone National Park

Sitting at 7,555 feet on the upper Grand Loop Road's southwest corner, Norris Campground sits near Norris Geyser Basin. A 10-minute walk connects the campground with the basin's boardwalks and trails. The geyser basin houses hot pools, steam vents, and Steamboat—the world's tallest geyser, which spouts to 380 feet. Porcelain Basin loops 1.6-mile through an austere landscape of colorful minerals, and Back Basin is a two-mile loop that houses the geysers, including the predictable Echinus, which begins eruptions with boiling water filling its basin. At the campground, the Museum of the National Park Ranger contains exhibits about early rangers, and anglers can fish for small brook trout in the confluence of the Gibbon River and Solfatara Creek. Hiking trails depart from the campground east to Ice Lake (4.3 miles) and north along Solfatara Creek. Another Ice Lake trailhead sits 3.5 miles east of Norris Junction. Don't carry a fishing rod to the barren lake.

Plan on arriving by 11am in midsummer to claim a site at this popular campground. Set in a loose pine and fir forest where you can see plenty of neighboring campers and surrounded by the large Norris meadows, the campground provides an excellent location for spotting moose, elk, bears, and bison. Choose from among sunny or shaded campsites. Large, flat spaces are available for tents at some sites. Loop A offers campsites that are more level and overlook the meadows while Loops B and C pitch on the hillside, sometimes posing a challenge for RVs.

Campsites, facilities: Norris has 100 RV or tent campsites. Two campsites are available for RVs up to 50 feet; five sites are available for RVs up to 30 feet. Three campsites are walk-in tent sites. Facilities include picnic tables, fire rings with grills, flush toilets, drinking water, bear boxes, garbage service, amphitheater for interpretive programs, and firewood and ice for sale. Leashed pets are permitted. A wheelchair-accessible toilet and campsites are available.

Reservations, fees: Reservations are not accepted. Campsites cost $20. Shared hiker and biker campsites cost $5 per person. Cash or check. Open mid-May-September.

Directions: From Norris Junction, drive 0.8 mile north on the Grand Loop Road, or from Mammoth, drive 20.2 miles south. Turn east and drive 0.2 mile into the campground. GPS Coordinates: N 44° 44.269' W 110° 41.623'

Contact: Yellowstone National Park, P.O. Box 168, Yellowstone, WY 82190-0168, 307/344-7381, www.nps.gov/yell.

29 CANYON

Scenic rating: 9

at Grand Canyon of the Yellowstone in Yellowstone National Park

BEST (

Canyon Campground, elevation 7,944 feet, sits just off the busy junction of Grand Loop Road and Norris Canyon Road at Canyon Village, which houses the Canyon Visitor Education Center, groceries, shopping, post office, restaurants, gas, vehicle repairs, and disposal station. The education center features live earthquake monitoring and other exhibits. The main attraction is the Grand Canyon of the Yellowstone, an immense colorful 1,200-foot-deep chasm with the Yellowstone River plunging down two huge waterfalls. Trails rim both sides of the canyon with overlooks at several points, accessed via connected trails or separate parking accesses. Multiple switchbacks and stairways climb down to platforms at the falls. Artist Point is the most photographed viewpoint. A bike lane runs on the road from the campground to canyon. Nearby, the trailhead goes two miles to Cascade Lake and further to Grebe Lake. At Dunraven Pass, hikers can climb the tallest peak in Yellowstone—Mt. Washburn. An evening drive south through Hayden Valley provides wildlife watching for bison, elk and sometimes wolves. Upstream and downstream from the canyon, the Yellowstone River offers fishing, but check restrictions as some sections are closed to fishing. Horseback trail rides are also available from Canyon Village.

The large Canyon Campground winds up a lodgepole forested hill with eleven loops. Four loops are for tents only. Leveling RVs and fitting into tight spots can prove challenging. Some private nooks tuck into the trees, but without shrubs neighbors are visible through the trunks. Although all loops have restrooms, showers (two included for each site with fee) are located in the launderette at the bottom of the hill, 0.75-mile away from Loops K and L. In midsummer, the campground fills every day; plan to arrive by 11am to claim a campsite.

Campsites, facilities: The campground has 200 RV and tent campsites and 73 campsites for tents only. RVs over 30 feet can fit in a limited number of campsites, but make reservations for large rigs to get a site. Facilities include picnic tables, fire rings with grills, flush toilets, drinking water, bear boxes, showers, firewood and ice for sale, amphitheater for interpretive programs, garbage service, launderette, disposal station, and campground hosts. Leashed pets are permitted. Wheelchair-accessible toilets and campsites are available.

Reservations, fees: Reservations are recommended (307/344-7901 for same day, 307/344-7311 or 866/439-7375 for advance, www.YellowstoneNationalParkLodges.com). Campsites cost $27, plus sales tax and a utility fee. Shared hiker and biker campsites cost $5 per person. Cash, check, or credit card. Open June-early September.

Directions: From Canyon Village Junction, drive 0.2 mile east on North Rim Drive. Turn left into the campground.

GPS Coordinates: N 44° 44.157' W 110° 29.319'

Contact: Yellowstone National Park, P.O. Box 168, Yellowstone, WY 82190-0168, 307/344-7381, www.nps.gov/yell.

30 FISHING BRIDGE RV

Scenic rating: 7

on Yellowstone Lake in Yellowstone National Park

At 7,751 feet in thick forest, Fishing Bridge flanks the north side of Yellowstone Lake. Contrary to its name, fishing is not permitted from the famous Fishing Bridge on the Yellowstone River; however, it is allowed about one mile downstream and on Yellowstone Lake. All native species are catch-and-release only. The one-mile Pelican Creek Nature Trail tours a marsh along Pelican Creek, where you can see American white pelicans and end at a black-sand beach on the lake. Fishing Bridge also has a grocery store, visitors center, restaurant, gas, and RV repair shop. A boat launch is available five miles southwest at Bridge Bay, although hand-carried watercraft can launch from picnic areas on the lake's north shore. Boat permits, available at visitors centers and backcountry offices, are required.

In a thick lodgepole forest, a paved road passes through the long campground loops,

© BECKY LOMAX

The Yellowstone River flows through the Grand Canyon of the Yellowstone and tumbles with several falls.

which all have paved, back-in campsites. Sites are close together, so privacy is minimal. Small patches of grass between the parking pads make up the campsites. Some campsites have one fir or lodgepole pine tree that offers a little shade; others are open and sunny. Little log tipis are available in a kids' play area. Located back in the woods, the campground is quiet once the generators turn off. The air at Fishing Bridge smells of sulfur.

Campsites, facilities: Fishing Bridge has 346 RV campsites for hard-sided vehicles only. No popup tent trailers or tent campers are allowed. RVs are limited to 40 feet. Hookups include water, sewer, and electricity up to 50 amps. Facilities include flush toilets (wheelchair-accessible), coin-op showers, launderette, garbage service, firewood for sale, and disposal station. Leashed pets are permitted.

Reservations, fees: Reservations are recommended (307/344-7901 for same day, 307/344-7311 or 866/439-7375 for advance, www.YellowstoneNationalParkLodges.com). RV sites cost $50, plus sales tax and a utility fee. Cash, check, or credit card. Open late May–late September.

Directions: From Yellowstone's east entrance, drive 27 miles west on the east entrance road, or from Fishing Bridge Junction, drive one mile east. Turn north into the campground. GPS Coordinates: N 44° 33.820' W 110° 22.167'

Contact: Yellowstone National Park, P.O. Box 168, Yellowstone, WY 82190-0168, 307/344-7381, www.nps.gov/yell.

31 BRIDGE BAY

Scenic rating: 9

on Yellowstone Lake in Yellowstone National Park

Located at 7,784 feet on the west side of Yellowstone Lake, Bridge Bay Campground and Marina sits on an idyllic sheltered lagoon off Bridge Bay. Bridge Bay includes a ranger station, store, and boat launch with docks, boat slips, trailer parking, and cement ramps. One-hour tours of Yellowstone Lake are available several times daily; the *Lake Queen* loops around Stevenson Island to see bald eagles and ospreys fish. Boat rentals (rowboats and motorboats), charter fishing and tour services, and a shuttle service to backcountry campsites are available. Paddlers will enjoy the shelter of the lagoon and bay, but should plan to avoid the lake's notorious afternoon winds. All boats require permits, available at the marina; no waterskiing or Jet Skiing. Separate one-mile trails for hikers and mountain bikers lead to Natural Bridge, a rhyolite rock arch 51 feet above Bridge Creek. You can climb to the top of the arch, but to protect the feature should not cross it. Bicyclists can also tour the scenic lakeshore drive around Gull Point.

Bridge Bay is Yellowstone's largest campground; in high summer it can hold a population bigger than many small towns in the Northern Rockies. Its huge front loops circle on a gentle, sunny sloped meadow above the lake. Many campsites overlook the water and Absaroka Mountains in the distance, but also include view of neighboring campers. Expect June's green grassy meadows to turn brown by August. Denser conifers cast more shade on back loop campsites. While Bridge Bay bustles during the day with marina traffic, it quiets at night.

Campsites, facilities: The campground has 432 RV or tent campsites. RV combinations are limited to 40 feet. As large RV parking pads are limited, RVs over 30 feet should reserve sites. Facilities include picnic tables, fire rings with grills, flush toilets, drinking water, bear boxes, garbage service, disposal station, firewood and ice for sale, amphitheater for evening ranger programs, and campground hosts. Leashed pets are permitted. Wheelchair-accessible toilets and campsites are available.

Reservations, fees: Reservations are recommended (307/344-7901 for same day, 307/344-7311 or 866/439-7375 for advance,

www.yellowstonenationalparklodges.com).
Campsites cost $23, plus tax and utility fee.
Shared hiker and biker campsites cost $5 per
person. Cash, check, or credit card. Open late
May-early September.

Directions: From the Fishing Bridge Junction
on Grand Loop Road, drive 3.5 miles south,
or from the West Thumb Junction, drive 17.5
miles north. Turn west into Bridge Bay for
0.2 mile, and turn right into the campground
entrance.

GPS Coordinates: N 44°32.195' W 110°
25.995'

Contact: Yellowstone National Park, P.O. Box
168, Yellowstone, WY 82190-0168, 307/344-
7381, www.nps.gov/yell.

32 GRANT VILLAGE

Scenic rating: 8

on Yellowstone Lake in Yellowstone National
Park

BEST (

On Yellowstone Lake, Grant Campground
sits at 7,733 feet on the south shore of West
Thumb—a huge bay larger than other lakes
in the park. Of the campgrounds around Yellowstone Lake, it is the closest to Old Faithful,
about 20 miles away. The sprawling Grant
Village complex houses a visitors center, restaurant, interpretive sightseeing tours, lodge,
general store, gas, showers, launderette, post
office, and marina that includes cement
ramps, docks, slips, and trailer parking. The
cold lake whips up a notorious chop in the
afternoons, so paddlers and anglers will want
to plan accordingly, but mornings and evenings can yield appealing water. All boats need
permits, available at the backcountry office at
the visitors center; no waterskiing or Jet Skiing. Nearby, West Thumb Geyser Basin has a
0.5-mile boardwalk trail to access hot springs,
Abyss Pool, and the Fishing Cone offshore,
where anglers used to cook their catch over
the steam. Also, hikers can grab a panoramic

view of the park's largest lake and Absaroka
Mountains by climbing the one-mile Yellowstone Lake Overlook Trail.

A paved road with paved parking pads
loops through this giant campground with
a midsummer population larger than some
Wyoming towns. In contrast to the other
large Yellowstone Lake campgrounds across
the highway from beaches, this one sits in
a lodgepole forest adjacent to the shoreline.
Trails lead to a large pebble and sand beach
for sunbathing or swimming. The campsites
sit close together under the partial shade of a
loose, sunny lodgepole forest. With no understory, you can see neighbors.

Campsites, facilities: The campground has
430 RV or tent campsites. RV combinations
are limited to 40 feet. With limited large RV
parking pads, RVs over 30 feet should reserve
sites. Facilities include picnic tables, fire rings
with grills, flush toilets, drinking water, bear
boxes, firewood for sale, garbage service, and
campground hosts. Showers, launderette, and
disposal station are available 0.5 mile south
in Grant Village. Leashed pets are permitted.
Wheelchair-accessible toilets and campsites
are available.

Reservations, fees: Reservations are recommended (307/344-7901 for same day,
307/344-7311 or 866/439-7375 for advance,
www.YellowstoneNationalParkLodges.com).
Campsites cost $27, plus tax and utility fee.
Shared hiker and biker campsites cost $5 per
person. Cash, check, or credit card. Open late
June-late September.

Directions: From West Thumb Junction,
drive south on Rockefeller Parkway for 1.8
miles, or from the park's south entrance, drive
22 miles north. Turn east into Grant Village
and drive one mile. Turn left and drive 0.5
mile to the campground.

GPS Coordinates: N 44° 23.654' W 110°
33.828'

Contact: Yellowstone National Park, P.O. Box
168, Yellowstone, WY 82190-0168, 307/344-
7381, www.nps.gov/yell.

33 FRANK ISLAND

Scenic rating: 8

on Yellowstone Lake in Yellowstone National Park

At 136 square miles, Yellowstone Lake is the second-largest freshwater lake in the world that is above 7,000 feet. That means cold water, 40-50°F, in summer. Frank Island is a unique place to camp in Yellowstone, but camping here does require a self-contained boat with a galley, berth, toilet, and anchor. The island itself is for day visitation only, but it's a good place to see bald eagles or ospreys. Because of nesting, shore landings are not permitted prior to August 15, except at the dock and picnic area, on the north side of the spit in the south bay, where a dock is available. Anglers fish for native cutthroat trout. All boats require permits, available at Bridge Bay or Grant Village; no waterskiing or Jet Skiing.

Boaters may camp at two anchorage locations within the eastern double cove of the island: one in the north bay and one in the south bay. Anchorage sites must be at least 100 feet from shore and 300 feet from the dock. The coves, which face east, are open to the lake's notorious afternoon winds, which can whip up five-foot waves, but also garner views of the Absaroka Mountains. Powerboats are limited to 45 mph on the lake.

Campsites, facilities: Overnight camping is not permitted on the island, but two anchorage spots are available. No facilities are provided at the anchorage sites, and only one boat, with a maximum of eight people, is permitted per site.

Reservations, fees: Reservations are accepted for backcountry campsites. Applications (available online) may be submitted with a nonrefundable $25 after January 1; reservation confirmations are issued starting April 1. Reservations are recommended for the coveted lake permits. At 48 hours or less before your trip, pick up free permits for backcountry campsites in person at Bridge Bay, Grant Village, or the south entrance backcountry office. Open June-October, depending on seasonal conditions.

Directions: To reach Frank Island, launch power boats from Bridge Bay for the 10-mile crossing.

GPS Coordinates: N 44° 24.795' W 110° 21.267'

Contact: Yellowstone National Park, P.O. Box 168, Yellowstone, WY 82190-0168, 307/344-7381, www.nps.gov/yell.

34 YELLOWSTONE LAKE

Scenic rating: 9

on Yellowstone Lake in Yellowstone National Park

Yellowstone Lake—the second-largest freshwater lake above 7,000 feet in the world—offers boat-in and hike-in camping on its east shore, three southern arms, and several bays east of West Thumb. You can launch boats from Grant Village or Bridge Bay; hand-carried watercrafts can also launch from Sedge Bay picnic area. The chilly (45°F) lake is notorious for daily afternoon winds with big whitecaps, so plan trips accordingly. Bridge Bay Marina (307/242-3893) provides a boat shuttle service for hikers and boaters mid-May-mid-September. For canoers and kayakers, the shuttle can save travel over open water. All boats require permits, available at Bridge Bay and Grant Village; no waterskiing or Jet Skiing. Many campsites link to hiking trails, and the park service advocates fishing for lake trout to help restore the cutthroat trout fishery.

These popular shoreline campsites are prized for their quiet, solitude, scenery, and wildlife-watching. The campsites sit back in the trees for protection, most within a few hundred feet of the shoreline. Some of the beaches garner views of the Absaroka Mountains to the east. Three locations with docks have three campsites each.

Campsites, facilities: Yellowstone Lake has 32 primitive tent campsites. Sites are limited to 8-12 people, depending on restrictions. Facilities include fire rings where campfires are permitted, bear boxes or poles, and pit toilets at some. Bring a 35-foot rope for hanging food, garbage, toiletries, and cooking gear. No drinking water is available; treat lake water. Pack out your trash. Pets are not allowed.

Reservations, fees: Reservations are accepted for backcountry campsites. Applications (available online) may be submitted with a nonrefundable $25 after January 1; reservation confirmations are issued starting April 1. Reservations are recommended for the coveted lake permits. At 48 hours or less before your trip, pick up free permits for backcountry campsites in person at Bridge Bay, Grant Village, or the south entrance backcountry office. Open June-October, depending on seasonal conditions; some campsites are closed because of bears until mid-July.

Directions: For launching from Grant Village, drive south from West Thumb Junction on Rockefeller Parkway for 1.8 miles, or from the park's south entrance, drive 22 miles north. Turn east into Grant Village, drive 0.9 mile, and turn right, following the signs to the boat launch. To launch from Bridge Bay, drive south from Fishing Bridge Junction on Grand Loop Road for 3.5 miles, or from the West Thumb Junction drive 17.5 miles north. Turn west into Bridge Bay for 0.2 mile to the marina.

GPS Coordinates for Bridge Bay: N 44° 32.026' W 110° 26.426'

GPS Coordinates for Grant Village: N 44° 23.520' W 110° 32.882'

Contact: Yellowstone National Park, P.O. Box 168, Yellowstone, WY 82190-0168, 307/344-7381, www.nps.gov/yell.

35 FLAT MOUNTAIN, SOUTH, AND SOUTHEAST ARMS

Scenic rating: 9
on Yellowstone Lake in Yellowstone National Park

BEST (

Yellowstone Lake offers paddlers and hikers access to three remote southern bays with views of the Absaroka Mountains, still snowcapped in early summer. Only hand-propelled watercraft are permitted; a few campsites allow sailboats to anchor. Launch from Grant Village to paddle 19 miles to Flat Mountain Arm or 33-35 miles into South Arm; launch from Sedge Bay picnic area on the lake's northeast corner to paddle the east shore for 20 miles into Southeast Arm. Watch for daily afternoon winds that whip the chilly (45°F) lake water into a chop of whitecaps. Bridge Bay Marina (307/242-3893) provides a boat shuttle service for hikers and boaters mid-May-mid-September. For canoers and kayakers, the shuttle saves paddling over open water. Hiking trails follow the shoreline, and the lake holds trout for fishing. All boats require permits, available at Bridge Bay or Grant Village; no waterskiing or Jet Skiing.

The popular campsites are prized for their quiet, solitude, scenery, wildlife-watching, and restrictions that exclude motorboats. The campsites are set back in the trees for protection, but most are within a few hundred feet of the shoreline; one site requires a 0.25-mile walk.

Campsites, facilities: Yellowstone Lake has 10 primitive tent campsites spread between the nonmotorized bays. Sites are limited to 8-12 people, depending on restrictions. Facilities include fire rings where campfires are permitted, bear boxes or poles, and pit toilets at some. Bring a 35-foot rope for hanging food, garbage, toiletries, and cooking gear. No drinking water is available; treat lake water. Pack out your trash. Pets are not allowed.

Reservations, fees: Reservations are accepted

for backcountry campsites. Applications (available online) may be submitted with a nonrefundable $25 after January 1; reservation confirmations are issued starting April 1. Reservations are recommended for the coveted lake permits. At 48 hours or less before your trip, pick up free permits for backcountry campsites in person at Bridge Bay, Grant Village, or the south entrance backcountry office. Open June-October, depending on seasonal conditions; seven campsites are closed because of bears until mid-July.

Directions: For launching from Grant Village, drive south from West Thumb Junction on Rockefeller Parkway for 1.8 miles, or from the park's south entrance, drive 22 miles north. Turn east into Grant Village, drive 0.9 mile, and turn right, following the signs to the boat launch. To launch from Bridge Bay, drive south from Fishing Bridge Junction on Grand Loop Road for 3.5 miles, or from the West Thumb Junction drive 17.5 miles north. Turn west into Bridge Bay for 0.2 mile to the marina.

GPS Coordinates for Bridge Bay: N 44° 32.026' W 110° 26.426'

GPS Coordinates for Grant Village: N 44° 23.520' W 110° 32.882'

Contact: Yellowstone National Park, P.O. Box 168, Yellowstone, WY 82190-0168, 307/344-7381, www.nps.gov/yell.

36 SHOSHONE LAKE

Scenic rating: 8
on Shoshone Lake in Yellowstone National Park

BEST

Campers access the solitude of Shoshone Lake's primitive campgrounds by hiking, canoeing, or kayaking. Motorized boats are not permitted. Launch boats from the ramp at Lewis Lake Campground to paddle across the lake and up the Lewis River Channel between the two lakes. The last channel requires wading in frigid water while dragging boats. Because of the long paddle, select a south shore site for the first night. Afternoon high winds on the lake are a daily occurrence, so plan to paddle early. All boats, including kayaks and canoes, need permits, available at Lewis Lake Campground. For hikers, the Howard Eaton, DeLacy, Dogshead, and Lewis Channel Trails connect to the trail that circles Shoshone Lake.

The remote, quiet popular campsites sprinkle along the north, west, and south shores of the lake, snuggled into the edge of the forest for protection from weather. Some campsites are for hikers only, some for boaters only, and some for both.

Campsites, facilities: The lake is rimmed with 21 tent campsites that each hold eight people maximum. Five campsites are accessed by trail only, 13 by boat only, and three via trail or water. These are primitive campsites, with no fires permitted. Facilities include pit or composting toilets and a bear pole or bar. Bring a 35-foot rope for hanging food, garbage, toiletries, and cooking gear. Pack out your trash. No pets are permitted.

Reservations, fees: Reservations are accepted for backcountry campsites. Applications (available online) may be submitted with a nonrefundable $25 after January 1; reservation confirmations are issued starting April 1. Reservations are recommended for the coveted lake permits. At 48 hours or less before your trip, pick up free permits for backcountry campsites in person at Bridge Bay, Grant Village, or the south entrance backcountry office. Open June 15-October, depending on seasonal conditions and bear restrictions.

Directions: From the south entrance to the park, drive 11 miles north, or from West Thumb Junction, drive 11 miles south. Turn west into the Lewis Lake boat launch.

GPS Coordinates: N 44° 22.378' W 110° 42.250'

Contact: Yellowstone National Park, P.O. Box

168, Yellowstone, WY 82190-0168, 307/344-7381, www.nps.gov/yell.

37 LEWIS LAKE

🥾 🏊 🚣 🛶 🎣 🐕 ♿ 🚐 ⛺

Scenic rating: 8

on Lewis Lake in Yellowstone National Park

BEST (

At 7,830 feet, Lewis Lake is the third-largest lake in the park. Its appeal rests in its quieter ambiance and less visited location. Adjacent to the campground, a boat dock, cement ramp, and trailer parking allow for launching onto the lake for pleasure boating or fishing for brown trout (no waterskiing or Jet Skiing). Lewis Lake is also the gateway to Shoshone Lake via the Lewis Lake Channel, but only canoes and kayaks are permitted up the channel into the larger lake. All boats require permits, available at Lewis Lake Campground. Driving north from the Tetons, this is the first Yellowstone National Park campground you'll reach tucked at the southeast corner of the lake. At the lake's northeast corner (about four miles away), two trails depart in opposite directions. An 11-mile loop goes up the Lewis Channel to Shoshone Lake and returns via the Dogshead Trail. Across the highway, a 7.5-mile trail heads to Heart Lake. For sightseers, Lewis Falls sits about one mile south on the road.

By park standards, Lewis Lake is one of the smaller campgrounds, although it is still larger than most Forest Service campgrounds. On a hillside, campsites are spaced out for privacy under the conifer canopy with choices of varying degrees of sunny or shaded sites. Narrow parking pads may pose difficulties for those not used to backing in RVs. Most of the daytime activity concentrates around the boat launch and beach with nights bringing quiet. This campground is the one of the last to fill in the park, but in peak season, all the sites can be taken by early afternoon.

Campsites, facilities: The campground has 85 RV or tent campsites. RVs are limited to 25 feet. Facilities include picnic tables, fire rings with grills, vault toilets, drinking water, garbage service, bear boxes, and boat launch. Generators are not permitted. Leashed pets are permitted. Wheelchair-accessible toilets and campsites are available.

Reservations, fees: Reservations are not accepted. Sites cost $15. Shared hiker and biker campsites cost $5 per person. Cash or check. Open mid-June-October.

Directions: From the south park entrance, drive 11 miles north on the Rockefeller Parkway, or from West Thumb Junction, drive 11 miles south. Turn west into the Lewis Lake boat launch and campground entrance.

GPS Coordinates: N 44° 16.875' W 110° 37.644'

Contact: Yellowstone National Park, P.O. Box 168, Yellowstone, WY 82190-0168, 307/344-7381, www.nps.gov/yell.

38 CAVE FALLS

🥾 🎣 🐕 ♿ 🚐 ⛺

Scenic rating: 9

on the Falls River in Caribou-Targhee National Forest

BEST (

At 6,200 feet in Caribou-Targhee National Forest, Cave Falls Campground requires a long drive through Idaho farmland and forest to reach this remote corner of Wyoming and Yellowstone National Park. The road ends in Yellowstone at Cave Falls—a cascade only 20 feet high, but spanning 250 feet wide. A five-minute walk leads to the falls, and a path climbs above to look down on it. A 1.5-mile trail leads farther to Bechler Falls (1.5 miles). The Falls and Bechler Rivers are home to rainbow trout. Depending on where you are fishing, you'll need a Wyoming or Yellowstone

© BECKY LOMAX

Cave Falls, a 250-foot-wide waterfall, tucks into the remote southwest corner of Yellowstone National Park.

fishing license. The Bechler Ranger Station in Yellowstone sits about two miles west, where multiple trails tour rivers in this remote corner of the park.

Set along the Falls River in the national forest, the campground lines up most of its campsites overlooking the river. You can prop a chair on the high bank's edge and watch the roaring river as the sunset glows on the rocky outcroppings opposite. Paths drop down the steep bank to the water, too. A tall forest of aspens, subalpine firs, and lodgepoles alternates with meadows of arrowleaf balsamroot and huckleberries. Campsites have a mix of shade, sun, and flat tent spaces. Plan on enjoying solitude.

Campsites, facilities: The campground has 22 RV or tent campsites. RVs are limited to 24 feet. Facilities include picnic tables, fire rings with grills, pedestal grills, vault toilets (wheelchair-accessible), drinking water, and bear boxes. Pack out your trash. Leashed pets are permitted.

Reservations, fees: Reservations are not accepted. Campsites cost $10. Extra vehicles cost $6. Cash or check. Open June-mid-September.

Directions: From five miles north of Ashton on Highway 47 in Idaho, drive east on Cave Falls Road (Greentimber Road or Forest Road 582) for 18 miles. At mile 5.5, the pavement ends and the bumpy ride begins. You'll hit pavement again at mile 16, where the road narrows and enters Wyoming. Turn right, drop 0.1 mile to the pay station, and swing right to the campsites. From Flagg Ranch, the 52-mile rugged, narrow, dirt Grassy Lake Road takes 2.5 hours to Cave Falls Campground. GPS Coordinates: N 44° 7.874' W 111° 0.896'

Contact: Caribou-Targhee National Forest, Island Park Ranger District, 3726 Hwy. 20, Island Park, ID 83429, 208/558-7301, www.fs.usda.gov/ctnf.

39 GRASSY LAKE PRIMITIVE

Scenic rating: 8

in Rockefeller Parkway and Caribou-Targhee
National Forest

BEST (

An old Native American and wagon route, the 52-mile Grassy Lake Road through remote wilderness connects Flagg Ranch, Wyoming with Ashton, Idaho, topping out at 7,306 feet. In winter, snowmobiles and dog sleds travel the route. In summer, once the road dries (usually by August), those with tenacity and sturdy rigs drive it. (Trailers are not recommended.) The dirt road is rocky and narrow, has few turn-outs, offers fewer views than one would expect, and will take 2.5 hours to drive. Mountain bikers can ride the road, too. Grassy Lake has a boat ramp and can be fished, paddled, or motored. On its east end, the Snake River is known for its trout fishery and can be floated with rafts and kayaks. Budget cuts in 2013 closed the designated campsites along this route; call for updates.

Eight tiny camps—prized for their quiet and solitude—are about one mile apart with large tent spaces. Facing east within 10 minutes from Flagg Ranch, camps 1-4 command outstanding views of the Snake River and Teton Wilderness peaks. Camps 1 and 2 sit on the river in sagebrush, willow, and grass bottomlands. Camps 3 and 4 sit on partly shaded open-forest bluffs overlooking the river. With forest and meadow views, camps 5-8 line the road as it climbs toward Grassy Lake. Camp 5 sits the farthest back from the road in green lodgepoles. Camps 6-8 sit closer to the road in forested settings, broken by meadows of yarrow and asters. Other primitive campsites sit at Grassy Lake and Lake of the Woods.

Campsites, facilities: Eight tiny camp-grounds with 14 RV or tent campsites between them line the first 10 miles from Flagg Ranch to Grassy Lake on Rockefeller Parkway. Camp 1 has four sites, camps 2-4 have two sites each, and camps 5-8 have one site each. Only small RVs are recommended. Facilities include picnic tables, fire rings with grills, vault toilets, bear boxes, and garbage service. Bring your own water. Seven additional primitive campsites sit in Caribou-Targhee National Forest at Grassy Lake and Lake of the Woods. The only facilities include rock fire rings. Leashed pets are permitted.

Reservations, fees: Reservations are not accepted. Camping is free. Open June-September.

Directions: From Flagg Ranch, Grassy Lake Road (Ashton-Flagg Ranch Road) heads west, crossing the Snake River. From Ashton, Idaho, the road begins two miles southeast of Ashton, heading east.

GPS Coordinates for the site nearest Flagg Ranch: N 44° 6.244' W 110° 41.233'

Contact: Grand Teton National Park, P.O. Drawer 170, Moose, WY 83102, 307/739-3300, www.nps.gov/grte/.

40 HEADWATERS

Scenic rating: 7

at Flagg Ranch in Rockefeller Parkway

At 6,849 feet at Flagg Ranch, Headwaters Campground is the only developed campground in Rockefeller Parkway between Yellowstone National Park and Grand Teton National Park. On the Snake River, the large tourist center (lodge, restaurant, grocery, and gas station) offers guided fly-fishing, lake kayaking, horseback riding, rafting trips, and interpretive programs. Skilled whitewater rafters, kayakers, and canoeists can put in at Southgate Launch, 0.5 mile south of the south entrance of Yellowstone, for three miles of Class III white water to the campground. The water mellows in the 10 miles from the ranch to Lizard Creek on Jackson Lake but requires route-finding through braided channels and paddling against strong lake winds. A non-motorized boat park permit is required ($10 for seven days), available at Moose and Colter Bay Visitor Centers. From the campground, you can fish the river, mountain bike Grassy Lake Road heading west, and hike to Huckleberry Lookout from Sheffield Creek one mile south.

The forested campground sits near the Snake River, with paths connecting to the riverfront. Campsites vary from fully shaded under large spruces and firs to partly sunny with mountain views. RV campsites have gravel pull-throughs wide enough for slide-outs and awnings. Because of the lack of understory, views include neighboring campers. The eastern loops sit closest to the highway, but traffic dwindles at night, and commercial trucking isn't permitted.

Campsites, facilities: The campground has 54 tent campsites and 96 RV campsites with hookups for sewer, water, and electricity up to 50 amps. RVs are limited to 60 feet. Facilities include picnic tables, fire rings, flush toilets, showers, drinking water, garbage service, launderette, and convenience store. Leashed pets are permitted. A wheelchair-accessible toilets and campsites are available.

Reservations, fees: Reservations are recommended. RV campsites cost $64 or $32 with park access passes. Tent campsites cost $35. Add on tax. Rates are for two adults. For each additional adult, add $5. Cash, check, or credit card. Open late May-September.

Directions: From Jackson Lake Junction in Grand Teton National Park, drive north on Highway 26/191/89 for 21 miles. From the south entrance to Yellowstone National Park, drive three miles south. Turn west into Flagg Ranch.

GPS Coordinates: N 44° 6.305' W 110° 40.091'

Contact: Headwaters Camping and RV, P.O. Box 187, Moran, WY 83013, 307/543-2861 or 800/443-2311, www.gtlc.com/headwaters-lodge.aspx

41 SHEFFIELD CREEK

Scenic rating: 8

near Teton Wilderness in Bridger-Teton National Forest

At 7,000 feet, Sheffield Creek Campground cuddles next to a small tributary of the nearby Snake River below the 9,615-foot Huckleberry Mountain in the Teton Wilderness. Sheffield Creek Trail (#027) climbs 2,600 feet in 5.5 miles from the campground to the Huckleberry Lookout, which is listed on the National Register of Historic Places. Outstanding views from the lookout include Jackson Lake, the Tetons, Yellowstone National Park, and Teton Wilderness. Mountain bikers can ride the Grassy Lake Road, departing from nearby Flagg Ranch. Fishing, rafting, kayaking, and canoeing are available on the Snake River, but be sure to get the appropriate permits from Grand Teton National Park.

Sheffield Creek offers sunny campsites with huge territorial views of the surrounding mountains, valley, and the Tetons to the south. A small stream runs west of the campground—one that you must drive through on the access road as no bridge crosses it. June may have too much water to cross; scout the water depth. Some years, the access isn't good until August. Because the campground is located in a grizzly bear recovery area, it may be closed temporarily to tents, tent campers, and tent trailers, allowing only hard-sided RVs, during high bear activity. Call to check on status first. Sheffield is a popular trailhead but quiets at night.

Campsites, facilities: The campground has five RV or tent campsites. RVs are limited to 30 feet. Facilities include picnic tables, fire rings with grills, vault toilet (wheelchair-accessible), horse facilities, drinking water, and bear box and food pole. Pack out your trash. Leashed pets are permitted.

Reservations, fees: Reservations are not accepted. Campsites cost $5 per unit (RV, trailer,

CAMPING IN GRAND TETON

Grand Teton National Park, which connects to Yellowstone via the John D. Rockefeller, Jr. Memorial Parkway, hosts high rugged spires shooting up from sagebrush meadows. A paved bike trail tours the valley floor while a myriad of hiking trails climb to high vistas in the mountains. Boaters can enjoy several lakes, including the biggest, **Jackson Lake.** A few smaller lakes allow for the quiet of only canoes and kayaks. On the park's south end, the National Elk Refuge is home to 5,000 wintering elk, and the town of Jackson offers shopping, art galleries, and restaurants. The area houses outfitters for rafting, fishing, hiking, horseback riding, mountaineering, and rock climbing.

The park strings its six large campgrounds along the east side of the mountain range and Jackson Lake. **Flagg Ranch** services campers on the parkway between the two parks. The surrounding Caribou-Targhee and Bridger-Teton National Forests also offer a few campgrounds within 15 minutes of the park. Of Teton's campgrounds, **Jenny Lake** is by far the most popular, due to its access to hiking trails that climb up canyons toward the Teton Crest and the tour boat that runs across the lake. **Signal Mountain, Colter Bay,** and **Lizard Creek Campgrounds** rim the east shores of Jackson Lake, a large dammed reservoir on the Snake River. **Gros Ventre Campground** borders the National Elk Refuge. Boaters, canoers, and kayakers can enjoy remote campsites on Jackson Lake and the smaller, more wind-protected Leigh Lake.

Colter Bay in Grand Teton offer hookups for RVs, while Jenny Lake caters to tent camping only and does not permit RVs.

or tent). Cash or check. Open late May-September. If weather permits, the campground can remain open later in fall, but without services.

Directions: From Jackson Lake Junction in Grand Teton National Park, drive north on Highway 26/191/89 for 20 miles. From the Flagg Ranch, drive one mile south. Turn east onto the dirt road south of the bridge over the Snake River and drive 0.3 mile southeast into to the campground.

GPS Coordinates: N 44° 5.592' W 110° 39.814'

Contact: Bridger-Teton National Forest, Buffalo Ranger District, Hwy. 26/287, Moran, WY 83013, 307/543-2386, www.fs.usda.gov/btnf.

42 LIZARD CREEK

Scenic rating: 9
on Jackson Lake in Grand Teton National Park

At the north end of Jackson Lake, Lizard Creek Campground, elevation 6,823 feet, stares across the lake at the jagged teeth of the northern Teton Mountains. While the campground offers enjoyment of the lakeshore (with several walk-in tent sites right on it), sometimes the lake level can drop so low that huge mudflats surrounds the campground. The lake harbors cutthroat and lake trout, but fishing from the campground varies depending on water levels. The campground has no boat launch, but with high water levels, you can launch hand-carried boats, rafts, kayaks, and canoes at a pullout about one mile south of the campground. Boat permits are required, available at Colter Bay Visitors Center.

The partly sunny hillside campground is prized for its quiet location and outstanding views. It offers less harried enjoyment of the lake compared to other lakefront campgrounds. A thick spruce, fir, and lodgepole forest aids privacy, which is greater in the upper loop. Many of the lower loop prime campsites overlook the lake and the Tetons. Most of the walk-in tent sites, located in the lower loop, sit on the lake. Claim a campsite early in the day.

Campsites, facilities: The campground has 43 RV or tent campsites and 17 walk-in tent campsites. RV size is limited to 30 feet. Facilities include picnic tables, fire rings with grills, drinking water, flush toilets, garbage service, bear boxes, hiker-biker shared campsites, amphitheater for interpretive programs, and campground hosts. Generators are permitted in the upper loop, but not the lower loop. Only one vehicle is permitted per site. Leashed pets are permitted. A wheelchair-accessible campsite is available.

Reservations, fees: Reservations are not accepted. Campsites cost $21. Shared hiker and biker campsites cost $5. Cash or check. Open early June-early September.

Directions: From Jackson Lake Junction, drive 14 miles north on Highway 89/191/287, or from the south entrance to Yellowstone, drive 10 miles south. Turn south onto the paved road for 0.1 mile into the campground.

GPS Coordinates: N 44° 0.350' W 110° 41.135'

Contact: Grand Teton National Park, P.O. Drawer 170, Moose, WY 83102, 307/739-3300, www.nps.gov/grte/.

43 PACIFIC CREEK

Scenic rating: 8

near Teton Wilderness in Bridger-Teton National Forest

Pacific Creek Campground perches at 7,000 feet on the edge of the Teton Wilderness—a 585,238-acre wilderness bordering Yellowstone and Grand Teton National Parks. The campground serves as a leap off point into the wilderness with the trail following Pacific Creek upstream. Anglers can find pools for fly-fishing for trout on the stream. For a day hike destination, hikers and anglers head eight miles to Gravel Lake, 0.4-mile-long lake southeast of rugged Pinyon Peak. The trail also provides hunting access in fall for big game.

Pacific Creek offers a mix of sunny and shady campsites under cottonwoods with territorial views of the surrounding mountains—even the tops of the Tetons in the distance. Pacific Creek flows east of the campground. Because the campground is located in a grizzly bear recovery area, it may be closed temporarily to tents, tent campers, and tent trailers, allowing only hard-sided RVs, during high bear activity. Call to check on status first. The trailhead is located here, so hikers and horse packers may come through the camp. Other than that, it's a quiet location.

Campsites, facilities: The campground has five RV or tent campsites. RVs are limited to 30 feet. Facilities include picnic tables, fire rings with grills, vault toilet, horse facilities, drinking water, and bear box and food pole. Pack out your trash. Leashed pets are permitted. Several free primitive campsites are also located on Pacific Creek after leaving the national park boundary.

Reservations, fees: Reservations are not accepted. Campsites cost $10 per unit (RV, trailer, or tent). Cash or check. Open late May-September. If weather permits, the campground can remain open later in fall, but without services.

Directions: From Moran Junction, head into Grand Teton National Park and turn north onto Rockefeller Parkway for 1.2 miles. From Jackson Junction, drive Rockefeller Parkway for 2.9 miles east. At the gravel Pacific Creek Road, turn north for eight miles to the campground entrance at the terminus.

GPS Coordinates: N 43° 56.357' W 110° 26.572'

Contact: Bridger-Teton National Forest, Buffalo Ranger District, Hwy. 26/287, Moran, WY 83013, 307/543-2386, www.fs.usda.gov/btnf.

44 TETON RANGE RESORT

Scenic rating: 8

in Moran

The Teton Range Resort, formerly called

Grand Teton RV, is a campground for convenience located just west of Moran Junction where one road goes north into Yellowstone National Park and the other road heads south into Grand Teton National Park. At 6,800 feet, the location away from the high-impact tourist areas and its views give it appeal. The campground sits behind a convenience store, restaurant, and gas station. Buffalo Fork circles in and around the campground. Anglers can wade-fish the stream, and when water levels are high enough, canoers can paddle it.

A handful of trees dot this sunny campground, but the trade-off is the view: From many campsites, the entire Teton Mountain range is visible across the horizon to the west. The ex-KOA campground is older, dusty, showing wear and tear, and the pool and hot tub were still closed in 2013.

Campsites, facilities: This campground has 160 RV campsites and 14 tent campsites. Sites can fit the largest RVs. Hookups are available for water, sewer, and electricity up to 50 amps. Facilities include picnic tables, fire rings, flush toilets, showers, drinking water, launderette, playground, convenience store, rental cars, and wireless Internet. Leashed pets are permitted.

Reservations, fees: Reservations are accepted. RV hookups cost $70-100. Tents cost $30-50. Rates cover four people; for each extra person, add $8; kids under six stay for free. Add on sales tax. Cash, check, or credit card. Open year-round.

Directions: From the Moran Junction, drive east on Highway 287 for 5.6 miles and turn south into the campground.

GPS Coordinates: N 43° 49.889' W 110° 24.123'

Contact: Teton Range Resort, 17800 Highway 287, Moran, WY 83013, 307/733-1980 or 800/563-6469, www.yellowstonerv.com.

45 HATCHET

Scenic rating: 7

near Moran Junction in Bridger-Teton National Forest

While Hatchet Campground isn't worth a visit as a destination in itself, its location provides a last-minute place to camp before reaching Grand Teton National Park and access to scenic fly-fishing and floating. The campground, elevation 6,800 feet, sits 0.2 mile west of the Buffalo Ranger Station and at the base of the dirt Hatchet Road, which climbs south along the foothills with dramatic views across the valley to the toothy Teton Mountains. The road, good for scenic drives, ATVs, hunting access, and mountain biking, also offers primitive campsites with big views overlooking the valley and the Tetons. The Buffalo Fork River parallels the highway heading west to its confluence with the Snake River—both trout fisheries. Paddling Jackson Dam to Pacific Creek on the Snake offers five miles of scenic, calm water. Buffalo Fork is closed to floating. Nonmotorized boats need a permit ($10 per week, $20 per season), available at the ranger station.

Rimmed with lodgepole pines and aspens, the sunny campground tucks its small campsites and small tent spaces around one loop. The best sites sit on the outside of the ring. Fireweed, wild roses, serviceberries, and sagebrush add to a short understory for some privacy. Sites 1 and 9 gaze north toward mountains, but unfortunately the highway is in sight, too. Given the campground's proximity to the highway, road noise is inevitable.

Campsites, facilities: The campground has nine RV or tent campsites. Sites can fit mid-sized RVs only. Facilities include picnic tables, fire rings with grills, pit toilets (wheelchair-accessible), drinking water, garbage service, and bear boxes. Leashed pets are permitted.

Reservations, fees: Reservations are not accepted. Campsites cost $10. Cash or check.

Open late May-September; however, if weather permits, campground stays open through fall without services.

Directions: From Moran Junction, drive east on Highway 26/287 for 8.3 miles. Turn south onto Hatchet Road (Forest Road 30160) and immediately left into the campground.

GPS Coordinates: N 43° 49.463' W 110° 21.323'

Contact: Bridger-Teton National Forest, Buffalo Ranger District, Hwy. 26/287, Moran, WY 83013, 307/543-2386, www.fs.usda.gov/btnf.

46 BOX CREEK

Scenic rating: 6

near Teton Wilderness in Bridger-Teton National Forest

Located in a valley of outfitters, Box Creek Campground at 7,000 feet is not a destination campground in itself, but one for access to the Teton Wilderness—a 585,238-acre wilderness bordering Yellowstone and Grand Teton National Parks. The trailhead campground is used mostly by horse-packers, with corrals, hitch rails, and stock ramps available. The Box Creek Trail climbs about five miles to 8,600 feet on Gravel Ridge. From the ridge, you can view the destruction from the 1987 Teton Tornado—the highest altitude recorded of a tornado touchdown. It cut a swath up to three miles wide across a 20-mile strip, snapping trees like toothpicks and uprooting others. Trout fishing is available in the Buffalo Fork River, and the area offers big game hunting.

The campground—set in aspens and pines—circles on the end of a large, grassy meadow. Several of the campsites have views of the forest and mountains. This sunny, little-used campground is ultra-quiet and secluded, but you'll see other campers, if any are there.

Campsites, facilities: The campground has six RV or tent campsites. RVs are limited to 30 feet. Facilities include picnic tables, fire grates, vault toilet (wheelchair-accessible), bear boxes, garbage service, and stock facilities. Drinking water is not available. Bring your own, or fill up at Turpin Meadows 1.3 miles east. Leashed pets are permitted.

Reservations, fees: Reservations are not accepted. Campsites cost $10 per unit (RV, trailer, or tent). Cash or check. Open late May-September, weather permitting.

Directions: From Moran Junction, drive east on Highway 26/287 for 3.4 miles and turn north onto Buffalo Valley Road for 8.7 miles. Turn north onto the narrow dirt road with no pullouts and climb 0.7 mile to the campground. Note: On Buffalo Valley Road, the only sign notes Box Creek Trailhead with no mention of the campground. An alternative route to the campground road departs Highway 26/287 at milepost 13, heading north on the gravel Forest Road 30050 for 4.2 miles to the bridge over the Buffalo Fork River and then one mile on pavement.

GPS Coordinates: N 43° 51.617' W 110° 17.680'

Contact: Bridger-Teton National Forest, Buffalo Ranger District, Hwy. 26/287, Moran, WY 83013, 307/543-2386, www.fs.usda.gov/btnf.

47 TURPIN MEADOW

Scenic rating: 8

near Teton Wilderness in Bridger-Teton National Forest

Turpin Meadow Campground, at 7,300 feet, sits across the Buffalo Fork River from Turpin Meadow Guest Ranch in a high valley facing the Teton Mountains. From the river, the road, and the trailhead, you can see Mount Moran and the Tetons in the distance, but not from the campground. The river is a popular trout fishery, but be aware of private property if you head downstream. Paths lead from the campground to the river, which can be wade-fished. A popular trailhead, often packed with horse trailers, sits northeast of the campground, a jump-off point into the Teton Wilderness. The Clear Creek Trail makes an 18-mile loop with the Box Creek Trail, and the Buffalo Fork Trail follows the river west to the confluence of its north and south forks, where the trail divides to climb to the Continental Divide National Scenic Trail.

The gravel campground road weaves through a young lodgepole and fir forest surrounded by a lodgepole fence and huge sagebrush meadows. The first part of the loop features sunny campsites across from the outfitter camping area; the campsites at the end of the loop are more shaded—especially site 12. Big tent spaces are available. Mountain bluebirds frequent the campground.

Campsites, facilities: The campground has 18 RV or tent campsites. Sites can fit mid-sized RVs only. Facilities include picnic tables, fire rings with grills, vault toilet (wheelchair-accessible), drinking water, garbage service, bear boxes, and stock facilities. Leashed pets are permitted.

Reservations, fees: Reservations are not accepted. Campsites cost $10. Cash or check. Open late May-September; however, if weather permits, the campground stays open through fall without services.

Directions: From Moran Junction, drive east on Highway 26/287 for 3.4 miles and turn north onto Buffalo Valley Road for 9.7 miles. Before the bridge over Buffalo Fork River, swing east onto the gravel road for 0.1 mile and veer right for 0.2 mile and turn right into the campground. An alternative route to the bridge departs Highway 26/287 at milepost 13, heading north on gravel Forest Road 30050 for 4.2 miles.

GPS Coordinates: N 43° 51.335' W 110° 15.947'

Contact: Bridger-Teton National Forest, Buffalo Ranger District, Hwy. 26/287, Moran, WY 83013, 307/543-2386, www.fs.usda.gov/btnf.

48 COLTER BAY

Scenic rating: 10

on Jackson Lake in Grand Teton National Park

Colter Bay, at 6,793 feet on Jackson Lake, sits north of islands and inlets that provide boating, windsurfing, paddleboarding, waterskiing, canoeing, kayaking, swimming, and fishing sheltered from the big lake winds. Jet Skis are not allowed, and all boats require permits, available at the visitors center. The campground is part of the large Colter Bay Village, which contains a visitors center, restaurants, gas, grocery, and marina with a cement boat ramp, boat slips, trailer parking, docks, guided fishing, lake tours, and boat rentals (canoes, kayaks, and motorboats). The lake holds a variety of species for sport anglers. The picnic area has a designated swimming beach. The revamped visitors center contains a new Indian arts exhibit. Hikers can walk a maze of gentle trails to short destinations such as Swan Lake, Heron Pond, and the Lakeshore Trail, the latter yielding spectacular views of Mt. Moran and the Tetons. Longer loops tour Hermitage Point. Trailheads to Two Ocean and Emma Matilda Lakes are also within five miles. Mountain bikers can ride the short path along the breakwater along the bay or get stunning mountain views from the Two Ocean Lake Road. Horseback riding is available just south at Jackson Lake Lodge.

Divided into an RV hookup section and non-hookup loops, this giant lodgepole forest campground sits on a lodgepole bluff above Jackson Lake, its size more akin to a housing development than a campground. In the non-hookup loops, pullover sites line up close together, but many have fire pits and picnic tables tucked in forest nooks with visibility of only a neighbor or two. Only a handful of campsites in either section get views of the lake or the Teton Mountains. Although it crowds in summer, you can find

Rental canoes, kayaks, and motorboats are available at Colter Bay on Jackson Lake.

breathing room in the off-season and quiet at night.

Campsites, facilities: The campground has 112 pull-throughs for large RVs with hookups for water, sewer, and electricity; 350 RV or tent campsites with no hookups, nine walk-in tent sites, shared hiker-biker campsites, and 11 group campsites. Facilities include picnic tables, fire pits with grills (non-hookup sites only), flush toilets, drinking water, disposal station, garbage service, bear boxes, and amphitheater for evening programs. Coin-op showers and launderette are available at Colter Bay Village. No tents, fires, or gas grills are permitted in the RV hookup campsites. Non-hookup loops include some generator-free zones. Leashed pets are permitted. Wheelchair-accessible facilities include toilets and campsites.

Reservations, fees: Reservations are accepted only for the RV hookup and group campsites (Grand Teton Lodge Company, 800/28-9988, 307/543-3100, www.gtlc.com). RV hookups cost $60. Non-hookup sites cost $21. Shared

hiker and biker campsites cost $8 per person. Cash, check, or credit card. Open late May-late September.

Directions: From Jackson Lake Junction, drive 5.5 miles north, or from the south entrance to Yellowstone National Park, drive 18.5 miles south. Turn south into Colter Bay and drive 0.6 mile. Turn right into the campground. GPS Coordinates: N 43° 54.533' W 110° 38.493'

Contact: Grand Teton National Park, P.O. Drawer 170, Moose, WY 83102, 307/739-3300, www.nps.gov/grte/.

49 JACKSON LAKE

Scenic rating: 10
on Jackson Lake in Grand Teton National Park

One of the largest high-altitude lakes in the United States at 6,772 feet, Jackson Lake is 15 miles long, 7 miles wide, and 438 feet deep. The lake tucks into the base of the jagged Teton Mountain Range with shoreline boat-in or hike-in campsites to get away from the crowds. The glacial lake trout waters are cold (only mid-50°F in August) and strong afternoon winds are common. Sailboats, windsurfers, and motorboats are permitted (No Jet Skis). Four boat launches rim the lake's east shore: Leeks Marina, Colter Bay Marina, Signal Mountain, and Spalding Bay. (Note: Budget cuts closed Spalding Bay in 2013. Call for status.) Hiking is available only from the Hermitage Point group campsite. Motorboat, canoe, and kayak rentals are available at Leeks Marina, Signal Mountain, and Colter Bay. Permits are required for boats; buy them at visitors centers.

Lake campsites are prized for their scenery, quiet, and solitude. Most campsites rim the lakeshore, set back into the trees for protection. Five campsites are on islands. Sites vary with sunrise or sunset views. Highly-prized ones face the Tetons.

Campsites, facilities: Jackson Lake has 10 individual tent campsites and five group tent campsites. Six people are allowed per campsite, except for group campsites, which can hold 12. Facilities include fire rings, bear boxes, and pit toilets, and a few campsites have tent platforms. No drinking water is available; bring your own, or treat lake water. Pets are not allowed in Jackson Lake campsites, except at Spalding Bay.

Reservations, fees: Reservation requests are accepted January 5-May 15. Applications are available online with a $25 nonrefundable fee. Then, 24 hours before your trip, obtain the required free overnight camping permits at the Craig Thomas and Colter Bay Visitor Centers or Jenny Lake Ranger Station. Boats must also have permits ($20 per week or $40 per season for motorized; $10 per week or $20 per season for nonmotorized). Purchase boat permits at Moose and Colter Bay Visitor Centers. Open June-October.

Directions: From Jackson Lake Junction, drive Highway 89/191/287 north to reach Colter Bay Marina in 5.5 miles or Leeks Marina in 6.3 miles. From Jackson Lake Junction, drive three miles south on Teton Park Road to reach Signal Mountain Marina. To reach Spalding Bay (a primitive launch for only single-axle trailers), drive north from North Jenny Lake Junction for 1.3 miles on Teton Park Road and turn northwest for 2.1 miles on dirt Spalding Bay Road.

GPS Coordinates for launch sites:
Leeks Marina: N 43° 55.797' W 110° 38.394'
Colter Bay Marina: N 43° 54.130' W 110° 38.611'
Signal Mountain Marina: N 43° 50.316' W 110° 36.976'
Spalding Bay: N 43° 49.446' W 110° 40.532'

Contact: Grand Teton National Park, P.O. Drawer 170, Moose, WY 83102, 307/739-3300, www.nps.gov/grte/.

50 SIGNAL MOUNTAIN

Scenic rating: 10
on Jackson Lake in Grand Teton National Park

BEST (

Signal Mountain Campground, at 6,802 feet, may command one of the best panoramic views of the jagged teeth of the Teton Mountains from its perch on the west shore of Jackson Lake. North of the campground, Signal Mountain Lodge houses a restaurant, convenience store, gas station, and marina with sailboat tours, guided fishing, and boat rentals (canoes, kayaks, and motorboats). Launching facilities sit south of the campground: cement boat ramp, dock, and trailer parking. The lake is popular for swimming, boating (no Jet Skis), fishing, waterskiing, kayaking, and canoeing, although be prepared for cold water and daily afternoon winds. Permits are required for all boats, available at park visitors centers. The steep 1.5-mile South Landing Trail connects the campground with the beach and boat launch. Driving tours along Teton Park Road often produce sightings of bugling elk in fall. The campground is named for the low mountain to the east. You can drive, bike, or hike to its summit for expansive views of the lake and Tetons. A 15-mile gravel road also parallels the Snake River eastward to Cottonwood—another option for wildlife-watching expeditions or mountain biking.

The campground loops around a hillside, where some of the campsites yield outstanding views of the lake and the Teton Mountains. A mix of fir and spruce provides some shade, but most of the campsites are sunny in midday. The campsites are small, with low brush creating partial privacy along with the trees. The narrow campground road and narrow parking pads can pose challenges for RV drivers unskilled in squeezing into tight spots. Loop 3 is generator-free. Because of its location and scenery, plan on arriving before noon to claim a campsite.

Campsites, facilities: The campground has 81 RV or tent campsites, four tent-only campsites, and one full hookup RV site (sewer, water, and electricity). RVs are limited to 30 feet. Facilities include picnic tables, fire rings with grills, flush toilets, drinking water, garbage service, amphitheater for evening programs, tent pads (30 sites), and disposal station. Only one vehicle is permitted per site. Leashed pets are permitted. A wheelchair-accessible toilet and campsite are available.

Reservations, fees: Reservations are not accepted. Campsites cost $21. RV site costs $55. Shared hiker and biker campsites cost $5. Cash or check. Open early May-early October.

Directions: From Jackson Lake Junction, drive south on Teton Park Road for three miles, or from Jenny Lake Visitor Center drive nine miles north. Turn west into Signal Mountain, continuing straight past the road heading right to the lodge to reach the campground.

GPS Coordinates: N 43° 50.488' W 110° 36.809'

Contact: Grand Teton National Park, P.O. Drawer 170, Moose, WY 83102, 307/739-3300, www.nps.gov/grte/.

51 LEIGH LAKE

Scenic rating: 10

between Jenny Lake and Jackson Lake in Grand Teton National Park

Leigh Lake, a small 250-acre lake tucked at 6,877 feet below the giant toothy Teton Mountains, is a popular kayak and canoe destination for camping. Only human-powered boats are permitted on the lake, making it a quiet place to enjoy nature. Paddle trips to Leigh Lake start at String Lake, a three-mile-long small, shallow lake. A narrow, rocky, shallow stream requiring a 600-foot portage links the two lakes. Trails loop around String Lake and along Leigh Lake's east shore. Two islands—Mystic and Boulder—sit in Leigh Lake, good destinations for exploration. The Tetons are known for strong afternoon winds; plan paddling schedules accordingly. All boats, including kayaks and canoes, require permits, available at the visitors centers and the Jenny Lake backcountry office.

These coveted campsites are set back into the forest on the east and west shores of Leigh Lake. They are prized for their quiet, solitude, wildlife-watching, and scenery. Those on the eastern shore can capture dramatic mountain reflections and sunsets on the water. Those on the western shore do not have trail access, thus guaranteeing more privacy.

Campsites, facilities: Leigh Lake has seven individual tent campsites, plus one group tent site. Six people maximum are allowed per permit, except at group sites, which can hold 12. Boaters may stay in a designated site for two consecutive nights. Facilities include fire pits, bear boxes, and pit toilets, and some sites have tent platforms. No drinking water is available; treat lake water. Pack out your trash. Pets are not allowed.

Reservations, fees: Reservation requests are accepted January 5-May 15. Applications are available online with a $25 nonrefundable fee. Then, 24 hours before your trip, obtain the required free overnight camping permits at the Craig Thomas and Colter Bay Visitor Centers or Jenny Lake Ranger Station. Open June-October.

Directions: From Teton Lake Road, turn west at North Jenny Lake Junction and drive 1.5 miles. Turn right at the sign for String Lake Trailhead. Drive 0.2 mile northwest, opting for the parking area on the left or the one where the road ends. Both require 170-foot portages to the shore.

GPS Coordinates: N 43° 47.173' W 110° 43.817'

Contact: Grand Teton National Park, P.O. Drawer 170, Moose, WY 83102, 307/739-3300, www.nps.gov/grte/.

From Jenny Lake, hikers loop through the Paintbrush-Cascade Canyons below the Grand Teton.

52 JENNY LAKE

Scenic rating: 10

on Jenny Lake in Grand Teton National Park

BEST (

At 6,789 feet, Jenny Lake claims front-row seating below the immense Teton Mountains with exceptional scenery. A ranger station and general store serve as the hub for hikers, bikers, mountain climbers, and boaters. Hikers will want to stay for days. Trails lead to short destinations: Hidden Falls, Inspiration Point, Leigh Lake, and Jenny Lake Loop. The 18-mile Paintbrush-Cascade Loop Trail draws those looking for dramatic high-elevation backcountry and access to rock climbing. A shuttle boat speeds canyon hikers across the lake. Other trailheads sit just south of Jenny Lake, accessed via Teton Park Road. While the lake offers fishing, you may line up along the shore with hordes of anglers. A tour boat circles the lake, and paddlers can rent canoes or kayaks. A gravel boat launch is available for human-powered watercraft or motorboats with 10 horsepower or less. Boating permits are required, available at the backcountry office. The campground offers wildlife-watching, often with male elk rounding up harems in fall. A paved bike trail runs from Jenny Lake to the Craig Thomas Discover Education Center and Jackson. The scenic Jenny Lake Drive also has a paved bike lane.

Jenny Lake—the most popular campground in the park—fills by 9am each day. Its campsites, strung through the loose hilly pine forest and glacial boulders—are roomy. Some are partly shaded, but the best sit in open meadows claiming big views of the Tetons. Campsites are not private, but the trade-off in views is worth it. Trails run from the campground to the visitors center, lake, and boat dock. After day visitors retreat, the area quiets at night. Listen in September for elk bugling.

Campsites, facilities: The campground has 50 tent campsites including several walk-in sites. Pop ups, trailers, truck campers, and generators are prohibited. Vehicles must be smaller than 8 feet wide and 14 feet long. Two tents, one vehicle or two motorcycles, and six people are the maximum allowed per site. Facilities include picnic tables, fire rings with grills, bear boxes, vault toilets, drinking water, shared hiker and biker campsites, and garbage service. Leashed pets are permitted. Wheelchair-accessible facilities include toilets and campsites.

Reservations, fees: Reservations are not accepted. Campsites cost $21. Shared hiker and biker campsites cost $8. Cash or check. Open mid-May-late September.

Directions: On Teton Park Road, drive toward Jenny Lake Visitor Center. Turn west, entering the visitors center complex, for 0.1 mile and turn right at the campground sign for 0.1 mile. GPS Coordinates: N 43° 45.220' W 110° 43.261'

Contact: Grand Teton National Park, P.O. Drawer 170, Moose, WY 83102, 307/739-3300, www.nps.gov/grte/.

At Jackson Hole Mountain Resort, visitors and hikers can take a tram up to the top of Rendezvous Mountain in the Tetons.

© BECKY LOMAX

53 JACKSON HOLE

Scenic rating: 8

in Jackson Hole

Sitting below the towering Teton Mountains, Jackson Hole Campground has convenience. Five miles north, hikers and sightseers can ride the iconic Jackson Hole Mountain Resort tram to the top of 10,450-foot Rendezvous Mountain for impressive views of the Jackson Hole valley and Grand Teton Mountain. Trails come back down the mountain or head into Grand Teton National Park. Lift-accessed mountain biking is also available at the resort. Across the highway from the campground, the Jackson Hole Community Pathway for runners, walkers, and cyclists connects with Teton Village, Moose, and Jackson.

Grassy campsites squeeze under mature cottonwoods and conifers for shade, but more open campsites grab prime views of the Teton Mountains. Larger RVs will feel cramped with low branches and narrow slots. Small tent sites tuck in between RV sites. Renovations in 2012 improved the gravel campground road and washrooms.

Campsites, facilities: This campground has 63 RV campsites, including eight tent campsites. RVs are limited to 40 feet. Hookups are available for water, sewer, and electricity up to 50 amps. Facilities include picnic tables, rock fire rings, flush toilets, showers, drinking water, launderette, camp store, wireless Internet, and disposal station. Leashed pets are permitted.

Reservations, fees: Reservations are accepted. RV sites cost $70-100. Tents cost $40-50. Rates cover four people; each extra person costs $8; kids under six stay for free. Add on sales tax. Cash, check, or credit card. Open May-mid-October.

Directions: From the junction of Highway 22 and Highway 390, drive north on Highway 390 (Moose Wilson Road) for 1.5 miles and turn right at the Fireside Resort sign. Or from Teton Village, drive 5.1 miles south and turn left.

GPS Coordinates: N 43° 31.222' W 110° 50.360'

Contact: Jackson Hole Campground, 2780 North Moose Wilson Road, Wilson, WY 83014, 307/732-2267, www.jacksonholecampground.com.

54 GROS VENTRE

Scenic rating: 8

on the Gros Ventre River in the south end of Grand Teton National Park

Gros Ventre Campground, at 6,568 feet, is not only the largest campground in Grand Teton National Park, but the closest national park campground to Jackson, about 12 miles south. The campground sits opposite the river from the National Elk Refuge, which attracts the largest collection of migrating elk each winter. Gros Ventre Road, a backroad cycling route, provides scenic opportunities for wildlife-watching for bison and elk. The campground's location is convenient for floating or fishing the lower stretches of the Snake River for 14 miles from Moose Landing to Wilson, which requires advanced boating skills. The Gros Ventre River, which flows past the campground, unfortunately often becomes a barren riverbed mid-July-September because of water diverted for irrigation.

The campground, which sits along the Gros Ventre River but with Black Butte blocking most of the Teton Mountains, sprawls its seven large loops on a flat sagebrush plateau beneath cottonwood trees for some shade. Paths lead to the river. Because of its road configurations and campsite parking pads, this campground is the best one in the national park for large trailers and RVs; it is also the last to fill up every day and often doesn't fill to capacity. Located several miles from the highway, the

campground is quiet, secluded, and a respite from busy downtown Jackson or the more popular tourist areas of the park. With no understory, campsites lack privacy.

Campsites, facilities: The campground has 350 individual RV and tent campsites and five large group sites. Two tents, two vehicles, and six people are the maximum allowed per site. The campsites can fit large RVs. Facilities include picnic tables, fire rings with grills, flush toilets, a disposal station, drinking water, an amphitheater for interpretive programs, and garbage service. Leashed pets are permitted. Wheelchair-accessible facilities include toilets and campsites.

Reservations, fees: Reservations are accepted only for group campsites (Grand Teton Lodge Company, 307/543-3100 or 800/628-9988). Campsites cost $21. Cash, check, or credit card. Open early May-early October.

Directions: From Gros Ventre Junction on Highway 89/191, turn northeast onto Gros Ventre Road for 4.6 miles. Turn south for 0.3 mile into the campground.

GPS Coordinates: N 43° 36.979' W 110° 39.979'

Contact: Grand Teton National Park, P.O. Drawer 170, Moose, WY 83102, 307/739-3300, www.nps.gov/grte/.

55 ATHERTON CREEK

Scenic rating: 8

in the Gros Ventre Mountains in Bridger-Teton National Forest

Atherton Creek Campground, elevation 7,000 feet, draws a varied boating crowd because of its location on the north shore of Lower Slide Lake in the colorful red- and orange-streaked Gros Ventre Mountains. Canoeists explore the shoreline, which has silvered trunks buried by water when the lake was formed by a 1925 landslide. Anglers fish for brook, lake, and cutthroat trout. Water-skiers weave a white trail across calm, blue water. When daily winds crop up, windsurfers hit the waves. The Gros Ventre Slide Geological Area still shows the track of the landslide, and an interpretive trail tells the story of the lake's creation. Mountain biking is an option on Gros Ventre Road, with bucolic views west of the Teton Mountains. A boat dock and ramp are available. May-July the Lower Gros Ventre River offers kayakers Class III-IV white water.

The sunny quiet hillside campground gleans a little shade from aspens, spruces, firs, and small willow bushes strung around its interconnected loops, which have back-in gravel parking pads. Sagebrush and wild roses complete the understory for campsites that range from shady and private to sunny and open. Sites 16 and 17 sit on the water, while sites 18 and 20 overlook the water; many of the other campsites have no view of the lake, but some have views of surrounding forest slopes. In the breeze, the aspen leaves clatter with a soothing background sound, but prepare for strong afternoon winds.

Campsites, facilities: The campground has 20 RV or tent campsites. Sites can fit midsized RVs only. Facilities include picnic tables, fire rings with grills, vault toilets (wheelchair-accessible), drinking water, garbage service, bear boxes, tent platforms, and campground hosts. Leashed pets are permitted.

Reservations, fees: Reservations are not accepted. Campsites cost $12. Cash or check. Open late May-September.

Directions: From Moose Junction, drive north 1.2 miles and turn east onto Antelope Flats Road for 3.2 miles. Turn south onto Lower Gros Ventre Road for 2.5 miles. Turn east onto Gros Ventre Road for 5.5 miles of bumpy paved road to the campground entrance on the right.

GPS Coordinates: N 43° 38.269' W 110° 31.333'

Contact: Bridger-Teton National Forest, Jackson Ranger District, 25 Rosencrans Ln., Jackson, WY 83001, 307/739-5400, www.fs.usda.gov/btnf.

56 RED HILLS AND CRYSTAL CREEK

Scenic rating: 8

in the Gros Ventre Mountains in Bridger-Teton National Forest

Sitting at 7,000 feet in the Gros Ventre Mountains of Bridger-Teton National Forest, Red Hill and Crystal Creek are a pair of small, older, adjacent campgrounds that allow exploration of the range facing the Teton Mountains. Red Hills is named for the red-orange sagebrush hills that create such a dramatic contrast in color. Crystal Creek Campground sits at the confluence of Crystal Creek with the Gros Ventre River. Both offer native cutthroat trout fishing, mountain biking on forest roads and nearby trails, and hiking. Trails run south along Crystal Creek into the Gros Ventre Wilderness, but only hikers may travel into the wilderness for climbing its 10,000-foot peaks, an important wildlife enclave for bighorn sheep, elk, and bears. Raft, kayaks, and canoes put in at the Warden Bridge to float eight miles of Class II-III rapids to Lower Slide Lake.

Both campgrounds squeeze in between the road and the river in a forest of spruces and firs. Willows line the riverbank. In Red Hills, sites 1, 2, 4, and 5 claim river frontage, with views of the red-orange hills surrounded by sagebrush. In Crystal Creek, sites 3 and 4 overlook the river, with big views of the richly colored countryside. The quiet, older campgrounds are popular with locals but rarely crowded.

Campsites, facilities: The campgrounds have 11 RV or tent campsites—five at Red Hills and six at Crystal Creek. Sites and the narrow campground roads can fit midsized RVs only. Red Hills has no turnaround. Facilities include picnic tables, fire rings with grills or rock fire rings, pit and vault toilets, drinking water, and bear boxes. Leashed pets are permitted.

Reservations, fees: Reservations are not

accepted. Campsites cost $10. Cash or check. Open late May-September, but Crystal Creek stays open into fall if weather permits.

Directions: From Moose Junction, drive north 1.2 miles and turn east onto Antelope Flats Road for 3.2 miles. Turn south onto Lower Gros Ventre Road for 2.5 miles. Turn east onto Gros Ventre Road for 10 miles of bumpy paved and dirt road. The campground entrances are on the left 0.4 mile apart.

Red Hills GPS Coordinates: N 43° 36.691' W 110° 26.266'

Crystal Creek GPS Coordinates: N 43° 36.643' W 110° 25.865'

Contact: Bridger-Teton National Forest, Jackson Ranger District, 25 Rosencrans Ln., Jackson, WY 83001, 307/739-5400, www.fs.usda.gov/btnf.

57 CURTIS CANYON

Scenic rating: 9

in the Gros Ventre Mountains in Bridger-Teton National Forest

Located at the north end of the Gros Ventre Mountains, the area around Curtis Canyon Campground has million-dollar views! At 7,000 feet on the east side of Jackson Hole, the area overlooks the Jackson Hole valley, National Elk Refuge, and the Teton Mountains. Across the road from the campground sits an overlook, a good place to walk in the evening to watch the sun set over the Tetons. The Curtis Canyon Road and spur forest roads attract mountain bikers and OHV riders. This is the closest Forest Service campground to the town of Jackson.

One prime campsite has the million-dollar view, like the overlook. The others cluster under a small forest of Douglas firs. Beneath the tree canopy, only tree trunks separate the grassy sites, letting you see the neighbors.

Campsites, facilities: The campground has 10 RV or tent campsites, plus two tent-only sites. A few parking pads can fit RVs up 40 feet, but small RVs will fit the narrow campground road, access road, overhanging trees, and parking pad width and angles better. Two pull-through sites are available. Facilities include picnic tables, fire rings with grills, vault toilets, drinking water, garbage service, firewood for sale, and bear boxes. Leashed pets are permitted.

Reservations, fees: Reservations are not accepted. Campsites cost $12 for one unit (RV, trailer, or tent). Cash or check. Open late May-September.

Directions: In Jackson, take Broadway east to its terminus at Nelson Drive and the National Elk Refuge Road. Turn north onto the gravel refuge road for 4.6 miles. Turn right onto Curtis Canyon Road for 2.6 miles to climb to the campground entrance on the right. Curtis Canyon Road is narrow, rocky, and has one sharp hairpin.

GPS Coordinates: N 43° 30.788' W 110° 39.672'

Contact: Bridger-Teton National Forest, Jackson Ranger District, 25 Rosencrans Ln., Jackson, WY 83001, 307/739-5400, www.fs.usda.gov/btnf.

58 VIRGINIAN RV PARK

Scenic rating: 6

in Jackson

The Virginian RV Park is the only campground in downtown Jackson, making it a campground of convenience about one mile from the downtown area with shopping, galleries, restaurants, park with antler arches, and famous cowboy western saloons. A free shuttle across the street runs to downtown Jackson. The campground is part of the Virginian Lodge, a motel complex with a restaurant, saloon, liquor store, hair salon, and heated outdoor pool and hot tub. Hiking and mountain biking trails weave around Snow

King Mountain, which looms to the south of town. The ski area at Snow King transforms in summer with the thrill of zipping down alpine slides and horseback riding.

The sunny parking lot-style campground sits behind the Virginian Lodge surrounded by commercial properties. Narrow small plots of grass separate the sites, which are about 20 feet wide. A handful of small trees offer minimal shade.

Campsites, facilities: This campground has 103 RV campsites. RVs are limited to 40 feet. The campground has 64 pull-throughs and 39 back-in slots with gravel parking pads and road. Hookups are available for water, sewer, cable TV, and electricity up to 50 amps. Facilities include picnic tables, flush toilets, showers, drinking water, launderette, and wireless Internet. Campers can use the swimming pool and hot tub at the lodge. Leashed pets are permitted.

Reservations, fees: Reservations are accepted. Campsites cost $65-70. A 6 percent sales tax is added. Cash, check, or credit card. Open May-mid-October.

Directions: From the junction of highways 22/189/89, drive east on West Broadway for three blocks and turn right.

GPS Coordinates: N 43° 28.358' W 110° 46.679'

Contact: Virginian RV Park, 750 West Broadway, Jackson Hole, WY 83001, 307/733-7189 or 800/321-6982, http://virginianlodge.com.

59 SNAKE RIVER PARK KOA

Scenic rating: 7

on the Snake River near Jackson

The Snake River Park KOA, elevation 5,090 feet, is a combination campground and white-water rafting outfitter on the Snake River between Hoback Junction and Jackson. Those

camping at the park can get 10 percent off white-water rafting trips or saddle and paddle trips. The corral is across the street from the campground. The campground is 20 minutes from the entrance to Grand Teton National Park and 15 minutes from Jackson. Fishing is available on the Snake River from the campground.

Tucked into a deep narrow canyon, the campground squeezes between the busy two-lane highway rumbling with commercial haul trucks and the Snake River. Tent campsites sit along Horse Creek and the river with partial shade and views. The sunny RV campsites are lined up in parking-lot fashion with mowed lawns between sites. Stairs lead from the campground to the sandy riverbank.

Campsites, facilities: This campground has 47 RV back-in campsites and 10 tent campsites. RVs are limited to 36 feet. Hookups are available for water, sewer, and electricity up to 50 amps. Facilities include picnic tables, fire rings with grills, flush toilets, showers, drinking water, a coin-op launderette, a game room, firewood for sale, playground, pet walk, convenience store, and wireless Internet. Leashed pets are permitted.

Reservations, fees: Reservations are accepted. RV hookups costs $81-89. Tents cost $41-45. Rates run less during spring and fall. Rates cover four people; each extra person costs $8; kids under six stay for free. A 6 percent sales tax is added. Cash, check, or credit card. Open mid-April-November.

Directions: On Highway 26/89/197/191, drive 12 miles south of Jackson or 1.5 miles north of Hoback Junction. Turn west into the campground.

GPS Coordinates: N 43° 20.450' W 110° 43.400'

Contact: Jackson South/Snake River KOA, 9705 S. Hwy. 89, Jackson, WY 83001, 307/733-7078 or 800/562-1878, www.srp-koa.com.

SOUTHERN YELLOWSTONE GATEWAYS

© BECKY LOMAX

Three national forests ring the southern boundaries of Yellowstone and Grand Teton National Parks. To the west, Caribou-Targhee National Forest offers spectacular "back-side" views of the Tetons. Campgrounds are smaller, more remote, and less crowded than in the national park. In the north, Island Park's plateau cradles lakes and rivers with more than 15 campgrounds. To the south and east, the Bridger-Teton National Forest surrounds Grand Teton's southern and eastern boundaries. Two high mountain ranges dominate: The Gros Ventre Mountains, with Granite Hot Springs and the Gros Ventre Landslide, while the Wind River Range contains Fremont Lake, Wyoming's second-largest natural lake. To the east, the Shoshone National Forest is the gateway from the Midwest. The Buffalo Bill Scenic Byway leads to Yellowstone's eastern entrance, where campgrounds line the arid corridor.

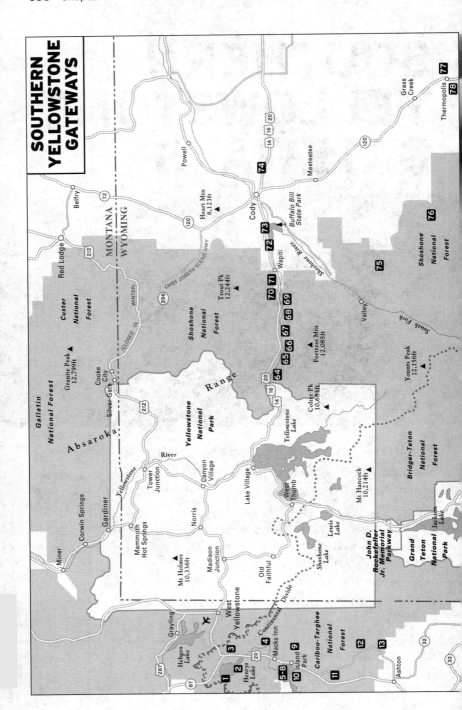

SOUTHERN YELLOWSTONE GATEWAYS

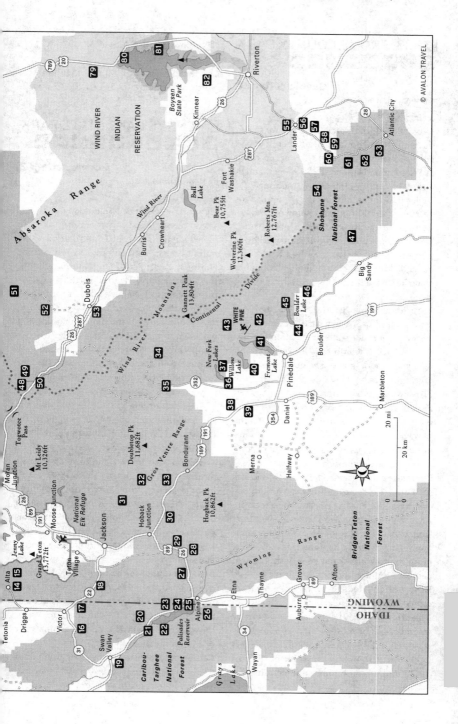

© AVALON TRAVEL

1 BILL FROME COUNTY PARK

🏊 🚣 �'' 🎣 🐕 ♿ 🚐 ⛺

Scenic rating: 7

on Henrys Lake, Idaho

At 6,450 feet, Bill Frome County Park sits on the west side of Idaho's 6,000-acre Henrys Lake about 15 miles from the west entrance to Yellowstone National Park. A boat launch includes a cement ramp, dock, mooring, and trailer parking. Henrys Lake is popular for boating, waterskiing, and fishing for Yellowstone cutthroat, brook, and rainbow trout. You can take a scenic 25-mile dirt-road drive west to Red Rocks Pass and Red Rocks National Wildlife Refuge. You can swim, but not much beach is available because of the boating facilities.

Surrounded by sagebrush prairie, the quiet campground uses a few small perimeter aspens to help shade some of the sunny campsites and act as windbreaks for the common strong afternoon gusts. The open area, however, provides big views of the lake and the surrounding mountains, including Sawtell Peak to the south and Black Mountain to the north. A single gravel road drops through the campground to the boat launch; all campsites line up on the grass and gravel back-in parking pads in close proximity.

Campsites, facilities: The campground has 35 RV or tent campsites that can accommodate large RVs. Facilities include some rock fire rings, vault toilets (wheelchair-accessible), boat launch, pet area, firewood for sale, and campground hosts. Drinking water is not available; bring your own. Pack out your trash. Leashed pets are permitted.

Reservations, fees: Reservations are not accepted. Camping is free. Open May-October.
Directions: From the junction of Highway 20 and Highway 87, drive north on Highway 87 for 5.1 miles. Turn west and follow Henrys Lake Drive around the west side of the lake for 2.7 miles. The campground entrance sits on the left.

GPS Coordinates: N 44° 38.997' W 111° 26.275'
Contact: Fremont County, 151 West 1st North, St. Anthony, ID 83445, 208/624-7332.

2 HENRYS LAKE STATE PARK

🥾 🚴 🏊 🚣 �'' 🎣 🐕 ♿ 🚐 ⛺

Scenic rating: 7

on Henrys Lake, Idaho

Henrys Lake State Park, elevation 6,470 feet, sits on the southeast corner of the 6,000-acre Henrys Lake north of Island Park and 15 miles from the west entrance to Yellowstone National Park. Within a 10-minute drive, the Targhee Creek Trailhead launches a 14-mile loop past five alpine lakes at the base of Targhee Peak. A paved bicycle and walking trail loops through the park, including the wheelchair-accessible Aspen Loop Nature Trail. Guided nature walks are available. A boat ramp allows for launching onto the lake for boating, waterskiing, paddling, and fishing. The lake harbors Yellowstone cutthroat, brook, and rainbow trout. The park also has good wildlife-watching: birds, pronghorn antelope, and moose. For kids, the park has a Junior Ranger Program.

Surrounded by wetlands and sagebrush prairie, the campground's two large paved loops are on the southeast shore of Henrys Lake, where few trees provide shade or act as windbreaks for the common strong afternoon gusts. The open area, however, provides big views of the lake and the surrounding mountains, including Sawtell Peak to the south and Black Mountain to the north. Paved back-in parking pads are surrounded by mowed lawn, with campsites spread out for privacy, although you will see everyone around your site. When the winds die down, you can hear a faint truck or two on the highway.

Campsites, facilities: The campground has 43 RV or tent campsites. RVs are limited to 40 feet. Hookups are available for electricity and water. Facilities include picnic tables, fire rings with grills, flush toilets, showers, drinking water, garbage service, disposal station, firewood for sale, horseshoe pits, interpretive programs, wireless Internet, boat launch, fish-cleaning station, and campground hosts. Leashed pets are permitted. Wheelchair-accessible facilities include toilets and one campsite.

Reservations, fees: Reservations are accepted (888/922-6743 or online). Campsites cost $18-24. Park entry costs $5. Add on 6 percent Idaho sales tax. Idaho residents can buy an annual $10 passport card that covers entry and gives discounts on camping fees. Cash, check, or credit card. Open late May-mid-October.

Directions: From the junction of Highway 87 and Highway 20, drive south toward Island Park for 1.2 miles and turn right at the state park sign for 1.7 miles to the park entrance station.

GPS Coordinates: N 44° 37.127' W 111° 22.315'

Contact: Henrys Lake State Park, 3917 East 5100 North, Island Park, ID 83429, 208/558-7532, www.parksandrecreation.idaho.gov.

3 VALLEY VIEW RV PARK

Scenic rating: 7

near Henrys Lake, Idaho

At 6,633 feet at the north end of Island Park, Valley View RV Park offers a convenient place to stay right on the highway for those traveling toward Yellowstone or wanting to explore the nearby Henrys Lake. Henrys Lake State Park, with a boat launch and trailer parking, sits 2.5 miles away for boating, fishing, waterskiing, canoeing, and kayaking. Nearby, the 14-mile Targhee Creek Trail loops past several forested lakes. South in Island Park, the Henry's Fork River offers fly-fishing, Harriman State Park has hiking and mountain biking trails, and scenic drives tour to Mesa Falls. The campground also sits 20 minutes

from the west entrance to Yellowstone National Park.

Baking in sun, the treeless campground offers no protection from the afternoon winds that crop up. That said, with the openness, all sites command views of the surrounding mountains, including Sawtell Peak. Some can see Henry's Lake in the distance. The campsites are level pull-throughs with small patches of grass between each site. From the campground's location by the highway, you will hear noise.

Campsites, facilities: The campground has 78 RV campsites. RVs are limited to 70 feet. Tents are allowed, too. Hookups include sewer, water, and electricity up to 50 amps. Facilities include picnic tables, flush toilets, drinking water, showers, launderette, and garbage service. Leashed pets are permitted.

Reservations, fees: Reservations are accepted. RV hookups cost $26-31. Tent sites cost $10 with no hookups or $14 with hookups. Rates are for two people. Cash or credit card. Open mid-May-September.

Directions: On Highway 20, locate Valley View RV Park 0.6-mile south of the junction with Highway 87.

GPS Coordinates: N 44° 37.614' W 111° 20.026'

Contact: Valley View RV Park, 5152 N Hwy 20, Island Park, ID 83429 208/558-7443 or 888/558-7443, http://valleyviewrv.com.

4 BIG SPRINGS

Scenic rating: 8

in Island Park in Caribou-Targhee National Forest

BEST (

At 6,400 feet, Big Springs Campground sits adjacent to Big Springs, an idyllic natural pool fed by snowmelt and rain that seeps through the Yellowstone plateau. The exceptionally clear water of the National Natural Landmark stays at 52°F year-round, providing habitat for trout, moose, bald eagles, and herons. Wheelchair-accessible trails connect the campground with the pond. A one-mile hiking-only trail (paved halfway) traverses downstream along the Henrys Fork of the Snake River. Big Springs does not permit wading, swimming, fishing, or boating along this route to protect the underwater gardens for spawning. One mile west of the campground, a river put-in allows paddlers to tour the four-mile National Recreation Water Trail, which is closed to fishing. Mountain bikers and ATV riders tour the nearby 42-mile dirt Union Pacific Railroad Right of Way Trail.

Set in a young lodgepole forest, the campground loops one paved road around its campsites, all with rough-paved pull-through parking. The campsites are spread out for privacy, and the lodgepoles are thick enough to shield sites from one another. At night, the quiet is broken only by the yipping of coyotes or the calls of herons. The spacious campsites vary between sunny (site 11) and partly shaded. Sites 1-3 view Big Springs Road.

Campsites, facilities: The campground has 15 RV or tent campsites and one large group campsite. RVs are limited to 32 feet. Facilities include picnic tables, fire rings with grills, cookstove pedestals, vault toilets (wheelchair-accessible), drinking water, garbage service, and campground hosts. Leashed pets are permitted.

Reservations, fees: Reservations are not accepted, except for the group campsite (877/444-6777, www.recreation.gov). Campsites cost $15. Extra vehicles cost $6. Cash or check. Open late May-mid-September.

Directions: From Highway 20, two entrances onto Big Springs Loop Road swing east to the campground. Coming from Henrys Lake, turn east at Island Park Village onto N. Big Springs Loop Road (Forest Road 059) for 4.3 miles mostly on dirt. Coming from Ashton, turn east at Mack's Inn onto S. Big Springs Loop Road for 4.7 paved miles. Locate the campground entrance south of the Big Springs Bridge.

GPS Coordinates: N 44° 29.849' W 111° 15.315'
Contact: Caribou-Targhee National Forest, Island Park Ranger District, 3726 Hwy. 20, Island Park, ID 83429, 208/558-7301, www.fs.usda.gov/ctnf.

5 FLAT ROCK

Scenic rating: 6
in Island Park in Caribou-Targhee National Forest, Idaho

At 6,400 feet, Flat Rock sits on the banks of the Henrys Fork of the Snake River, a blue-ribbon trout fishery. A five-minute walk leads to Mack's Inn, where you can rent canoes, kayaks, and rafts. Outfitters for fishing and horseback riding are nearby, as well as groceries, restaurants, and gas. The campground also sits at the lower end of the Henrys Fork of the Snake River National Recreation Water Trail—a four-mile paddle. Fishing is not permitted on the trail until Henrys Fork Outlet Creek; however, fishing is permitted along the riverbank at the campground, and you can launch hand-carried watercrafts from the campground. The river harbors native Yellowstone cutthroat, plus rainbow and brook trout. On Sawtell Peak, the six-mile Rock Creek Basin Trail climbs over the Continental Divide into the scenic rocky basin. For bicyclists on Highway 20, the campground is one of the most convenient with its short access.

The campground is divided into lower and upper loop (A and B loops). Loop B has electrical hookups in sites 1-9; the Loop A includes sites along the river (18-23). You can pick from sunny or shady campsites under lodgepole pines, and the grassy meadows between campsites bloom with asters in August. You'll see several other campsites from your picnic table, and both loops pick up substantial highway noise.

© BECKY LOMAX

The Henrys Fork of the Snake River is a waterway for floating and wildlife-watching.

Campsites, facilities: The campground has nine RV campsites with electrical hookups (one is a double site) and 32 tent or RV campsites. RVs are limited to 32 feet. Facilities include picnic tables, fire rings with grills, cookstove pedestals, vault and flush toilets (wheelchair-accessible), drinking water, garbage service, and campground hosts. Leashed pets are permitted.

Reservations, fees: Reservations are accepted (877/444-6777, www.recreation.gov). Hookups cost $20. The double site costs $40. Non-hookup campsites cost $15. Extra vehicles cost $6. Cash or check. Open late May-mid-September.

Directions: From Highway 20 south of Mack's Inn at milepost 393, turn west into the campground.

GPS Coordinates: N 44° 29.993' W 111° 20.316'

Contact: Caribou-Targhee National Forest, Island Park Ranger District, 3726 Hwy. 20, Island Park, ID 83429, 208/558-7301, www.fs.usda.gov/ctnf.

6 COFFEE POT

Scenic rating: 7

in Island Park in Caribou-Targhee National Forest, Idaho

Located at 6,300 feet, Upper Coffee Pot sits on the Henrys Fork of the Snake River, a blue-ribbon trout stream. Kayakers, rafters, and canoeists can float the river one mile from Mack's Inn to the campground or five miles to the campground, starting at the upper end of the Henrys Fork of the Snake River National Recreation Water Trail. However, all boaters must take out at the campground because of the dangerous rapids downstream. Fishing is not permitted on the water trail until the confluence with the Henrys Fork Outlet Creek, but fishing is permitted at the campground. A 2.5-mile hiking trail tours the shoreline from the campground southeast to Coffee Pot Rapids. Mountain bikers and ATV riders can ride the network of old Forest Service roads around the campground.

The campground lines up in two sections along the river. The right loop contains electrical sites (8-15). Nine campsites overlook the river, but all campsites have quick access to it. Campsites at the end of each loop turnaround have the most privacy. The loose lodgepole forest and grassy meadow campground has sunny and partly shaded sites that are close enough that you'll see neighboring campers. With its location away from the highway, the only sound in the campground is the river.

Campsites, facilities: The campground has eight RV campsites with electrical hookups (one site is double) plus five RV or tent campsites. RVs are limited to 50 feet. Facilities include picnic tables, fire rings with grills, vault toilets (wheelchair-accessible), drinking water, garbage service, and campground hosts. Leashed pets are permitted.

Reservations, fees: Reservations are accepted (877/444-6777, www.recreation.gov). Hookups cost $20. Campsites cost $15. The double site costs $40. Extra vehicles cost $6. Cash or check. Open late May-mid-September.

Directions: From 0.5 mile south of Mack's Inn on Highway 20, turn west onto Forest Road 130 at milepost 392.5. Drive one mile and turn right onto Forest Road 311. Drive 0.4 mile. Turn right, and drive 0.2 mile to the campground.

GPS Coordinates: N 44° 29.442' W 111° 21.974'

Contact: Caribou-Targhee National Forest, Island Park Ranger District, 3726 Hwy. 20, Island Park, ID 83429, 208/558-7301, www.fs.usda.gov/ctnf.

7 MCCREA BRIDGE

Scenic rating: 6

in Island Park in Caribou-Targhee National Forest, Idaho

At 6,200 feet, McCrea Bridge Campground sits where the Henrys Fork of the Snake River flows into the northeast arm of Island Park Reservoir, formed by a 1,250-foot-long dam built in 1938. The campground has a boat launch with four docks and a cement ramp, which allows access to the reservoir for boating, waterskiing, paddling, and fishing for kokanee salmon, rainbow trout, and Yellowstone cutthroat trout. Water levels drop in late summer; call the Forest Service to check on levels. Mountain bikers can tour the maze of forest roads in the area.

Sitting on the narrow arm of the reservoir, the campground flanks a western-facing hillside of lodgepole and sagebrush and looks across at summer homes. The campground has two interconnected gravel loops, with the A loop closest to the water. Three sites (3, 4, and 6) overlook the water. Several sites (2, 3, 4, 10, and 12) are wide open and sunny; the others have partial shade and some privacy created from the forest. Although the campground is removed from the trucking noise on Highway 20, the Yale-Kilgore Road is a main thoroughfare for accessing private homes on the reservoir. Most of the campsites are gravel back-ins.

Campsites, facilities: The campground has 25 RV or tent campsites. Five are double sites. RVs are limited to 32 feet. Facilities include picnic tables, fire rings with grills, vault toilets (wheelchair-accessible), drinking water, garbage service, boat launch, and campground hosts. Leashed pets are permitted.

Reservations, fees: Reservations are accepted (877/444-6777, www.recreation.gov). Campsites cost $15. Double campsites cost $30. Extra vehicles cost $6. Cash or check. Open late May-mid-September.

Directions: From Highway 20 two miles north of the Island Park Ranger Station, turn west onto Yale-Kilgore Road at milepost 389.2. Drive 2.1 miles and turn south before the bridge into the campground.

GPS Coordinates: N 44° 27.758' W 111° 24.043'

Contact: Caribou-Targhee National Forest, Island Park Ranger District, 3726 Hwy. 20,

Island Park, ID 83429, 208/558-7301, www.
fs.usda.gov/ctnf.

8 BUTTERMILK

Scenic rating: 6

in Island Park in Caribou-Targhee National
Forest, Idaho

Buttermilk Campground, elevation 6,200 feet,
sits on the tip of a peninsula on Island Park
Reservoir's east end. The campground is the
biggest on the reservoir—empty on weekdays
in early and late season, but hopping busy in
peak summer. The campground's boat launch,
with five docks, a double-side concrete ramp,
and trailer parking, accommodates those getting onto the reservoir for boating, waterskiing, paddling, and fishing. Anglers go after
kokanee salmon, rainbow trout, and Yellowstone cutthroat trout. Mountain bikers and
ATVers ride the local network of forest roads.

Buttermilk spreads the partly shaded campsites out, but you can see through the trees
to the neighbors. Although the access to the
campground is via paved road, the campground loops and parking pads, mostly back-
ins, are gravel. Only three sites in loop A and
five sites in loop B have peek-a-boo views of
the water through the trees. After the boating
stops, the campground is quiet at night. Paths
cut from the campground loops to the water.

Campsites, facilities: The campground has
47 RV or tent campsites, five double campsites,
and one group site. (As of 2013, only 25 are
available to the public.) One additional RV
campsite (site 38) has a hookup for electricity.
RVs are limited to 45 feet. Facilities include
picnic tables, fire rings with grills, vault toilets
(wheelchair-accessible), drinking water, tent
platforms, garbage service, a boat launch, and
campground hosts. Leashed pets are permitted.

Reservations, fees: Reservations are accepted (877/444-6777, www.recreation.gov).
Campsites cost $15. The electrical hookup site

costs $20, and double sites cost $30. Extra
vehicles cost $6. Cash or check. Open late
May-mid-September.

Directions: From Highway 20 two miles
north of the Island Park Ranger Station, turn
west onto Yale-Kilgore Road at milepost 389.2.
Drive 1.9 miles and turn south onto Buttermilk Road for 2.5 miles. Turn right into the
campground.

GPS Coordinates: N 44° 25.934' W 111°
25.568'

Contact: Caribou-Targhee National Forest,
Island Park Ranger District, 3726 Hwy. 20,
Island Park, ID 83429, 208/558-7301, www.
fs.usda.gov/ctnf.

9 BUFFALO

Scenic rating: 7

in Island Park in Caribou-Targhee National
Forest, Idaho

At 6,200 feet, Buffalo is the largest national
forest campground in the Island Park area
and the one that sees the most visits. The
campground sits right on the Buffalo River,
where anglers go after a variety of trout. A
wheelchair-accessible boardwalk and fishing
platforms sit adjacent to the G loop. Kayakers, canoeists, tubers, and rafts float the river.
Boaters, water-skiers, and anglers can access
Island Park Reservoir via the Island Park boat
ramp, two miles from the campground. Cyclists on Highway 20 use this campground
for its convenience to the highway. Evening
interpretive programs include appearances by
Smokey Bear.

A paved road winds through the seven
loops of Buffalo Campground with paved
pull-through or back-in parking pads. Surrounded by grass, fireweed, and purple asters,
the campsites are partly shaded by doghair
lodgepole and aspens, which also make the
sites semiprivate. A and B loops sit closest to
the highway, which rumbles with commercial

trucking. Loops A, D, F, and G each have a handful of campsites that border the river, although trees, serviceberries, and willows block some views. G5 has the best river view.

Campsites, facilities: The campground has 127 RV or tent campsites, including 12 sites with electricity, four double campsites, and one group site. RVs are limited to 45 feet. Facilities include picnic tables, fire rings with grills, flush and vault toilets (wheelchair-accessible), drinking water, tent platforms, garbage service, an amphitheater for interpretive programs, and campground hosts. Leashed pets are permitted.

Reservations, fees: Reservations are accepted (877/444-6777, www.recreation.gov). Campsites cost $15. Electrical hookups cost $20; double sites cost $40. Extra vehicles cost $6. Cash or check. Open late May–mid-September.

Directions: On Highway 20, drive 0.25 mile north of the Island Park Ranger Station to milepost 387.5. Turn east off the highway into the campground.

GPS Coordinates: N 44° 25.571' W 111° 22.119'

Contact: Caribou-Targhee National Forest, Island Park Ranger District, 3726 Hwy. 20, Island Park, ID 83429, 208/558-7301, www.fs.usda.gov/ctnf.

10 BOX CANYON

🏃🚴🛶⛵🚣🎣🐕♿🚐⛺

Scenic rating: 7

in Island Park in Caribou-Targhee National Forest, Idaho

Located at 6,320 feet, Box Canyon sits on the Henrys Fork of the Snake River. Trout anglers favor the blue-ribbon fishery for its wild Yellowstone cutthroat and rainbow trout. In this section, the river is catch-and-release only with barbless hooks. Box Canyon is also a favorite section of the river for rafts, kayaks, and experienced canoeists with its Class II rapids. The two-hour float goes from the Island Park Dam Road launch to Last Chance. Mountain bikers tour the maze of dirt Forest Service roads in the area, and hikers can walk Box Canyon via a three-mile trail along its rim.

Box Canyon is one of the best campgrounds in Island Park for those who like privacy and seclusion. One gravel loop accesses all the campsites with gravel back-in parking pads. Set back from the highway, the quiet campground has spacious campsites tucked into shade of lodgepoles and Douglas firs. The large, grassy sites spread out for privacy surrounded by purple asters, huckleberries, and serviceberries. Several campsites sit near the river, without views of the water, but with paths cutting through the trees to the riverbank.

Campsites, facilities: The campground has 19 RV or tent campsites, including two double sites. RVs are limited to 32 feet. Facilities include picnic tables, fire rings with grills, vault toilets (wheelchair-accessible), drinking water, garbage service, tent platforms, and campground hosts. Leashed pets are permitted.

Reservations, fees: Reservations are not accepted. Campsites cost $15; double campsites cost $30. Extra vehicles cost $6. Cash or check. Open late May–mid-September.

Directions: From Highway 20 one mile south of the Island Park Ranger Station, turn west at milepost 386 onto the gravel Forest Road 134 for 0.4 mile. Turn right onto Forest Road 284 for one mile to reach the campground entrance. GPS Coordinates: N 44° 24.584' W 111° 23.799'

Contact: Caribou-Targhee National Forest, Island Park Ranger District, 3726 Hwy. 20, Island Park, ID 83429, 208/558-7301, www.fs.usda.gov/ctnf.

11 RIVERSIDE

🏃🚴🛶🚙🚣🎣🐕♿🚐⛺

Scenic rating: 8

in Island Park in Caribou-Targhee National Forest, Idaho

BEST (

At 6,200 feet, Riverside is Island Park's

southernmost campground. It sits five miles south of Harriman State Park ($4 for entrance), a wildlife refuge where you can see elk, moose, sandhill cranes, and trumpeter swans. The park is also renowned for its blue-ribbon fishery, and it holds 20 miles of trails for hikers and mountain bikers. Guided horseback trail rides and tours of historical ranch buildings are also available. From the campground, you can fish the Henrys Fork of the Snake River. Upstream of the campground is catch-and-release only with barbless hooks. Downstream of the campground there's a two-fish limit. Expert boaters can launch from the campground to float Cardiac Canyon to Hatchery Ford; less skilled boaters should float the upstream section seven miles from Last Chance to take out at the campground.

The campground sprawls in several interconnected loops. The A sites line up along the river, with many of them overlooking the water and the volcanic rockfalls flanking the opposite shore. While many of these grab the views, they do so at a cost to privacy as they are more sunny and open amid small stands of aspens and lodgepoles. Those seeking privacy and shade will find both in the hillside camps of loops B and C under tall lodgepoles. The river froths here, filling the campground with its sound.

Campsites, facilities: The campground has 56 RV or tent campsites, plus one double site and one group campsite. (As of 2013, only 34 sites are available to the public.) Fifteen sites have paved parking pads and patios that are wheelchair-accessible. RVs are limited to 35 feet. Facilities include picnic tables, fire rings with grills, cookstove pedestals, vault toilets, drinking water, garbage service, and campground hosts. Leashed pets are permitted. Wheelchair-accessible toilets are available.

Reservations, fees: Reservations are accepted (877/444-6777, www.recreation.gov). Campsites cost $15. Double sites cost $30. Extra vehicles cost $6. Cash or check. Open late May-mid-September.

Directions: From Highway 20 about 16 miles

north of Ashton, turn east off the highway at milepost 375.6. Head southeast on the narrow, rough-paved Forest Road 304 for 0.8 mile to the campground entrance.

GPS Coordinates: N 44° 15.999' W 111° 27.482'

Contact: Caribou-Targhee National Forest, Island Park Ranger District, 3726 Hwy. 20, Island Park, ID 83429, 208/558-7301, www.fs.usda.gov/ctnf.

12 GRANDVIEW

Scenic rating: 9

in Island Park in Caribou-Targhee National Forest, Idaho

BEST (

Located on the Mesa Falls Scenic Byway at 5,900 feet, Grandview perches on the lip of a deep canyon that houses the Henrys Fork of the Snake River where it roars through Mesa Falls. A four-wheel-drive road drops from the

© BECKY LOMAX

Lower Mesa Falls on the Henrys Fork of the Snake River

back of the campground 0.5 mile to the river for fishing, rafting, or kayaking. The route also makes a good hike, since the climb back up gains 500 feet in elevation. From the campground, a two-minute walk leads to the overlook for the 65-foot-high Lower Mesa Falls, but the larger 114-foot-high and 300-foot-wide Upper Mesa Falls thunders about a mile upstream, looking like a smaller clone of Niagara Falls. At the site ($5 or federal access passes), paths lead to decks overlooking various points of the falls, including the lip.

The campground sits in a loose forest of fir, aspen, and lodgepole trees with brushy mountain ash and willows lending a thick understory. The short gravel road puts the partly shaded campsites close to each other, but the underbrush lends privacy. Once the day traffic on the scenic byway disappears, the campground is so quiet that you can hear the faint roar of Lower Mesa Falls below in the canyon.

Campsites, facilities: The campground has nine RV or tent campsites (two are double sites). RVs are limited to 28 feet. Facilities include picnic tables, fire rings with grills, cookstove pedestals, electrical hookups, vault toilets (wheelchair-accessible), drinking water, garbage service, and campground hosts. Leashed pets are permitted.

Reservations, fees: Reservations are not accepted. Campsites cost $20. Double sites cost $40. Extra vehicles cost $6. Cash or check. Open from late May-October.

Directions: From Highway 20 one mile north of Harriman State Park, turn east onto the Mesa Falls Scenic Byway (also Route 47 and Forest Road 294) and drive south for 14 miles. Or from Ashton, drive the byway 16 miles northeast. The campground entrance is on the southwest side of the byway adjacent to Lower Mesa Falls Overlook and 0.5 mile southeast from the entrance to Upper Mesa Falls. GPS Coordinates: N 44° 10.506' W 111° 18.837'

Contact: Caribou-Targhee National Forest, Island Park Ranger District, 3726 Hwy. 20, Island Park, ID 83429, 208/558-7301, www.fs.usda.gov/ctnf.

13 WARM RIVER

Scenic rating: 6

in Island Park in Caribou-Targhee National Forest, Idaho

BEST

At 5,200 feet along the Mesa Falls Scenic Byway, Warm River Campground sits adjacent to a tiny burg of three houses. The river's slow-moving water is popular for swimming, floating with tubes, paddling, and rafting. Fed by water from the Yellowstone plateau via underground springs, the clear water maintains a year-round temperature of 50°F. Wading anglers go after native trout, and a wheelchair-accessible fishing platform is available. The campground is also the south entrance to the 42-mile Railroad Right of Way Trail, which includes one tunnel, with its first two miles open only to hikers and mountain bikers.

Surrounded by sagebrush and aspen slopes, the popular campground tucks into a lush river corridor. Many of the grassy campsites sit right on the Warm River. Mature willows provide shade for some of the sites, but the lack of understory allows you to see other campers. The campground is in several sections: a collection of shady RV sites, walk-in tent sites, a large group pavilion, and a sunny loop of campsites accessed via a narrow bridge across the river. Once the byway traffic dies at night, the campground quiets to the sound of the river and birds.

Campsites, facilities: The campground has 13 RV campsites, 12 tent campsites, one double site, and one group site. RVs are limited to 40 feet. Facilities include picnic tables, fire rings with grills, pedestal grills, cookstove pedestals, vault toilets, drinking water, garbage service, horseshoe pits, tent pads, and campground hosts. Leashed pets are permitted.

Wheelchair-accessible facilities include toilets and one campsite with electricity (site 13).

Reservations, fees: Reservations are accepted (877/444-6777, www.recreation.gov). Campsites cost $15. The double site costs $30. Extra vehicles cost $6. The accessible electrical hookup site costs $19-21. Cash or check. Open late May-mid-September.

Directions: From Highway 20 one mile north of Harriman State Park, turn east onto the Mesa Falls Scenic Byway (also Route 47 and Forest Road 294) and drive south for 20 miles. At milepost 8.9, turn east along the river and drive 0.5 mile into the campground. From Ashton, you can also head north on the byway for about nine miles to reach the campground. GPS Coordinates: N 44° 7.208' W 111° 18.814'

Contact: Caribou-Targhee National Forest, Island Park Ranger District, 3726 Hwy. 20, Island Park, ID 83429, 208/558-7301, www.fs.usda.gov/ctnf.

14 REUNION FLATS

Scenic rating: 9

in the Teton Mountains in Caribou-Targhee National Forest, Wyoming

Located at 6,900 feet, Reunion Flats sits on the west flank of the Teton Mountains. It is the closest campground to Grand Targhee Resort, which offers summer scenic lift rides, horseback riding, and lift-accessed mountain biking and hiking. You'll stare at Grand Teton from Targhee's slopes. The resort's annual bluegrass festival takes place in late August. Trailheads into the Jedediah Smith Wilderness and Grand Teton National Park depart 1.8 miles to the east near Teton Canyon Campground. Because of the Yellowstone cutthroat trout's spawning, fishing is not permitted in Teton Creek until July 1.

While a pine, fir, and aspen forest surrounds the campground, many of the grassy sites are open, allowing big views of Teton

Canyon and the tips of the Teton Mountains in the distance. Paths connect to Teton Creek, which runs past the campground. The spacious sites have flat, roomy spots for tents. Unfortunately, the individual sites sit in between the large group camping sites, but if large groups are not present, the campground is very quiet.

Campsites, facilities: The campground has four RV or tent campsites, one tent campsite, and three large group sites. RVs are limited to 60 feet. Facilities include picnic tables, fire rings with grills, vault toilets (wheelchair-accessible), drinking water, and garbage service. Leashed pets are permitted.

Reservations, fees: Reservations are accepted (877/444-6777, www.recreation.gov). Campsites cost $12. Group sites cost $50. Extra vehicles cost $6. Cash or check. Open late May-September.

Directions: From Highway 33 in Driggs, Idaho, turn east at Little Street/Ski Hill Road for one mile to a Y intersection. Bear left onto Ski Hill Road and go 5.6 miles, passing Alta and the state line into Wyoming, to the campground sign. Turn right onto the gravel Forest Road 009 and drive 2.7 miles, turning right into the campground. GPS Coordinates: N 43° 45.449' W 110° 57.032'

Contact: Caribou-Targhee National Forest, Teton Basin Ranger District, 515 S. Main, Driggs, ID 83422, 208/354-2312, www.fs.usda.gov/ctnf.

15 TETON CANYON

Scenic rating: 9

in the Teton Mountain in Caribou-Targhee National Forest, Wyoming

At 6,960 feet, Teton Canyon Campground sits on the edge of the Jedediah Smith Wilderness on the west flank of the Teton Mountains. En route to the campground, the scenic drive, which enters Wyoming, lends views of Grand

Teton National Park's rugged panorama of peaks. From the campground, a popular trailhead departs into the wilderness via the South and North Forks of Teton Creek. Reach Alaska Basin Lakes in seven miles, Grand Teton National Park in nine miles, or 11,106-foot Table Mountain in six miles for views of the Grand Teton. Stock facilities sit 0.1 mile west of the campground. Surrounding granitic rock outcroppings and cliffs have rock-climbing routes. Teton Creek is closed to fishing until July 1.

The campground's two interconnected loops provide different environments. The southern loop weaves through a thick conifer forest that shades the campsites dark, keeping them cool and protected from the elements. Teton Creek flows nearest sites 6-8, and most of the sites are gravel back-ins. The open understory permits some views of nearby campers. Campsites in the north loop ring an open wildflower field dotted with only a handful of aspens. While the open sites, most of which are pull-throughs, do not afford privacy, they command views of the canyon's cliffs and sweeping mountain slopes. The trailhead draws in day hikers, but at night, the campground is ultra quiet.

Campsites, facilities: The campground has 20 RV or tent campsites. RVs are limited to 24 feet. Facilities include picnic tables, fire rings with grills, vault toilets, drinking water, garbage service, and campground hosts. Bring your own firewood. Leashed pets are permitted.

Reservations, fees: Reservations are accepted (877/444-6777, www.recreation.gov). Campsites cost $12. The double site costs $24. Extra vehicles cost $6. Cash or check. Open late May-September.

Directions: From Highway 33 in Driggs, Idaho, turn east at Little Street/Ski Hill Road for one mile to a Y intersection. Bear left onto Ski Hill Road and go 5.6 miles, passing Alta and the state line into Wyoming, to the campground sign. Turn right onto the gravel Forest Road 009 and drive 4.3 miles, turning right into the campground.

GPS Coordinates: N 43° 45.411' W 110° 55.258'

Contact: Caribou-Targhee National Forest, Teton Basin Ranger District, 515 S. Main, Driggs, ID 83422, 208/354-2312, www.fs.usda.gov/ctnf.

16 PINE CREEK

Scenic rating: 8

in the Big Hole Mountains in Caribou-Targhee National Forest, Idaho

At 6,600 feet, Pine Creek sits nearly at the summit of Pine Creek Pass over the Big Hole Mountains. A trail along the crest of the Big Hole Mountains departs northward just west of the pass. Hikers use the trail for its expansive views across the Teton Valley to the Grand Teton and Teton Mountains. Mountain bikers ride the 17 miles across the crest trail to the Horseshoe Canyon Trailhead west of Driggs.

The curvy gravel campground road and back-in gravel parking pads may pose difficulties for those with large trailers, but spacious, spread-out campsites make it appealing. A mixed forest of firs, lodgepoles, and aspens provides a thick overhead canopy for shade. Pink wild roses and a brushy understory shield the campground from the highway, but Pine Creek Summit is not a major thoroughfare for trucking, so night traffic is minimal. Sites 1 and 2 sit closest to the road. Two of the campsites have small bridges crossing the creek to their tables and tent spaces.

Campsites, facilities: The campground has 10 RV or tent campsites. RVs are limited to 30 feet. Facilities include picnic tables, fire rings, and vault toilets. No water is available; bring your own. When the creek through the campground is running, treat its water. Pack out your trash. Leashed pets are permitted.

Reservations, fees: Reservations are not accepted. Campsites cost $8. Extra vehicles cost $5. Cash or check. Open late May–mid-September.

Directions: From Victor, drive Highway 31 southwest for six miles. Turn left into the campground. Coming from Swan Valley, locate the campground entrance about 0.7 mile on the east side of Pine Creek Pass.

GPS Coordinates: N 43° 34.388' W 111° 12.322'

Contact: Caribou-Targhee National Forest, Teton Basin Ranger District, 515 S. Main, Driggs, ID 83422, 208/354-2312, www.fs.usda.gov/ctnf.

17 MIKE HARRIS

Scenic rating: 8

in the Big Hole Mountains in Caribou-Targhee National Forest, Idaho

At 6,560 feet, Mike Harris Campground sits in the Big Hole Range south of Victor. At the bottom of the long, 10 percent grade climb over Teton Pass, the campground is popular with hikers and mountain bikers. With the trailhead departing from the 90-degree bend in the campground entrance road, the Mikesell Canyon Trail (#049) climbs four miles to the top of 8,987-foot Oliver Peak for views of the southern Teton Mountains. Another four-mile stretch crosses the state line into Wyoming to connect with Mosquito Pass on the Teton Crest. Stream fishing is available in Trail Creek adjacent to the highway.

The one gravel campground loop tucks under a green canopy of firs, lodgepole pines, and aspens, with two gravel pull-throughs and the remainder back-in parking pads. Meadows of grass, paintbrush, and fireweed weave through the trees, which partly shade the campsites. The roomy campsites are spread out for privacy, but spaces for tents are small. With its proximity to the highway, morning and evening noise is abundant with the commuter traffic from the Teton Valley to Jackson Hole.

Campsites, facilities: The campground has 10 RV or tent campsites. RVs are limited to 30 feet. Facilities include picnic tables, fire rings with grills, pedestal grills, vault toilets (wheelchair-accessible), bear boxes, garbage service, and a campground host. No drinking water is available; treat stream water. Leashed pets are permitted.

Reservations, fees: Reservations are accepted (877/444-6777, www.recreation.gov). Campsites cost $8. Extra vehicles cost $5. Cash or check. Open mid-May–mid-September.

Directions: From Victor, drive southeast on Highway 33 for 3.8 miles. At milepost 153.5, turn west for 300 feet, and turn south for 0.3 mile, arcing right into the campground. Coming from Teton Pass, locate the turnoff 1.5 miles northwest of the Idaho-Wyoming state line.

GPS Coordinates: N 43° 33.371' W 111° 4.136'

Contact: Caribou-Targhee National Forest, Teton Basin Ranger District, 515 S. Main, Driggs, ID 83422, 208/354-2312, www.fs.usda.gov/ctnf.

18 TRAIL CREEK

Scenic rating: 8

in Big Hole Mountains in Caribou-Targhee National Forest, Wyoming

Located at 6,600 feet, Trail Creek Campground sits in the Big Hole Mountains on the highway over Teton Pass. It is convenient for those traveling over the pass to reach Grand Teton and Yellowstone National Parks, but those who drive the steep road with trailers will feel its 10 percent grade. The trailhead at Coal Creek Meadows leads through the Jedediah Smith Wilderness to the Teton Crest Trail, with views north to the Grand Teton. A three-mile steady climb reaches the meadows. Cyclists traveling over Teton Pass use this campground for its convenience to the highway, and mountain bikers use the nearby national forest trails.

The campground road parallels the highway, squeezed by traffic on the north and Trail Creek on the south. Most of the campsites are open to the highway, which buzzes with commuters traveling between Teton Valley and Jackson Hole in the morning and evening. At night, after the traffic dies down, you can hear the creek. The sunny campsites have little privacy; however, a few snuggled against the aspen and fir forest carve out little private nooks. Surrounded by pink fireweed in midsummer, the grassy campsites are spread out, with big, flat tent spaces available. Six of the campsites have gravel pull-through parking pads.

Campsites, facilities: The campground has 10 RV or tent campsites. RVs are limited to 40 feet. Facilities include picnic tables, fire rings with grills, vault toilets (wheelchair-accessible), bear boxes, garbage service, drinking water, and campground hosts. Leashed pets are permitted.

Reservations, fees: Reservations are accepted (877/444-6777, www.recreation.gov). Campsites cost $8. Extra vehicles cost $5. Cash or check. Open mid-May–September.

Directions: From Victor, drive southeast on Highway 33 for 5.6 miles. At milepost 155, turn south into the campground. Coming from Teton Pass, locate the turnoff 3.5 miles past the Coal Creek Meadows pullout. GPS Coordinates: N 43° 32.462' W 111° 2.477'

Contact: Caribou-Targhee National Forest, Teton Basin Ranger District, 515 S. Main, Driggs, ID 83422, 208/354-2312, www.fs.usda.gov/ctnf.

19 FALLS

Scenic rating: 7

on the Snake River in Caribou-Targhee National Forest, Idaho

At 5,282 feet, Falls Campground sits on old river bars that once were under the Snake River, but now form a series of wooded islands—home to eagles, deer, and moose. The river is a favorite for anglers, canoers, kayakers, and rafters. Nearby Conant Boat Ramp offers a place to launch for floating, and anglers can fish from the campground. Nearby, the falls that gives the campground its name tumbles from Falls Creek 60 feet over a travertine outcrop into the river. The river's edge is a favorite spot for photographing the falls.

The quiet campground sits on a cottonwood-covered river bar where a small braid of the Snake River flows past several grassy campsites. One double campsite has views of the river spur while others have short trails through the brush to access it. You'll have your choice of partly shaded and sunny campsites. A few pull-through sites are available.

Campsites, facilities: The campground has 16 RV or tent campsites, five double campsites, one tent site, and one large group campsite. RVs are limited to 45 feet. Facilities include picnic tables, fire rings with grills, vault toilets, drinking water, garbage service, firewood for sale, and campground hosts. Leashed pets are permitted.

Reservations, fees: Reservations are accepted (877/444-6777, www.recreation.gov). Campsites cost $12. Extra vehicles cost $6. Double campsites cost $24. Cash or check. Open May–September.

Directions: Coming from Idaho Falls on Highway 26, drive 45 miles and turn right just before the bridge crossing the Snake River. Coming from Swan Valley, drive west on Highway 26 for 3.4 miles to the bridge crossing the Snake River and turn left. Drive Forest Road 058 for 2.4 miles and turn north into the campground. GPS Coordinates: N 43° 25.957' W 111° 21.749'

Contact: Caribou-Targhee National Forest, Palisades Ranger District, 3659 E. Ririe Hwy., Idaho Falls, ID 83401, 208/523-1412, www.fs.usda.gov/ctnf.

20 PALISADES CREEK

Scenic rating: 7

in the Snake River Mountains in
Caribou-Targhee National Forest, Idaho

At 5,550 feet, Palisades Creek Campground
snuggles into the Palisades Creek Canyon
at the base of 10,000-foot-high peaks of the
Snake River Range. It houses the most popular
trail in the range, busy on hot summer days
when hikers head to the cool subalpine lakes
for fishing and swimming. A gentle trail leads
four miles to Lower Palisades Lake, surrounded by willow brush, and continues through
Waterfall Canyon to the larger Upper Palisades
Lake with its scenic shoreline (7.5 miles total).
The trailhead departs from the east side of
the campground. A stock ramp is available
at the separate trailhead for horses. You can
often see mountain goats on the canyon cliffs
high above the trail and moose at the lakes.
Anglers enjoy the lakes and Palisades Creek
for its native cutthroat trout.

The tiny campground tucks its loop into
a shady forest of mixed conifers at the bottom of the Palisades Creek Canyon. The creek
runs adjacent to the campground. Underbrush
and small trees contribute to the privacy of
the campsites. Once day hikers depart, the
campground is very quiet, prized by those who
seek solitude.

Campsites, facilities: The campground has
five RV or tent campsites and two double
campsites. RVs are limited to 22 feet. Facilities include picnic tables, fire rings with grills,
vault toilets, drinking water, garbage service,
firewood for sale, and campground hosts.
Leashed pets are permitted.

Reservations, fees: Reservations are not accepted. Campsites cost $12. Extra vehicles cost
$6. Double campsites cost $24. Cash or check.
Open May-September.

Directions: On Highway 26, drive 7.1 miles
south of Swan Valley. Turn north onto Palisades Creek Road (Forest Road 255) for two
dirt miles to the campground entrance, passing
the hiker parking for the trailhead just before
the entrance. Coming from the south on the
highway, locate the turnoff 3.7 miles north of
Palisades Dam.

GPS Coordinates: N 43° 23.803' W 111°
12.892'

Contact: Caribou-Targhee National Forest,
Palisades Ranger District, 3659 E. Ririe Hwy.,
Idaho Falls, ID 83401, 208/523-1412, www.
fs.usda.gov/ctnf.

21 RIVERSIDE PARK

Scenic rating: 7

on the Snake River in Caribou-Targhee
National Forest

Riverside Park, elevation 5,400 feet, sits on
the South Fork of the Snake River below Palisades Dam. Fishing is available right from
the campground. The river in this stretch,
referred to as the South Fork, is renowned for
its fly-fishing, which runs from early July in
to autumn. Drift boats full of anglers fishing
for trout float from the dam downstream to
Swan Valley. The Class II river also works
for scenic floats in rafts, kayaks, tubes, and
canoes. American pelicans, sandhill cranes,
golden eagles, and moose frequent the area.
Designated as a National Important Bird
Area, the river corridor is home to the largest riparian cottonwood forest in the West,
which provides habitat for 126 bird species, including 21 raptors. A boat ramp is
also available for launching onto the nearby
Palisades Reservoir.

The campground squeezes in between the
river and the highway, with road noise pervasive. Built on a flat river bar, the location
offers roomy campsites with big, flat, raised
gravel tent platforms. The electrical hookup
sites are very open, sunny, back from the river,
and lined up in parking-lot fashion. The other
campsites sit partly shaded on a loop in the

cottonwoods down by the river. Several sites overlook the river.

Campsites, facilities: The campground has 22 RV or tent campsites, plus 10 double campsites. Pull-through sites can accommodate large RVs. Nine RV campsites have electrical hookups. Facilities include picnic tables, fire rings with grills, flush and vault toilets (wheelchair-accessible), drinking water, garbage service, firewood for sale, tent platforms, disposal station ($5), and campground hosts. Leashed pets are permitted.

Reservations, fees: Reservations are not accepted. Campsites cost $12 for single sites and $24 for double sites. Electrical hookups cost $17. Extra vehicles cost $6. Cash or check. Open May-September.

Directions: On Highway 26, drive eight miles south of Swan Valley. At milepost 387, turn west into the campground. Coming from the south on the highway, locate the turnoff one mile north of Palisades Dam.

GPS Coordinates: N 43° 20.424' W 111° 12.319'

Contact: Caribou-Targhee National Forest, Palisades Ranger District, 3659 E. Ririe Hwy., Idaho Falls, ID 83401, 208/523-1412, www.fs.usda.gov/ctnf.

22 CALAMITY

Scenic rating: 7

on Palisades Reservoir in Caribou-Targhee National Forest, Idaho

Located at 5,660 feet, Calamity Campground is the largest of the campgrounds on Palisades Reservoir, dividing the Snake River and Caribou Mountains. The campground sits on the northwest corner of the reservoir, south of Palisades Dam. Warnings on the dam will note concerns for motorists and campers on the gravel access road where it passes through a landslide. The reservoir is popular for fishing, swimming, boating, waterskiing, paddling, and sailing. The boat launch includes concrete ramps, a dock, and trailer parking. The campground's location across the reservoir from the highway makes it quieter than other reservoir campgrounds and it has huckleberries in season.

Built on a steep hillside with constructed steps and gravel terraces for campsites, the campground has three loops. The spacious campsites have big, flat spaces for tents with a forest of aspen, fir, and lodgepoles adds partial shade and privacy to some sites; others are sunny with views of the reservoir. You can hear faint trucking noise from the highway across the reservoir. Loop C, on a steeper hillside with more privacy, has the best views.

Campsites, facilities: The campground has 40 RV or tent campsites and one double campsite. RVs are limited to 40 feet. Facilities include picnic tables, fire rings with grills, vault toilets (wheelchair-accessible), drinking water, garbage service, firewood for sale, boat launch, and campground hosts. Leashed pets are permitted.

Reservations, fees: Reservations are accepted (877/444-6777, www.recreation.gov). Campsites cost $12. Double sites cost $24. Extra vehicles cost $6. Cash or check. Open May-September.

Directions: From Alpine Junction, where Highway 26 and Highway 89 join on the Snake River, drive 18.5 miles northwest on Highway 26. At milepost 388, turn west over the dam on Bear Creek Road (Forest Road 058) and drive one mile of rough dirt road, veering left into the campground. Coming from the north on the highway, locate the turnoff at Palisades Dam.

GPS Coordinates: N 43° 19.641' W 111° 12.922'

Contact: Caribou-Targhee National Forest, Palisades Ranger District, 3659 E. Ririe Hwy., Idaho Falls, ID 83401, 208/523-1412, www.fs.usda.gov/ctnf.

23 BIG ELK CREEK

🚶 🚴 🏊 ⛵ 🛶 🎣 🐎 ♿ 🚐 ⛺

Scenic rating: 7

on Palisades Reservoir in Caribou-Targhee
National Forest, Idaho

At 5,680 feet, Big Elk Creek Campground sits on Palisades Reservoir in a forested side canyon below the 10,000-foot-high peaks of the Snake River Mountains. The campground sits on an arm of the reservoir that fills with water in early summer, but dwindles to a dry basin in late summer. It is close enough to launch boats from two nearby primitive ramps or the concrete ramps at Blowout or Calamity Campgrounds. The reservoir is popular for fishing, swimming, boating, waterskiing, paddling, and sailing. The campground's location in a side canyon makes it quieter than the Palisades campgrounds right on the highway. Big Elk Creek Road terminates 0.4 mile farther at a trailhead with a stock ramp. A gentle trail for hikers, bikers, and horseback riders heads up the creek canyon, reaching Dry Canyon in 2.5 miles, Hells Hole Canyon in 3.4 miles, and Idaho-Wyoming border in 4.5 miles.

The grassy campground loops on an open, sunny, south-facing gentle slope. A few conifers sprinkle through the campground but provide minimal shade. Surrounded by a large sagebrush field, the wide-open sites garner big views of the Big Elk Creek drainage, but at the cost of privacy, and some sites are quite close together. A gravel road loops through the campground to access gravel and grass parking pads. Overflow primitive camping is available at Little Elk Creek boat ramp.

Campsites, facilities: The campground has 10 RV or tent campsites, plus five double sites and three large group campsites. RVs are limited to 22 feet. Facilities include picnic tables, fire rings with grills, vault toilets (wheelchair-accessible), drinking water, garbage service, firewood for sale, and campground hosts. Leashed pets are permitted.

Reservations, fees: Reservations are only accepted for group campsites (877/444-6777, www.recreation.gov). Campsites cost $12. Double sites cost $24. Large group sites cost $50. Extra vehicles cost $6. Cash or check. Open May-September.

Directions: From Alpine Junction, where Highway 26 and Highway 89 join on the Snake River, drive 15.1 miles northwest on Highway 26. At milepost 390.8, turn north onto Big Elk Creek Road (Forest Road 262) and drive 1.6 miles. The campground entrance is on the left. Coming from the north on the highway, locate the turnoff about 3.4 miles southeast of Palisades Dam.

GPS Coordinates: N 43° 19.331' W 111° 7.051'

Contact: Caribou-Targhee National Forest, Palisades Ranger District, 3659 E. Ririe Hwy., Idaho Falls, ID 83401, 208/523-1412, www.fs.usda.gov/ctnf.

24 BLOWOUT

🚴 🏊 ⛵ 🛶 🎣 🐎 ♿ 🚐 ⛺

Scenic rating: 7

on Palisades Reservoir in Caribou-Targhee
National Forest, Idaho

At 5,800 feet, Blowout Campground is situated on the northeast side of the 16,000-acre Palisades Reservoir, surrounded by steep forested mountains. With its location, it is one of the most popular campgrounds on the lake. Fed by the Snake River, the reservoir, which is known for wind and summer thunderstorms, is popular for fishing, swimming, boating, waterskiing, paddling, and sailing. The campground's large boat launch includes a double-wide concrete ramp, dock, and trailer parking. The reservoir harbors cutthroat, brown, and lake trout, along with kokanee salmon. Thanks to its location on the highway, cross-country cyclists find this campground convenient. In fall, the hillsides around the lake light up with color—especially when the aspens turn gold.

The aspen and lodgepole forest provides partial shade for the tight campsites with gravel back-in parking pads; you'll have your pick between sites overlooking the reservoir and varying amounts of privacy. Only small spaces for tents are available. Unfortunately, sites 2 and 15 plop next to the highway and chain-link fence. This campground picks up road noise during the night from commercial trucking on the highway. Overflow parking for large RVs is available at the boat launch.

Campsites, facilities: The campground has 11 RV or tent campsites, plus four double campsites. RVs are limited to 32 feet. Facilities include picnic tables, fire rings with grills, vault toilets (wheelchair-accessible), drinking water, garbage service, boat launch, firewood for sale, and campground hosts. Leashed pets are permitted.

Reservations, fees: Reservations are not accepted. Campsites cost $12. Double sites cost $24. Extra vehicles cost $6. Cash or check. Open mid-May-mid-September.

Directions: From Alpine Junction, where Highway 26 and Highway 89 join on the Snake River, drive 12 miles northwest on Highway 26. At milepost 394, turn south into the campground. Coming from the north on the highway, locate the campground entrance about 6.5 miles southeast of Palisades Dam. GPS Coordinates: N 43° 17.131' W 111° 7.350'

Contact: Caribou-Targhee National Forest, Palisades Ranger District, 3659 E. Ririe Hwy., Idaho Falls, ID 83401, 208/523-1412, www.fs.usda.gov/ctnf.

25 ALPINE

Scenic rating: 7

on Palisades Reservoir in Caribou-Targhee National Forest, Wyoming

Located at 5,692 feet, Alpine Campground sits at the head of the 16,000-acre Palisades Reservoir, surrounded by steep forested mountains. Anglers will need to ensure they have the appropriate state licenses depending on where they drop in lines. The reservoir, fed by the Snake River, is shallow along the shoreline near the campground. When the lake water level drops low in late August, the area in front of the campground can become a muddy maze of braided streams. The reservoir is popular for fishing, swimming, paddling, and boating. The closest boat ramp is in the town of Alpine. Another is located midlake on the east side at Indian Creek. The reservoir harbors cutthroat, brown, and lake trout along with kokanee salmon. Because of its location on the highway, cross-country cyclists find this campground convenient.

The campground tucks into a loose lodgepole pine, aspen, and spruce forest, which admits partial and full sun to campsites. Contrary to the surrounding steep hillsides, the campground is in flatter terrain. High undergrowth blooming with pink fireweed under the forest canopy gives the roomy, grassy campsites privacy. With the highway so close—a commercial trucking route—road noise enters the campground.

Campsites, facilities: The campground has 16 RV or tent campsites, plus six double campsites and three large group campsites. RVs are limited to 45 feet. Facilities include picnic tables, fire rings with grills, vault toilets (wheelchair-accessible), drinking water, firewood for sale, garbage service, and campground hosts. Leashed pets are permitted.

Reservations, fees: Reservations are accepted (877/444-6777, www.recreation.gov). Campsites cost $12. Double sites cost $24. Group campsites cost $50. Extra vehicles cost $6. Cash or check. Open late May-mid-September.

Directions: From Alpine Junction, where Highway 26 and Highway 89 join on the Snake River, drive two miles northwest on Highway 26. At milepost 402, turn south into the campground. Coming from the north on the highway, look for the campground entrance 0.5 mile southeast of Forest Road 402. GPS Coordinates: N 43° 11.817' W 111° 2.483'

Contact: Caribou-Targhee National Forest, Palisades Ranger District, 3659 E. Ririe Hwy.,

Idaho Falls, ID 83401, 208/523-1412, www.fs.usda.gov/ctnf.

26 MCCOY CREEK

Scenic rating: 7

on Palisades Reservoir in Caribou-Targhee National Forest, Idaho

Located at 5,682 feet in the Caribou Mountains, McCoy Creek Campground sits where McCoy Creek flows into the 16,000-acre Palisades Reservoir. Owing to the campground's location at the head of the lake, the lake water drops low in August, leaving bare slopes rimming the reservoir. A primitive boat ramp off the second campground spur works for launching hand-carried watercraft like canoes, kayaks, and rafts. The reservoir harbors cutthroat, brown, and lake trout along with kokanee salmon, and anglers can fish McCoy Creek, too. Swimmers can cool off at the reservoir.

Two separate gravel spurs with turnarounds form the campground. Partly shaded to sunny campsites tuck into a mixed conifer forest. The location at the southeast corner of the reservoir defines quiet because of its distance from the highway.

Campsites, facilities: The campground has 17 RV or tent campsites. RVs are limited to 25 feet. Facilities include picnic tables, fire rings with grills, vault toilets (wheelchair-accessible), drinking water, firewood for sale, garbage service, and campground hosts. Leashed pets are permitted.

Reservations, fees: Reservations are not accepted. Campsites cost $12. Extra vehicles cost $6. Cash or check. Open May-September.

Directions: From Alpine Junction, where Highway 26 and Highway 89 join on the Snake River, drive southeast on Highway 89 for 3.7 miles. Turn right onto Salt River-McCoy Road (Forest Road 087) and drive 6.7 miles to the first campground entrance

on the right. The second entrance sits 0.25 mile further.

GPS Coordinates: N 43° 11.075' W 111° 6.080'

Contact: Caribou-Targhee National Forest, Palisades Ranger District, 3659 E. Ririe Hwy., Idaho Falls, ID 83401, 208/523-1412, www.fs.usda.gov/ctnf.

27 WOLF CREEK

Scenic rating: 8

in Snake River Canyon in Bridger-Teton National Forest

In the Wyoming Range, Wolf Creek Campground sits at 5,800 feet at the southwest end of the Snake River Canyon. The canyon walls narrow, forcing the campground to climb a hillside, but this Class III stretch of river through the canyon, designated as Wild and Scenic, is favored by kayakers and rafters for eight miles of white water. Taco Hole kayak playboat area is 3.5 miles northwest of the campground. Anglers on the shore or in drift boats go after brown and Yellowstone cutthroat trout. Outfitters for fishing and rafting are available in Hoback Junction. The Wolf Creek Trailhead, 1.5 miles east of the campground, leads eight miles to Red Pass on the west side of 9,483-foot Wolf Mountain. The campsite's highway location is convenient for cross-country cyclists.

The campground does not afford enjoyment of the river from campsites, but a few paths across the highway lead to the shore. On a hillside, the campsites have views of the highway, power lines crossing above the campground, and the river. The gravel road accesses three loops with gravel parking pads. Loop C climbs the farthest above the highway, with its upper campsites having views of the cliffs across the canyon. A few firs for shade sprinkle across the sagebrush hillside, blooming with fireweed and mountain hollyhock.

Campsites, facilities: The campground has 20 RV or tent campsites. RVs are limited to midsized rigs. Facilities include picnic tables, fire rings with grills, vault toilets (wheelchair-accessible), drinking water, bear boxes, garbage service, tent platforms, and campground hosts. Leashed pets are permitted.

Reservations, fees: Reservations are not accepted. Campsites cost $15. Cash or check. Open late June-August.

Directions: On Highway 26/89/6, from Hoback Junction drive southwest for 16 miles, or from Alpine drive seven miles northeast. At milepost 124.9, turn north into the campground.
GPS Coordinates: N 43° 11.931' W 110° 54.017'

Contact: Bridger-Teton National Forest, Jackson Ranger District, 25 Rosencrans Ln., Jackson, WY 83001, 307/739-5400, www.fs.usda.gov/btnf.

28 STATION CREEK

Scenic rating: 8
in Snake River Canyon in Bridger-Teton National Forest

Located at 5,800 feet in the Wyoming Range, the popular Station Creek Campground sits midway in the Snake River Canyon. The canyon walls narrow, forcing the campground onto a bluff above the river without access to the shore. The Class III stretch of river through the canyon, designated as Wild and Scenic, is favored by kayakers and rafters for its eight miles of white water, which peaks in early June. Water rips through Big Kahuna, Lunch Counter, and Ropes rapids. The campground is convenient for floaters as it sits midway between the put-in at West Table launch site and take-out at Sheep Gulch. Taco Hole, a kayak playboat area with a 30-foot-wide wave hole and the accompanying Burrito Hole, sits 0.5 mile west. Anglers, floating the upper section

of the river in drift boats, go after brown and Yellowstone cutthroat trout. Station Creek Trail departs across the highway. Outfitters for fishing and rafting are available in Hoback Junction. The highway location is convenient for cross-country cyclists.

Station Creek Campground sits high above the Snake River on a bluff, with half of its campsites (3-10) overlooking the river. The drop to the river is so steep that fences rim the ledges. Lodgepole pines and firs shade the campsites, which are ringed with meadows of fireweed. The sites sit within view of neighboring campers, and road noise competes with the roar of the river.

Campsites, facilities: The campground has 16 RV or tent campsites and a large group campsite across the highway. RVs are limited to midsized rigs. Facilities include picnic tables, fire rings with grills, pedestal grills, vault toilets (wheelchair-accessible), drinking water, bear boxes, garbage service, tent platforms, and campground hosts. Leashed pets are permitted.

Reservations, fees: Reservations are only accepted for the large group site (877/444-6777, www.recreation.gov). Campsites cost $15. Cash or check. Open late May-August.

Directions: On Highway 26/89/6, from Hoback Junction drive southwest for 12 miles, or from Alpine drive 11 miles northeast. At milepost 128.7, turn south into the campground.
GPS Coordinates: N 43° 12.296' W 110° 50.074'

Contact: Bridger-Teton National Forest, Jackson Ranger District, 25 Rosencrans Ln., Jackson, WY 83001, 307/739-5400, www.fs.usda.gov/btnf.

29 EAST TABLE CREEK

Scenic rating: 8
in Snake River Canyon in Bridger-Teton National Forest

At 5,800 feet in the Wyoming Range, East

Table Campground sits toward the upper end of the Snake River Canyon. Even though this is the only Snake River Canyon campground that accesses the water, boat launching is not permitted from the campground. Instead, launch from the huge West Table boat ramp west of the campground or for hand-carried watercraft, use the adjacent East Table primitive boat ramp. The river, designated as Wild and Scenic, is calmer above the campground, where anglers float drift boats from Hoback Junction to fish for brown and Yellowstone cutthroat trout. You can also fish from the shore along the campground and wade-fish in late summer. Below the campground, an eight-mile stretch of Class III white water amuses kayakers and rafters. Outfitters for fishing and rafting are available in Hoback Junction. The campground's highway location is convenient for cross-country cyclists, and hikers can access the East Table Creek Trail across the highway.

The campground sits on a large, aspen- and lodgepole-covered river bar crisscrossed with paths leading to the water. Eight campsites overlook the river. Tall, mature pines shade many of the campsites, but with little understory, you'll see neighbors. Road noise competes with the sound of the river. If the campground is full, you can use the primitive overflow sites and walk-in tent campsites across the highway, but no services are available. Hunters can reserve the overflow site in fall (307/739-5427).

Campsites, facilities: The campground has 18 RV or tent campsites. RVs are limited to midsized rigs. Facilities include picnic tables, fire rings with grills, pedestal grills, vault toilets (wheelchair-accessible), drinking water, bear boxes, garbage service, tent platforms, and campground hosts. Leashed pets are permitted.

Reservations, fees: Reservations are not accepted. Campsites cost $15. Cash or check. Open late May-August.

Directions: On Highway 26/89/6, from Hoback Junction drive southwest for 11 miles, or from Alpine drive 12 miles northeast. At milepost 130, turn south into the campground.

GPS Coordinates: N 43° 12.762' W 110° 48.459'

Contact: Bridger-Teton National Forest, Jackson Ranger District, 25 Rosencrans Ln., Jackson, WY 83001, 307/739-5400, www.fs.usda.gov/btnf.

30 HOBACK

Scenic rating: 8

in Hoback Canyon in Bridger-Teton National Forest

In the Gros Ventre Range, Hoback Campground tucks at 6,200 feet into deep gray- and red-cliffed Hoback Canyon, where ospreys fish the Hoback River. Trout fishing runs sluggish during June runoff, but during the salmon fly hatch in early July, fishing picks up. Designated Wild and Scenic, the Hoback froths with Class I-III white water through the canyon. You can put in at the campground and take out at Hoback Junction, or put in at Granite Creek and take out at the campground. Because of its white-water sections, this river requires some skill to navigate by kayak or raft. This highway campground attracts cross-country cyclists, and across the highway, a trail climbs partway up Cream Puff Peak.

Tucked under big spruce, firs, and aspens, the campground squeezes in between the highway and the river; a couple campsites, such as site 7, suffer right near the highway noise. Open, sunny campsites are interspersed with partly shaded campsites, offering campers a choice. Those in the open garner views of the canyon walls. Five sites enjoy river frontage. A paved road loops through the campground with paved back-in parking pads.

Campsites, facilities: The campground has 13 RV or tent campsites. RVs are limited to midsized rigs. Facilities include picnic tables, fire rings with grills, pedestal grills, vault toilets (wheelchair-accessible), drinking water, bear boxes, garbage service, and campground hosts. Leashed pets are permitted.

Reservations, fees: Reservations are not accepted. Campsites cost $15. Cash or check. Open late May-September.

Directions: From Hoback Junction, drive eight miles southeast on Highway 189/191. At milepost 155.5, turn south into the campground.

GPS Coordinates: N 43° 16.876' W 110° 35.628'

Contact: Bridger-Teton National Forest, Jackson Ranger District, 25 Rosencrans Ln., Jackson, WY 83001, 307/739-5400, www.fs.usda.gov/btnf.

31 GRANITE CREEK

Scenic rating: 9

in the Gros Ventre Mountains in Bridger-Teton National Forest

BEST (

Located at 6,870 feet, Granite Creek Campground lies below the massive Open Door rock slab, a slice of orange rock with a horizontal hole like a doorway. Granite Hot Springs (307/734-7400, open late May-October) and Granite Falls sit within one mile. The hot springs (with a changing room, restrooms, and outdoor cement pool built by the CCC in 1933) heats to 93°F in the summer, when rains and snowmelt dilute the hot water, and to 112°F in the winter. Primitive hot pools also sit below Granite Falls. Granite Creek flows past the campground, although its thick willows make wade-fishing for Yellowstone cutthroat trout and mountain whitefish more difficult. Granite Creek Trail runs along the opposite side of the river from the bridge south of the campground two miles to the falls and hot springs before continuing farther north into the Gros Ventre Wilderness. Rafting and kayaking—best late May-mid-June—start at the wooden bridge seven miles up the road from the highway.

Granite Creek Hot Springs is a pool constructed in 1933 by the Civilian Conservation Corps in Bridger-Teton National Forest.

© BECKY LOMAX

Several campsites on the campground's three loops have views of the Open Door. Large lodgepoles and subalpine firs shade most of the campsites, except for a handful of sunny, open sites in loop A. The sites are spaced out for privacy—many with spacious tent areas—but with forest pine needle and duff floors, the minimal vegetation between sites lets you see neighboring campers. Despite the narrow high elevation canyon, sandhill cranes fly in over the willows around the creek, squawking as they land.

Campsites, facilities: The campground has 53 RV or tent campsites. RVs are limited to midsized rigs. Facilities include picnic tables, fire rings with grills, pedestal grills, vault toilets (wheelchair-accessible), drinking water, bear boxes, garbage service, tent platforms, and campground hosts. Leashed pets are permitted.

Reservations, fees: Reservations are not accepted. Campsites cost $15. Cash or check. Open late May-September.

Directions: From Hoback Junction, drive 11 miles southeast on Highway 189/191. Turn north onto bumpy dirt Granite Creek Road (Forest Road 30500) for 8.6 miles to the campground entrance on the right.

GPS Coordinates: N 43° 21.567' W 110° 26.802'

Contact: Bridger-Teton National Forest, Jackson Ranger District, 25 Rosencrans Ln., Jackson, WY 83001, 307/739-5400, www.fs.usda.gov/btnf.

32 GRANITE CREEK PRIMITIVE

Scenic rating: 9

in the Gros Ventre Mountains in Bridger-Teton National Forest

Located 6,400 to 6,850 feet, Granite Creek primitive campsites are popular for their beauty, solitude, and quiet as well as options for camping in shoulder seasons when Granite Creek Campground is closed. Granite Hot Springs (307/734-7400, open late May-October) and Granite Falls (with primitive hot pools at the base) sit at the end of the 10-mile dirt road. From the hot springs, Granite Creek Trail runs two miles along the river south past the falls and also north into the Gros Ventre Wilderness. At primitive campsites, anglers wade-fish for Yellowstone cutthroat trout and mountain whitefish in Granite Creek. Rafters and kayakers float the river's bottom seven miles, best from late May to mid-June.

All campsites command river frontage along Granite Creek. The first few sit within sight of the road, but the upper ones tuck into private locations behind aspens, firs, and pines. Some have sweeping views of the Gros Ventre Mountains at the end of the drainage. Many of the spur accesses are narrow and rough; scout them first.

Campsites, facilities: The area has 12 RV or tent campsites; some can accommodate midsized RVs. Facilities include rock fire rings. Bring your own drinking water, or treat creek water. Pack out your trash. Use Leave No Trace principles for managing human waste. Pets are permitted.

Reservations, fees: Reservations are not accepted. Camping is free. Open May-early November.

Directions: From Hoback Junction, drive 11 miles southeast on Highway 189/191. Turn north onto the bumpy dirt Granite Creek Road (Forest Road 30500). Locate the entrances to the primitive campsites on the right side of the road along the seven miles after milepost 1.3 and 1.3 miles before the end of the road, where a sign denotes the end of primitive camping.

GPS Coordinates: N 43° 17.833' W 110° 30.115' (first primitive site)

Contact: Bridger-Teton National Forest, Jackson Ranger District, 25 Rosencrans Ln., Jackson, WY 83001, 307/739-5400, www.fs.usda.gov/btnf.

33 KOZY

Scenic rating: 8

in Hoback Canyon in Bridger-Teton National Forest

At 6,500 feet in the Gros Ventre Mountains, tiny Kozy Campground tucks into deep gray- and red-cliffed Hoback Canyon, where ospreys fish the Hoback River. Trout fishing runs sluggish during June runoff, but during the salmon fly hatch in early July, fishing picks up. Designated Wild and Scenic, the Hoback froths with Class I-III white water through the canyon. You can put in at the campground and take out at Hoback Junction, or put in at Bondurant and take out at the campground. Considering its white-water sections, this river requires some skill to navigate by kayak or raft. West of the campground, the Shoal Creek trail climbs to a falls, a lake, and the Gros Ventre Wilderness. The campground attracts cross-country cyclists because of the highway location.

The tiny campground, with a paved road and parking pads, nestles in Hoback Canyon, squeezed between the highway and the river. It's close to the highway, and even the river can't drown out the trucking noise at night. Surrounded by sagebrush and pine slopes, the campground tucks several of the campsites into the loose forest, but you can still see the highway as well as other campers. Five sites claim river frontage. At the end of the turnaround loop, one site offers the most privacy.

Campsites, facilities: The campground has eight RV or tent campsites. RVs are limited to midsized rigs. Facilities include picnic tables, fire rings with grills, pedestal grills, vault toilets (wheelchair-accessible), drinking water, bear boxes, and garbage service. Leashed pets are permitted.

Reservations, fees: Reservations are not accepted. Campsites cost $12. Cash or check. Open late May-mid-September.

Directions: From Hoback Junction, drive 13 miles southeast on Highway 189/191. At milepost 151.9, turn north into the campground. GPS Coordinates: N 43° 16.217' W 110° 31.021'

Contact: Bridger-Teton National Forest, Jackson Ranger District, 25 Rosencrans Ln., Jackson, WY 83001, 307/739-5400, www.fs.usda.gov/btnf.

34 GREEN RIVER LAKE

Scenic rating: 10

in the Wind River Mountains in Bridger-Teton National Forest

Green River Lake Campground, elevation 8,080 feet, is a prized spot for campers on Lower Green River Lake. Stunning views at the lake often yield reflections of the blocky Squaretop Mountain, and rugged peaks over 11,000-feet that surround the campground. With stock facilities available, trails depart for several destinations, including one only for hikers and horseback riders that saunters in three gentle miles to Upper Green River Lake in the Bridger Wilderness. It is also part of the Continental Divide Trail. Mountain bikers can access trail outside the wilderness and old forest roads. Anglers can fish for trout in the Green River and the lakes. Using a primitive ramp, boaters and paddlers can launch onto the two-mile-long Green River Lake. When conditions are right, paddlers can travel upstream into Upper Green River Lake, paddling or pulling canoes or kayaks while walking streamside. Swimmers should prepare for chilly water in the lake.

Prepare for thick mosquitoes and biting flies at this remote quiet campground, tucked in a lush green valley around two loops. While lodgepoles occlude views of the lake from most campsites, several campsites command views of Squaretop Mountain and surrounding peaks—scenery worth giving up sheltered privacy to enjoy. A trail descends from the lower loop to the beach of Green River Lake. Primitive and overflow camping is also available at many sites along the Green River on the way up to Green River Lakes; campers at these dispersed sites should use previous fire rings, treat water taken from the river, pack out trash, and use Leave No Trace responsibility with human waste.

Campsites, facilities: The campground has 39 RV or tent campsites plus three large group campsites. RVs are limited to 35 feet. Facilities include picnic tables, fire rings with grills, vault toilets, drinking water, bear boxes, and campground hosts. Pack out your trash. Leashed pets are permitted. Wheelchair-accessible toilets are available.

Reservations, fees: Reservations are accepted only for the group campsites (877/444-6777, www.recreation.gov). Campsites cost $12. Cash or check. Open mid-June-mid-September.

Directions: From seven miles west of in Pinedale on Highway 191, turn north onto State Highway 352 for 28 miles where the pavement ends, and the gravel road becomes Forest Road 650. Drive for 23 miles, staying to the right of the river at junctions, to the campground entrance on the right.

GPS Coordinates: N 43° 18.905' W 109° 51.808'

Contact: Bridger-Teton National Forest, Pinedale Ranger District, 29 E. Fremont Lake Rd., Pinedale, WY 82941, 307/367-4326, www.fs.usda.gov/btnf.

35 WHISKEY GROVE

Scenic rating: 8

in the Wind River Mountains in Bridger-Teton National Forest

Whiskey Grove Campground sits at 7,720 feet along the Upper Green River. Anglers can fish the Green River for brook and rainbow trout. The nearby Kendall Warm Springs (no swimming or fishing) harbors dace, a tiny fish

listed on the Endangered Species List for its rarity. The fish lives in the 85°F spring water that streams down into the Green River. The campground sits just south of a fork with two scenic back-road drives in the Wind River Mountains. One route follows the Green River to Green River Lakes. The other crosses the mountains over the 9,664-foot Union Pass.

The campground sits on the south rim of an oxbow in the Green River. A pine forest casts partial shade on the campground, but with little undergrowth, you'll see some neighbors. Several sites have river frontage, with views of the water.

Campsites, facilities: The campground has nine RV or tent campsites. RVs are limited to 35 feet. Facilities include picnic tables, fire rings, vault toilets, and drinking water from a hand pump. Pack out your trash. Leashed pets are permitted.

Reservations, fees: Reservations are not accepted. Campsites cost $7. Cash or check. Open mid-June-mid-September.

Directions: From seven miles west of in Pinedale on Highway 191, turn north onto State Highway 352 for 28 miles where the pavement ends, and the gravel road becomes Forest Road 650. Drive three miles and turn left into the campground.

GPS Coordinates: N 43° 15.337' W 110° 1.550'

Contact: Bridger-Teton National Forest, Pinedale Ranger District, 29 E. Fremont Lake Rd., Pinedale, WY 82941, 307/367-4326, www.fs.usda.gov/btnf.

36 NEW FORK LAKE

Scenic rating: 8

in the Wind River Mountains in Bridger-Teton National Forest

New Fork Lake Campground sits at the foot of a scenic lake at 7,850 feet. New Fork Lake tucks into a steep-walled canyon that descends from Dome Peak following the route of a glacier. While you can launch hand-carried canoes or kayaks from the campground, a cement boat ramp with trailer parking sits partway up the lake, requiring a 1.5-mile drive, and serving to launch motorized boats (no Jet Skis permitted). In the lake, anglers go after a variety of trout as well as kokanee salmon. Several beaches at the lake's foot offer places for family water play and swimming.

The campground tucks its one loop in a grove of aspens that chatter in the breeze. The sites are all back-ins, and the narrow loop can pose problems for some RVs; scouting is advised. A few campsites have views of the lake and dramatic canyon, but all gain privacy from the thick understory.

Campsites, facilities: The campground has 15 RV or tent campsites plus one large group campsites. RVs are limited to 30 feet. Facilities include picnic tables, fire rings with grills, vault toilets, and campground hosts. Bring your own drinking water, or treat lake water. Pack out your trash. Leashed pets are permitted. Wheelchair-accessible toilets are available.

Reservations, fees: Reservations are accepted (877/444-6777, www.recreation.gov). Campsites cost $7. Cash or check. Open June-mid-September.

Directions: From seven miles west of in Pinedale on Highway 191, turn north onto State Highway 352 for about 14 miles. Turn right onto the gravel New Fork Lake Road for 3.3 miles. Turn right onto Forest Road 753 for 0.1-mile and left into the campground.

GPS Coordinates: N 43° 4.950' W 109° 57.966'

Contact: Bridger-Teton National Forest, Pinedale Ranger District, 29 E. Fremont Lake Rd., Pinedale, WY 82941, 307/367-4326, www.fs.usda.gov/btnf.

37 NARROWS

Scenic rating: 9

in the Wind River Mountains in Bridger-Teton National Forest

At 7,900 feet, the Narrows Campground overlooks New Fork Lake, a lake nearly split in two by a pair of peninsulas. You can swim the narrow waterway—only a couple hundred feet—that separates the two peninsulas, but be prepared for cold water. The lake tucks into a steep-walled canyon that descends from Dome Peak following the route of a glacier. A cement boat ramp with trailer parking sits one mile before the campground, offering a place to launch motorboats, canoes, and kayaks (no Jet Skis permitted). In the lake, anglers go after a variety of trout as well as kokanee salmon. A trailhead with stock facilities departs from the campground to head up the lake and into the Bridger Wilderness.

The quiet hillside campground flanks the north slope at the Narrows. Most of the campsites overlook the lake and garner views of the canyon and mountains at the head of the lake. Amid aspens, the campground's two spurs pack the grassy campsites close to each other.

Campsites, facilities: The campground has 18 RV or tent campsites. RVs are limited to 30 feet. Facilities include picnic tables, fire rings with grills, vault toilets, drinking water, and campground hosts. Leashed pets are permitted. Wheelchair-accessible toilets are available.

Reservations, fees: Reservations are accepted (877/444-6777, www.recreation.gov). Campsites cost $12. Cash or check. Open June-mid-September.

Directions: From seven miles west of in Pinedale on Highway 191, turn north onto State Highway 352 for about 14 miles. Turn right onto the gravel New Fork Lake Road for four miles. Veer right for two miles along the lake until the road terminates in the campground.

GPS Coordinates: N 43° 6.288' W 109° 56.557'

Contact: Bridger-Teton National Forest, Pinedale Ranger District, 29 E. Fremont Lake Rd., Pinedale, WY 82941, 307/367-4326, www.fs.usda.gov/btnf.

38 GREEN RIVER WARREN BRIDGE ACCESS AREA

Scenic rating: 8

on the Green River

BEST (

Located between 7,600 and 8,000 feet, the Green River floats through a series of convoluted oxbows in its gentle descent through the valley from the Wind River Mountains. Nine miles of mini campgrounds line the river's western shore at 12 developed river access points. During early-summer high water, the river runs at Class I-II, good for canoes, rafts, drift boats, and kayaks. Late-summer low water may require negotiating gravel bars. In this reputable fishery, anglers go after rainbow, brown, and Yellowstone cutthroat trout via wade-fishing or by boat in the river. Boat ramps—which work for standard trucks and cars with trailers—are provided at four of the river access sites. Most vehicles can reach the river access sites, but wet, muddy conditions may require four-wheel drive, and many require steep descents.

The sunny campgrounds offer quiet places away from hordes of people. But in the height of the boating season, you will see plenty of river traffic and day-use visitors. At night, the campgrounds are very quiet. Sagebrush prairies cover the slopes around the campgrounds, with brushy willows along the riverbanks. Be ready to cope with biting blackflies.

Campsites, facilities: The river access area has 12 locations on the west side of the Green River with 23 RV or tent campsites. Five of the river accesses (3, 4, 7, 10, and 12) can accommodate large RVs; the others can only fit RVs less than 31 feet. Vehicles must be parked at least 50 feet from the water. Facilities include picnic tables, fire rings with grills, vault toilets, and boat ramps at sites 1, 2, 4, and 12. Drinking water is not available. Bring your own, or treat river water. Pack out your trash. Leashed pets are permitted.

Reservations, fees: Reservations are not accepted. Camping is free. Open mid-May-September.

Directions: From 20 miles north of Pinedale on Highway 191, turn east onto the gravel road north of Warren Bridge over the Green River. Road conditions vary, depending on the season. The 12 river access locations are on the right side of the road in the nine miles upstream from Warren Bridge.

GPS Coordinates for first site: N 43° 1.713' W 110° 6.365'

Contact: Bureau of Land Management, Pinedale Field Office, 1625 W. Pine St., Pinedale, WY 82941, 307/367-5300, www.blm.gov/wy/st/en/field_offices/Pinedale/recreation/developed_sites.html.

39 WARREN BRIDGE

Scenic rating: 8

on the Green River

At 7,250 feet, Warren Bridge Campground sits on a broad sagebrush prairie between the Wind River Mountains and the Wyoming Range. It flanks the upper Green River en route to its confluence in Utah with the Colorado River. Across Warren Bridge, a gravel road parallels the Class I and II river upstream with 12 different places to launch drift boats, kayaks, rafts, or canoes. High water runs in early summer, but even as the water level drops, the river remains floatable through August. September flows may require pulling boats over shallow gravel bars. Wildlife—particularly sage grouse and pronghorn antelope—use the prairies around the river. Anglers go after rainbow, Yellowstone cutthroat, and brown trout in the Green.

Warren Bridge Campground is adjacent to the highway, where commercial trucking delivers noise to the campground at night. Only the howling wind can drown out the highway. The sagebrush and purple lupine plateau can be hot or windy, but the treeless campground offers big views of the Wyoming Range and the Wind River Mountains. The wide-open prairie offers no natural fences between sites, but they are spaced out for privacy.

Campsites, facilities: The campground has 16 RV or tent campsites. Large RVs can fit in the pull-through sites. Facilities include picnic tables, fire rings with grills, pedestal grills, vault toilets (wheelchair-accessible), drinking water, disposal station, and campground hosts. Leashed pets are permitted.

Reservations, fees: Reservations are not accepted. Campsites cost $10. Use of the waste disposal costs $5. Cash or check. Open mid-May-September.

Directions: From 20 miles north of Pinedale on Highway 191, turn southwest into the campground at milepost 120—just south of the bridge over the Green River.

GPS Coordinates: N 43° 1.076' W 110° 7.109'

Contact: Bureau of Land Management, Pinedale Field Office, 1625 W. Pine St., Pinedale, WY 82941, 307/367-5300, www.blm.gov/wy/st/en/field_offices/Pinedale/recreation/developed_sites.html.

40 WILLOW LAKE

Scenic rating: 7

in the Wind River Mountains in Bridger-Teton National Forest

Willow Lake Campground offers a way to explore a less visited lake. The 4.5-mile-long glacially carved lake sits in a more arid basin

from neighboring lakes. A primitive ramp allows for launching onto the lake for boating, paddling, or fishing. Swimming is okay here. Anglers also enjoy fly-fishing in Willow Creek. The head of the lake touches the Bridger Wilderness, and trails access peaks, lakes, and the interior mountains. The campground is popular with hunters.

This unmaintained campground is not for everyone as the Forest Service does little upkeep. Nevertheless, its location offers quiet and solitude at the foot of the lake where sagebrush surrounds campsites tucked into aspen groves.

Campsites, facilities: The campground has six RV or tent campsites. RVs are limited to 25 feet. Facilities include picnic tables, fire pits, pit toilets, and boat launch. Bring your own drinking water, or treat lake water. Leashed pets are permitted.

Reservations, fees: Reservations are not accepted. Camping is free. Open June-early September.

Directions: In Pinedale, take Jackson Street north until it turns into Willow Lake Road. Drive about 10 miles to the national forest boundary. After the boundary, veer left and drive about four miles to the lake on a rough gravel road. Find the campground entrance on the southwest shore.

GPS Coordinates: N 42° 59.334' W 109° 43.936'

Contact: Bridger-Teton National Forest, Pinedale Ranger District, 29 E. Fremont Lake Rd., Pinedale, WY 82941, 307/367-4326, www.fs.usda.gov/btnf.

41 FREMONT LAKE

Scenic rating: 8

in the Wind River Mountains in Bridger-Teton National Forest

Fremont Lake Campground, elevation 7,500 feet, sits on the east shore of Fremont Lake, where the landscape changes from sagebrush prairie to forest. The nine-mile-long and 600-foot-deep, glacier-carved lake, which supplies Pinedale's water, is the second-largest natural lake in Wyoming. The lake is popular for boating, sailing, waterskiing, Jet Skiing, swimming, kayaking, canoeing, and fishing for lake, rainbow, and brown trout. The newly reconstructed boat launch has a concrete ramp, dock, and trailer parking. Sandy swimming beaches rim part of the campground shore. Mornings bring calm water; winds usually pick up in the afternoon with whitecaps, and late afternoon thunderstorms are common. Accessible by boat, short hiking trails into the Bridger Wilderness depart from the head of the lake. The location of the campground near the lake's upper canyon blocks views of the snow-covered peaks of the Wind River Range; drive or boat to the lake's south end for the stunning views.

Reconstructed in 2013 with upgraded toilets, a group campsite, and pull-throughs for larger RVs, the campground—the largest in the Pinedale area—offers a mix of shaded, partly shaded, and sunny campsites with paved parking aprons sprawled in several loops along the lakeshore hillside. A mixed forest of Douglas fir, junipers, spruce, and aspens provides the shade for some sites; others are surrounded by brushy growth of wild roses, sagebrush, balsamroot, and willows. From some campsites, you can the neighbors; very few campsites have lake views.

Campsites, facilities: The campground has 54 RV or tent campsites. RVs are limited to 45 feet. Facilities include picnic tables, fire rings with grills, vault and pit toilets, drinking water, boat launch, and campground hosts. Leashed pets are permitted. Wheelchair-accessible facilities include toilets and six campsites.

Reservations, fees: Reservations are highly recommended (877/444-6777, www.recreation.gov). Campsites cost $12. Cash or check. Open late May-early September.

Directions: From Highway 191 in Pinedale, turn northeast onto Fremont Lake Road for

Fremont Lake, the second largest natural lake in Wyoming, tucks into the Wind River Mountains.

four miles. At the T junction, turn left for 0.2 mile. At the Y junction, turn right for 3.1 miles to the campground entrance on the left. GPS Coordinates: N 42° 56.415' W 109° 47.814'

Contact: Bridger-Teton National Forest, Pinedale Ranger District, 29 E. Fremont Lake Rd., Pinedale, WY 82941, 307/367-4424, www.fs.usda.gov/btnf.

42 HALF MOON LAKE

Scenic rating: 7

in the Wind River Mountains in Bridger-Teton National Forest

Half Moon Lake Campground sits at 7,600 feet on the three-mile-long lake. A boat ramp on the north shore, located 0.2 miles from the campground, includes room for trailer parking and launching motorboats, canoes, or kayaks. Hiking trails depart from the road's end at the lake's northeast corner; the trail tours around the head of the lake, climbing over the ridge, connecting with Fayette Lake (3 miles), and linking with trails into the Bridger Wilderness. Families can enjoy the sandy beach at the campground for swimming and playing in the water. The narrow winding Skyline Drive is worth the nine-mile drive up to Elkhart Park for the views of the Wind River Mountains and Bridger Wilderness; from there, a 10-mile-round trip trail leads to Photographer's Point.

The campground curls one main loop in the willows on the west end of the lake. The trees and brush leave the campsites with no views of the lake. However, several campsites sit very close to lake, where the sandy beach offers a place to swim, fish, and moor boats. The tight campground loop cramps large RVs, and overgrowth scrunches places for setting up tents.

Campsites, facilities: The campground has 15 RV or tent campsites and one tent-only site. RVs are limited to 40 feet. Facilities include picnic tables, fire rings, vault toilets, and boat launch. Bring your own drinking water, or treat lake water. Leashed pets are permitted.

Reservations, fees: Reservations are not accepted. Camping costs $7. Open June–early September.

Directions: From Highway 191 in Pinedale, turn northeast onto Fremont Lake Road for four miles. Continue straight onto Skyline Drive for 3.8 miles. Turn right and drive on the dirt Forest Road 114 for 1.1 miles and turn right to reach the campground entrance.

GPS Coordinates: N 42° 56.206' W 109° 45.666'

Contact: Bridger-Teton National Forest, Pinedale Ranger District, 29 E. Fremont Lake Rd., Pinedale, WY 82941, 307/367-4326, www.fs.usda.gov/btnf.

43 TRAIL'S END

Scenic rating: 8

in the Wind River Mountains in Bridger-Teton National Forest

At 9,300 feet, Trail's End Campground has the distinction of being the highest vehicle-accessed campground in the Wind River Mountains. Also known as Elkhart, the area is a leap off point into the Bridger Wilderness, with alpine wildflower meadows interspersed with forests splayed out on gray rocky monoliths. Trails depart for lakes and connect eventually with the Continental Divide. Anglers may want to hike two miles to Long Lake to fish for trout. But the best day hike destination heads five miles to Photographer's Point, where expansive views include rugged peaks over 13,000 feet. Horse facilities including corrals are available at the trailhead. During the summer, the Forest Service maintains an information A-frame at Elkhart. The campground attracts hunters in fall.

Be ready for the high elevation of this campground. Just walking to the toilet will tucker you out if you aren't acclimatized to the altitude. In midsummer, the campground can fill up; plan to arrive early to get a spot. Otherwise, you can camp in several primitive sites on Skyline Drive. While plenty of spectacular views await hikers, those sticking to the campground will see mostly meadows and forest rather than peaks. Be ready for voracious mosquitoes.

Campsites, facilities: The campground has eight RV or tent campsites. RVs are limited to 20 feet. Facilities include picnic tables, fire rings, vault toilets, and drinking water. Leashed pets are permitted.

Reservations, fees: Reservations are not accepted. Camping costs $12. Open June–mid-September, depending on snow.

Directions: From Highway 191 in Pinedale, turn northeast onto Fremont Lake Road for four miles. Continue straight onto Skyline Drive for about 12 miles until the road's end. GPS Coordinates: N 43° 0.324' W 109° 45.151'

Contact: Bridger-Teton National Forest, Pinedale Ranger District, 29 E. Fremont Lake Rd., Pinedale, WY 82941, 307/367-4326, www.fs.usda.gov/btnf.

44 BOULDER LAKE (BLM)

Scenic rating: 5
in the Wind River Mountains

At 7,300 feet, the BLM Boulder Lake Campground is located at the foot of the four-mile-long Boulder Lake on the north side of the dam. Anglers can fish the creek below the dam and the lake, which is surrounded by dry sagebrush foothills broken by rocky outcroppings. You can launch hand-carried watercraft from primitive ramps, but larger boats must launch from the boat ramp on the west end of the lake accessed via the Boulder Lake Road. Boulder Creek, which flows west from the lake's dam, tumbles about 1.5 miles down to Stokes Crossing, located on the south side of the stream.

Both campgrounds are quite primitive and raw in comparison to the USFS Boulder Lake Campground at the head of the lake. The dirt sites at both campgrounds have full sun, territorial and water views, no shade, and are subject to wind. Rocks and sagebrush surround the campsites.

Campsites, facilities: Boulder Lake Campground has four RV or tent campsites. Stokes Crossing Campground has two campsites. RVs are limited to 40 feet. Facilities include picnic tables, fire rings with grills, and vault toilets. Bring your own drinking water, or treat lake and creek water. Pack out your trash. Leashed pets are permitted.

Reservations, fees: Reservations are not accepted. Camping is free. Open late May-mid-October.

Directions: From Boulder (south of Pinedale),

drive north on Burnt Lake Road for seven miles to Boulder Lake Campground. For Stokes Crossing, drive east on State Route 353 for 2.4 miles. Turn north onto the dirt and gravel Boulder Lake Road (Forest Road 125) for five miles. Turn left at the Stokes Crossing sign.

GPS Coordinates: N 42° 50.250' W 109° 42.303'

Contact: Bureau of Land Management, Pinedale Field Office, 1625 W. Pine St., Pinedale, WY 82941, 307/367-5300, www.blm.gov/wy/st/en/field_offices/Pinedale/recreation/developed_sites.html.

45 BOULDER LAKE (USFS)

Scenic rating: 7
in the Wind River Mountains in Bridger-Teton National Forest

At 7,300 feet, Boulder Lake Campground is located at the head of the four-mile-long Boulder Lake. But the campground actually sits on Boulder Creek, which runs into the lake. Anglers can fish the creek and the lake, which is surrounded by dry sagebrush foothills broken by rocky outcroppings. You can launch hand-carried watercraft into the creek or at the lake's head, but larger boats must launch from the primitive boat ramps on the west end of the lake. For access to the Bridger Wilderness, the Boulder Creek Trailhead with horse corrals sits adjacent to the campground. Trails loop to a myriad of lakes including Burnt, Blueberry, and Lovatt Lakes. Another trail wanders up the Boulder Canyon to the Continental Divide. Swimmers can enjoy the lake.

One campground loop circles through a mixed forest of aspens, lodgepole pine, and willows. A few of the grassy, private campsites have views of the lakes while others pick up territorial views. The location at the end of the road guarantees nighttime quiet.

Campsites, facilities: The campground has

20 RV or tent campsites. RVs are limited to 40 feet. Some pull-through sites are available. Facilities include picnic tables, fire rings, vault toilets, and lantern holders. Bring your own drinking water, or treat lake water. Pack out your trash. Leashed pets are permitted.

Reservations, fees: Reservations are not accepted. Camping costs $7. Open June-mid-October.

Directions: From Boulder (south of Pinedale), drive east on State Route 353 for 2.4 miles. Turn north onto the dirt and gravel Boulder Lake Road (Forest Road 125) for six miles. At a fork, veer right for 4.5 miles to the campground entrance across the creek.

GPS Coordinates: N 42° 51.406' W 109° 37.039'

Contact: Bridger-Teton National Forest, Pinedale Ranger District, 29 E. Fremont Lake Rd., Pinedale, WY 82941, 307/367-4326, www.fs.usda.gov/btnf.

46 SCAB CREEK

Scenic rating: 6

in the Wind River Mountains

At 8,200 feet in the southern Wind River Range foothills, the Scab Creek Campground is mostly used by those launching into the Bridger Wilderness. From the trailhead, the route bolts with a steep grunt for two miles, but moderates into more gentle grades after entering the wilderness. Anglers hike the 2.5 miles to Divide Lake for fishing, and horseback riders cruise farther to a series of high alpine lakes along the Continental Divide. Above the campground, a jumble of rocky buttresses provide habitat for marmots, and about 45 minutes up the trail, rock climbers scale a popular 400-foot granite slab known as the Scab Creek Buttress.

The ultra quiet campground gains partial shade from a loose lodgepole and aspen forest.

In early summer, elk frequent the grass, sagebrush, and wildflower meadows that surround the campground. A horse camp was added to accommodate those traveling with stock. Be prepared for heavy mosquitoes and black flies in summer, but enjoy the brilliant stars from this altitude.

Campsites, facilities: The campground has nine RV or tent campsites. RVs are limited to 31 feet. Facilities include picnic tables, fire rings with grills, and vault toilets. Bring your own drinking water, or treat creek water. Pack out your trash. Leashed pets are permitted.

Reservations, fees: Reservations are not accepted. Camping is free. Open May-mid-November, snow permitting.

Directions: From Boulder (south of Pinedale), drive east on State Route 353 for seven miles. Turn north onto the gravel Scab Creek Road for 1.4 miles. Veer left and go 7.3 curvy miles that climb to the campground at the road's end.

GPS Coordinates: N 42° 49.247' W 109° 33.162'

Contact: Bureau of Land Management, Pinedale Field Office, 1625 W. Pine St., Pinedale, WY 82941, 307/367-5300, www.blm.gov/wy/st/en/field_offices/Pinedale/recreation/developed_sites.html.

47 BIG SANDY

Scenic rating: 7

in the Wind River Mountains in Bridger-Teton National Forest

BEST (

At 9,100 feet in the southern Wind River Range, remote Big Sandy Campground requires hours of laborious, bumpy dirt-road driving to reach it. Despite the rough roads, you'll arrive to parking areas brimming with 50-60 cars because of the popular trailhead, which accesses both the Bridger and Popo Agie Wildernesses, lakes for fishing, and the Cirque

© BECKY LOMAX

High elevation Jackass Pass accesses Cirque of the Towers in the Popo Agie Wilderness.

of the Towers rock-climbing area. Day hikes lead to three small lakes within 3.5 miles, Big Sandy Lake (5.3 miles), and Jackass Pass (7.7 miles), the latter with stunning views into the Cirque of the Towers. Horse facilities (corrals, ramps, and hitch rails) are available. Big Sandy River flows past the campground, offering wade-fishing for brook and Yellowstone cutthroat trout.

Despite the number of cars, the campground is quiet. Grassy campsites vary between sunny and open with views of vehicles to shaded under mature lodgepoles within earshot of the river. All have large flat spaces for tents. The three spacious campsites at the end of the turnaround may see each other, but not the hordes of vehicles, plus they are shaded from the late afternoon heat. Campers not acclimatized to high elevation will feel shortness of breath at the altitude.

Campsites, facilities: The campground has 12 RV or tent campsites. Some grassy parking pads can accommodate midsized RVs, but leveling is difficult and the access road brutal.

Facilities include picnic tables, fire rings with grills or fire pits, pit and vault toilets, and bear boxes. Drinking water is not available. Bring your own, or treat river water. Leashed pets are permitted.

Reservations, fees: Reservations are not accepted. Campsites cost $7. Cash or check. Open mid-June-early September.

Directions: From Highway 191 south of Pinedale, drive 19 miles east on Highway 353 to where pavement ends. Turn east onto Big Sandy Elkhorn Road for 8.6 miles. Turn east onto the Lander Cutoff Road for seven miles. Turn north onto Big Sandy Road for 10 miles. Plan on one hour to drive the rugged, narrow Big Sandy Road. From Highway 28 at South Pass, you can also drive the dirt Lander Cutoff Road for 25 miles to reach Big Sandy Road. GPS Coordinates: N 42° 41.258' W 109° 16.283'

Contact: Bridger-Teton National Forest, Pinedale Ranger District, 29 E. Fremont Lake Rd., Pinedale, WY 82941, 307/367-4326, www.fs.usda.gov/btnf.

© BECKY LOMAX

Brooks Lake sits high on Wyoming's Continental Divide.

48 BROOKS LAKE

Scenic rating: 10

in the Absaroka Mountains in Shoshone
National Forest

BEST (

Located at 9,100 feet, Brooks Lake sits on the
Continental Divide, squeezed between large
orange buttresses of rock. The campground
looks across the lake to the Pinnacles, spires
that capture the alpenglow of the setting sun.
The Continental Divide Trail departs from
the lake, and trails loop around the Pinnacles.
Trails also lead to Upper Jade Lake, Upper
Brooks Lake, and Rainbow Lake. At the
campground, a primitive boat ramp aids those
launching small boats (motors are okay) for
paddling the shoreline of the 234-acre lake or
fishing for rainbow and brook trout. The lake
has exceptionally clear water in early summer,
but as it overturns at the end of August, it takes
on a green cast from algae. Historical Brooks
Lake Lodge sits behind the campground, with
its horses grazing near the lake.

Recent thinning, to control fungus in the
pine trees at the ultra-quiet campground,
changed some of the campsites from deep
shade to partial shade. Two short gravel spurs
and one gravel loop make up the campground,
with the loop offering sites 10-13 overlooking
the lake and pinnacles. Most of the loop sites
are open, close together, and substitute privacy
for stunning location; the spur campsites are
more private. You will feel the high elevation
walking from the lake back to your campsite.

Campsites, facilities: The campground has
13 RV or tent campsites. RVs are limited to 32
feet. Facilities include picnic tables, fire rings
with grills, vault toilets, bear boxes, garbage
service, and campground hosts. Drinking
water is not available; treat lake water. (You
can also get potable water one mile east at
Pinnacles Campground.) Leashed pets are
permitted.

Reservations, fees: Reservations are not accepted. Campsites cost $10. Cash or check.
Open July-early September.

Directions: On Highway 26/287, drive 22
miles west from Dubois or 33 miles east from

Moran Junction. At milepost 33, turn north onto Brooks Lake Road (Forest Road 515). Drive four miles and veer left at the fork. At the signed junction, turn left for 0.6 mile, and turn sharp right at Brooks Lake Lodge, dropping 0.2 mile to the lake.

GPS Coordinates: N 43° 45.017' W 110° 0.320'

Contact: Shoshone National Forest, Wind River Ranger District, 1403 W. Ramshorn, Dubois, WY 82513, 307/455-2466, www.fs.usda.gov/shoshone.

49 PINNACLES

🚶 🚴 🏊 🛶 🚐 🚤 🐎 🚗 ⛺

Scenic rating: 10

in the Absaroka Mountains in Shoshone National Forest

BEST (

Located at 9,142 feet, Pinnacles Campground nestles below an orange butte of fantastical pinnacles—hence its name. The Pinnacles are a photographer's delight, best shot in late afternoon and evening light. The campground also sits on Brooks Lake and borders its outlet creek. The Continental Divide Trail departs from the lake, and trails loop around the Pinnacles. Trailheads within two miles also lead to Bonneville Pass and the Pinnacles. You can launch boats, canoes, and kayaks from Brooks Lake Campground one mile to the west. Both the lake and the creek have rainbow and brook trout along with splake, a cross between the two. The lake has exceptionally clear water in early summer, but as it overturns at the end of August, it takes on a green cast from algae. Be ready at this high elevation for afternoon thunderstorms.

In contrast to nearby Brooks Lake Campground, Pinnacles offers more private, shadier campsites spread out across a bigger area. The hilly campground has one loop with some campsites tucked directly under the Pinnacles (site 10 grabs a good view of them) and six campsites overlooking Brooks Lake (these can

be windy). The ultra-quiet campground in the mixed subalpine fir and pine forest has both gravel pull-through and back-in parking pads. Sites 1 and 2 are positioned for snippets of Pinnacle views, but with traffic at the entrance.

Campsites, facilities: The campground has 21 RV or tent campsites. RVs are limited to 32 feet. Facilities include picnic tables, fire rings with grills, vault toilets, bear boxes, drinking water, garbage service, and campground hosts. Leashed pets are permitted.

Reservations, fees: Reservations are not accepted. Campsites cost $15. Cash or check. Open late June–mid-September.

Directions: On Highway 26/287, drive 22 miles west from Dubois or 33 miles east from Moran Junction. At milepost 33, turn north onto Brooks Lake Road (Forest Road 515). Drive four miles and veer left at the fork for 0.3 mile. At the signed junction, turn right, crossing the bridge into the campground.

GPS Coordinates: N 43° 45.114' W 109° 59.740'

Contact: Shoshone National Forest, Wind River Ranger District, 1403 W. Ramshorn, Dubois, WY 82513, 307/455-2466, www.fs.usda.gov/shoshone.

50 FALLS

🚶 🚴 🛶 🚐 🚤 🐎 ♿ 🚗 ⛺

Scenic rating: 8

in the Absaroka Mountains in Shoshone National Forest, Wyoming

Falls Campground, elevation 8,366 feet, sits just east of Togwotee Pass on Wyoming's Centennial Scenic Byway. The campground is one convenient for cyclists touring the highway and those needing a campground before hitting Grand Teton National Park, 40 minutes west. An interpretive wheelchair-accessible trail leads to an overlook of the falls that gives the campground its name. Hiking trails, boating, canoeing, and fishing are available five miles to the north at Brooks Lake.

The campground's location on the busy highway explains the hum of vehicle noise. However, the road is not a major trucking thoroughfare, so traffic does quiet somewhat after dark. The partly shaded campsites tuck under a loose mixed forest of pines and subalpine firs in two loops. Neighboring campsites are visible, but not stacked close like a parking lot. Gravel back-in and pull-through parking spurs access the campsites, some of which grab snippets of views of the Pinnacles to the north.

Campsites, facilities: The campground has 54 campsites. Loop A is geared toward RVs with 20 campsites with electrical hookups, and loop B is geared more toward tent campers with 34 sites, including five walk-ins. RVs are limited to 32 feet. Facilities include picnic tables, fire rings with grills, vault toilets, bear boxes, drinking water, garbage service, and campground hosts. Leashed pets are permitted. Wheelchair-accessible facilities include toilets and campsites.

Reservations, fees: Reservations are not accepted. Campsites cost $15, or $20 with electricity. Cash or check. Open mid-June-late September.

Directions: On Highway 26/287, drive 22.5 miles west from Dubois or 32.5 miles east from Moran Junction. At milepost 32.5, turn southeast off the highway onto the campground road. GPS Coordinates: N 43° 42.409' W 109° 58.248'

Contact: Shoshone National Forest, Wind River Ranger District, 1403 W. Ramshorn, Dubois, WY 82513, 307/455-2466, www.fs.usda.gov/shoshone.

51 DOUBLE CABIN

Scenic rating: 9

in the Absaroka Mountains in Shoshone National Forest

At 8,100 feet, Double Cabin Campground

enjoys seldom seen views of the Absaroka Mountains because it is long miles from the highway. But those who go here must be prepared for the tedious slow driving on the single-lane access road that is rough in places. The campground sits at the confluence of Frontier Creek and Wiggins Fork pour from the Washakie Wilderness, offering fly-fishing for trout. Several trails for hikers and horseback riders lead into the wilderness, which surrounds the campground. The Frontier Creek Trail #818 leads seven miles to a petrified forest.

For utter quiet far from a highway, the campground provides a remote hideaway. The campsites tuck under a forest of spruce and lodgepoles in one loop. Most of the campsites have spectacular views of the surrounding rugged peaks that climb more than 11,000 feet high.

Campsites, facilities: The campground has 14 RV or tent campsites. RVs are limited to 32 feet. Facilities include picnic tables, fire rings with grills, vault toilets (wheelchair-accessible), bear boxes, drinking water, garbage service, tent pads, and campground hosts. Leashed pets are permitted.

Reservations, fees: Reservations are not accepted. Campsites cost $15. Cash or check. Open late May-late September.

Directions: From Dubois, drive north on Horse Creek Road (Forest Road 285), which turns into a gravel road before four miles. At seven miles, veer right at the fork and continue for three miles. Turn right and drive for two miles. Veer right (Forest Road 285) and drive for 13 miles to the campground. GPS Coordinates: N 43° 48.396' W 109° 33.646'

Contact: Shoshone National Forest, Wind River Ranger District, 1403 W. Ramshorn, Dubois, WY 82513, 307/455-2466, www.fs.usda.gov/shoshone.

52 HORSE CREEK

Scenic rating: 7

in the Absaroka Mountains in Shoshone
National Forest

At 7,700 feet, Horse Creek Campground
flanks the arid southern slopes of the Absaroka Mountains. From the campground, you
can see only the lower sagebrush-, grass-, and
forest-covered rounded foothills rather than
the rocky peaks of the high Absarokas. Horse
Creek runs parallel to the campground, offering a place for anglers to go fly-fishing. The
stream usually clears of runoff sediments by
July, with the remainder of summer and early
fall offering decent fly-fishing.

With its location far from town and the
highway, the campground gives campers a
place to find quiet. The campsites have a mix
of shade and sun: some tuck into forested
nooks for privacy while others that are more
open garner territorial views. Lodgepole pines
and brush separate the campsites. Paths lead
to the stream for wading or fishing.

Campsites, facilities: The campground has
nine RV or tent campsites. RVs are limited to
32 feet. Facilities include picnic tables, fire
rings with grills, vault toilets (wheelchair-
accessible), bear boxes, drinking water, and
garbage service. Leashed pets are permitted.

Reservations, fees: Reservations are not accepted. Campsites cost $15. Cash or check.
Open late May-late September.

Directions: From Dubois, drive north on
Horse Creek Road (Forest Road 285) for 10
miles. (Around four miles, the road turns to
gravel and can be rough.) Turn north into the
campground.
GPS Coordinates: N 43° 40.003' W 109°
38.133'

Contact: Shoshone National Forest, Wind
River Ranger District, 1403 W. Ramshorn,
Dubois, WY 82513, 307/455-2466, www.
fs.usda.gov/shoshone.

53 WIND RIVER KOA

Scenic rating: 6

in Dubois

At 6,917 feet, the Wind River KOA makes
a good base camp for exploring the Wind
River Mountains to the south or the Absaroka Mountains to the north. It also makes
for a place to camp en route to Yellowstone
and Grand Teton National Parks. The Wind
River flows past the campground, offering
trout fishing and riverside relaxation, and
with the campground's location in town, you
can walk to shops and restaurants. Dubois is
a cowboy town with rodeos, square dances,
and western celebrations during the summer.

Only a few small cottonwood trees for shade
cluster in a portion of the grassy campground
where narrow sites line up in parking lot fashion. The sunny campground affords an easy
place for satellite reception. Many campsites
capture views of the Wind River Mountains.

Campsites, facilities: The campground
has 43 RV campsites and 14 tent campsites.
RVs are limited to 80 feet. There are 17 pull-
though sites for big RVs. Hookups include
water, sewer, and electricity up to 50 amps.
Three RV sites cater to equestrians with horse
corrals. Two of the tent sites have electricity
and water. Facilities include picnic tables, fire
rings with grills, flush toilets, showers, launderette, drinking water, indoor swimming
pool (late May-early September), game room,
playground, wireless Internet, cable TV, camp
store, and firewood for sale. Leashed pets are
permitted.

Reservations, fees: Reservations are accepted
(800/562-0806). Hookups cost $48-54. Tent
sites cost $28-32. Rates cover two people. For
extra campers, add $4-6. Kids under six stay
free. Open mid-May-September.

Directions: From Highway 26 in Dubois, turn
south on Riverton Street and drive one block
to the campground entrance straight ahead.

GPS Coordinates: N 43° 31.949' W 109° 38.148'

Contact: Dubois/Wind River KOA, 225 Welty Street, Dubois, WY 82513, 307/445-2238, www.koa.com.

54 DICKINSON CREEK

🚶 🚣 🏕 🚐 ⛺

Scenic rating: 9

in the Wind River Mountains in Shoshone National Forest

At 9,358 feet, Dickinson Creek Campground sits just outside the Popo Agie Wilderness in Dickinson Park between Black Mountain and Dishpan Butte. Trails for hikers and horseback riders lead to high alpine lakes. Anglers head to Shoshone Lake to fish for trout. Access to the campground is over private Wind River Indian Reservation Lands. All persons in the vehicle are required to purchase tribal fishing licenses to cross the reservation. They are available at Hines Store. Stunning mountain views accompany the drive to the campground.

This little visited campground can guarantee quiet and solitude, miles from the hubbub of civilization. A loose forest of lodgepoles shades some of the campsites, and the campground forest is surrounded by the expansive meadows of Dickinson Park. Some of the campsites garner views of the wilderness peaks. Campers not acclimatized to high elevation may feel shortness of breath. Be prepared for voracious mosquitoes and daily afternoon thunderstorms.

Campsites, facilities: The campground has 15 RV or tent campsites. RVs are limited to 20 feet. Facilities include picnic tables, cook grates, and vault toilets. No drinking water is available; treat creek water. Pack out your trash. Leashed pets are permitted.

Reservations, fees: Reservations are not accepted. Campsites cost $15. Cash or check. Open May-November, snow permitting.

Directions: From Lander, drive Highway 287

northwest for 15 miles, or from Fort Washakie, drive 0.7 miles south. At Hines General Store, turn west onto Trout Creek Road for 5.5 miles. Go straight through the intersection and drive for 17 miles on Moccasin Creek Road. Veer left at forks to stay on Moccasin Creek Road, which turns into Forest Road 329 at the forest boundary. Through the Wind River Indian Reservation, the narrow, rocky dirt road with no turnouts can beat up RVs. Be prepared to handle flat tires and other vehicle emergencies. GPS Coordinates: N 42° 50.188' W 109° 3.423'

Contact: Shoshone National Forest, Washakie Ranger District, 333 E. Main St., Lander, WY 82520, 307/332-5460, www.fs.usda. gov/shoshone.

55 SLEEPING BEAR RV PARK

🐕 🚴 ♿ 🚐 ⛺

Scenic rating: 6

in Lander

At 5,491 feet, the Sleeping Bear RV Park and Campground sits on the southern edge of Lander, home to NOLS (Northwest Outdoor Leadership School). Visitors to Lander can explore the Museum of the American West, take in a rodeo, check out casinos, or hook up with guides for fishing, rock climbing, and horseback riding. Downtown Lander includes a few galleries, shops, and restaurants. The local 18-hole golf course flanks the campground, and Sinks Canyon State Park sits just southwest of town.

Given the highway location and the nearby airport, you'll hear traffic and airplanes in the campground. Gravel back-in and pull-through RV sites line up with minimal privacy in parking lot fashion, and tent camping flanks the north perimeter. Some permanent residents live in the campground. Grassy campsites have full sun; a few trees dot the center island of RV sites. Views span the Wind River Range and the lights of Lander at night.

Campsites, facilities: The campground has 45 RV campsites and 10 tent campsites. RVs are limited to 65 feet. Hookups include water, sewer, and electricity up to 50 amps. Facilities include picnic tables, fire rings, flush toilets (wheelchair-accessible), showers, launderette, drinking water, splash park, playground, wireless Internet, dog run, propane and firewood for sale, disposal station, and camp store. Leashed pets are permitted.

Reservations, fees: Reservations are accepted. Hookups cost $25-39. Tent sites cost $21. Rates cover two people. For extra campers, add $2-4. Kids under six stay free. Open year-round.

Directions: On Highway 287, drive south in Lander for 0.5 mile past Buena Vista Drive. Turn right into the park.

GPS Coordinates: N 42° 49.485' W 108° 43.139'

Contact: Sleeping Bear RV Park and Campground, 515 E. Main Street, Lander, WY 82520, 307/332-5159 or 888/757-2327, www.sleepingbearrvpark.com.

56 PIONEER RV PARK

Scenic rating: 6

in Lander

At 5,491 feet, the Sleeping Bear RV Park and Campground sits on the southern edge of Lander, home to NOLS (Northwest Outdoor Leadership School). Visitors to Lander can explore the Museum of the American West, take in a rodeo, or hook up with guides for fishing, rock climbing, and horseback riding. Downtown Lander includes a few galleries, shops, and restaurants. The local 18-hole golf course flanks the campground, and Sinks Canyon State Park sits just southwest of town.

At this location on the highway, you'll hear traffic and airplanes, as the airport sits nearby. The sunny, treeless campground consists of gravel pull-through RV sites lined up with minimal privacy in parking lot fashion, but the owners take great care to keep the lawns green and potted flowers blooming. A long strip of lawn flanks all campsites, and views span the Wind River Range.

Campsites, facilities: The campground has 22 RV campsites. RVs are limited to 90 feet. Hookups include water, sewer, and electricity up to 50 amps. Facilities include picnic tables, launderette, drinking water, and wireless Internet. No showers or toilets. Leashed pets are permitted.

Reservations, fees: Reservations are accepted. Hookups cost $28. Open May-September.

Directions: On Highway 287, drive one mile south of Lander to Sunflower Street and turn right.

GPS Coordinates: N 42° 48.879' W 108° 42.751'

Contact: Pioneer RV Park, 176 Sunflower Street, Lander, WY 82520, 307/332-0155 or 888/875-5238, www.pioneerrv.com.

57 SAWMILL

Scenic rating: 8

in the Wind River Mountains

At 6,200 feet in Sinks Canyon State Park, Sawmill is one of two state park campgrounds in the narrow, arid sagebrush canyon. Sinks Canyon, an Ice Age feature, acquired its name from the disappearance of the Middle Fork of the Popo Agie River (pronounced po-PO-zha). The river enters a limestone cave and sinks underground only to emerge 0.25 mile lower in a pool called The Rise. The park's visitors center (open Labor Day-Memorial Day) sits 0.5 mile up the highway, where hikers can access the one-mile Popo Agie Nature Trail and the four-mile Canyon Loop Trail. The Sinks area is near the visitors center; a 0.25-mile trail leads to The Rise. Fishing is available in portions of the Popo Agie River but not permitted in The Rise pond.

Tucked along the roaring, boulder-strewn river in the canyon bottom, Sawmill is a small, sunny campground right on the highway. However, traffic dwindles after dark, as the road is a forest access rather than a trucking route. A few cottonwoods lend partial shade, and several campsites are open to the road. Tent space is limited in the very small and cramped sites. The campground is best suited as an overflow site for Popo Agie Campground one mile southwest. A wildlife-watching area—visible from several campsites—sits on the opposite side of the highway. Look for bighorn sheep and golden eagles.

Campsites, facilities: The campground has four RV or tent campsites that can fit small RVs. Facilities include picnic tables, fire rings with grills, vault toilets (wheelchair-accessible), drinking water, playground, and garbage service. Leashed pets are permitted.

Reservations, fees: Reservations are not accepted. Campsites cost $10 for Wyoming residents, $17 for nonresidents. Rates include day-use fees. Cash or check. Open May-September.

Directions: From Lander, drive south on Highway 131 for six miles. At milepost 7, turn left into the campground.

GPS Coordinates: N 42° 45.423' W 108° 47.982'

Contact: Sinks Canyon State Park, 3079 Sinks Canyon Rd., Lander, WY 82520, 307/332-6333 or 307/332-3077, http://wyoparks.state.wy.us.

58 POPO AGIE

Scenic rating: 8

in the Wind River Mountains

In Sinks Canyon State Park, Popo Agie Campground (pronounced po-PO-zha), elevation 6,750 feet, is the largest of the two state park campgrounds in the narrow, arid sagebrush canyon housing the Middle Fork of the Popo Agie River. Sinks Canyon, an Ice Age feature, acquired its name from the disappearance of the river, which enters a limestone cave and sinks underground only to emerge 0.25 mile lower in a pool called The Rise. The park's visitors center (open Labor Day-Memorial Day) sits 0.5 mile down the highway. The Sinks cavern is near the visitors center; a 0.25-mile trail leads to The Rise. From the campground, a bridge crosses the river to access the one-mile Popo Agie Nature Trail and the four-mile Canyon Loop Trail. Fishing for rainbow trout is available in portions of the Popo Agie River but not permitted in The Rise pond. Rock climbers tackle several routes in Sinks Canyon.

Set in junipers, cottonwoods, and sagebrush, the sunny campground squeezes in between the highway and the river. The roar of the river with early summer high runoff drowns out vehicle noise from the highway, which, as a forest access, is not used for commercial trucking. A paved road winds through the campground, connecting paved parking pads. Most sites can only accommodate small tents. The campground offers a mix of privacy, with some sites very open and others more sheltered with privacy. Sites 13, 15, 16, 19, and 20-23 overlook the river.

Campsites, facilities: The campground has 21 RV or tent campsites plus three walk-in tent sites. RVs are limited to 35 feet, although one site can fit a 45-footer. Facilities include picnic tables, fire rings with grills, vault toilets (wheelchair-accessible), drinking water, and garbage service. Leashed pets are permitted.

Reservations, fees: Reservations are not accepted. Campsites cost $10 for Wyoming residents, $17 for nonresidents. Rates include day-use fees. Cash or check. Open May-September.

Directions: From Lander, drive south on Highway 131 for seven miles. At milepost 8.2, turn left into the campground.

GPS Coordinates: N 42° 44.560' W 108° 49.206'

Contact: Sinks Canyon State Park, 3079 Sinks Canyon Rd., Lander, WY 82520, 307/332-6333 or 307/332-3077, http://wyoparks.state.wy.us.

59 SINKS CANYON

Scenic rating: 8

in the Wind River Mountains in Shoshone
National Forest

At 6,850 feet in Sinks Canyon, Sinks Canyon Campground squeezes between the Middle Fork of the Popo Agie River and the canyon highway. Sinks Canyon, an ice age feature, acquired its name from the disappearing river, which enters a limestone cave and sinks underground only to emerge 0.25 mile lower in a pool called The Rise. The state park visitors center (open Labor Day-Memorial Day), The Sinks, and The Rise sit one mile down the highway. Fishing for rainbow trout is available along the river. From the campground, a bridge crosses the river to access the four-mile Canyon Loop Trail. From Bruces picnic area 1.5 miles southeast, a trail leads 1.6 miles to Popo Agie Falls, a series of roaring cascades. Bicyclists and scenic drivers also tour the Loop Road, which climbs above the campground in a series of switchbacks and continues 33 miles to Highway 28. The pavement ends after eight miles. Sinks Canyon also attracts rock climbers.

In a thin forest of aspens, lodgepoles, and junipers, the sunny campground tucks between the highway and the river. Most of the campsites are open to the highway, but the views also yield sights of the streaked canyon walls and the split habitat of the canyon's sagebrush north slopes and forested south slopes. The highway—a forest access road—sees traffic in midsummer but quiets after dark, as the route is not used for commercial trucking. The river, which is strewn with large boulders, roars in early summer. Tenters find more space here than at the two nearby state park campgrounds; sites 1-3 offer shaded walk-in sites for tents.

Campsites, facilities: The campground has 11 RV or tent campsites and three walk-in tent campsites. RVs are limited to 20 feet. Facilities include picnic tables, fire rings with grills, vault toilets (wheelchair-accessible), drinking water, bear boxes, garbage service, firewood for sale, tent platforms, and campground hosts. Leashed pets are permitted.

Reservations, fees: Reservations are not accepted. Campsites cost $15. Cash or check. Open May-November, but services are shut off October 1.

Directions: From Lander, drive Highway 131 eight miles southeast. Turn left into the campground at milepost 9.
GPS Coordinates: N 42° 44.197' W 108° 50.160'

Contact: Shoshone National Forest, Washakie Ranger District, 333 E. Main St., Lander, WY 82520, 307/332-5460, www.fs.usda.gov/shoshone.

60 WORTHEN MEADOWS

Scenic rating: 8

in the Wind River Mountains in Shoshone
National Forest

At 8,850 feet, Worthen Meadows Campground sits on the south shores of cold Worthen Meadows Reservoir, which provides water for the city of Lander. Surrounded by large granite boulders and lodgepoles, the reservoir is named for the high elevation sagebrush and lupine meadows in the area. A trailhead accesses Roaring Fork, Stough Creek Lakes, and the Sheep Bridge Trail in Popo Agie Wilderness. Anglers go after brook and rainbow trout in the reservoir, best fished from a boat, and the small lake offers canoers and kayakers a place to paddle. Water levels can drop in the reservoir by late summer; call the Forest Service for status. Mountain bikers tour the dirt Loop Road (Hwy. 131) to Louis Lake.

The campground is divided into two sections—one sitting on each side of the boat ramp. The Lakeside loop has 20 campsites, with sites 9, 10, and 12-15 overlooking the reservoir. The partly shaded campsites tuck under aspens and lodgepoles with whortleberry and pine needle duff forest floors. Eight sites sprawl around the Hilltop loop on a peninsula, with sites 4 and 5 overlooking the water. Sites are spread out for privacy, but the lack of understory allows visibility of neighboring campers from some campsites. Both gravel pull-through and back-in sites are available. The campground is extremely quiet, except for the loud squawking of Clark's nutcrackers.

Campsites, facilities: The campground has 28 RV or tent campsites. RVs are limited to 24 feet. Facilities include picnic tables, fire rings with grills, vault toilets (wheelchair-accessible), drinking water, bear boxes, garbage service, tent platforms, and campground hosts. Leashed pets are permitted.

Reservations, fees: Reservations are not accepted. Campsites cost $15. Cash or check. Open July-September.

Directions: From Lander, drive Highway 131 (also known as The Loop or Louis Lake Road) for 16 miles south, climbing up the series of Loop switchbacks. Turn right at the signed junction and the end of the pavement onto Forest Road 302. Drive 2.4 miles, veering left at the youth camp and the unmarked entrance to the reservoir. Turn right into the campground. GPS Coordinates: N 42° 41.885' W 108° 55.721'

Contact: Shoshone National Forest, Washakie Ranger District, 333 E. Main St., Lander, WY 82520, 307/332-5460, www.fs.usda.gov/shoshone.

61 FIDDLERS LAKE

Scenic rating: 8

in the Wind River Mountains in Shoshone National Forest

At 9,400 feet, the remote 57-acre Fiddlers Lake houses a beaver lodge, yellow water lilies, brook trout, boat ramp, boat dock, and campground. The lake, which is stocked annually with rainbow trout, is cold, retaining ice often through May. It's best for small boats and canoes. With stock facilities, the trailhead to Christina Lake (#721)—a scenic popular fishing lake—is 0.5 mile south on The Loop. The 4.3-mile trail climbs to the lake. The same trailhead also leads four miles into the Popo Agie Wilderness to Upper Silas Lake. A 0.7-mile trail, one mile north of Fiddlers Lake, climbs to Blue Ridge Lookout, an abandoned fire lookout at 9,998 feet with views of the Wind River Range. Mountain bikers ride The Loop road.

If you're looking for solitude and quiet, Fiddlers Lake offers both in abundance. The campground sprawls along the north and west sides of the idyllic lake, with sunny or shaded campsites spread out for privacy; however, some sites are open to the campground road. Sites 5, 7, 8-10, and 18-20 overlook the lake. Many of the lake sites have pull-over gravel parking pads; the other campsites have back-ins. The surrounding lodgepole forest is broken by grassy meadows of purple lupine and white yarrow. Campers not acclimatized to high elevation will feel shortness of breath at the altitude.

Campsites, facilities: The campground has 16 RV or tent campsites and four walk-in tent sites. RVs are limited to 40 feet. Facilities include picnic tables, fire rings with grills, benches, pedestal grills, vault toilets (wheelchair-accessible), drinking water, bear boxes, garbage service, tent platforms, and campground hosts. Leashed pets are permitted.

Reservations, fees: Reservations are not accepted. Campsites cost $15. Cash or check. Open June-September, snow permitting.

Directions: From Lander, drive Highway 131 (also known as The Loop or Louis Lake Road) for 21 miles southeast. The last five miles are on a narrow dirt road. Turn right and drive 0.3 mile into the campground. GPS Coordinates: N 42° 38.047' W 108° 52.823'

Contact: Shoshone National Forest, Washakie Ranger District, 333 E. Main St., Lander,

WY 82520, 307/332-5460, www.fs.usda.gov/shoshone.

62 LITTLE POPO AGIE

Scenic rating: 7

in the Wind River Mountains in Shoshone National Forest

At 8,800 feet, Little Popo Agie (pronounced po-PO-zha) sits on the east side of the Wind River Range. A long, rough dirt road drive is required to reach it. Compared to the other three developed lake campgrounds on The Loop, this one sits near the Little Popo Agie River, which spills from Christina Lake. Trout fishing is available a three-minute walk from the campground near the single-lane bridge crossing the river. Watch for black bears and moose along the river. Hiking trails are available within 2-3 miles at Fiddlers and Louis Lakes. One mile south of the campground, the adjacent Maxon Basin loops with mountain-bike and ATV trails.

The four sites are located around the circumference of a gravel parking lot of this older, quiet, little-used campground surrounded by lodgepole and aspen trees. Whortleberries and lupines cover the ground, and some willow brush grows nearby, but the partly shaded campsites are open to each other. Ponds in the area can produce prodigious mosquitoes in July, but they abate by the end of August.

Campsites, facilities: The campground has four RV or tent campsites. RVs are limited to 16 feet. Facilities include picnic tables, fire grates, vault toilet (wheelchair-accessible), and garbage service. Drinking water is not available. Bring your own, or treat creek water. (You can also get water at Fiddlers Lake Campground two miles northwest.) Leashed pets are permitted.

Reservations, fees: Reservations are not accepted. Camping is free. Open July-September.

Directions: From Lander, drive Highway 131 (also known as The Loop or Louis Lake Road) for 23.5 miles. The last 7.5 miles are on a narrow, rough dirt road. Turn right into the campground.

GPS Coordinates: N 42° 36.503' W 108° 51.298'

Contact: Shoshone National Forest, Washakie Ranger District, 333 E. Main St., Lander, WY 82520, 307/332-5460, www.fs.usda.gov/shoshone.

63 LOUIS LAKE

Scenic rating: 8

in the Wind River Mountains in Shoshone National Forest

Remote small Louis Lake, elevation 8,600 feet, offers boating, fishing, and swimming, but be prepared for cold water. The high elevation lake retains ice until late May. A boat launch with a ramp, dock, and trailer parking is available on the campground entrance road, and picnic areas with sandy swimming beaches sit on the opposite side of the lake. The Louis Lake Lodge runs a tiny camp store on the lake's west shore, rents canoes, kayaks, and fishing boats, and guides horseback tours. A Forest Service guard station also sits on the lake. A trail leads 4.5 miles to Christina Lake and 1.7 miles farther to Atlantic Lake in the Popo Agie Wilderness. Two miles north, mountain-bike and ATV trails also loop through Maxon Basin.

The quiet campground tucks at the bottom of a tall talus slope in a loose forest of aspens and lodgepoles. The small sunny sites are clustered close together with sites 6 and 7 overlooking the lake. A trickling stream, which flows only in early summer, runs through the campground loop.

Campsites, facilities: The campground has nine RV or tent campsites. RVs are limited to 24 feet. Facilities include picnic tables, fire rings with grills, vault toilets (wheelchair-accessible), bear boxes, and garbage service.

Drinking water is not available; treat lake water. Leashed pets are permitted.

Reservations, fees: Reservations are not accepted. Campsites cost $10. Cash or check. Open June-September.

Directions: From Lander, drive Highway 131 (also known as The Loop or Louis Lake Road) 26.5 miles (the final 10.5 are dirt). Watch for ATVs on the road, which narrows to one lane frequently. Turn left and drive 0.8 mile through giant potholes into the campground. Trailers may have trouble with some of the deeper potholes. Louis Lake can also be reached via an eight-mile drive on Forest Road 300 from Highway 28.

GPS Coordinates: N 42° 35.522' W 108° 50.624'

Contact: Shoshone National Forest, Washakie Ranger District, 333 E. Main St., Lander, WY 82520, 307/332-5460, www.fs.usda.gov/shoshone.

64 THREEMILE

Scenic rating: 8

in the Absaroka Mountains in Shoshone National Forest

On the North Fork of the Shoshone River, Threemile Campground, elevation 6,700 feet, allows the quickest access into Yellowstone National Park from the Buffalo Bill Scenic Byway. Debating whether to camp here or push on into the park? Consider that the drive to Fishing Bridge Campground requires more than an hour. Threemile snuggles into the narrow canyon between the Absaroka Mountains and Washakie Wilderness. From the campground, anglers wade-fish the river for rainbow, brown, and Yellowstone cutthroat trout. Rafters and kayakers put in here to float the Class I-III white water. As the river level drops throughout the summer in front of the campground, sand and rock bars form beaches. Sitting one mile west, Pahaska Tepee Resort features a

lodge built by Buffalo Bill Cody in 1904. The resort offers trail rides and has a convenience store, gas, restaurant, bar, and gift shop. The 22-mile Pahaska Trail (#751) leads hikers and horse-packers into the Absaroka Mountains.

The campground was thinned to remove beetle-killed trees, leaving much of it wide open and sunny. Views from many of the campsites span the forested hills and the river; however, they also now include the highway and other campsites. Road noise is pervasive in the campground, but it does quiet down at night. Thick cow parsnip meadows surround the campground.

Campsites, facilities: The campground has 20 RV campsites. RVs are limited to 32 feet. With the prevalence of bears, only hard-sided camping units are permitted (no tents, tent pop-ups, or tent trailers). Facilities include picnic tables, fire rings with grills, vault toilets (wheelchair-accessible), drinking water, lantern poles, bear boxes, garbage service, and campground hosts. Leashed pets are permitted.

Reservations, fees: Reservations are accepted (877/444-6777, www.recreation.gov). Campsites cost $15. Cash or check. Open late May-early September.

Directions: On the Buffalo Bill Scenic Byway (Hwy. 14/16/20), drive three miles east of Yellowstone National Park or 47.5 miles west of Cody. Turn south into the campground.

GPS Coordinates: N 44° 29.783' W 109° 56.854'

Contact: Shoshone National Forest, Wapiti Ranger District, 203A Yellowstone Ave., Cody, WY 82414, 307/527-6921, www.fs.usda.gov/shoshone.

65 EAGLE CREEK

Scenic rating: 6

in the Absaroka Mountains in Shoshone National Forest

At 6,500 feet on the North Fork of the

Shoshone River, Eagle Creek Campground allows quick access into Yellowstone National Park, about six miles west. The 10-mile Eagle Creek Trail (#755) departs from the campground, crossing the North Fork on a hiker and horse bridge, heading into the Washakie Wilderness. From the campground, anglers wade-fish both the river and Eagle Creek for rainbow, brown, and Yellowstone cutthroat trout. Rafters and kayakers drive 10 minutes west to put in at Pahaska Tepee to float the Class I-III North Fork of the Shoshone. As the river level drops in front of the campground, sand and rock bars form beaches.

Eagle Creek sits in a loose lodgepole and juniper forest with meadows of hollyhock, cow parsnips, fireweed, harebells, and black-eyed susans. Wild roses are thick enough to scent the air. The two loops are crammed in between the river and the highway, which, unfortunately, adds vehicle noise that you can hear above the sound of the river. You can also see the highway from a few campsites in the left loop. All of the campsites in the left loop have river frontage, although some of the views include cabins across the river. About half of the right loop's campsites overlook the river. You'll have your choice of sunny or partly shaded campsites. Recent thinning projects have removed many of the beetle-killed trees, giving the campground a fresher, more open appearance.

Campsites, facilities: The campground has 20 RV campsites. RVs are limited to 40 feet. Because bears are prevalent, only hard-sided camping units are permitted (no tents, tent pop-ups, or tent trailers). Facilities include picnic tables, fire rings with grills, vault toilets (wheelchair-accessible), drinking water, bear boxes, lantern hangers, garbage service, and campground hosts. Leashed pets are permitted.

Reservations, fees: Reservations are not accepted. Campsites cost $15. Cash or check. Open mid-May-September.

Directions: On the Buffalo Bill Scenic Byway (Hwy. 14/16/20), drive seven miles east of Yellowstone National Park or 43.8 miles west of

Cody. Turn south off the highway into the campground.

GPS Coordinates: N 44° 28.312' W 109° 53.298'

Contact: Shoshone National Forest, Wapiti Ranger District, 203A Yellowstone Ave., Cody, WY 82414, 307/527-6921, www.fs.usda.gov/shoshone.

66 NEWTON CREEK

Scenic rating: 8

in the Absaroka Mountains in Shoshone National Forest

Located at 6,300 feet along the North Fork of the Shoshone River, Newton Creek is the last campground en route toward Yellowstone National Park that allows tents, tent trailers, and bicycle-touring campers. All campgrounds upriver require hard-sided camping units. The campground is popular for fishing, rafting, and kayaking on the Class I-III North Fork of the Shoshone River; however, fishing is closed below Newton Creek April-June because of spawning trout. (Upriver, there's no closure.) The surrounding canyon walls often have bighorn sheep grazing in early summer. On a spur road one mile east, the Blackwater National Recreation Trail climbs four miles to a memorial for 15 firefighters who died fighting a blaze in 1937. The Mummy Cave archeological site is also nearby.

Newton Creek also defines the abrupt shift from the arid sagebrush and juniper forest to the thicker Douglas fir and pine forests of the Absaroka Mountains. Two gravel loops weave around the sagebrush, wild rose, grass, and pine needle duff floor. The spacious campsites include large flat spaces for tents, and a small creek bisects the left loop campsites. Over half of the campsites have river frontage, either sitting adjacent to it or overlooking it from a small bluff. Views include the dramatic pinnacles across the river. While this campground

Anglers head to campgrounds along the North Fork of the Shoshone River for its reputable fishing.

is popular for its ambiance, it comes with highway noise, which dwindles after dark.

Campsites, facilities: The campground has 31 RV and tent campsites. RVs are limited to 40 feet. Facilities include picnic tables, fire rings with grills, vault toilets (wheelchair-accessible), drinking water, bear boxes, garbage service, and campground hosts. Leashed pets are permitted.

Reservations, fees: Reservations are not accepted. Campsites cost $15. Cash or check. Open mid-May-September.

Directions: On the Buffalo Bill Scenic Byway (Hwy. 14/16/20), drive 14.5 miles east of Yellowstone National Park or 36 miles west of Cody. Turn south off the highway into the campground.

GPS Coordinates: N 44° 27.148' W 109° 45.472'

Contact: Shoshone National Forest, Wapiti Ranger District, 203A Yellowstone Ave., Cody, WY 82414, 307/527-6921, www.fs.usda.gov/shoshone.

67 REX HALE

Scenic rating: 7

in the Absaroka Mountains in Shoshone National Forest

At 6,100 feet, along the North Fork of the Shoshone River, Rex Hale is one of the last two campgrounds en route toward Yellowstone National Park that allows tents, tent trailers, and bicycle touring campers. The campground is popular for fishing, rafting, and kayaking on the Class I-III North Fork of the Shoshone River; however, fishing is closed along the campground section April-June because of spawning trout. The surrounding canyon walls often have bighorn sheep grazing in early summer. On a spur road 1.5 miles away, the Blackwater National Recreation Trail climbs four miles to a memorial for 15 firefighters who died fighting a blaze in 1937.

The wide, open sagebrush plateau blooming with yellow clover in July offers neither privacy nor shade, but it is popular because of the electrical hookups at the campsites. Only a few fir, pines, and junipers dot the campground, allowing every campsite to have big canyon views, which unfortunately includes the highway. Highway noise dies down somewhat at night as the route is not a major trucking thoroughfare. Ten campsites overlook the river, and large spaces for tents are available.

Campsites, facilities: The campground has 30 RV and tent campsites. RVs are limited to 40 feet. Facilities include picnic tables, lantern hangers, fire rings with grills, vault toilets (wheelchair-accessible), drinking water, hookups for electricity, bear boxes, garbage service, a group campfire area for interpretive programs, and campground hosts. Leashed pets are permitted.

Reservations, fees: Reservations are accepted (877/444-6777, www.recreation.gov). Campsites cost $20 for electrical hookups and $15 without hookups. Cash or check. Open late May-mid-September.

Directions: On the Buffalo Bill Scenic Byway (Hwy. 14/16/20), drive 16 miles east of Yellowstone National Park or 34 miles west of Cody. Turn south off the highway into the campground.

GPS Coordinates: N 44° 27.241' W 109° 43.745'

Contact: Shoshone National Forest, Wapiti Ranger District, 203A Yellowstone Ave., Cody, WY 82414, 307/527-6921, www.fs.usda.gov/shoshone.

68 CLEARWATER

Scenic rating: 8

in the Absaroka Mountains in Shoshone National Forest

BEST (

Along the North Fork of the Shoshone River, Clearwater Campground, elevation 6,000 feet, is aptly named, for after spring runoff, the river runs with very clear water. The river, which wraps under a rusty-orange cliff wall opposite the campground, attracts anglers wade-fishing for rainbow, brown, and Yellowstone cutthroat trout, but because of spawning trout, fishing here is closed April-June. As the river level drops during the summer, large sandy and pebble beaches form along the campground. The Class I-III river works for floating in a raft or kayak usually through July. The tent-only campground works well for cyclists touring the highway. The campground tucks next to the river on an open sagebrush plateau under a mix of limber pine, junipers, and cottonwoods. The sparse trees allow for big views of the dramatic canyon walls from many of the grassy, sunny campsites. Several sites overlook the river. The open campsites allow views of neighboring campers, and vehicle noise from the highway seeps into the campground.

Campsites, facilities: The campground has 11 tent campsites. Facilities include picnic tables, fire rings with grills, vault toilets, bear boxes, garbage service, and campground hosts. Drinking water is not available; treat river water. Leashed pets are permitted.

Reservations, fees: Reservations are not accepted. Campsites cost $10. Cash or check. Open late May-early September.

Directions: On the Buffalo Bill Scenic Byway (Hwy. 14/16/20), drive 20 miles east of Yellowstone National Park or 31 miles west of Cody. Turn south off the highway into the campground.

GPS Coordinates: N 44° 27.678' W 109° 40.101'

Contact: Shoshone National Forest, Wapiti Ranger District, 203A Yellowstone Ave., Cody, WY 82414, 307/527-6921, www.fs.usda.gov/shoshone.

69 ELK FORK

Scenic rating: 6

in the Absaroka Mountains in Shoshone National Forest

Located at 6,000 feet along Elk Fork Creek, Elk Fork Campground is popular with horsepackers and hunters. Across the Buffalo Bill Scenic Byway from Wapiti Campground, it also offers an alternative for tenters who may not want to be around so many RVs. At the back of the campground, a popular horsepacking trail follows Elk Fork Creek upstream into the Washakie Wilderness. Horse facilities at the trailhead include trailer parking, corrals, and a stock ramp. Elk Fork Creek is closed to fishing, but across the highway, anglers can wade-fish the North Fork of the Shoshone River for trout after July 1 (it is closed April-June for spawning trout). Rafters, kayakers, and skillful canoeists can float the river, which runs with Class I-III white water. Hunters use the campground in fall.

Surrounded by an arid sagebrush canyon, the grassy campground with junipers, willows, and fireweed contrasts with a lush cottonwood bottomland on the east side of Elk Fork Creek. The partly shaded or sunny campsites are spread out for privacy; however, many are open enough to see neighboring campsites. The paved campground road connects with paved parking pads, most of which are back-ins. With the campground's proximity to the highway, you'll hear traffic, but it does die down at night.

Campsites, facilities: The campground has 13 RV or tent campsites. RVs are limited to 22 feet. Facilities include picnic tables, fire rings with grills, vault toilets, bear boxes, garbage service, and campground hosts. No drinking water is available; treat creek water. Leashed pets are permitted.

Reservations, fees: Reservations are not accepted. Campsites cost $10 when services are available in summer; otherwise free. Cash or check. Open year-round.

Directions: On the Buffalo Bill Scenic Byway (Hwy. 14/16/20), drive 22 miles east of Yellowstone National Park or 29 miles west of Cody. At milepost 22.4 just east of the bridge over Elk Fork, turn south off the highway into the campground.

GPS Coordinates: N 44° 27.828' W 109° 37.701'

Contact: Shoshone National Forest, Wapiti Ranger District, 203A Yellowstone Ave., Cody, WY 82414, 307/527-6921, www.fs.usda.gov/shoshone.

70 WAPITI

Scenic rating: 8

in the Absaroka Mountains in Shoshone National Forest

At 6,000 feet along the North Fork of the Shoshone River, Wapiti Campground is named for the elk herds that inhabit the valley. Across the highway at Elk Fork Campground, a popular horse-packing trail follows Elk Fork Creek upstream into the Washakie Wilderness. The river attracts anglers wade-fishing for its wild trout (rainbow and Yellowstone cutthroat), but because of spawning trout, fishing here is closed April-June. The North Fork of the Shoshone River runs with Class I-III white water, navigated usually through July in a raft or kayak.

Surrounded by red canyon walls with dramatic eroded spires, the popular, well-maintained, partly shaded campground's two loops sit under tall cottonwoods and junipers on each side of the forest road that crosses the river. Campsites are spread out for privacy, plus tall brush makes some ultra-private. Ten sites overlook the river; for the remainder of the campsites, paths access the river. As the river level drops throughout the summer, sandy beaches grow larger. Passing vehicles on the highway can be heard, but traffic dwindles at night as the route is not a major trucking thoroughfare.

Campsites, facilities: The campground has 21 RV sites and 19 RV or tent campsites. RVs are limited to 50 feet. Facilities include picnic tables, fire rings with grills, vault toilets, drinking water, hookups for electricity, bear boxes, garbage service, and campground hosts. Leashed pets are permitted. Wheelchair-accessible facilities include toilets and campsites.

Reservations, fees: Reservations are accepted (877/444-6777, www.recreation.gov). Campsites cost $20 with electrical hookups and $15 without hookups. Cash or check. Open mid-May-September.

Directions: On the Buffalo Bill Scenic Byway (Hwy. 14/16/20), drive 22.5 miles east of Yellowstone National Park or 28.5 miles west of Cody. At milepost 22.5, turn north off the highway onto Sweetwater Creek Road (Forest Road 423) for 0.1 mile. Campground loops sit on both sides of the road.

GPS Coordinates: N 44° 27.932' W 109° 37.458'

Contact: Shoshone National Forest, Wapiti Ranger District, 203A Yellowstone Ave., Cody, WY 82414, 307/527-6921, www.fs.usda.gov/shoshone.

71 BIG GAME

Scenic rating: 7

on the North Fork of the Shoshone River in
Shoshone National Forest

At 5,900 feet along the North Fork of the Shoshone River, Big Game Campground is surrounded by sagebrush hills broken by eroded
orange pinnacles. The Wapiti Wayside, 0.5
mile west of the campground, offers interpretive information on grizzly bears. The river attracts fly-fishers for its wild trout, but because
of spawning trout, fishing here is closed April-
June. The river runs with Class I-III white
water, runnable usually through July in a raft
or kayak. Canoeists can paddle part of the
river. As river levels drop during the summer,
a large pebble and sand bar forms between the
campground and the water.

Compared to the arid surrounding hillsides,
the campground is lush—partly shaded by
giant willow trees, junipers, and lodgepoles
with privacy created by short brushy willows.
This vegetation means none of the sites overlook the river, but paths weave through the
brush to the bank. Some open, grassy sites have
views of the pinnacles. A few pull-through
gravel parking pads are available for RVs, and
flat spaces are available for tents. Because the
sites are squeezed between the highway and
the river, the sound of passing vehicles enters
the campground, but it dwindles at night as
the route is not a major trucking thoroughfare.

Campsites, facilities: The campground has
16 RV or tent campsites. RVs are limited to 32
feet. Facilities include picnic tables, fire rings
with grills, pit toilets, bear boxes, garbage service, and campground hosts. Drinking water
is not available; treat river water. (You can
also get potable water 0.5 mile west at Wapiti
Campground.) Leashed pets are permitted.

Reservations, fees: Reservations are accepted (877/444-6777, www.recreation.gov).
Campsites cost $10. Cash or check. Open
mid-June-mid-September.

Directions: On the Buffalo Bill Scenic Byway
(Hwy. 14/16/20), drive 23 miles east of Yellowstone National Park or 28 miles west of
Cody. At milepost 23.1, turn north off the
highway into the campground.
GPS Coordinates: N 44° 27.715' W 109°
36.439'

Contact: Shoshone National Forest, Wapiti
Ranger District, 203A Yellowstone Ave., Cody,
WY 82414, 307/527-6921, www.fs.usda.gov/
shoshone.

72 NORTH FORK

Scenic rating: 7

in Buffalo Bill State Park

At 5,500 feet, North Fork Campground sits at
the confluence of Trout Creek and the North
Fork of the Shoshone River about 36 miles
from Yellowstone National Park's east entrance
station. Buffalo Bill Reservoir is less than one
mile to the east. An east-end boat launch
nearby allows for fishing, boating, paddling,
and waterskiing, plus the reservoir's consistent
winds make it popular for windsurfing. The
campground's Trout Creek Nature Trail, a
0.25-mile walk, tours riparian habitat on Trout
Creek. About four miles west, the Four Bears
Trail explores the eroded badlands country
for 4.5 miles to a ridgeline viewpoint below
Four Bears Mountain. The North Fork of the
Shoshone River contains Class I-III water for
rafting, canoeing, and kayaking and is floated best in June. The river is closed to fishing
April-June for spawning trout.

The North Fork campground with lush,
mowed, green lawns is strikingly opposite from
the arid North Shore Bay Campground, but
as at its sister campground, every campsite has
views of the surrounded eroded hills. A few
short cottonwood trees rim the three paved
loops, but the trees aren't tall enough to yield
shade or provide wind breaks. Most of the
campsites have paved pull-through parking

pads. While the campground sits on the Shoshone River, none of the campsites overlook the water. You can hear the highway, but wind can drown out traffic.

Campsites, facilities: The campground has eight RV campsites with hookups for water and electricity, 55 RV or tent campsites, and six tent-only walk-in sites. RVs are limited to 50 feet. Facilities include picnic tables, fire rings with grills, vault toilets, drinking water, garbage service, playground, disposal station, and campground hosts. Leashed pets are permitted. Wheelchair-accessible facilities include toilets and three campsites with water and electrical hookups.

Reservations, fees: Reservations are accepted (877/996-7275, http://travel.wyo-park.com). Campsites cost $10 for Wyoming residents and $17 for nonresidents. Cash, check, or credit card. Open May-September.

Directions: From Cody, drive west for 13 miles on the Buffalo Bill Scenic Byway (Hwy. 14/16/20) toward Yellowstone National Park. At milepost 36.7, turn south off the highway and drive 0.1 mile. Turn right into the campground entrance.

GPS Coordinates: N 44° 29.174' W 109° 19.935'

Contact: Buffalo Bill State Park, 47 Lakeside Rd., Cody, WY 82414, 307/587-9227, http://wyoparks.state.wy.us/.

73 NORTH SHORE BAY

Scenic rating: 8

in Buffalo Bill State Park

North Shore Bay Campground, elevation 5,500 feet, sits on the north shore of Buffalo Bill Reservoir about 42 miles from Yellowstone National Park's east entrance station. Surrounded by eroded sandstone formations, the reservoir draw locals for its fishing, boating, paddling, windsurfing, swimming, and waterskiing. The campground's boat launch includes a cement ramp, dock, and fish-cleaning station. Anglers go after rainbow, brown, lake, and Yellowstone cutthroat trout. The wheelchair-accessible Eagle Point Trail, which will eventually traverse the north shore, is in the Eagle Point Day Use Area four miles east. Buffalo Bill Dam maintains a museum open to the public, and the walk across the dam lets you view the Shoshone Canyon gorge from above.

The campground, with a paved road and paved parking pads at most of its campsites, squeezes its three loops in between the reservoir and the highway. Even though the highway is a major traffic route into Yellowstone, it does not serve as a major trucking highway; much of the noise diminishes after dark. The arid campground sits on a natural sparse grass and sagebrush plateau exposed to the wind and sun with only a handful of small cottonwoods. Half of the campsites overlook the lake, which makes it popular, and all of the campsites have views encompassing the rock spires to the north. The tent-only sites sit on a terraced hillside with windscreens.

Campsites, facilities: The campground has seven RV campsites with hookups for electricity and water, 32 RV or tent campsites, and five tent-only walk-in sites. Large RVs are okay, although midsized and smaller ones will have more choices. Facilities include picnic tables, fire rings with grills, vault toilets, drinking water, garbage service, boat launch, disposal station, and park personnel on-site in the entrance station. Leashed pets are permitted. Wheelchair-accessible facilities include toilets and three campsites.

Reservations, fees: Reservations are accepted (877/996-7275, http://travel.wyo-park.com). Campsites cost $10 for Wyoming residents and $17 for nonresidents. Cash, check, or credit card. Open May-September.

Directions: From Cody, drive west for nine miles on the Buffalo Bill Scenic Byway (Hwy. 14/16/20) toward Yellowstone National Park. Locate the entrance to the campground at milepost 42 on the south side of the highway.

GPS Coordinates: N 44° 30.095' W 109° 14.234'

Contact: Buffalo Bill State Park, 47 Lakeside Rd., Cody, WY 82414, 307/587-9227, http://wyoparks.state.wy.us/.

74 CODY KOA

Scenic rating: 5

near Cody

At 5,097 feet just east of Cody, the KOA is convenient for visiting sights in town. Buffalo Bill Historical Center wraps five museums about the West (including the life of Buffalo Bill Cody) under one roof. The Cody Rodeo, the longest-running rodeo in the United States, runs every night June-August with bull riding, calf roping, and barrel racing. (The KOA provides a shuttle to the rodeo.) Cody also is home to local outfitters for white-water river rafting, fishing, and horseback riding. The Shoshone River, west of Cody, froths with Class II-III white water through Red Rock Canyon for rafters and kayakers, with water runnable through September. Nearby Beck Lake offers fishing for kids.

The open, sunny campground affords an easy place for satellite reception. Only a few small cottonwood trees cluster in the mowed lawn campground for a bit of shade. Located outside of town, the campground is removed from the hubbub of town but has highway noise, which does include some commercial trucking.

Campsites, facilities: The campground has 161 RV campsites and 12 tent campsites. RVs are limited to 80 feet. Hookups include water, sewer, and electricity up to 50 amps. Facilities include picnic tables, fire rings with grills, flush toilets, showers, coin-operated launderette, drinking water, playground, basketball, horseshoe pits, jumping pillow, swimming pool, hot tub, wading pool, game room, dog playground, wireless Internet, cable TV, patios,

camp store, firewood and propane for sale, and disposal station. Leashed pets are permitted.

Reservations, fees: Reservations are accepted (800/562-8507, www.koa.com). Hookups cost $45-70. Tent sites cost $29. Rates cover two people. For extra campers, add $4-6. Kids under six stay free. Taxes and a resort fee will be added on. Open May-September.

Directions: From Cody, drive three miles east on Highway 14/16/20, passing the airport. Turn left into the campground.

GPS Coordinates: N 44° 30.775' W 109° 0.487'

Contact: Cody KOA, 5561 Greybull Hwy., Cody, WY 82414, 307/587-2369, www.codykoa.com.

75 JACK CREEK

Scenic rating: 8

in the Absaroka Mountains in Shoshone National Forest

Located about 7,600 feet along the Greybull River, Jack Creek Campground sits in terrain that looks like the southwest. Cliffy and arid, large buttes of the Absaroka Mountains rise up above the forested river valley. One trail follows the Greybull River for miles upstream, eventually connecting into the Washakie Wilderness, while other trails climb along tributaries. The trails attract hikers, hunters, anglers, and horseback riders, and stock facilities are available at the trailhead. Anglers consider the Greybull River a fly-fishing mecca. The river harbors native fish such as Yellowstone cutthroat trout and mountain whitefish.

The campground sits literally at the end of the road; that alone guarantees night time quiet. A mixed forest provides shade, and many sites sidle up to the river.

Campsites, facilities: The campground has seven RV or tent campsites. RVs are limited to 30 feet, but most of the spurs are smaller. Facilities include picnic tables, fire rings, and vault toilets. No drinking water is available; treat river water. Pack out your trash. Leashed pets are permitted.

Reservations, fees: Reservations are not accepted. Camping is free. Open mid-May-October.

Directions: From Meeteetse, drive State Highway 290 southwest for 11 miles. Take the dirt and gravel Forest Road 208 east for eight miles and veer left at the junction for another eight miles.

GPS Coordinates: N 44° 6.606' W 109° 21.125'

Contact: Shoshone National Forest, Greybull Ranger District, 203A Yellowstone Ave., Cody, WY 82414, 307/527-6921, www.fs.usda.gov/shoshone.

76 BROWN MOUNTAIN/ WOOD RIVER

Scenic rating: 8

in the Absaroka Mountains in Shoshone National Forest

Located about 7,400 feet in the Wood River Valley, Brown Mountain and Wood River Campgrounds sit about two miles apart, cowering under the tall Absaroka Mountains. The pair of campgrounds attracts anglers fishing for trout in the Wood River, horseback riders, hikers, hunters, and ghost town fans. Nearby trails follow tributaries upstream from Wood River. Below 12,000-foot peaks, the ghost town of Kirwin tucks on a hillside just below timberline. Find it 16-18 miles west of the campgrounds on a rough road suitable only for four-wheel drives or mountain bikes. By the early 1900s, the mining town held 200 inhabitants. Today, historical preservation efforts work toward saving its remaining 38 buildings.

The long gravel drive to the campgrounds guarantees that you'll fall asleep to the sound of the river rather than the sounds of civilization. The forested campgrounds provide shade with some campsites enjoying river frontage.

Campsites, facilities: Wood River has five RV or tent campsites with a maximum RV length of 30 feet. Brown Mountain has seven RV or tent campsites; most of the sites can fit RVs up to 16 feet, and one site has a 40-foot parking spur. Facilities include picnic tables, fire rings, and vault toilets. No drinking water is available; treat river water. Pack out your trash. Leashed pets are permitted.

Reservations, fees: Reservations are not accepted. Camping is free. Open mid-May-October.

Directions: From Meeteetse, drive State Highway 290 southwest for about seven miles. Turn left at Wood River Road (4DT) and drive 16 dirt and gravel miles to Wood River Campground on the left. Continue 2.5 miles further to Brown Mountain Campground on the left. Wood River GPS Coordinates: N 43° 55.923' W 109° 7.888'

Brown Mountain GPS Coordinates: N 43° 56.136' W 109° 10.756'

Contact: Shoshone National Forest, Greybull Ranger District, 203A Yellowstone Ave., Cody, WY 82414, 307/527-6921, www.fs.usda.gov/shoshone.

77 FOUNTAIN OF YOUTH RV PARK

Scenic rating: 6

outside Thermopolis

At 4,300 feet, Thermopolis is home to natural hot mineral springs. At the Fountain of Youth RV Park north of town, the Sacajawea Hot Springs flows at 128°F pumping out 1.3 million gallons a day. It feeds a large 235-foot-long and 75-foot-wide soaking pool, which is kept at 100°F. A bathhouse, lounge chairs, and benches flank the pool. Thermopolis State

Park sits about 2.5 miles south with a bathhouse, outdoor hot pool, hiking, and fishing. Two private concessionaires run additional indoor and outdoor hot pools with waterslides.

Pull-through RV sites have gravel parking pads set amid grass and shade trees. The campground squeezes between the highway and the railroad tracks, so bring earplugs to aid sleeping. The Bighorn River flows on the other side of the railroad tracks.

Campsites, facilities: The campground has 62 RV campsites. RVs are limited to 50 feet. Tenting is available in an overflow area. Hookups include water, sewer, and electricity up to 50 amps. Facilities include picnic tables, flush toilets, showers, drinking water, playground, large mineral pool, launderette, wireless Internet, horseshoes, dog trail, and camp store. Leashed pets are permitted. A toilet and the pool are wheelchair-accessible.

Reservations, fees: Reservations are accepted. Hookups cost $39-42. Tent sites cost $35. Rates cover two people. For extra campers, add $6 each. Open year-round.

Directions: From Thermopolis, drive north on Highway 20 for 1.9 miles and turn east into the campground.

GPS Coordinates: N 43° 40.425' W 108° 12.330'

Contact: Fountain of Youth RV Park, 250 N. Highway 20, Thermopolis, WY 82443, 307/864-3265, www.fountainofyouthrvpark.com.

78 WYOMING GARDENS RV PARK

Scenic rating: 6

in Thermopolis

At 4,300 feet, Thermopolis is home to hot springs. At Thermopolis State Park, the natural hot springs pumps out more than 8,000 gallons per day of mineral water. While the hot water steaming down rainbow-colored terraces reaches 135°F, water for bathing in the free bathhouse is 104°F. (Rental towels and swimsuits do have a fee, though.) With a bison herd on site, the park flanks the Bighorn River, crossed by a suspension footbridge, and 6.2 miles of hiking trails tour the grounds. Anglers fish the river for trout. Trails and a fishing pier are wheelchair-accessible. Two private hot spring businesses offer indoor and outdoor swimming pools, hot tubs, and slides. From the campground on the south end of town, you can walk downtown for shopping and restaurants, but the state park and hot pools sit 1.8 miles away on the north end of town.

Pull-through RV sites have gravel parking pads separated by grass picnic strips and shade trees. Each of the tent sites has its own water and electricity services, plus woods chips for tent pads. A Mexican restaurant is also on the premises.

Campsites, facilities: The campground has 11 RV campsites and four tent campsites. Large RVs are okay, but call to check availability. Hookups include water, sewer, and electricity up to 50 amps. Facilities include picnic tables, pedestal grills (bring your own charcoal), flush toilets, showers, drinking water, sandbox, trampoline, and wireless Internet. A launderette sits across the street. Leashed pets are permitted.

Reservations, fees: Reservations are accepted. Hookups cost $28-31. Tent sites cost $18. Rates cover two people. For extra campers, add $2 each. Kids under five stay free. Open year-round.

Directions: In Thermopolis, go south on Highway 20 where it turns west into Shoshoni Street. Drive two blocks and turn right.

GPS Coordinates: N 43° 38.325' W 108° 12.910'

Contact: Wyoming Gardens RV Park, 720 Shoshoni Street, Thermopolis, WY 82443, 307/864-2778 or 307/921-0151, www.wyominggardensrvpark.com.

79 UPPER AND LOWER WIND RIVER

Scenic rating: 8

in Boysen State Park

In the southern Owl Creek Mountains, Boysen State Park—Wyoming's largest state park—sits on the Wind River Canyon Scenic Byway. It contains the 20-mile-long Boysen Reservoir spilling north through Boysen Dam into Wind River Canyon. The reservoir is popular for boating, water-skiing, fishing, paddling, and swimming. Anglers catch ling, walleye, perch, crappie, and trout. Fishing is available in the Wind River, too. Lower and Upper Wind River Campgrounds squeeze between the highway and the Wind River, tucked into the canyon below the dam at 4,600 feet. Lower Wind River Campground is the site where the original dam stood.

The campgrounds have lawns and some shade trees, but you can find open sites with views of the canyon walls and its geological features. The canyon is home to bighorn sheep, which you can sometimes see from the campsites. Expect to hear trucking and railroad noise drowning out the sound of the river, and prepare for strong winds through the canyon. Pull-through sites are available, and large RV parking areas can accommodate multiple rigs.

Campsites, facilities: Together, the two campgrounds have 100 RV or tent campsites. Large RVs are okay. Facilities include picnic tables, fire rings with grills, vault toilets, drinking water, garbage service, playgrounds, disposal station (at park headquarters), and campground hosts in summer. Leashed pets are permitted. Wheelchair-accessible facilities include toilets and four campsites (three in lower, one in upper).

Reservations, fees: Reservations are accepted (877/996-7275, http://travel.wyo-park.com). Campsites cost $10 for Wyoming residents and $17 for nonresidents. Rates include day-use fees. Cash, check, or credit card. Open mid-May-mid-September.

Directions: From Boysen Dam at the north end of Boysen State Park, drive north on Highway 20 for 1.4 miles to the upper campground or 1.9 miles to the lower campground. Find the entrances on the left.

Lower Campground GPS Coordinates: N 43° 26.478' W 108° 10.344'

Upper Campground GPS Coordinates: N 43° 26.044' W 108° 10.645'

Contact: Boysen State Park, 15 Ash Street, Shoshoni, WY 82649, 307/876-2796, http://wyoparks.state.wy.us/.

80 BRANNON/TAMARASK/ MARINA

Scenic rating: 6

in Boysen State Park

In the southern Owl Creek Mountains, Boysen State Park—Wyoming's largest state park—sits on the Wind River Canyon Scenic Byway. It contains the 20-mile-long Boysen Reservoir, which spills at the north through Boysen Dam into Wind River Canyon. Surrounded by arid sagebrush hills, the reservoir attracts boaters, water-skiers, anglers, paddlers, and swimmers. Anglers catch ling, walleye, perch, crappie, and trout. Brannan, Tamarask, and the Boysen Marina line up adjacent to each other along the northeastern shore of the reservoir, all three with camping zones. A sandy swimming beach is available along with full marina services, concrete boat ramps, docks, boat slips, moorings, fuel, and fishing licenses.

The campgrounds and marina overlook the reservoir, but back up to the highway and the railroad, which contribute a significant amount of noise. With virtually no trees in the sunny campgrounds, winds whip through the area. The campground sites vary between individual grass sites and large cement parking lots.

Campsites, facilities: The campgrounds

have 65 RV or tent campsites. Large RVs are okay. Facilities include picnic tables, fire rings with grills, vault toilets, drinking water, garbage service, playgrounds, disposal station (at park headquarters), and campground hosts in summer. Leashed pets are permitted. Wheelchair-accessible facilities include toilets and campsites.

Reservations, fees: Reservations are not accepted. Campsites cost $10 for Wyoming residents and $17 for nonresidents. Rates include day-use fees. Cash, check, or credit card. Open mid-May–mid-September.

Directions: In Boysen State Park, locate Brannon Drive on the east side of Highway 20 about 0.25 mile north of park headquarters or 0.8 mile south of the dam. Brannon Drive accesses the campgrounds and marina. Brannon GPS Coordinates: N 43° 26.478' W 108° 10.344'
Tamarask GPS Coordinates: N 43° 26.044' W 108° 10.645'

Contact: Boysen State Park, 15 Ash Street, Shoshoni, WY 82649, 307/876-2796, http://wyoparks.state.wy.us/.

81 TOUGH CREEK

Scenic rating: 5

in Boysen State Park

On the Wind River Canyon Scenic Byway, Boysen State Park is Wyoming's largest state park with the 20-mile-long Boysen Reservoir. Surrounded by arid sagebrush hills, the reservoir attracts boaters, water-skiers, anglers, paddlers, and swimmers. Anglers fish for ling, walleye, perch, crappie, and trout. Tough Creek Campground is located on the east side of the reservoir on a narrow long spit rimmed with sandy beaches. A concrete boat ramp and dock are available. Two other primitive overflow campgrounds sit west of Shoshoni: Poison Creek and Lakeside. Lakeside has a boat ramp.

Plan for strong winds to pummel this campground at times since it has minimal trees for wind protection. Contrary to the state park campgrounds further north, Tough Creek offers quiet. Pavement ends at the parking area with most of the campsites on dirt road spurs. Many campsites overlook the water; some have private beaches.

Campsites, facilities: The campground has 67 RV and tent campsites. Large RVs are okay. Facilities include picnic tables, fire rings with grills, vault toilets, drinking water, garbage service, playground, picnic shelters at 15 sites, and disposal station (at park headquarters). Leashed pets are permitted. Wheelchair-accessible facilities include toilets and campsites.

Reservations, fees: Reservations are accepted only for the group camping shelter (877/996-7275, http://travel.wyo-park.com). Campsites cost $10 for Wyoming residents and $17 for nonresidents. Rates include day-use fees. Cash, check, or credit card. Open mid-May–mid-September.

Directions: In Boysen State Park, drive 6.7 miles south from park headquarters on Highway 20. Turn right onto Tough Creek Road and drop 1.6 miles, crossing the railroad tracks and going to the end of the narrow peninsula. GPS Coordinates: N 43° 19.807' W 108° 9.144'

Contact: Boysen State Park, 15 Ash Street, Shoshoni, WY 82649, 307/876-2796, http://wyoparks.state.wy.us/.

82 BOYSEN WEST SIDE PRIMITIVE

Scenic rating: 5

in Boysen State Park

Boysen State Park on the Wind River Canyon Scenic Byway is Wyoming's largest state park with the 20-mile-long Boysen Reservoir. Surrounded by arid sagebrush hills, the reservoir attracts boaters, water-skiers, anglers, paddlers, and swimmers. Anglers fish for ling, walleye, perch, crappie, and several species of trout. Small primitive campgrounds cluster among the bays and peninsulas on the rugged west side of the reservoir. Cottonwood Bay, the furthest north, requires the longest drive and sits on the south shore of one of the reservoir's largest bays. Loop 1 road accesses campsites closer to reach in South Muddy, Fremont Bay, Libby Point, and Sandy Hills Loop; Loop 2 road scatters campsites in Trout Bay, Cottonwood Bay, Sand Mesa, Wilson Bay, and North Muddy. Fremont and Cottonwood Bays have the only boat ramps on the reservoir's west side. Fremont Bay, to closest to access, has a playground for kids. Stop at park headquarters to pick up a state park brochure with a map to help with locating west side campgrounds.

These quiet, primitive, sunny campsites offer a place to be off by yourself. Many have private beaches. Some have a few cottonwood trees for shade; others are dusty and dry. Tenters should choose locations with trees for wind protection.

Campsites, facilities: Loop 1 has 20 RV or tent campsites. Loop 2 has 30 RV or tent campsites. Smaller and midsized RVs are best.

Facilities including picnic tables and fire pits are limited to specific locations. Toilets are only available at Cottonwood Bay, Trout Bay, Sand Mesa, North Muddy, South Muddy, Sandy Hills, and Fremont Bay. Drinking water is only available at Fremont and Cottonwood Bays. A disposal station is at park headquarters. Leashed pets are permitted.

Reservations, fees: Reservations are not accepted. Campsites cost $10 for Wyoming residents and $17 for nonresidents. Rates include day-use fees. Cash, check, or credit card. Open mid-May–mid-September.

Directions: From Shoshoni, drive four miles west on Highway 26 to the bridge over the head of the reservoir. From the bridge, continue west for one mile to Bass Lake Road and turn north. To access Loop 1, veer right. To access Loop 2, veer left, staying on Bass Lake Road for 8.2 miles to West Shore Drive. The loops are mostly gravel and dirt roads.

GPS Coordinates of Fremont Bay: N 43° 15.871' W 108° 11.725'

Contact: Boysen State Park, 15 Ash Street, Shoshoni, WY 82649, 307/876-2796, http://wyoparks.state.wy.us/.

IDAHO PANHANDLE

© BECKY LOMAX

Lakes define the Idaho Panhandle. Most developed campgrounds cluster around four large lakes and the rivers that feed them. The Selkirk Mountains cradle Priest Lake, which is encompassed by state and national forests. Its 72-mile shoreline is rimmed with campgrounds—more than the other three lakes combined. Islands offer boat-in camping, while Priest Lake State Park and Idaho Panhandle National Forest campgrounds line the shore. The Clark Fork River feeds Lake Pend Oreille—Idaho's biggest lake. Where the national forest borders the waterway, campgrounds offer boating and fishing. Lake Coeur d'Alene is the easiest lake to reach, but public access is limited to only a few campgrounds. The North Fork of the Clearwater River fills Dworshak Reservoir with 54 miles of waterway for boating, fishing, and swimming through July 4.

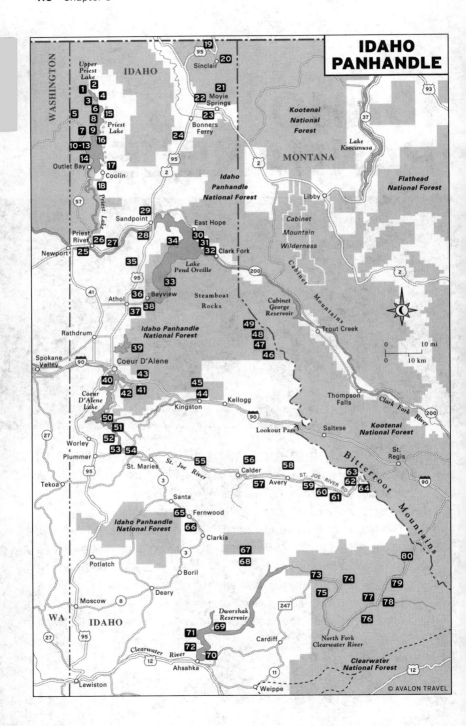

1 NAVIGATION

Scenic rating: 9

on Upper Priest Lake in Idaho Panhandle National Forest

BEST

Located at 2,500 feet on the west shore of Upper Priest Lake in the Selkirk Mountains, Navigation is the most remote lakeshore hike-in, bike-in, or boat-in campground in the Priest Lake area. The 3.5-mile-long Upper Priest Lake is a forested lake devoid of summer homes. Hikers, mountain bikers, and horseback riders access it via the 8.1-mile Navigation Trail (#291). Boaters and paddlers reach it via the 2.5-mile Thorofare, a slow-moving slough rife with wildlife between Priest Lake and Upper Priest Lake. Powerboats are restricted to no-wake speed. From Priest Lake, paddlers portage 50 feet across the sand to avoid the jetty. Boaters, including paddlers, launch from the free boat ramp south of Beaver Creek Campground. A longer drive up Priest Lake's east side leads to Lionhead Campground's boat ramp, which charges a fee. Paddlers have two other launches on the west side: One is a short canoe portage from Beaver Creek Campground (fee), but to avoid Priest Lake winds, park at the Navigation Trailhead (free) to portage 1,000 feet directly onto the Thorofare. To reach Navigation requires six miles of paddling. Upper Priest Lake is catch-and-release fishing only.

The quiet campground sits on the northwest end of Upper Priest Lake among firs and pines, where it has views from the beach of the Selkirk Mountains and sunrises. The campground does not have a dock, but the sandy beach provides a good place to beach boats overnight. Of the four upper lake campgrounds, this one is prized for the most wilderness feel.

Campsites, facilities: The campground has four tent campsites. Facilities include picnic tables, fire rings with grills, vault toilets, and bear boxes, but no drinking water. You can haul water from nearby Deadman Creek or the lake, but treat it. Pack out all trash. Leashed pets are permitted.

Reservations, fees: Reservations are not accepted. Camping is free, but two launch sites charge fees. The Forest Service charges $7 to use the short canoe portage and parking at Beaver Creek Campground. Lionhead Campground charges an entrance fee of $5. Cash or check. Open May-October.

Directions: From Priest River, drive 39 miles north on Highway 57 to Nordman. Turn right onto Reeder Bay Road (Forest Road 2512) for 12 miles to Beaver Creek Campground.

GPS Coordinates: N 48° 47.653' W 116° 54.472

Contact: Idaho Panhandle National Forest, Priest Lake Ranger District, 32203 Hwy. 57, Priest River, ID 83856, 208/443-2512, www.fs.usda.gov/ipnf.

2 TRAPPER CREEK

Scenic rating: 8

on Upper Priest Lake in Idaho Panhandle National Forest

Located on Upper Priest Lake's east shore at 2,500 feet, Trapper Creek is one of the more remote lakeshore hike-in, bike-in, or boat-in campgrounds in the Selkirk Mountains. With no summer homes, the forested lake has a wilderness feel. Hikers, mountain bikers, and horseback riders access it via the 4.3-mile Upper Priest Lake Trail (#302). Boaters, canoeists, and kayakers enter Upper Priest Lake via the 2.5-mile Thorofare, convoluted oxbows filled with bald eagles and birds, to reach the smaller 3.5-mile-long lake north of Priest Lake. Powerboats are restricted to no-wake speed. From Priest Lake, paddlers portage 50 feet across the sand to avoid the jetty. Boaters, including paddlers, launch from the free boat ramp south of Beaver

Creek Campground. (A longer drive up Priest Lake's east side leads to Lionhead Campground's boat ramp, where a fee is charged.) Paddlers have two other launches: One is a short canoe portage from Beaver Creek Campground (fee), but to avoid Priest Lake winds, park at the Navigation Trailhead (free) to portage 1,000 feet directly onto the Thorofare. To reach Trapper Creek requires about 5.5 miles of paddling. Upper Priest Lake and the upper Priest River are catch-and-release fishing only.

The quiet campground with campsites spread out for privacy sits on the northeast side of Upper Priest Lake facing Plowboy Mountain and the sunsets. The campsites are tucked into the forest edge of the lake, which offers protection from winds. The sandy beach makes it easier to pull canoes and kayaks from the lake.

Campsites, facilities: The campground has five tent campsites. Facilities include picnic tables, fire rings with grills, vault toilets, and bear boxes, but no drinking water. Haul water from nearby Trapper Creek or the lake, but treat it. Pack out all trash. Leashed pets are permitted.

Reservations, fees: Reservations are not accepted. Camping is free, but two sites charge launch fees. The Forest Service charges $7 to use the short canoe portage and park at Beaver Creek Campground. Lionhead Campground charges a $5 entrance fee. Cash or check. Open May-October.

Directions: From Priest River, drive 39 miles north on Highway 57 to Nordman and turn right onto Reeder Bay Road (Forest Road 2512) for 12 miles to Beaver Creek Campground. GPS Coordinates: N 48° 47.858' W 116° 53.957'

Contact: Idaho Panhandle National Forest, Priest Lake Ranger District, 32203 Hwy. 57, Priest River, ID 83856, 208/443-2512, www.fs.usda.gov/ipnf.

🔒 PLOWBOY

Scenic rating: 9

on Upper Priest Lake in Idaho Panhandle National Forest

Located at 2,500 feet on the west shore of Upper Priest Lake, the boat-in Plowboy Campground faces the Selkirk Mountains on the woodsy lake devoid of summer homes. Hikers, mountain bikers, and horseback riders access it via the three-mile rolling Navigation Trail (#291). Boaters, canoeists, and kayakers enter Upper Priest Lake via the 2.5-mile Thorofare, the slough connecting the upper lake to the lower lake. Powerboats are restricted to no-wake speed. From Priest Lake, paddlers portage 50 feet across the sand to avoid the jetty. Boaters, including paddlers, launch from the free boat ramp south of Beaver Creek Campground. (A longer drive up Priest Lake's east side leads to Lionhead Campground's boat ramp, which charges a fee.) Paddlers have two other launches: One is a short canoe portage from Beaver Creek Campground (fee), but to avoid Priest Lake winds, park at the Navigation Trailhead (free) to portage 1,000 feet directly onto the Thorofare. To reach Plowboy requires 3.5 miles of paddling. Upper Priest Lake is catch-and-release fishing only.

Facing the Selkirk Mountains, the campground sits on the southeast side of Upper Priest Lake, a half-mile from Geisingers Campground on the opposite side of the Thorofare. Plowboy gets more traffic than the campgrounds on the upper end of the lake because hikers use it as a destination to see the upper lake, but at night it quiets. The shaded campsites tuck into the mixed forest for privacy and protection from winds.

Campsites, facilities: The campground has four tent sites. Facilities include picnic tables, fire rings with grills, vault toilets, and bear boxes, but no drinking water. Treat lake water. Pack out all trash. Leashed pets are permitted.

Reservations, fees: Reservations are not accepted. Camping is free, but two launch sites charge fees. The Forest Service charges $7 to use the short canoe portage and park at Beaver Creek Campground. Lionhead Campground entrance costs $5. Cash or check. Open May-October.

Directions: From Priest River, drive 39 miles north on Highway 57 to Nordman and turn right onto Reeder Bay Road (Forest Road 2512) for 12 miles to Beaver Creek Campground. GPS Coordinates: N 48° 46.196' W 116° 52.832'

Contact: Idaho Panhandle National Forest, Priest Lake Ranger District, 32203 Hwy. 57, Priest River, ID 83856, 208/443-2512, www.fs.usda.gov/ipnf.

▟ GEISINGERS

Scenic rating: 8

on Upper Priest Lake in Idaho Panhandle National Forest

Located at 2,500 feet on Upper Priest Lake's south end, Geisingers Campground—accessed only by hiking or by boat—sits in the Selkirk Mountains. Woodsy Upper Priest Lake is devoid of summer homes. Hikers, mountain bikers, and horseback riders access it on Upper Priest Lake Trail (#302) via Trapper Creek Campground. Boaters, canoeists, and kayakers enter Upper Priest Lake via the 2.5-mile Thorofare, a slow-moving river that links with Priest Lake. From Priest Lake, paddlers portage 50 feet across the sand to avoid the jetty. Boaters, including paddlers, launch from the free boat ramp south of Beaver Creek Campground. (A longer drive up Priest Lake's east side leads to Lionhead Campground's boat ramp, where there's a fee.) Paddlers have two other launches: One is a short canoe portage from Beaver Creek Campground (fee), but to avoid Priest Lake winds, park at the Navigation Trailhead (free) to portage 1,000 feet directly onto the Thorofare. To reach Geisingers requires 3.25 miles of paddling. Upper Priest Lake is catch-and-release fishing only.

The campground sits under hemlocks and pines on the south side of Upper Priest Lake at the outlet. Located at the end of the Thorofare, the campground sees lots of day traffic, is good for people watching, but quiets at night. The view from the beach spans the entire 3.5-mile length of the lake with a backdrop of mountains. Ancient rusted relics from early logging days can be found around the camp.

Campsites, facilities: The campground has two tent sites. Facilities include one picnic table, fire rings with grills, vault toilets, and bear boxes, but no drinking water. Treat lake water. Pack out all trash. Leashed pets are permitted.

Reservations, fees: Reservations are not accepted. Camping is free, but two launch sites charge fees. The Forest Service charges $7 to use the short canoe portage and park at Beaver Creek Campground. Lionhead Campground charges an entrance fee of $5. Cash or check. Open May-October.

Directions: From Priest River, drive 39 miles north on Highway 57 to Nordman and turn right onto Reeder Bay Road (Forest Road 2512) for 12 miles to Beaver Creek Campground (where you can launch your boat). The Upper Priest Lake Trail #302 (through Trapper Creek Campground) accesses the campground on a mountain bike, horseback, or on foot. GPS Coordinates: N 48° 45.948' W 116° 51.844'

Contact: Idaho Panhandle National Forest, Priest Lake Ranger District, 32203 Hwy. 57, Priest River, ID 83856, 208/443-2512, www.fs.usda.gov/ipnf.

▟ STAGGER INN

Scenic rating: 7

northwest of Priest Lake in Idaho Panhandle National Forest

Up a long stretch of washboard gravel road, Stagger Inn Campground garnered its name

© BECKY LOMAX

The 2.5-mile Thorofare waterway connects Upper and Lower Priest Lake.

from the manner in which the 1926 firefighters stumbled into fire camp after trekking from Nordman on Priest Lake's west side without a road. Today, the campground, elevation 3,200 feet, is adjacent to Granite Falls and Roosevelt Grove of the Ancient Cedars Scenic Area. Granite Falls tumbles with crashing and frothing white water through its carved canyon. A two-minute walk leads to the base of the falls, but a one-mile loop trail (#301) tours higher for a dramatic look at the lower falls and then a peek at the upper falls. The cedar grove, named after Teddy Roosevelt, was nearly destroyed in a 1926 fire, but two small stands of the giants remain, some up to 12 feet in diameter and averaging 800 years old. Explore the upper grove off the trail, reached via one mile of walking from the top of the loop trail.

Tucked under lush cedars with a forest floor of ferns, the campground sits in the other surviving grove. The area has one small loop that doubles as the parking lot and picnic area for grove visitors during the day and acts as a primitive quiet campground at night. The heavy cedar canopy makes the campground dark and shady.

Campsites, facilities: The campground has four RV or tent campsites that can accommodate small RVs. Facilities include picnic tables, fire ring, and a vault toilet (wheelchair-accessible). Bring your own water, or treat creek water. Haul the water from lower downstream where access is safer. Leashed pets are permitted.

Reservations, fees: Reservations are not accepted. Camping is free. Open late May-September.

Directions: From Priest River, drive 37 miles north on Highway 57 to Nordman. Continue north for 1.6 miles until the pavement ends and the road turns into Forest Road 302. Drive another 10.7 miles on the rough dirt road to reach the campground on the left.

GPS Coordinates: N 48° 46.006' W 117° 3.671'

Contact: Idaho Panhandle National Forest, Priest Lake Ranger District, 32203 Hwy. 57, Priest River, ID 83856, 208/443-2512, www.fs.usda.gov/ipnf.

6 BEAVER CREEK

Scenic rating: 9

on Priest Lake in Idaho Panhandle National Forest

BEST (

Located at 2,500 feet the farthest north of the drive-to campgrounds on the west side of Priest Lake, Beaver Creek is a good location for enjoy watersports—swimming, fishing, boating, and paddling. It is in the best vicinity to boat the Thorofare to Upper Priest Lake. The narrow, flatwater river provides wildlife-watching for moose, ospreys, bald eagles, and bears. To avoid running aground, be sure to follow the channel markers when entering and exiting the Thorofare. Powerboats take the Thorofare at no-wake speeds, while kayakers paddle its 2.5 miles. Several hiking trails depart from the campground. Navigation Trail (#291) heads in three miles to Upper Priest Lake and then continues on for another five miles up the lake. Lakeshore Trail (#294) begins near the swimming area and travels south along the shoreline to dispersed campsites.

Tucked under lush cedars and hemlocks, the popular campground has two paved loops with paved parking aprons, some of which are double-wide. Campsites 13, 15, 33, and 34 sit closest to the lake, but views of the water are blocked. While the campsites are large and spaced out, you can still see the neighbors through the trees. From the sandy swimming beach, the views span the Selkirk Mountains, including Lookout Mountain. Find the boat launch on a gravel spur road south of the campground.

Campsites, facilities: The campground has 41 RV or tent campsites and one group site. RVs are limited to 60 feet. Facilities include picnic tables, fire rings with grills, drinking water, vault toilets (wheelchair-accessible), campground hosts, firewood for sale, swimming area, canoe portage, and boat launch. Leashed pets are permitted.

Reservations, fees: Reservations are accepted (877/444-6777, www.recreation.gov). Campsites cost $18. An extra vehicle costs $8. Cash or check. Open late May-September.

Directions: From Priest River, drive 39 miles north on Highway 57 to Nordman and turn right onto Reeder Bay Road (Forest Road 2512) for 12 miles to Beaver Creek Campground.

GPS Coordinates: N 48° 44.153' W 116° 51.695'

Contact: Idaho Panhandle National Forest, Priest Lake Ranger District, 32203 Hwy. 57, Priest River, ID 83856, 208/443-2512, www.fs.usda.gov/ipnf.

full hookups. The outpost has a store that sells fishing licenses and camping supplies, a restaurant, a bar, and a lodge. While no recreation is available at the campground, plenty is in the vicinity. Seven miles south is a golf course, and 2.7 miles west is Reeder Bay on Priest Lake. The lake attracts visitors for fishing, boating, waterskiing, paddling, and swimming; boat launches are north of Reeder Bay. Nearby, the 4.2-mile Kalispell-Reeder Bay multiuse trail (#365) for mountain bikers, hikers, horses, and trail motorcycles runs south to Kalispell Bay. The campground is popular with hunters in fall.

In 2012, the campground tripled in size. The older section lines up 12 sites on a broad grassy swath backed up to forest. The newer section curves 27 back-in campsites around a grassy loop. Half of the sites sit adjacent to forest while the others sit in the middle of the loop or at its end next to a dusty clearing. A community fire pit is available.

Campsites, facilities: The campground has 39 RV campsites. RVs are limited to 50 feet. Hookups include water, sewer, and electricity. Other amenities include flush toilets, showers, and launderette. Leashed pets are permitted.

Reservations, fees: Reservations are accepted. Campsites cost $25. Cash, check, or credit card. Open May-October.

Directions: From Priest River, take Highway 57 north for 39 miles to Nordman and turn left at the Nordman Store.

GPS Coordinates: N 48° 37.849' W 116° 56.793'

Contact: Priest Lake Lodge and Campground, Priest Lake, ID 83856, 208/443-2538.

7 PRIEST LAKE LODGE

Scenic rating: 6

near Priest Lake

Located in Nordman, a tiny remote outpost west of Priest Lake, Priest Lake Lodge and Campground offers a place for RVers to have

8 NORTH SHORE PRIEST LAKE

Scenic rating: 9

on Priest Lake in Idaho Panhandle National Forest

Priest Lake's north half has hike-in or boat-in

campgrounds on its west shore at 2,500 feet in the bottleneck where the lake narrows to one mile across. They are only accessed by boat, kayak, or canoe from the water, or by foot, horse, or mountain bike on the Lakeshore Trail. For water access, launch from the Reeder Bay public boat launch on the west side or Indian Creek Campground on the east side. You can also launch from farther north at Beaver Creek on the west side or Lionhead Campground on the east side. For trail access, the heavily used Lakeshore Trail (#294) runs seven miles along the lakeshore, paralleling Forest Road 2512. Its southern trailhead sits on the Copper Bay Cutoff Road (milepost 4.7), and the north end is at the Beaver Creek Campground (milepost 12). Two other trailheads are spaced out on side roads at mileposts 4.9 and 7.8. Spur paths cut off the Lakeshore Trail to reach the campground beaches. Trail entrances for Bottle Bay and Teacher Bay are signed with small pullouts for parking.

This string of developed lakefront campgrounds runs from Distillery Bay to Tule Bay. Primitive campsites are also sprinkled in between the developed campgrounds. Most campsites overlook the lake, with flat spaces for tents under the partial shade of firs and cedars. Some of the primitive campsites are very private. Those at Teacher and Bottle Bays have less privacy and attract more campers.

Campsites, facilities: Tule Bay has seven tent campsites; Bottle Bay has 10 tent sites. Tripod, Distillery, and Teacher Bay have two or three tent sites each. Facilities at the five developed campgrounds include vault toilets, picnic tables, and fire rings with grills. Primitive campsites have only rock fire rings. None of the campsites have drinking water; treat lake water. Pack out your garbage. Leashed pets are permitted.

Reservations, fees: Reservations are not accepted. Campsites are free. Open May- October.

Directions: From Priest River, drive 37 miles north on Highway 57 to Nordman and turn

right onto Reeder Bay Road (Forest Road 2512). In the next 12 miles heading north toward Beaver Creek Campground, this road accesses boat launches and trailheads for reaching the north shore campgrounds.

GPS Coordinates for Bottle Bay: N 48° 42.154' W 116° 51.934'

Contact: Idaho Panhandle National Forest, Priest Lake Ranger District, 32203 Hwy. 57, Priest River, ID 83856, 208/443-2512, www.fs.usda.gov/ipnf.

9 REEDER BAY

Scenic rating: 9

on Priest Lake in Idaho Panhandle National Forest

Halfway up Priest Lake's west side at 2,500 feet, Reeder Bay Campground offers a place to enjoy boating, fishing, paddling, and swimming. It squeezes in between a few small resorts on Reeder Bay east of Nordman, where you can buy propane and minor camping supplies. The bay sits south of the Priest Lake bottleneck, where the span narrows to one mile across. Beginning on the Reeder Bay side of the mountain, the Lakeview Mountain Trail (#269) is a 5.3-mile trek up and over the mountain to Highway 57 for hikers, mountain bikers, horses, and trail motorcycles. The summit requires a 1,500-foot climb but does not afford views until you drop 0.25 mile down the west side to a marked junction to a rocky viewpoint. The 4.2-mile Kalispell-Reeder Bay Trail (#365) is a multiuse trail for mountain bikers, hikers, horses, and trail motorcycles that runs south to Kalispell Bay.

The campground sits under a heavy canopy of huge cedar trees—indicative of the moisture this area receives. The paved campground road loops beneath the cedars, with large sites spread out for privacy. Reeder also has the most waterfront campsites of any of the west-side campgrounds: Sites 14-24 all have views and lake frontage. You can see Chimney Rock poking up in the Selkirks across the lake. The campground does not have a boat launch, but you can carry kayaks or canoes to the shore. Launch larger boats just north of the campground.

Campsites, facilities: The campground has 24 RV or tent campsites. RVs are limited to 45 feet. Site 16 can fit a 50-foot RV; site 14 can fit a 60-foot RV. Facilities include picnic tables, fire rings with grills, pedestal grills, vault toilets (wheelchair-accessible), drinking water, and campground hosts. Leashed pets are permitted.

Reservations, fees: Reservations are accepted (877/444-6777, www.recreation.gov). The waterfront sites cost $20. Sites 1-13 cost $18. An extra vehicle costs $8. Cash or check. Open mid-May-September.

Directions: From Priest River on Highway 57, go 37 miles north to Nordman. Turn right onto Reeder Road and drive 2.6 miles to the campground entrance on the right.

GPS Coordinates: N 48° 37.850' W 116° 52.979'

Contact: Idaho Panhandle National Forest, Priest Lake Ranger District, 32203 Hwy. 57, Priest River, ID 83856, 208/443-2512, www.fs.usda.gov/ipnf.

10 KALISPELL ISLAND

Scenic rating: 9
on Priest Lake in Idaho Panhandle National Forest

BEST (

Kalispell Island, the largest, most popular of the Priest Lake boat-in islands, is completely public property, best accessed from the west side. The island at 2,500 feet also sits opposite the Indian Rock pictographs, which are best seen from the water. A 2.5-mile trail circles the island between all of the campgrounds, with views of the Selkirk Mountains to the east.

The island has two day-use sites and 13 waterfront campgrounds, including one large group site at Three Pines. The smallest campgrounds—Shady and Peninsula—have two campsites each. An island host cabin at West Shores is flagged for visibility from the water. Kalispell boat launch has a free SCAT machine boaters may use to clean and sanitize portable toilets, including five-gallon buckets and ammo boxes. Most of the campsites are tucked into the forest for wind protection, but they overlook the lake.

Campsites, facilities: Kalispell Island campgrounds have 52 tent campsites. Facilities include picnic tables, fire rings with grills, and vault toilets at Schneider, North Cove, Silver Cove, Silver, Three Pines, and Rocky Point. Portable toilets, including self-contained boat toilets, are required for camping at West Shores, Selkirk, Shady, Peninsula, and Cottonwood, which have privacy screens for setting up privies. Island rangers will check for these. No drinking water is available: bring your own, or treat lake water. Pack out your garbage to the Kalispell boat launch dumpster. Leashed pets are permitted.

Reservations, fees: Reservations are accepted only for the group campsites (877/444-6777, www.recreation.gov). Campsites cost $10 per night. Pay for campground fees at the boat launch or in the fee collection tubes located on the island at the Kalispell host site, Schneider, Silver Cove, Three Pines, Rocky Point, and North Cove. Parking for island campers at Kalispell boat launch is free for one car and one launch. Additional vehicles cost $5 for the first day and $3 per day thereafter. Cash or check. Open May-October.

Directions: From Priest River, drive 31 miles north on Highway 57 to Kalispell Bay Road. Turn right and drive 1.7 miles to the Kalispell boat launch on the right.

GPS Coordinates: N 48° 34.191' W 116° 54.445'

Contact: Idaho Panhandle National Forest, Priest Lake Ranger District, 32203 Hwy. 57, Priest River, ID 83856, 208/443-2512, www.fs.usda.gov/ipnf.

11 BARTOO ISLAND

Scenic rating: 9

on Priest Lake in Idaho Panhandle National Forest

At 2,500 feet, Bartoo Island is a boat-in oblong island southeast of Kalispell Island on Priest Lake's west side. Those paddling or boating to the island will cross an expanse of open water between Kalispell and Bartoo, broken only by the miniature Papoose Island. Respect the strip of private property on the north side.

The island has two day-use sites, six waterfront campgrounds, and the Sunrise group site. For ultra privacy, head to Solo Two, Bartoo Solo, or Cedars—all with single campsites. When launching from the Kalispell boat launch, you can check which sites are available. An island host cabin near Cedars is flagged for visibility from the water. The Kalispell boat launch has a free SCAT machine boaters may use to clean and sanitize portable toilets, including five-gallon buckets and ammo boxes.

Campsites, facilities: Bartoo campgrounds have 22 tent campsites plus one group campsite at Sunrise. Facilities include picnic tables and fire rings with grills (except for the solo sites). Sunshine campground has the only vault toilet. Those staying at other sites (North Bartoo, Solo Two, South Bartoo, Bartoo Solo, Sunrise group site, and Cedars) are required to have self-contained toilets in boats or portable toilets—labeled with the owner's name, address, phone number, and driver's license number. Privacy screens for setting up privies are available at the campsites. Drinking water is not available: bring your own, or treat lake water. Pack out your garbage. Leashed pets are permitted.

Reservations, fees: Reservations are accepted only for the group campsite (877/444-6777, www.recreation.gov). Campsites cost $10. Pay for your campsite at the boat launch or in the fee tubes at North Bartoo, South Bartoo, and

Sunshine. Parking for island campers at Kalispell boat launch is free for one car and one launch. Additional vehicles cost $5 for the first day and $3 per day thereafter. Cash or check. Open May-October.

Directions: From Priest River, drive 31 miles north on Highway 57 to Kalispell Bay Road. Turn right and drive 1.7 miles to the Kalispell boat launch on the right.
GPS Coordinates: N 48° 32.652' W 116° 53.050'

Contact: Idaho Panhandle National Forest, Priest Lake Ranger District, 32203 Hwy. 57, Priest River, ID 83856, 208/443-2512, www.fs.usda.gov/ipnf.

12 LUBY BAY

Scenic rating: 9

on Priest Lake in Idaho Panhandle National Forest

On Priest Lake's west side at 2,500 feet, Luby Bay provides a place to enjoy lake activities, fishing, and hiking. It links onto the six-mile Beach Trail (#48) along the shoreline, which is for hikers only. The 5.3-mile Woodrat Trail (#235) for hikers and mountain bikers cruises through the forest, paralleling Forest Road 237. A half-mile south of the campground is the Priest Lake Museum and Visitor Center. While you can launch canoes or kayaks from the campground, a public launch sits 0.8 mile north for larger boats.

Set on both sides of the access road, Luby Bay Campground has two looping sections with a paved road. Because of the hillside on lower Luby, some of the campsites cram together and have less privacy than those at upper Luby. Sites 1-11 sit near the waterfront, with sites 7, 9, 10, and 11 boasting high-demand lake frontage. Upper Luby tucks lusher campsites into the hemlock-cedar forest and has more level, spacious sites. Sites 27-40 are large with room for tents. Sites 47-54 can

© BECKY LOMAX

Moose inhabit Priest Lake and its surrounding mountains.

accommodate bigger rigs. Trails, including one paved, lead to the long sandy beach.

Campsites, facilities: Luby Bay has 52 RV or tent sites. RVs are limited to 65 feet. Facilities include picnic tables, fire rings with grills, pedestal grills, flush and vault toilets, some double-wide parking pads, garbage service, drinking water, amphitheater for interpretive programs, campground hosts, and disposal station. Leashed pets are permitted. Wheelchair-accessible facilities include toilets and more than 15 campsites.

Reservations, fees: Reservations are accepted (877/444-6777, www.recreation.gov). Waterfront sites cost $20; other sites cost $18. An extra vehicle costs $8. The disposal station costs $7 (but you can drive about 10 minutes south to the Priest River Information Center to use free disposal stations). Cash or check. Open mid-May-early October.

Directions: From Priest River, drive 28.6 miles north on Highway 57 to Luby Bay Road (Forest Road 1337). Turn right and drive 1.3 miles to West Lakeshore Road (Forest Road 237). Turn left and drive 0.6 mile to the campground. Lower Luby Bay campground is to the right, and Upper Luby Bay campground is to the left.

GPS Coordinates: N 48° 32.925' W 116° 55.532'

Contact: Idaho Panhandle National Forest, Priest Lake Ranger District, 32203 Hwy. 57, Priest River, ID 83856, 208/443-2512, www. fs.usda.gov/ipnf.

13 OSPREY

Scenic rating: 9

on Priest Lake in Idaho Panhandle National Forest

On the southwest side of Priest Lake at 2,500 feet, Osprey Campground is a quick access, popular campground to enjoy watersports, swimming, fishing, and boating. It sits right on the hiker-only six-mile Beach Trail (#48) that runs from Outlet Campground to Luby Bay. Mountain bikers can tour forest roads.

You can launch hand-carried watercraft from the campground, but the nearest boat launch is about five miles north. Within a 10-minute drive, you'll find the Priest Lake Golf Course, Priest Lake Museum and Visitor Center, and Priest Lake Marina. RVers looking for a disposal station can find a free one at the Priest Lake Information Center five miles south.

The campground road is paved, with gravel parking aprons. Compared to Outlet and Lower Luby campgrounds, Osprey has very spacious sites with lots of privacy because of their distance from each other. The campground's one loop sits under a mixed canopy with a heavy dose of cedars. Sites 8-15 claim premium waterfront views, although sites 14 and 15 across the road have peek-a-boo views through the trees rather than beach frontage. Trails from the campground access the shoreline.

Campsites, facilities: Osprey has 16 RV or tent campsites. RVs are limited to 20 feet. Facilities include picnic tables, raised tripod fire pans on cement pads, flush toilets (wheelchair-accessible), drinking water, garbage collection, and campground hosts. Leashed pets are permitted.

Reservations, fees: Reservations are accepted (877/444-6777, www.recreation.gov). Waterfront sites cost $18. Other sites cost $16. Extra vehicles cost $8. Cash or check. Open June-early September.

Directions: From Priest River, go 26 miles north on Highway 57. At milepost 26, turn right onto Outlet Bay Road. Drive 0.5 mile and turn left at the sign onto the dirt West Lakeshore Drive (Forest Road 237). Drive one mile and turn right into the campground. GPS Coordinates: N 48° 30.455' W 116° 53.340'

Contact: Idaho Panhandle National Forest, Priest Lake Ranger District, 32203 Hwy. 57, Priest River, ID 83856, 208/443-2512, www.fs.usda.gov/ipnf.

14 OUTLET BAY

Scenic rating: 9

on Priest Lake in Idaho Panhandle National Forest

As you drive north on the west side of Priest Lake, Outlet Bay at 2,500 feet is the first campground on the lake with views of the Selkirk Mountains. The location is convenient for those who want to explore both sides of the lake; the road to the east side sits less than four miles south on Highway 57. The Beach Trail (a hiker-only trail) runs six miles from the campground to Luby Bay along the shoreline. The popular 5.3-mile Woodrat Trail (#235), for mountain bikers and hikers, also departs across the road from the campground entrance. Paddlers in rafts or kayaks aiming for the Class II-III white water of Priest River can start paddling from Outlet Campground. One mile of flat water leads to a dam requiring a portage before hitting the Binarch Rapids section. Larger boats for sightseeing, waterskiing, or fishing must launch from the public launch five miles north.

Tucked under tall cedars, the shady campground reconstructed in 2011 has large sites but only small paved parking pads. The narrow, curvy campground road loops through tight trees. Prime waterfront campsites (3-5, 24-27) have peek-a-boo views of the lake. A few sites, which are best for tents, are paired to work for two parties camping together in two sites.

Campsites, facilities: Outlet Bay has 27 RV or tent campsites. RVs are limited to 35 feet, but most sites can only fit RVs 25 feet or less. Facilities include picnic tables, fire rings with grills, flush toilets (wheelchair-accessible), drinking water, campground hosts, and garbage service. Leashed pets are permitted.

Reservations, fees: No reservations are accepted. Waterfront campsites cost $18. Other campsites cost $16. Extra vehicles cost $8. Cash or check. Open late May-early September.

Directions: From Priest River, go 26 miles north on Highway 57. At milepost 26, turn right onto Outlet Bay Road. Drive 0.5 mile and turn left onto the dirt West Lakeshore Drive—also known as the Forest Road 237—at the sign. Drive 0.5 mile and turn right into the campground.

GPS Coordinates: N 48° 29.958' W 116° 53.616'

Contact: Idaho Panhandle National Forest, Priest Lake Ranger District, 32203 Hwy. 57, Priest River, ID 83856, 208/443-2512, www.fs.usda.gov/ipnf.

15 LIONHEAD

Scenic rating: 8
in Priest Lake State Park on Priest Lake

Located on Squaw Bay at 2,500 feet on Priest Lake's east side, Lionhead Campground is named for large, rocky Lions Head Peak in the Selkirk Mountains to the east. The campground is the one farthest north on the state park side of the lake, but the location is convenient for paddling up the Thorofare or hiking and mountain biking to Upper Priest Lake. The campground has an intricate web of trails, and the three-hour hike up to Lookout Lake and Mountain yields views of the Selkirk Mountains. A dock and ramp serves for launching boats for sightseeing, boating, waterskiing, and fishing. The south-facing swimming beach is a favorite because of its 0.25-mile-long sandy shore with oodles of room for sunbathing. The sheltered bay gets less wind than the central lake corridor.

The East Lakeshore access road turns to gravel several miles before Lionhead, and the parking aprons for the campsites are gravel. Eleven campsites sit in the trees in a prime waterfront location overlooking the beach.

Most campsites have ample room for tents. The thick forest canopy shades most campsites, but depending on understory, some have privacy or can see neighbors.

Campsites, facilities: The campground has 47 RV or tent campsites. RVs are limited to 25 feet. Facilities include picnic tables, fire rings with grills, drinking water, vault toilets (wheelchair-accessible), boat launch with dock, swimming beach, campground rangers, firewood for sale, and amphitheater for naturalist presentations. The Lionhead Group Campsite has a cabin with a kitchen and nine RV hookup sites with electricity. Leashed pets are permitted.

Reservations, fees: Reservations are accepted (888/922-6743 or online). Campsites cost $12-18. Park entrance costs $5 per vehicle. Add on a 6 percent Idaho tax. Idaho residents can buy the $10 State Parks Passport for unlimited entry and camping discounts. Cash, check, or credit card. Open early May-late October.

Directions: From Priest River, drive 22 miles north on Highway 57. Turn right at Dickensheet Road, staying on that to Coolin, and turning right onto East Lakeshore Road. The drive from Highway 57 to Lionhead entrance is 26 miles.

GPS Coordinates: N 48° 43.918' W 116° 49.371'

Contact: Priest Lake State Park, 314 Indian Creek Park Rd., Coolin, ID 83821, 208/443-2200, http://parksandrecreation.idaho.gov.

16 INDIAN CREEK

Scenic rating: 8
on Priest Lake's east shore in Priest Lake State Park

BEST (

On the east side of Priest Lake at 2,500 feet about halfway up, the popular Indian Creek Campground sits on the protected south bay of Cape Horn at the base of the Selkirk

© BECKY LOMAX

Sundance Lookout towers above Priest Lake.

Mountains. Both beaches on either side of the park are lined with summer homes. The campground offers forest hiking to places like the Old Flume, a three-mile-long path for loggers in the 1940s and 1950s to shoot logs down to the bay. The campground is also the closest for hiking to Hunt Lakes, Mount Roothaan, and the dramatic Chimney Rock. Some trails are open to mountain biking. In winter, the park becomes a base for snowmobilers. The campground's attraction is its huge, long sandy beach with a buoyed-off area for swimming. The boat launch area has a dock, cement ramp, and large paved parking lot for trailers. Anglers go after trophy-sized lake trout.

The campsites tuck into a loose mixed cedar forest with the burbling Indian Creek running by some. A paved road loops through the campground: One loop curves near the beach while the White Pine campsites snuggle on two loops back in the woods.

Campsites, facilities: The campground has 73 RV campsites and 20 tent campsites.

RVs are limited to 40 feet. Hookups include water, sewer, and electricity up to 50 amps. Facilities include picnic tables, fire rings with grills, drinking water, flush toilets, showers, disposal station, amphitheater for interpretive programs, horseshoes, basketball, camp store, swimming beach, and boat launch. Pack out your trash. Leashed pets are permitted. Wheelchair-accessible facilities include toilets and two campsites.

Reservations, fees: Reservations are highly recommended (888/922-6743 or online). Hookup sites cost $24-26. Other sites cost $12-18. Park entrance costs $5 per vehicle. Add on 6 percent Idaho tax. Idaho residents can buy the $10 State Parks Passport for entrance and camping discounts. Cash, check, or credit card. Open all year.

Directions: From Priest River, drive 22 miles north on Highway 57 and turn right at the Dickensheet Road. Stay on that to Coolin and turn right onto East Lakeshore Road. From Highway 57 to Indian Creek entrance is 17 miles.

GPS Coordinates: N 48° 36.686' W 116° 49.816'

Contact: Priest Lake State Park, 314 Indian Creek Park Rd., Coolin, ID 83821, 208/443-2200, http://parksandrecreation.idaho.gov.

17 HUNT CREEK PRIMITIVE

Scenic rating: 6

in Priest Lake State Forest in the Selkirk Mountains

On the east side of Priest Lake at 2,650 feet, Hunt Creek primitive campground sits on a large, previously logged plateau in the Selkirk Mountains. The dirt access road continues farther to the trailhead to Hunt Lakes, requiring a one-hour drive and a 90-minute hike. The route passes through a boulder field where you must follow orange dots on the rocks. The campground is also adjacent to Hunt Creek

Hunt Creek Falls roars on the east side of Priest Lake.

Falls, in a gorgeous mossy gorge. In spring the falls roar with water roiling through the multiple cascades. Rough log benches allow you to sit and listen.

A rough, rocky dirt road loops around the plateau holding the campsites. Most of the large campsites sit on sunny, grassy areas surrounded by brush and shaded by only a few pines. The first campsite, however, is easier to access and set under the trees with more shade and a forest duff floor.

Campsites, facilities: The campground has four primitive RV or tent campsites that can fit small RVs. Facilities include rock fire rings. Use Leave No Trace practices here for human waste, and pack out your trash. Bring your own water. The gorge is slippery at the falls; do not attempt to get water here. Pets are permitted.

Reservations, fees: Reservations are not accepted. Camping is free. Open April-November.

Directions: From Priest River, drive 22 miles to the Dickensheet Road, turning right and heading toward Coolin. At Coolin, turn right

to follow the East Lakeshore Road four miles to the dirt Forest Road 23. Turn right, heading up the steep hill. Turn left at the state lands sign. You'll find the first campsite on the right and the others sprawled around the loop.

GPS Coordinates: N 48° 33.799' W 116° 49.481'

Contact: Priest Lake State Park, 314 Indian Creek Park Rd., Coolin, ID 83821, 208/443-2200, http://parksandrecreation.idaho.gov.

18 DICKENSHEET

Scenic rating: 7

on Priest River in Priest Lake State Park

Located on Priest River between Binarch and Chipmunk Rapids, Dickensheet is the southernmost campground in the Priest Lake Area. The river, which you can float or fish, starts at the lake and ends at the town of Priest River at the Mudhole Campground and the confluence with the Pend Oreille River.

Sections of Class II and III rapids litter the river; Binarch and Eight Mile Rapids are the most hazardous in high water. The river has seven accesses: Outlet Campground, the put-in below the dam, Dickensheet, Saddlers Creek, and the take-out at Mudhole are just off Highway 57; White Tail Butte Landing and Big Creek are reached via the East Side and West Side Roads. At the south end of the campground, a small parking area accommodates boat trailers. A connector trail departs from camp, crossing the river on the old bridge, to link up with the West Priest Lake Trails. You can scout the rapids just below the camp via mountain bike or by hiking on the Chipmunk Rapids National Recreation Trail at the Priest Lake Information Center, a five-minute drive away.

Tucked under cedar trees right next to the road and river, Dickensheet is a cramped, small campground, but perfect for those who float the river as you can launch right from the campground. The sites have little privacy. Three sites enjoy riverfront.

Campsites, facilities: Dickensheet has 11 RV or tent campsites. RVs are limited to 28 feet. Facilities include picnic tables, fire pits with grills, and vault toilet (wheelchair-accessible), but no drinking water. Treat river water. Pack out your trash. Leashed pets are permitted.

Reservations, fees: Reservations are accepted (888/922-6743, http://parksandrecreation. idaho.gov). Campsites cost $12-18. Park entrance costs $5 per vehicle. Add on a 6 percent Idaho tax. Idaho residents can buy the $10 State Parks Passport for unlimited entry and camping discounts. Open May-September.

Directions: From Priest River, drive 22 miles north on Highway 57. Turn right onto Dickensheet Road and drive one mile, crossing Priest River. The campground sits immediately on the right.

GPS Coordinates: N 48° 27.115' W 116° 53.989'

Contact: Priest Lake State Park, 314 Indian Creek Park Rd., Coolin, ID 83821, 208/443-2200, http://parksandrecreation.idaho.gov.

19 ROBINSON LAKE

Scenic rating: 7

on Robinson Lake in Idaho Panhandle National Forest

Near the Canadian border at 2,600 feet, tiny Robinson Lake provides a quiet place to swim or paddle on summer days. The 60-acre lake is best for nonmotorized boats, and a small boat ramp on the north shore helps with launching (although the campground sits on the southwest shore). Anglers can fish the lake or nearby streams. A two-mile interpretive trail loops around the lake through different wildlife habitats. Wildlife sightings can include moose, elk, and eagles.

The campsites sit around one loop and one spur on a forested hillside above Robinson Lake. The mixed forest offers shade, but with little undergrowth, you'll see neighbors between the trees. You can hear songbirds, the squawk of waterfowl, and the tapping of woodpeckers.

Campsites, facilities: The campground has 10 RV or tent campsites. RVs are limited to 27 feet. Facilities include picnic tables, fire rings with grills, vault toilets, drinking water, tent pads, and campground hosts. Pack out your trash. Leashed pets are permitted. Wheelchair-accessible facilities include toilets and three campsites.

Reservations, fees: No reservations are accepted. Campsites cost $8. Cash or check. Open May-October.

Directions: From Bonners Ferry, drive north on Highway 95 to Mount Hall Junction. Veer right on Highway 95 and drive east for 8.7 miles. Turn north onto Forest Road 448 for 0.3 miles to the campground.

GPS Coordinates: N 48° 58.135' W 116° 12.982'

Contact: Idaho Panhandle National Forest, Bonners Ferry Ranger District, 6286 Main St., Bonners Ferry, ID 83805, 208/267-5561, www.fs.usda.gov/ipnf.

20 COPPER CREEK

Scenic rating: 7

on Moyie River in Idaho Panhandle National
Forest

Sitting at 2,600 feet in the Purcell Mountains
on the east bank of the Moyie River, Cooper
Creek is a favorite for anglers, river rafters, and
kayakers. The river harbors rainbow, brook,
and westslope cutthroat trout. You can float
three miles from the Canadian border to Copper Creek, or put-in at Copper Creek to float
18 miles to the take-out upstream of the Moyie
Falls Dam. From Copper Creek to Meadow
Creek, the Class II rapids work for canoes,
with shallow, rocky riffles. Below Meadow
Creek, the river enters a canyon containing two
Class III rapids requiring technical skills at old
Eileen Dam and Hole-in-the-Wall. About two
miles from the campground, a 1.5-mile trail
leads to Copper Falls, where a ribbon of water
plunges 225 feet in two pitches over a rocky
lip. In winter, the waterfall freezes to become
a lure for ice climbers.

The campsites sit around one loop on a
forested hillside above the Moyie River, but
none with river frontage. The mixed forest
offers partial shade and some privacy between
sites. The sound of passing trains filters into
the camp from across the river.

Campsites, facilities: The campground has
16 RV or tent campsites. RVs are limited to 35
feet. Facilities include picnic tables, fire rings
with grills, vault toilets, and drinking water.
Pack out your trash. Leashed pets are permitted. Wheelchair-accessible facilities include
toilets and three campsites.

Reservations, fees: No reservations are accepted. Campsites cost $6. Cash or check.
Open mid-May-September.

Directions: From the Canadian border at
Eastport, drive 0.8 mile south on Highway
95 to the campground sign and turn east onto
Copper Creek Road (Forest Road 2517). From
Bonners Ferry, drive Highway 95 north for
29.8 miles and turn east onto Forest Road
2517. Drive the dirt, single-lane road for 0.6
mile to the signed campground entrance on
the right. The road has pullouts in case you
meet an oncoming vehicle.

GPS Coordinates: N 48° 59.123' W 116°
10.074'

Contact: Idaho Panhandle National Forest,
Bonners Ferry Ranger District, 6286 Main
St., Bonners Ferry, ID 83805, 208/267-5561,
www.fs.usda.gov/ipnf.

21 MEADOW CREEK

Scenic rating: 8

on Moyie River in Idaho Panhandle National
Forest

Sitting at 2,300 feet in the Purcell Mountains
on the west side of the Moyie River where it
oxbows around the campground, Meadow
Creek is favored by river rafters and kayakers
in May and June. From the put-in at Copper
Creek to the take-out upstream of the Moyie
Falls Dam is 18 miles. The section from Copper Creek Campground to Meadow Creek is
filled with Class II rapids, but skilled canoeists
can navigate its smaller, rocky rapids. Below
Meadow Creek, the river dives into a canyon
with two technical Class III rapids—old Eileen Dam and Hole-in-the-Wall—best left to
skilled white-water river rafters and kayakers.
For anglers, the river also harbors rainbow,
brook, and westslope cutthroat trout, along
with mountain whitefish. Four miles south
of the campground, the 1.3-mile Queen Lake
Trail (#152) leads to huckleberry-picking
opportunities.

The quiet campground with gravel parking
aprons sits in a thick pine and birch forest in
two loops surrounded by the river. Some of
the campsites right on the river are walk-in
sites best for tents. As water levels drop during
the summer, sandbars open up the shoreline.

Campsites, facilities: The campground has

22 RV or tent campsites. RVs are limited to 35 feet. Facilities include picnic tables, fire rings with grills, vault toilets, and drinking water. Pack out your trash. Leashed pets are permitted.

Reservations, fees: No reservations are accepted. Campsites cost $6. Cash or check. Open mid-May-September.

Directions: From Bonners Ferry, drive north three miles on Highway 95 to the junction with Highway 2. Turn right and drive 2.5 miles to Meadow Creek Road. Turn north and drive 10 miles to the signed campground entrance on the right.

GPS Coordinates: N 48° 49.193' W 116° 8.889'

Contact: Idaho Panhandle National Forest, Bonners Ferry Ranger District, 6286 Main St., Bonners Ferry, ID 83805, 208/267-5561, www.fs.usda.gov/ipnf.

22 SMITH LAKE

Scenic rating: 7

on Smith Lake in Idaho Panhandle National Forest

Sitting at 3,000 feet in a mixed forest, the tiny Smith Lake is small enough to swim across and only a half-mile long. It has a dock for swimming, and a separate dock for the boat ramp. The small size of the lake makes it best for nonmotorized boats, canoes, and kayaks. Fishing is available in the lake, and a trail loops around the lake for hiking. Watch for moose. Plenty of forest roads in the vicinity work for mountain biking.

The older campground in a mature forest puts its campsites in tight proximity to each other, but a bit of undergrowth adds a semblance of privacy. Some of the facilities show wear, and the campsites are large enough to accommodate tents. You'll wake to the call of loons in the morning.

Campsites, facilities: The campground has seven RV or tent campsites. RVs are limited to small sizes. Facilities include picnic tables, fire rings with grills, vault toilets, and drinking water. Pack out your trash. Leashed pets are permitted.

Reservations, fees: No reservations are accepted. Camping is free. Open mid-May-September.

Directions: From Bonners Ferry, drive north three miles on Highway 95 to the junction with Highway 2. Stay on Highway 95 for 2.2 miles further and turn right onto Smith Lake Road for 2.3 miles to the campground. (On Smith Lake Road, turn left and then veer right to stay on the main road.)

GPS Coordinates: N 48° 46.732' W 116° 15.852'

Contact: Idaho Panhandle National Forest, Bonners Ferry Ranger District, 6286 Main St., Bonners Ferry, ID 83805, 208/267-5561, www.fs.usda.gov/ipnf.

23 TWIN RIVERS CANYON RESORT

Scenic rating: 8

on the Kootenai River near Bonners Ferry

At the confluence of the Kootenai and Moyie Rivers in the Purcell Mountains, Twin Rivers Canyon Resort has the advantages of two rivers on its borders. The Moyie River Overlook and bridge—one of the highest in the state—sits a half-mile to the west. This bridge offers terrific views of the river and dam. River rafters and kayakers tackle the Moyie's rapids, and those looking to float the bigger, slower waters of the Kootenai can rent a raft for the day for self-guided floating. A shuttle service transfer rafters to an upriver launching area to float back down to the park. Anglers go after 20-pound trout in the Kootenai, and you can fish along the banks of the Moyie. A dock is available for swimmers and anglers. Adjacent to the campground is the new Twin Rivers Fish Hatchery and visitors center, operated by the Kootenai Tribe to get sturgeon and burbot back in the river.

Campground recreation includes mini-golf, picnicking, playground for small children, basketball/pickleball court, softball diamond, volleyball court, and horseshoe. Lightly shaded campsites are available in pull-through and back-in sites, and the tenting campsites line up nearest the Moyie River.

Campsites, facilities: The campground has 50 RV campsites and 16 tent campsites. Large rigs are okay. Hookups include 30-amp electricity, water, and sewer. Facilities include picnic tables, fire rings, flush toilets, showers, convenience store, launderette, firewood for sale, wireless Internet, covered pavilion with gas barbecues, and boat ramp. Leashed pets are permitted.

Reservations, fees: Reservations are accepted. Hookups cost $30-32. Tent campsites cost $20. Cash or credit card. Open April-October.

Directions: From Moyie Springs, drive one mile east on Highway 2 and turn right onto Twin Rivers Road, or from the border with Montana, drive nine miles west on Highway 2 and turn left. Follow the road as it switchbacks down to the river.

GPS Coordinates: N 48° 43.147' W 116° 11.022'

Contact: Twin Rivers Canyon Resort, 1823 Twin Rivers Rd., Moyie Springs, ID 83845, 208/267-5932 or 888/258-5952, www.twin-riversresort.com.

24 BLUE LAKE RV RESORT

🏊 🛶 🛥 🎣 🐕 ♿ 🚐 ⛺

Scenic rating: 6

near Bonners Ferry

Located in the Purcell Trench—the lowlands between the Purcell and Selkirk Mountains—Blue Lake is a tiny, spring-fed lake in a private resort. The 20-acre Blue Lake RV Resort has a lakeside deck, tiered amphitheater, and wood-fired sauna. The small lake has a dock for swimming and fishing for rainbow trout, catfish, and brown bluegill, and the resort permits nonmotorized boats, canoes, and kayaks on the lake. Kayaks and paddleboats are available for rent. A golf course is in Bonners Ferry.

A gravel road loops through the grassy, treed campground; parking pads are gravel and close together. Some sites garner partial shade from tall conifers; others sit in full sun. Many of the big-rig sites have views of the lake. Tent campsites tuck into the trees right on the lake.

Campsites, facilities: The campground has 36 RV campsites and six tent campsites. RVs are limited to 70 feet. Hookups are available for water, sewer, and electricity up to 50 amps. Facilities include picnic table, fire rings, flush toilets (wheelchair-accessible), showers, wireless Internet, launderette, propane and firewood for sale, off-leash pet run, clubhouse with wine bar, and disposal station. The resort also rents boutique pole tents. Two leashed pets are permitted; inquire about breeds not allowed.

Reservations, fees: Reservations are accepted. Hookups cost $30-47. Tent campsites cost $10 plus $5 for each person. Rates are for two adults and two children. For extra people, add $3-5. Extra vehicles and boats cost $5. Open April-October.

Directions: From Sandpoint, drive north on Highway 95 for 22 miles to milepost 498. Turn left onto Blue Lake Road across the railroad. Or from Bonners Ferry, drive 5.5 south on Highway 95 to reach Blue Lake Road. Drive 0.25 mile to the south end of the lake.

GPS Coordinates: N 48° 34.877' W 116° 23.290'

Contact: Blue Lake Resort RV Park, 242 Blue Lake Rd., Naples, ID 83847, 208/946-3361, www.bluelakervresort.com.

25 ALBENI COVE RECREATION AREA

Scenic rating: 7

on the Pend Oreille River

BEST (

At the Idaho-Washington border, the Pend Oreille River backs up into a slow-moving lake by Albeni Falls Dam, elevation 2,000 feet. Upstream from the dam, Albeni Cove Recreation Area sits on the south shore where high water can close the boat ramp and swim beach during May and June. After high water abates, the facilities attract boaters, water-skiers, anglers, paddlers, and swimmers. The sandy cove is home to bald eagles, ospreys, bears, deer, skunks, and porcupines while the water holds bass, Kokanee salmon, and trout. On Highway 2 on the north side of the river, the Albeni Falls Dam Visitor Center has exhibits on history and natural history, plus offers tours of the dam daily Memorial Day to Labor Day.

Albeni Cove is the smallest of the Pend Oreille River campgrounds. It tucks its small campsites on a shady, east-facing hillside with built-up platforms among firs, cedars, and pines overlooking the cove. Two large sandy spits create the cove and are great places to explore.

Campsites, facilities: Albeni Cove has 10 RV or tent campsites and four tent-only sites. RVs are limited to 40 feet. Facilities include picnic tables, fire rings with grills, drinking water, flush toilets (wheelchair-accessible), showers, boat ramp, swimming beach, and interpretive programs. Leashed pets are permitted.

Reservations, fees: Reservations are accepted (877/444-6777, www.recreation.gov). Campsites cost $18 per night. An extra vehicle costs $10. Open mid-May-early September.

Directions: From Priest River, drive six miles west, crossing into Washington and continuing two miles across the Pend Oreille River to Newport, Washington. Turn south onto State Avenue, crossing on an overpass over the railroad tracks, and then left onto 4th Street, which will turn into Albeni Cove Road. The pavement becomes a rough dirt road as it crosses back into Idaho. Stay on it, veering left at the fork in the road. At the power lines the road turns back to pavement into the campground.

GPS Coordinates: N 48° 10.594' W 116° 59.984'

Contact: Army Corps of Engineers, 2376 E. Hwy. 2, Oldtown, ID 83882, 208/437-3133.

26 PRIEST RIVER RECREATION AREA (MUDHOLE)

Scenic rating: 6

on the Pend Oreille River

BEST (

Located at 2,000 feet on the east edge of the town of Priest River, the Priest River Recreation Area earned a nickname—the Mudhole—for its large beach in a protected bay where Priest River meets the Pend Oreille River. However, the water isn't muddy. The water runs clear most of the year, and the fine sand beach enlarges as water levels drop in August. Hot summer days see scads of day-use visitors for swimming, boating, paddling, and fishing. The adjacent Priest River Wildlife Area adds bird-watching—especially for ospreys, songbirds, and waterfowl. The nine-hole Ranch Club Golf Course sits two miles west, as do grocery stores and gas. Anglers and boaters head out on both rivers; kayakers and canoeists enjoy the slough along the Pend Oreille River southeast of the campground. It is also the last take-out for those rafting or kayaking the white water on Priest River. The campground has a large, grassy baseball and soccer field.

Tucked under shady pines and hemlocks, the campground squeezes in between the highway and the railroad, so be ready for some noise rather than hoping for the quiet of wilderness. Sites 10-13 sit closest to the river. Campsites 12 and 13 also sit on a side spur from the one main campground loop. The entrance gate is locked 10pm-7am on weekends and holidays, so make reservations for this popular campground.

Campsites, facilities: The campground has 20 RV or tent campsites. RVs are limited to 60 feet. Facilities include picnic tables, fire rings with grills, flush toilets (wheelchair-accessible), showers, drinking water, garbage service, disposal station, campground hosts, boat ramp, playground, and swimming beach. Leashed pets are permitted.

Reservations, fees: Reservations are accepted (877/444-6777, www.recreation.gov). Campsites cost $18. An extra vehicle costs $10. Open mid-May-late September.

Directions: From the town of Priest River, drive one mile east on Highway 2, crossing Priest River. The campground is on the right. From Sandpoint, you'll reach the campground entrance in 21 miles on Highway 2.

GPS Coordinates: N 48° 10.720' W 116° 53.398'

Contact: Army Corps of Engineers, 2376 E. Hwy. 2, Oldtown, ID 83822, 208/437-3133.

27 RILEY CREEK RECREATION AREA

🚶 🚴 🏊 🛶 🎣 🛥 🐕 ♿ 🚐 ⛺

Scenic rating: 7

on the Pend Oreille River

Of the campgrounds located on the Pend Oreille River, Riley Creek is the largest, tucked at 2,000 feet the base of the Selkirk Mountain foothills along Highway 2. With water on three sides, Riley Creek sits at the end of a peninsula in the Pend Oreille River, facing west, making it a prime location for boating, Jet Skiing, fishing, paddling, hiking, bicycling, and swimming. However, it is also adjacent to waterfront homes rather than wilderness. A multilane cement boat ramp, dock, boat basin for mooring, fishing pier, and parking for boat trailers aid those heading out on the water. A bicycling and hiking trail also

loops through the recreation area, and a large grassy field is available for Frisbee, football, and soccer games, plus horseshoes, volleyball, and basketball.

Campsites cluster around two loops under a thick evergreen canopy for shade. They are close enough together that you can see neighboring campers, but tree trunks help to act as privacy shields. The campground locks the park gates 10pm-7am for security. Railroad and highway noise creeps into the campground after it quiets at night. Riley Creek is popular, requiring a noon arrival on weekends and holidays.

Campsites, facilities: The campground has 67 RV or tent campsites. RVs are limited to 35 feet. Hookups include water and electricity up to 50 amps. Facilities include picnic tables, fire rings with grills, flush toilets (wheelchair-accessible), showers, disposal station, boat launch, garbage service, horseshoe pits, firewood for sale, amphitheater programs, campground hosts, and swimming beach. Leashed pets are permitted.

© BECKY LOMAX

Osprey are common around the Pend Oreille River and Lake Pend Oreille.

Reservations, fees: Reservations are accepted (877/444-6777, www.recreation.gov). Campsites cost $18 per night. An extra vehicle costs $10. Cash or check. Open mid-May-early September.

Directions: From Priest River, go eight miles east on Highway 2. Or from Sandpoint, drive 14 miles west on Highway 2. In Laclede, turn south onto Laclede Ferry Road for 0.4 mile. Then, turn right onto Riley Creek Park Road for 0.9 mile to the entrance.

GPS Coordinates: N 48° 9.594' W 116° 46.249'

Contact: Army Corps of Engineers, 2376 E. Hwy. 2, Oldtown, ID 83822, 208/437-3133.

28 SPRINGY POINT RECREATION AREA

Scenic rating: 6

on Lake Pend Oreille

On Lake Pend Oreille at 2,000 feet, Springy Point is the only public campground on the west arm where the lake flows into the Pend Oreille River. Its north-facing beach and small bay are protected by Springy Point. With its location off the main lake, the bay is more protected than the open, windy expanses. The sandy beach is divided into two sections—the buoyed swimming beach reached by a trail and the boat launch area with a small cement ramp and dock. En route to the campground, the paved access road passes large waterfront homes and summer cabins—indicative of the number of boaters you'll encounter in the area. A 10-minute drive puts you right in downtown Sandpoint for restaurants, gas, groceries, and shopping.

The campground squeezes onto a heavily treed slope. Two paved campground loops curve through narrow openings between the trees. Only smaller RVs and trailers can fit through these. Even though underbrush provides fences between some of the campsites, most are crammed in close together with little privacy. In the Birch loop, campsites 23 and 24 sit right above the boat ramp area, with log rails keeping campers from falling down the steep hill. In Cedar loop, several campsites have snippets of lake views through the trees.

Campsites, facilities: The campground has 37 RV or tent campsites, plus one tent-only site. RVs are limited to 35 feet. Facilities includes picnic tables, fire rings with grills, flush toilets (wheelchair-accessible), showers, drinking water, disposal station, garbage service, campground hosts, boat ramp, boat trailer parking, and swimming beach. Leashed pets are permitted.

Reservations, fees: Reservations are accepted (877/444-6777, www.recreation.gov). A campsite costs $18. An extra vehicle costs $10. Cash or check. Open mid-May-early October.

Directions: From Sandpoint, go 1.5 miles south on Highway 95 and turn right onto Lakeshore Drive for three miles to the entrance on the right.

GPS Coordinates: N 48° 14.164' W 116° 35.207'

Contact: Army Corps of Engineers, 2376 E. Hwy. 2, Oldtown, ID 83882, 208/437-3133.

29 BONNER COUNTY FAIRGROUNDS

Scenic rating: 7

in Sandpoint

Bonner County Fairgrounds, elevation 2,137 feet, upgraded their campground facilities. While the campground is convenient for attending events at the fairgrounds, including equestrian competitions, rodeos, and the county fair in August, you don't have to attend events to stay in the fairground campground. Tucked at the bottom of the Schweitzer Mountain road, the fairground offers the closest place to camp to visit Schweitzer Mountain Resort. Summer recreation at the resort features scenic lift rides, horseback rides, mountain biking, hiking, huckleberry picking, ziplining, and kid fun. The campground is also convenient for visiting Sandpoint for shopping and dining or Lake Pend Oreille for swimming, boating, paddling, and fishing.

One loop of the campground rings a large grassy island with a pavilion and barbecue grills; the other fills inside and outside with campsites. On the north end of the fairgrounds, the campground loops with paved interior roads and offers shady or sunny campsites divided by lawns. While the campground tucks back in trees, some noise seeps in as it is within a few blocks of the highway, railroad tracks, and an airport.

Campsites, facilities: The campground has 33 RV campsites. RVs are limited to 47 feet; one site runs 54 feet. Hookups include sewer, water, and electricity up to 50 amps. Facilities include picnic tables, flush toilets, showers, drinking water, wireless Internet, disposal station, and campground hosts. Leashed pets are permitted.

Reservations, fees: Reservations are accepted. Campsites cost $25. Open year-round.

Directions: From downtown Sandpoint, drive north on Highway 95 for about two miles and turn left onto Schweitzer Cutoff Road. Drive to the T in the road and turn right onto North Boyer Road and left into the fairgrounds and campground.

GPS Coordinates: N 48° 18.721' W 116° 33.550'

Contact: Bonner County Fairgrounds Campground, 4203 N. Boyer Rd., Sandpoint, ID 83864, 208/263-8414, www.co.bonner.id.us/fairgrounds.

30 SAM OWEN RECREATION AREA

Scenic rating: 8

on Lake Pend Oreille in Idaho Panhandle National Forest

BEST (

On the north shore of Lake Pend Oreille

at 2,100 feet, Sam Owen Recreation Area sits on the David Thompson Game Preserve. Drive slowly to avoid deer. From the campground, interpretive trails lead to the day-use area and boat-launch area. The boat ramp allows for launching onto the lake for boating, waterskiing, paddling, and fishing for monster kamloops rainbow trout. Hiking and mountain biking are available on trails outside of Hope; those looking for a big view of the lake should climb the 7,009-foot Scotchman Peak. A three-mile steep ascent leads to its summit—the tallest in the area—where mountain goats live and the site of an old lookout.

Campsites tuck back under a thick canopy of pines, cedars, and firs back from the water. A paved road winds through the campground, but the parking aprons are gravel. Very little underbrush separates the campsites; however, they are set apart from each other, and some of the large old-growth trunks form barriers between the sites. The campsites surround four loops, with Skipping Stone loop (sites 29-43) the closest to the beach. Red Sun loop sits behind the day-use area and boat ramp. Dancing Shadow and Scented Leaf loop are farther back uphill in the woods.

Campsites, facilities: The campground has 79 RV or tent campsites, plus one RV-only site. RVs are limited to 45 feet. Facilities include picnic tables, fire rings with grills, drinking water, flush toilets (wheelchair-accessible), disposal station, campground hosts, firewood for sale, an amphitheater for naturalist programs, swimming beach, and boat launch. Leashed pets are permitted.

Reservations, fees: Reservations are accepted (877/444-6777, www.recreation.gov). Premium sites near the lake cost $20. All others cost $18. An extra vehicle costs $8. Boat launching costs $8. Disposal station costs $7. Cash or check. Open May-September.

Directions: From Hope, drive two miles east on Highway 200 and turn right onto Peninsula Road. Drive 0.8 mile, swinging left at the fork, and turn right onto Sam Owen Road.

GPS Coordinates: N 48° 13.185' W 116° 17.048'

Contact: Idaho Panhandle National Forest, Sandpoint Ranger District, 1500 Hwy. 2, Sandpoint, ID 83864, 208/263-5111, www.fs.usda.gov/ipnf.

31 BEYOND HOPE RESORT

Scenic rating: 8

on Lake Pend Oreille

East of Sandpoint and Hope on a peninsula at 2,100 feet, Beyond Hope Resort enjoys the north shore of Lake Pend Oreille. The campground is also located on the David Thompson Game Preserve: wildlife sightings such as deer and ospreys are common. The resort centers on its marina, which offers protected boat mooring. The lake provides 148 square miles of water for boating, waterskiing, fishing, and paddling, and a sandy swimming beach sits adjacent to the marina. The resort sponsors free music every Sunday during the summer. Local roads on the peninsula are good for bicycle tours.

The campground splits on both sides of the access road, with mostly back-in campsites, dirt and gravel interior roads, and dirt or grass parking pads. A handful of trees provide a little shade at some campsites. Tent sites 5-7 tuck on the edge of trees with more privacy than the tent sites near the road.

Campsites, facilities: The campground has 60 RV campsites and seven tent campsites. RVs are limited to 40 feet. Hookups include water and electricity up to 30 amp. Facilities include picnic tables, portable fire pits for tent sites, drinking water, flush toilets, showers, launderette, playground, wireless Internet, restaurant, marina, and sewage pump out service. Leashed pets are permitted.

Reservations, fees: Reservations are accepted. Hookups cost $45. Tent sites cost $30.

Boat slips cost $35-40. Open late May-early September.

Directions: From Hope, drive two miles east on Highway 200 and turn right onto Peninsula Road. Drive 1.2 miles, swinging left at the fork. Locate the campground just south of Hill Drive.

GPS Coordinates: N 48° 12.879' W 116° 17.054'

Contact: Beyond Hope RV Park, 1267 Peninsula Rd., Hope, ID 83836, 208/264-5251, www.beyondhoperesort.com.

32 ISLAND VIEW RESORT

Scenic rating: 8

on Lake Pend Oreille

East of Sandpoint and Hope at 2,100 feet on the north shore of Lake Pend Oreille, Island View Resort is aptly named, for it looks out on a few of the northern islands, the nearest of which is Memaloose Island. The campground sits on the David Thompson Game Preserve: deer, ospreys, and sometimes bald eagles are common sights. Because of the game preserve, drive or bicycle slowly on the paved access road. The glacially-formed Lake Pend Oreille provides 148 square miles of water for boating, waterskiing, paddling, fishing, and swimming. The resort has a small marina formed by a narrow, rocky, treed reef just offshore. A small, primitive boat launch sits just east of the resort.

The office sits right on the waterfront, with a handful of pull-in campsites for RVs on both sides. These spots have prime lake views; however, they are virtually parking stalls perpendicular to the shore and just inches from each other. All of the other sites are across the street in a grassy setting under firs and pines with more room. The open sites afford little privacy, but have a bucolic setting among the nearby small farms. Instead of individual campsite fire rings, a community fire pit with benches is available in the grass near the beach. Some long-term residents also stay here.

Campsites, facilities: The campground has 61 RV campsites. RVs are limited to 40 feet. Hookups include water, sewer, and electricity. Facilities include picnic tables, flush toilets, showers, community fire pit, launderette, store, cable TV hookups, and propane gas. Leashed pets are permitted.

Reservations, fees: Reservations are accepted. Hookups cost $40. Open year-round.

Directions: From Hope, drive two miles east on Highway 200 and turn right onto Peninsula Road. Drive 1.7 miles, swinging left at the fork. Locate the campground just south of Sunray Drive.

GPS Coordinates: N 48° 12.555' W 116° 17.284'

Contact: Island View Resort, 1767 Peninsula Rd., Hope, ID 83836, 208/264-5509.

33 WHISKEY ROCK

Scenic rating: 7

on Lake Pend Oreille

Remote on Lake Pend Oreille's east shore, Whiskey Rock Campground at 2,000 feet offers a place for swimming, fishing, boating, waterskiing, and paddling. While the legends about Whiskey Rock are many—a transfer point for rum runners, a maroon site for three days for a pair of pioneers with only a jug of whiskey—the bay today holds a few lodges and summer homes. The campground demands a tough drive: The dirt road is littered with potholes, steep drops, curves, and switchbacks, requiring over an hour to drive. Some campers boat across the lake to reach the campground, launching from Garfield Bay on the west side about 13 miles to the north. A dock is available for boat-in campers and a ramp for launch. Because of the area's location on the lake, Whiskey Rock can get hammered by winds; secure all boats overnight. Hiking

and mountain biking are available on Packsaddle Mountain.

Located at the base of Packsaddle, the largest mountain surrounding Lake Pend Oreille, the partially forested campground has three campsites right on the lake. The others sit back in the woods. From the campground, trails lead to the water, the day-use picnic area with a sandy beach for swimming, viewpoints of the lake, and a cove.

Campsites, facilities: The campground has nine RV or tent campsites. RVs are limited to 16 feet. Facilities include picnic tables, fire rings with grills, vault toilets, and drinking water. Pack out your trash. Leashed pets are permitted.

Reservations, fees: No reservations are accepted. Camping is free. Open May-September.

Directions: From Sandpoint, drive 27 miles east on Highway 200 to Clark Fork. Turn right onto Stephen Road and drive across the Clark Fork River. Take the first right at the Sportsman Access sign and follow Forest Road 278 (also called Johnson Creek Road) for 2.5 miles. Turn right onto the dirt road to reach the dock and fishing access. Boaters should head to Garfield Bay. Drive south out of Sandpoint on Highway 95 for 5.3 miles. Turn left at Sagle Road and drive 7.1 miles. At the fork, veer right onto Garfield Bay Road and drive 1.2 miles to the road's end.

GPS Coordinates: N 48° 3.086' W 116° 27.247'

Contact: Idaho Panhandle National Forest, Sandpoint Ranger District, 1500 Hwy. 2, Sandpoint, ID 83864, 208/263-5111, www.fs.usda.gov/ipnf.

34 GREEN BAY

Scenic rating: 7

on Lake Pend Oreille

Green Bay Campground, elevation 2,000 feet on Lake Pend Oreille, offers a small, primitive campground for watersports enjoyment. The lake attracts boaters, water-skiers, paddlers, and anglers. Boaters can launch in Garfield Bay, where ramps, docks, and trailer parking are available (none are at the campground). A two-mile motor or paddle connects with the beach at the campground. Boat-in campers should beach boats securely at night because winds can crop up.

The south facing campground on a forested slope offers a quiet place with a remote feel for enjoying Lake Pend Oreille. Shaded campsites spread out above the swimming beach.

Campsites, facilities: The campground has 11 RV or tent campsites. Sites and the access road can fit only small, compact RVs. Facilities include picnic tables, fire rings, and vault toilets. No drinking water is available; treat lake water. Pack out your trash. Leashed pets are permitted.

Reservations, fees: No reservations are accepted. Camping is free. Open May-September.

Directions: From the boat launch at Garfield Bay on Lake Pend Oreille, take Garfield Bay Road east for 0.25 miles. Veer left onto the Cut Off Road for 0.4 miles. Turn right onto Forest Road 532 for 0.3 mile. Turn left onto Green Bay Road (Forest Road 2672) for 0.9-mile. Veer right for 0.6 mile to the campground. The Forest Service discourages RVs and trailers on the last 1.5 rough miles.

GPS Coordinates: N 48° 10.688' W 116° 24.333'

Contact: Idaho Panhandle National Forest, Sandpoint Ranger District, 1500 Hwy. 2, Sandpoint, ID 83864, 208/263-5111, www.fs.usda.gov/ipnf.

35 ROUND LAKE STATE PARK

Scenic rating: 6

south of Sandpoint

South of Sandpoint at the 142-acre Round Lake State Park, a small 58-acre lake is the remnant of a depression made by Ice Age glaciers chewing on the landscape. Fed by Cocolalla Creek, the lake at 2,100 feet is named appropriately, for it is round. The shallow lake—37 feet at its deepest point—warms up much more than its larger neighbor, Lake Pend Oreille, making it a favorite for swimming. A two-mile nature trail tours the lake. Ringed with grasses and water lilies, the lake chimes with bullfrog choruses in the evening, and it attracts songbirds, herons, deer, raccoons, and porcupines. For anglers, it is also home to brook trout, largemouth bass, pumpkinseed sunfish, yellow perch, and black crappie. Only electric boats and hand-powered watercraft are permitted. In winter, the lake offers ice fishing, ice skating, and cross-country skiing. The ski and snowshoe trail converts to a hiking and mountain-biking trail in summer.

The campground, with its narrow, looping road, sits on the north side of the lake. Campsites cluster under the shade of huge cedars, hemlocks, and Douglas firs. Filtered sunlight reaches the campsite floors, which are covered with forest duff and cones. The dirt back-in campsites are very close together with little underbrush; you can see several other campsites.

Campsites, facilities: The campground has 16 RV campsites with electricity and 35 RV or tent campsites. RVs are limited to 24 feet. Facilities includes picnic tables, fire rings, flush toilets, showers, drinking water, disposal station, boat ramp and dock, canoe rentals, guided walks, educational campfire programs, horseshoes, firewood for sale, and swimming beach. Leashed pets are permitted. Wheelchair-accessible facilities include toilets and two campsites.

Reservations, fees: Reservations are accepted (888/922-6743 or online). Campsites with electricity cost $22; other campsites cost $16. Park entrance costs $5 per vehicle. Add on a 6 percent Idaho tax. Idaho residents can buy the $10 State Parks Passport for unlimited entry and camping discounts. Open year-round, but water turned off in winter.

Directions: From Sandpoint drive 10 miles south on Highway 95, or from Coeur d'Alene go north on Highway 95 approximately 34 miles. Turn west onto Dufort Road, driving two miles to the campground entrance to the south.

GPS Coordinates: N 48° 9.913' W 116° 38.246'

Contact: Round Lake State Park, 1880 W. Dufort Rd., Sagle, ID 83860, 208/263-3489, http://parksandrecreation.idaho.gov.

36 SILVERWOOD THEME PARK

Scenic rating: 5

near Coeur d'Alene

The largest theme park in the Northern Rockies, Silverwood Theme Park and Boulder Beach sits 15 minutes north of Coeur d'Alene. Campers who stay at the RV park can purchase discounted tickets for the theme park and beach. The theme park has 65 rides, including monster roller coasters and white-water river splash rides. Its other attractions include a 1915 steam engine train, a Victorian village of restaurants and souvenir shops, magic and ice shows, and climbing trees. Boulder Beach features water slides, wave pools, springs, creeks, and a cabana island.

With gravel roads looping through the campground and gravel parking pads, campsites sprawl throughout the park-like grassy grounds under a thick, shady canopy of pines and firs. The open area beneath the canopy affords little privacy from neighbors. Loops A, B, C, and D sit farthest away from the highway, while loops E, F, and sites 99-115 on the main loop are adjacent to the highway. The campground connects to the theme park via a pedestrian tunnel and also has an overflow camping area minus hookups. You can hear the highway, railroad, and theme park in the campground.

Campsites, facilities: The campground has 132 RV campsites and 71 tent campsites. Large RVs are okay. Hookups are available for water, sewer, and electricity up to 30 amps. Facilities include picnic tables, flush toilets, showers, drinking water, launderette, propane, volleyball courts, horseshoes, and camp store. Fires are not permitted. RV sites can also fit one or two tents. Leashed pets are permitted in the campground, but not in the theme park.

Reservations, fees: Reservations are accepted. Hookups cost $40; tent campsites cost $31. Add on 6 percent Idaho tax. Cash or credit cards. Open daily June-early September. Open weekends and holidays in May and early September-October. Note: Boulder Beach is only open June-early September.

Directions: From Coeur d'Alene, drive north on Highway 95 for 15 miles. The campground is on the east side of the highway opposite the theme park to the west.

GPS Coordinates: N 47° 54.465' W 116° 42.048'

Contact: Silverwood Theme Park and Boulder Beach, 27843 N. Hwy. 95, Athol, ID 93801, 208/683-3400, www.silverwoodthemepark. com.

37 NORTH IDAHO ALPINE COUNTRY RV PARK

Scenic rating: 4

north of Coeur d'Alene

Located 10 miles north of Coeur d'Alene, this campground works for Highway 95 travelers looking to be out of the I-90 corridor bustle between Post Falls and Coeur d'Alene. The campground is seven miles south of Silverwood Theme Park. It is not a destination in itself, but it can provide overflow camping for Silverwood or even Farragut State Park. Recent highway reconstruction added a newly paved bike trail adjacent to the road.

The campground sits off the four-lane

highway behind a gas station and minimart. Although the store blocks the campground from the highway, some traffic noise creeps in, especially from the trains, which toot their horns as they pass the road crossing. Bring earplugs if you're a light sleeper. The campground's gravel road loops through a parked-out, grassy, no privacy setting with firs and willows for shade. The tent-only sites (1-6) sit in their own loop adjacent to a large pet area.

Campsites, facilities: The campground has 19 RV campsites and six tent campsites. RVs are limited to 70 feet. Hookups are available for water, sewer, and electricity up to 50 amps. Facilities include picnic tables, pedestal grills, flush toilets (wheelchair-accessible), showers, drinking water, wireless Internet, and minimart. Leashed pets are permitted.

Reservations, fees: Reservations are accepted. Hookups cost $32. Tent campsites cost $18. Cash or credit card. Open mid-April-mid-October.

Directions: From I-90 in Coeur d'Alene, take Exit 12 and head north on Highway 95 for 10 miles. Find the store and campground on the east side of the highway.

GPS Coordinates: N 47° 49.785' W 116° 46.740'

Contact: Alpine Country Store and RV Park, 17568 N. Hwy. 95, Hayden Lake, ID 83835, 208/772-4305, www.nirvpark.com.

38 FARRAGUT STATE PARK

Scenic rating: 7

on Lake Pend Oreille

At 2,064 feet, Farragut State Park, which used to be the world's second largest naval training station, is now a 4,000-acre park covering a huge knoll between two bays at the southwest end of Lake Pend Oreille. It features several campgrounds, swimming, boat launch, fishing, disc golf courses, orienteering course, model airplane field, sand volleyball courts,

horseshoes, and 40 miles of trails for hiking, mountain biking, and horseback riding. Lake Pend Oreille attracts boaters, water-skiers, paddlers, and anglers.

Campsites sit on forested slopes well above the shore. Some sites are open and sunny; others tuck under partial mixed conifer shade. All are close together. Gilmore, Snowberry, Redtail, and Nighthawk areas contain serviced RV sites. Whitetail has only tent sites. The Ward Primitive area (no services, tables, or fires) permits self-contained RVs to park for the night; tents are not permitted. Snowberry and Whitetail sit nearest the boat launch, disc golf courses, and disposal station. Gilmore is closer to the visitors center and Beaver Bay Beach. The Corral campsite section is for those traveling with stock.

Campsites, facilities: The park has 156 RV serviced campsites, 61 RV or tent campsites, six equestrian campsites, and seven group sites. RVs are limited to 60 feet. Hookups are available for water and electricity. Facilities include picnic tables, fire rings, flush toilets, drinking water, showers, tent pads, campground hosts, boat ramp, and disposal station. Companion sites that permit more than eight people and double the equipment are also available. Leashed pets are permitted. Wheelchair-accessible facilities include toilets and five campsites.

Reservations, fees: Reservations are accepted (888/922-6743 or online). Campsites with hookups cost $30; other campsites cost $23. Companion campsites cost $37. RV camping in the Ward Primitive area costs $12. Park entrance costs $5 per vehicle. Add on a 6 percent Idaho tax. Idaho residents can buy the $10 State Parks Passport for unlimited entry and camping discounts. Cash, check, or credit card. The park is open all year with camping available late March-early November, but water is available only mid-April-mid-October.

Directions: Drive Highway 95 to Athol, about 15 minutes north of Coeur d'Alene. From Athol, turn east onto Highway 54 and drive four miles to the park entrance sign. Drive 0.2

mile farther to reach the visitors center on the south side of the road for camper registration. GPS Coordinates for Camper Registration: N 47° 57.068' W 116° 36.219'

Contact: Farragut State Park, 13550 E. Hwy. 54, Athol, ID 83801, 208/683-2425, http:// parksandrecreation.idaho.gov.

39 MOKINS BAY

Scenic rating: 7

on Hayden Lake in Idaho Panhandle National Forest

Located at 2,250 feet, Mokins Bay Campground tucks into the forest on the Hayden Lake's east side. The 3,800-acre lake is no wilderness retreat; it is built up along most of the shoreline with waterfront homes and cabins. While you can walk 0.1 mile to look at Mokins Bay filled with water lilies, the campground does not offer beach or boat facilities. The closest boat launch is at Sportman Park at the north end of the lake, which is popular for boating, waterskiing, paddling, and fishing. Anglers fish for bass, crappie, and trout.

The shady campground offers campsites with gravel parking pads tucked into a thick pine forest. The area is fairly quiet.

Campsites, facilities: The campground has 15 RV or tent campsites. RVs are limited to 30 feet. Facilities include picnic tables, fire rings with grills, vault and pit toilets, garbage service, campground hosts, horseshoe pit, and drinking water from hand pumps. Leashed pets are permitted.

Reservations, fees: Reservations are accepted (877/444-6777, www.recreation.gov). Campsites cost $16. An extra vehicle costs $8. Cash or check. Open May-September.

Directions: From Coeur d'Alene, drive north on Highway 95 for six miles. Turn east onto Lancaster Road and drive about four miles until the road makes a 90-degree turn north to become East Hayden Lake Road. Follow

East Hayden Lake Road for about seven curvy miles to Mokins Bay Road (Several roads will veer off, but stay on main road). Turn left for 0.1 mile to campground entrance.

GPS Coordinates: N 47° 47.014' W 116° 39.862'

Contact: Idaho Panhandle National Forest, Coeur d'Alene River Ranger District, 2502 E. Sherman Ave., Coeur d'Alene, ID 83814, 208/664-2318, www.fs.usda.gov/ipnf.

40 BLACKWELL ISLAND RV RESORT

Scenic rating: 4

in Coeur d'Alene

Located on the Spokane River, this city-surrounded, RV-only campground is convenient for those traveling I-90 and needing to pop off the freeway for the night. The location on the Spokane River gives boating access to Lake Coeur d'Alene, but the area is more protected than the open lake. The campground has 500 feet of sand and pebble beach for swimming. A boat launch accesses the river or lake for fishing, waterskiing, paddling, and sightseeing. You can rent pontoon boats, canoes, and water toys. Across the river, the paved 24-mile North Idaho Centennial Trail for walkers and bicyclists parallels the river to the Washington border and also connects in 1.5 miles with downtown Coeur d'Alene. Downtown has golfing (including a floating green), dining, shopping, art walks, boat cruises, parasailing, and live theater concerts. Cedars Floating Restaurant sits across the river from the campground.

A paved road weaves through the sunny, open campground, which is landscaped with tiny grassy islands, young trees, and gravel parking pads. The open sites yield no privacy, and while the campground overlooks the Spokane River, it also views industrial and residential areas. Most of the sites are pull-throughs, and some 40-foot-wide sites accommodate slide-outs. You'll hear noise from the adjacent highway and the railroad tracks across the river. Bring earplugs if you are a light sleeper.

Campsites, facilities: The campground has 182 RV campsites. RVs are limited to 60 feet. Hookups are available for water, sewer, electricity up to 50 amps, and cable TV. Facilities include flush toilets (wheelchair-accessible), showers, wireless Internet, launderette, propane, minimart, game room, boat launch and moorage, a playground, dog walk, and swimming beach. Leashed pets are permitted.

Reservations, fees: Reservations are accepted. Campsites cost $50-60, plus 6 percent Idaho tax. Cash or credit card. Open April-mid-October.

Directions: From I-90 in Coeur d'Alene, take Exit 12. Drive south on Highway 95 for 1.5 miles, driving over the Spokane River. Turn east onto Marina Drive and take the first left to reach the park entrance on the left.

GPS Coordinates: N 47° 40.844' W 116° 48.160'

Contact: Blackwell Island RV Park, 800 S. Marina Dr., Coeur d'Alene, ID 83814, 208/665-1300 or 888/571-2900, www.idahorvpark.com.

41 LAKE COEUR D'ALENE CAMPING RESORT

🏃 🚴 🛶 🎣 🛥 🐕 💧 🚐 ⛺

Scenic rating: 6

on Lake Coeur d'Alene

At 2,650 feet in the Coeur d'Alene Mountains, Lake Coeur d'Alene Camping Resort provides waterfront fun on Wolf Lodge Bay. Adjoining Lake Coeur d'Alene via no-wake zone wetland ponds and a river, this camping resort can be a destination by itself. Launch small, hand-carried watercraft, canoes, and kayaks from the campground's ramp, but for larger boats, a public boat ramp sits 0.5 mile west. The campground also rents paddleboats, canoes, and powerboats. The 25-mile-long lake offers plenty of places for boating, waterskiing, and fishing. The paved, 24-mile North Idaho Centennial Trail for walking and bicycling along the lake starts at Higgens Point, about two miles to the west.

The campground has two parts, split by the access road—a primitive tent section that sprawls adjacent to the water, and an RV section that climbs up the terraced slope that houses the swimming pool, adults-only hot tubs, and showers. The grassy, open tent sites are partly shaded by willows and divided by thigh-high rail fences. A few walk-in tent sites sit on peninsulas right on the water. The RV terraces are both back-in and pull-through; some are quite narrow, cramming in two RVs. The campground is close enough to the freeway to hear truck noise.

Campsites, facilities: The campground has 47 RV campsites and 39 tent campsites. RVs are limited to 60 feet. Hookups include water, sewer, and electricity up to 50 amps. Facilities include picnic tables, fire barrels, flush toilets, showers, wireless Internet, cable TV hookups, camping cabins, drinking water, disposal station, launderette, volleyball, horseshoes, propane, camp store, playground, swimming pool, hot tubs, café, and firewood for sale. Leashed pets are permitted in the RV campsites, but not tent campsites.

Reservations, fees: Reservations are accepted. Hookups run $32-43. Tent sites cost $27-30. Six people are permitted in each site. Rates are based on two people; for each additional person, add $3. Boat mooring and extra vehicles cost $10 per night. Cash or credit card. Open April-September.

Directions: From I-90 east of Coeur d'Alene, take Exit 22. Turn south for 0.5 mile, crossing the wetlands and the lake. Take the first left onto E. Wolf Lodge Bay Road. Drive 0.2 mile to the campground. Find the office to the right.

GPS Coordinates: N 47° 37.163' W 116° 38.629'

Contact: Lake Coeur d'Alene Camping Resort, 10588 E. Wolf Lodge Bay Rd., Coeur d'Alene, ID 83814, 208/664-4771 or 888/664-4471, www.campcda.com.

42 BEAUTY CREEK

Scenic rating: 7

near Coeur d'Alene Lake in Idaho Panhandle National Forest

Located at 2,100 feet on the east side of Coeur d'Alene Lake, Beauty Creek Campground sits on Beauty Creek, rather than on the lake. The campground squeezes in between the tall, forested ridges of the Coeur d'Alene Mountains flanking Beauty Bay. The Mineral Ridge public boat launch is less than two miles east, and the lake offers boating, waterskiing, paddling, and fishing. This campground sits along the Lake Coeur d'Alene Scenic Byway, a slow, curvy paved road touring the lake's east side. Bicyclists on the byway need to watch for narrow-to-nonexistent shoulders. From the campground, the five-mile Caribou Ridge National Recreation Trail climbs the ridge above to two overlooks of the lake. Other nearby trails include the Mineral Ridge Scenic Area National Recreation Trail, a 3.3-mile interpretive path with 22 educational stations, and the 0.5-mile Beauty Bay Recreation Area trail for a soaring lake view. The 4.6-mile Mt. Coeur d'Alene Viewpoint trail is for hikers and mountain bikers.

Snuggled into the mixed forest along Beauty Creek, the quiet campground has two types of campsites. Those at the front sit in open grassy sites that have little privacy from each other. With more trees and thick underbrush, the sites at the back half are more secluded—particularly sites 14, 16, 17, 18, and 19. A few sites have cabanas over their picnic tables. The access road, campground road, and parking pads are paved.

Campsites, facilities: The campground has

20 RV or tent campsites. RVs are limited to 50 feet. Facilities include picnic tables, fire rings with grills, vault toilets (wheelchair-accessible), garbage service, campground hosts, and drinking water. Leashed pets are permitted.

Reservations, fees: Reservations are accepted (877/444-6777, www.recreation.gov). Campsites cost $18. An extra vehicle costs $8. Cash or check. Open mid-May-late September.

Directions: From I-90 east of Coeur d'Alene, take Exit 22 and drive 2.3 miles southeast on Lake Coeur d'Alene Scenic Byway (Route 97). Turn left onto Forest Road 438. Drive 0.6 mile to the campground entrance on the right. GPS Coordinates: N 47° 36.451' W 116° 40.151'

Contact: Idaho Panhandle National Forest, Coeur d'Alene River Ranger District, 2502 E. Sherman Ave., Coeur d'Alene, ID 83814, 208/664-2318, www.fs.usda.gov/ipnf.

43 WOLF LODGE

Scenic rating: 6

in the Coeur D'Alene Mountains

At 2,150 feet in the Coeur d'Alene Mountains, Wolf Lodge Campground sits adjacent to I-90, making a convenient place to overnight for those traveling the freeway. A public boat launch is about two miles west on Coeur D'Alene Lake. The paved, 24-mile North Idaho Centennial Trail for walking and bicycling along the lake starts at Higgens Point, about four miles to the west. In the campground creek, you can swim or paddle canoes, but fishing is not permitted since it is a spawning creek.

The campground sits in a grassy meadow on a creek with trees for shade, but without underbrush, the sites have little privacy from each other. By midsummer, the creek shrinks down considerably. Some of the campsites are open with clear shots of the sky for satellite reception, and the proximity to the freeway adds traffic noise. Tent sites 1-16 and 31-33 border the creek.

Campsites, facilities: The campground has 57 RV campsites and 34 tent campsites. RVs are limited to 70 feet. Hookups include water, sewer, and electricity up to 50 amps. Facilities include picnic tables, fire rings, flush toilets (wheelchair-accessible), showers, volleyball, badminton, horseshoes, shuffleboard, launder-ette, camp store, three-wheeled bike and canoe rentals, and wireless Internet. Six people are permitted per site. Leashed pets are permitted.

Reservations, fees: Reservations are accept-ed. Sites with hookups cost $31-39. Tent sites cost $25-28. Rates are based on two people; for each additional person, add $3. Extra vehicles, boats, and trailers cost $5 each. Cash or credit card. Open mid-May-September.

Directions: From I-90 at the east end of Lake Coeur d'Alene, take Exit 22. Drive to the free-way's north side and turn east onto Frontage Road for 1.75 miles, passing the Wolf Lodge Inn and Steakhouse. The campground en-trance is on the left and crosses over the creek. GPS Coordinates: N 47° 37.829' W 116° 36.982'

Contact: Wolf Lodge Campground, 12329 E. Frontage Rd., Coeur d'Alene, ID 83814, 866/664-2812 or 208/664-2812, www.wol-flodgervcampground.com.

44 ALBERT'S LANDING RIVER RESORT

🏃 🚲 ⛵ 🏊 🛶 🎣 🐕 🚐 ⛺

Scenic rating: 6
in the Bitterroot Mountains

At 2,180 feet, Albert's Landing River Resort enjoys 900 feet of riverfront on the North Fork of the Coeur d'Alene River. The funky throwback resort provides services to river floaters with a shuttle running frequently on weekends to upriver locations to launch for floating or fishing. The lazy lower river is popular for tubing, canoeing, kayaking,

rafting, paddleboarding, and fishing from drift boats. The resort rents tubes and paddleboards. South of the campground, the 72-mile Trail of the Coeur d'Alenes parallels the freeway. The paved path for runners, walkers, and cyclists go both east and west. In fall, the resort serves as a basecamp for hunters.

The campground has a mix of sunny open sites and shady to partly-shaded sites. More than half of the campsites flank the river; oth-ers cluster around a large grassy field. Parking pads don't exist; you just park on the grass.

Campsites, facilities: The campground has 44 RV campsites and 20 tent campsites. RVs are limited to 40 feet. Hookups include electricity up to 50 amps. Facilities include communal fire pits, flush toilets, showers, drinking water, volleyball, tetherball, horseshoes, store, bar, and firewood for sale. Leashed pets are permitted.

Reservations, fees: Reservations are ac-cepted. RV sites run $25-35. Tent sites cost $20. Rates are based on four people; for each additional person, add $3. Extra vehicles cost $5. Pets cost $1. Cash or credit card. Open year-round.

Directions: From I-90, take Exit 43 at Kingston. Drive north on the Coeur d'Alene River Road for 1.9 miles. Turn right onto Old River Road, which will swing around to cross the river on a bridge and go 0.1 to the campground.

GPS Coordinates: N 47° 34.276' W 116° 15.258'

Contact: Albert's Landing River Resort, 418 Old River Road, Kingston, ID 83839, 208/682-4179, www.albertslanding.com.

45 BUMBLEBEE

🏊 🚐 ⛵ 🐕 ♿ 🚐 ⛺

Scenic rating: 7
in the Bitterroot Mountains in Idaho Panhandle National Forest

Near the Little North Fork Coeur D'Alene River at 2,200 feet, Bumblebee Campground has the shortest access, hence its popularity. The campground sits within walking distance to the river, where anglers enjoy fly-fishing for rainbow and cutthroat trout. Three miles away, the North Fork of the Coeur D'Alene River provides floating for rafts, tubes, kayaks, and canoes. The five-mile section of river that ends at the Bumblebee Bridge gets packs with floaters on hot summer days.

The two quiet campground loops offer different types of campsites, some flanking Bumblebee Creek: the south loop tucks under a thick forest canopy with heavily-shaded campsites while the north loop offers several meadow campsites with territorial views (and views of neighboring campers, too). While the campground loops are paved, parking spurs are gravel. Plenty of primitive campsites are also available along the Little North Fork Coeur D'Alene River; you can use these if the campground is full.

Campsites, facilities: The campground has 25 RV or tent campsites and one large group campsite. RVs are limited to 45 feet, but one 80-foot pull-through is available in the south loop. Facilities include picnic tables, fire rings with grills, vault toilets (wheelchair-accessible), drinking water from hand pumps, disposal station, and campground hosts. Leashed pets are permitted.

Reservations, fees: Reservations are accepted (877/444-6777, www.recreation.gov). Campsites cost $16. An extra vehicle costs $8. Cash or check. Open May-September.

Directions: From I-90 between Cataldo and Pinehurst, take Exit 43 at Kingston and drive north for 5.8 miles on Forest Road 9 (Coeur D'Alene River Road). Turn left onto the Little North Fork Road (Forest Road 209) and drive about three miles. Turn right onto Forest Road 796 for 0.1 mile to the campground entrance on the right and left.

GPS Coordinates: N 47° 38.064' W 116° 16.888'

Contact: Idaho Panhandle National Forest, Coeur d'Alene River Ranger District, 173 Commerce Ave., Smelterville, ID 83868, 208/783-2100, www.fs.usda.gov/ipnf.

46 BERLIN FLAT

Scenic rating: 7

in the Bitterroot Mountains in Idaho Panhandle National Forest

Sitting on Shoshone Creek at 2,794 feet, Berlin Flat Campground provides a remote place to enjoy one of the upper tributaries of the Coeur D'Alene River drainage. On the surrounding mountain slopes, a patchwork of logged stands shows various stages of regrowth in the heavily timbered forest. Anglers can fish Shoshone Creek. Up the nearby Falls Creek drainage and side roads, hikers and mountain bikers can trot along the Hulliman Ridge Trail #578 to the Idaho-Montana border.

The long drive from the Interstate guarantees quiet and solitude at this small mixed forest campground set above a creek. Gravel parking spurs ring the gravel loop, and a short trail drops to the creek.

Campsites, facilities: The campground has nine RV or tent campsites. RVs are limited to midsized. Facilities include picnic tables, fire rings with grills, vault toilets (wheelchair-accessible), and drinking water from a hand pump. Pack out your trash. Leashed pets are permitted.

Reservations, fees: No reservations are accepted. Campsites cost $16. An extra vehicle costs $8. Cash or check. Open May-September.

Directions: From I-90 between Cataldo and Pinehurst, take Exit 43 at Kingston and drive north for 23 miles on Forest Road 9 (Coeur D'Alene River Road). From Prichard, cross Prichard Creek and continue north on Forest Road 208 for six miles. Then, turn right to follow Shoshone Creek north for 6.6 miles on Forest Road 412 (Shoshone Creek Road) and veer left for 0.9 mile. These forest roads are paved, except for about two miles.

GPS Coordinates: N 47° 47.599' W 115°
57.147'
Contact: Idaho Panhandle National Forest,
Coeur d'Alene River Ranger District, 173
Commerce Ave., Smelterville, ID 83868,
208/783-2100, www.fs.usda.gov/ipnf.

47 KIT PRICE

Scenic rating: 8
in the Bitterroot Mountains in Idaho Panhandle
National Forest

Sitting on the North Fork of the Coeur
D'Alene River at 2,540 feet, Kit Price Campground is the nearest in a line-up of three
campgrounds within nine miles on this popular recreational river. Fly-fishing for catch-and-
release cutthroat trout, anglers wade in to get
away from the shoreline brush. The river access
site at the end of the campground offers a place
to launch or take out boats. Floaters tackle the
river with rafts, canoes, kayaks, and tubes,
but educate yourself about the river: Most of
the river runs with Class I and II water, but
less skilled floaters and tubers should avoid
the Class III rapids. You can put in upriver
at Devil's Elbow or Big Hank Campgrounds
to float back to Kit Price or float south to
Prichard Bridge. In the area, hiking trails go
to Centennial Falls, Shadow Falls, and Settler's
Grove of Ancient Cedars, a stand of ancient
trees growing 10 feet in diameter that were
skipped over by the 1910 fire. The area also
offers mountain biking.

Three loops comprise this campground with
pavement for the access road, campground
loops, and parking spurs. Small sunny meadows rim parts of the campground, giving
neighboring sites territorial views. Most of
the campsites are shaded under dense forest.
The campground serves as a river access site
for day use, bringing a bustle on hot summer
days, but it quiets at night.

Campsites, facilities: The campground has
53 RV or tent campsites, including one large
group site. RVs are limited to 45 feet. Facilities include picnic tables, fire rings with grills,
vault toilets (wheelchair-accessible), drinking
water, and campground hosts. A disposal station is available at Shoshone Work Center,
three miles south of the campground. Leashed
pets are permitted.
Reservations, fees: Reservations are accepted
(877/444-6777, www.recreation.gov). Campsites cost $16. An extra vehicle costs $8. Cash
or check. Open May-September.
Directions: From I-90 between Cataldo and
Pinehurst, take Exit 43 at Kingston and drive
north for 23 miles on Forest Road 9 (Coeur
D'Alene River Road). From Prichard, cross
Prichard Creek and continue north on Forest
Road 208 for about 9.5 miles to the camp-
ground entrance on the right.
GPS Coordinates: N 47° 44.413' W 116°
0.480'
Contact: Idaho Panhandle National Forest,
Coeur d'Alene River Ranger District, 173
Commerce Ave., Smelterville, ID 83868,
208/783-2100, www.fs.usda.gov/ipnf.

48 DEVIL'S ELBOW

Scenic rating: 8
in the Bitterroot Mountains in Idaho Panhandle
National Forest

Sitting on the North Fork of the Coeur
D'Alene River at 2,600 feet, Devil's Elbow
Campground is the middle in a string of three
campgrounds in nine miles on this popular
recreational river. Fly-fishing for catch-and-
release cutthroat trout, anglers wade in to get
away from the shoreline brush. The river access site at the end of the campground offers
a place to launch or take out boats. Floaters
tackle the river with rafts, canoes, kayaks,
and tubes, but educate yourself about the

river: Most of the river runs with Class I and II water, but less skilled floaters and tubers should avoid the Class III rapids. You can put in upriver at Big Hank for a lazy float back to the campground. In the area, hiking trails go to Centennial Falls, Shadow Falls, and Settler's Grove of Ancient Cedars, a stand of ancient trees growing 10 feet in diameter that were skipped over by the 1910 fire. The area also offers mountain biking.

Repaving in 2012 spruced up the campground road and parking spurs. Several campsites now offer wide enough parking spurs for two vehicles. Shady campsites rim one loop tucked into a dense lodgepole pine forest. The end of the campground serves as a river access site for day use, bringing a bustle on hot summer days, but the campground quiets at night.

Campsites, facilities: The campground has 20 RV or tent campsites, including one large group site. RVs are limited to 30 feet, except for two larger pull-through sites. Facilities include picnic tables, fire rings with grills, vault toilets (wheelchair-accessible), drinking water from hand pumps, and campground hosts. A disposal station is available at Shoshone Work Center, three miles south of Kit Price Campground. Leashed pets are permitted.

Reservations, fees: Reservations are accepted (877/444-6777, www.recreation.gov). Campsites cost $16. An extra vehicle costs $8. Cash or check. Open May-September.

Directions: From I-90 between Cataldo and Pinehurst, take Exit 43 at Kingston and drive north for 23 miles on Forest Road 9 (Coeur D'Alene River Road). From Prichard, cross Prichard Creek and continue north on Forest Road 208 for about 13 miles to the campground entrance on the right.

GPS Coordinates: N 47° 46.275' W 116° 1.991'

Contact: Idaho Panhandle National Forest, Coeur d'Alene River Ranger District, 173 Commerce Ave., Smelterville, ID 83868, 208/783-2100, www.fs.usda.gov/ipnf.

49 BIG HANK

Scenic rating: 8

in the Bitterroot Mountains in Idaho Panhandle National Forest

Flanking the North Fork of the Coeur D'Alene River at 2,700 feet, Big Hank Campground is the furthest of three campgrounds within nine miles on this popular recreational river. Fly-fishing for catch-and-release cutthroat trout, anglers wade in to get away from the shoreline brush. A river access site adjacent to the campground offers a place to launch or take out boats. Floaters tackle the river with rafts, canoes, kayaks, and tubes, but educate yourself about the river: Most of the river runs with Class I and II water, but less skilled floaters and tubers should avoid the Class III rapids. You can put in at Big Hank to float downstream to Devil's Elbow Campground. In the area, hiking trails go to Centennial Falls, Shadow Falls, and Settler's Grove of Ancient Cedars, a stand of ancient trees growing 10 feet in diameter that were skipped over by the 1910 fire. The area also offers mountain biking.

A paved access road, paved campground road, and paved parking spurs make this quiet campground popular with RVers. About half of the campsites back up to the river with trails running through the brush to the shoreline. Most of the sites are shady with partial sunlight breaking through the trees.

Campsites, facilities: The campground has 30 RV or tent campsites. RVs are limited to 40 feet. Facilities include picnic tables, fire rings with grills, vault toilets (wheelchair-accessible), drinking water from hand pumps, and campground hosts. A disposal station is available at Shoshone Work Center, three miles south of Kit Price Campground. Leashed pets are permitted.

Reservations, fees: Reservations are accepted (877/444-6777, www.recreation.gov). Campsites cost $16. An extra vehicle costs $8. Cash or check. Open May-September.

Directions: From I-90 between Cataldo and Pinehurst, take Exit 43 at Kingston and drive north for 23 miles on Forest Road 9 (Coeur D'Alene River Road). From Prichard, cross Prichard Creek and continue north on Forest Road 208 for 19 miles to the campground entrance on the left.

GPS Coordinates: N 47° 49.407' W 116° 5.961'

Contact: Idaho Panhandle National Forest, Coeur d'Alene River Ranger District, 173 Commerce Ave., Smelterville, ID 83868, 208/783-2100, www.fs.usda.gov/ipnf.

50 BELL BAY

Scenic rating: 9

on Lake Coeur d'Alene in Idaho Panhandle National Forest

On the east side of Lake Coeur d'Alene, Bell Bay Campground overlooks the lake. A trail leads from the campsites down to two boat docks for mooring, but the closest public boat launch is at Harrison, a 12-minute drive south. For bicyclists, runners, and walkers, Harrison also has trailheads for the paved 72-mile Trail of the Coeur d'Alenes, which meanders through pastoral farmland, wetlands housing abundant nesting birds, and Lake Coeur d'Alene's shoreline to the Chacolet Bridge.

The campground is divided into upper and lower sections, one mile apart and connected via the Bell Bay Trail. The lower section sits above the lake in a mixed forest; a steep trail descends to the water. Six sites overlook the lake with site 15 commanding seclusion and a prime lake view. While the access road requires washboard gravel driving, the campground road and parking pads are paved. The rougher upper loop is used for large groups and overflow when available.

Campsites, facilities: The campground has 26 RV and tent campsites, four boat campsites, and one large group site. RVs are limited to 40 feet. Facilities include picnic tables, fire rings with grills, vault toilets (wheelchair-accessible), drinking water, campground hosts, and garbage service. Leashed pets are permitted.

Reservations, fees: Reservations are accepted (877/444-6777, www.recreation.gov). Campsites cost $16 in the lower loop and $14 in the upper loop. Extra vehicles cost $8. Cash or check. Open mid-May–mid-September.

Directions: From I-90 east of Coeur d'Alene, take Exit 22. Drive south on the Lake Coeur d'Alene Scenic Byway (Route 97) for 25 slow, curvy miles. At East Point Road, turn west for three miles. After 0.7 mile of pavement, you'll hit two miles of gravel before reaching pavement again. At the entrance, follow the left fork for 0.9 mile down steep switchbacks to the lower loop.

GPS Coordinates: N 47° 28.410' W 116° 50.668'

Contact: Idaho Panhandle National Forest, Coeur d'Alene River Ranger District, 2502 E. Sherman Ave., Coeur d'Alene, ID 83814, 208/664-2318, www.fs.usda.gov/ipnf.

51 HARRISON

Scenic rating: 7

on Lake Coeur d'Alene

On the east side of Lake Coeur d'Alene, the tiny town of Harrison springs to life in summer. The town centers on the Gateway Marina with boating facilities: trailer parking, slips, docks, rentals, jetty, and ramps. The lake provides swimming, boating, waterskiing, paddling, and fishing. For bicyclists, runners, and walkers, the paved 72-mile Trail of the Coeur d'Alenes crosses behind the campground. To the east, it meanders through pastoral farmland, wetlands housing abundant nesting birds, and to the south, it tours along Lake Coeur d'Alene's shoreline to the Chacolet Bridge. Harrison also includes a bike shop with rentals, several restaurants, and an ice cream shop.

The campground is at the city beach and a marina. The RV spaces line up in a parking lot, and a grassy lawn serves as a space for tents without separated sites. The tent lawn sits right on the beach.

Campsites, facilities: The campground has 20 RV campsites and room for 10 tents. RVs are limited to 35 feet. Facilities include flush toilets, a few picnic tables, coin-op showers, drinking water, disposal station, campground hosts, and garbage service. Leashed pets are permitted.

Reservations, fees: Reservations are accepted. RV campsites cost $35-42. Tent campsites cost $15. Cash or check. Open May-September.

Directions: In Harrison on the east side of Coeur d'Alene Lake, drive Highway 97 south through town and turn right at Harrison Street. Drive one block and drop down into the campground, beach, and marina area. GPS Coordinates: N 47° 27.242' W 116° 47.232'

Contact: City of Harrison, P.O. Box 73, Harrison, ID 83814, 208/689-3393, www.cityofharrisonidaho.com.

52 CHACOLET

Scenic rating: 8
in Heyburn State Park on Lake Coeur d'Alene

Heyburn State Park flanks a series of small lakes that connect to the south end of Lake Coeur d'Alene, surrounded by the Coeur d'Alene Indian Reservation. In Heyburn State Park, Chacolet Campground—which sits on Chacolet Lake, although most campers think they are on the larger lake—is popular for boating, hiking, and biking. For boaters, water-skiers, paddlers, and anglers, the campground has a marina with a boat ramp, dock, and moorage. The cruise boat *Idaho* also departs from the marina. The Plummer

Point swimming area is 0.9 mile from the campground and easily reached via the Trail of the Coeur d'Alenes, a paved 72-mile trail for bicyclists, runners, and walkers. Departing from the campground, most cyclists ride across the Chacolet Bridge to tour Lake Coeur d'Alene's east shoreline. Bird-watchers will enjoy nesting ospreys from the Chacolet Bridge. Within two miles, trailheads depart for the Plummer Creek Marsh interpretive boardwalk for wildlife-watching opportunities, the three-mile Indian Cliffs Trail, and the one-mile, hiking-only CCC Nature Trail. Over 12 miles of mountain-biking trails also loop through the park.

Chacolet, the least developed of the park's three campgrounds, has small, cramped together, sloped, and partially shaded campsites. A dusty dirt road loops through the quiet campground, and most of the small, narrow parking pads are back-ins that can accommodate only smaller RVs. Some of the sites have peek-a-boo lake views.

Campsites, facilities: The campground has

Walkers, runners, and bikers can tour the Chacolet Bridge.

38 RV or tent campsites. RVs are limited to 18 feet. Facilities include picnic tables, fire pits with grills, flush toilets (wheelchair-accessible), drinking water, campground hosts, tent pads, and garbage service. Leashed pets are permitted.

Reservations, fees: Reservations are accepted (888/922-6743 or online). Campsites cost $19. Park entrance costs $5 per vehicle. Add on a 6 percent Idaho tax. Idaho residents can buy the $10 State Parks Passport for unlimited entry and camping discounts. The park is open year-round, but Chacolet is only open mid-May-mid-September.

Directions: From Coeur d'Alene, drive south on Highway 95 for 34 miles to Plummer. Turn east onto Highway 5 for 6.4 miles to Hawley's Landing. Turn north and drive west through the parking lot onto the Chacolet Road for 1.9 miles. Veer left at the fork for 0.2 mile and again left at the junction at the cabins for 0.2 mile, staying on Upper Chacolet Road. GPS Coordinates: N 47° 22.594' W 116° 45.816'

Contact: Heyburn State Park, 1291 Chacolet Rd., Plummer, ID 83851, 208/686-1308, http://parksandrecreation.idaho.gov/.

53 HAWLEY'S LANDING

Scenic rating: 8

in Heyburn State Park on Lake Coeur d'Alene

BEST (

The 5,500-acre Heyburn State Park, created in 1908, is the oldest park in the Northwest. Surrounded by Coeur d'Alene Indian Reservation, it houses small lakes connected to Lake Coeur d'Alene. Hawley's Landing sits on Chatcolet Lake in a western red cedar and hemlock forest mixed with drier tall ponderosa pines, some 400 years old. One mile east, boaters, waterskiers, and anglers can launch at the Rocky Point Marina or rent rowboats, kayaks, canoes, and paddleboats. A one-mile bicycle ride on a paved road connects to the 72-mile Trail of the Coeur d'Alenes. A 0.6-mile hiking trail tours the lakeshore and meets with the Plummer Creek Marsh interpretive trail, where you can see muskrats, great blue herons, and loons. Other mountain-biking and hiking trailheads are one mile away, as is the Plummer Point swimming beach. In winter, cross-country skiers and snowshoers tour the park's trails.

The shady campsites are cramped; neighbors are squeezed close together, and some sites are on slopes where a picnic table cannot sit flat. Most of the small, narrow gravel parking pads are back-ins, but a few are pull-throughs. With a common parking lot, four of the sites are walk-ins for tents, with the best views overlooking the lake. Some sites have no hookups while others have partial or full hookups. You'll hear nearby trains.

Campsites, facilities: The campground has 36 RV or tent campsites and four tent-only walk-in sites. RVs are limited to 40 feet. Hookups are available for water and electricity up to 30 amps, with sewer available at only a couple sites. Facilities include picnic tables, fire pits with grills, flush toilets (wheelchair-accessible), showers, tent pads at 16 sites, disposal station, firewood for sale, drinking water, interpretive programs, campground hosts, and garbage service. Leashed pets are permitted.

Reservations, fees: Reservations are accepted (888/922-6743 or online). Campsites cost $21-27. Park entrance costs $5 per vehicle. Add on a 6 percent Idaho tax. Idaho residents can buy the $10 State Parks Passport for unlimited entry and camping discounts. The park is open year-round, but Hawley's Landing is only open April-October.

Directions: From Coeur d'Alene, drive south on Highway 95 for 34 miles to Plummer. Turn east onto Highway 5 and turn left into Hawley's Landing at milepost 6.4 and swing right into the campground. GPS Coordinates: N 47° 21.303' W 116° 46.229'

Contact: Heyburn State Park, 1291 Chacolet Rd., Plummer, ID 83851, 208/686-1308, http://parksandrecreation.idaho.gov/.

54 BENEWAH LAKE

Scenic rating: 7

in Heyburn State Park on Benewah Lake

Heyburn State Park includes Benewah Lake, which connects to Chacolet Lake via the St. Joe River. Chacolet Lake in turn connects with Lake Coeur d'Alene. The connected waterways lead many campers to mistakenly think they are still on Lake Coeur d'Alene. Boaters will find a boat ramp, dock, and trailer parking just before the campground. Benewah Lake harbors islands, a railroad trestle, and wetlands, which offer protection and good destinations for canoeists, kayakers, anglers, and birdwatchers. A 0.4-mile walking or mountain-biking trail departs from the campground for touring the shoreline or fishing. At its location on the east end of Heyburn, most of the park's hiking, mountain-biking, and horse trails—along with the 72-mile paved Trail of the Coeur d'Alenes—sit about 10 minutes to the west.

As at all three of Heyburn's campgrounds, camping at Benewah provides an excellent location for enjoying the lake, but there's no privacy in its three loops. The forested campsites scrunch so close to each other that you can hear the snores in the neighbors' tent. Nine sites have lake views. Passing train sounds carry into the campground. Some sites have no hookups while others have partial or full hookups.

Campsites, facilities: The campground has 26 RV campsites plus 19 RV or tent campsites, and four tent-only sites. RVs are limited to 40 feet. Hookups are available for water, sewer, and electricity up to 30 amps. Facilities include picnic tables, fire rings with grills, flush toilets (wheelchair-accessible), showers, disposal station, drinking water, campground hosts, firewood for sale, and garbage service. Leashed pets are permitted.

Reservations, fees: Reservations are accepted (888/922-6743 or online). Campsites cost $21-27. Park entrance costs $5 per vehicle. Add on a 6 percent Idaho tax. Idaho residents can buy the $10 State Parks Passport for unlimited entry and camping discounts. Cash or check. The park is open year-round, but Benewah is only open mid-May–mid-September.

Directions: From Coeur d'Alene, drive south on Highway 95 for 34 miles to Plummer to reach Highway 5. Or from St. Maries, turn west on Highway 5. At milepost 11.8, turn north onto Benewah Lake Road and drive 1.3 miles, veering left at the trailer park. GPS Coordinates: N 47° 20.976' W 116° 41.222'

Contact: Heyburn State Park, 1291 Chacolet Rd., Plummer, ID 83851, 208/686-1308, http://parksandrecreation.idaho.gov/.

55 SHADOWY ST. JOE

Scenic rating: 7

on the St. Joe River in Idaho Panhandle National Forest

BEST (

East of St. Maries at 2,100 feet, the lower St. Joe River—nicknamed the Shadowy St. Joe—gathers its headwaters from the Bitterroot Mountains along the Idaho-Montana border. The blue-ribbon trout fishery holds cutthroat, rainbow, brook, and bull trout. In its lower stretches, the water calms into deep slow-moving flats traveling about 0.5 mile per hour, where the river is popular for motorboats and floating with rafts, canoes, and kayaks. From St. Joe City (don't let the name fool you; it's just a hamlet), the river runs for 31 miles to reach Chacolet and Coeur d'Alene Lakes. The river here has the reputation of being the world's highest navigable river; tugs haul logs to Coeur d'Alene mills.

Shadowy St. Joe Campground tucks between the road and the river. With only a few trees—cottonwoods and birch—the open, grassy, sunny campground offers minimal shade. Hit it around July 4 and the surrounding green grass will be as tall as a human. The campsites, however, are mowed. The campground—with a paved road and paved parking pads—also has a boat ramp, dock, and trailer parking. Sites 10-12 border the river, but with the tall grass and brush, they don't offer views of it.

Campsites, facilities: The campground has 14 RV or tent campsites. RVs are limited to 45 feet. Facilities include picnic tables, fire rings with grills, vault toilet (wheelchair-accessible), drinking water, garbage service, campground hosts, and boat launch. Leashed pets are permitted.

Reservations, fees: No reservations are accepted, and camping costs $6. Cash or check. Open late May-early September.

Directions: From St. Maries, drive north on State Route 3 to the outskirts of town to find the paved St. Joe River Road (Forest Road 50). Drive 10 miles east. The campground entrance sits on the right.

GPS Coordinates: N 47° 19.490' W 116° 23.622'

Contact: Idaho Panhandle National Forest, St. Joe Ranger District, 222 S. 7th Street, St. Maries, ID 83861, 208/245-2531, www.fs.usda.gov/ipnf.

56 BIG CREEK

Scenic rating: 7

in the St. Joe Mountains in Idaho Panhandle National Forest

On Big Creek, a tributary of the St. Joe River, Big Creek Campground sits at 2,380 feet—once the site of a Civilian Conservation Corps camp. Today OHV riders, anglers, and hikers use the campground to explore the St. Joe Mountains of the Bitterroots. Anglers go fly-fishing for trout in Big Creek. Trailheads to various hiking destinations are within a few miles of the campground. Hunters use

the campground as a base for fall hunting. The upper creek attracts expert whitewater rafters and kayakers for the Class III-IV rapids in spring; the lower five miles from the first bridge is a Class I-II float. Check with the Forest Service for current conditions.

This quiet campground sits on one long side road in a mixed forest that shades most of the campsites. Trails lead from several riverfront campsites to the water, but tall grass and brush block views of the river from the campsites. Some sites grab snippets of territorial views of the surrounding Big Creek canyon.

Campsites, facilities: The campground has nine RV or tent campsites. RVs are limited to small rigs. Facilities include picnic tables, fire rings with grills, vault toilets (wheelchair-accessible), and drinking water. Pack out your trash. Leashed pets are permitted.

Reservations, fees: No reservations are accepted. Camping is free. Open May-September.

Directions: From the St. Joe River Road (Forest Road 50) at Calder, drive the county road for 4.5 miles east. Then turn north on to Big Creek Road (Forest Road 537) for three miles to the campground entrance on the left.

GPS Coordinates: N 47° 18.286' W 116° 7.124'

Contact: Idaho Panhandle National Forest, St. Joe Ranger District, 222 S. 7th Street, St. Maries, ID 83861, 208/245-2531, www.fs.usda.gov/ipnf.

57 HUCKLEBERRY

Scenic rating: 7

on the St. Joe River in Idaho Panhandle National Forest

On the lower St. Joe River, Huckleberry Campground sits about midway in between the tiny burgs of Calder and Avery. It is the only campground on the St. Joe River with serviced sites. This section of river is mixed with Class I and II water—gentle for canoeing, rafting, and float tubing. The St. Joe maintains a reputation as a prime trout fishery. It harbors endangered bull trout and cutthroat trout whose numbers are declining because of hybridization with other trout. Both trout are catch-and-release only. The surrounding national forest is also popular with elk hunters.

Squeezed in between the road and the river, the long, narrow, sunny campground packs almost half of its sites along the riverfront. The campground, having a paved road and parking pads, sits in two sections. Some pull-through sites are available. The mowed-lawn sites with few trees have little to block the view of the road or other campers. With the proximity to the St. Joe River Road, busy traffic passes most of the day but quiets somewhat at night.

Campsites, facilities: The campground has 33 RV or tent campsites. RVs are limited to 40 feet. Hookups are available for electricity and water. Facilities include picnic tables, fire rings with grills, vault toilets (wheelchair-accessible), garbage service, horseshoe pits, disposal station, gravel tent pads, campground hosts, and drinking water. Three sites are for groups. Leashed pets are permitted.

Reservations, fees: No reservations are accepted. Campsites cost $14 for tents and $18 for hookups. A second vehicle costs $5. Use of disposal station costs $5. Cash or check. Open year-round.

Directions: From the north side of St. Maries on Highway 3, drive east on the St. Joe River Road (Forest Road 50). At milepost 29.5, turn north at the sign into the campground entrance, about five miles past Calder.
GPS Coordinates: N 47° 16.056' W 116° 5.326'

Contact: Bureau of Land Management, Coeur d'Alene Field Office, 3815 Schreiber Way, Coeur d'Alene, ID 83815, 208/769-5000, www.blm.gov.

58 TELICHPAH

Scenic rating: 7

in the St. Joe Mountains in Idaho Panhandle National Forest

On the remote North Fork of the St. Joe River at 2,800 feet, the renamed Telichpah may be identified on some older maps as North Fork St. Joe or Squaw Creek Campground. The North Fork River lures anglers for 18-inch cutthroat trout. In May-June, rafters and kayakers tackle the river's Class III rapids. The four-mile Squaw Creek Trail #196 departs from the campground. For mountain bikers, the campground is the closest to Pearson (a 20-minute drive), the lower trailhead of the Route of the Hiawatha bike trail. The 15-mile railroad grade trail has 10 tunnels and seven trestles ($10 for adults and $6 for kids), and you can shuttle to the top to ride down ($6-9). En route to Pearson, you'll drive through seven tunnels—all single-lane and a scenic drive in itself. Honk to alert oncoming traffic, and turn on lights for safety.

This quiet campground in three sections sits on a lodgepole-covered hillside that permits some views of the surrounding North Fork of the St. Joe River canyon. Filtered sunlight reaches the campsite floor made of forest duff and cones. There's very little underbrush, so you'll see neighboring campers through the trees. The section with sites 7-14 sits nearest the river.

Campsites, facilities: The campground has 14 RV or tent campsites, including one large group site. Some sites can fit small RVs. Facilities include picnic tables, fire rings with grills and benches, tent pads, and vault toilets (wheelchair-accessible), but no drinking water. Treat river water. Pack out your trash. Leashed pets are permitted.

Reservations, fees: No reservations are accepted. Camping is free. Open late May-October.

© BECKY LOMAX

The 15-mile Route of the Hiawatha bike trail passes over seven trestles.

Directions: From Avery on the St. Joe River Road (Forest Road 50), drive north on dusty, washboarded Moon Pass Road (Forest Road 456) for six miles to the high bridge over the North Fork of the St. Joe River. At the north-west corner of the bridge, drop onto Old Moon Pass Road for one mile. It plummets in a single lane to the river. Turn right and cross the river to the campground entrance. Trailers are not recommended on Old Moon Pass Road, and the road narrows to single-lane through several tunnels. You can also access this area from Wallace.

GPS Coordinates: N 47° 17.825' W 115° 46.504'

Contact: Idaho Panhandle National Forest, St. Joe Ranger District, 222 S. 7th Street, St. Maries, ID 83861, 208/245-2531, www.fs.usda.gov/ipnf.

59 TURNER FLAT

Scenic rating: 8

on the St. Joe River in Idaho Panhandle National Forest

Turner Flat Campground sits at 2,700 feet on the upper St. Joe River, a nationally designated Wild and Scenic River that attracts rafters and kayakers in spring. The river runs with four miles of Class III-IV whitewater from the campground through Skookum Canyon to Packsaddle. Trips can run until mid-July when water levels drop. Check with the Forest Service for current river conditions. No boat ramp is available, but you can carry boats to and from the river. After the river clears of runoff, anglers fish the St. Joe for trout, fly-fishing by wading for the best success. Hunters use the campground as a base for fall big game hunting.

This remote, quiet campground enjoys the St. Joe River frontage with the sounds of the river. Sites on the west end are more open, allowing for views of the river, sunshine, and neighbors. Sites on the east end have more shade, tucked under the trees and separated from the river by shoreline brush. If the campground is full, numerous primitive free camping spots along the river are available.

Campsites, facilities: The campground has 10 RV or tent campsites, plus one group campsite. RVs are limited to 40 feet. Facilities include picnic tables, fire rings with grills, vault toilets (wheelchair-accessible), and drinking water from a hand pump. Pack out your trash. Leashed pets are permitted.

Reservations, fees: No reservations are accepted. Campsites cost $6. Cash or check. Open May-October, although water is usually not available until June.

Directions: From Avery on the St. Joe River Road (Forest Road 50), drive 8.6 paved miles east to the campground entrance on the right. GPS Coordinates: N 47° 14.217' W 115° 39.387'

Contact: Idaho Panhandle National Forest, St. Joe Ranger District, 222 S. 7th Street, St. Maries, ID 83861, 208/245-2531, www. fs.usda.gov/ipnf.

60 TIN CAN FLAT

Scenic rating: 8

on the St. Joe River in Idaho Panhandle National Forest

On the upper St. Joe River, Tin Can Flat Campground sits on a forested river bar at 2,750 feet. The St. Joe River, a nationally designated Wild and Scenic River, attracts rafters and kayakers in spring. In the Tin Can Flat stretch, you can float the river usually until mid-July when water levels drop. No boat ramp is available at the campground; most floaters launch at accesses upstream and take out at Turner Flat Campground. Check river conditions first with the Forest Service. After runoff clears from the river, anglers catch-and-release

cast for trout, including bull trout, cutthroat, and rainbow. Hunters use the campground as a base for fall big game hunting.

After dark when road travel diminishes, the campground enjoys quiet and the sound of the river. Most campsites tuck into the dense conifer forest that offers shade. Several sites get views of the river, and distance from neighbors lends privacy. If the campground is full, plenty of free primitive campsites are available along the river upstream.

Campsites, facilities: The campground has 11 RV or tent campsites. RVs are limited to 50 feet. Facilities include picnic tables, fire rings with grills, benches, vault toilets (wheelchair-accessible), tent pads, and drinking water from a hand pump. Pack out your trash. Leashed pets are permitted.

Reservations, fees: No reservations are accepted. Campsites cost $6. Open May-October, although water not available until June.

Directions: From Avery on the St. Joe River Road (Forest Road 50), drive 11 paved miles east to the campground entrance on the right. GPS Coordinates: N 47° 13.818' W 115° 37.335'

Contact: Idaho Panhandle National Forest, St. Joe Ranger District, 222 S. 7th Street, St. Maries, ID 83861, 208/245-2531, www. fs.usda.gov/ipnf.

61 CONRAD CROSSING

Scenic rating: 8

on the St. Joe River in Idaho Panhandle National Forest

Conrad Crossing sits at 3,300 feet on the upper St. Joe River, a nationally designated Wild and Scenic River that attracts rafters and kayakers in spring. From the campground, where you can carry boats to the water for launching, the river runs seven miles with Class II-IV whitewater to Bluff Creek Bridge. Wave trains build to the Class IV Tumbledown Rapid that drops over a ledge into a clear green pool—usually runnable until mid-June when water levels drop. Check river conditions first with the Forest Service. In the later season after the runoff clears, anglers fish the St. Joe for trout. The campground, named for the river ford here used by gold prospectors, sits on the Old Montana Trail, an Indian route through the St. Joe that tromped over the Bitterroot Mountains to Montana. A small segment of the old trail heads out from the upper campground. Several other trails in the area climb Whitetail, Conrad, and Mosquito Peaks. Hunters use the campground as a base for fall big game hunting. The campground is also near the Gold Creek-Little Joe Road that connects the St. Joe River Valley through the Bitterroot Mountains to St. Regis, Montana.

This remote, quiet campground enjoys the St. Joe River frontage in a mature forest of cedars and firs. The campground separates on both sides of the access road with three of the campsites adjacent to the river and the other five above the road. The river campsites get the advantage of river views and sounds, but one of the sites sees frequent traffic of boat launchers during the rafting season. If the campground is full, you can camp in primitive free sites along the river.

Campsites, facilities: The campground has eight RV or tent campsites. RVs are limited to small rigs. Facilities include picnic tables, fire pits, vault toilets, and drinking water. Pack out your trash. Leashed pets are permitted.

Reservations, fees: No reservations are accepted. Camping is free. Open May-October, but water is not available until June.

Directions: From Avery on the St. Joe River Road (Forest Road 50), drive 30 paved miles east to the campground entrance on the right. Or from St. Regis, Montana, drive the Little Joe Road (Forest Road 282) to the Idaho border, where it turns into Gold Creek Road (Forest Road 388). Turn right on the St. Joe River Road and drive 1.4 miles west to the campground entrance.
GPS Coordinates: N 47° 9.510' W 115° 25.008'

Contact: Idaho Panhandle National Forest, St. Joe Ranger District, 222 S. 7th Street, St. Maries, ID 83861, 208/245-2531, www.fs.usda.gov/ipnf.

62 FLY FLAT

Scenic rating: 8

on the St. Joe River in Idaho Panhandle National Forest

At 3,460 feet, Fly Flat Campground sits on the upper St. Joe River. In spring, rafters and kayakers run 10 miles of the Class III rapids from Spruce Tree Camp to Gold Creek, passing the campground. The float season wraps up usually by mid-June when water levels drop. Call the Forest Service for current conditions. As the river clears from runoff, anglers show up for fly-fishing, wading to avoid the brushy banks. Hikers can access nearby trails, such as the Fly Creek Trail (#629) and climb to Peggy Peak (#28). Hunters use the campground in fall as a base for big game hunting. The campground also provides quick access to the Gold Creek-Little Joe Road that connects the St. Joe River Valley through the Bitterroot Mountains with St. Regis, Montana.

The remoteness of the campground off the main St. Joe River Road guarantees quiet, solitude, and hearing the sound of the river. A mixed mature larch, pine, and cedar forest shades most of the campsites on the flat river bar. Short trails lead through brush to the river. If the campground fills, primitive free campsites are also available along the river.

Campsites, facilities: The campground has 14 RV or tent campsites. RVs are limited to 60 feet. Facilities include picnic tables, fire rings with grills, vault toilets, and drinking water from a hand pump. Pack out your trash. Leashed pets are permitted.

Reservations, fees: No reservations are accepted. Camping is free. Open late May-October, but water is not available until June.

Directions: From Avery on the St. Joe River Road (Forest Road 50), drive 29 paved miles east and turn right on the single-lane Red Ives Road (Forest Road 218) for 3.5 miles to the campground entrance on the right. Or from St. Regis, Montana, drive the Little Joe Road (Forest Road 282) to the Idaho border, where it turns into Gold Creek Road (Forest Road 388). Turn left at the Gold Creek Bridge onto Red Ives Road to reach the campground.

GPS Coordinates: N 47° 6.836' W 115° 23.464'

Contact: Idaho Panhandle National Forest, St. Joe Ranger District, 222 S. 7th Street, St. Maries, ID 83861, 208/245-2531, www.fs.usda.gov/ipnf.

63 SPRUCE TREE

Scenic rating: 8

on the St. Joe River in Idaho Panhandle National Forest

On the upper St. Joe River, Spruce Tree Campground sits at 3,750 feet. At the end of the road, the campground serves as the start of rafting and kayaking on the St. Joe River. In spring, floaters run 10 miles of the Class III rapids from Spruce Tree Camp to Gold Creek. The float season wraps up usually by mid-June when water levels drop. Call the Forest Service for current conditions. As the river clears from runoff, anglers show up for fly-fishing bull, cutthroat, and rainbow trout. The St. Joe River Trail (#48) continues from the campground upstream to access headwaters in the Bitterroot Mountains. The Red Ives Information Center with historical ranger buildings sits about two miles north of the campground. Hunters use the campground in fall as a base for big game hunting.

With a vehicle, you can't get any further off the road than this. The remoteness of the campground at the end of the road guarantees quiet and solitude. You'll hear the sound of the river and birds. A mature larch and pine forest shades most of the campsites; a few open sites get more sun. In midsummer, you can wade the river crossing downstream to get to a large flat river bar meadow rife with animal trails.

Campsites, facilities: The campground has nine RV or tent campsites. RVs are limited to 35 feet. Facilities include picnic tables, fire rings with grills, vault toilets, and drinking water from a hand pump. Pack out your trash. Leashed pets are permitted.

Reservations, fees: No reservations are accepted. Camping is free. Open late May-October, but water is not available until June.

Directions: From Avery on the St. Joe River Road (Forest Road 50), drive 29 paved miles east and turn right on the single-lane Red Ives Road (Forest Road 218) for about 12 miles to the campground entrance on the right. Or from St. Regis, Montana, drive the Little Joe Road (Forest Road 282) to the Idaho border, where it turns into Gold Creek Road (Forest Road 388). Turn left at the Gold Creek Bridge onto Forest Road 218.

GPS Coordinates: N 47° 2.338' W 115° 20.823'

Contact: Idaho Panhandle National Forest, St. Joe Ranger District, 222 S. 7th Street, St. Maries, ID 83861, 208/245-2531, www.fs.usda.gov/ipnf.

64 CAMP 3

Scenic rating: 7

in the Clearwater Mountains in Idaho Panhandle National Forest

Sitting at 3,220 feet, Camp 3 flanks Marble Creek, a tributary of the St. Joe River. Anglers can fish the creek for trout. Fishing is best done by wading to get away from the brushy banks. Hikers and horseback riders can tour the nearby 11-mile Marble Creek Trail (#261)

to pick huckleberries in midsummer. With many logging roads, the area is popular with OHV riders, and hunters look for big game in fall. Getting to the campground from the St. Joe River requires a long, curvy drive on gravel and dirt roads up Marble Creek. The north end of the road houses the Marble Creek Interpretive Site, commemorating logging history. The south end near Hobo Pass features the Hobo Cedar Grove with a self-guided nature trail through immense centuries-old cedars that have survived fires and logging.

The small, remote, creekside campground offers quiet and solitude, but it is also a favorite of the backwoods motorsports crowd bringing daytime noise of motorized bikes and ATVs. The campground sits in a meadow adjacent to the creek with mostly open and sunny campsites. You'll see territorial views of forested slopes and the neighbors.

Campsites, facilities: The campground has four RV or tent campsites. Limit RVs to mid-sized. Facilities include picnic tables, fire rings with grills, vault toilets, corral, and stock ramp, but no drinking water. Bring your own, or treat creek water. Leashed pets are permitted.

Reservations, fees: Reservations are not accepted. Camping is free. Open May-September.

Directions: From St. Maries, drive east on the St. Joe River Road (Forest Road 50) for 33 miles to Marble Creek Road (Forest Road 312). Turn south and drive Marble Creek Road for 11.5 miles (other roads veer off; stay on the main road). Steer right onto Hobo Pass Road for 2.7 miles and drop down the steep switchbacks into the campground.

GPS Coordinates: N 47° 7.790' W 116° 6.172'

Contact: Idaho Panhandle National Forest, St. Joe Ranger District, St. Maries Office, 222 S. 7th St., St. Maries, ID 83861, 208/245-2531, www.fs.usda.gov/ipnf/.

65 EMERALD CREEK

Scenic rating: 7

in the Clearwater Mountains in Idaho Panhandle National Forest

Emerald Creek, a tributary of the St. Maries River in the Clearwater Mountains, is known for its gemstones. Located four miles southwest of the campground, the Emerald Creek Garnet Area (open 9am-5pm Friday-Tuesday, Memorial Day-Labor Day) is best known for star garnets, the 12-sided crystals that are found only in Idaho and India. A 0.5-mile hike reaches the site, and permits for collecting are available: $10 for adults, $5 for children ages 6-12. Buckets, shovels, and two sluices are available for screening and washing. You can keep up to five pounds of garnets daily, but bring a bag or container for your gems. You can also fish Emerald Creek, and the area is popular with OHV riders.

The campground at 2,800 feet is a welcome reprieve from crowded, cramped campgrounds because the thick Douglas fir and pine forest yields privacy. Campsites spread out surrounded by lush thimbleberry undergrowth. Some of the sites are fully shaded; others see filtered sunlight during the day. Despite the gravel road access, the campground loop is paved, with gravel back-in parking pads. Its distance from the highway makes this a very quiet campground.

Campsites, facilities: The campground has 18 RV or tent campsites. RVs are limited to 45 feet. Facilities include picnic tables, fire rings with grills, vault toilets (wheelchair-accessible), drinking water, garbage service, and campground hosts. Leashed pets are permitted.

Reservations, fees: Reservations are not accepted. Camping costs $6. Cash or check. Open May-September.

Directions: From St. Maries, drive south on Highway 3 for 25 miles. Turn west at the signed turnoff onto Forest Road 447 to drive the five miles to the campground entrance. After 0.3 mile, the pavement ends. Continue on the washboard gravel road, veering left at 3.3 miles. From here, the road narrows, with pullouts for passing. Find the campground entrance on the left.

GPS Coordinates: N 47° 0.463' W 116° 19.560'

Contact: Idaho Panhandle National Forest, St. Joe Ranger District, St. Maries Office, 222 S. 7th St., Ste. 1, St. Maries, ID 83861, 208/245-2531, www.fs.usda.gov/ipnf/.

66 CEDAR CREEK

Scenic rating: 5

in the Clearwater Mountains in Idaho Panhandle National Forest

The area along Highway 3 is timber country, dotted by small towns, like Clarkia, that depend on the forest for their economic base. Huge bare swaths flank mountaintops where logging operations have clear-cut portions of the Idaho Panhandle National Forest. The tiny campground is more a convenient place to stay while driving or bicycling Highway 3 than a destination. Cedar Creek Campground sits at 2,800 feet in elevation, with access to the St. Maries River for fishing. Clarkia, three miles south, has groceries and gas.

The campground has a small day-use area, plus small campsites. Sunny site 1 sits within sight of the highway with no room for a tent. Site 2 has flat space for a tent. Site 2 and 3 are tucked back in the woods with more privacy. Cottonwoods, firs, pines, and hawthorns partially shade them. Sites 1 and 2 have short gravel parking pads that are wide enough for two cars.

Campsites, facilities: The campground has three RV or tent campsites. RVs are limited to small rigs. Facilities include picnic tables, fire rings with grills, and a vault toilet (wheelchair-accessible), but no drinking water. Bring your own water, or treat river water. Pack out your trash. Leashed pets are permitted.

Reservations, fees: Reservations are not accepted. Camping is free. Open May-September.

Directions: From Clarkia on Highway 3, drive three miles north, turning left into the campground before crossing the St. Maries River. From St. Maries, take Highway 3 southeast for 27 miles to the campground entrance right after the bridge.

GPS Coordinates: N 47° 3.043' W 116° 17.298'

Contact: Idaho Panhandle National Forest, St. Joe Ranger District, St. Maries Office, 222 S. 7th St., St. Maries, ID 83861, 208/245-2531, www.fs.usda.gov/ipnf/.

67 ELK CREEK

Scenic rating: 6

in the Clearwater Mountains in Clearwater National Forest

At 2,800 feet, Elk Creek Campground sits one mile north of the town of Elk River—a funky backwoods village with cafés, groceries, lodging, bars, and gas north of Dworshak Reservoir. The area is a favorite haunt for ATV riders, offering dusty rides on a web of dirt national forest roads. Forest Road 382 north from Elk River houses short 0.5- to 1-mile scenic hikes. Three waterfalls at Elk Creek Falls plummet through a deep basalt gorge, and Morris Creek Cedar Grove protects 90 acres of old-growth trees up to 500 years old, including an 18-foot-diameter giant red cedar is 3,000 years old. For anglers, Elk Creek harbors brook trout. Five minutes from the campground, Elk Creek Reservoir offers boating, fishing, and canoeing. The campground, sits at the north end of the Elk River Backcountry Byway, a curvy scenic half-gravel, half-paved, steep graded road along Dworshak Reservoir's east side.

A mixed pine and fir forest lends filtered shade to this campground, which was built in 2006. While the gravel road and several double-wide parking pads accommodate RVs, the campsites themselves are small—most with very little room for tents. The sites are open to the campground road but spaced out from each other to afford privacy.

Campsites, facilities: The campground has 14 RV or tent campsites. RVs are limited to 40 feet. Hookups are available for electricity. In addition, an overflow parking lot with electrical hookups fits 10 additional camping vehicles. Facilities include picnic tables, fire rings with grills, drinking water from hand pumps, vault toilets, and campground hosts. Pack out your trash. Leashed pets are permitted. A wheelchair-accessible toilet and campsite are available.

Reservations, fees: Reservations are accepted (877/444-6777, www.recreation.gov). Campsites cost $15. Extra vehicles cost $2. Cash or check. Open May-October.

Directions: From Elk River, take Dent Road out of town and veer immediately left. Drive 0.7 mile and turn right and then immediately left to reach the campground entrance. GPS Coordinates: N 46° 47.581' W 116° 10.337'

Contact: Clearwater National Forest, Palouse Ranger District, Potlatch Ranger Station, 1700 Hwy. 6, Potlatch, ID 83855, 208/875-1131, www.fs.usda.gov/nezperceclearwater.

68 ELK CREEK RESERVOIR

Scenic rating: 8

in the Clearwater Mountains in Clearwater National Forest

Sprawled along Elk Creek Reservoir, this camping area combines seven different types of campsites—lakeshore, forest, grassy, and parking lot. The reservoir has a dock for swimming and a primitive boat launch (electric motors only permitted), and the water harbors largemouth and smallmouth bass, bluegill, and stocked rainbow trout. The town of Elk River, with cafés, groceries, and gas, is a mecca for summer ATV riders and winter snowmobilers exploring the miles of trails and roads in the Clearwater National Forest. Forest Road 382 north from Elk River houses natural sightseeing: short 0.5- to 1-mile hikes to three waterfalls in a basalt gorge at Elk Creek Falls Recreation Area, 500-year-old trees in the Morris Creek Cedar Grove, and a 3,000-year-old giant red cedar. This reservoir sits as the northern gateway to the curvy Elk River Backcountry Byway, which links by steep gravel grades with Dent Acres, Dworshak Reservoir, and Orofino. Between here and Dent Acres, the washboarded gravel road throws steep, nearly 10 percent grade climbs and descents at drivers. Don't be fooled by the map; the road is not straight, but snakes the entire way.

Several different units make up the campground sprawled along one mile of the reservoir's western shore. You'll find open gravel parking lots suited for the largest RVs overlooking the reservoir, shaded campsites tucked under trees on the shoreline, grassy and treed tent sites across the road, and a series of more private campsites across the road in the forest.

Campsites, facilities: The campground has 64 RV and tent campsites. Some can fit the largest RVs. Facilities include picnic tables, fire rings (rock or metal rings with grills), and vault or pit toilets (wheelchair-accessible). Bring your own drinking water. If you choose to use reservoir water, filter or boil it first. Leashed pets are permitted.

Reservations, fees: Reservations are accepted by phone or online. Campsites cost $8-10. Extra vehicles cost $3. A park host comes around to collect the fees. Cash or check. Open mid-April-October.

Directions: Find the various units between mileposts 36 and 37 on the Elk River Backcountry Byway. GPS Coordinates: N 46° 46.518' W 116° 10.309'

Contact: Elk River Recreation District, P.O. Box 82, Elk River, ID 83827, 208/826-3468, www.elkriverrecreation.com.

69 DENT ACRES

🏊 🛶 🚤 🚣 🐴 🎣 🚴 ♿ 🚐 ⛺

Scenic rating: 9
on Dworshak Reservoir in Clearwater National Forest

BEST (

When you drive into Dent Acres, the campground host can tell whether you came on the Elk River Backcountry Byway via the gravel road from Elk River or on the paved road from Orofino. The dust on the vehicle is testament to the route. Regardless of the access, you will travel miles of steep curvy grades—despite the appearance on some maps of the road being a straight line. Located on the north shore of Dworshak Reservoir's eastern arm and surrounded by the Clearwater National Forest, the campground sits about 10 minutes from Dent Bridge, which crosses the reservoir. The reservoir is popular in early summer for bass and kokanee salmon fishing, boating, waterskiing, and paddling before water levels drop low. The campground accommodates boaters with a large paved trailer parking area, cement boat ramp, dock, and fish-cleaning station. Unfortunately, you can't swim at the boat launch area, and much of the remaining shoreline is steep and rocky. Most people swim from their boats. The reservoir is usually at full pool through July 4.

Largest of the east side campgrounds, Dent Acres sits on a sunny, grassy south-facing hillside with three paved loops and a few token trees between the open sites. All campsites except site 43 are paved pull-throughs. This popular campground books out months in advance for holiday weekends and is a hunter's favorite in fall. Most of the picnic tables are covered with small shade canopies.

Campsites, facilities: The campground has 50 RV or tent campsites. RVs are limited to 35 feet. Hookups include water, sewer, and electricity up to 50 amps. Facilities include picnic tables, fire rings with grills, flush toilets, showers, summer campground hosts, disposal station, tent pads, playground, summer garbage service, marine pump-out station, and weather station. Pack out your trash in the off-season. Leashed pets are permitted. Wheelchair-accessible facilities include toilets and all campsites.

Reservations, fees: Reservations are accepted (877/444-6777, www.recreation.gov). Campsites cost $18. Cash, check, or credit card. Open early April–November.

Directions: From Dent Acres Bridge on the Elk River Backcountry Byway, climb one mile north up the curvy road and turn south at the recreation area sign. Descend 1.9 miles on the steep, curvy, gravel road.

GPS Coordinates: N 46° 37.638' W 116° 13.183'

Contact: U.S. Army Corps of Engineers, P.O. Box 48, Ahsahka, ID 83520, 208/476-1255 or 800/321-3198 (recorded reservoir information), www.nww.usace.army.mil.

70 CANYON CREEK

🏊 🛶 🚤 🚣 🐴 ♿ 🚐 ⛺

Scenic rating: 8
on Dworshak Reservoir in Clearwater National Forest

Dworshak Reservoir is popular in spring and summer for boating. With the lake at full pool around July 4, most of the campgrounds fill up, including this remote one on the east side of the reservoir about halfway between Orofino and Dent Bridge. Once you depart the paved Elk River Backcountry Byway, a long gravel drive leads to the 96-acre campground, dropping from the ranchland to the reservoir on a narrow, curvy road in its last miles. Use second or first gear for the final very steep descent to avoid the burning brake smell. Via water, the campground sits about seven miles from Big

Eddy marina. The primitive campground has a single-lane boat ramp with a dock in a sheltered bay. The reservoir attracts boaters for sightseeing, swimming, waterskiing, and fishing. The campground's bay offers sheltered paddling.

The quiet campground tucks under a shady canopy of trees and the steep wall of the reservoir's gorge. Sunlight finds the area late in the day. Most of the sites are close together in the open loop under the trees for protection from lake winds, but three campsites above the shoreline have great sunset views. Some of the campsites in the middle of the loop have large, flat tent spaces.

Campsites, facilities: The campground has 17 RV or tent campsites. RVs are limited to 22 feet. Facilities include picnic tables, fire pits with grills, and vault toilets (wheelchair-accessible). Pack out your garbage. No drinking water is available; bring your own, or treat lake water. Leashed pets are permitted.

Reservations, fees: Reservations are not accepted. Camping is free. Open May-November.

Directions: From Orofino, drive 11 miles north on Elk River Road via Wells Bench and Eureka Ridge Road, following the signs to Canyon Creek Campground. From the turnoff at Elk River Backcountry Byway, drive west through scenic Palouse ranchland for eight miles on a gravel road. At 3.9 miles, turn right and continue as the road plummets to the campground.

GPS Coordinates: N 46° 33.364' W 116° 14.005'

Contact: U.S. Army Corps of Engineers, P.O. Box 48, Ahsahka, ID 83520, 208/476-1255 or 800/321-3198 (recorded reservoir information), www.nww.usace.army.mil.

71 DWORSHAK MINI-CAMPS

Scenic rating: 7

on Dworshak Reservoir

At 1,610 feet, Dworshak Reservoir offers 17,090 acres of water for boat-in campers to explore. Primitive campsites rim the reservoir, with some on the main channel and others on more protected side bays. The reservoir is popular in early summer for boating, waterskiing, paddling, swimming, and fishing for bass and kokanee salmon before water levels drop low. The Big Eddy boat launch and marina accommodates boaters with a large paved trailer parking area, cement boat ramp, docks, and fish-cleaning station. The reservoir is usually at full pool through July 4, but call for specific reservoir levels. On your way to Big Eddy, stop at the Dworshak Dam Visitor Center (open daily in summer, weekdays in off-season) to get more details on the locations of the camps.

Dworshak Reservoir rims with 175 miles of shoreline. Sprinkled around the reservoir on both sides are primitive, designated campsites. Most have some trees for shade and wind protection. You can choose sites on the eastern shore with sunset views or sites on the western shore with sunrise views. Some of the locations have multiple campsites, so you might have neighbors; others offer solitude.

Campsites, facilities: The reservoir has 72 primitive tent-only sites. Facilities include fire rings with grills and some tent pads. Bring your own drinking water, or treat lake water. Follow leave no trace principles for human waste, or take a containment system. Leashed pets are permitted.

Reservations, fees: Reservations are not accepted. Camping is free. Open year-round, but inaccessible in snow.

Directions: From Orofino, drive north for four miles to Ahsahka. Continue north on Cavendish Road (Route 7) for 0.7 mile and turn right onto Viewpoint Road. Drive 2.5 miles to Big Eddy launch and marina.

GPS Coordinates: N 46° 31.641' W 116° 18.387'

Contact: U.S. Army Corps of Engineers, P.O. Box 48, Ahsahka, ID 83520, 208/476-1255 or 800/321-3198 (recorded reservoir information), www.nww.usace.army.mil.

The 54-mile-long Dworshak Reservoir offers boating, waterskiing, and fishing.

7 2 FREEMAN CREEK

Scenic rating: 8

in Dworshak State Park on Dworshak Reservoir

At 1,650 feet, Freeman Creek Campground sits in Dworshak State Park on the west side of Dworshak Reservoir. The reservoir is popular in early summer for boating, waterskiing, paddling, and fishing for bass and kokanee salmon before water levels drop low. The campground accommodates boaters with a large paved trailer parking area, cement boat ramp, docks, and fish-cleaning station. Canoes and kayaks are available for rent. The park offers plenty of beach area for swimming. The reservoir is usually at full pool through July 4. Hiking and mountain biking trails tour the park.

Looping with paved interior roads and paved parking pads (34 pull-throughs), the campground sits on a sunny, grassy west-facing hillside overlooking the reservoir. The tent camping loops enjoy close proximity to the water, while serviced campsites sit up on the hillside. Trails connect with the boat launch and beach.

Campsites, facilities: The campground has 25 tent-only sites, 36 RV or tent campsites, 46 RV hookup sites, and a large group campsite. RVs are limited to 35 feet. Hookups include water and electricity up to 50 amps. Facilities include picnic tables, fire rings with grills, flush toilets, showers, disposal station, tent pads, playground, amphitheater, volleyball, horseshoes, garbage service, wireless Internet, boat launch, and firewood for sale. Leashed pets are permitted. Wheelchair-accessible facilities include toilets and two campsites.

Reservations, fees: Reservations are accepted (888/922-6743 or online). Campsites cost $19 for tents or dry camping and $27 for hookups. Entry to the park costs $5 per vehicle. Idaho residents can purchase state park passports for $10 for unlimited entry and camping discounts. Cash, check, or credit card. Open year-round, but inaccessible in snow.

Directions: From Orofino, drive north for four miles to Ahsahka. Continue northwest on the Cavendish Road (Old Hwy. 7) for 11 miles. Turn right on Freeman Creek Road for 10 miles to the Freeman Creek unit of the park. GPS Coordinates: N 46° 34.484' W 116° 16.793'

Contact: Dworshak State Park, 9934 Freeman Creek, Lenore, ID 83541, 208/476-5994 or 800/321-3198 (recorded reservoir information), http://parksandrecreation.idaho.gov.

73 AQUARIUS CREEK

Scenic rating: 8

on the North Fork of the Clearwater River in Clearwater National Forest

BEST (

At 1,700 feet, the remote Aquarius Creek Campground sits south of the 30,000-acre Mallard-Larkins Pioneer Area, a proposed wilderness area. The area skyrockets 5,000 feet off the valley floor into high alpine cliffs, glacial cirques, and 21 lakes. The six-mile Smith Ridge Trail (#240), which climbs Larkin Peak, departs about 14 miles from the campground. From the campground, a multiuse trail runs downriver. Aquarius Creek is the only North Fork of the Clearwater River campground accessed via pavement, which ends right after the campground. Several good swimming holes sit just east of the campground. Anglers enjoy fly-fishing the river for wild trout. Early in summer, the river runs with big Class III-V whitewater for rafters and kayakers, but by August floaters can tube on the river above Aquarius. The campground is the last take out on the river, as the road goes no farther downstream. Hunters use the campground in fall for big game hunting.

Aquarius sits on the north side of the river adjacent to the bridge. All of the campsites line up along the river; those at the back of the campground have more shade from the thicker cedars and alders. Sites 1-5 garner more sunshine with sites 2 and 3 having large flat areas for tents. From their location at the end, surrounded by patches of thimbleberry, elderberry, and ferns, sites 7-9 feature more privacy.

Campsites, facilities: The campground has nine RV or tent campsites, plus two group campsites at adjacent Purple Beach. RVs are limited to 21 feet. Facilities include picnic tables, fire rings with grills, drinking water, and vault toilets (wheelchair-accessible). Pack out your trash. Leashed pets are permitted.

Reservations, fees: Reservations are not accepted. Campsites cost $7. Cash or check. Open May-October.

Directions: From Headquarters, drive north on Forest Road 247 for 25 miles to reach the North Fork of the Clearwater River. Cross the bridge over the river and turn into the campground entrance on the right. You can also reach the campground from Pierce by driving 29 miles on Forest Road 250 to Bungalow junction and then turning west onto Forest Road 247 for 27 miles.

GPS Coordinates: N 46° 50.463' W 115° 37.128'

Contact: Clearwater National Forest, North Fork Ranger District, 12730 Hwy. 12, Orofino, ID 83544, 208/476-4541, www.fs.usda.gov/nezperceclearwater.

74 NORTH FORK OF THE CLEARWATER RIVER PRIMITIVE

Scenic rating: 8

on the North Fork of the Clearwater River in Clearwater National Forest

BEST (

The North Fork of the Clearwater River runs for 45 miles, paralleled by narrow dirt forest roads. Primitive dispersed camps line the entire river corridor, popular for fishing, mountain biking, hiking, rafting, kayaking, canoeing, and float tubing. These afford free places to camp in the utmost solitude. Three primitive campgrounds—Riviara, Bungalow, and Death Creek—also offer multiple sites and toilets.

Look for the undeveloped sites where you see unmarked spur roads turn right or left off the road. Some sit on shaded bluffs overlooking the river; others access sunny, rocky, river bar campsites. Do not drive blindly on the spurs; walk them first to be sure you can turn around or back out. Locate Riviara (it's signed) under alders and cedars along a sunny rocky river bar between Aquarius Creek and Washington Creek. Find the unsigned grassy and partially shaded Bungalow campsites on both sides of Orogrande Creek on the south side of the bridge over the North Fork at the junction of Forest Roads 247 and 250. Locate the unsigned, heavily shaded Death Creek camp north of the road and river between Weitas Creek and Noe Creek.

Campsites, facilities: The corridor contains around 30 primitive dispersed campsites, plus three primitive campgrounds with flat spaces for tents: Riviara (three sites), Bungalow (four sites), and Death Creek (six sites). Some of the campsites can fit RVs up to 25 feet. All of the campsites have rock fire rings; use them rather than making new ones. The three primitive campgrounds also have vault or pit toilets. No drinking water is available. Bring your own, or treat river water. Pack out your trash. Leashed pets are permitted.

Reservations, fees: Reservations are not accepted. Camping is free. Open May-November.

Directions: From Headquarters, drive north on Forest Road 247 for 25 miles to reach the North Fork of the Clearwater River. Cross the river on the bridge and turn right. You can also reach the river from Pierce, by driving 29 miles on Forest Road 250 to Bungalow junction and then turning west onto Forest Road 247 or east onto Forest Road 250.

GPS Coordinates: N 46° 37.854' W 115° 30.486' (Bungalow)

Contact: Clearwater National Forest, North Fork Ranger District, 12730 Hwy. 12, Orofino, ID 83544, 208/476-4541, www.fs.usda.gov/nezperceclearwater.

75 WASHINGTON CREEK

Scenic rating: 8

on the North Fork of the Clearwater River in Clearwater National Forest

BEST (

Along the North Fork of the Clearwater River, Washington Creek sits at 2,100 feet on the opposite side of the river from the dusty road. The Wild and Scenic River runs with big Class III-V rafting and kayaking whitewater in June, but drops low enough for float tubes by August. Deep water pools above the entrance bridge and runs shallower past the campground with big rocky bars. The river provides top-notch trout fishing. The Washington Ridge Trail (#600) departing from the campground reaches Hornby Creek Road in three miles, but goes farther to Elk Mountain.

Washington Creek, the largest of the North Fork's campgrounds, tucks its shaded campsites under tall cedars and alders. In early summer, wild roses and syringa—Idaho's state flower—bloom along the river. Sites 2-8 overlook the river across the campground road. Sites 9, 11, and 13 have their own waterfront. The group campsite sits on an open grassy area with plenty of flat space for tents. The campsites at the back of the campground tuck under heavier shade.

Campsites, facilities: The campground has 23 RV or tent campsites plus one small group campsite. RVs are limited to 60 feet. Facilities include picnic tables, fire rings with grills, drinking water, vault toilets, campground hosts, and a horseshoe pit. Pack out your trash. Leashed pets are permitted.

Reservations, fees: Reservations are not accepted. Campsites cost $7. The small group campsite costs $15. Cash or check. Open May-September.

Directions: From Pierce, drive 29 miles up the half-paved, half-gravel, narrow, curvy French Mountain Road, also known as Forest Road 250, to Bungalow junction. Cross the North Fork of the Clearwater River on the bridge and turn left. Drive seven miles west on the narrow, single-lane washboard and potholed gravel road. Be prepared to back up into turnouts for passing vehicles. At the campground sign, cross the North Fork on the single-lane bridge to enter the campground. You can also arrive via Headquarters by driving 25 miles northeast on Forest Road 247, crossing the bridge at Aquarius, and then continuing east and south for 20 miles.

GPS Coordinates: N 46° 42.111' W 115° 33.380'

Contact: Clearwater National Forest, North Fork Ranger District, 12730 Hwy. 12, Orofino, ID 83544, 208/476-4541, www.fs.usda. gov/nezperceclearwater.

76 WEITAS CREEK

Scenic rating: 7

on the North Fork of the Clearwater River in Clearwater National Forest

Weitas Creek Campground sits at 2,350 feet on the confluence of the North Fork of the Clearwater River and Weitas Creek. After the June whitewater rafting and kayaking season abates, the North Fork runs with shallow riffles here around small grassy islands. You can fish both waterways, plus float both on rafts, kayaks, canoes, or float tubes. A multiuse trailhead departs from the back of the campground for Hemlock Butte. The road south from the campground connects to the Lolo Motorway, the historic trail of the Nez Perce and the Lewis and Clark expedition. Note: In 2011, the Forest Service closed the access bridge to the campground because of safety concerns, leaving the campground only accessible from the Lolo Motorway or by rafts. As of 2013, no plans for repairs have been announced. Check with the Forest Service for current status.

The quiet campground sits in tall grass and lady ferns under large cedar trees that admit filtered sunlight. Ox-eye daisies and self-heal flowers bloom in early July. Three of the sites sit on Weitas Creek, but those along the North Fork of the Clearwater River have larger flat spaces for tents. After driving across the bridge, find one private campsite to the left and five of the sites to the right.

Campsites, facilities: The campground has six RV or tent campsites. RVs are limited to 18 feet. Facilities include picnic tables, fire rings with grills, and a pit toilet, but no drinking water. Bring your own water; or treat river water. Pack out your trash. Leashed pets are permitted. Another six primitive campsites sit on the north side of the bridge.

Reservations, fees: Reservations are not accepted. Camping is free. Open late May-September.

Directions: From Pierce, drive 29 miles up the half-paved, half-gravel, narrow, curvy French Mountain Road (Forest Road 250) to Bungalow junction. Cross the North Fork of the Clearwater River on the bridge and turn right. Drive five miles east on the narrow, single-lane washboard and potholed gravel road. Be prepared to back up into turnouts for passing vehicles. At the campground sign, cross the North Fork on the single-lane, rusty bridge to enter the campground.

GPS Coordinates: N 46° 38.161' W 115° 25.918'

Contact: Clearwater National Forest, North Fork Ranger District, 12730 Hwy. 12, Orofino, ID 83544, 208/476-4541, www.fs.usda. gov/nezperceclearwater.

77 NOE CREEK

Scenic rating: 7

on the North Fork of the Clearwater River in Clearwater National Forest

Located at 2,500 feet along the North Fork of the Clearwater River, Noe Creek is a campground that grants solitude and quiet, guaranteed by its long, bumpy, dusty access. The

North Fork of the Clearwater River contains westslope cutthroat, bull, brook, and rainbow trout, along with kokanee salmon. After the spring whitewater rafting and kayaking season abates, the river is gentle enough for beginner floaters—rafts, kayaks, canoes, or float tubes. Departing up Mush Creek five miles from the campground, the trail to Pot Mountain Ridge (#144) climbs 1,000 feet for views of the drainage.

A gravel road drops through the campground, with a small turnaround loop at the end. All of the campsites enjoy the sound of the river and overlook the water. Site 6 has the best views. Those tucked deep under the shade-giving firs and larch have short trails through the lady ferns and thimbleberry to reach the beach. The road is visible from most of the sites, but the sites are spaced out for privacy.

Campsites, facilities: The campground has six RV or tent campsites, including one small group site for four vehicles. RVs are limited to 22 feet. Facilities include picnic tables, fire rings with grills, hand pump for drinking water, and vault toilets (wheelchair-accessible). Pack out your trash. Leashed pets are permitted.

Reservations, fees: Reservations are not accepted. Campsites cost $7. The small group campsite costs $15. Cash or check. Open late May–September.

Directions: From Pierce, drive 29 miles up the half-paved, half-gravel, narrow, curvy French Mountain Road (Forest Road 250) to Bungalow junction. Cross the North Fork of the Clearwater River on the bridge and turn right. Drive 10.3 miles east on the narrow, single-lane washboard and potholed gravel road. Be prepared to back up into turnouts for passing vehicles. The campground sits on the south side of the road on the river.

GPS Coordinates: N 46° 41.091' W 115° 21.985'

Contact: Clearwater National Forest, North Fork Ranger District, 12730 Hwy. 12, Orofino, ID 83544, 208/476-4541, www.fs.usda.gov/nezperceclearwater.

78 KELLY FORKS

Scenic rating: 8

on the North Fork of the Clearwater River in Clearwater National Forest

At 2,700 feet, Kelly Forks sits at the confluence of Kelly Creek with the North Fork of the Clearwater River and adjacent to Kelly Forks Ranger Station. Only those who really want to see the area suffer the miles of bumpy dirt road to reach Kelly Forks, but they are rewarded with beauty, solitude, and quiet. Despite its name, Kelly Creek is really a blue-ribbon trout river, loaded with 12- to 15-inch westslope cutthroat trout, plus a few mountain whitefish and rainbow trout. Fishing is equally good on the North Fork of the Clearwater River. Once the big spring whitewater rafting and kayaking season abates, the river is gentle enough for canoes and float tubes. Hiking and mountain-biking trails are available up the Kelly Creek and North Fork drainages; Flat Mountain is one of the more scenic destinations.

The Kelly Forks Campground sits on Kelly Creek rather than on the North Fork of the Clearwater River. Sites 6, 7, 8, 10, 14, and 15 have creek frontage, with trails to the shore. Alive with the sounds of songbirds into July, a mixed forest of firs and alders provides shade for most of the campsites, while a healthy dose of thick brush adds privacy. You'll hear only the creek and river. The narrow campground road and dirt parking pads are tight for some RVs.

Campsites, facilities: The campground has 14 RV or tent campsites, plus one small group site for four vehicles. RVs are limited to 40 feet. Facilities include picnic tables, fire rings with grills, drinking water, vault toilets, campground hosts, and interpretive programs. Pack out your trash. Leashed pets are permitted.

Reservations, fees: Reservations are not accepted. Campsites cost $7. The group campsite costs $15. Cash or check. Open late May–early September.

Directions: From Pierce, drive 29 miles up the half-paved, half-gravel, narrow, curvy French Mountain Road (Forest Road 250) to Bungalow junction. Cross the North Fork of the Clearwater River on the bridge and turn right. Drive 18 miles east on the narrow, single-lane washboard and potholed gravel road. Be prepared to back up into turnouts for passing vehicles. The campground sits on the right-hand side of the road 0.25 mile past the Kelly Forks Ranger Station.

GPS Coordinates: N 46° 43.017' W 115° 15.284'

Contact: Clearwater National Forest, North Fork Ranger District, 12730 Hwy. 12, Orofino, ID 83544, 208/476-4541, www.fs.usda.gov/nezperceclearwater.

79 HIDDEN CREEK

Scenic rating: 7
on the North Fork of the Clearwater River in Clearwater National Forest

Along the North Fork of the Clearwater River at 3,350 feet, Hidden Creek Campground is worth the scenic drive through Black Canyon. Steep, forested mountains rise more than 3,000 feet from the river. Putting down miles of dirt road exploration, you can continue on the route over the Bitterroot Mountains into Superior, Montana, on I-90. Anglers relish the campground and setting for fly-fishing in the North Fork River, which holds a reputation for abundant wild trout. Hunters use the campground in fall as a base for big game hunting.

Quiet Hidden Creek Campground tucks into old-growth cedar trees, giving campsites shade and a sacred feel. You'll hear the river as you go to sleep at night and wake to the sound of birds. Several campsites have river frontage, a few more sites garner snippets of territorial views.

Campsites, facilities: The campground has 13 RV or tent campsites and one group campsite. RVs are limited to 40 feet. Facilities include picnic tables, fire rings with grills, vault toilets, and a hand pump for drinking water. Pack out your trash. Leashed pets are permitted.

Reservations, fees: Reservations are not accepted. Camping costs $7. Open May-October, although water is only available mid-June-mid-September.

Directions: From Pierce, drive 29 miles up the half-paved, half-gravel, narrow, curvy French Mountain Road (Forest Road 250) to Bungalow junction. Cross the North Fork of the Clearwater River on the bridge and turn right. Drive 18 miles east on the narrow, single-lane washboard and potholed gravel road. Be prepared to back up into turnouts for passing vehicles. At Kelly Forks, turn north onto Black Canyon Road (a continuation of FR 250) for 11 miles to the campground entrance on the right. Because of Black Canyon Road's single-lane with turnouts, the Forest Service discourages trailers. The campground can also be accessed from Superior on I-90 in Montana. GPS Coordinates: N 46° 49.905' W 115° 10.721'

Contact: Clearwater National Forest, North Fork Ranger District, 12730 Hwy. 12, Orofino, ID 83544, 208/476-4541, www.fs.usda.gov/nezperceclearwater.

80 CEDAR CREEK

Scenic rating: 7
on the North Fork of the Clearwater River in Clearwater National Forest

Along the North Fork of the Clearwater River at 3,600 feet, the remote Cedar Creek Campground is used only by those who relish long backcountry rough drives to reach destinations of solitude. The campground sits at the confluence of Long Creek and the North Fork, with fly-fishing for wild trout in both waterways. The Idaho Centennial Trail, a backcountry primitive road and trail route, passes the campground. The 900-mile trail makes a huge loop along the crest of the Bitterroot Mountains in the Clearwater National Forest. Hunters use the campground in fall for big game hunting. Forest Road 250 continues northeast to cross the Bitterroot Mountains into Superior, Montana.

Cedar Creek Campground sits along the river with campsites enjoying the sound of burbling water. Meadows lend airiness and territorial views of the surrounding forested mountains. Clumps of firs lend protection, shade, and privacy.

Campsites, facilities: The campground has five RV or tent campsites. RVs are limited to 25 feet. Facilities include picnic tables, fire rings with grills, and vault toilets. No drinking water is available; bring your own, or treat river water. Pack out your trash. Leashed pets are permitted.

Reservations, fees: Reservations are not accepted. Camping is free. Open May-October.

Directions: From Pierce, drive 29 miles up the half-paved, half-gravel, narrow, curvy French Mountain Road (Forest Road 250) to Bungalow junction. Cross the North Fork of the Clearwater River on the bridge and turn right. Drive 18 miles east on the narrow, single-lane washboard and potholed gravel road. Be prepared to back up into turnouts for passing vehicles. At Kelly Forks, turn north onto Black Canyon Road (Forest Road 250) for 18 miles. Around mile 17, turn left after the first two bridges and cross the bridge over the North Fork to reach the campground. Because of Black Canyon Road's single-lane with turnouts, the Forest Service discourages trailers. The campground can also be accessed from Superior on I-90 in Montana.

GPS Coordinates: N 46° 52.354' W 115° 4.612'

Contact: Clearwater National Forest, North Fork Ranger District, 12730 Hwy. 12, Orofino, ID 83544, 208/476-4541, www.fs.usda.gov/nezperceclearwater.

EASTERN CENTRAL IDAHO

© STACEY BENGTSON

Eastern-central Idaho attracts campers for its rugged scenery and wild big rivers, much of which are accessible only by hiking, horseback riding, rafting, and kayaking. Vehicle-accessible campgrounds line rivers to the north and south of the roadless regions. The Lochsa and Selway Rivers border the north, while the Salmon River rims the south. All three provide corridors loaded with national forest campgrounds that offer hiking, mountain biking, fishing, rafting, kayaking, canoeing, and floating. Two wilderness areas make up the vast mountainous expanse between the Lochsa and Salmon Rivers: the Selway-Bitterroot Wilderness and the Frank Church-River of No Return Wilderness. The Sawtooth National Recreation Area extends camping south over Galena Pass to Sun Valley, where you can mountain bike or walk portions of the 18-mile Harriman Trail from campgrounds flanking the Big Wood River.

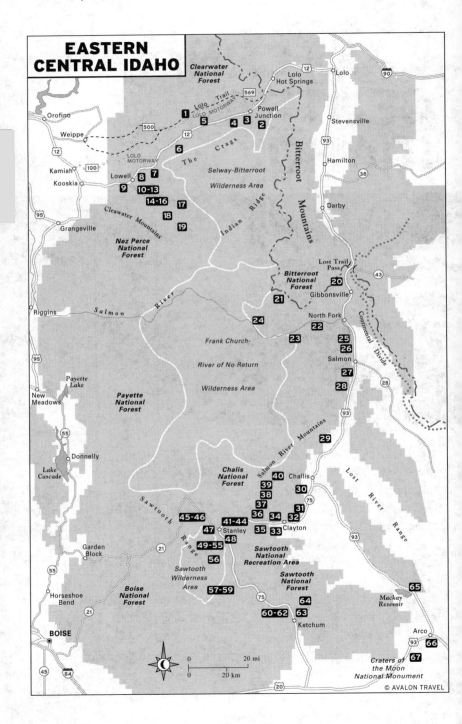

EASTERN CENTRAL IDAHO

© AVALON TRAVEL

1 LOLO MOTORWAY AND TRAIL

🚶 🚲 🛶 🐕 🚐 ⛺

Scenic rating: 9

in the Bitterroot Mountains in Clearwater National Forest

A primitive ridgetop road topping out at 6,800 feet, the 73-mile Lolo Motorway follows the Lolo Trail National Historic Landmark paralleling Highway 12 and the Lochsa River. Western tribes used the mountainous trail to reach buffalo hunting grounds; eastern tribes used it to reach salmon-fishing streams. Lewis and Clark used the trail, and in 1877, the Nez Perce followed it to flee General Howard's army. When the Civilian Conservation Corps built the road on the route in the 1930s, the Lolo Motorway (Forest Road 500) became a winding dirt thoroughfare through lodgepole and ponderosa forests alternating with green meadows and interpretive sites. Most of the single-lane road is rocky and steep. It is good for mountain bikes, and with only a few pullover spots, the Forest Service discourages trailers. You'll need a sturdy high-clearance vehicle, good tires, a full-sized spare, and the wits to back up a long distance when you meet an oncoming car. Protruding rocks, trees, and branches can scrape large vehicles. Watch for large potholes, downed trees, rocks, and early snowstorms. Check current road conditions before you depart, and gas up the car. You'll find no services.

Plan for 2-5 days to drive the trail. No developed campgrounds exist, but you'll find plenty of primitive campsites. Use previous fire rings to avoid additional scars on the landscape.

Campsites, facilities: None of the primitive campsites have any facilities besides a rock fire ring. RVs are limited to 23 feet. Pack out your trash, and take drinking water along. Treat lake or creek water. A scant handful of toilets can be found, but most campers will need to follow Leave No Trace ethics for human waste. Leashed pets are permitted.

Reservations, fees: No reservations are accepted. Camping is free. The motorway generally is snow free by July 4 and open until the snows bury it.

Directions: From the Powell area, access the Lolo Motorway via Parachute Hill Road (Forest Road 569). From the Wilderness Gateway area, connect via Saddle Camp Road (Forest Road 107). From the Kamiah area, locate the access to Forest Road 100 at the junction of Highway 12 and the Kamiah bridge over the Clearwater River.

GPS Coordinates at Powell Junction: N 46° 34.746' W 114° 43.121'

Contact: Clearwater National Forest, Powell Ranger District, 192 Powell Road, Lolo, MT 59847, 208/942-3113, www.fs.usda.gov/nezperceclearwater.

2 WHITE SANDS

🚶 🏊 🛶 🎣 🚐 🛥 🐕 ♿ 🚐 ⛺

Scenic rating: 7

on the Lochsa River in Clearwater National Forest

At 3,500 feet in the Bitterroot Mountains, White Sands sits on a forested sandy bar adjacent to the confluence of the Crooked Fork and the Wild and Scenic Lochsa River. The Lochsa is popular in spring for rafting and kayaking; this stretch of river has Class II and III rapids, and you can put in to the river on the bridge over the Lochsa. Crooked Fork also has a short, highly technical Class III-V two-mile section for rafting and kayaking from Hopeful Creek to Brushy Creek. Fishing is catch-and-release only for trout in the Lochsa, but on Crooked Fork, you can keep two trout over 14 inches per day. Fishing is also permitted in the small pond between the campground and the bridges. The campground also marks the beginning of the Elk Summit road, a bumpy, dusty scenic 20-mile

RIVER CAMPING AND RECREATION

National Wild and Scenic Rivers bounce between raging white water and streams running clear enough to see trout swim. For river camping, pack the fishing tackle, rafts, canoes, and kayaks.

Forming the northern boundary of the wilderness, the 70-mile-long **Lochsa River** churns in its upper stretches from the Bitterroot Mountains with huge sustained rapids that have the reputation of flipping boats. In addition to its Class IV white water, the river also runs with riffles that give it its blue-ribbon trout stream status. Highway 12 offers easy access to most of the river, with campgrounds every few miles along its length. The corridor also resounds with history, as it served as the route of Lewis and Clark heading west and the Nez Perce traveling to and from buffalo lands. Their routes followed the ridges above the Lochsa, now known as the Lolo Motorway—a 73-mile single-lane dirt road with primitive camping.

Converging with the Lochsa River, the **Selway River** rips through the heart of the Selway-Bitterroot Wilderness, flowing 60 miles. The river's blue-ribbon trout fishing comes from its crystalline waters filled with westslope cutthroat trout. While the upper river requires a flight or horse-packing trip into the wilderness for rafting the Class IV white-water rapids, the more sedate lower Selway parallels a rough dirt road, giving campers easy access for floating or fishing. Vehicle-accessible campgrounds line the

drive. Elk Summit has moose and views of the Selway-Bitterroot Wilderness. The 1.5-mile Walton Lakes Trail (#79) departs from Forest Road 362 to drop into a glacier-carved cirque. During heavy fire seasons, Forest Service crews use the campground in late summer, closing it to the public.

A dusty gravel road accesses the campground, which has one potholed dirt loop with short dirt parking pads. All of the sites line up adjacent to the Lochsa River, with short trails to the shore. Sites 1 and 2 have prime river views. Most of the sites, except for 6 and 7, are spread out for privacy under a mixed forest canopy. Some campsites have been opened up to more sun after removal of bark beetle-killed trees.

Campsites, facilities: The campground has seven RV or tent campsites. The campsites fit small RVs only. Facilities include picnic tables, fire rings with grills, vault toilets (wheelchair-accessible), hand pump for drinking water, and garbage service. Leashed pets are permitted.

Reservations, fees: Reservations are not accepted. Campsites cost $8. An extra vehicle costs $2. Cash or check. Open mid-May-September.

Directions: From Kooskia, drive 89 miles east on Highway 12, or from Lolo Pass, drive 11 miles west. Locate the road heading to Elk Summit at milepost 163.2 on the south side of the highway. Drive one mile downhill on the washboarded, gravel Forest Road 111. The entrance to the campground sits on the right just before bridge.

GPS Coordinates: N 46° 30.470' W 114° 41.198'

Contact: Clearwater National Forest, Powell Ranger District, 192 Powell Road, Lolo, MT 59847, 208/942-3113, www.fs.usda.gov/nezperceclearwater.

3 POWELL

Scenic rating: 8

on the Lochsa River in Clearwater National Forest

Powell Campground, at 3,400 feet in the Bitterroot Mountains, sits on a side spur in between Lochsa Lodge and the Powell Ranger Station. You can get gas, fishing gear, and route up to the wilderness boundary east of Selway Falls.

To the south, the 425-mile **Main Salmon River** curves northward from the Sawtooth Mountains and turns west, cutting through the Frank Church-River of No Return Wilderness en route to the Snake River. Portions are calm enough for canoes; other stretches cut through steep-walled, narrow canyons with white-water drops. The Salmon River attracts anglers for its trout, steelhead, and chinook salmon. Many federal campgrounds line the river for fishing and floating access, and campgrounds increase in number in the canyon northeast of Stanley—a summer hub for rafting, fishing, horseback riding, and mountain biking.

The **Salmon River,** which originates in the 217,088-acre Sawtooth Wilderness, flows through a valley of ranches at the base of the ragged Sawtooth Mountains, which top 10,000 feet. Small streams tumble from the glacier-carved peaks, forming lakes that attract campers for stunning scenery, boating, and swimming on sandy beaches. Kayakers and canoeists ply the waters, along with water-skiers and anglers. The Sawtooth National Recreation Area includes trails for hikers and horseback riders that head to wilderness destinations of alpine lakes. Mountain climbers ascend to jagged summits, while rock climbers aim for the Sawtooths' granite faces. Mountain bikers tour reams of national forest trails surrounding the Sawtooth Mountains.

minimal groceries at Lochsa Lodge, and the ranger station has maps and handouts on hiking trails. Powell is popular in spring for rafting and kayaking on the Wild and Scenic Lochsa; this stretch of river has Class II and III rapids, but the campground has no river put-in. The river here is catch-and-release only for trout. Powell is also a jump-off point for driving the primitive Lolo Motorway, the historic Nez Perce and Lewis and Clark Trail, via the Parachute Hill Road. The Lewis and Clark Trail #25 goes through the campground, and the Powell Complex Trail (1.5 mile) tours the forested area.

The campground tucks under large firs and pines in two loops. Loop A houses the sites with electrical hookups and has campsites crammed in close to each other. Some of the sites are more open, and half have river frontage. Loop B campsites have more privacy and two campsites have river frontage. The campground road is paved, as are the parking pads, most of which are back-ins.

Campsites, facilities: The campground has 33 RV campsites with electrical hookups and 10 RV or tent campsites without hookups.

RVs are limited to 40 feet at most sites, but two 200-foot pull-throughs are available. Facilities include picnic tables, fire rings with grills, flush and vault toilets (wheelchair-accessible), drinking water, campground hosts, garbage service, and an amphitheater with interpretive programs. Leashed pets are permitted.

Reservations, fees: Reservations are accepted (877/444-6777, www.recreation.gov). Campsites cost $8. Campsites with hookups cost $15. An extra vehicle costs $2. Cash or check. Open mid-May-early November.

Directions: From Kooskia drive 88 miles east on Highway 12, or from Lolo Pass drive 12 miles west. Locate the road to Powell at milepost 161.8 on the south side of the highway. Drive 0.2 mile past the entrance to Lochsa Lodge and continue toward the ranger station, turning right at the campground sign. GPS Coordinates: N 46° 30.701' W 114° 43.247'

Contact: Clearwater National Forest, Powell Ranger District, 192 Powell Road, Lolo, MT 59847, 208/942-3113, www.fs.usda.gov/nezperceclearwater.

4 WENDOVER AND WHITEHOUSE

🥾 🚴 🏊 🛶 🏖 🛶 〰️ 🐕 ♿ 🚐 ⛺

Scenic rating: 8

on the Lochsa River in Clearwater National Forest

BEST (

Located at 3,300 feet in the Bitterroot Mountains, Wendover and Whitehouse Campgrounds sit adjacent to each other on the Lochsa River. Lewis and Clark stopped at the sites on September 15, 1805. The campgrounds are popular for rafting and kayaking with this stretch of river having Class II and III rapids. But neither campground has river launches. The river here is catch-and-release only for wild trout. Six miles west, the one-mile Warm Springs Trail crosses the Lochsa to Jerry Johnson Hot Springs. Two of the natural pools can be used year-round, but the waterfall pools are submerged under spring's high runoff until late summer. The rock-ringed pools are open 6am-8pm. The campground is three miles west of Lochsa Lodge, where gas, minimal groceries, and a restaurant are available. About 12 miles west, the 1.2-mile Colgate Licks National Recreation Trail tours a fire zone and natural wildlife mineral lick.

Both campgrounds spread out under a thick canopy of cedars, pines, and firs with a handful of campsites enjoying river frontage and private beaches. For the other campsites, trails lead to the beach for fishing or enjoying the water. Wild roses, corn lilies, and bear grass bloom in July, and a jungle of brushy willows add privacy to the campsites. The campground roads and back-in parking pads are paved with loop turnarounds at the terminus aiding trailers.

Campsites, facilities: Wendover has 26 RV or tent campsites, and Whitehouse has 13 RV or tent campsites. RVs are limited to 45 feet. Facilities include picnic tables, fire rings with grills, vault toilets (wheelchair-accessible), hand pumps for drinking water, garbage service, and campground hosts. Leashed pets are permitted.

Reservations, fees: No reservations are accepted. Campsites cost $8. An extra vehicle costs $2. Cash or check. Open late May-September.

Directions: From Kooskia, drive 84 miles east on Highway 12 or from Lolo Pass, drive 16 miles west. Locate the turnoff into Wendover at milepost 158.1 and Whitehouse at 158.3 on the south side of the highway.

Wendover GPS Coordinates: N 46° 30.624' W 114° 47.001'

Whitehouse GPS Coordinates: N 46° 30.488' W 114° 46.714'

Contact: Clearwater National Forest, Powell Ranger District, 192 Powell Road, Lolo, MT 59847, 208/942-3113, www.fs.usda.gov/nezperceclearwater.

5 JERRY JOHNSON

🥾 🏊 🛶 🚐 🛶 〰️ 🐕 ♿ 🚐 ⛺

Scenic rating: 8

in the Bitterroot Mountains in Clearwater National Forest

At 3,100 feet, Jerry Johnson was popular for its nearby hot springs. Call the Forest Service to check on status; a dwindling budget has kept the campground closed in recent years. Three natural rock-ringed soaking pools sit across the Lochsa River from the campground along Warm Springs Creek, about a 20-minute hike from the campground. Two of the pools can be used year-round (6am-8pm), but the waterfall pools submerge under early summer runoff. The campground used to be popular for spring rafting and kayaking on the Lochsa River's Class II and III rapids and summer for catch-and-release trout fishing. Two miles west, the 1.2-mile Colgate Licks National Recreation Trail tours a fire zone and natural wildlife mineral lick.

The campground lost summer popularity after the Forest Service removed its diseased trees, leaving an open, sunny, hot hillside overlooking the highway. As of 2013, the Forest Service is considering permanent closure.

Campsites, facilities: The campground has 19 RV or tent campsites. Large RVs are okay. Facilities include picnic tables, fire rings with grills, vault toilets (wheelchair-accessible), and drinking water. Pack out your trash. Leashed pets are permitted.

Reservations, fees: No reservations are accepted. Campsites cost $8. An extra vehicle costs $2. Cash or check. Call to check on seasonal status.

Directions: From Kooskia, drive 76 miles east on Highway 12. Locate the turnoff into the campground at milepost 150.5 on the north side of the road. The campground sits about 24 miles west of Lolo Pass.

GPS Coordinates: N 46° 28.548' W 114° 54.319'

Contact: Clearwater National Forest, Powell Ranger District, 192 Powell Road, Lolo, MT 59847, 208/942-3113, www.fs.usda.gov/nezperceclearwater.

Campgrounds along the Lochsa River attract river rafters for the big water.

© STACEY BENGTSON

6 WILDERNESS GATEWAY

Scenic rating: 9

on the Lochsa River in Clearwater National Forest

BEST (

Located at 2,100 feet in the Bitterroot Mountains, Wilderness Gateway is so named for its access south into the Selway-Bitterroot Wilderness. As the largest campground in the Lochsa drainage, it sits away from the highway on the river's south bank where water churns white through a boulder garden. Rafting or kayaking here requires technical expertise, and boats can be launched from the campground. In late May, onlookers sit in lawn chairs above Lochsa Falls just to watch the carnage of rafts flipping in the Class IV rapid. Adjacent to the campground, a trail outfitter offers horseback rides. Several trails depart from the campground: The Downriver Trail (0.5 mile) leads to an overlook of the river, a birding trail (one mile) loops around the campground, and the Lochsa

Peak Trail (15 miles) heads into the wilderness. Fishing for trout upstream of the bridge over the Lochsa is catch-and-release only, but below the bridge and in Boulder Creek, you can keep trout. About one mile from the campground is the Lochsa Historical Ranger Station.

With four paved loops, the campground divides across both sides of Boulder Creek. Loop C has campsites right on the Lochsa River, with the remaining partly shaded campsites under a mixed forest of firs and pines flanked by thimbleberry bushes. Loop D, equipped with hitching rails, feeders, and a stock ramp, is only for campers with horses. The birding trail runs behind loops A and B.

Campsites, facilities: The campground has 85 RV or tent campsites and four tent-only sites. RVs are limited to 55 feet. Facilities include picnic tables, fire rings with grills, flush and vault toilets, drinking water, amphitheater with interpretive programs, campground hosts, disposal station, and garbage service. Leashed pets are permitted. Wheelchair-accessible toilets are available.

Reservations, fees: Reservations are accepted (877/444-6777, www.recreation.gov). Campsites cost $8. An extra vehicle costs $2. Cash or check. Open early May-late September.

Directions: From Kooskia, drive 48 miles east on Highway 12. Locate the bridge crossing the Lochsa at milepost 122.2 on the south side of the road. (The bridge is about 52 miles west of Lolo Pass.) After crossing the wide two-lane bridge, drive less than 0.1 mile to the campground.

GPS Coordinates: N 46° 20.531' W 115° 18.531'

Contact: Clearwater National Forest, Lochsa Ranger District, 502 Lowry Street, Kooskia, ID 83539, 208/926-4274, www.fs.usda.gov/nezperceclearwater.

7 KNIFE EDGE

Scenic rating: 8

on the Lochsa River in Clearwater National Forest

On the curvy, paved, two-lane Northwest Passage Scenic Byway, Knife Edge Campground is a river access site at 1,700 feet for those putting in or taking out from the Lochsa River. The rapids in this stretch of the river run Class III and IV, requiring technical skills to avoid rocks even at lower water levels. Right in front of the campground, the river flows deeper where the canyon narrows. Anglers can fish from the campground for trout, steelhead, and salmon. Built in the 1920s, the Lochsa River Historical Trail has its Split Creek Trailhead 2.5 miles east on the highway. It runs 16 miles east to the Sherman Creek Trailhead near the Lochsa Historical Ranger Station and offers views of the Lochsa Canyon. The path is also part of the Idaho Centennial Trail. Several other trailheads sit within two miles, too. Hunters use the campground in fall for big game hunting in the surrounding Bitterroot Mountains.

Squeezed in between the river and the highway, the campground has shaded sites under a canopy of cedars and firs. Two parking pads are small pull-throughs. Sites 3 and 5 have river frontage. As a river access site, the campground includes a place to launch rafts and kayaks, plus a trailer turnaround and parking space. Given its proximity to the highway, noise from long-haul trucks competes with that of the river at night.

Campsites, facilities: The campground has five RV or tent campsites. Small RVs are okay. Facilities include picnic tables, fire rings with grills, vault toilets (wheelchair-accessible), tent pads, and garbage service. No drinking water is available. Bring your own, or treat river water. Leashed pets are permitted.

Reservations, fees: No reservations are accepted. Camping is free. Open April-November.

Directions: From Kooskia, drive 34 miles east on Highway 12. Locate the campground on the south side of the highway at milepost 108.7. The campground sits about 66 miles west of Lolo Pass.

GPS Coordinates: N 46° 13.631' W 115° 28.471'

Contact: Clearwater National Forest, Lochsa Ranger District, 502 Lowry Street, Kooskia, ID 83539, 208/926-4274, www.fs.usda.gov/nezperceclearwater.

8 APGAR CREEK

Scenic rating: 8

on the Lochsa River in Clearwater National Forest

At 1,600 feet in the Bitterroot Mountains on the curvy paved two-lane Northwest Passage Scenic Byway, Apgar Creek sits on a rock and sand bar on the Lochsa River. The campground is across the road from the Apgar Creek Trailhead; the trail (#111) grunts up 2,800 feet in 4.3 miles for views of the Coolwater Ridge area. This section of the Lochsa River flattens out compared to its upper reaches, but Class II-IV rapids still require experience to navigate in rafts and kayaks. Anglers go after trout in the river's calmer pools, which double as swimming holes. Because of its location on the highway, the campground works for cyclists crossing Lolo Pass.

Pinched in between the river and the highway, the campground loops under western red cedars with minimal sword fern undergrowth, allowing you to see your neighbors. Sites 5-7 are more shaded than sites 1-4, which have river frontage with peek-a-boo views. Site 1 is a walk-in tent site with a private area along the river. A group fire pit surrounded by benches is available on an open patch of grass with views of the forested mountains and river. A trail accesses the river between campsites 4 and 5. Its proximity to the highway means noise seeps in at night from long-haul trucks.

Campsites, facilities: The campground has seven RV or tent campsites. The narrow dirt road and dirt back-in parking pads are suitable only for smaller RVs. Facilities include picnic tables, fire rings with grills, vault toilets (wheelchair-accessible), drinking water, and garbage service. Leashed pets are permitted.

Reservations, fees: No reservations are accepted. Campsites cost $8. An extra vehicle costs $2. Cash or check. Open Memorial Day weekend-early September.

Directions: From Kooskia, drive 30 miles east on Highway 12. Turn into the campground on the south side of the highway at milepost 104.3. The campground sits about 70 miles west of Lolo Pass.

GPS Coordinates: N 46° 12.847' W 115° 32.200'

Contact: Clearwater National Forest, Lochsa Ranger District, 502 Lowry Street, Kooskia, ID 83539, 208/926-4274, www.fs.usda.gov/nezperceclearwater.

9 WILD GOOSE

Scenic rating: 8

on the Middle Fork of the Clearwater River in Clearwater National Forest

BEST (

Located at 1,500 feet on the banks of the Middle Fork of the Clearwater River, Wild Goose Campground is popular for its sandy beaches and its ease of access en route to Lolo Pass. The campground sits within a few miles either direction of rafting companies that guide trips on the Selway and the Lochsa Rivers, both designated Wild and Scenic Rivers. The tamer Middle Fork of the Clearwater, also a designated national Wild and Scenic River, runs 22 miles with Class I and II water—gentle enough for canoes and float tubes. Thanks to the campground's close proximity to the confluence of the Selway and the Middle Fork, you can launch rafts, float tubes, and canoes from the Selway's lower stretches and float back to camp. A float downriver to Kooskia (pronounced KOOS-kee by the locals) is a 21-mile adventure. The river is also known for its 15-pound steelhead.

Squeezed between the highway and the river, the coveted campground lines up all but one of its campsites along the riverfront under large cedar trees. Two stairways lead to the sandy beaches along the swift-moving river. The proximity of the highway adds noise from long-haul trucks during the night. Site 6, on the turnaround loop, is geared for groups, with two double-long picnic tables and a huge fire ring with three benches. Most of the sites—accessed by the narrow campground road with short parking pads—have flat spots for tents.

Campsites, facilities: The campground has six RV or tent campsites. Most are only suitable for RVs under 30 feet, but leveling may be difficult in some sites. Facilities include picnic tables, fire rings with grills, vault toilets (wheelchair-accessible), drinking water, and garbage service. Leashed pets are permitted.

Reservations, fees: Reservations are not accepted. Campsites cost $8. An extra vehicle costs $2. Cash or check. Open Memorial Day weekend-early September.

Directions: From Kooskia, drive 21 miles east on Highway 12. Locate the campground on the south side of the highway at milepost 95.4. The campground sits about 79 miles west of Lolo Pass.

GPS Coordinates: N 46° 8.147' W 115° 37.525'

Contact: Clearwater National Forest, Lochsa Ranger District, 502 Lowry Street, Kooskia, ID 83539, 208/926-4274, www.fs.usda.gov/nezperceclearwater.

10 JOHNSON BAR

Scenic rating: 8

on the Selway River in Nez Perce National Forest

BEST (

Johnson Bar, at 1,515 feet, is the first in a long string of campgrounds running up the Selway River, a designated Wild and Scenic River. Its sandbar is popular for swimming, and the river is tamer here than at its upper end. May and June runoff makes for good kayaking and rafting. After water levels drop in July, the lower river works for canoeing, rafting, and float tubing. Even without a boat ramp, you can launch rafts, kayaks, and canoes easily from several locations in the campground. Extra parking areas for trailers are available. Catch-and-release anglers go after trout, chinook salmon, and steelhead in this outstanding fishery. The historical Fenn Ranger Station—open weekdays for visitor information—is 0.6 mile southwest of the campground. Across from the ranger station, Fenn Pond, with its boardwalk and wheelchair-accessible trail, is stocked annually with rainbow trout. The pond is great for teaching kids to fish.

The Selway Road is paved to the campground entrance, but the campground roads and parking pads are gravel. The campground is a combination of large, open, grassy fields and partially shaded sites flanked with mixed deciduous trees and cedars. Five sites have riverfront locations, but these are mostly open with little privacy. The group campsite sits in a large grassy field. A few treed sites are more private in their own loop. Be cautious about rattlesnakes.

Campsites, facilities: The campground has nine RV or tent campsites, plus a large group site. RVs are limited to 20 feet. Facilities include picnic tables, fire rings and grills, vault and portable toilets, drinking water, and garbage service. Leashed pets are permitted. Wheelchair-accessible facilities include a toilet and campsites.

Reservations, fees: Reservations are not accepted, except for the group site (877/444-6777, www.recreation.gov). If the group site is not reserved, it is available for anyone to use. Camping costs $6. An extra vehicle costs $2. Cash or check. Open mid-May-mid-September.

Directions: From Lowell on Highway 12, turn southeast onto the Selway Road (Forest Road 223). Drive to milepost 4. The campground entrance is on the right.

GPS Coordinates: N 46° 6.123' W 115° 33.430'

Contact: Nez Perce National Forest, Moose Creek Ranger District, 831 Selway Rd., Kooskia, ID 83539, 208/926-4258, www.fs.usda.gov/nezperceclearwater.

11 CCC CAMP

Scenic rating: 7

on the Selway River in Nez Perce National Forest

Located at 1,550 feet, the CCC Camp on the Selway Road works as a spillover campground for crowded holiday weekends. The easily accessed riverbank across the road from the campground has a large sandbar that increases

© STACEY BENGTSON

Fenn Pond has rainbow trout stocked for fishing.

in size as the river level drops during the summer. The bar is popular for day use for swimming, fishing, and floating with rafts, kayaks, canoes, and tubes. Fishing on the Selway is catch-and-release only. Adjacent to the campground, the six-mile-long CCC Trail (#734) for hikers and horses only, ascends 4,000 feet in elevation to the Coolwater Ridge Road 317 on an open bear grass ridge with views of the Selway. The trailhead includes a stock ramp and hitching post.

The campground, shaded by tall cedars, has large flat spaces for tents. Several sites sit between the campground loop road and the Selway Road in full view of all passing vehicles, but with great views of the river. A walk-in campsite is more secluded under larger cedars on a raised bench above the campground loop with peek-a-boo views of the river.

Campsites, facilities: The campground has six primitive RV or tent campsites. Midsized RVs are okay. Facilities include a wheelchair-accessible vault toilet and a few fire rings. You can get water for drinking from the river across the road, but treat it first. You can also get potable water at nearby O'Hara or Johnson Bar Campgrounds. Pack out your trash. Leashed pets are permitted.

Reservations, fees: Reservations are not accepted. Camping is free. Open late April-October.

Directions: From Lowell on Highway 12, turn southeast onto the Selway Road, also called Forest Road 223. Drive to milepost 6. The campground is on the left and is unsigned. GPS Coordinates: N 46° 5.447' W 115° 31.217'

Contact: Nez Perce National Forest, Moose Creek Ranger District, 831 Selway Rd., Kooskia, ID 83539, 208/926-4258, www. fs.usda.gov/nezperceclearwater.

12 O'HARA BAR

Scenic rating: 8

on the Selway River in Nez Perce National Forest

BEST (

O'Hara Bar sits at 1,550 feet at the confluence

of O'Hara Creek with the Selway River, a designated Wild and Scenic River. The riverside location makes it convenient for fishing, rafting, kayaking, or floating right from camp, and the bar has a mix of sand, river rocks, and grass. The Selway is catch-and-release fishing only. O'Hara, the largest of the Selway campgrounds, is also the last campground upriver accessed via pavement. A one-mile interpretive trail tours up O'Hara Creek, home to beavers, belted kingfishers, and ospreys. Efforts to improve the stream restored chinook salmon, trout, and steelhead spawning to the once fishless creek, which was damaged from timber harvesting and road building sediments. You can also drive or mountain bike the dirt Hamby Road 3.5 miles to hike the 2.1-mile O'Hara Creek trail. A steep, six-mile trail (#335) climbs from the campground to Stillman Point, an old fire lookout.

The paved campground loop road has paved back-in parking pads. Over half of the campsites have Selway River frontage; river views through the lush thimbleberries, yews, and sword ferns vary. Cedars and alders shade most of the sites, too. Sites 26-32 are grassy, more open, and sunnier. Despite the campground's rainforest appearance, be cautious of rattlesnakes. Many of the sites include large, flat spaces for tents. Because of its location across the river from the Selway Road, the campground is quiet.

Campsites, facilities: The campground has 32 RV or tent campsites. RVs are limited to 45 feet. Facilities include picnic tables, fire rings with grills, vault toilets, hand pumps for drinking water, garbage service, and campground hosts. Leashed pets are permitted. Wheelchair-accessible facilities include toilets and campsites.

Reservations, fees: Reservations are accepted (877/444-6777, www.recreation.gov). Campsites cost $10. An extra vehicle costs $3. Cash or check. Open mid-May-late September.

Directions: From Lowell on Highway 12, turn southeast onto the Selway Road (Forest Road 223). Drive to milepost 7 and turn right onto the bridge. After crossing over the Selway River, take an immediate left for 0.1 mile to the campground.

GPS Coordinates: N 46° 5.106' W 115° 30.895'

Contact: Nez Perce National Forest, Moose Creek Ranger District, 831 Selway Rd., Kooskia, ID 83539, 208/926-4258, www.fs.usda.gov/nezperceclearwater.

13 RACKLIFF

Scenic rating: 7

on the Selway River in Nez Perce National Forest

At 1,580 feet, Rackliff is the first campground up the Selway River Road after leaving the pavement. The road narrows at milepost 7, offering a rough, curvy, jouncing ride for its remaining 12 miles upriver. Many aiming for the upper campgrounds give up after one mile of washboards and potholes to camp here instead. Large sandbars both up- and downriver from the campground work for fishing, swimming, rafting, kayaking, canoeing, and floating. Fishing in the Selway is catch-and-release only. The Rackliff Ridge Trail (#702) climbs a steep six miles to Coolwater Lookout.

This shaded campground tucked under thick firs and cedars is best for tents only. The tight, dirt-road access, narrow parking areas, and cramped turnaround space don't lend themselves to RV maneuvering. Most of the sites have flat spaces to accommodate large tents. Some of the sites have room for more than one tent. The campground—in two parts on both sides of Rackliff Creek—sits on a bench above the road and has peek-a-boo views of the river. Access to the river requires dropping across the road and climbing down the short bank.

Campsites, facilities: The campground has six tent campsites. Facilities include picnic tables, fire rings with grills, and vault toilets, but no drinking water. Bring your own, or treat creek water. Pack out your trash. Leashed pets are permitted.

Reservations, fees: Reservations are not accepted. Campsites cost $5. Open mid-May-mid-September.

Directions: From Lowell on Highway 12, turn southeast onto the Selway Road (Forest Road 223). After milepost 7, the road turns to gravel and narrows to one lane with turnouts. Drive to milepost 7.9. The first part of Rackliff sits on the left before Rackliff Creek, and the second half is on the left after the creek. The campground sign is difficult to see tucked in the brush.

GPS Coordinates: N 46° 5.146' W 115° 29.897'

Contact: Nez Perce National Forest, Moose Creek Ranger District, 831 Selway Rd., Kooskia, ID 83539, 208/926-4258, www.fs.usda.gov/nezperceclearwater.

14 TWENTYMILE BAR, SLIDE CREEK, AND TWENTYFIVE MILE BAR

Scenic rating: 7

on the Selway River in Nez Perce National Forest

Between 1,590 and 1,660 feet, three primitive free campgrounds are for those looking for solitude to enjoy the Wild and Scenic Selway River. In this section, the river widens into shallow riffles alternating with slower deeper pools for fishing and swimming. Large gravel bars make great midsummer beaches. This section of the river works for float tubing, rafting, and canoeing in midsummer, but rafting and kayaking are best in the early summer high white-water runoff. Fishing is catch-and-release only with several species of trout in the river.

Twentymile Bar Campground sits on a dirt-road spur above the Selway Road and the river. One site with room for small tents sits on the left, virtually in the parking lot; a more spacious walk-in site sits just uphill on the right. It has room for a large tent. Both sites are heavily shaded under a mixed forest with peek-a-boo views of the water. Slide Creek is a walk-in campground with both sites on a rocky, sandy bar right on the river. It is one place you can camp with your tent door just a few feet from the water. From the parking pullouts on the Selway Road, drop 30 feet down the steep embankment trails to the bar. One site is protected under cedars and firs; the other is grassy, more open, and sunny. The first pullout can only accommodate a small vehicle; the second pullout can fit trucks and bigger cars. An alternative primitive site is available above the road on the creek other sites fill. Twentyfive Mile Bar requires a steep descent down a narrow road to reach the large sandy bar on the river where private campsites tuck under large cedars separated by thimbleberry bushes. The access is suitable for small RVs, but not trailers.

Campsites, facilities: Twentymile Bar has two tent campsites. Slide Creek has two tent campsites. Twentyfive Mile Bar has three RV or tent campsites. Facilities include some picnic tables, rock or metal fire rings, and vault or pit toilet, but no drinking water. Bring water with you, get it from O'Hara or Johnson Bar, or treat river water. Pack out your trash. Leashed pets are permitted.

Reservations, fees: Reservations are not accepted. Camping is free. Open May-September.

Directions: From Lowell on Highway 12, turn southeast onto the Selway Road (Forest Road 223). After milepost 7, the road turns to gravel and narrows to one lane with turnouts. These campgrounds are not signed in advance on the road. Drive to milepost 9.5 to look for the entrance of the Twentymile Bar road spur on the left. Drive to milepost 10.5 to find the Slide Creek sign on the right-hand side near a small pullout, followed by the larger parking pullout farther down the road. Drive to milepost 15.1 for the steep road descending to Twentyfive Mile Bar.

Twentymile Bar GPS Coordinates: N 46° 5.222' W 115° 27.909'

Slide Creek GPS Coordinates: N 46° 5.037' W 115° 27.062'

Twentyfive Mile Bar GPS Coordinates: N 46° 4.379' W 115° 22.589'

Contact: Nez Perce National Forest, Moose Creek Ranger District, 831 Selway Rd., Kooskia, ID 83539, 208/926-4258, www.fs.usda.gov/nezperceclearwater.

15 BOYD CREEK

Scenic rating: 8

on the Selway River in Nez Perce National Forest

Boyd Creek, at 1,610 feet, is a tributary of the Wild and Scenic Selway River. The western trailhead to the 23-mile-loop East Boyd-Glover-Roundtop National Recreation Trail (#703 and #704) departs across the Selway Road from the campground. The trail is open to hikers, mountain bikers, motorbikes, and horseback riders. A stock ramp and hitching post are available. Access to the Selway River shoreline for fishing, swimming, or floating is via the lower campsites. In May and June, the Selway offers white-water rafting and kayaking, while midsummer is tamer. Fishing is catch-and-release only.

The campground has two parts. Two sites (1 and 2) are on a cedar and hemlock bluff overlooking the river and adjacent to the Selway Road. One is on an open grassy knoll, while the other is tucked under the trees with a large cement pad. Access the remaining sites (3-6) by dropping down a steep, narrow gravel road to the river level. Sites 3, 4, and 6 have river frontage. Site 3 is the most secluded as a walk-in tent site. Sites 5 and 6 sit very close together on an open, sunny bench—a good option for two parties traveling together.

Campsites, facilities: The campground has six RV or tent campsites. RVs are limited to 20 feet. Facilities include picnic tables, fire rings with grills, and a vault toilet, but no drinking water. Bring your own, or pick it up at O'Hara or Johnson Bar. Pack out your trash. Leashed pets are permitted.

Reservations, fees: Reservations are not accepted. Campsites cost $5. Cash or check. Open May-September.

Directions: From Lowell on Highway 12, turn southeast onto the Selway Road (Forest Road 223). After milepost 7, the road turns to gravel and narrows to one lane with turnouts. Drive to milepost 10.8. The campground is on the right in two parts—the upper sites off Selway Road and the lower sites on the river.

GPS Coordinates: N 46° 4.866' W 115° 26.565'

Contact: Nez Perce National Forest, Moose Creek Ranger District, 831 Selway Rd., Kooskia, ID 83539, 208/926-4258, www.fs.usda.gov/nezperceclearwater.

16 GLOVER

Scenic rating: 7

on the Selway River in Nez Perce National Forest

At 1,690 feet along the Wild and Scenic Selway River, Glover Campground sits far up the jarring washboarded and potholed single-lane Selway Road. (Watch for ATVers on the road.) While the lesser-used campground sits on a sloped plateau above the road, trails cut below the road to a large rocky bar along the river for fishing, swimming, and floating. The river attracts kayakers and rafters in May and June, followed by rafters, canoeists, and tube floaters in summer. Fishing on the Selway is catch and release only for trout—rainbow, cutthroat, bull, and eastern brook. The eastern trailhead to the 23-mile-loop East Boyd-Glover-Roundtop National Recreation Trail (#703 and

#704) departs across the Selway Road from the campground. It's open to hikers, mountain bikers, motorbikes, and horses. A stock ramp and hitching post are available.

Access to the campground requires a steep climb up a narrow road with a sharp hairpin. The hairpin turn is not suitable for trailers or large RVs, but smaller rigs such as trucks with campers can negotiate the sharp corner. One campsite sits on Glover Creek at the end of the hairpin. The others are sprinkled around an open grassy hillside with a few cedars for partial shade. One campsite at the upper end tucks along Glover Creek. Two along the edge of the plateau have views of the river.

Campsites, facilities: The campground has seven campsites. RVs must be small. Facilities include picnic tables, fire rings with grills, and vault toilet, but no drinking water. Bring water with you, get it from O'Hara or Johnson Bar when you drive upriver, or treat creek water. Pack out your trash. Leashed pets are permitted.

Reservations, fees: Reservations are not accepted. Campsites cost $5. Open May-September.

Directions: From Lowell on Highway 12, turn southeast onto Selway Road (Forest Road 223). After milepost 7, the road turns to gravel and narrows to one lane with turnouts. Drive to milepost 15.1. Look for a steep road climbing up to the left.

GPS Coordinates: N 46° 4.147' W 115° 21.795'

Contact: Nez Perce National Forest, Moose Creek Ranger District, 831 Selway Rd., Kooskia, ID 83539, 208/926-4258, www.fs.usda.gov/nezperceclearwater.

17 RACE CREEK
🚶 🛶 🎣 🐾 🚐 ⛺

Scenic rating: 7
on the Selway River in Nez Perce National Forest

Over 12 miles of narrow, bumpy dirt-road driving is required to reach Race Creek. At 1,760 feet only a few miles from the Selway-Bitterroot Wilderness boundary, Race Creek is a springboard for those accessing the wilderness on either foot or horseback on the Selway-Bitterroot Trail (#4). As a wilderness entrance, it also has a stock ramp, hitch rail, and feeding trough. Moose Creek Ranger Station, which is not staffed full-time, sits one mile back on the road. Only catch-and-release fishing is permitted in the Selway River, which is home to a variety of trout—rainbow, cutthroat, bull, and eastern brook.

Race Creek is not a campground one enjoys as a destination (go for Slims Camp or Selway Falls instead), but rather for utilitarian reasons. The campground is made up of parking-lot terraces crammed with cars and Forest Service trucks because of the popular wilderness entry point here. Most campers are preparing to follow the trail as it continues up the river 25 miles into the Selway-Bitterroot Wilderness. One campsite sits under cedars across from the toilet, and another tucks into an alcove of firs and thimbleberries. Located right on the river under a few trees for protection, the best site is a walk-in tent site below the parking area.

Campsites, facilities: The campground has seven RV or tent campsites. RVs must be small. Facilities include picnic tables, fire rings with grills, and vault toilet, but no drinking water. Bring water with you, get it from O'Hara or Johnson Bar when you drive upriver, or treat river water. Pack out your trash. Leashed pets are permitted.

Reservations, fees: Reservations are not accepted. Campsites cost $5. Open May-September.

Directions: From Lowell on Highway 12, turn southeast onto the Selway Road (Forest Road 223). After milepost 7, the road turns to gravel and narrows to one lane with turnouts. Drive to milepost 19.5, where the road ends.

GPS Coordinates: N 46° 2.653' W 115° 17.032'

Contact: Nez Perce National Forest, Moose Creek Ranger District, 831 Selway Rd., Kooskia, ID 83539, 208/926-4258, www.fs.usda.gov/nezperceclearwater.

18 SELWAY FALLS

🚵 🏊 🎣 🐕 🚐 ⛺

Scenic rating: 7

in the Clearwater Mountains in Nez Perce
National Forest

One reason to drive the 12 miles of bumpy
gravel road to Selway Falls Campground is to
see Selway Falls. The falls—broken by titanic
boulders—roar at a deafening volume in early
summer high water. Even after the river level
drops in summer, the white water still churns
through here. Fishing is catch-and-release only,
and no fishing is permitted between the cable
car below the falls and the bridge. At 1,760
feet, the campground is about a mile to the
southwest on the Meadow Creek tributary of
the Selway. The Meadow Creek drainage is
lush with sword ferns and vine maples. The
campground is also popular with ATV riders and mountain bikers, who continue on to
Falls Point (7 miles) and Elk City (30 miles).
A large swimming sandbar sits between the
campground and the bridge above the falls.

The campground sprawls its campsites
along the Meadow Creek Road. The first four
sites are near one toilet, and the last three are
near another. All of the sites are open to the
road, but most are quite shaded under western
red cedar trees with large flat spaces for tents.
Campsite 4's hillside has scarring from ATVs
and motorcycles. Trailers may have trouble
turning around.

Campsites, facilities: The campground has
seven RV or tent campsites. RVs must be small.
Facilities include picnic tables, fire rings with
grills, and vault toilets, but no drinking water.
Bring water with you, get it from O'Hara or
Johnson Bar when you drive upriver, or treat
creek water. Pack out your trash. Leashed pets
are permitted.

Reservations, fees: Reservations are not
accepted. Campsites cost $5. Cash or check.
Open late May-early September.

Directions: From Lowell on Highway 12, turn
southeast onto Selway Road (Forest Road 223).

After milepost 7, the road turns to gravel and
narrows to one lane with turnouts. Drive to
milepost 18.5 and turn right onto the one-lane
bridge. After crossing the Selway, continue 0.7
mile on narrow, potholed dirt Meadow Creek
Road to the campground.

GPS Coordinates: N 46° 2.382' W 115° 17.708'

Contact: Nez Perce National Forest, Moose
Creek Ranger District, 831 Selway Rd.,
Kooskia, ID 83539, 208/926-4258, www.
fs.usda.gov/nezperceclearwater.

19 SLIMS CAMP

🥾 🚵 🏊 🎣 🐕 🚐 ⛺

Scenic rating: 8

in the Clearwater Mountains in Nez Perce
National Forest

Located at 1,780 feet, Slims Camp sits far
up the Selway drainage on Meadow Creek.
Departing from the campground loop, the
Meadow Creek Trail (#726) climbs 15 miles
up the drainage and fords the creek to reach
Meadow Creek Cabin, which you can rent.
The first three miles are open to motorcycles
and mountain bikes, but the trail permits
only hikers and horses after that. From the
campground, Forest Road 290 continues on
for 12 more miles from Slims Camp to Indian
Hill Lookout, perched on the boundary of the
Selway-Bitterroot Wilderness. Trout fishing is
permitted in Meadow Creek.

The campground tucks into a lush, shady
cedar forest of thimbleberries, elderberries,
and ferns. The two campsites on the river have
large, flat grassy areas for tents and privacy.
The loop at the end of the campground makes
it easier to turn around. The campground is
also more private than Selway Falls.

Campsites, facilities: The campground has
two RV or tent campsites. RVs should be small.
Facilities include picnic tables, fire rings with
grills, and vault toilet, but no drinking water.
Bring water with you, get it from O'Hara or
Johnson Bar when you drive upriver, or treat

creek water. Pack out your trash. Leashed pets are permitted.

Reservations, fees: Reservations are not accepted. Camping is free. Open late May-early September.

Directions: From Lowell on Highway 12, turn southeast onto the Selway Road (Forest Road 223). After milepost 7, the road turns to gravel and narrows to one lane with turnouts. Drive to milepost 18.5 and turn right onto the one-lane bridge. After crossing the Selway, continue 1.6 miles on narrow, potholed dirt Meadow Creek Road, past the Selway Falls campsites and crossing the creek on a single-lane bridge to reach Slims Camp.

GPS Coordinates: N 46° 1.837' W 115° 17.417'

Contact: Nez Perce National Forest, Moose Creek Ranger District, 831 Selway Rd., Kooskia, ID 83539, 208/926-4258, www.fs.usda.gov/nezperceclearwater.

20 TWIN CREEK

Scenic rating: 7

in the Bitterroot Mountains in Salmon-Challis National Forest

At 5,100 feet on the Lewis and Clark National Historic Trail, Twin Creek Campground sits five minutes off the Salmon River Scenic Byway (Hwy. 93) in a forested side canyon. Its location south of Lost Trail Pass makes it the closest campground to the Idaho-Montana border. Fishing is available on the North Fork of the Salmon River along the highway and in Twin Creek adjacent to the campground. Find easy access to the river via the paved loop of the old highway across from Forest Road 449. Paths through the woods access Twin Creek.

Set in a diverse forest of Douglas firs and ponderosas, the partly shaded campground sprouts with a lush ground cover of snowberry, Oregon grape, and bear grass. The spacious campsites—including one large, double campsite—feature huge flat spaces for tents.

Since the forest lacks a midstory, one or two other campsites are visible even though they are spread out for privacy around the two loops. The location in a side canyon off the highway contributes to nighttime quiet. Twin Creek runs through the woods south of the campground.

Campsites, facilities: The campground has 40 RV or tent campsites. RVs are limited to 35 feet. Facilities include picnic tables, fire rings with grills, pedestal grills, vault toilets (wheelchair-accessible), drinking water, garbage service, stock ramps, and campground hosts. Leashed pets are permitted. Horses are also permitted in the campground.

Reservations, fees: Reservations are not accepted. Campsites cost $10. Cash or check. Open May-October, but services available only late May-September.

Directions: From Highway 93 between Gibbonsville and Lost Trail Pass (Idaho-Montana border), turn west at milepost 342.4 onto Forest Road 449. Drive for 0.5 mile, passing the picnic area, and turn left at the camping sign into the campground.

GPS Coordinates: N 45° 36.517' W 113° 58.253'

Contact: Salmon-Challis National Forest, North Fork Ranger District, 11 Casey Road, North Fork, ID 83466, 208/865-2700, www.fs.usda.gov/scnf/.

21 HORSE CREEK HOT SPRINGS

Scenic rating: 5

in the Bitterroot Mountains in Salmon-Challis National Forest

At 6,050 feet, Horse Creek Hot Springs survived a fire that swept through the area in 2011. Although miles of burned timber surround the campground, low greenery is coming back, including wildflowers. For those who suffer through the long bumpy, dusty dirt road access, the hot springs is a reward. The hot springs sit along the main road around the corner 0.25 miles from the campground. You can soak in two places—inside the small bathhouse shack or in the shallow natural lower pool, both a short walk from the parking area. A covered changing area is available. With sandy bottoms, the shack pool hangs around 102°F while the lower pool cools from that. The area is also popular with the ATV crowd.

The Forest Service stripped the campground of its burned timbers after the fire, leaving it completely open to the hot summer sun. You'll see neighboring campers, but don't have to worry about trees toppling on you in high winds. At this distance into the mountains, the campground quiets at night.

Campsites, facilities: The campground has nine RV or tent campsites. RVs are limited to 35 feet. Facilities include picnic tables, fire rings with grills, vault toilet (wheelchair-accessible), and drinking water. Pack out your trash. Leashed pets are permitted.

Reservations, fees: Reservations are not accepted. Campsites cost $10. Cash or check. Open May-October, but services available only late May-September.

Directions: From North Fork on Highway 93, turn west onto the Salmon River Road (Forest Road 30) and drive 14 miles. Turn north onto Forest Road 38 for eight miles. Turn west onto Forest Road 44 for 10.8 miles. Turn southwest onto Forest Road 65 for 3.6 miles. To reach the campground, turn left for 0.2 miles. Stay on the main road to reach hot springs parking lot immediately after the left turn to the campground.

GPS Coordinates: N 45° 30.246' W 114° 27.578'

Contact: Salmon-Challis National Forest, North Fork Ranger District, 11 Casey Road, North Fork, ID 83466, 208/865-2700, www.fs.usda.gov/scnf/.

22 SPRING CREEK

Scenic rating: 7

on the Salmon River in Salmon-Challis National Forest

At 3,400 feet on the Salmon River, Spring Creek Campground is a popular river access site for floating and fishing on the longest free-flowing river in the United States. It's the first designated campground on the drive down the Wild and Scenic River, and one of the quickest river accesses to reach, hence its high traffic. The fishery holds rainbow and cutthroat trout, plus steelhead. Rafters and kayakers put in at Spring Creek to float 10 miles downstream through splashy Class III rapids to Cove Creek. The river access has a primitive boat ramp for launching. The Salmon River Road is littered with primitive campsites that can be used as backup if the campground is full. The Salmon River area shows evidence of the 2012 Mustang Fire with charred and silvered trees.

The campground tucks between the road and the river on a fairly open river bar. Because the campground is also a river access site, it can see heavy traffic during the day. But at night it quiets. Most of the campsites flank a long shady spur to the east, but one campsite sits on the west river access spur. The northern slopes above the campground burned in 2012.

Campsites, facilities: The campground has five RV or tent campsites. RVs are limited to 35 feet. Facilities include picnic tables, fire rings with grills, vault toilet, and drinking water. Pack out your trash. Leashed pets are permitted.

Reservations, fees: Reservations are not accepted. Campsites cost $10. Cash or check. Open May-October, but services available only late May-September.

Directions: From North Fork on Highway 93, turn west onto the Salmon River Road (Forest Road 30) and drive 18 miles to the campground on the left. Note: Pavement ends one mile before the campground.

GPS Coordinates: N 45° 23.525' W 114° 15.095'
Contact: Salmon-Challis National Forest, North Fork Ranger District, 11 Casey Road, North Fork, ID 83466, 208/865-2700, www.fs.usda.gov/scnf/.

23 EBENEZER BAR

Scenic rating: 6

on the Salmon River in Salmon-Challis National Forest

At 3,140 feet in the Salmon River Mountains, Ebenezer Bar Campground is a popular river access site for floating and fishing. Once a Civilian Conservation Corps camp, it requires a long haul up the Wild and Scenic River, the longest free-flowing river in the United States. The fishery holds rainbow and cutthroat trout, plus steelhead. Rafters and kayakers put in at Ebenezer to float 12 miles downstream to Corn Creek, the last take out before the Frank Church-River of No Return Wilderness. At the campground, the river access has a primitive boat ramp for launching. The Salmon River Road is littered with primitive campsites that can be used as backup if the campground is full. The Salmon River area shows evidence of the 2012 Mustang Fire with charred and silvered trees.

The sunny, dusty campground splits on both sides of the Salmon River Road. Cement foundations and fruit trees recall its CCC past with interpretive signs. Upper loop campsites work better for tents while the lower loop sites can fit RVs. The campsites sit on a bench above the river, but without views of it. Because the campground is also a river access site, it can see heavy traffic during the day. But at night it quiets. The northern slopes above the campground burned in 2012.

Campsites, facilities: The campground has five RV or tent campsites and six tent campsites. RVs are limited to 45 feet. Facilities include picnic tables, fire rings with grills, vault toilet (wheelchair-accessible), and hand pumps for drinking water. Pack out your trash. Leashed pets are permitted.

Reservations, fees: Reservations are not accepted. Campsites cost $10. Cash or check. Open May-October, but services available only late May-September.

Directions: From North Fork on Highway 93, turn west onto the Salmon River Road (Forest Road 30) and drive about 34 miles to the campground on the left. Note: Pavement ends at mile 17; the remainder is a dusty, bumpy, single-lane road with turnouts.

GPS Coordinates: N 45° 18.299' W 114° 30.960'

Contact: Salmon-Challis National Forest, North Fork Ranger District, 11 Casey Road, North Fork, ID 83466, 208/865-2700, www.fs.usda.gov/scnf/.

24 CORN CREEK

Scenic rating: 7

on the Salmon River in Salmon-Challis National Forest

At 2,950 feet in the Salmon River Mountains, Corn Creek Campground is busy place for floating and fishing. As a jump off into the Frank Church-River of No Return Wilderness, it sees hoards of floaters and jet boats launching for week trips (permits required; primitive ramp and dock available). It is also the last take-out for those rafting and kayaking along the Salmon River Road. The campground requires a long haul up the Wild and Scenic River, the longest free-flowing river in the United States. The fishery holds rainbow and cutthroat trout, plus steelhead. Hikers and equestrians can head into the wilderness on the Salmon River Trail; stock facilities are available at the trailhead. Corn Creek is also a Native American archeological site. The Salmon River area shows evidence

© BECKY LOMAX

Lewis and Clark camped at Tower Rock on their journey along the Salmon River.

of the 2012 Mustang Fire with charred and silvered trees.

One large campground loop tucks into an arid Ponderosa pine forest between the road and the river. At night, the campground is quiet, but during the day, river rafters are busy preparing to float into the wilderness. Several campsites overlook the river; another few sit adjacent to Corn Creek. The eastern slopes above the campground burned in 2012. The campground fills with those preparing to launch the next day; if it fills, you can find plenty of primitive free campsites sprinkled along the river upstream.

Campsites, facilities: The campground has 17 RV or tent campsites. RVs are limited to 38 feet. Facilities include picnic tables, fire rings with grills, vault toilet, and a hand pump for drinking water. Pack out your trash. Leashed pets are permitted.

Reservations, fees: Reservations are not accepted. Campsites cost $10. Cash or check. Open March-October, but services available only June-September.

Directions: From North Fork on Highway 93, turn west onto the Salmon River Road (Forest Road 30) and drive about 46 miles to the campground on the left. Note: Pavement ends at mile 17; the remainder is a dusty, bumpy, single-lane road with turnouts.
GPS Coordinates: N 45° 22.189' W 114° 41.128'
Contact: Salmon-Challis National Forest, North Fork Ranger District, 11 Casey Road, North Fork, ID 83466, 208/865-2700, www.fs.usda.gov/scnf/.

25 TOWER ROCK

Scenic rating: 7

on the Salmon River

The Salmon River flows north past Tower Rock, a site where Lewis and Clark camped on their journey through the area in 1805. Surrounded by arid, orange-colored sagebrush hills, the rock outcropping towers above the campground. Its sandstone eroded 57 million years ago into the blocky prow. Nearby, the Tower Creek Pyramids, named by William Clark, stand in tribute to the unique geology of the area. Boating facilities at the campground include two cement ramps and trailer parking to aid those floating the Class II Salmon River with rafts, kayaks, canoes, and drift boats. Fishing for steelhead and trout is available in the campground from two wheelchair-accessible fishing platforms. A large osprey nest is on site, as well as historical and geological interpretive displays.

Sitting on a wide-open flat river bar at 3,770 feet, the sunny campground borders a trailer park; however, it is fenced off to minimize views into neighboring yards. With no trees, the mowed-lawn campground with its paved loop road and paved parking pads affords no privacy, but it does provide views of the river from some of the campsites. Tucked between the river and the highway, the campground picks up the sound of the river and the two-lane highway. Site 5 includes a tent platform.

Campsites, facilities: The campground has six RV or tent campsites. RVs are limited to 28 feet. Facilities include picnic tables, fire rings with grills, pedestal grills, vault toilets (wheelchair-accessible), garbage service, one tent platform, and boat ramp, but no drinking water. Bring your own or purify river water. Leashed pets are permitted.

Reservations, fees: Reservations are not accepted. Campsites cost $5. An extra vehicle costs $2. Cash or check. Open May-October.

Directions: From Salmon, drive north on Highway 93 for about 11 miles and turn west at milepost 315 into the campground.

GPS Coordinates: N 45° 18.716' W 113° 54.391'

Contact: Bureau of Land Management, Salmon Field Office, 1207 S. Challis St., Salmon, ID 83467, 208/756-5400, www.blm.gov/id/.

26 MORGAN BAR

Scenic rating: 7

on the Salmon River

Backed up against sagebrush hills of the Salmon River Mountains to the west, Morgan Bar sits at 3,850 feet on a former homestead and still has a remnant orchard. The Class II Salmon River flows north past the campground, with the 10,000-foot-high Beaverhead Mountains to the east. In early summer, they are still covered in snow. The campground also sits on the Lewis and Clark National Historic Trail. A hiking and mountain biking trail loops around a wetland pond and tours a mile along the Salmon River. A cement boat ramp aids launching canoes, kayaks, rafts, and drift boats onto the river for floating and fishing.

The sunny campground has the advantage of sitting across the river and fields away from the highway, so river sounds provide the backdrop for its campsites. The mowed-grass

campground's one gravel loop circles through thickets of willows and a few cottonwoods for a bit of shade. Most of the campsites have views of the Beaverhead Mountains. Sites 1-3 line up in a field without views of the river. Site 4 claims privacy at the east end of the loop, with both views and partial shade. Sites 7-9 overlook the river.

Campsites, facilities: The campground has eight RV or tent campsites. RVs are limited to 28 feet. Facilities include covered picnic tables, fire rings with grills, vault toilets (wheelchair-accessible), drinking water, garbage service, horseshoes, volleyball, firewood for sale, and campground hosts. Leashed pets are permitted.

Reservations, fees: Reservations are not accepted. Campsites cost $5. An extra vehicle costs $2. Cash or check. Open May-September.

Directions: From Highway 93 about seven miles north of Salmon, turn west at milepost 309 onto Diamond Creek Road. Drive 0.5 mile on pavement and veer left where the road turns to gravel. Drive 0.3 mile to a Y, taking the right fork. Drive 1.3 miles and turn right into the campground.

GPS Coordinates: N 45° 15.171' W 113° 54.464'

Contact: Bureau of Land Management, Salmon Field Office, 1207 S. Challis St., Salmon, ID 83467, 208/756-5400, www.blm.gov/id/.

27 SHOUP BRIDGE

Scenic rating: 6

on the Salmon River

Located at 4,038 feet on the south side of the Shoup Bridge over the Salmon River, the campground is one of the popular launch points for floating the Class II river. The surrounding arid slopes, covered with sagebrush, flank the bucolic river corridor, which is rimmed with small ranches and farms. A cement boat ramp helps those launching kayaks, canoes, rafts, and drift boats. Fishing for steelhead requires barbless hooks; only hatchery steelhead—identified by a clipped adipose fin—may be kept. The campground is convenient to Salmon (five miles north) for gas, groceries, ice, and fishing supplies. Fishing and floating outfitters are also based in Salmon, as are outfitters for horseback riding and hunting. The town is the birthplace of Sacajawea and on the Lewis and Clark National Historic Trail. It also houses the developed Salmon Hot Springs (open year-round, 248 Hot Springs Rd., Salmon, ID 83467, 208/756-4449, fee charged).

Tucked under big shady cottonwood trees, the tiny mowed-lawn campground sits among the highway, the river, and the bridge. Noise from passing vehicles comes with the territory; however, the highway is only a two-laner. A paved road loops through the campground, which squeezes its paved parking pads for campsites very close together. Site 3 claims waterfront.

Campsites, facilities: The campground has five RV or tent campsites. RVs are limited to 28 feet. Facilities include picnic tables, fire rings with grills, pedestal grills, vault toilets (wheelchair-accessible), drinking water, and garbage service. Leashed pets are permitted.

Reservations, fees: Reservations are not accepted. Campsites cost $5. An extra vehicle costs $2. Cash or check. Open April-October.

Directions: From Highway 93 about five miles south of Salmon, turn west at milepost 299.4 into the campground.

GPS Coordinates: N 45° 5.877' W 113° 53.601'

Contact: Bureau of Land Management, Salmon Field Office, 1207 S. Challis St., Salmon, ID 83467, 208/756-5400, www.blm.gov/id/.

28 WILLIAMS LAKE

Scenic rating: 7

near Williams Lake in the Salmon River Mountains

On the arid sagebrush-covered eastern edge of the Salmon River Mountains, Williams Lake, elevation 5,400 feet, sits in a pocket formed about 6,000 years ago. A landslide—most likely triggered by an earthquake—blocked Lake Creek, damming up the flow to create the lake. Today, homes surround two sides of the lake. A boat launch is 1.5 miles west of the campground. Boat launch facilities include a steep cement ramp and trailer parking. Boaters, water-skiers, canoeists, kayakers, and swimmers use the lake, as well as anglers going after rainbow trout. The fish are reputedly large—up to two pounds. The trailhead for Thunder Mountain National Historic Trail sits two miles west of Williams Lake, an option for hikers and mountain bikers.

Despite its name, the campground has no lake frontage or lake views. It sits on a small, loose-forested parcel northeast of the lake. The single-lane dirt road through the campground gets more eroded at its far end, prompting overuse at the larger upper sites. Mature firs lend partial shade to many of the sites, which have forest duff floors surrounded by burnt-red boulders or grass. Large, flat tent spaces are available, as well as peek-a-boo views of cliffs above the campground on sagebrush hills. Given its distance from the highway, the campground is quiet. With grass and three kinds of sagebrush, the campground's open midstory admits views of neighboring campsites.

Campsites, facilities: The campground has 11 RV or tent campsites. RVs are limited to 28 feet. Facilities include picnic tables, fire rings with grills, vault toilets (wheelchair-accessible), drinking water, and garbage service. Leashed pets are permitted.

Reservations, fees: Reservations are not accepted. Campsites cost $5. An extra vehicle costs $2. Cash or check. Open late May-October.

Directions: From Highway 93 about four miles south of Salmon, turn west at milepost 299.4 across the one-lane Shoup Bridge over the Salmon River. At 0.7 mile, turn left onto Williams Lake Road. Drive 3.6 miles to where the road turns to gravel and climbs another 2.7

miles to a junction. Turn right and drive 0.4 mile uphill. Turn left into the campground. GPS Coordinates: N 45° 1.472' W 113° 57.914'

Contact: Bureau of Land Management, Salmon Field Office, 1207 S. Challis St., Salmon, ID 83467, 208/756-5400, www.blm.gov/id/.

29 COTTONWOOD

Scenic rating: 7

on the Salmon River

Sitting at 4,680 feet along the north-flowing Salmon River, Cottonwood Campground provides river access for floaters and anglers in a section of canyon surrounded by arid, sagebrush slopes. A large sandbar south of the boat launch provides access to a swimming hole. The boat launch area—a cement ramp with trailer parking—aids those launching drift boats, rafts, kayaks, and canoes for the Class II water. You can put in at the campground to float 17 miles to Kilpatrick take-out, or put in upriver at Spring Gulch to float six miles back to the campground. Anglers go after trout and steelhead in the river. Cronks Canyon Hot Springs, an undeveloped rock pool on the Salmon River, sits five miles north of the campground.

As the name implies, the campground sits under mature cottonwood trees, which provide shade for some of the campsites; however, sunny, open campsites are also available. Brushy willows separate some of the sites—particularly those that back up to the highway—into private niches. Mowed lawn surrounds the paved pull-through and back-in parking pads. Sites 1-4 and 6-8 overlook the river. Sites 1-3 line up very close together. Sites 5, 8, 9, and 11 have tent platforms; sites 8 and 9 are walk-in tent sites. With the highway above the campground, the road noise is less obnoxious, but still audible.

Campsites, facilities: The campground has 11 RV or tent campsites, plus two walk-in tent campsites. RVs are limited to 65 feet. Facilities include picnic tables, fire rings with grills, pedestal grills, vault toilets, drinking water, disposal station, garbage service, horseshoe pits, boat ramp, two tent platforms, and summer campground hosts. Leashed pets are permitted. Wheelchair-accessible facilities include toilets and campsites.

Reservations, fees: Reservations are not accepted. Campsites cost $10. Use of the disposal station costs $3. Cash or check. Open year-round.

Directions: From Highway 93 about 14 miles north of Challis, turn west at milepost 261.3 into the campground.

GPS Coordinates: N 44° 40.103' W 114° 4.752'

Contact: Bureau of Land Management, Challis Field Office, 1151 Blue Mountain Rd., Challis, ID 83226, 208/879-6200, www.blm.gov/id/.

30 BAYHORSE

Scenic rating: 7

on the Salmon River

Named for an old mining community in the area, Bayhorse Campground sits at 5,177 feet on the upper Salmon River, tucked into a narrow, arid, sagebrush-walled canyon on the southeast edge of the Salmon River Mountains. The campground provides boating, kayaking, canoeing, and fishing access to Class II portions of the Upper Salmon River between Stanley and Challis. A cement boat ramp and trailer parking are available. Two miles southwest of the campground and accessed via rough dirt roads, Deadman Hole Recreation Site contains a deep swimming pool below a rocky cliff. Put in at East Fork to float nine miles back to Bayhorse, or float downstream from the campground for two miles to Dugway or eight miles to the Challis Bridge to take out. Outfitters for rafting, fishing, and horseback riding are in Challis, 10 miles north. ATVers ride the Bayhorse Trails, a series of old mining roads.

The wide-open, sunny campground loops with three interconnected gravel roads through the river bar. Mowed lawns surround the level, gravel parking pads, and grass has started to invade the gravel tent platforms—both provide large flat spaces for tents. Brushy willows and sage line the riverbank, with a few aspens and cottonwoods along the perimeter. Because of the proximity to the two-lane highway, the campground garners noise from passing vehicles—even above the sound of the river. Sites 5 and 7-11 overlook the river. Power lines cross the upper end of the campground.

Campsites, facilities: The campground has 11 RV or tent campsites. RVs are limited to 45 feet. Facilities include picnic tables, fire rings with grills, pedestal grills, vault toilets (wheelchair-accessible), drinking water, garbage service, boat ramp, and summer campground hosts. Leashed pets are permitted.

Reservations, fees: Reservations are not accepted. Campsites cost $10. Cash or check. Open year-round.

Directions: From Highway 75 about 10 miles southwest of Challis, turn west at milepost 237 into the campground.

GPS Coordinates: N 44° 23.130' W 114° 15.634'

Contact: Bureau of Land Management, Challis Field Office, 1151 Blue Mountain Rd., Challis, ID 83226, 208/879-6200, www.blm.gov/id/.

31 DEADMAN HOLE

Scenic rating: 6

on the Salmon River

At 5,257 feet on the Upper Salmon River, Deadman Hole Campground sits on an open river bar below the sagebrush slopes of the Salmon River Mountains. The site is mainly

for floating and fishing access for the river. A new cement boat ramp is available for launching drift boats, rafts, kayaks, or canoes onto the Class II river. The river also attracts anglers for trout and steelhead. The hole here is a deep pool for swimming located upstream from the campground, but be cautious of the high water eddy and driftwood. Off a side road near the campground, the 0.5-mile Malm Gulch Interpretive Trail tours past 50-million-year-old petrified sequoia trees. Fences surround the 10-foot-diameter stumps to protect them.

Sitting on an arid strip of land between the highway and the river, this sunny campground had a facelift in 2012, bringing it up to par with the other BLM sites on the river. The new campsites feature four pull-overs and one back-in. Four of the campsites flank the river. No shade is available on the sagebrush river bar. Watch for rattlesnakes.

Campsites, facilities: The campground has five RV or tent campsites. RVs are limited to 25 feet. Facilities include covered picnic tables, fire rings with grills, vault toilets (wheelchair-accessible), hand pump for drinking water, and boat ramp. Pack out your trash. Leashed pets are permitted.

Reservations, fees: Reservations are not accepted. Camping is free. Open year-round.

Directions: From Highway 75 about nine miles north of Clayton and 14 miles southwest of Challis, turn west into the campground.

GPS Coordinates: N 44° 20.704' W 114° 16.102'

Contact: Bureau of Land Management, Challis Field Office, 1151 Blue Mountain Rd., Challis, ID 83226, 208/879-6200, www.blm.gov/id/.

32 EAST FORK

Scenic rating: 6

on the Salmon River

At 5,373 feet on the confluence of the East

Fork of the Salmon River with the Upper Salmon River, the campground provides access to both rivers for floating and fishing. A primitive boat ramp sits on the highway's south side on the East Fork for launching rafts, kayaks, and canoes onto the Class II Salmon River. On the Upper Salmon, you can paddle from East Fork seven miles to Deadman Hole, or from Torrey's Bar 16 miles back to the campground. You can also float 22 miles of the East Fork, which has been nominated for designation as a national Wild and Scenic River. Put in at Little Boulder Creek and take out at the campground. Within three miles up the East Fork canyon, a trail departs for Jimmy Smith Lake, a 1.2-mile hike. The Snake Ridge ATV trail, also a route for mountain bikers, connects with the national forest. The East Fork also accesses hot springs and is the eastern portal for hiking and mountain biking in the White Cloud Mountains.

Sitting on a willow and cottonwood bluff above both rivers, the campground offers sunny or partly shaded campsites surrounded by mowed lawn. Sites offer views of the dry, sagebrush canyon hills. Several sites overlook the East Fork, while others overlook the Salmon. Two tent camping sites overlook both rivers. Sites 8 and 9 have big views of the highway bridge, too. Despite the sound of the rivers, the noise of passing vehicles invades the campground, but the number of vehicles lessens substantially at night. Watch for rattlesnakes in the campground.

Campsites, facilities: The campground has eight RV or tent campsites, plus three tent campsites. RVs are limited to 45 feet. Facilities include covered picnic tables, fire rings with grills, vault toilets (wheelchair-accessible), drinking water, garbage service, boat ramp, and summer campground hosts. Leashed pets are permitted.

Reservations, fees: Reservations are not accepted. Campsites cost $10. Cash or check. Open year-round.

Directions: From Highway 75 about four miles north of Clayton and 19 miles southwest

of Challis, turn west at milepost 227 into the campground.

GPS Coordinates: N 44° 16.042' W 114° 19.582'

Contact: Bureau of Land Management, Challis Field Office, 1151 Blue Mountain Rd., Challis, ID 83226, 208/879-6200, www.blm.gov/id/.

33 HOLMAN CREEK

Scenic rating: 6

near the Salmon River in Sawtooth National Recreation Area

Sitting at 5,625 feet on Holman Creek, the campground is the first Forest Service campground lining the Upper Salmon River when you drive west. Tucked into a sagebrush canyon below a Douglas fir forest, the campground is convenient for travelers but doesn't provide the river access that many of the other Upper Salmon River campgrounds do. Anglers can reach the river by walking across the highway to the south bank, but no developed river access exists. A primitive boat launch is 0.25 mile west. Expert rafters and kayakers float the Class IV river from Sunbeam to Holman Creek. A trail for hikers and mountain bikers loops south on Holman Creek.

At the entrance, the campground seems to have little appeal thanks to power lines overhead and the highway between the campsites and the river. But drive the gravel road past the first six sunny, open sagebrush campsites, and the campground runs a spur of four campsites south into a narrow, forested side canyon along Holman Creek. Sites 8-10 have short bridges that cross the creek to reach their tables, fire pits, and tent spaces. Site 8 is also a double campsite at double the price. The spur campsites are shadier, cooler, and quieter than those in front, but the front sites claim the views of the canyon. Large tent spaces are available at many of the sites.

Campsites, facilities: The campground has eight RV or tent campsites, and two tent-only campsites. RVs are limited to 45 feet. Facilities include picnic tables, fire rings with grills, vault toilets (wheelchair-accessible), hand pumps for drinking water, and garbage service. Leashed pets are permitted.

Reservations, fees: Reservations are not accepted. Campsites cost $10. An extra vehicle costs $4. Cash or check. Open year-round, but services only mid-May-early September.

Directions: From Stanley, take Highway 75 for 24 miles east, passing Sunbeam, and turn south into the campground.

GPS Coordinates: N 44° 14.945' W 114° 31.822'

Contact: Sawtooth National Forest, Stanley Ranger Station, HC 64 Box 9900, Stanley, ID 83278, 208/774-3000, www.fs.usda.gov/sawtooth/.

34 WHISKEY FLATS

Scenic rating: 5

on the Salmon River in Sawtooth National Recreation Area

Sitting at 5,666 feet, Whiskey Flats is one of the more primitive river bar campgrounds along the Upper Salmon River. Expert boaters can raft or kayak this Class IV section of river from below Sunbeam to Holman Creek, and fishing is available from the riverbanks. On the east side of the bridge, Slate Creek Road (Forest Road 666) terminates in eight miles at a trailhead. A 0.25-mile walk leads to rustic Slate Creek hot springs. The road and springs both have problems with spring flooding; call the Forest Service for conditions before driving.

The tiny, wide-open campground sits on a tall grass and sagebrush bench with a couple cottonwoods, junipers, and firs. Be prepared for a rough, eroded dirt loop through the sunny campground. From any site, you can see campers at all the others and will hear the highway. Site 1 sits on the river, the farthest from the highway, but it still has views of the highway bridge. Sites 2 and 4 can see the river across the campground road. Site 3, which overlooks the river, is the closest to the highway bridge. Large tent spaces are available.

Campsites, facilities: The campground has four RV or tent campsites. RVs are limited to midsized rigs. Facilities include picnic tables, fire rings with grills, and vault toilet. No drinking water is available; treat river water. Pack out your trash. Leashed pets are permitted.

Reservations, fees: Reservations are not accepted. Campsites cost $10. Extra vehicles $4. Double campsites cost $20. Cash or check. Open March-November, but serviced only late May-September.

Directions: From Stanley, head east on Highway 75 for 22 miles, passing Sunbeam. Just before the Whiskey Flats Bridge at milepost 213.3, turn north onto a dirt road. Swing immediately right into the campground loop.

GPS Coordinates: N 44° 15.295' W 114° 33.182'

Contact: Sawtooth National Forest, Stanley Ranger Station, HC 64 Box 9900, Stanley, ID 83278, 208/774-3000, www.fs.usda.gov/sawtooth/.

35 UPPER AND LOWER O'BRIEN

Scenic rating: 7

on the Salmon River in Sawtooth National Recreation Area

BEST (

Located at 5,900 feet on the Upper Salmon River, the O'Brien campgrounds are popular because of their location across the river from the highway. Expert boaters can raft or kayak this Class IV section of river to Holman Creek, and fishing for trout or steelhead is available from the riverbanks. Mountain bikers can tour the forest road that parallels the river and the highway for seven miles east. The nearby Warm Spring Trail climbs to Garland Lakes in the White Cloud Mountains. Sunbeam, with guided white-water rafting and gold dredge tours, sits two miles west, and Sunbeam Hot Springs are one mile farther west. Sunbeam is also the access for the Yankee Fork and the historical Custer Motorway, a 46-mile gravel mining road with two ghost towns.

Both the upper and lower campgrounds sit on flat river bar benches; however, the upper sits above the river along rapids and the lower sits at river level with a rocky beach and only small riffles. Douglas firs and lodgepoles lend shade to both campgrounds; however, a couple of sunny sites are available, too. With the highway high above the campgrounds, the sound of the river is more pervasive than the sound of vehicles. Big, flat spaces for tents are available. At least half of the campsites in both campgrounds overlook the river, and sites are spaced out for privacy, although you'll see neighboring campers.

Campsites, facilities: The campgrounds have 19 RV or tent campsites, including a few double campsites. RVs are limited to 35 feet in the upper campground and small rigs in the lower campground. Facilities include picnic tables, fire rings with grills, pit toilets (wheelchair-accessible), and hand pumps for drinking water. Pack out your trash. Leashed pets are permitted.

Reservations, fees: Reservations are not accepted. Campsites cost $13. Double campsites cost $26. An extra vehicle costs $5. Cash or check. Open mid-May-November, but serviced until early September. Lower campground closes mid-August for streamside vegetation restoration.

Directions: From Highway 75 east of Sunbeam between Stanley and Challis, turn south at milepost 204.3 to drop on the steep, narrow dirt Robinson Bar Road (Forest Road 454) to cross the Salmon River on a one-lane bridge. Find the upper campground entrance on the left 0.3 mile from the highway and the lower

campground entrance on the left 0.2 mile farther.
GPS Coordinates for Upper O'Brien: N 44° 15.558' W 114° 41.926'
GPS Coordinates for Lower O'Brien: N 44° 15.423' W 114° 41.668'
Contact: Sawtooth National Forest, Stanley Ranger Station, HC 64 Box 9900, Stanley, ID 83278, 208/774-3000, www.fs.usda.gov/sawtooth/.

36 BLIND CREEK

Scenic rating: 7

on the Yankee Fork River in Salmon-Challis National Forest

At 5,990 feet, Blind Creek Campground is the first campground up the Yankee Fork River from the confluence with the Salmon River. Its location one mile from Sunbeam makes it popular for touring the Sunbeam Dam Interpretive Site to see the remnants of the dam installed in 1910. It provided power for mining up the Yankee Fork, and the subsequent breaching of the dam in 1934 permitted the return of salmon and steelhead to spawning grounds. Sunbeam also offers Gold Dredge Tours and Upper Salmon River rafting trips. The Sunbeam hot springs—natural undeveloped springs—are one mile west on the highway. The Yankee Fork and Salmon Rivers are both favorites for rafting and kayaking, but the Class IV water below Sunbeam is for experts only. For anglers, habitat rehabilitation efforts have improved fishing in the Yankee Fork, which contains trout, mountain whitefish, steelhead, and salmon.

The tiny campground tucks its five campsites on a forested plateau 15 feet above the river, where the sound of rushing water pervades the campsites. Unfortunately, you'll also hear cars driving up the Yankee Fork to its ghost towns. Rimmed with gray boulders and a lush understory of thimbleberry, fireweed, and wild roses, the campsites overlooking the river (2-4) have some privacy. Aspens, firs, and spruce partly shade the sites. Sites 1 and 5 border the road. Site 2 is a double site.

Campsites, facilities: The campground has five RV or tent campsites. RVs are limited to 32 feet. Facilities include picnic tables, fire rings with grills, and vault toilets (wheelchair-accessible). No drinking water is available; treat river water. Pack out your trash. Leashed pets are permitted.

Reservations, fees: Reservations are not accepted. Camping costs $5. Double campsites cost $10. Open June-September.

Directions: From Sunbeam at milepost 202.5 on Highway 75 between Challis and Stanley, turn north onto Yankee Fork Road (Forest Road 013). Drive north for 1.1 mile, turning east into the campground.

GPS Coordinates: N 44° 16.856' W 114° 43.952'

Contact: Salmon-Challis National Forest, Challis-Yankee Fork Ranger District, HC 63 Box 1669 Hwy. 93, Challis, ID 83226, 208/879-4100, www.fs.usda.gov/scnf/.

37 FLAT ROCK

Scenic rating: 7

on the Yankee Fork River in Salmon-Challis National Forest

At 6,115 feet, Flat Rock Campground sits along the Yankee Fork River and the rugged 46-mile gravel Custer Motorway. A scenic forest drive upriver leads to two ghost mining towns—Custer and Bonanza City. The river is a favorite of rafters and kayakers. For anglers, habitat rehabilitation efforts have improved fishing in the Yankee Fork, which contains trout, mountain whitefish, steelhead, and salmon.

Located along the opposite side of the road from the Salmon River, the two quiet campgrounds function as one campground. Set close to the road, Flat Rock has a six-campsite loop and the Flat Rock extension has three campsites. Both have an open understory that admits views of neighboring campers as well as passing vehicles. Site 5 garners the most privacy.

Campsites, facilities: The campgrounds have 9 RV or tent campsites. RVs are limited to 32 feet. Facilities include picnic tables, fire rings with grills, vault toilets (wheelchair-accessible), and a hand pump for drinking water. Pack out your trash. Leashed pets are permitted.

Reservations, fees: Reservations are not accepted. Campsites cost $10. Cash or check. Open late May-September.

Directions: From Sunbeam on Highway 75 between Challis and Stanley, turn north at milepost 202.5 onto Yankee Fork Road (Forest Road 013). Drive north for two miles to Flat Rock Campground and 0.2 mile further to Flat Rock Extension Campground.

GPS Coordinates: N 44° 17.411' W 114° 43.106'

Contact: Salmon-Challis National Forest, Challis-Yankee Fork Ranger District, HC 63 Box 1669 Hwy. 93, Challis, ID 83226, 208/879-4100, www.fs.usda.gov/scnf/.

38 POLE FLAT

Scenic rating: 7

on the Yankee Fork River in Salmon-Challis National Forest

At 6,150 feet, Pole Flat Campground sits along the Yankee Fork River and the rugged 46-mile gravel Custer Motorway. A scenic drive upriver leads to two ghost mining towns—Custer and Bonanza City. The campground sits the opposite side of the road from the river with paths accessing the bank. Rafters and kayakers put in on the river here to float downstream to the Salmon River. For anglers, habitat rehabilitation efforts have improved fishing in the Yankee Fork, which contains trout, mountain whitefish, steelhead, and salmon.

With one loop flanking a steep hillside, the popular quiet campground offers shaded or sunny campsites with large tent spaces. A mixed loose forest of firs, lodgepoles, spruce, and aspens lend peek-a-boo views of gray talus slopes and spires in the canyon. Unfortunately, power lines also pass overhead. Two double campsites at double the price are available.

Campsites, facilities: The campground has 10 RV or tent campsites. RVs are limited to 32 feet. Facilities include picnic tables, fire rings with grills, vault toilets (wheelchair-accessible), tent pads, and drinking water. Pack out your trash. Leashed pets are permitted.

Reservations, fees: Reservations are not accepted. Campsites cost $10. Cash or check. Open late May-September.

Directions: From Sunbeam at milepost 202.5 on Highway 75 between Challis and Stanley, turn north onto Yankee Fork Road (Forest Road 013). Drive north for three miles to the campground entrance on the right.

GPS Coordinates: N 44° 18.197' W 114° 43.188'

Contact: Salmon-Challis National Forest, Challis-Yankee Fork Ranger District, HC 63 Box 1669 Hwy. 93, Challis, ID 83226, 208/879-4100, www.fs.usda.gov/scnf/.

39 CUSTER

Scenic rating: 7

on the Yankee Fork River in Salmon-Challis National Forest

At 6,660 feet, Custer Campground sits along the Yankee Fork River and the rugged 46-mile gravel Custer Motorway. The mining ghost town of Custer is nearby with a museum open in summers. Self-guided walking tours lead through the one-block town that hit its boom in the 1890s. Bonanza, another mining boomtown sits two miles south from the

Custer townsite. You can also tour the Yankee Fork Gold Dredge. For anglers, habitat rehabilitation efforts have improved fishing in the Yankee Fork, which contains trout, mountain whitefish, steelhead, and salmon.

Tucked into an arid forest, the quiet campground sits on the Yankee Fork in a section of the canyon with rugged rock formations. A turnaround loop at the end of the campground aids RVs. The river is not visible from campsites, and it requires a steep descent to reach the shoreline.

Campsites, facilities: The campground has six RV or tent campsites. RVs are limited to 32 feet. Facilities include picnic tables, fire rings with grills, and vault toilet (wheelchair-accessible), but no drinking water. Bring your own, or treat river water. Pack out your trash. Leashed pets are permitted.

Reservations, fees: Reservations are not accepted. Camping is free. Open late May-September.

Directions: From Sunbeam on Highway 75 at milepost 202.5 between Challis and Stanley, turn north onto Yankee Fork Road (Forest Road 013). Drive north for 11 miles to the campground entrance on the left.

GPS Coordinates: N 44° 23.955' W 114° 39.838'

Contact: Salmon-Challis National Forest, Challis-Yankee Fork Ranger District, HC 63 Box 1669 Hwy. 93, Challis, ID 83226, 208/879-4100, www.fs.usda.gov/scnf/.

40 EIGHTMILE

Scenic rating: 7

on the Yankee Fork River in Salmon-Challis National Forest

At 6,835 feet, tiny Eightmile Campground sits along the Yankee Fork River and the rugged 46-mile gravel Custer Motorway. This campground is the farthest upriver from Sunbeam, and connects on a rugged road over

Pine Summit with Challis. It's attractive for its remote setting at the confluence of Eight-mile Creek and the Yankee Fork River. For anglers, habitat rehabilitation efforts have improved fishing in the Yankee Fork, which contains trout, mountain whitefish, steelhead, and salmon.

The small campground sits among the road, the river, and the creek, making the sound of water pervasive. As the Yankee Fork water drops, the river bar beach grows bigger. The forest lends partial shade to the campsites, which have views of the surrounding canyon.

Campsites, facilities: The campground has two RV or tent campsites. RVs are limited to 16 feet. Facilities include picnic tables, fire rings with grills, and vault toilet (wheelchair-accessible), but no drinking water. Bring your own, or treat river water. Pack out your trash. Leashed pets are permitted.

Reservations, fees: Reservations are not accepted. Camping is free. Open late May-September.

Directions: From Sunbeam on Highway 75 at milepost 202.5 between Challis and Stanley, turn north onto Yankee Fork Road (Forest Road 013). Drive for 14 miles to the campground entrance on the right.
GPS Coordinates: N 44° 25.593' W 114° 37.268'

Contact: Salmon-Challis National Forest, Challis-Yankee Fork Ranger District, HC 63 Box 1669 Hwy. 93, Challis, ID 83226, 208/879-4100, www.fs.usda.gov/scnf/.

41 MORMON BEND

Scenic rating: 7

on the Salmon River in Sawtooth National Recreation Area

BEST (

Sitting at 6,100 feet on the Upper Salmon River, Mormon Bend is a popular site for rafting and kayaking the Class III-IV white-water section of the river from the campground to Sunbeam Dam. The campground has a cement boat ramp and trailer parking available. You can float from Stanley to the campground, or from the campground to Torrey's Hole before Sunbeam. (Total distance from Stanley is about 13 miles.) From the campground to Yankee Fork, the river is closed to floating mid-August-late September. For anglers, the river harbors trout and steelhead. Across the river from the campground there are natural undeveloped hot springs, which are best in fall and reached by wading the river. The Basin Creek Hot Springs (also called Kem or Cove hot springs) are 1.5 miles east on the highway. Hunters use the campground in fall.

Logging in the campground because of beetle kill opened up the sagebrush and small pine campsites to more sun and, unfortunately, to the highway, too. Views now include the surrounding arid slopes of the canyon. Although several campsites line up along the river, only sites 6 and 7 actually have views of the water because of heavy willows and brush. Most of the sites off the paved campground loops are paved back-ins, and sites 1 and 2 on a side spur offer no trailer turnaround. In spring, the campground packs out with kayakers and rafters, and in fall, with hunters. Arrive early to claim a campsite. Expect to hear road noise above the sound of the river.

Campsites, facilities: The campground has 13 RV or tent campsites, plus two tent-only sites. RVs are limited to 40 feet. Facilities include picnic tables, fire rings with grills, vault toilets, hand pumps for drinking water, garbage service, tent platforms, firewood for sale, and campground hosts. Leashed pets are permitted. Wheelchair-accessible facilities include toilets and campsites.

Reservations, fees: Reservations are not accepted. Campsites cost $13. Double campsites cost $26. An extra vehicle costs $5. Cash or check. Open March-November, but only serviced in summer.

Directions: From Highway 75 about seven miles east of Stanley, turn south at milepost 196.1 into the campground.

GPS Coordinates: N 44° 15.737' W 114° 50.529'

Contact: Sawtooth National Forest, Stanley Ranger Station, HC 64 Box 9900, Stanley, ID 83278, 208/774-3000, www.fs.usda.gov/sawtooth/.

42 RIVERSIDE

Scenic rating: 7

on the Salmon River in Sawtooth National Recreation Area

At 6,125 feet, Riverside is one of three campgrounds sitting close together on the Salmon River Scenic Byway on the Upper Salmon River. Part of the campground squeezes between the highway and the river; the other portion sits north of the highway. Rafters and kayakers float the Class III-IV river from Stanley to Mormon Bend or farther to Torrey's Hole west of Sunbeam. Anglers fish for trout, chinook salmon, and steelhead; check fishing regulations for catch-and-release regulations and seasonal closures for spawning.

Sprawled around paved loops set on either side of the highway, this campground has views of the surrounding sagebrush and forest canyon, but also the two-lane highway with its accompanying noise. Those areas with views of the river also look across to private homes and cabins along the river. The grass and sagebrush sites sit under a thinned-out lodgepole forest; both sunny and partly shaded sites are available. With no midstory, you'll see neighboring campers. While anyone can camp on either side, the upper loop has longer parking pads for RVs and the lower loop bigger flat spots for tents.

Campsites, facilities: The campground has 18 RV or tent campsites. RVs are limited to 38 feet. Facilities include picnic tables, fire rings with grills, vault toilets (wheelchair-accessible), hand pumps for drinking water, garbage service, and campground hosts. Leashed pets are permitted.

Reservations, fees: Reservations are not accepted. Campsites cost $13. An extra vehicle costs $5. Cash or check. Open mid-May–mid-August.

Directions: From Highway 75 about six miles east of Stanley, turn south or north at milepost 195.2 into the campground. Loops sit on both sides of the highway.

GPS Coordinates: N 44° 15.945' W 114° 51.029'

Contact: Sawtooth National Forest, Stanley Ranger Station, HC 64 Box 9900, Stanley, ID 83278, 208/774-3000, www.fs.usda.gov/sawtooth/.

43 CASINO CREEK

Scenic rating: 7

on the Salmon River in Sawtooth National Recreation Area

At 6,120 feet, Casino Creek has the advantage of being on the south side of the Upper Salmon River, in contrast to most of the other campgrounds in the vicinity. Anglers fish for trout and steelhead. The river attracts rafters and kayakers. Although the campground doesn't have a good launch ramp, you can launch up or downstream from the campground. The Big Casino Creek (#646) trailhead for hikers, mountain bikers, and horse-packers sits at the end of the campground. It is equipped with a stock ramp and hitch rail. The trail provides a strenuous 19-mile mountain-bike loop with Little Casino Creek in the White Cloud Mountains.

A lodgepole fence with gates for access lines the willow-covered riverbank. Accessed via a dirt road, the sagebrush- and lupine-filled campground sits on a dry river bar in a loose lodgepole forest with gravel back-in parking pads. Most of the sites are sunny and open. Sites 1-8, 10 and 11 overlook the river. Site 8 is a double site at double the price, and sites 18 and 19 sit uphill on a bench with walk-in tent sites. Site 17 has the most privacy. Even though the campground sits across the river from the highway, you'll hear the sound of vehicles.

Campsites, facilities: The campground has 17 RV or tent campsites, plus two walk-in tent sites. RVs are limited to 35 feet. Facilities include picnic tables, fire rings with grills, vault toilets, and drinking water from a hand-cranked well. Bring your own water as back up because of the taste. Pack out your trash. Leashed pets are permitted.

Reservations, fees: Reservations are not accepted. Campsites cost $13. Double campsites cost $26. An extra vehicle costs $5. Cash or check. Open mid-May-early September.

Directions: From Highway 75 about 5.5 miles east of Stanley, turn south onto Forest Road 651, crossing the Upper Salmon River. Drive 0.2 mile on a potholed dirt road to the campground pay station.

GPS Coordinates: N 44° 15.338' W 114° 51.327'

Contact: Sawtooth National Forest, Stanley Ranger Station, HC 64 Box 9900, Stanley, ID 83278, 208/774-3000, www.fs.usda.gov/sawtooth/.

44 SALMON RIVER

Scenic rating: 7

on the Salmon River in Sawtooth National Recreation Area

BEST (

Located at 6,150 feet, Salmon River Campground is the first of three campgrounds in a row heading east on the Salmon River Scenic Byway along the Upper Salmon River. Part of the campground squeezes between the highway and the river; the other portion sits north of the highway. Rafters and kayakers float the 13-mile, Class III-IV river from Stanley to Mormon Bend or farther to Torrey's Hole west of Sunbeam. Anglers fish for trout, chinook salmon, and steelhead; check fishing regulations for catch-and-release regulations and seasonal closures for spawning. Outfitters for rafting and fishing are in Stanley. Elkhorn hot springs (also called Boat Box), offering a wooden tub and rock-rimmed, user-built pools, are 1.5 miles to the west on the river.

Sprawled around paved loops set on both sides of the highway, this sunny campground has views of forested slopes to the south across the river and arid sagebrush slopes to the north. A few lodgepoles provide shade, but the open sagebrush meadows and tight campsites lend no privacy. You'll see neighboring campers, hear the highway, and see the road. The lower loop sits on the river with many campsites overlooking the water.

Campsites, facilities: The campground has 30 RV or tent campsites. RVs are limited to 50 feet. Facilities include picnic tables, fire rings with grills, vault toilets (wheelchair-accessible), hand pumps for drinking water, garbage service, and campground hosts. Leashed pets are permitted.

Reservations, fees: Reservations are not accepted. Campsites cost $15. Double campsites cost $30. An extra vehicle costs $5. Cash or check. Open March-November, but riverside campsites close in mid-August to protect streamside vegetation.

Directions: From Highway 75 about four miles east of Stanley, turn south or north at milepost 193.8 into the campground. Loops sit on both sides of the highway.

GPS Coordinates: N 44° 14.958' W 114° 52.175'

Contact: Sawtooth National Forest, Stanley Ranger Station, HC 64 Box 9900, Stanley, ID 83278, 208/774-3000, www.fs.usda.gov/sawtooth/.

45 STANLEY LAKE INLET

Scenic rating: 9

in the Sawtooth Mountains in Sawtooth National Recreation Area

BEST (

Stanley Lake, which sits at 6,500 feet at the

north end of the jagged Sawtooth Mountains, offers fishing, boating, water-skiing, and paddling (no Jet Skis). Boats can launch at the lake's primitive ramp adjacent to the Stanley Lake Inlet Campground, located at the west end of the lake. Anglers go after trout, including mackinaw. A sand and pebble beach makes for good swimming. From the west end of the lake, trails depart into the Sawtooth Wilderness with Bridal Veil Falls (3.5 miles) as the closest destination. Stock facilities are available at the trailhead, plus one mile of trail is gravel for wheelchair-accessibility. Mountain bikers head to the 11.5-mile Elk Mountain Loop.

The quiet campground with gravel parking pads sits along the shoreline of Stanley Lake. It has three parts: a left spur that has campsites overlooking the lake, a right spur that flanks the beach, and the boat ramp spur that includes sites that back into the trees. Spindly lodgepoles lend partial shade to the campsites, but the forest has no midstory to add privacy beyond the tree trunks. Look for mountain bluebirds around the campsites.

Campsites, facilities: The campground has 14 RV or tent campsites. RVs are limited to 50 feet. Facilities include picnic tables, fire rings with grills, vault toilets (wheelchair-accessible), drinking water, garbage service, firewood for sale, and campground hosts. Leashed pets are permitted.

Reservations, fees: Reservations are not accepted. Campsites cost $15. An extra vehicle costs $5. Cash or check. Open year-round, but services only late May-October.

Directions: From 4.6 miles north of Stanley on Highway 21, turn west at milepost 125.9 onto the paved Stanley Lake Road (Forest Road 455). Drive 3.6 miles and turn left at the head of the lake. Turn immediately left into the campground.

GPS Coordinates: N 44° 14.785' W 115° 3.891'

Contact: Sawtooth National Forest, Stanley Ranger Station, HC 64 Box 9900, Stanley, ID 83278, 208/774-3000, www.fs.usda.gov/sawtooth/.

46 STANLEY LAKE AND LAKEVIEW

Scenic rating: 10

in the Sawtooth Mountains in Sawtooth National Recreation Area

Stanley Lake, which sits at 6,500 feet at the north end of the jagged Sawtooth Mountains, offers fishing, boating, water-skiing, paddling, and swimming (No Jet Skis). Boats can launch at the lake's primitive west end ramp, but hand-carried crafts can launch from the day-use area between Lakeview and Stanley Lake Campgrounds. Anglers can fish for trout and mackinaw. From the west end of the lake, trails depart into the Sawtooth Wilderness with Bridal Veil Falls (3.5 miles) as the closest destination. Stock facilities are available at the trailhead, plus one mile of trail is gravel for wheelchair-accessibility. Mountain bikers head to the 11.5-mile Elk Mountain Loop. A scenic overlook sits in the day-use loop between the two campgrounds. Additional dispersed campsites are available on the east end of the lake, accessed via rough, potholed dirt roads from Stanley Lake Road.

On a bluff overlooking the lake, the pair of quiet campgrounds sits adjacent to each other with views of McGown and Mystery Mountains, rising up over 9,000 feet to reflect in the lake on calm days. Split on both sides of a day-use loop, the campgrounds with gravel parking pads have several spurs that end in turnaround loops. Aspens and lodgepoles lend partial shade to the sunny campsites, which give up privacy in favor of views. Trails lead to the shoreline.

Campsites, facilities: The campgrounds have 24 RV or tent campsites, including several double campsites. RVs are limited to 45 feet. Facilities include picnic tables, fire rings with grills, vault toilets (wheelchair-accessible), hand pumps for drinking water, garbage service, and campground hosts. Leashed pets are permitted.

© BECKY LOMAX

Stanley Lake offers wading, swimming, fishing, and boating.

Reservations, fees: Reservations are accepted (877/444-6777, www.recreation.gov). Campsites cost $15. Double campsites cost $30. An extra vehicle costs $5. Cash or check. Open May-October, but serviced only in summer.

Directions: From 4.6 miles north of Stanley on Highway 21, turn west at milepost 125.9 onto the paved Stanley Lake Road (Forest Road 455). Drive 3.1 miles and turn left. At the first campground junction, go straight to reach Stanley Lake Campground, which has reserved sites, and turn right to reach Lakeview Campground.

GPS Coordinates: N 44° 14.971' W 115° 3.295'

Contact: Sawtooth National Forest, Stanley Ranger Station, HC 64 Box 9900, Stanley, ID 83278, 208/774-3000, www.fs.usda.gov/sawtooth/.

47 IRON CREEK

Scenic rating: 7

in the Sawtooth Mountains in Sawtooth National Recreation Area

BEST (

At 6,700 feet, Iron Creek is one of the few Sawtooth Mountain campgrounds that does not sit on a lake. Campers use this campground as a leap-off point into the Sawtooth Wilderness Area. The trailhead, which is equipped with a stock ramp and hitch rail, leads 5.5 miles and 1,700 feet in elevation to stunning Sawtooth Lake. Steep switchbacks finish the trail into the scenic lake, flanked by the 10,190-foot Mount Regan. The lake harbors rainbow trout. You can also access Alpine Lake from this trailhead.

The campground tucks one loop into a spindly lodgepole forest, the remaining healthy pines left after removal of the larger beetle-killed trees. The pines do contribute partial shade to the campsites. After the loop passes the trailhead, the campsites line up along the creek.

Most of the campsites are open to the road, and neighboring campers are visible. On weekends there's a stream of vehicles to the popular trailhead, which can see 40 people a day in summer, but at night, the campground quiets.

Campsites, facilities: The campground has nine RV or tent campsites. RVs are limited to small rigs. Facilities include picnic tables, fire rings with grills, vault toilets, hand pump for drinking water, and garbage service. Leashed pets are permitted.

Reservations, fees: Reservations are not accepted. Campsites cost $13. An extra vehicle costs $5. Cash or check. Open May-October, but only serviced in summer.

Directions: From 2.1 miles north of Stanley on Highway 21, turn south onto Iron Creek Road (Forest Road 619) and drive 2.7 miles of dirt to the campground loop.

GPS Coordinates: N 44° 11.983' W 115° 0.350'

Contact: Sawtooth National Forest, Stanley Ranger Station, HC 64 Box 9900, Stanley, ID 83278, 208/774-3000, www.fs.usda.gov/sawtooth/.

48 SUNNY GULCH

Scenic rating: 9

on the Salmon River in Sawtooth National Recreation Area

At 6,450 feet along the Upper Salmon River, Sunny Gulch is a convenient campground for visiting the town of Stanley. Fishing and rafting outfitters are headquartered in town, plus groceries, ice, and gas are available. A seasonal bakery is worth a stop in summer. For cyclists traveling through the Sawtooth National Recreation Area, this campground is the only one located on the highway between Stanley and Galena Pass to the south. The Upper Salmon River harbors rainbow trout, steelhead trout (mid-March-April), and chinook salmon (until late July). Trails within a 10-minute drive

depart into the White Clouds or Sawtooth Mountains. Mountain-biking trails are also available near Redfish Lake. If Sunny Gulch and the Redfish Lake campgrounds fill up, a primitive overflow camping area sits south of Sunny Gulch Campground. A disposal station is available at the ranger station 1.1 miles north of the campground.

The sunny campground sits surrounded by sagebrush, grass, and a loose lodgepole forest with peek-a-boo views of the Sawtooth Mountains and White Cloud foothills. Through the open forest, much of the campground is visible, but so are the dramatic peaks. A paved road makes two loops around the campground with paved parking pads that are mostly back-ins. While the campground does hear highway noise, sites at the back overlooking the river canyon also hear the river. Sites 35, 37-39, 42, 44, and 45 not only sit farthest from the highway, but also overlook the river. A lodgepole fence divides the campsites from the abrupt canyon edge. The loop with campsites 27-45 sits on a higher plateau with bigger views.

Campsites, facilities: The campground has 45 RV or tent campsites. RVs are limited to 35 feet. Facilities include picnic tables on cement pads, fire rings with grills, cookstove pedestals, vault toilets (wheelchair-accessible), hand pumps for drinking water, garbage service, tent platforms, firewood for sale, and campground hosts. Leashed pets are permitted.

Reservations, fees: Reservations are accepted (877/444-6777, www.recreation.gov). Campsites cost $16. Double campsites cost $32. An extra vehicle costs $5. Cash or check. Open May-October.

Directions: From 3.6 miles south of Stanley on Highway 75, turn northeast into the campground at milepost 185.8.

GPS Coordinates: N 44° 10.431' W 114° 54.624'

Contact: Sawtooth National Forest, Stanley Ranger Station, HC 64 Box 9900, Stanley, ID 83278, 208/774-3000, www.fs.usda.gov/sawtooth/.

49 CHINOOK BAY AND MOUNTAIN VIEW

Scenic rating: 9

in the Sawtooth Mountains in Sawtooth National Recreation Area

Located at 6,500 feet on tiny Little Redfish Lake, these adjacent campgrounds sitting at the base of the rugged Sawtooth Mountains fill every night. The lake, which does not permit motorboats, is small enough to avoid the big whitecaps of the larger lake. Hand-carried watercraft can be launched from both campgrounds. Since the lake is so shallow, it does not offer the same quality of fishing as Redfish Lake, but fish pass through its waters. Mountain bikers tour the 12-mile Decker Flat Loop, which parallels Highway 75. The Redfish complex, 1.5 miles south, includes hiking trailheads, boat launches, horseback rides, bicycle and boat rentals, convenience store, launderette, showers, disposal station, and lodge with restaurant.

Lodgepole pines dominate the two adjacent grass and sagebrush campgrounds, but they are sparse enough for sun. With little mid-story, neighboring campers are visible. Of all the Redfish complex campgrounds, these two are the noisiest—vehicles can be heard on the highway and the Redfish entrance road. Some sites even have views of the road. Both campgrounds, however, garner dramatic views of Heyburn Mountain. In Mountain View, sites 2, 3, and 4 grab prime views of the jagged Sawtooths. In Chinook Bay, sites 9 and 11 pick up lake views with sites 4, 5, 7, and 8 lining up along the riverbank. Power lines pass over a few sites in Chinook Bay.

Campsites, facilities: The campgrounds have 19 RV or tent campsites. RVs are limited to 40 feet. Facilities include picnic tables, fire rings with grills, flush toilets (wheelchair-accessible), drinking water, garbage service, firewood for sale, and campground hosts. Leashed pets are permitted.

Reservations, fees: Reservations are not accepted. Campsites cost $16. Double campsites cost $32. An extra vehicle costs $5. Cash or check. Open May-October, but serviced summers only.

Directions: From 4.3 miles south of Stanley on Highway 75, turn southwest at milepost 185 onto Redfish Lake Road (Forest Road 214). Drive 0.4 mile to Chinook Bay Campground entrance and 0.1 mile farther to Mountain View Campground. Both entrances are on the right.

Chinook Bay GPS Coordinates: N 44° 9.847' W 114° 54.215'

Mountain View GPS Coordinates: N 44° 9.711' W 114° 54.269'

Contact: Sawtooth National Forest, Stanley Ranger Station, HC 64 Box 9900, Stanley, ID 83278, 208/774-3000, www.fs.usda.gov/sawtooth/.

50 POINT

Scenic rating: 10

in the Sawtooth Mountains in Sawtooth National Recreation Area

Tucked below the jagged Sawtooth Mountains on Redfish Lake's northwest side, Point Campground is popular for its location, views, boating, kokanee salmon fishing, and big sandy swimming beach with a dock. It is also the closest Redfish complex campground to the lodge, boat tours, and bicycle, kayak, and boat rentals. Horseback rides, showers, launderette, visitors center, and a disposal station are also available within one mile. Bench Lakes trail (3.4 miles) departs near the campground entrance, climbing 1,200 feet to lakes filled with yellow-blooming lily pads. The nearby Decker Trail gives mountain bikers 12 miles of riding. Hand-carried watercraft can launch from the campground or picnic area, but the launch for larger boats sits on the lake's opposite side.

The campground splits on both sides of the

Trails and off-trail scrambles criss-cross the Sawtooth Mountains.

day-use picnic area. Skinny lodgepoles provide partial shade for the grassy campsites but are also open enough for views of the lake and Sawtooth Mountains as well as neighboring campers. Sites 1-8 are walk-in sites for tents only. Handcarts are available to transfer camping gear to the campsites from the parking area. Sites 11, 12, 14, 16, and 17 overlook the water in the eastern loop. While Redfish Lake hums with the noise of motorboats during the day, at night the campground is quiet.

Campsites, facilities: The campground has nine RV or tent campsites plus eight walk-in tent sites. RVs are limited to camper vans and trucks with campers only. No motorhomes, trailers, or pop-up tent trailers are permitted. Facilities include picnic tables, fire rings with grills, cookstove pedestals, flush and vault toilets (wheelchair-accessible), drinking water, bear boxes, tent platforms, garbage service, firewood for sale, and campground hosts. Leashed pets are permitted.

Reservations, fees: Reservations are advised (877/444-6777, www.recreation.gov). Campsites cost $16. Double campsites cost $32. An

extra vehicle costs $5. Cash or check. Open late May–mid-September.

Directions: From 4.3 miles south of Stanley on Highway 75, turn southwest at milepost 185 onto Redfish Lake Road (Forest Road 214). Drive 1.7 miles and turn right for 0.7 mile, passing the lodge. The road terminates at the campground.

GPS Coordinates: N 44° 8.399' W 114° 55.535'

Contact: Sawtooth National Forest, Stanley Ranger Station, HC 64 Box 9900, Stanley, ID 83278, 208/774-3000, www.fs.usda.gov/sawtooth/.

51 GLACIER VIEW

Scenic rating: 9

in the Sawtooth Mountains in Sawtooth National Recreation Area

North of Redfish Lake at 6,575 feet, Glacier View is somewhat a misnomer. While a monstrous glacier carved the lake basin, the Sawtooth Mountains have no active glaciers remaining today. The campground has access to the lake at the North Shore picnic area, which sits across the road with stunning views of the Sawtooths and a sandy swimming beach. Canoes and kayaks can launch from the picnic area, but larger boats must drive 0.9 mile south to the boat launch. The lake, which is best fished from boats, harbors several species of trout plus kokanee salmon. It is also a favorite for water-skiing, sailing, and paddling. The 12-mile Decker Mountain Bike Loop is nearby, and trailheads depart for hikers from various locations around the lake—some for destinations in the Sawtooth Wilderness Area. Bicycle and boat rentals, horseback rides, boat tours, disposal station, convenience store, visitors center, launderette, and showers all sit within two miles.

Set on a knoll above the lake, Glacier View campsites rim three paved loops in a loose lodgepole forest that is open enough for views of the Sawtooth or White Cloud Mountains. With only short vegetation between the trees—sagebrush, lupines, and grass—views include neighboring campers. The A loop overlooks the outlet stream drainage, and paths connect to the banks. Since the campground is set back from the lakeshore, it is quieter than the Redfish campgrounds with lake frontage.

Campsites, facilities: The campground has 65 RV or tent campsites, including eight double campsites. RVs are limited to 50 feet. Facilities include picnic tables on paved pads, fire rings with grills, pedestal grills, flush toilets (wheelchair-accessible), drinking water, tent platforms, garbage service, firewood for sale, three small playgrounds, and campground hosts. Leashed pets are permitted.

Reservations, fees: Reservations are advised (877/444-6777, www.recreation.gov). Campsites cost $16. Double campsites cost $32. An extra vehicle costs $5. Cash or check. Open late May-mid-September.

Directions: From 4.3 miles south of Stanley on Highway 75, turn southwest at milepost 185 onto Redfish Lake Road (Forest Road 214). Drive 2.2 miles, swinging east at the lake. Turn left into the campground and drive 0.1 mile uphill to the pay station.

GPS Coordinates: N 44° 8.746' W 114° 54.906'

Contact: Sawtooth National Forest, Stanley Ranger Station, HC 64 Box 9900, Stanley, ID 83278, 208/774-3000, www.fs.usda.gov/sawtooth/.

52 OUTLET

Scenic rating: 10

in the Sawtooth Mountains in Sawtooth National Recreation Area

BEST (

Located at 6,500 feet on Redfish Lake's northeast shore, Outlet Campground sits on a sandy bay with views of Mount Heyburn and the Grand Mogul—two of the Sawtooth Mountains' more dramatic peaks. The campground also has a day-use picnic area, with a buoyed swimming beach. Canoes and kayaks can launch from the picnic area, but larger boats must drive 0.6 mile south to the boat launch. The lake attracts water-skiers, sailors, and paddlers, and is best fished from boats. It harbors several species of trout, kokanee salmon, and sockeye salmon. The 12-mile Decker Mountain Bike Loop and the hiking trail to the end of the lake depart 0.7 mile south. Bicycle and boat rentals, horseback rides, boat tours, disposal station, convenience store, visitors center, launderette, and showers all sit within two miles.

With paved interior roads and parking pads, the long, narrow campground squeezes between the lake and the busy road, which accesses two more campgrounds plus the boat launch for Redfish Lake. Young lodgepole pines partly shade the spacious campsites, many of which have peek-a-boo views of the lake and Mount Heyburn. Sagebrush and grasses cover the ground surrounding the campsites. At the campground's north end, sites are more open, and views include neighboring campers. At the southern end, the trees are thicker, allowing more privacy. Sites 8, 11, 13, and 15 sit nearest the water.

Campsites, facilities: The campground has 19 RV or tent campsites, including seven double campsites. RVs are limited to 45 feet. Facilities include picnic tables on cement pads, fire rings with grills and pot hangers, cookstove pedestals, vault toilets, drinking water, tent pads, garbage service, firewood for sale, and campground hosts. Leashed pets are permitted. Wheelchair-accessible facilities include toilets and campsites.

Reservations, fees: Reservations are advised (877/444-6777, www.recreation.gov). Campsites cost $16. Double campsites cost $32. An extra vehicle costs $5. Cash or check. Open late May–mid-September.

Directions: From 4.3 miles south of Stanley on Highway 75, turn southwest at milepost 185 onto Redfish Lake Road (Forest Road 214). Drive 2.5 miles, swinging east around the head of the lake. Turn right and immediately left into the campground.

GPS Coordinates: N 44° 8.602' W 114° 54.682'

Contact: Sawtooth National Forest, Stanley Ranger Station, HC 64 Box 9900, Stanley, ID 83278, 208/774-3000, www.fs.usda.gov/sawtooth/.

53 MOUNT HEYBURN

🥾🚲🏊🛶🛥️🎣🐎👤♿🚐⛺

Scenic rating: 9

in the Sawtooth Mountains in Sawtooth National Recreation Area

Mount Heyburn Campground, which sits at 6,600 feet on the east side of Redfish Lake, is popular with boaters, water-skiers, paddlers, and sailors. The campground sits opposite the Mount Heyburn day-use picnic area. The day-use area houses the lake's boat launch, with docks, cement ramp, trailer parking, and buoyed swimming area with a sandy beach. Best fished from boats, the lake harbors kokanee salmon, sockeye salmon, and several species of trout. It is also popular for water-skiing. The 12-mile Decker Mountain Bike Loop and the hiking trail to the end of the lake depart 0.3 mile south. Bicycle and boat rentals, horseback rides, boat tours, disposal station, convenience store, visitors center, launderette, and showers sit within 2.5 miles.

Mount Heyburn Campground tucks into a lodgepole forest. Its one large, paved loop is treed with a thin forest of spindly lodgepole pines—all that remain after logging the campground clean of beetle-killed trees. Sagebrush and wild grass surround the campsites, which are now sunny and open. Some have views to the road. The campground's location off the lake makes it quieter than some of the other Redfish campgrounds, and it tends to fill up later than the others.

Campsites, facilities: The campground has 20 RV or tent campsites. RVs are limited to 40 feet. Facilities include picnic tables, fire rings with grills, vault toilets (wheelchair-accessible), drinking water, garbage service, three small playgrounds, firewood for sale, and campground hosts. Leashed pets are permitted.

Reservations, fees: Reservations are not accepted. Campsites cost $16. Double campsites cost $16. An extra vehicle costs $5. Cash or check. Usually, either Mt. Heyburn or Sockeye Campground stays open year-round; otherwise, open late May–early September.

Directions: From 4.3 miles south of Stanley on Highway 75, turn southwest at milepost 185 onto Redfish Lake Road (Forest Road 214). Drive 3.1 miles, swinging east around the lake past Outlet Campground. At the boat launch, turn left into the campground.

GPS Coordinates: N 44° 8.155' W 114° 54.934'

Contact: Sawtooth National Forest, Stanley Ranger Station, HC 64 Box 9900, Stanley, ID 83278, 208/774-3000, www.fs.usda.gov/sawtooth/.

© BECKY LOMAX

Rental boats are available at Redfish Lake at the dock at the lodge.

54 SOCKEYE

🥾 🚴 🏊 🎣 🛶 🚤 🐕 ♿ 🚐 ⛺

Scenic rating: 10

in the Sawtooth Mountains in Sawtooth National Recreation Area

BEST (

Sockeye Campground, named for the salmon stocked in Redfish Lake, sits at 6,500 feet on the east shore of the Sawtooth Mountains' largest lake. The campground entrance is 0.1 mile from Mount Heyburn day-use picnic area, which houses the docks, cement boat ramp, trailer parking, and a buoyed swimming area with a sandy beach. Adjacent to campsite 20, a trailhead departs for Redfish Ridge, Decker Flat, Redfish Lake inlet, the 12-mile Decker Mountain Bike Loop, and lakes in the Sawtooth Wilderness. Bicycle and boat rentals, horseback rides, boat tours, disposal station, visitors center, convenience store, launderette, and showers sit less than three miles north of the campground.

Sockeye Campground gains appeal because it sits at the road's terminus. While noise from motorboats on the lake enters the campground during the day, it quiets at night. The campground looks across the lake to Mount Heyburn, and a lodgepole fence borders the water, permitting access to the rocky shoreline only at certain places to prevent habitat damage and guard sockeye salmon spawning. Sites 1-5 have views of the water from across the campground road, but sites 6, 7, 9, 12, 14, and 15 overlook the lake through lodgepoles. The thinned doghair lodgepole forest permits views of neighboring campers, but the campsites are spread out. Most of the campsites are sunny with only a little shade.

Campsites, facilities: The campground has 22 RV or tent campsites, including six double campsites, plus one tent-only site. RVs are limited to 35 feet. Facilities include picnic tables on cement pads, fire rings with grills, campstove pedestals, vault toilets (wheelchair-accessible), drinking water, garbage service, tent platforms, firewood for sale, and campground hosts. Leashed pets are permitted.

Reservations, fees: Reservations are not accepted. Campsites cost $8. An extra vehicle costs $5. Cash or check. Usually, either Mt. Heyburn or Sockeye Campground stays open year-round; otherwise, open late May-early September.

Directions: From 4.3 miles south of Stanley on Highway 75, turn southwest at milepost 185 onto Redfish Lake Road (Forest Road 214). Drive 3.2 miles, swinging east around the lake until the road ends at the campground. GPS Coordinates: N 44° 8.106' W 114° 55.041'

Contact: Sawtooth National Forest, Stanley Ranger Station, HC 64 Box 9900, Stanley, ID 83278, 208/774-3000, www.fs.usda.gov/sawtooth/.

55 REDFISH INLET

Scenic rating: 10

in the Sawtooth Mountains in Sawtooth
National Recreation Area

BEST (

Tucked below the jagged Mount Heyburn on
Redfish Lake's southwest side, Redfish Inlet
Campground requires a boat or five-mile
hike to reach. From the Mount Heyburn
boat launch on the lake's opposite side, the
crossing is three miles. From the lodge at the
north end of the lake, the crossing is five miles.
Motorboats, canoes, and kayaks are available
to rent at the lodge, and a boat shuttle service
runs about five times per day to the transfer
camp. When crossing the lake, look for the
Guardians of the Lake, the large rocks flanking both sides. Securely beach canoes, kayaks,
and boats overnight for safety from winds.
From the camp, a 0.5-mile walk leads to Lily
Lake. Trails circle Redfish Lake and head up
Redfish Lake Creek into the Sawtooth Wilderness. The south slopes of Mount Heyburn
contain the Redfish Slab rock-climbing routes.
For anglers, the lake harbors kokanee salmon
and rainbow trout.

The campground sits back in the forest on
the north side of Redfish Lake Creek. The
sites sprinkle across an open forest flat bench
with peek-a-boo views of the lake and Grand
Mogul. Sites are partly shaded by lodgepole
pines, many of which have been damaged by
pine bark beetles. The campsites are within
sight of each other and trails. During the day,
the area hums with activity as the tour boat
disgorges visitors on its dock, but nighttime
is exceptionally quiet.

Campsites, facilities: The campground has
six tent campsites. Facilities include picnic
tables, fire rings with grills, bear boxes, and
a vault toilet. Drinking water is not available. Bring your own, or treat lake or creek
water. Pack out your trash. Leashed pets are
permitted.

Reservations, fees: Reservations are not
accepted. Camping is free. Open mid-June–
mid-September.

Directions: From 4.3 miles south of Stanley
on Highway 75, turn southwest at milepost
185 onto Redfish Lake Road (Forest Road
214). Drive 3.1 miles, swinging east around
the lake to the boat launch on the right.

GPS Coordinates: N 44° 5.955' W 114° 57.180'

Contact: Sawtooth National Forest, Stanley
Ranger Station, HC 64 Box 9900, Stanley,
ID 83278, 208/774-3000, www.fs.usda.gov/
sawtooth/.

56 PETTIT LAKE

Scenic rating: 9

in the Sawtooth Mountains in Sawtooth
National Recreation Area

BEST (

On other Sawtooth Mountain lakes, no summer homes line the shores. On 395-acre Pettit Lake, elevation 7,000 feet, homes string
along the south lakeshore and the point with
the campground, which is on the northeastern end. A boat launch is available 0.5 mile
southeast, but canoes and kayaks can launch
from the campground to tour the shallow east
bays. The lake harbors rainbow, brook, and
cutthroat trout. At the adjacent Tin Cup Trailhead, the hiking trail departs for Yellow Belly
Lake (2.7 miles) or Alice Lake (6.3 miles). The
18-mile Toxaway-Pettit Loop strings together
a series of lakes through 10,000-foot peaks
of the Sawtooth Wilderness. Listen for loons
on the lake.

Surrounded by low sagebrush, grass, and
lupine, the campground sits on two loops
on a shallow east-side bay with only a couple
of campsites having snippets of water views.
Circling under skinny lodgepoles, the campground weaves campsites close together in
mostly open, non-private locations, the result
of logging beetle-killed trees. Sites 1-3 unfortunately sit under power lines and along
the campground road that leads to the busy

trailhead. Sites 4-6 sit adjacent to trailhead parking, but sites 7-13, located on the left loop, sit nearer the lake. A lodgepole fence surrounds the campground, with gates to access the water. The campsites have large, flat tent spaces.

Campsites, facilities: The campground has 13 RV or tent campsites, including three double campsites. RVs are limited to 45 feet. Facilities include picnic tables, fire rings with grills, vault toilets (wheelchair-accessible), hand pump for drinking water, garbage service, firewood for sale, and campground hosts. Leashed pets are permitted.

Reservations, fees: Reservations are not accepted. Campsites cost $12. Double campsites cost $24. An extra vehicle costs $5. Cash or check. Open year-round, but serviced only in summer.

Directions: From Highway 75 about 17 miles south of Stanley, turn west at milepost 171.3 onto the gravel Pettit Lake Road (Forest Road 208). Expect some small potholes and washboards. Drive 1.6 miles to a junction with the picnic area and boat launch. Turn right and drive 0.5 mile to the campground pay station. GPS Coordinates: N 43° 59.099' W 114° 52.141'

Contact: Sawtooth National Forest, Stanley Ranger Station, HC 64 Box 9900, Stanley, ID 83278, 208/774-3000, www.fs.usda.gov/sawtooth/.

57 ALTURAS LAKE INLET

Scenic rating: 9

in the Sawtooth Mountains in Sawtooth National Recreation Area

At 7,036 feet in the southern Sawtooth Mountains, Alturas Lake Inlet Campground sits at the west end of Alturas Lake in one of the best locations for swimming. Visitors opt for camping here as a quieter alternative to the Redfish complex crowds. Canoes and kayaks can launch from the day-use beach, which has a sandy buoyed swimming area. The developed boat launch for boaters, water-skiers, and anglers is 1.3 miles east at Smokey Bear Campground. Mountain bikers can ride up the valley along Alturas Lake Creek—partway on road, part on trail. With a trailhead one mile north of the lake, the Cabin Creek Lakes Trail climbs a steep 1,998 feet in 4.5 miles. Watch for loons, ospreys, and tundra swans on the lake.

The quiet campground with dirt interior roads tucks into the forest between the forest road heading up the valley to trailheads, the day-use picnic area at the lake's head, and Alturas Lake Creek. The sunny campground sits in a loose, open forest of firs and lodgepoles, but in a lush zone that fosters mosquitoes. A few trails whack through the willow brush to the creek, and a trail leads to the beach at the picnic area. Flat spaces for tents are available. Sites at the west end have views up the valley across the meadows.

Campsites, facilities: The campground has 27 RV or tent campsites, including five double campsites. RVs are limited to 40 feet. Facilities include picnic tables, fire rings with grills, vault toilets (wheelchair-accessible), drinking water, garbage service, firewood for sale, and campground hosts. Leashed pets are permitted.

Reservations, fees: Reservations are accepted (877/444-6777, www.recreation.gov). Campsites cost $15. Double campsites cost $30. An extra vehicle costs $5. Cash or check. Open late May-early September.

Directions: From Highway 75 about 21 miles south of Stanley, turn east onto Alturas Lake Road (Forest Road 205) at milepost 167.5. Drive 4.8 miles and turn left and then immediately right into the campground. GPS Coordinates: N 43° 54.396' W 114° 52.813'

Contact: Sawtooth National Forest, Stanley Ranger Station, HC 64 Box 9900, Stanley, ID 83278, 208/774-3000, www.fs.usda.gov/sawtooth/.

Alturas Lake, in the Sawtooth National Recreation Area, offers fishing, boating, and swimming.

58 NORTH SHORE

Scenic rating: 9

in the Sawtooth Mountains in Sawtooth National Recreation Area

In the southern Sawtooth Mountains, North Shore Campground sits at 7,050 feet on the north shore of Alturas Lake. It sits west of Smokey Bear Campground, which has the lake's one developed boat launch, equipped with a dock, cement ramp, and boat trailer parking. Motorboats are permitted on the lake, but not personal watercraft. The lake, which frequently sees afternoon winds, supports a fish population of rainbow and cutthroat trout as well as kokanee salmon. Mountain biking is permitted on the forest roads in the area that connect to Pettit Lake, and hiking trails tour the lakeshore and launch into the Sawtooth Wilderness. Sandy beaches are available for swimming near the boat launch. Visitors opt for camping at Alturas as a quieter alternative

to the busy Redfish complex. Watch for bald eagles, ospreys, and grebes on the lake.

North Shore is a quiet campground with dirt roads situated on a hillside rimmed with only a few tall firs and lodgepole pines lending snippets of shade. Grass and sagebrush meadows make up most of the sunny campground. Campsites in meadow areas glean big views up the valley to the southern Sawtooth Mountains. Flat tent spaces are available. Some of the campsites overlook the lake. Trails connect with the shore.

Campsites, facilities: The campground has 15 RV or tent campsites. RVs are limited to 50 feet. Facilities include picnic tables, fire rings with grills, vault toilets (wheelchair-accessible), drinking water, garbage service, firewood for sale, and campground hosts. Leashed pets are permitted.

Reservations, fees: Reservations are not accepted. Campsites cost $15. An extra vehicle costs $5. Cash or check. Open late May–early September.

Directions: From Highway 75 about 21 miles

south of Stanley, turn east onto paved Alturas Lake Road (Forest Road 205) at milepost 167.5. Drive 3.7 miles and turn left into the campground.

GPS Coordinates: N 43° 55.195' W 114° 51.969'

Contact: Sawtooth National Forest, Stanley Ranger Station, HC 64 Box 9900, Stanley, ID 83278, 208/774-3000, www.fs.usda.gov/sawtooth/.

59 SMOKEY BEAR

Scenic rating: 9

in the Sawtooth Mountains in Sawtooth National Recreation Area

At the south end of the Sawtooth Mountains, Smokey Bear Campground sits at 7,050 feet on the north shore of Alturas Lake. The campground has the lake's one developed boat launch, equipped with a dock, cement ramp, and boat trailer parking. Motorboats are permitted on the lake, but not personal watercraft. The lake supports a fish population of rainbow and westslope cutthroat trout as well as kokanee salmon. The lake frequently sees afternoon winds. Mountain biking is permitted on the forest roads in the area that connect to Pettit Lake, and hiking trails tour the lakeshore. Sandy beaches are available for swimming. Visitors opt for camping at Alturas as a quieter alternative to the busy Redfish complex. Watch for loons and tundra swans on the lake in spring and fall.

The quiet Smokey Bear campground used to be thick forest, but pine beetles killed many of the trees, which have been subsequently logged out. Much of the campground receives sun. With gravel pull-through or back-in parking pads, campsites with forest duff floors are surrounded by doghair lodgepoles that only lend a bit of shade. Several of the sites are spacious with flat sites for tents, but

neighbors are still visible. Sites 4-7 and 10 overlook the lake.

Campsites, facilities: The campground has 11 RV or tent campsites, including three double campsites. RVs are limited to 16 feet. Facilities include picnic tables, fire rings with grills, vault toilets (wheelchair-accessible), drinking water, and garbage service. Leashed pets are permitted.

Reservations, fees: Reservations are not accepted. Campsites cost $15. Double campsites cost $30. An extra vehicle costs $5. Cash or check. Open all year, but serviced late May-early September.

Directions: From Highway 75 about 21 miles south of Stanley, turn east onto paved Alturas Lake Road (Forest Road 205) at milepost 167.5. Drive 3.5 miles, and turn left into the campground. Campsites sit to the right of the pay station and the boat launch to the left.

GPS Coordinates: N 43° 55.263' W 114° 51.757'

Contact: Sawtooth National Forest, Stanley Ranger Station, HC 64 Box 9900, Stanley, ID 83278, 208/774-3000, www.fs.usda.gov/sawtooth/.

60 EASLEY AND BOULDER VIEW

Scenic rating: 8

on the Big Wood River in Sawtooth National Recreation Area

BEST (

At 6,600 feet along the Big Wood River and the Sawtooth Scenic Byway, neighboring Easley and Boulder View Campgrounds are popular for the adjacent developed hot springs. Run by the Idaho Baptist Convention, the swimming complex (open Memorial Day-Labor Day, 208/726-7522, www.cathedralpines.org) has a full-size chlorine-free swimming pool, two 98°F hot tubs, and changing rooms with showers. Views from the pools include the Boulder Mountains. The campground also sits on the 18.8-mile Harriman Trail, a double-track hiking, mountain biking, and horseback riding trail that connects SNRA Headquarters with Galena, where more mountain-biking and hiking trails are available. The Big Wood River is known for its rainbow and brook trout fishery.

Boulder View and Easley Campgrounds sit across the river from each other. Easley spreads out private campsites along one dirt road with a small turnaround loop at the end while Boulder View campsites rim a more compact loop. Both are in an open aspen forest with a few Douglas firs and pines contributing partial shade to some of the campsites. Some sites have views of the rugged Boulder Mountains. With the Big Wood River flowing through willow bogs between them, the area can buzz with mosquitoes. Highway sounds are audible.

Campsites, facilities: Together, the campgrounds have 20 RV or tent campsites, including several double sites. RVs are limited to 50 feet. Facilities include picnic tables, fire rings with grills, vault toilets (wheelchair-accessible), drinking water, garbage service, firewood for sale, and campground hosts. Leashed pets are permitted.

Reservations, fees: Reservations are accepted for Easley (877/444-6777, www.recreation.gov). Campsites cost $12. Double campsites cost $24. An extra vehicle costs $5. Cash or check. Open mid-May–mid-September.

Directions: From Highway 75 about 12 miles north of downtown Ketchum, turn south at milepost 142.4 onto Forest Road 160. Drive 0.2 mile and turn right into the campground. Boulder View Campground can also be reached via the highway turnoff 0.5 mile north of the Easley turnoff.

GPS Coordinates: N 43° 46.775' W 114° 32.185'

Contact: Sawtooth National Forest, Sawtooth National Recreation Area Headquarters, 5 North Fork Canyon Road, Ketchum, ID 83340, 208/727-5000, www.fs.usda.gov/sawtooth/.

61 WOOD RIVER

Scenic rating: 7

on the Big Wood River in Sawtooth National Recreation Area

On the Sawtooth Scenic Byway, Wood River Campground, elevation 6,360 feet, sits on the Big Wood River, a rainbow trout fishery tumbling from Galena Pass and surrounded by steep-sloped peaks climbing above 9,000 feet. The campground also sits on the 18.8-mile Harriman Trail, a double-track trail for hiking, mountain biking, and horseback riding. The trail passes through the campground, linking 2.5 miles south to SNRA Headquarters and 16.3 miles north to Galena, where another network of mountain-bike and hiking trails is available. A nature trail also tours the forest from the back of the campground.

This campground, set in a deep forest, fills up fast because of its location and ambience. A thicker forest of aspens, lodgepoles, and Douglas firs shades many of the campsites, although some of the dying pines may be removed in the future. The campground also sits on the opposite side of the river from the highway. Unfortunately, those sites along the river also hear the highway and view it, too. Sites at the back of the campground have more shade and a bit more privacy backing up to the forest slope. The campground also has a paved road but a mix of paved and dirt parking pads—only two of which are pull-throughs. A handful of sites garner views up valley.

Campsites, facilities: The campground has 25 RV or tent campsites, five tent-only campsites, and one large group campsite. RVs are limited to 40 feet. Facilities include picnic tables, fire rings with grills, vault toilets (wheelchair-accessible), drinking water, garbage service, double campsites, firewood for sale, an amphitheater for interpretive programs, and campground hosts. Leashed pets are permitted.

Reservations, fees: Reservations are accepted

for the group campsite only (877/444-6777, www.recreation.gov). Campsites cost $12. Double campsites cost $24. An extra vehicle costs $5. Cash or check. Open May-October.

Directions: About 10 miles north of downtown Ketchum, turn south off Highway 75 at milepost 138.4 and drive 0.1 mile across the single-lane bridge over the Big Wood River into the campground.

GPS Coordinates: N 43° 47.614' W 114° 27.459'

Contact: Sawtooth National Forest, Sawtooth National Recreation Area Headquarters, 5 North Fork Canyon Road, Ketchum, ID 83340, 208/727-5000, www.fs.usda.gov/sawtooth/.

62 NORTH FORK

Scenic rating: 6
on the Big Wood River in Sawtooth National Recreation Area

At 6,265 feet on the Sawtooth Scenic Byway, the North Fork Campground is named for the river flowing into the Big Wood River just downstream of the campground; however, the campground does not sit up the North Fork Canyon but rather on the main Big Wood River surrounded by sagebrush. It is the nearest campground to Ketchum, where rafting, fishing, and horseback riding outfitters are headquartered. The Big Wood River harbors rainbow trout for fishing. The campground's popularity is due to its placement on the south end of the Harriman Trail, an 18.8-mile double-track trail for hiking, mountain biking, and horseback riding. The trail parallels the river and highway running from SNRA Headquarters to Galena. The nearest destination is Baker Creek at seven miles.

Located in between the highway and the river, the campground's two loops circle through an aspen forest dotted with a few dying pines. Sites are partly shaded by the trees; brushy willows add privacy to some campsites, while others are more open with wildflower meadows. The sounds of both the river and the highway pervade the campground, along with winds that cause the aspen leaves to clack together in song. Ten campsites sit adjacent to the river. The small spread out campsites have small tent spaces. Some with views of low sagebrush slopes of the Boulder Mountains.

Campsites, facilities: The campground has 28 RV or tent campsites. RVs are limited to 40 feet. Facilities include picnic tables, fire rings with grills, vault toilets (wheelchair-accessible), drinking water, garbage service, firewood for sale, double campsites, and campground hosts. Leashed pets are permitted.

Reservations, fees: Reservations are accepted (877/444-6777, www.recreation.gov). Campsites cost $12. Double campsites cost $24. An extra vehicle costs $5. Cash or check. Open mid-May-mid-September.

Directions: On Highway 75 about eight miles north of downtown Ketchum, turn south at milepost 136.6 into the campground.

GPS Coordinates: N 43° 47.292' W 114° 25.475'

Contact: Sawtooth National Forest, Sawtooth National Recreation Area Headquarters, 5 North Fork Canyon Road, Ketchum, ID 83340, 208/727-5000, www.fs.usda.gov/sawtooth/.

63 MURDOCK

Scenic rating: 7
in the North Fork Canyon in Sawtooth National Recreation Area

At 6,400 feet, Murdock Campground sits in the North Fork Canyon along the North Fork of the Big Wood River. The river, which flows past the campground on the opposite side of the road, provides rainbow and brook trout habitat. Mountain bikers ride the North Fork Canyon Road to access single-track trails. The Murdock Trailhead, adjacent to the campground's south side, is equipped with a stock ramp and hitch rails. The trail follows Murdock Creek for 3.5 miles. A disposal station is on North Fork Canyon Road, 0.7 mile from the entrance.

One dirt road loops through the sunny campground, which tucks under a few aspens and large lodgepoles for shade in a sage and grass meadow. South of the campground, a large meadow (good for wildlife watching) allows views down-valley for sites 1-4, which border it. On the north end of the campground, sites 9 and 10 grab views up the valley. The open forest permits seeing neighboring campers. Even though the campground is adjacent to North Fork Canyon Road and Murdock Trailhead, the campground quiets at night.

Campsites, facilities: The campground has 11 RV or tent campsites. RVs are limited to midsized rigs. Facilities include picnic tables, fire rings with grills, vault toilets (wheelchair-accessible), drinking water, garbage service, firewood for sale, and a campground host. Leashed pets are permitted.

Reservations, fees: Reservations are not accepted. Campsites cost $12. An extra vehicle costs $5. Cash or check. Open May-October.

Directions: From Highway 75 about eight miles north of downtown Ketchum, turn north at milepost 136.4 onto North Fork Canyon Road (Forest Road 146). Drive north past the Sawtooth National Recreation Area Headquarters for 1.4 miles to the campground entrance on the right. (Pavement turns to dirt at 0.4 mile. Be ready for potholes and a single-lane bridge.)

GPS Coordinates: N 43° 48.289' W 114° 25.244'

Contact: Sawtooth National Forest, Sawtooth National Recreation Area Headquarters, 5 North Fork Canyon Road, Ketchum, ID 83340, 208/727-5000, www.fs.usda.gov/sawtooth/.

64 CARIBOU

Scenic rating: 6

in the North Fork Canyon in Sawtooth National Recreation Area

At 6,500 feet in the North Fork Canyon, Caribou Campground sits between North Fork Canyon Road and the North Fork of the Big Wood River. The river supports a rainbow and brook trout fishery. Trails for hiking, mountain biking, and horseback riding tour up all three forks of the river drainage: the East Fork, the North Fork, and the West Fork. Access these trails within four miles of the campground at the end of North Fork Canyon Road. A disposal station is on North Fork Canyon Road, 0.7 mile from the entrance.

Caribou is a quiet campground where you can listen to the sound of the river, which flows along its west side. Set in a loose forest of Douglas firs and lodgepole pines (some dying from beetle infestations), the campground offers partial shade with views of forested slopes. Large, flat spaces are available for tents. Sites 1, 3, 5, and 7 sit on the river side of the campground, which has a dirt-road loop with back-in parking pads. With only low grass and brush between the trees, neighboring campers are visible. Paths lead to the river.

Campsites, facilities: The campground has seven RV or tent campsites. RVs are limited to 22 feet. Facilities include picnic tables, fire rings with grills, vault toilets (wheelchair-accessible), and garbage service, but no drinking water. Drinking water is available at nearby Murdock Campground. Leashed pets are permitted.

Reservations, fees: Reservations are not accepted. Campsites cost $12. An extra vehicle costs $5. Cash or check. Open May-October. Fees drop in mid-September when services are limited.

Directions: From Highway 75 about eight miles north of downtown Ketchum, turn north at milepost 136.4 onto North Fork Canyon

Road (Forest Road 146). Drive north for two miles. (Pavement turns to dirt at 0.4 mile. Be ready for potholes and a single-lane bridge.) Turn left onto the single-lane campground road for 0.1 mile.

GPS Coordinates: N 43° 48.813' W 114° 25.450'

Contact: Sawtooth National Forest, Sawtooth National Recreation Area Headquarters, 5 North Fork Canyon Road, Ketchum, ID 83340, 208/727-5000, www.fs.usda.gov/sawtooth/.

65 JOE T. FALLINI

Scenic rating: 6

on Mackay Reservoir

At 6,100 feet below the Lost River Mountains, Joe T. Fallini Campground is a renovated recreation site for anglers and boaters on the north shore of Mackay Reservoir. The Lost River Mountains contain 12,000-foot-tall peaks, including Mt. Borah, the highest in Idaho. Mackay Reservoir attracts boaters, sightseers, waterskiers, Jet Skiers, swimmers, and anglers. The fishery houses Kokanee salmon, a variety of trout, and ice fishing in winter. The boating access includes a cement ramp, trailer parking, and docks. A paved interpretive trail connects the two campground loops.

The newly revamped campground, complete with paved interior roads through the two loops and paved parking pads, sits in a treeless desert-like environment surrounded by dust and sagebrush. Eight of the RV campsites and all tent campsites come with shade shelters. The open campground gives you big views of the Lost River Range and your neighboring campers. Be prepared for wind.

Campsites, facilities: The campground has 18 RV campsites, 4 double RV campsites, and 4 tent campsites. RVs are limited to 60 feet. Facilities include picnic tables, fire rings with grills, vault toilets, drinking water, garbage service, disposal station, and summer campground hosts. Leashed pets are permitted. Wheelchair-accessible facilities include toilets and seven campsites.

Reservations, fees: Reservations are not accepted. Campsites cost $6 for tents, $10 for tents with water service, $14 for water and electric hookups, and $16 for double campsites (plus $4 for each hookup). Cash or check. Open year-round.

Directions: From Challis, drive southeast on Highway 93 for about 49 miles. Or from Mackay, drive northwest on Highway 93 for six miles. The campground is on the south side of the road.

GPS Coordinates: N 43° 57.682' W 113° 40.772'

Contact: Bureau of Land Management, Challis Field Office, 1151 Blue Mountain Rd., Challis, ID 83226, 208/879-6200, www.blm.gov/id/.

66 CRATERS OF THE MOON KOA

Scenic rating: 7

near Craters of the Moon National Monument

At 5,300 feet in Arco, Craters of the Moon KOA sits 18 miles north of the visitors center and the entrance to the Craters of the Moon National Monument, a monstrous lava flow that is part of the Yellowstone volcanic complex. Eight major volcanic eruptions formed 25 cones and 60 lava flows in the 618-square-mile lava field. A seven-mile scenic drive (good for biking) and trails explore cones, craters, tree molds, and long lava tubes. Permits are required to visit the lava tube caves. With a 1950s look, the small town of Arco, the first city to be powered by atomic energy, has a couple of restaurants, gas, and groceries.

The KOA serves as an oasis in the dry, high desert. Lawns surround campsites, which have

© BECKY LOMAX

Visitors can tour underground lava tubes in Craters of the Moon National Monument.

gravel pull-through or back-in sites, and large leafy trees add partial shade to a handful of campsites in the otherwise the sunny, open, breezy location. Some campsites have views of the surrounding mountains, which can be covered by snow in spring. During the summer, the KOA adds ice cream socials and free movie showings.

Campsites, facilities: The campground has 49 RV campsites and five tent campsites. RVs are limited to 90 feet. Hookups include water, sewer, cable TV, and electricity up to 50 amps. Facilities include picnic tables, group fire pit, flush toilets, drinking water, showers, wireless Internet, swimming pool, propane and firewood for sale, camp store, launderette, disposal station, playground, dog playground, horseshoes, and banana bike rentals. Leashed pets are permitted.

Reservations, fees: Reservations are accepted. Hookups cost $37-45. Tent sites cost $25-32. Cash, check, or credit card. Open May-October.

Directions: From Hwy. 93/26/20 in Arco, turn south at Pickle's Place onto County Road

and drive 0.4 mile to the campground entrance on the left.

GPS Coordinates: N 43° 37.606' W 113° 17.750'

Contact: Craters of the Moon/Arco KOA, 2424 North 3000 West, Arco, ID 83213, 208/527-8513 or 800/562-3408, www.koa. com.

67 LAVA FLOW

Scenic rating: 8

in Craters of the Moon National Monument and Preserve

BEST (

At 5,870 feet in Craters of the Moon National Monument and Preserve, Lava Flow Campground puts campers right in the midst of unique geology, part of the same volcanic activity that created the Yellowstone Caldera. Eight major volcanic eruptions formed 25 cones and 60 lava flows in the 750,000-acre monument, creating a wild land of cones, craters, tree molds, and tubes. Hiking trails tour the moon-like landscape. The 3.5-mile North Crater Flow Trail departs from the campground to cross one of the youngest lava flows and climb through the crater. Visitors can explore caves formed in the lava, including the 800-foot-long Indian Tunnel (permit required). For a scenic drive or bicycle ride, the paved seven-mile Loop Road tours the lava field with interpretive overlooks to see volcanic features.

Located within walking distance to the visitors center, the campground lets campers stay in the lava flow. Blocky black lava rocks surround every sunny campsite built on lava gravel parking pads. Mounds of block lava separate some campsites into private nooks. A few sparse pine and junipers dot the campground, but only providing sporadic shade. Prepare for wind.

Campsites, facilities: The campground has 51 RV or tent campsites. RVs are limited to 50 feet. Facilities include picnic tables, pedestal grills (bring your own charcoal), flush and vault toilets, drinking water, amphitheater for interpretive programs, and garbage service. Leashed pets are permitted. Wheelchair-accessible facilities include toilets and one campsite.

Reservations, fees: Reservations are not accepted. Campsites cost $10 in summer and $6 in shoulder seasons. Cash or check. Open May-November.

Directions: From Craters of the Moon visitors center, drive 0.25 miles up the Loop Road and turn right into the campground.

GPS Coordinates: N 43° 27.669' W 113° 33.470'

Contact: Craters of the Moon National Monument, PO Box 29, Arco, ID 83213, 208/527-1335, www.nps.gov/crmo.

RESOURCES

RESERVATIONS
National Recreation Reservation Service

The National Recreation Reservation Service (NRRS) books reservations for federal campgrounds in Montana, Wyoming, and Idaho. While not all campgrounds offer reservations, the Forest Service, Bureau of Land Management, and National Park Service each offer some campgrounds on the NRRS reservation system:

877/444-6777 or international 518/885-3639
TDD 877/833-6777
www.recreation.gov

State Parks
Montana State Parks
855/922-6768
http://montanastateparks.reserveamerica.com

Idaho State Parks
888/922-6743
http://idahostateparks.reserveamerica.com

Wyoming State Parks
877/996-7275
http://wyoparks.state.wy.us/reservations

NATIONAL RESOURCES
Passes

The annual interagency pass—America the Beautiful—grants access to federal recreation lands that charge entrance fees. The $80 pass ($10 for seniors and free to disabled U.S. citizens and military personnel) provides entrance to national parks, Bureau of Land Management areas, U.S. Wildlife Refuges, and U.S. Forest Service lands. For seniors and disabled citizens, the passes also grant half-price camping fees. Passes may be purchased at entrance stations or online.

America the Beautiful National Pass
888/275-8747
http://store.usgs.gov/pass/index.html

National Park Service Sites
Big Hole National Battlefield
16425 Highway 43 W.
Wisdom, MT 59761
406/689-3155
www.nps.fov/biho

Craters of the Moon National Monument
P.O. Box 29
Arco, ID 83213
208/527-1335
www.nps.gov/crmo.

Glacier National Park
P.O. Box 128
West Glacier, MT 59936
406/888-7800
www.nps.gov/glac

Grand Teton National Park
P.O. Drawer 170
Moose, WY 83012
307/739-3300
www.nps.gov/grte

Grant-Kohrs Ranch National Historic Site
266 Warren Lane
Deer Lodge, MT 59722
406/846-2070
www.nps.gov/grko

Ice Age Floods National Geologic Trail
Ice Age Floods Institute
c/o Columbia River Exhibition of History, Science, and Technology
95 Lee Street
Richland, WA 99352
509/954-4242 or 509/685-0788
www.iafi.org/trail.html

Lewis and Clark National Historic Trail
601 Riverfront Drive
Omaha, NE 68102
402/661-1804
www.nps.gov/lecl

Nez Perce National Historic Trail
12730 Highway 12
Orofino, ID 83544
208/476-8334
www.fs.usda.gov/npnht

Sawtooth National Recreation Area Visitor Center
5 North Fork Canyon Road
Ketchum, ID 83340
208/727-5000 or 800/260-5970
www.fs.usda.gov/sawtooth/

Yellowstone National Park
P.O. Box 168
Yellowstone National Park, WY 82190
307/344-7381
www.nps.gov/yell

National Forests

Many national forests keep current campground information on their websites. On the road, contact the district ranger stations for updated information. You can also get maps and camping, hiking, boating, fishing, and hunting information at the district offices.

BEAVERHEAD-DEERLODGE NATIONAL FOREST

Supervisor's Office
420 Barrett Street
Dillon, MT 59725
406/683-3900
www.fs.usda.gov/bdnf

Butte Ranger District
1820 Meadowlark
Butte, MT 59701
406/494-2147

Jefferson Ranger District
3 Whitetail Road
Whitehall, MT 59759
406/287-3223

Madison Ranger Station
5 Forest Service Road

Ennis, MT 59729
406/682-4253

Pintler Ranger District
88 Business Loop
Philipsburg, MT 59858
406/859-3211

Wisdom Ranger District
P.O. Box 238
Wisdom, MT 59761
406/689-3243

Wise River Ranger District
P.O. Box 100
Wise River, MT 59762
406/832-3178

BITTERROOT NATIONAL FOREST

Supervisor's Office
1801 N. First Street
Hamilton, MT 59840
406/363-7100
www.fs.usda.gov/bitterroot

Darby Ranger District
712 N. Main
Darby, MT 59829
406/821-3913

Stevensville Ranger District
88 Main Street
Stevensville, MT 59870
406/777-5461

Sula Ranger District
7338 Highway 93 S.
Sula, MT 59871
406/821-3201

West Fork Ranger District
6735 West Fork Road
Darby, MT 59829
406/821-3269

BRIDGER-TETON NATIONAL FOREST

340 N. Cache Street

Jackson, WY 83001
307/739-5500
www.fs.usda.gov/btnf

Buffalo Ranger District
P.O. Box 278
Moran, WY 83013
307/543-2386

Jackson Ranger District
25 Rosencrans Lane
Jackson, WY 83001
307/739-5400

Pinedale Ranger District
29 E. Fremont Lake Road
Pinedale, WY 82941
307/367-4326

CARIBOU-TARGHEE NATIONAL FOREST
Supervisor's Office
1405 Hollipark Drive
Idaho Falls, ID 83401
208/524-7500
www.fs.usda.gov/ctnf

Ashton Ranger District
P.O. Box 858
Ashton, ID 83420
208/652-7442

Dubois Ranger District
127 W. Main
Dubois, ID 83423
208/374-5422

Island Park Ranger District
3726 Highway 20
Island Park, ID 83429
208/558-7301

Palisades Ranger District
3659 E. Ririe Highway
Idaho Falls, ID 83401
208/523-1412

Teton Basin Ranger District
515 S. Main
Driggs, ID 83422
208/354-2312

CUSTER NATIONAL FOREST
Supervisor's Office
1310 Main Street
Billings, MT 59105
406/255-1400
www.fs.usda.gov/custer

Beartooth Ranger District
HC 49, Box 3420
Red Lodge, MT 59068
406/446-2103

FLATHEAD NATIONAL FOREST
Supervisor's Office/Tally Lake Ranger District
650 Wolfpack Way
Kalispell, MT 59901
406/758-5200
www.fs.usda.gov/flathead

Hungry Horse and Glacier View Ranger Districts
10 Hungry Horse Drive
Hungry Horse, MT 59919
406/387-3800

Spotted Bear Ranger District
Spotted Bear, MT
406/758-5376

Swan Lake Ranger District
200 Ranger Station Road
Bigfork, MT 59911
406/837-7500

GALLATIN NATIONAL FOREST
Supervisor's Office
P.O. Box 130
Bozeman, MT 59771
406/587-6701
www.fs.usda.gov/gallatin

Bozeman Ranger District
3710 Fallon Street, Suite C
Bozeman, MT 59718
406/522-2520

Gardiner Ranger District
805 Scott Street
Gardiner, MT 59030
406/848-7375

Hebgen Lake Ranger District
P.O. Box 520
West Yellowstone, MT 59758
406/823-6961

Yellowstone Ranger District
Big Timber Office
P.O. Box 1130
225 Big Timber Loop Road
Big Timber, MT 59011
406/932-5155

Yellowstone Ranger District
Livingston Office
5242 Highway 89 S.
Livingston, MT 59047
406/222-1892

HELENA NATIONAL FOREST
Supervisor's Office and Helena Ranger District
2880 Skyway Drive
Helena, MT 59602
406/449-5201 and 406/449-5490
www.fs.usda.gov/helena

Lincoln Ranger District
1569 Highway 200
Lincoln, MT 59639
406/362-7000

Townsend Ranger District
415 S. Front
Townsend, MT 59644
406/266-3425

IDAHO PANHANDLE NATIONAL FOREST
Supervisor's Office

3815 Schreiber Way
Coeur d'Alene, ID 83815
208/765-7223
www.fs.usda.gov/ipnf

Bonners Ferry Ranger District
6286 Main Street
Bonners Ferry, ID 83805
208/267-5561

Coeur d'Alene Ranger District
Silver Valley Office
173 Commerce Drive
Smelterville, ID 83868
208/783-2100

Coeur d'Alene River Ranger District
Fernan Office
2502 E. Sherman Avenue
Coeur d'Alene, ID 83814
208/664-2318

Priest Lake Ranger District
32203 Highway 57
Priest River, ID 83856
208/443-2512

Sandpoint Ranger District
1602 Ontario Street
Sandpoint, ID 83864
208/263-5111

St. Joe Ranger District
Avery Office
34 Hoyt Drive
Avery, ID 83802
208/245-4517

Clarkia Office
54495 Highway 3
Clarkia, ID 83812
208/245-1134

St. Maries Office
222 S. 7th Street, Suite 1
St. Maries, ID 83861
208/245-2531

KOOTENAI NATIONAL FOREST
Supervisor's Office
31374 US Highway 2
Libby, MT 59923
406/293-6211
www.fs.usda.gov/kootenai

Cabinet Ranger District
Trout Creek Ranger Station
2693 Highway 200
Trout Creek, MT 59874
406/827-3533

Fortine Ranger District
Murphy Lake Ranger Station
12797 Highway 93 S.
Fortine, MT 59918
406/882-4451

Libby Ranger District
Canoe Gulch Ranger Station
12557 Highway 37
Libby, MT 59923
406/293-7773

Rexford Ranger District
Eureka Ranger Station
949 Highway 93 N.
Eureka, MT 59917
406/296-2536

Three Rivers Ranger District
Troy Ranger Station
12858 Highway 2
Troy, MT 59935
406/295-4693

LEWIS AND CLARK NATIONAL FOREST
Supervisor's Office
1101 15th Street N.
Great Falls, MT 59401
406/791-7700
www.fs.usda.gov/lcnf

Augusta Information Station
405 Manix Street

Augusta, MT 59410
406/562-3247

Lewis and Clark Interpretive Center
4201 Giant Spring Road
Great Falls, MT 59403
406/727-8733

Rocky Mountain Ranger District
1102 Main Avenue NW
Choteau, MT 59422
406/466-5341

LOLO NATIONAL FOREST
Fort Missoula, Building 24
Missoula, MT 59804
406/329-3750
www.fs.usda.gov/lolo

Missoula Ranger District
Fort Missoula, Building 24
Missoula MT 59804
406/329-3814

Ninemile Ranger District
20325 Remount Road
Huson, MT 59846
406/626-5201

Plains-Thompson Falls Ranger District
408 Clayton
Plains, MT 59859
406/826-3821

Seeley Lake Ranger District
3583 Highway 83
Seeley Lake, MT 59868
406/677-2233

Superior Ranger District
209 W. Riverside
Superior, MT 59872
406/822-4233

NEZ PERCE-CLEARWATER NATIONAL FOREST
Supervisor's Office

104 Airport Road
Grangeville, ID 83530
208/983-1950
www.fs.usda.gov/nezperceclearwater

Lochsa Ranger District
502 Lowry Street
Kooskia, ID 83539
208/926-4274

Moose Creek Ranger District
Fenn Ranger Station
831 Selway Road
Kooskia, ID 83539
208/926-4258

North Fork Ranger District
12730 Highway 13
Orofino, ID 83544
208/476-4541

Powell Ranger District
192 Powell Road
Lolo, MT 59847
208/942-3113

Red River Ranger District
Elk City Ranger Station
300 American River Road
Elk City, ID 83525
208/842-2150

Salmon River Ranger District
Slate Creek Ranger Station
304 Slate Creek Road
White Bird, ID 83554
208/839-2211

SALMON-CHALLIS NATIONAL FOREST
Supervisor's Office
1206 S. Challis Street
Salmon, ID 83467
208/756-5100
www.fs.usda.gov/scnf

Challis-Yankee Fork Ranger District
HC 63, Box 1669, Highway 93

Challis, ID 83226
208/879-4100

North Fork Ranger District
11 Casey Road
North Fork, ID 83466
208/865-2700

SAWTOOTH NATIONAL FOREST
Supervisor's Office
2647 Kimberly Road E.
Twin Falls, ID 83301
208/737-3200
www.fs.usda.gov/sawtooth

Ketchum Ranger District
206 Sun Valley Road
Ketchum, ID 83340
208/622-5371

Sawtooth National Recreation Area
Stanley Ranger Station
HC 64, Box 9900
Stanley, ID 83278
208/774-3000

SHOSHONE NATIONAL FOREST
Supervisor's Office
808 Meadowlane Avenue
Cody, WY 82414
307/527-6241
www.fs.usda.gov/shoshone

**Clarks Fork Canyon, Wapiti,
and Greybull Ranger Districts**
203A Yellowstone Avenue
Cody, WY 82414
307/527-6921

Washakie Ranger District
333 E. Main Street
Lander, WY 82520
307/332-5460

Wind River Ranger District
1403 W. Ramshorn
Dubois, WY 82513
307/455-2466

National Wildlife Refuges

Kootenai National Wildlife Refuge
287 Westside Road
Bonners Ferry, ID 83805
208/267-3888
www.fws.gov/refuges

Lee Metcalf National Wildlife Refuge
4567 Wildfowl Lane
Stevensville, MT 59870
406/777-5552
www.fws.gov/refuges

Lost Trail National Wildlife Refuge
6295 Pleasant Valley Road
Marion, MT 59925
406/858-2211
www.fws.gov/refuges

National Elk Refuge
P.O. Box 510
Jackson, WY 83001
307/733-9212
www.fws.gov/nationalelkrefuge

Pablo, and Ninepipe National Wildlife Refuges and National Bison Range
58355 Bison Range Road
Moiese, MT 59824
406/644-2211
www.fws.gov/bisonrange

Red Rocks National Wildlife Refuge
27650B South Valley Road
Lima, MT 59739
406/276-3536
www.fws.gov/redrocks

Bureau of Land Management

Idaho Bureau of Land Management
1387 S. Vinnell Way
Boise, ID 83709
208/373-4000
www.blm.gov/id

Montana Bureau of Land Management
5001 Southgate Drive
Billings, MT 59101
406/896-5000
www.blm.gov/mt

Wyoming Bureau of Land Management
5353 Yellowstone Road
Cheyenne, WY 82009
307/775-6256
www.blm.gov/wy

STATE RESOURCES
Montana

Montana Department of Transportation
2701 Prospect Avenue
Helena, MT 59620
Road conditions: 800/226-7623
www.mdt.mt.gov/travinfo

Montana Fish, Wildlife, and Parks
1420 E. 6th Avenue
Helena, MT 59620
406/444-2535
www.fwp.mt.gov

Montana Office of Tourism
301 S. Park Avenue
Helena, MT 59620
800/847-4868
www.visitmt.com

Idaho

Idaho Division of Tourism
700 W. State Street
Boise, ID 83720
208/334-2470 or 800/847-4843
www.visitidaho.org

Idaho Fish and Wildlife
600 S. Walnut
Boise, ID 83712
208/334-3700
www.fishandgame.idaho.gov

Idaho Parks and Recreation
5657 Warm Springs Avenue
Boise, ID 83716

208/334-4199
www.parksandrecreation.idaho.gov

Idaho Transportation Department
3311 W. State Street
Boise, ID 83707
Road conditions: 888-432-7623
www.511.idaho.gov

Wyoming
Wyoming Department of Transportation
5300 Bishop Boulevard
Cheyenne, WY 82009
Road conditions: 888/996-7623
www.wyoroad.info

Wyoming Game and Fish
5400 Bishop Boulevard
Cheyenne, WY 82006
307/777-4600
http://wgfd.wyo.gov

Wyoming State Parks
2301 Central Avenue
Cheyenne, WY 82002
307/777-6323
http://wyoparks.state.wy.us

Wyoming Office of Tourism
5611 High Plains Road
Cheyenne, WY 82007
307/777-7777 or 800/225-5996
www.wyomingtourism.org

NATIVE AMERICAN RESERVATIONS
Blackfeet Nation
1 Agency Square
Browning, MT 59417

406/338-7521
www.blackfeetnation.com

Coeur d'Alene Indian Reservation
850 A Street
Plummer, ID 83851
208/686-1800
www.cdatribe-nsn.gov

Confederated Salish and Kootenai Tribes
51383 Highway 93 N.
Pablo, MT 59855
406/675-2700
www.cskt.org

Wind River Indian Reservation
P.O. Box 538
Fort Washakie, WY 82514
307/856-0706
www.windriver.org

MAPS
Beartooth Publishing
Regional recreation maps for southern Montana and northwestern Wyoming; maps include latitude and longitude grids, trail mileages, and campgrounds.
406/585-7205 or 800/838-1058
www.beartoothpublishing.com

National Geographic Trails Illustrated
Maps can be purchased for Glacier, Grand Teton, and Yellowstone National Parks.
800/962-1643
www.natgeomaps.com

USGS
Topographical maps for Montana, Wyoming, and Idaho.
888/275-8747
www.usgs.gov

Index

www.moon.com

DESTINATIONS | ACTIVITIES | BLOGS | MAPS | BOOKS

MOON.COM is ready to help plan your next trip! Filled with fresh trip ideas and strategies, author interviews, informative travel blogs, a detailed map library, and descriptions of all the Moon guidebooks, Moon.com is all you need to get out and explore the world—or even places in your own backyard. While at Moon.com, sign up for our monthly e-newsletter for updates on new releases, travel tips, and expert advice from our on-the-go Moon authors. As always, when you travel with Moon, expect an experience that is uncommon and truly unique.

MOON IS ON FACEBOOK—BECOME A FAN!
JOIN THE MOON PHOTO GROUP ON FLICKR

YOUR ADVENTURE STARTS HERE

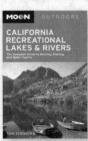
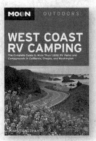

JUL 2 3 2014

MOON MONTANA, WYOMING & IDAHO CAMPING

Avalon Travel
a member of the Perseus Books Group
1700 Fourth Street
Berkeley, CA 94710, USA
www.moon.com

Editors: Leah Gordon, Sabrina Young
Series Manager: Sabrina Young
Copy Editor: Carolyn Cotney
Production and Graphics Coordinator:
   Lucie Ericksen
Cover Designer: Lucie Ericksen
Map Editor: Mike Morgenfeld
Cartographer: Stephanie Poulain

ISBN-13: 978-1-61238-742-0
ISSN: 1532-1142

Printing History
1st Edition – 2001
3rd Edition – May 2014
5 4 3 2 1

Front cover photo: Otokomi Lake, Glacier National Park © Becky Lomax
Title page photo: Mountain goats in Glacier National Park © Becky Lomax
Front matter photos: pages 4-7: © Becky Lomax
Back cover photo: © Al Valeiro / Getty Images

Printed in Canada by Friesens

Keeping Current

We are committed to making this book the most accurate and enjoyable camping guide to the region. You can rest assured that every campground in this book has been carefully reviewed in an effort to keep this book as up-to-date as possible. However, by the time you read this book, some of the fees listed herein may have changed and campgrounds may have closed unexpectedly.

If you have a favorite gem you'd like to see included in the next edition, or see anything that needs updating, clarification, or correction, please drop us a line. Send your comments via email to feedback@moon.com, or use the address above.